LABOR RADICAL

LABOR
RADICAL

FROM THE WOBBLIES TO CIO

A PERSONAL HISTORY

LEN DE CAUX

BEACON PRESS   BOSTON

TO CAROLINE

ACKNOWLEDGMENTS

I am most grateful: To Carl Haessler, kind, caustic, and ever-helpful, who bravely damned the flood of my reminiscence and tried to channel it to useful ends. To the Louis M. Rabinowitz Foundation, whose generous aid-without-strings gave me time to write. To Angus Cameron and Carl Marzani, who helped me to get started. To the many persons young and old, left and right (some mightn't like the company, if I listed all), who read my manuscript at various stages—the younger contributing impatient comment on our mistakes, the older shared memories and seasoned advice. To my ever-present and much-loved children, whose interruptions brought me down to earth. To the mentioned and unmentioned hundreds I've known in the movement (we, too, called it that), who furnished the substance of this book. Thanks again.

CONTENTS

LABOR RADICAL

VIEWPOINT

Chapter One

I WANT TO JOIN THE WORKING CLASS

Harrow, Belfast and World War I could tell
enough of the viewpoints of a landed gentry
and the bourgeoisie to make one look toward
the working class.

An explorer first climbing to Harrow-on-the-Hill might fancy himself out of this world. Wherever he topped The Hill's backbone, its long, curving, undulating High Street, he'd start seeing things.

Like a flying saucer, a broadbrimmed, flat straw hat would flit into sight—little more than inch-high in the center and anchored by elastic around the back of a pimply, pink-faced boy's head. Below it blue blazer and gray flannel pants. The apparition would ignore the explorer or cast an icy glance. It would dart or stroll to join others of its kind. Curious accents of Harrow slang would lilt from the self-absorbed group. Any stranger must know at once he didn't belong and wasn't wanted.

On a Sunday, coveys of sleek black silk tophats would appear atop boys big and small. Eton collars and shortcut jackets for the smaller. On the bigger, tailcoats, stiff white shirts, black bow ties, striped dark pants—fit for a West End waiter or swell.

The First World War broke out when I entered Harrow School in the fall of 1914. It made little impact on customs generations old, or on the Harrow ideology I absorbed during my four years. The boys maintained and enforced the status quo, with teenage tyranny.

From American junior-high youngsters I learned the word "chop." A parent could chop one down by no more than a greeting in the presence of schoolmates. A boy could chop himself down by doing anything unusual that invited ridicule. "Chop" became adjective and noun, as well as verb, for anything that caused a boy to lose face. The "chop" taboo might apply to any detail of attire, speech, behavior. Its bans were arbitrary and ever-changing, in line with current fads.

At Harrow, I recall no word like "chop." The dictates of conformity were rigid, everlasting, all-embracing. The American boy who dared to be "chop" might draw laughs or sneers, perhaps some minor hazing. But home was a privileged sanctuary where he could act as chop as he liked. At Harrow, the boys punished infractions of their age-old rules both physically and psychologically. There was no sanctuary.

On my first day I unwittingly broke two rules. I left the bottom button of my blazer unbuttoned—a privilege reserved for the second year. Bumped off the narrow, crowded sidewalk, I tried walking in the street—which only bloods might do. The gibes I drew were penalty enough. I never repeated a known offense. I found security at last in knowing every detail of every rule . . . never to be in doubt about what "just isn't done."

The American teenage conformities, in clothes and gadgetry, were geared to the profit requirements of mass production. They conditioned herd impulses and thought controls useful for the capitalist manipulation of a supposedly democratic society. At Harrow, the more intricate conformities revealed a distinctly feudal hangover. The new boy learned at once to expect no equality or democracy. Status and privilege were all-important. In an ordered sequence of time, one might climb above the lowest rungs of the social ladder. But those on top were born to rule —rocketed past the ladder-plodders by their innate superiority.

On the top were the "bloods." These could strut (at Harrow a loungy stroll) down the center of High Street, with tophat at arrogant angle, silk-covered lapels, maybe a rolled brolly for cane. As they passed, the common herd drew back in whispering awe, some fawning for a condescending smile. The bloods had real power. They had small-boy fags who shined their shoes, cleaned their rooms, made their tea and toast, and waited on their whims. Some were "heads of Houses" or held high rank therein. Each House where the boys lived had its hierarchy, and boy-made rules more intimate and compelling than those of The

School at large. Their boy rulers were potentates, authorized to "whop" the unruly.

Most bloods rose to power through cricket and football. To this elite every Harrow boy had the right to aspire; realistically, he had to be born with the requisite physique and dexterity. The future blood was recognizable from his first year. The adult authorities appointed monitors—chosen for character and leadership, they said, and even taking classwork into account. But in line with the British creed of victory-through-playing-field, almost any blood could become a monitor; it didn't follow any monitor could be a blood. The new boy who confused the self-made (by study) monitor with a real blood to the manor born, was soon put wise: "Him! He's no blood. He's just a groise."

If the blood was at the top of the heap, the groise was at the bottom. Groises were always looking for hiding places—all too few in a goldfish bowl like the boys' Harrow—where they might read or study unobserved. They led a double life, publicly professing interest in games to cover up their studious iniquities. Groises became conspiratorial. They plotted for chances at bookish indulgence and covertly helped each other out of jams—the while they proclaimed due public contempt for all groises. But great was the joy, when at some secret rendezvous, groise met groise in uninhibited mental conspiracy.

Few groises had the imagination or daring to challenge their stigma. Most felt guilty, tried to reform, and learned to cover up when they backslid. Only in my last (17-18) year did I meet fellow groises without pretense among ourselves. To a remote and concealed alcove in the Library we would sneak one by one. There we relished whispered wisecracks about bloods, games-goofy masters, and Harrow ideology.

Peters helped to spell things out for me. He was an awkward, gangling, long-nosed youth, top boy in a topmost class—and used to being first. He had little muscle and poor coordination. A natural groise, it might seem. Peters vehemently rejected the aspersion. He insisted he studied little and couldn't help getting high marks, he was born that way. Peters joined the anti-groise pack, even tried to lead it—ideologically.

If Harrow was to produce men qualified as well as entitled to rule, Peters held, there must be no namby-pamby sentimentality about the inferior. The true aristocrat (ruler by virtue of being best) should be strong, agile, well-favored, with character to command respect and obedience—one naturally looked up to by others. Which Harrow men best met these tests? Obviously the bloods. The groise was their opposite—homely, weak, hopeless at games, too timid to be a positive leader. Proof of the pudding: Who at Harrow was more despised than the groise?

Good brains were all right, Peters conceded, if they didn't make bookworms. But the mental equipment of most bloods was adequate for British purposes. They had to run an established system by proved and easily learned rules—not experiment with doubtful innovations. If the groise really had good brains, he need spend little time on study and could devote himself to the more important character-building aspects of Harrow life. The groise showed himself mentally inferior by having to study so hard. He sought perverted compensation for his lack of social standing—thus only making himself the more despised. He became embittered and might turn to crazy nostrums like socialism.

Peters imparted this philosophy to me over long periods in the same classes with him—by insinuation, side remarks and reactions, and sometimes quite coherent expression. I developed a mental image of this homely all-knees-and-elbows galoot surrounded by Harrow bloods and telling them how superior "we" are. I thought of him when, years later, I saw gnome Goebbels proclaiming the superiority of his Nordic supermen.

Rating Peters a conservative, I was surprised to find him become known for a doctrine deemed disturbingly radical. It happened in a top class that dabbled in Greek philosophy and might even discuss politics. Not English party politics, however, on which there was no division. All Harrovians were assumed to be Tory (Conservative party). If any Liberal lurked among us, he'd hardly admit it.

One Liberal did expose himself while I was at Harrow. It was on Speech Day (Commencement). Old Harrovians of wealth, title, military, or political prominence were honored guests. Some made little speeches in Latin in the auditorium. Afterwards the boys gathered at the foot of long stone steps to watch and acclaim emerging celebrities. One was a stocky, red-faced man who stepped out jauntily from the Speech Room. He stopped to grin and wave to the boys below. A low, grumbling murmur ran through them. A boo was heard. It broke the dam of what "isn't done." Soon catcalls drowned handclaps. There were cries of "traitor."

The un-Harrovian old Harrovian was the Right Honorable Winston Churchill. Long suspect of conspiring to cater to the common people, Churchill had recently switched from the Conservative to the Liberal party—though it was not to be for long.

The politics in our classroom had percolated through the sands of time from ancient Greece. It concerned forms of government—monarchy, theocracy, tyranny, oligarchy, plutocracy, aristocracy, democracy. I include democracy because I secretly sympathized with the idea. It had no open advocates. Like American Birchers, the boys seemed to see it as perversion of government, breakdown of authority and tradition, mob rule.

In those years before the Russian revolution, the word "communism" had a faded early-Christian flavor; "democracy" was the equivalent epithet. An old lady I once boarded with would beat her cane on the floor—even spat once—at mention of the word. When servants were impertinent, mail full of bills, dishes dirty, fires dead in grate, tradespeople demanding, she'd growl: "That's what we get for letting democracy run wild!"

A few romantics were strong for monarchy, absolute monarchy, the Divine Right of Kings. They grew misty-eyed over "Charles the Martyr," the beheaded King Charles I. They hated the Roundheads as forerunners of democracy. One was for tyranny, arguing that a "tyrannos" was better than a king to keep the people down, win wars, promote the national glory. A tyrant had to be forceful to seize power, while a king might be weak, decadent, hampered by tradition.

Theocracy found no support. The boys believed in God—a most sound British institution. Religion had its place—in church on Sunday. It helped keep the lower classes in their place. Clergymen had their place. (How feudal the constant stress on place!) The clergyman's place was well above the servants' quarters—closer to that of an estate manager—but well below the seats of power.

Oligarchy was the obvious favorite. To the boys it meant that they and their families should stay on top. They paid homage to The Throne as to God. Too many Harrow generations had fought for God, King, and Empire to permit any caddish flippancy about this trinity. "The King" was more of a throat-choker than the Americans' "Mother." Most Harrow boys were raised by nannies and had only a bowing acquaintance with "the Mater." Most were also realistic enough to know that in England neither Divinity nor Royalty actually ruled, while an oligarchy did.

In drawing modern inference, three trends emerged. The Left—a small shaky minority—halfheartedly defended British parliamentarism. True it let a low demagogue like Lloyd George get elected (he had called their like the aristocracy's "litters"). But it also saved England from horrors like the French Revolution. Most members of Parliament were of the Harrow-Eton, Oxford-Cambridge stripe. Even in politics, a gentleman should be more than a match for a lower-class upstart. The Center were not so sure that landed gentlemen and old Harrovians could hold their own in a free-for-all. They called for more curbs on democracy to entrench the ruling class. The Right were for more extreme measures, such as abolishing the House of Commons to give all power to a hereditary House of Lords.

"Inky" (the master) noted the prevailing sentiment for oligarchy, and for aristocracy as its best form. In root meaning, he stressed, the word was not limited to a titled aristocracy, as in England, but left room for differences on who were "the best" and so entitled to rule. He assigned Peters to write a summing-up paper.

Before letting Peters read his paper, Inky expressed some misgivings. It was really too "modern" and "controversial" for a classical paper, he said. So the boys listened with close attention, but also with growing murmurs of dissent. At the end, restrained Harrovian hell broke loose.

Advancing aristocracy as the best form of government, Peters developed his own ideas on "rule by the best." Rule by a titled and landed aristocracy was outdated, he said bluntly. (Mutters of "Shame.") That was a good form of government. Peters paid due Harrovian tribute to the Golden Age of feudalism, but said that it was gone. Decadence was also possible in a hereditary aristocracy. Here Peters trod delicately, to avoid personal offense. Still some insisted afterwards he'd been bounder enough to imply dim-witted degeneracy from aristocratic intermarriage.

Peters advocated an infusion of new blood in the aristocracy. If a brilliant cricketer, or general, or statesman arose from the common people, might he not as one of the best have title to rule? Some nodded. But as he went on, there was grumbling hardly quelled by Inky's frowns.

Among those pushing to the top, Peters said, were manufacturers, merchants, financiers—the men of money. Plutocracy was a vulgar, brutal form of government. (Whispers of "Hear, hear!") But the go-ahead capitalists were able, forceful men, with power to command—qualities needed by a ruling class. Weren't they as much entitled to rule as landowners who just inherited their wealth? (A mutter: "Talks like a bloody Liberal!")

Those who wanted rule by the best had two alternatives: They could insist that money power didn't make for "the best," and engage in ruinous conflict with the men of money. Or they could redefine "the best" to include the money-men, and make them allies. The second, said Peters, was much the wiser course; and, he added slyly, it was happening anyhow.

As he stopped, several boys were on their feet.

"I say, sir," said one, "we've had to listen to this bilge, but we don't have to agree with it, do we?"

Another: "I should say not."

A daring: "I think there's a lot in what Peters says."

Inky was calm, sarcastic as ever. "Nobody invited your comments," he said. "It takes a certain intellectual capacity—not apparent in this group—to agree or disagree with a reasoned approach to any subject. As to bilge, Jackson, I believe the word refers to stale water in the hull of a ship. I'll expect you to look up the Greek word for bilge, and to use it hereafter whenever you feel driven to such vulgar expression."

Inky was restraining the lunges of boys disturbed in dream-drenched sleep. Their dreamworld—like the magnolia-scented memory-myths of the American South—never really existed. They clung to it the more. I knew about it from childhood through Mother.

Mother held there were just two classes. Ladies and gentlemen, on the one hand, common people on the other; or more baldly, the upper class and the lower class. Though modesty and breeding forbade her to press the point, I got the impression Mother herself was in the upper of the two classes. We children were only conditionally so . . . insofar as we took after her side of the family, not Father's. Mother came from a landed "county family" in once rural Essex. Father's father had been but a bank manager in the grimy industrial Midlands. To Mother, bankers ranked with "tradespeople" and all others who vulgarly haggled and scrabbled for money.

The idea was a laggard, even in her time—certainly in New Zealand, where I was born and raised. Yet even there I learned from others too, how things looked to a landed gentry. When Father, as Vicar of Waipawa, took some of us kids along on long journeys by horse-trap to minister to big sheep-run owners in his parish, we reveled in their gracious living—with servants and hired hands to do the work, with comfort and rich food, with lots of leisure for fun and games. I was too young for politics, but I'm sure my older sisters drew logical conclusion: The way of the gentry was best. Marry a man of property . . . have horses to ride, one of the first motor cars, no housework to do. To preserve this way of life, vote tory, true-blue conservative, be ever on guard against roundheads, levelers, socialists, tradespeople, all with envious designs on the gentry's good thing.

In the Harrow boys' dreamworld, real ladies and gentlemen —a genuine elite, an aristocracy by Inky's definition—lived gallantly, generously, chivalrously, patriotically. In refined and civilized living, in sense of social obligation, they set an example to all mankind. They were obedient to authority, loyal to superiors, comradely with equals, considerate of inferiors, charitable to the poor and weak. They set the interests of the team, the school, the class, the country, ahead of any selfish individual interests.

Like the biblical lilies, this upper class did not toil, let alone spin, nor render any particular productive service. Yet a Solomon might envy their array—at the Ascot races, a Buckingham Palace reception, or the Harrow-Eton cricket match at Lords. Where did their money come from? One didn't speak of things like that, any more than of toilet doings or physical sex. It was vulgar to talk about money. Presumably the Pater or the Mater owned some land or stocks or something. Only a money-grubbing tradesman would inquire.

This upper class had long ruled to the great glory of Merrie England and the British Empire. Now envious upstarts and lower classes threatened it. Not decent country folk who did their work and paid their rent. Trouble stemmed from the miserable millions spawned by a satanic factory system.

The poor workers were themselves all right. They needed the help, by jove, that real gentlemen could give them. All others were out to exploit them. Not only grinding employers, but also trade-union and socialist agitators who wanted to overthrow everything. In the boys' attitude to labor, however, I early detected some contradiction. When workers struck or otherwise "rose" rebelliously, it was held they should be "shot down." Asking if this was really the gentlemanly thing to do, I got the argument that lethal measures were kinder in the long run.

Tradespeople threatened the upper class—and personally too. So demanding about tailor bills and such! And vulgar about money! All they think and talk about . . . and some, y'know, even have more than we have!

Worst in a way were the newly rich, the capitalists—with their filthy smoke-belching factories . . . their machine-mad pushing ahead over everything . . . trying to make money rule everywhere. Socially too, an awful bore, rather disgusting. Trying to push into clubs where they weren't wanted, to buy their way into the upper class.

Yet all the boys knew the real world wasn't like their dream-world. Even at Harrow, names advertised for lowly articles and services were cropping up among those of princes and nabobs from other lands, English aristocrats and county families, Army and Navy, the well-bred well-to-do.

If some resented the sons of the new-rich among them, I didn't hear them say so. Paradoxically, Harrow was to this degree a leveler. Every boy, rich or not, titled or commoner, foreign or English, was run through the same wringer. He was judged only by Harrow-made standards.

Even before Harrow, I had wondered about the viewpoint of those who were not comfortably ensconced on top of the heap. Reaching puberty in the grim, gray city of Belfast, where poverty popped out at every corner, I added social reflection to my other confusions.

In search of out-of-the-way cinemas, I took long walks through narrow grimy streets walled by solid blocks of joined houses whose doors opened right onto them. Children spilled out to play in the gutters, scrawny, pale, poorly clothed . . . starved, if not for food, at least for the comforts and treats that made life livable to me.

On these streets lived workers of the shipyards, factories, textile mills, of Ireland's biggest industrial city. From them came stories of brick-and-bottle battles, bombings, shootings, bloody brawls. I thought the poor were rising against the rich . . . until I learned that Protestants were fighting against Catholics, Orangemen against Sinn Feiners.

Into our middle-class neighborhood came little clusters of kids begging. Peaked and pallid, in odd-sized, castoff clothes, barefoot in the cold or with worn-through shoes, they hung around grocery stores whining for food from emerging customers. They knocked at the doors of homes and peered in hungrily at the comforts within.

I prayed to God for explanation. He gave me none. So I turned to his walking delegate, my father, to register my beef against social injustice. Father, then employed by the Church Missionary Society, had lots to say. He took me hill climbing with him, and we talked.

Poverty?

Deplorable. But the Bible says the poor we have with us always.

Is God responsible?

Yes, God is responsible for everything.

Why did God create poverty?

To try men's souls. Without it, the poor would have no incentive to better themselves through work and thrift; the rich no exercise for the virtue of charity.

How about the poor going on strike for more money, like the miners and railwaymen do? Is that a good idea?

No.

Why not?

God made the rich man in his castle, the poor man at the gate. He made masters and men—the men to obey the masters, commoners to obey kings, children to obey parents. If workmen rebel against their masters, they defy God's law.

What if the workmen don't get enough for their families to live on?

A hypothetical question. Actually the men who keep striking make more money than most—they're just greedy for more.

But suppose it's really strike-or-starve like they say?

Rebellion against lawful authority is never justified. If the employers can't pay more wages, as they evidently can't, then the workmen must tighten their belts and manage as best they can.

If Father was as callous as I recall here, this may be said. He was a fighter. If his presumptuous little son was trying to drive him into a logical corner, he'd not appease or retreat. He'd stand his ground, even if later he might regret a lack of ministerial unction.

On our next hike above the smoke and soot of Belfast, to hilltops where the sun sometimes shone, Father tried to interest me in charity work, and I pursued a new angle. If the poor shouldn't strike, and the rich wouldn't give them more, how about passing laws to even things up?

Father conceded that New Zealand had laws like this that some thought good. But there was grave danger of the poor becoming lazy and thriftless if coddled too much. And, of course, it was sheer robbery for the law to take from the rich to give to the poor.

"Why?" I objected, being an early Robin Hood fan.

"Because that leads straight to socialism."

"I know socialism's pretty awful, but why d'you think it's so bad?"

"In the first place, it would never work. It's against human nature. You know my story about the socialist agitator and the Irishman. . . ."

"Yes, yes," I said hastily. But Father was not to be denied. He went through all the things the Irishman was willing to share. He laughed heartily, as always, at the punchline: "Git away wid ya, ye know I got two pigs."

Father warned of the menace of socialism. This was 1914; the communist menace came later. There were actually people pushing for socialism, he said . . . called themselves the Labor party.

"Some things they say don't sound so bad——" I began.

Father was alerted. "You must have heard some socialist propaganda. Don't let them fool you." He stopped walking and tapped my arm.

"D'you know how much I get paid a year?"

"I don't know. Not more than £400, is it?"

"Not enough for us to live as we do . . . you children going to the best schools, and all that. The rest of the money comes from your mother. She gets almost as much from her inheritance as I get from my salary. If Labor ever came to power, they'd take away your mother's money . . . 'nationalization' they call it. You'd suffer as much as any."

The war? I took it in stride, as did Harrow. Questions arose but were not encouraged, still less answered. My family was duly patriotic. It had always held the Germans to be clean, decent, civilized people (wasn't our King really a German?). After war was declared, my elder brother came home saying they were "dirty Huns."

"Why?" I asked.

"What d'you mean 'why'? Don't you know we're at war?"

"Well, does that change the Germans?"

"What do you think?" He grinned. "Watch out you don't get mobbed."

Harrow held aloof from the mob hysteria stirred by the "gutter press." It read (or pretended to) the stodgy *Morning Post*, a deplorer more than a denouncer. Eggheads took the dignified *Times*. Popular jingo papers like the *Daily Mail* were read on the sly . . . a big infra dig, y'know.

Harrow did its bit. It activated its Officers Training Corps. It sent many to the snootier regiments. It engraved many new names on the Honor Roll of Harrow's war dead. It carried on . . . kept the home fires burning, cherished British traditions for the boys to return to. It discussed war aims and reasons no more than did the British army when I joined it.

While I was in the Royal Field Artillery, some papers and politicians started yakking that the troops should be told what the war was about. Whitehall issued a directive. Grumbling that the war was being bogged down with paperwork, our commanding officer referred it to a colonel, who couldn't make it out and passed it to a major. No bookworm either, he gave the assignment to a lieutenant as "last from school."

Lieutenant Black was a brisk young man, trim and slim, with close-cropped mustache. He marched us off the parade ground to an army classroom.

"Men," he said, "I've been stuck with a silly job. We've been fighting Germany for three years, and I'm supposed to tell you what the war's about and why we're fighting. I'm not going to make a speech about democracy, rights of small nations, war to end war, and all that. You know that's a lot of tommyrot. There's only one issue in this war: Either Germany wins or we do. And, by God, we've bloody well got to win!"

He stopped and glanced around for reaction. There were none. "Any questions?" No response. We had a chance to get off an hour early. Anyone asking questions would have been mobbed. "All right. Dismissed!"

Through the war years, there was a German boy with me at Harrow. I disliked Baum, but not as a German. I had a sneaking sympathy for the underdog Germans . . . defeated every day in the papers, abused, insulted, the poor devils never seemed to stand a chance. But Baum was no underdog. Older and bigger than I, he was sullenly arrogant. He hunted with the hounds— against the groises, against the lower classes. If others said strikers should be "shot down," Baum would add, ". . . like bloody dogs." Me he ignored, or tried to bully.

Baum didn't speak about the war. The other boys avoided the subject in his presence. Behind his back, they were curious.

"Did you see how Baum looked when the war came up in class?"

"No, I thought he was just bored, like the rest of us."

"Stuffy shouldn't have talked against the Germans, with him there."

"Oh, I don't know. After all we are at war. Baum's got to know he's in an enemy country."

"But isn't he supposed to be on our side? He'd be interned, wouldn't he, if he were on the German side?"

"He has to pretend he's on our side. But you've got to hand it to him—he won't say a word one way or the other, he's not going to crawl."

"I wonder which side he's really on. I mean, in his own heart."

"He's bound to be on the German side. After all, he *is* a gentleman. Just can't get away to fight for them. If we were Germans, we'd jolly well be patriotic on their side, wouldn't we? Baum's not such a cad as to turn against his own country."

That was Harrow lore all right. My country right or wrong, so who cared about rights and wrongs? War was a periodical, if rather deadly, sporting event. Like the Harrow-Eton cricket match . . . except you couldn't tell who the enemy would be from war to war. Patriotism dictated your side: to fight to the death against equally patriotic enemies.

It was enough to make me an internationalist. Imbued first with the idea that free trade could bring a warless world economy, I turned briefly to the Liberal party . . . only to find its leader, David Lloyd George, the biggest of war-frothing jingos.

His postwar election slogans: "Hang the Kaiser!" "Make Germany Pay!" "Britain for the British!"

The vision lasted long enough, however, to create for me a vaporous image of United States President Woodrow Wilson—with his 14 points, his self-determination, his democracy, his League of Nations—as world prophet of internationalism. When Wilson drove through London streets, I yelled and waved and cheered with most un-British abandon. Then came the Treaty of Versailles, and the drawn out "pf-f-ft" of the League of Nations.

Myself I didn't do badly out of the war. An Army grant was added to scholarships won on leaving Harrow and for entrance to Hertford College, Oxford—enough to cover fees and living expenses for four years. Before "going up," I had nearly a year to fill in. I taught school and tutored, then spent a long summer in France. During this pleasant letdown, at last—a curiously delayed reaction— I became revolted with the war.

This bloody, brutal, stupid war had made no sense at all, except to war profiteers on both sides, I concluded. I was enraged at the propaganda that bamboozled millions of decent people into hating and slaughtering each other for four long years. I began to question all thought patterns and institutions once taken for granted. Patriotism, religion, government, weren't they all parts of the same murderous moronic con game?

No mixer, I was little aware how many of my postwar generation were going through a similar process of revulsion, challenge, rejection. We had been bidden to fight for God, King, and Country, or for God, Kaiser, and Country. The King/Kaiser-Country stuff had made me an internationalist. The God stuff went deeper. I worked my way hard and long through religion—finally to come out on the other side. Then I looked for the social and political answers. By the time I entered Oxford, in the fall of 1919, I was emotionally and mentally conditioned to become a red.

Oxford was mellow indeed to a green apple from New Zealand. The gray, moist atmosphere. Rare sunshine soft as first snow. Weathered walls. Sky-pointing spires. A week-long Sunday quiet, broken by gently chiming bells. All conspired to relax, to ripen.

The life was softly suited to my taste. As a Scholar I rated good rooms. Bedroom and cot were small, narrow, ascetic. The study-living room made up. It was large, wainscoted, carpeted, with big fireplace. All around the walls were bookshelves. With bibliophilic zeal, I filled them up. On the low, deep, Oxonian wicker armchairs, with enough cushions, one could stretch out horizontally before an open fire and laze bookishly in full content.

My typical day was as I chose. Breakfast in the college dining hall, in my rooms, or in a nearby tearoom where I could scan the morning papers by a crackling fire. Then a pleasant walk through Oxford streets to a lecture or two. Within my classical field I could pick my lectures. Most were a grinding bore with their dreary grammatics, glosses, and quibbling commentaries. I skipped most. But not the lectures of Gilbert Murray.

An alabaster-smooth little man with silvery fringe, Murray was a Liberal not a Tory. He related the Greek classics to modern ideas and ideals. He was a humanist. He treated the classics as literature, not torturous mental discipline. Murray was also a lowercase liberal. Mildly but devastatingly, he debunked the hidebound in religion, politics, morality. He glorified individual freedom. He was democrat, libertarian, internationalist.

One thing stuck in my craw. The ancient Athenians, whose liberalism Murray extolled, didn't share it with their slaves— whom Murray barely took into account. In his own politics, by the same token, he took little account of the British working class and its labor movement. His Liberal party was the merchants and manufacturers party. His freedoms were for them, and for intellectuals removed from toil, more than for the poverty-stunted many who most needed freedom from want and exploitation.

The afternoon was for exercise—in my case meandering by placid streams and along far-wandering footpaths. Then the main social event, afternoon tea. One might have it in the Common Room and meet students one didn't ordinarily run into. A time for mixing, kidding, argument. Or one might have tea in his own rooms, inviting friends with common interests.

We talked of life, of love (not much), of ourselves, of the outside world, and chiefly—in my rooms—of which side we were on in its struggles. We reached for truth's elusive slippery tentacles. Almost we might have hold of one—only to realize suddenly that time, like truth, had slipped away . . . and we'd have to run to the dining hall for dinner.

This was a dignified occasion. Gowned dons on a dais. Gowned and restrained undergrads at the long tables of a medieval hall. Rituals, as when a big silver tankard of ale passed from lip to lip—paid for by someone guilty of "talking shop" at dinner. The rest of the evening was for individual study, outside entertainment, debates, club meetings.

The life was easy, interesting, mildly stimulating. It was so soft I felt trapped—by my own inclinations. Oxford only seemed aloof. It was part of a setup designed to perpetuate the privileges of the upper classes, to promote their economic and imperial interests. Oxford took the thoughtful, treated them well, and turned their thoughts toward some cozy niche in the establishment. At best it produced no more than Gilbert Murrays. I was on guard. I could hardly be snared in the thought-cage of the landed gentry. For me, Harrow had sprung as well as set that trap. The bourgeoisie was more wily with its lures, but I wanted none of them. There were other class viewpoints. I'd made my choice and hoped to stick by it.

James Ramsay MacDonald, as Labor party leader, was patron of the Oxford Labor Club when I joined; his undergrad son Malcolm, a leading light.

Malcolm was impressive—for our callow crowd, politically mature. He was calm and reasonable in debate. He avoided abuse, emotion, too obvious demagogy. He was positive, seemingly sure of himself. In embryo, the coming Colonial Secretary, governor, diplomat, pillar of empire. Malcolm argued against the "wild men," but not as enemies. Like a psychiatrist, he tried to understand them, to gain their confidence, to strike responsive chords. He invited them—red ties, cantankerous manners, and all—to his political afternoon teas in his rooms.

Malcolm's rightwing Laborite line was more persuasive to

me than that of his more emotional father. Neither inspired me. When one burns to right the world's wrongs, it's a letdown to hear leaders counsel caution, a step at a time, the inevitability of gradualness . . . seemingly more eager to hold back impatient ranks than to fight the foe. I was for the young-men-in-a-hurry. Yet I had a lurking hunch that, practically speaking, Malcolm might be right. My approach had been along the Fabian road.

The Russian revolution shook me out of old ruts. It enlisted all my sympathies. But the terminology of Bolshevism was foreign to me. The socialist doctrine I heard in the Independent Labor party was rooted less in Marxism than in nonconformist Christian ethics, democratic populism, utopian collectivism. This insular socialism grew from the working class, however. It's champion Keir Hardie was in some ways a British Gene Debs. It was linked with unionism and strikes. Practicing, if not preaching, class struggle, it had to encounter Marxist ideas.

In the labor circles I first entered, Marxism was taboo. Rightwingers frowned on it and fought it. Center and left might ape Marxist terms when dealing with continental European colleagues. Their tone was condescending, as toward a theoretical system they hadn't bothered to study because it was pedantic, dogmatic, and—let's face it—un-British.

To me the Russian revolution was doubly foreign. The country and its ways were more remote than the furthest reaches of Africa and Asia—of which I'd heard from missionaries and other agents of the far-flung British empire. The Bolsheviks were not only Russian in many allusions, they also used Marxist terms that had been carefully censored from me.

The very word "revolution" was disreputable to British ears. It was "going a bit far." Why can't those chaps be civilized like we are? Our police don't even carry guns. We settle things by voting. That's why we've never had a revolution and never will. When the Bolsheviks went on to speak of "proletarian dictatorship," that was going a bit too far!

Yet one big idea was clear even to a native New Zealander from the wilds of Waipawa. A hideous tyranny—byword the world over for dire oppression—had been overthrown, and the workers of factory and farm proclaimed on top. They'd bow no more to czars or feudal lords—or capitalists either, they added—

but try to run the country for those who did its useful work. Some years later, in the dark hayloft of a North Dakota farm, I was one of a harvest crew that started to talk about the Russian Revolution. A big impassive Finn, who seldom spoke, suddenly chuckled out: "In Roossia, rich man work!"

To my youthful confusion, the Fabians had offered soothing language smooth to the coddled taste. I started with the *Fabian Essays* of Sidney and Beatrice Webb, H.G. Wells, George Bernard Shaw, Annie Besant, as compiled by the Fabian Society. The Fabians took their name from the Roman general Fabius Cunctator (the Delayer), who avoided decisive battle, trying gradually to wear down the enemy. They aimed to make socialism respectable in England, shunning "shocking" words and ideas, particularly Marxist ones. They rejected revolution in favor of evolution. They produced a made-in-Britain socialism so vague that almost any step might be said to lead to it—a great convenience for Labor party politicians.

Parliamentary democracy, the Fabians held, opened the door to socialism . . . already here in post office, schools, sewers, power, and light. As public ownership proved its benefits, Britons would vote to extend it to more industries and services, until Britain became a socialist country. To the workers, their unions and cooperatives, and especially their party, the Fabians paid the respect due to likeliest sponsors. But they shunned a class approach. Capitalists (to be well compensated) should also see the light and come to vote for socialism. The civil service, by public-spirited efficiency, could do more for socialism than any other group.

The tranquilizers and bland diet of Fabianism could not long appease the appetites of my impetuous youth. Nor could I quite see our ruling class (the term meant something to a Harrovian if not to a Fabian) yielding gently to a democratic decision for real socialism. My sympathies soon turned to the wild men of labor, the ginger groups, the "Bolshies."

I began to explore radical thought, from the Guild socialism of G.D.H. Cole to the anarchism of Kropotkin and interpretations of Russian Bolshevism by Nikolai Bukharin and R.W.P. Postgate. Gradually I got an inkling of Marxian ideas on the class structure of society, historical materialism, the working class. With British insularity, I got it at secondhand, only later turning to the writings of Marx, Engels, Lenin.

One concept took deep root—that the working class was the class with most reason to challenge capitalist power and most capable of achieving power itself. Yet in England, of all countries, anti-Marxism had largely suppressed this simple idea. Here was a clearly defined working-class majority, highly organized in unions, cooperatives, a labor political party. It lacked only a consciousness of class power and purpose . . . unlike the class-conscious ruling classes I knew so well.

Having decided to recognize the working class, however, the earnest would-be socialist of Oxford faced a personal problem. How to identify with a class to which he didn't belong?

It wrenched the imagination to link Oxford's budding socialists with any kind of labor. Pink-faced, soft-handed, lankily awkward, they were too academic, unpractical, work-shy, to know a nut from a bolt.

This never failed to amuse the Tory undergrads, who made the zealous Laborite the butt of much Common-Room humor . . . about "loving labor but hating work," or socializing with the "lower class." To the Tories, that was as thinkable as social equality between black and white to American white southerners. I recall one red-faced defender of British tradition protesting: "You wouldn't want your sister to marry a navvy (laborer)!"

The only workers with whom Oxford undergrads came in regular contact were in the service trades—notably the men servants ("scouts") who cleaned their rooms, made beds, fetched food, and waited on them. The Tories deemed it the cream of the jest to josh the Labor neophyte on his behavior toward his scout. This got under the skin of some and led to embarrassing efforts to get scouts to sit down and talk, to stay to tea as well as bring it. The Tories claimed the scouts resented both the "familiarities" and the "socialist talk."

My own labor contacts were simpler and more rewarding. There was in Oxford a labor college, Ruskin College. Supported by philanthropists of the Workers Education Association, Rus-

kin was not Marxist like WEA's rival, the National Council of
Labor Colleges. But its students were workers who came from
the unions and were supposed to return to them.

Through Ruskin friends, I came to join the Independent
Labor party, engage in strike activities, and find interests more
absorbing than conventional Oxford life. Most Ruskin men were
"political." That is, food, sex, sports, personal affairs, didn't absorb all their attention. They read and talked eagerly of the
mighty urgencies of a changing world, of labor doings in Britain,
of the revolutionary wave sweeping Europe.

I spent my 1920 summer on the continent, knowing enough
French, German, and Italian at least to read posters and papers
and to get some idea about the spreading strikes and incipient
revolutions.

While I was in Italy, the workers occupied the factories. I
saw red flags—and some black flags of the anarcho-syndicalists—
flying over many plants. I saw company names painted over, and
signs that these were now "socialist factories" of "the people" or
"the workers." "Evviva Lenin," "Evviva il Rivoluzione," were
among the slogans scrawled everywhere.

These Italian takeovers preceded by 15 years the American
sitdown strikes that accompanied and assured the birth of CIO.
The Italian workers went beyond the limited CIO objective of
closing down plants till a strike was won. They tried to keep their
plants in operation. The idea spread that this was the social revolution.

Excitedly I scanned the Italian labor papers—rightwing Socialist, leftwing Socialist (no Communist party yet), trade
union, anarchist. In the plants solidarity and revolutionary fervor
ran high. I saw the faces at the windows, the demonstrations of
support. I heard the cheering, the singing of Bandiera Rossa and
the Internazionale. In the leaders' press, confusion and division.
Rightwing leaders urged evacuation. The anarchists talked revolution with vague flamboyance. Union leaders urged holding out
for certain demands. Leftwing Socialists added political to economic demands and projected hazy "revolutionary perspectives."

A united, determined, disciplined workers' revolutionary
party, it seemed to me, with the popular support evident in the
1920 upheaval, might have turned Italy toward socialism. As it

was, Premier Giolitti, "the Fox," found an easy henhouse to raid. Wheedling, bribing, conceding, compromising, Giolitti got the workers out of the plants. Immediately their display of power was deflated like a pricked balloon.

Meanwhile, Benito Mussolini was waiting offstage for his big ham act. I barely noted Italian press items about black-shirted rowdies, calling themselves Fascisti, who marched around pulling stunts like those of latter-day American Nazis. Once restored to command, the scared capitalists opened their coffers to this crew. Two years later, Mussolini marched on Rome—over the prostrate body of a divided labor movement.

That same summer, while I was abroad, British trade union-ists were setting up Councils of Action and threatening a general strike, to block armed intervention against the Soviet Union.

Those were stirring times. At Oxford, the events made less stir than the spoons in ten thousand teacups between four and five. The university was relapsing into its agelong somnolence.

Each morning I devoured the papers for exciting news. To the library I went for interpretive articles and books. Out Iffley Road I hiked to a little socialist bookstore for radical papers . . . among them those of jostling rivals in the newly forming communist movement. My head full to bursting of vital news and views, I looked for someone to discuss them with. I tired of stale undergrad reactions:

The Tory: "Oh, I say, old chap, you have got it bad! Why don't you get a red tie and a soapbox? Did you hear the latest one about the Bolshies nationalizing women? It seems Margot Asquith——"

The Liberal: "This stuff will all blow over. Always happens after wars, till people settle down again. I don't even bother to read about it."

The Laborite: "Hm-m-mn . . . yes, indeed. May be a lot to what you say. Good thing British workmen aren't so excitable . . . too much common sense. Of course, I suppose you can't blame those blokes on the continent——"

So off to Ruskin College I'd flee . . . to young men really interested in these events, and eager and able to discuss them. Not all were. I began to identify labor types. Some were flabby, inhibited, looking outside labor for their future. Others tried cautiously to toe the line of their union sponsors. But the positive ones were positive indeed. I recall three.

Red was a short, wiry, volcanic, Durham miner. (His actual nickname was Ginger—not girlish in England, but suggesting a spunky redhead.) Red usually wore a scarf over collarless shirt, in deliberately working-class style. When he wore a tie, it was a flaming red.

Unlike other Ruskinites, mostly reserved, Red tried to shock. He'd barge into Labor Club meetings pugnaciously glaring around, and take the floor repeatedly. Red's line was far left —or so he intended. He denounced the capitalists and all their minions, including bourgeois undergrads, whose soft parasitism he contrasted with the workers' university-of-hard-knocks. Given to passionate armswinging outbursts, he'd look around elated at the wild applause . . . until he realized it was Oxonian irony and restrained himself.

On the whole, Red was taken seriously. To Tories and Liberals, he was the wild-eyed agitator, the Bolshy, who sent shivers down the bourgeois spine. To Oxford Laborites, he was an emotional extremist needing to be restrained by people like themselves. Malcolm MacDonald frequently invited him to his tea parties and seemed to be making headway with him.

Red's harshest critics were Ruskin mates who tagged him a showoff, knowing little, thinking less, and lining up with the reformist right in a showdown. His behavior, they said, was inverted fawning on the bourgeoisie.

If Red was a phony, who then, I asked, was a real red? Another Ruskinite, L.M. Cox, was pointed out. A Welch coal miner, he was broad-shouldered, solidly muscular, bigger than most miners. A boxer or football player, one might think, but for a rugged, bespectacled face serious to the point of grimness. Cox was studious—usually with books under his arm. He rarely spoke at the Labor Club, and then but briefly, to make a limited point. On social occasions, he didn't mix readily.

Other Ruskinites called Cox a thinker, who had the political answers, or would try to work them out with you. A practical socialist and revolutionary. Why wasn't Cox in the ILP then, I asked, and more vocal on the left? I was told he'd come to Ruskin for education denied him by a working-class childhood; that he set little stock on Oxford undergrad goings-on; that the party he was interested in was the coming Communist party.

Of all the reputed "Bolshies," Cox was the first actual communist I met. From across the Atlantic in later years, I read frequent mention of his name, both as a communist and as a writer on working-class life.

My third Ruskinite, Bob Johnson, was also headed in the communist direction. He was as smooth as the other two were roughhewn. Bob was a machinist—at work a shop steward of the Amalgamated Society of Engineers (later Amalgamated Engineering Union). He was easy-mannered, quiet in dress and behavior. Friendly and ready to listen, he had a soft-sell approach. Bob was my sponsor, leader, political nurse, in the ILP branch.

International affiliation was then much at issue. The Second International had broken down in the First World War, with German, British, and other parties each supporting their own imperialists. The Second's social democrats had also opposed social revolution after the war—even, as in Germany, turning guns against workers' uprisings. Inspired by the Russian Revolution, many socialist parties were now joining the communists in a Third International.

In my branch, Bob led the fight for ILP affiliation with the Third International. He was well-informed and persuasive, but couldn't prevail over caution and apathy. None answered Bob's arguments, and many said privately they agreed with him. But pressures from the top prevailed, and Bob was voted down. Years later, after most of its lefts had joined the Communist party, the ILP disposed of the issue with a "$2\frac{1}{2}$ International."

A bus strike finally got our rather ingrown branch out of its shell, with Bob in the lead. The strike shook up Oxford. It intruded on teatime talk. It disturbed academic composure. Few undergrads patronized the buses, but all missed the bumblebee buzz of the lumbering two-deckers. Labor Club members were active in support. The Tory crowd—denouncers of strikes—were squeamish about this little one on their doorstep, and the poverty-line wages it protested. The Liberals were liberal.

At one open-air rally, I heard a speaker with an American accent. With strong and serious face, he looked and lectured like an embryo college president . . . but did it on a strike soapbox. He was one to deplore strikes, but this one he felt compelled to support—with thoughtful counsel anyhow. He was Felix Morley, a Rhodes scholar, later prominent as editor and author in the United States, maturing from youthful liberal to conservative spokesman.

My strike chores gave me entrance into union meetings and workers' homes. As an outside sympathizer, I was welcomed but treated with reserve. I hated being an outsider. I envied the comradeship of those who, sharing a common lot, were joined in common struggle. The union branch chairman—a tall, mustached bus driver who developed from diffidence into effective strike leadership—kept calling me "sir." It rankled.

I'd chosen sides—the workers' side. Some reasons:
- It seemed a lousy deal that those who did the hardest work should have the hardest lot—while employers, landlords, businessmen, coupon-clippers, got away with the swag.
- In the microcosm of a strike, I'd seen organization, comradeship, discipline, mutual aid, emerging to good social purpose.
- Out of the workers' struggles—and the capacities they developed—the power should come to transform society, to make it serve the needs of the many rather than the profits of the few.
- Ruling classes up to now had fattened on poverty, exploitation, colonialism, imperialist aggression, and war. The working class coming to power should have no comparable interest.

But having chosen sides, what was I going to do about it?

My undergrad friends looked to careers in professions suited to their background and education—in capitalist institutions, under ruling-class direction. On the side, they hoped discreetly to further their social ideals. Gently but aptly they kidded me on the vehemence with which I was determined to devote my life, I didn't know how, to doing I didn't know what, for a movement to which I didn't belong.

From the feeling of not belonging germinated a fantasy, a

daydream. What if I actually could belong to the movement as a worker myself?

In the English circles of my upbringing, socially hard-and-fast lines were drawn around the working class. I'd look ridiculous, I felt, if I tried to cross them. Continental Europe was as bad. In the colonies, "gentlemen" sometimes did manual work; they didn't become workers. Then there was the United States. . . .

A Canadian socialist friend told me class lines were often crossed in the United States. A student might work his way through college on manual jobs. To work with one's hands even brought kudos. The pioneers had done it before becoming landowners and capitalists and sending their sons to Harvard and Yale. Politicians bragged of past calluses.

American students at Oxford were the first to whom I broached my dream of becoming a worker. The English reacted as I expected. They were incredulous. They suppressed their mirth or laughed outright. "You? Ridiculous!" The Americans didn't bat an eyelid.

Not all the Americans understood my motives. Art Mosk, for instance: "Bully idea, old man! Start at the bottom. Learn your business in a practical way. You'll soon be on the way up." Felix Morley was more abstract. I doubt he "concretized" what I had in mind. He suggested I might find the *Nation* and *New York Times* better for my study of the United States than the *Liberator* and Socialist Labor party literature I'd picked up in England.

Daniel DeLeon and his SLP, incidentally, seemed to impress Britishers more than Americans. To many ILP socialists, he offered the first Marxist-angled offset to their own imprecise ideologies. In Washington in the Forties, New Zealand's Labor Premier Peter Fraser wanted at once to discuss DeLeon with me when he learned of my CIO connection.

S. Stephenson Smith, a Rhodes scholar from Oregon, readily got my point, though not agreeing with it. Experience of working-class life was important, he conceded, in devoting oneself to the labor movement. But one didn't have to get it at first hand. "There are plenty of ways of getting it vicariously," he said. With western directness, Smith said that in the United

States I could do exactly what I had in mind. He saw nothing screwy or romantic about wanting to live the part you wish to play; about matching belief with action, theory with practice.

Smith gave me practical advice, and three introductory letters. These were my only links between old world and new when, in early spring of 1921, I brushed from me the cobwebs of Oxford and emigrated to the United States.

In leaving, I cast one backward glance. Having scraped through "Moderations" with enough honors to continue my scholarships, I was expected to go on to "Greats"—still Latin-Greek classical, with emphasis on philosophy. My tutor told me I was now free to drop classics, as I wanted, and suggested I look into "Modern Greats." I did—with an errant thought I might study Marxism. The reading lists dispelled it. Dozens of readings from anti-Marxist books; none on the Marxian side, except for a section of Marx's *Capital* on British working-class conditions during the Industrial Revolution, included as a historical reference.

My backward glance didn't turn me into a pillar of salt; it did harden my heart against staying in this academic Sodom-Gomorrah.

There was just to pack and go. The "packing" meant disposing of all trappings of my bourgeois past. A self-made proletarian, I intended to take with me only a small light suitcase of personal effects. Books? All had to go. I assigned them to the least book-loving of my friends, with a lingering thought to get them back if ever I recrossed the Atlantic and class lines. Clothes? Disdainfully my scout consented to dispose of them. One item alone had value—a quite new dinner-jacket suit.

Mosk was interested. We were of like size and shape. He offered to buy my tuxedo, though advising me to take it along. "We're as formal as the English on lots of occasions," he said. I told him I wanted to join the working class, not to preserve my bourgeois identity; evening clothes would be inappropriate. Mosk was confused, but unconvinced. He muttered something about "plumbers making more money than. . . ." So, before my intimates, I swore an oath that if ever again I wore this "emblem of the ruling class," I did hereby disown the person who would bear my name.

The radical press was then indignantly spoofing union leaders who affected upper-class ways. Rightwing J.H. Thomas, Railwaymen's leader, had been photographed at the Ascot races in gray topper, frock coat, and other super-toff gear. Frank Hodges, Miners' leader, had spoken at Oxford in formal tails-and-stiff-shirt—to Red's disgust. I anticipated the worst, and was not surprised when in 1923 Hodges, as fraternal delegate to the AFL convention, set its redbaiting red-purge tone with a virulent anticommunist speech; and later joined the employers, as director of several companies.

Later, in the United States, my class interpretation of the tuxedo got this much support. While I was working for the Brotherhood of Locomotive Engineers in Cleveland, my Canadian socialist friend of Oxford days visited me. He pointed to a nearby office window which mine overlooked. "In that office," he said, "Art Mosk is working for the Chamber of Commerce. He had 'American-Plan,' open-shop, antiunion slogans, and literature all around him. And, d'you know, when I visited him yesterday at his house, he was dressed for dinner in your tuxedo."

Alas for my oath and my interpretations—the time was to come when, as a Washington newspaperman, I got and wore another tuxedo . . . to attend a reception at the Soviet embassy.

I missed the grand entrance to the New World . . . New York harbor, Statue of Liberty, world-famous skyline. My old tub, the all-steerage S.S. *Haverford*, full of east European immigrants, entered miles of greasy brackish water with naught to lift the eyes, and landed me at Philadelphia.

While the ship pitched and tossed for two weeks on and off course over a stormy North Atlantic, rumors of revolution had reached us. When we left England, the Miners had been locked out, and Railway and Transport Workers were ready to strike in sympathy. In midocean word spread—supposedly from telegraph messages the ship picked up—that a Triple Alliance strike had become a general strike, and then a revolution. Some said British

Soviets of Workers and Soldiers were installed in the Houses of Parliament. Others more vaguely passed the word that England had gone socialist, with labor on top and the rich and toffs skedaddling.

Actually, the big strike was called off at the last moment in what was called the Black Friday fiasco. Key leaders in the "betrayal" were well-dressed J.H. Thomas and Frank Hodges—the latter repudiated by his own union.

Passengers and crew I talked with were matter-of-fact about the assumed revolution.

"It had to happen. I always said it would. It'll be a good thing for the poor people."

"Won't mean much to my folks. They been doing all right anyhow."

"I don't know. If I gotta be robbed, I'd as soon a rich bloke did it. He's got his already—not so greedy as some of them union leaders. . . ." This from a crew member, bitter at his union's leader Havelock Wilson.

"Come off it, 'Arry! This is the revolution . . . any robbin' to be done, we'll do it." General laughter.

The only American, a Boston streetcarman returning from an old-country visit: "You can't blame them, the way things are there. But I don't think it'll happen in America. A man's got more chance to get ahead."

At Philadelphia, the immigration formalities, in a barracksy building, were hard and bare . . . in 1921 still largely perfunctory. I walked downtown from the docks. A long walk past warehouses, factories, slums. No antilitter measures then. Paper scraps whirled in the wind. Eddying dust choked my throat. Decaying debris stank in the gutters. Gobs of spittle and snot shone slimily. An ugly, dirty country it seemed.

My heart sang as I strode along. I hadn't looked for streets paved with gold, gutters flowing with milk and honey. I sought no asylum from persecution. A refugee from unearned ease and privilege, I'd fled a land I deemed more free and democratic (though little enough) than the United States.

I was a Daniel entering a capitalist den. I knew of America's wealth, her millionaires, moneymaking chances, higher wages. I'd also heard of Elbert Gary's 12-hour day in steel, of "Cossacks" riding down strikers, of huddled slums, lynchings of black people, the Ludlow massacre.

I'd come to join the working class in a country where class struggle was more brazenly brutal than in England or New Zealand. To enter it by way of prisonlike warehouses and plants, past overflowing slums, through dust and dirt . . . wasn't that a fitting baptism for my new life?

As I marched into the hinterland of darkest America, all I had was the clothes I wore, the underwear in my grip, the $50 I'd had to show to immigration. How much more proletarian, thought I, can one get? I was to find out.

I moved on to New York. Fascinated by the strange sights, sounds, smells, tastes, and behaviors of this amazing city, I soon squandered my $50 sampling its novelties. Then for the first time, I was up against the problem of how to eat without money or job.

I thought of my three letters. One was to a man on the Seattle *Union Record*. Another to a Chicago labor editor, of the *New Majority*. The third contact fortunately was closer—Frank Tannenbaum, of New York.

Tannenbaum was a swarthy young man, cordial and first-naming at once. A graduate of the lower East Side's school of hard knocks, he had earlier won fame and prison by leading homeless unemployed into churches. He was now enjoying more formal education, and was to become author of many books of social content.

Just married to a charming young girl, Tannenbaum was exuberant. After treating me to a dinner that filled a two-day gap, hand-in-hand and starry-eyed they walked me up Broadway to the Capitol theater, then the latest and fanciest showplace for the populace. I exclaimed at the theater's glittering delights. "Only in America," Frank enthused, "can ordinary common people get all of this—and all for 35 cents."

He and I were like lighted ships that pass in the night and blare friendly greetings. Tannenbaum was on his way from poverty to higher education in a land of boundless opportunity for the smart, the white, the lucky. "Ideas, ideas, ideas!" he exulted. "That's what I want to live with. There's the world I want to explore." I was headed in the other direction. I'd left a world of ideas—ideas of a privileged class, I felt. I wanted to explore the world he'd known and was happy to leave.

Because we were headed in opposite directions, I found it hard to signal how dire was my need of a job. Tannenbaum said he couldn't help, but he'd make me an appointment with someone who might, Dr. Horace Meyer Kallen of the New School for Social Research.

Tannenbaum must have given me an undeserved buildup. For the next day, in Dr. Kallen's office, I found myself an unworthy exhibit of Oxford learning amid some really learned Americans. I blushfully disremember the discussion, and how I tried to get it down to my earthly need. Even when it edged down from the stratosphere, it orbited in the academic atmosphere of college appointments.

At last I forced a splashdown . . . that I wanted any old job I could eat on. Then—not that it gave me any satisfaction—it was I who had the wise men of Gotham on the defensive. There was silence—broken only by the tapping of pipes and one discreet withdrawal. Someone hazarded:

"Maybe he could become a newsy?"

I quaked to think of selling papers on New York's streets . . . shy as I was, with Oxford accent, still mystified by American money. Bravely I asked what to do, where go, whom see, to be a newsy. Again silence—broken by someone else remembering an appointment.

In the end Dr. Kallen—human and direct with one in need —rescued me. He gave me a letter to Mr. Edward Brentano, of the bookshop firm.

Mr. Brentano was in conference. His secretary referred me to a superintendent, who soon asked the dread What-can-you-do question and gleaned from my evasions the real answer Nothing-at-all. He firmly advised me there was "no suitable position" for one with my background; and even a less suitable floor-boy job at $15 a week was not for such as me.

Realizing past privilege could be a handicap, I thereafter found virtue—in line with my intent—in going through the same routines as any other penniless immigrant. Pounding the pavement. Help-wanted ads and signs. Turndown after turndown, in a time of much unemployment. Getting hungrier and hungrier—until I dropped on the sidewalk.

Like other immigrants (supposedly), I finally got my break. The police picked up my unconscious body and took it to Bellevue Hospital. There I got free bed and board, and when I emerged, a steer that landed me in a busboy job at a YWCA cafeteria at $7 a week, with meals.

My next job jumped me to $17 a week—without meals, alas —as an office clerk for the Onyx Hosiery Company, on Broadway. It was pretty soft. Secure on a regular salary, I began to enjoy American life. I made friends, paid visits, went to meetings and shows, made labor contacts.

But it was a comedown from my purpose. I had to do something about it.

During this clerical interlude, I found a mentor in Frank Anderson. A lanky, pale-faced westerner, he was a researcher at the Bureau of Industrial Research . . . who quickly let you know he'd once been a lumberjack.

With Frank I took long walks through the New York I wanted to know—East Side slums, Bowery, Harlem, radical centers, scenes of labor unrest and activity. He introduced me to labor educators, editors, lawyers, economists at the Civic Club. I best recall the brooding presence of Dr. W.E.B. Du Bois, a natural center around whom others revolved.

This was the heyday of the needle trades as unions of social significance. Clothing was the city's largest industry. It had grossly sweated swarms of immigrants from eastern Europe. When these began to organize and strike, they showed a fighting spirit hard to match. Their leaders—largely Jewish—included refugees from czarist tyranny who had learned about organization in a revolutionary socialist movement.

It was a dynamic combination—extreme exploitation, fighting spirit, radical leadership. The great strikes were emotional, inspirational, with some messianic preaching of socialism. Liberals rallied to them, against the venomous attacks of redbaiting reaction. The Amalgamated Clothing Workers, Ladies Garment, Fur Workers, Cloth Hat, Cap & Millinery, and other unions broke through to success this way.

The new-unionism wave after the 1889 London dock strike and the American CIO in the Thirties both showed that successful union revivalism is not narrowly trade-conscious. It is class-conscious in the sense of promoting the cause of all workers. It is a breakthrough favorable to new ideas, new tactics, new forms of union and political activity. In the early Twenties, the needle unions were showing these signs.

But the socialist movement was weak and badly split. A rightwing was veering, through anticommunism, toward abandonment of socialist ideas. A leftwing was heading toward the embryo communist movement. Needle union leaders, and liberals flocking to them, looked wistfully toward Britain—wishing they had an American counterpart to its union-based Labor party.

In education, research, public relations, health, welfare, culture, the needle unions were alert and pioneering. They welcomed expert outside help. Many of the Civic Club members worked directly or indirectly for them. Most were competent and intelligent, less interested in money than in labor as a cause. They were the so-called "intellectuals of the labor movement" . . . and some unduly self-conscious about this role.

The intellectuals wanted to extend the scope of their labor services. But unlike the more radical Jewish union leaders, the Tammany-type, Irish-Catholic leaders of other New York unions had no use for them. They saw them as pinkos, reds, or meddling do-gooders—butting into job areas reserved for relatives or deserving henchmen of incumbent officers. As old line business unionists, they were uninterested in new techniques.

Even in the unions that welcomed them, the intellectuals suffered some expert needling. The Jewish leaders had intellectual pretensions themselves, setting undue stock on formal education, envying the college-trained. There was malice in the kidding they used to put intellectuals in their place—a place far removed from competition for union leadership.

So there was much emotion, if little real issue, in the many discussions of the time on "the intellectual in the labor movement." A real issue might sometimes sneak in, however, as to how far unions should be narrowly trade-conscious, economist, or more broadly social and political, if not class-conscious—and so subject to more mental stress.

After my soft spell in New York, I had to find a way of reverting to my original purpose. Frank Anderson suggested I do like Powers Hapgood, a Harvard man who'd wanted to become integrated in the labor movement. Young, strong, adventurous, Hapgood broke away by "bumming around the country." Going from one labor job to another, he ended up as a coal miner.

I had no idea what bumming-around meant. In English slang "bum" meant butt, rump, arse; it was indelicate to inquire. After Frank introduced me to Powers, I gathered that both had somehow traveled in the trucks of goods trains—called "freight cars" in the United States.

"Do they charge a lower fare?" I asked.

The two laughed. "No, nothing at all."

I was puzzled. English goods trains carried only crew or men in charge of animals. Powers hadn't been so employed. Frank said I needed no job to "ride the freights"; it was known as "beating your way." This must be illegal—trespassing at least. My friends didn't look like lawbreakers.

Bashful about my ignorance, I hesitated to ask direct questions but hinted I'd like to hear more about this curious method of travel. Frank and Powers responded readily with much talk about hopping freights, riding the blinds, riding the rods; about gondolas, flats, boxcars, empties, cabooses; about brakies, shacks, hoggers, dicks, bulls, boes.

The words were less familiar than Greek to me. One point I got, that thousands of workers headed in this way for western harvest fields each year, and anyone could join them. This, thought Frank, might introduce me to working-class life. I could pick up labor jobs, wash dishes if hungry. After harvest, I'd have a stake to last till I got a steady job.

How to get started? Powers suggested I go to the Bowery and get a railroad job agent to ship me out as a gandydancer (track laborer). After this much start westward, I could start hopping the freights. My talk with Powers was brief. It left me with some confusing questions about which Frank was rather vauge. One thing I had to know.

"If I go to a Bowery job agent like this and ask him to ship me out on a labor job, won't he just laugh?"

Frank looked at my stiff straw hat, white shirt, well-pressed summer suit, pink face, soft white hands . . . and he laughed.

"First thing to do," he said, "is to buy a blue workshirt and pair of overalls. Then——" He was off with practical advice.

As we parted, Frank had an afterthought. "A brand new shirt and overalls may make you conspicuous. Better soak the overalls and muss them up."

Two days later, I'd cashed my last check from the Onyx Hosiery Company. I had made a scouting trip to the Bowery. I'd soaked and mussed my new workclothes, adding a little mud—a touch of my own. Early in the morning, without shaving (another touch of mine), I sneaked out avoiding the landlady. I'd paid my rent, but I was self-conscious about my overalls.

As I walked down the Bowery, my knees buckled. My breath was hard to control. There was a tightening in my diaphragm. There was no turning back.

Chapter Two

RIDING THE RAILS

*In harvest fields and camps, the fame of the
Wobblies lingered on. From them came the
one-union ideas, the songs, the spirit of class
struggle and rank-and-file democracy that
CIO inherited.*

I slung pick and shovel over my shoulder as I saw the
other men do. I carried them to the toolshed and dumped them,
as they did. I joined them in the half-mile hike back to camp
—and tried to walk like they did.

There was the rub. Stiff overalls scraped tender skins. Muscle rubbed muscle. Knees wobbled. Feet dragged. I couldn't
match their stride.

"Ahi, paisano!" an Italian shouted back. "You okay?"

"Just a bit stiff." I grinned. "I'm okay."

Okay I was. My limp was a triumphal march. I couldn't
stretch my fingers. Red spots showed on burning, blistering
palms. These hands the commissary man had taken in his and
chuckled, "You won't last a day!" I had. I'd lasted a full 10-hour
day of steady pick-and-shovel work. At 40¢ an hour, I'd earned
$4—by the toil of my hands and the sweat of my brow.

That last day in New York, I didn't go to a railroad agent,
but to a job shark with a sign, "Laborers Wanted for Road
Work." He didn't care what I looked like or could do. He sized
me up—correctly—for six bucks. I also paid railroad fare to New
Milford, Pennsylvania.

The camp was a few miles out of town. An abandoned
farmhouse where we were fed, a big barn where the laborers
slept. As bidden, I reported to the commissary man—big, fat,

aproned, greasy. I'd feared rejection, but he liked my looks, my hands, my fee receipt . . . $3 of it for him, I guessed.

The first day it was enough to survive. Then came the problem of getting by. We were removing dirt for highway leveling. The few-score laborers were Italians, recent immigrants. They laughed at my awkwardness, as they gave me tips on handling pick and shovel; on softening up imbedded stones and roots; on varying routines, water-trips, comfort-stops, to last through the day.

The American foreman was not amused. Trying to get production out of me, he put me next to an Italian boy of 15 and said I ought to do at least as well as the kid. I didn't. The boy was stocky and muscular. He applied exactly enough effort, but no more, to each motion. He worked with a rhythm I couldn't match.

The foreman didn't yell at me, nor was he friendly. His tone was different than toward the Italians. The American bosses barked at the Italians like top sergeants. If they condescended to relax with them, it was in the manner familiar to me of "superiors" patronizing "inferiors," and would sooner or later include a sharp reminder not to presume. With the American craftsmen there was some social equality, some joshing fro as well as to. The drifter who came to camp for a meal more than a job, if he was white and spoke American, was addressed in the same kind of tone I was. It implied: "You may be a bum or a dumb punk, but at least you're one of us."

How did the Italians feel about things? They spoke little English, but I had a smattering of Italian. I heard them gripe less than the Americans—more used to rough treatment perhaps, and consoled by what they saw as a great chance to make money. We worked six full 10-hour days, with only Sunday off. None shared my wish for some time off on Saturday. Some wished we could work Sunday too—a wasted day, hanging around camp or a strange, dead, small town. Better to add another $4 to our $18 a week ($24 less $6 for board). They loved to calculate how much they made in Italian money—looking forward to spending it in Italy, for a well-fed sociable life among warm, kindly people.

The few American-speaking workers in camp were much grimmer. The truck and equipment operators lived or lodged in town, but with the drifters who came and went we were enough to make a group of our own around an outside fire. Here the men laughed and kidded less than the Italians, and cussed much more. They hated the super, the strawbosses, above all the commissary man . . . the "belly-robber," suspect as in most camps of being paid much more for food than the cost of the hog-swill he served. Pie-in-the-sky for these Americans was more in the past than the future. They liked to brag how much money they'd made during the war, and how lavishly they'd thrown it around on broads and booze.

One angle to the talk made me prick up my ears.

There was a new drifter in camp. Beating his way in from the west, he said. He was sun-baked, tall, rangy—automatically addressed as Slim. He cussed the swill and asked how things were. We told him.

"You know what you need here?" said Slim, reaching for his Bull Durham.

"Yeah?" we encouraged. He rolled a cigarette and spat into the fire.

"What you need is a bunch of Wobblies should roll into camp."

"What's Wobblies?" asked one of the men.

Slim glared at him. "Where you been all your life? Them's IWWs. You know, Inter . . . Inder . . . aw hell, everybody knows the Wobblies. Workers of the World, or something, except they don't like work."

"Ain't they reds?" the man asked.

"I don't know nothing about that," said Slim. "Nor I ain't no Wobbly myself. Who the hell are you, the camp stoolie?" Slim got up as if to go.

"No offense," said the man. "I didn't know, never been out west."

Slim shot a few expert gobs into the fire, then sat down again.

"I just heard tell about the Wobblies. Any camp they don't

like conditions, they won't work. Yeah, I . . W . . W." He chuckled. "I Won't Work—that's what it should stand for."

Another drifter broke in. "I heard about them. Really
wrecked up some camps, didn't they? What d'you think they'd
do, if they come here?"

"We-e-ell," Slim reflected. "First thing, that there belly-robber . . . They might take and pitch him in the river. Then——"

It was quite a game. Others too had ideas on "wrecking the
camp." What the Wobblies might do, they said. But the IWW
was soon forgotten. Except to the two westerners, it was hardly
even a myth.

I didn't like the talk. It seemed unfair to the IWW. I'd
heard and read a lot about it—as organizer of exploited workers
neglected by the AFL . . . leader of militant strikes and free-
speech fights . . . victim of sadistic acts of suppression. Migratory workers without home or vote—caring little for election politics or the "sewer socialism" of the Socialist party—were drawn
to the IWW. Its direct or job action made more sense to footloose workers always having to change jobs than the prolonged
bargaining and binding contracts of homeguard unions. The ultimate aim was to organize all workers into One Big Union which
should take over and run industry—with no more to be seen of
capitalists and politicians than their heels.

As to "sabotage," that could cover a wide range of tactics—
from the monkey wrench (successor to the French "sabot," or
wooden shoe) in the machine, through British "ca' canny" and
American "go slow," to the "work to rule" tactic of rail unions,
tying up transportation through literal obedience to redtape
rules. Echoes of the Socialist party debate on sabotage had long
since died away, I gathered a reformist wing, including Socialist
officeholders (the "politicians" of IWW contempt), had used
this as a verbal issue to drum out more revolutionary elements
identified with Big Bill Haywood and the IWW.

In any case, if the IWW practiced sabotage—and in later
years it issued disclaimers—it was as an organized tactic for
"striking on the job," not the individual acts of destruction that
conspicuously marked all American struggle, and were usually
done by persons who'd never heard the word sabotage. Yet the
IWW was constantly made a public scapegoat for rough-and-

ready violence linked more to the frontier tradition then to any labor or radical theory.

At the moment, however, I was less interested in spittoon philosophy—as the Wobblies called it—than in getting from the two westerners some tips on beating my way to the harvest.

I lay on the ground near the railroad track, peering through dewdamp foliage at the glistening rays of a rising sun. The moment for action had come, and I was wondering if I was more coward or fool.

Nobody had spelled out just where and how I should board my first freight. Should I keep away from the yards? "Unh-h? Guess so, with you so green." Must I then get on a moving freight? "It's okay to catch her on the fly . . . if you can." I had concluded I must do it away from town where I couldn't be seen, at a spot where freights had to move slowly . . . up a steep hill, for instance.

I'd started out fine. I had a stake of thirty dollars earned on the road job. This I mailed to myself, General Delivery, Buffalo. Aside from a $2 bill sewed into my overalls, I carried only silver change—lest I be frisked while I slept. I shipped my suitcase to Buffalo by American Express. I left camp feeling light and free as a bird.

I headed for the Lackawanna tracks, swinging my arms. Warming up, I took off my coat and slung it over my shoulder, holding its neck in my hand as I'd seen the westerners do. I tried to slouch along as they did. Reaching the tracks, I didn't walk the ties. I followed country roads near the tracks, skirting through woods and fields at times. There were always hills ahead. When I reached them, they seemed to flatten out.

The countryside was new to me and lovely. I enjoyed walking, but by late afternoon I was tired. Coming to the highest hill yet, around which the tracks corkscrewed, I decided this would have to be it. By now I had crossed from Pennsylvania into New York state. At the foot of the thickly wooded hill was a cool blue lake. No sign of house or human. I'd take it easy until dark— have a dip in the lake and a snooze.

Alone with nature, and hungry now, I hunted for berries to eat. I slept on the warm woodsy ground, till the stars winked through the treetops and the earth was no longer warm.

In the daylight I'd seen few freight trains. Now in the still of moonless night I heard afar their bellows, their rush, their rumble. I shivered. They were the strangest of monsters, and I had to mount one. I forced myself up. I pushed through the thicket to the track. As I neared the rails, a tremor ran through them. One of those bellows was at hand, puffing and snorting. Its headlight shot around the curves like flame from a dragon's nostrils. The earth shook before it.

This one, I decided, I'd sit out.

It labored as it mounted the hill. I took courage. Then it was upon me. The roar was deafening. The boxcars swayed dizzily. The speed seemed little abated. I tried to picture myself running alongside, on that uncertain gravel, grabbing for some hardly visible handhold.

I told myself—with little conviction—I'd make the next one . . . after a long time, no doubt. But now I didn't want them, the freights followed one after the other. I didn't like their looks, or their speed. I reconsidered. Why had I waited till dark? Why not wait till daylight?

It wasn't so cozy going back to sleep. Nothing to keep me warm. The damned lake was breathing up a damp mist. It was better at least than trying to grab a freight. I slept.

Now that I was awake, I had no more excuses. The birds chirped carelessly. Green leaves shimmered in the delicate rays of a rising sun. The mist was lowering to the level of the lake. In this beautiful unmindful world, I was a condemned man. Down to the tracks I drove myself. I'd grab the first freight, I ordered. Halfheartedly I ran alongside. Each handhold was beyond reach before I could summon courage to grasp at it.

If condemned, I was self-condemned. Now I set the time for execution. The next one . . . I'd rush and grab it, if it killed me. I rushed. I grabbed. The boxcar kicked back. It pitched me into the ditch. I lay stunned . . . but not too stunned to rise again and savor one solace of defeat. I'd tried. I'd been defeated. I could relax.

Back to the highway of old-style vagabondage. To hell with the freights! Let brasher, fleeter men than I do battle and be bruised.

Happy just to be walking, I headed west—toward Buffalo. No rushing speedways, thruways, freeways then. Tramping along quiet roads I sniffed the greenery, the new-mown hay; harkened to mooing cows, bickering birds, the crow of a tardy rooster. Life lay ahead. I had no appointments. Why not keep on walking? True, I might be a year late for the harvest, but . . .

"Hi there, stranger, want a ride?" Puzzled I looked around. A farmhand in horse-drawn wagon had come out of a side road.

He was as natural, thought I, as the future communist man might be. Between spits of chewing tobacco he talked, easy and friendly. Didn't pry into who I was, what up to. He'd have done the same for anyone. When we parted, I was no longer "stranger." "Goodbye, friend," said he, "and good luck."

I walked on greatly encouraged. The next town was ten miles away—too far to reach by nightfall. I thought to sleep by the way, in a nice warm haystack. Again I was surprised. This time by a truck horn and the driver's voice: "Climb aboard, bud." What a friendly people! In England, they passed the stranger by. Their bourgeois motto, "Mind your own business."

The truckdriver took me two towns further. We had coffee in a diner, and he insisted on paying.

I'd never heard of "hitchhiking." Later I heard hobos talk of "hitting the highway." It was little favored. Too slow and uncertain compared to the freights. My first two rides I held to be a surprising fluke.

It was lonesome and pitch-dark on the country road I took from the town where the truckdriver dropped me. I meant to walk as far as I could before hunting a haystack. No traffic. No sounds but the rustling of trees, some snuffles and snorts from livestock, and the yelps of two dogs barking at each other across the empty spaces.

Or was that all? From far behind, weren't there faint padding sounds? Perhaps some cows on the road. I stopped to listen through the darkness. It was human footsteps, for soon I heard low voices.

I wasn't going to walk through the night with unknown persons behind. Once I might have feared footpads, after my money. But now! What had I to lose? I sat down by the road and waited for the strangers.

Two figures approached, a bigger, a smaller. I stood up and said "Hi!" The bigger lit a match. He looked me over.

"Thought you might be a dick," he said. "Where you headed?"

"Buffalo. How about you?"

"No place in particular. You got the makings?"

I had. Anderson and Hapgood had told me a sack of Bull Durham tobacco and cigarette papers would make me popular on the road. Seeing me as awkward as the kid with him at rolling my own, Buck, a youth around 20, rolled cigarettes for the three of us.

"How you figurin' to get to Buffalo?" he asked.

"By freight," I lied. Lest he ask what then I was doing on that road, I added, "Thought I'd find a haystack to sleep in."

"A haystack! Shi-i-it!" sneered Buck. He tried to spit across the road, but his gob fell feebly short. I was reassured.

"Not that I'd pass up a good hayloft on a cold night," Buck resumed, more conciliatory. He drew the kid aside to whisper with him. When he turned back to me, he was friendly.

"Whaddya say we string along, bud?" he asked. "I got an aunt in Buffalo. The Kid don't care where he goes. We come from Jamestown. I took a rap there. The Kid got throwed out on his ass by his old man. You're green . . . ain't been long in this country. I can put you wise."

With a guide, it was all quite simple. Buck led us to a water tank, where all freights stopped to water up. We didn't take the first one. It had no empty boxcars, and Buck wanted a good sleep. When the next stopped, we walked up and down to pick a boxcar that suited him. A brakeman came within a hundred yards. I nudged Buck and pointed.

"Hell, he don't care," said Buck. "He ain't no bull."

After we climbed in, the brakey passed our open door. We pulled back. He didn't look in.

The floor was hard. I shivered with cold as night went on. We rolled around. Each time the train stopped, it shook us awake. In motion, there was rhythm to its rocking; the yukety-yuk-yukety-yuk of its wheels lulled one easily to sleep. For me a night of high achievement. I'd come a long way from Harrow and the bourgeoisie. Tonight I'd found a magic carpet to carry me fantastically further.

By Buffalo I was a loner again. My two companions vanished the second night. Interested only in my Bull Durham, I thought, and my few nickels for coffee. Then I doubted that much calculation. As we rolled along, legs dangling from boxcar door, we had talked. About food . . . women . . . the Kid about parents. Buck bragged of minor crimes. Showing off. In stealthily slipping away, he might have wanted to look like he was "on a job." I didn't believe it. Aimless was the word. They didn't want to go to Buffalo, or anywhere. Any chance might have diverted them in any direction. Buck too, like the Kid, was running away.

At Buffalo I had money waiting, and clean clothes. I rented a room, filled up on food, took in a show. I started to look for a job. Two places I haunted. A public employment office and the USSB—U.S. Shipping Board, also known as U-Starvation-Son-of-a-Bitch—which controlled hiring on Great Lakes boats and might get me as far as a Lake Michigan port.

In both big bare halls, scores of men sat waiting on hard benches or leaned against walls. Job calls seldom came . . . and then only for a handful chosen by some mysterious system—favoritism, the others said. The unchosen came back day after day and waited hour after hour, showing little interest in the rare job calls. There was no unemployment insurance—not till the late Thirties. One could only hope, or stop hoping, for a job.

I came back too. I tried waiting hour after hour—but with none of the patience of the experienced unemployed. It was intolerable to do nothing for so long in such a bleak setting of human dejection. On the road one could lie down to snooze. There were open air, sunshine, the stars at night. There was movement, and changing scenery.

I shipped my grip and remaining money to Chicago. Off to

the west Buffalo yards I went—this time with some idea of what I was about.

At Ashtabula, Ohio, I got off a New York Central freight before it passed the depot. My clothes were clean when I left Buffalo. I'd washed up at a stop on the way. I thought I could pass muster walking into town. At the depot a burly man in business suit stood apart from the waiting passengers. As I passed, he nudged me with his elbow.

"Where the hell d'you think you're going?" he asked.

"What's it to——?" I stopped. He spoke with authority—and looked it. "Just heading into town for some coffee," I added mildly.

"Yeah? Where you from?"

"Buffalo."

"Where you headed?"

"Cleveland."

The man looked me over. I fidgeted, uncertain. Obviously a railroad bull. He couldn't have seen me getting off the freight. I had my rights. There wasn't anything he could do. Or was there?

"Keep your ass off this railroad. I'm warning you." He turned away.

"Okay, okay, I will. Sure will."

I recognized in my tone a cheerful assent learned from the Italians on the road gang. Bosses demanded you both obey . . . and like it.

As I started off, the bull nodded me back. He put his hand on my arm, almost kindly. After all, as there, I was "one of us"—white, English-speaking.

"Tell you what you do, kid. You know where the Nickel Plate is?" I didn't. He gave me directions to a bridge. "Their freights stop under that bridge. You can make one easy. Now you go and do just that."

I thanked the bull and turned away. He shot after me:

"But keep to hell away from the New York Central!"

By the time I reached Cleveland, I was as furtive as the most nervous hobo. With boxcar door open only a slit, I rode as far as the Old Depot yards on the lakefront. There I kept out of sight, trying to muster courage to go into town. In good shape at Ashtabula, I couldn't pass. Now I had a layer of grime, a rip in my overalls, a drop in my stomach in place of self-confidence. I'd heard the lowdown on cops, from the low down.

"Keep away from that burg, the suckin' cops is awful mean there."

What can they do, I wondered, if you're breaking no law, just walking around out of luck? The answers came before I asked.

In any town, a cop might stop a bo at any time.

How could he tell you were one?

A laugh. They smell it. Then they look at your hands. No calluses, you're a bo, not a working man.

So! What can they do?

Plenty. Take you in for questioning and give you the works. Rough you up right on the street, if they don't like your looks—say you started it. Run you out of town. Vag you (jail for vagrancy). Pin some rap on you, if they need a patsy.

What if you've got enough dough to say you're looking for eats or a room?

A big laugh. Look, if you got any dough, you ain't no bo. Why, for a buck you can buy one of them cops for yourself.

I found a diner near the yards. A cup of coffee and a wash gave me courage. If I had cop trouble in town, I still had enough to blow up to four bits for a flop . . . or maybe a meal and an all-night movie.

I walked to Public Square, then up Euclid Avenue. Bright lights blazed and twinkled. Movie theaters glittered. Delicious restaurants beckoned, their prices sneered. Through well-fed, well-dressed crowds I moved . . . no part of them. Nobody bothered me. A few stared. A plump man came out of a restaurant picking his teeth. He dodged away from me as from a panhandler. I turned back, crossing Public Square to a skid row section west of it. Standing undecided on a corner, I saw a cop coming.

"Hey, you!" He twirled his club. "What d'you think you're up to?"

"Just waiting for a streetcar."

It slipped out . . . typical of hobo retorts—corny, snotty, racy at times, obscene if possible, never servile.

"Wise guy!" sniffed the cop. He turned away but stayed on the corner.

Why not? I thought. Might be worth the price of a coffee-and-sinker. Getting on a streetcar, I waved to the cop and stuck out my tongue. I rode to the end of the line. Then I started walking—due west.

I'd had my bellyful of the freights. But walking wasn't going to get me far. Sooner or later I'd have to head back to them. Was I getting aimless too? Still, walking was a relief. To my right, I heard Lake Erie lapping. I went to the cliff's edge and looked out. The water was sullenly still in the dark, starless night. Once I liked to stroll on the shore at night, poetic, romantic, philosophical. Now I thought about drowning.

I turned back to the road and tried to keep my mind on the houses to my left. Smooth rolling lawns. Trimmed shrubs. Flower beds. Beyond them, lighted living rooms in full view. In an English suburb, blinds would be down, curtains drawn. High hedges would hide the lawns. No passing stranger dare pry into the Englishman's home, his castle.

A table spread for a late meal. A man lounging in armchair, in shirtsleeves and slippers. Children snuggling up—or cutting up. Pampered pets. Comfort, security, affection. It looked good, from the outside.

From the outside—that was it. I was on the outside looking in, for once. I played with the thought. I was playing with life. I didn't have to be on the outside, I'd chosen to be. Even now I might knock on a door and hear a motherly woman say: "Why, under all that dirt, he's just a nice clean cut American boy. John, give him enough for a meal and a room, and have him come to your office tomorrow. We can speak to the minister——"

Or—a glimmer of doubt—might she not take one glance through the window, bolt the door, and call the police to report a prowler?

And suppose I weren't nice, clean-cut, "American." What if I were colored, foreign-speaking, with slum mannerisms? I thought of Stephenson Smith's "vicarious experience." Maybe that was all I could get.

At the moment I wanted a place to sleep—and not vicariously. I walked on and on. No sign of haystack, barn, or empty shed. Then I recalled Anatole France's epigram that the law, in its majestic equality, forbids rich as well as poor to beg in the streets or sleep under bridges. I slept under a bridge.

As I drew closer to Chicago, I had more company—including a partner. He called himself Spike; others called him Squirt, Kid, Punk. We boarded our last freight to Chicago in the Fort Wayne yards. I closed the boxcar door. Squirt opened it and stuck out his head.

"Hey, Limey," he called. "Get a load of this."

Blinking into the sunlight, I saw a man in a straw hat. I pulled back fast. "Go on, look," said Squirt. "He ain't no bull, he's a bo. Can you feature that lid!"

It was a new stiff straw, worn at a cocky angle, a la Maurice Chevalier . . . a Chevalier in overalls!

Came the thud up front, and the jolt ran back from car to car. Just before our door jerked shut, I saw the man break from a stroll to a lope.

"Whaddya bet he lost that lid climbin' aboard?" said Squirt. He rolled the door back and sat down, legs dangling. "Now I seen everything."

"Ain't as funny as you sleepin' in that broken-down buggy," said I.

"Look who's talkin'," he jeered. "You sleepin' in that coalshed. Now look at ya!"

By the first time we stopped, Squirt and I were tired of talking about hash—any kind, all kinds. My Bull Durham was gone. We'd rolled the last shreds of tobacco from butts Squirt had picked up. We were sitting against the wall, not even looking out, when we heard the gravel crunch. We scrambled for the corners. A straw hat poked in.

"If it ain't The Hat himself!" said Squirt, with a wink at me.

The man stood cool in the sunshine. Around forty, he was the plump kind—if he'd had it softer. For an outdoor stiff, his

face was pale. He looked us over, then walked on. The hog
squealed, and the man turned back. Before the jolt hit our car,
he took off his straw and put it in first. Then he climbed in. His
overalls had a rip, right in the rump.

"Say, Hat," asked Squirt, "you ain't got a coffin-nail or the
makin's?" He wanted to wisecrack, but wasn't too sure of the
guy.

"No, kid, wisht I had," said Hat, not looking up. He was
fussing over his hat, wiping the sweatband, breathing on the
straw to rub off soot.

"Quite a lid you got there," said Squirt. "Headin' for Hollywood?"

Hat plunked his straw on his head and got up. Squirt
backed out of his way. Hat went and spat out the door. Then he
was ready to talk.

"Where you fellers headed?" he asked. To the harvest, I
said, while Squirt gave him one of his stories—the one about his
old man working in the Chicago stockyards and might get him a
job. Hat sat down again, and took his hat in his hands as he
talked.

"Me, I got nothin' to worry about. Just had a run of bad
luck. I was doin' fine, money to burn—and more where it come
from. Then I gets to drinkin'. One night I'm rolled by a broad."
Hat puckered his lips, as if thinking. Then he shot a gob of spit
clear across the car and out the door. "Yeah, it musta been her.
Though I didn't remember nothin'. After that, I get vagged in
that lousy burg."

Squirt looked sideways at me. Hat turned on him. "You
heard what I said, kid. Just a vag-rap, that's all." He said it like it
might have been something fancier. Either way, he couldn't fool
Squirt, who never believed anything.

"I didn't say nothin', big shot," said Squirt, deadpan.

Hat's face reddened. "Look here, you punks. I don't have to
take no shit from you. I don't want no stinkin' blood-and-guts
job in the Yards. Nor I ain't gonna break my back pitchin'
bundles . . . like when I was green. I don't have to. I got connections—see?"

"What's your racket, Hat?" asked Squirt.

"Never you mind." Hat cooled off. "Once I hit Chi I'm all set. Soon be in the dough. Look me up and don't act smart, and I'll get you drunk."

We were making good time, across the Indiana flatlands. The sun beat down on the boxcar. What with the heat, the rocking, the yukety-yuk-yukety-yuk, we all got drowsy. Hat was first to stretch out. He wrapped his hat in a newspaper. He rolled up his coat for a pillow. Now we saw the soles of his shoes, they were worn through.

When he dozed off, Squirt had to have his joke. He crept over and made as if to reach for the straw. Hat stirred. Squirt backed up and shuffled back. "Bet he sleeps eyes open to guard his lid," said he.

Asleep or awake, Hat seemed to know what was going on. As soon as Squirt dozed off, he nodded me over to him. He spoke in a low voice:

"Guess you're okay, Limey. I'm gonna let you in on a good thing. You ain't been long enough in this country to know a guy don't have to be on the bum here—not if he's smart and someone shows him the ropes. With me, you can go places. But you gotta ditch that fresh punk partner of yours. Whaddya say, kid?"

"Could be," I said. "What's your angle?"

Hat lay back, not even looking at me. "Ever see them big hotels around the Loop? Pretty soft for them rich bastards. How'd you like to shack up in a . . . 'suite,' they say, with a doll? Ride up Michigan Avenue in a long car, with a big seegar?"

"Sounds okay." I couldn't help yawning. I'd heard lots of that talk on the road—and I hadn't caught much sleep in the coalshed.

The yawn got Hat's goat. He raised up and poked me with a finger.

"See here, Limey. You're still wet behind the ears. I been around. They ain't one of them bastards got rich by workin'. You know where they got theirs? Took it from the suckers that break their back workin'. Look at that there Squirt . . . thinks he's so smart——"

Squirt was snoring. Hat went on:

"So that punk gets a job in the Yards, like his old man. He works his ass off, but can't save nothing. Comes another depression, all they got is a kick in the pants. I know, 'cause I tried it. But not no more."

"You ain't one of them reds?" I asked. I didn't think so. Most down-and-outers had a radical slant. I had yet to hear some radical conclusions.

"Me? Hell, no," Hat replied. "I always say workin' men got strong backs and weak heads—ain't got sense enough to stick together. I like this country the way it is. A man's got a chance to make good, if he's smart and looks out for hisself. Once you're on top, you got everything."

"How about you and me?" I asked, wishing he'd let me sleep.

"I was comin' to that, kid. Like I said, when I get to Chi, I'm all set. I got connections I can hit up for . . . five or ten bucks, easy. You said you was headin' for the harvest. Maybe that ain't a bad idea."

"But you said you wasn't figurin' on working."

"Nor I ain't. First thing I get is a deck of cards."

"I can't handle cards—never could."

"I don't give a shit. Don't want you to touch 'em—leave that to me. Don't even want you to know me. Get that, kid?" Hat squinted at me, then winked. "We ain't never seen each other before. Get it? You're just a green Limey punk, don't know his ass from a knothole. You don't know nothin'—just our little code. I get a game goin' with some suckers. You happen to mosey up and kibitz. You get it, kid?"

"But who's got any dough beating his way to the harvest?" I wasn't so green I didn't know that.

"They's one born every minute," said Hat, as if he didn't hear me. He lay back, tapping on his hat. Then he lifted his head again.

"So we hire out, to get with a harvest crew. But not for long. Soon as there's hands paid off, we hit the jungles. Then there's pickin's."

My eyes closed. I was half asleep when Hat poked me again. He had another angle. He came at it like a dog sniffing around a post.

"With our stake, Limey, first thing we get is some high-class duds. You ain't a bum no more when you got a fancy suit, Eyetalian shoes, and . . . a hat." He patted his straw. "Take you——"

He propped up his head to look me over. His mouth formed silent words. His face got close . . . I could have thrown up at the stink of his breath.

"You'll look okay . . . when you're all dolled up. There's rich guys goes for a clean-appearin' punk . . . that looks a bit soft——"

"Suck you!" I said. "I ain't so soft."

Hat grinned foolishly. "Take it easy, kid. Don't get me wrong. I'm strictly for the broads, and you ain't no pansy. Nor that ain't my idea of a good racket. Was just showin' there's lots of ways to turn a quick buck."

After he reckoned I'd cooled off, Hat began burbling again:

With our dough from this deal, and all slicked up, we'll head back to Chi . . . ridin' the cushions, by Christ. We'll get one of them suites . . . no more boxcars . . . no more flophouses. We got what it takes. But we ain't blowin' it all, nossir. Once you got dough, there's plenty ways to make more of the same. The more you got, the less chances you gotta take. 'Fore you know it, we'll be buyin' into a nice business . . . strictly on the up and up. We'll be sittin' pretty, kid . . ."

Hat's voice got so dreamy I went to sleep to its drone.

We slept till Gary. Then we slept some more. When next we woke, the train was slowing down in the wastelands outside Chicago.

I thought of Dante's approaches to hell. No green fields. No hills or streams. No life or habitation. Flatlands covered with swamps and trash dumps. Sooty smoke smarted the eyes, dried nostrils and lips. Afar oil-stinking refineries, the hellish glare, the shooting flames of steel mills.

Hat was refreshed. He shook out his jacket and brushed himself off. He polished his hat with his sleeve and stuck it jauntily on his head.

"Chicago, here I come!" he said, as he moved to the door.

Hat stuck out his head, looking for a place to jump. But the train was still moving, and as he held to the side of the door, it picked up speed again. As it rounded a curve, a gust of wind blew off the straw hat. It smashed on the rails and bounced brokenly down the track.

I thought Hat would jump after it. His face was so startled it was comical. Squirt burst out laughing. Even I snickered.

"I knowed that was gonna happen," Squirt chortled. "Never heard of a guy tryin' to beat his way in a straw hat!"

Too licked to snap back, Hat just turned around and sat down. He passed his hand gingerly over the little bald spot on his head as if it were a fresh bump. He muttered some curses, then turned sullen.

When the freight finally came to a full stop outside the yards, we all jumped out and headed for the highway. "Better string out," said Squirt, "we'll never get a ride together." He held back, while Hat and I walked on. After he hooked a ride, I gave Hat a chance for the next one, telling him to stop while I went ahead.

Hat didn't stop. He didn't answer. With his bare head he looked different, slouching along. We got a ride anyhow—in the back of an empty truck. It dumped us half a mile from the Loop. Hat hadn't spoken a word, but as we started walking again, he muttered: "I was just shittin' about being all set in Chicago. Can't hit up no one . . . not the way I look."

We neared the skid row section of South State Street . . . could see the lights of the penny-in-the-slot palaces, the hole-in-the-wall movies, the greasy spoons, the flophouses.

"It's a suckin' shame . . ." Hat had revived enough to start beefing. Suddenly he pulled away and started across the street. He jerked his head for me to follow. When I caught up, he grabbed me with shaky hand.

"For Chrissakes, Hat," I growled, "what's eatin' you?"

"Din't you see that cop starin' at us?" he hissed from the corner of his mouth.

"So what!"

"I'm telling you, kid, them Chicago cops is plenty mean."

"You're askin' for it. Whyn't you pull yourself together?"

"Gawd, what I wouldn't give for a cup of coffee!" groaned Hat.

"I still got enough for that," I told him.

Hat stared at me. "Well, what're we waitin' for?"

When we sat back, the coffee working on us, Hat shook a finger at me and said, "Listen here, kid, I got another angle——"

I laughed outright. Hat looked startled, then grinned sourly. "Aw, what the hell!"

As we left the quick-and-dirty, Hat asked, "Okay, wise guy, what's next?"

"Why not ride up Michigan Avenue in a . . . ?"

"That's it," Hat broke in. "Come on, Limey, I'll show you the sights."

He led me to Michigan Avenue and we turned north. Across from the big buildings on our left were stretches of lawn ringed with shrubbery, with the Illinois Central tracks in back, and beyond them Lake Michigan. It was a warm evening. People lay all over the grass . . . some lovers, some relaxing and cooling off, the rest looking as destitute as we did.

By midnight most of those with homes had left. We stayed on with many who spread out newspapers to lie on and later to use as covers. Hat was soon asleep. I lay listening to the purr and pause of the stream of cars along the avenue . . . watching the lights glimmer or go out in the mountainous range of office buildings, hotels, clubs . . . looking around at the human litter every few yards up and down the cropped lawns.

The chill of the hours before dawn awoke me. My newspapers were soggy with dew. The hundreds of human paper piles were now but scores. In the distance, I could see two cops going from pile to pile.

There was no sign of Hat. I was not surprised. I felt through my clothes for the small change I'd had. Not a cent was left. Again I wasn't surprised. When the sun rose and offices opened, I could get the money and grip I'd sent ahead from Buffalo. No one had taken my shoes. I could walk around and see the sights of Chicago before it awoke.

East met West on West Madison Street. Here came men like my partners until now . . . youngsters and oldsters, running away . . . unemployed hardly hoping for jobs . . . tramps . . .

an eastern trickle into a broader stream. From the west came migrants of muscle and skill. Men who built railroads and maintained the tracks. Harvesters who followed the crops for thousands of miles. Lumberjacks. Laborers who did the hard and heavy work, and then left others to build fortunes on the foundations they laid.

From dawn to dark, and later, these men lined both sides of West Madison for miles. They milled around job agencies, restaurants, erstwhile saloons, poolrooms, flophouses. Many sat on the sidewalks with feet in gutter, or squatted with backs against the building walls.

Around the missions gathered a different element, more anchored, hopeless, derelict. Older faces, wrinkled, bleary-eyed, twitching, faces still familiar on the skid row of any American city.

The roosting lines weren't as static as those I'd seen in New York on the approaches to Brooklyn Bridge, or sunning themselves in European towns. On West Madison, in 1921, the sitters came and went, and there was an undercurrent of discontent. The western migrants of railroad, range, and labor camp who sat and spat kept changing from day to day, from hour to hour. They talked and cussed . . . and mostly in American. A few read papers or leaflets. In the center of West Madison—at 1001—was the headquarters of the IWW, Industrial Workers of the World.

It was a roomy corner building. On the ground floor, the IWW printshop—there in 1923, I know; in 1921 I vaguely recall a meeting hall. On upper floors, the offices of a fair-sized labor organization. Here elected leaders—rotated annually—administered the IWW, aided by a more permanent staff. They issued the famous Red Card and accounted for $1 dues. They published the weekly paper *Industrial Solidarity*, the monthly magazine *Industrial Pioneer*.

To this headquarters came aggressive men from the camps —IWW job delegates, the fabled Wobblies. They came from "the point of production," they said, reporting on job actions, bringing dues, and literature money. They soon left again—with IWW supplies—to join the daily, hourly exodus from West Madison Street to the far reaches of the West.

On West Madison I had my being until I left Chicago. A

hobo was not conspicuous. Prices competed for the transient trade. If one sign said "Coffee an'—5¢," another lunchroom might retort "Coffee and 2 donuts—5¢." Hot cakes and coffee for 10¢ could be undercut by offering "a real stack" (more than two) or adding a sausage or rasher of bacon. Lunchrooms had specials, loss leaders. With luck, one might find "today only" corned beef and cabbage for 15¢ with "all bread you can eat."

One thing I found hard to do on West Madison was sleep. My first try was typical. The flophouse boasted "separate rooms." They were small cages with tin walls topped by wire netting . . . to admit light from the ceiling of a big dormitory, and ventilation from whiffs of many-odored air circulated by human movement.

There was "real linen" as advertised—sheets and pillowslip on the creaky cot. I lit a match to examine it. The sheets bore marks of bedbugs killed in battle—redly telling of missions accomplished. Other-colored splotches testified to the victors' manhood. On the pillow, a crushed cockroach . . . plus marks of sweat, hair grease, and dried saliva. I removed the linen and shoved it under the bed. I wrapped myself in the blanket—too dark to tell tales. Later I learned to lie fully clothed on top of the covers, wrapping myself in clean newspapers.

Instead of sheep, I counted the shufflings, mutterings, cussings, as each cubicle was occupied. In this tune-up, I noted the remarkable acoustics of the big hall's thinly tintinnabulating partitions.

Then the symphony began. It started pianissimo with the winds—belches, groans, farts, incipient snores. It rose in a crescendo of tubercular coughing, bibulous slurping, snorting and snoring, a vomit, and many-stringed cot-creaking. After a climax of nightmare yells, partition-pounding, and cries of protest, a brief intermission called by the night clerk. Then on again, till dawn's early light brought the quiet of windless exhaustion.

On West Madison I attended my first IWW meeting . . . a homey experience, it turned out. The speaker had a Yorkshire accent as throat-sticking as Yorkshire pudding. He was George

Hardy, IWW general secretary until rotated out of office, and now back from England on a speaking tour.

Chunky, rough in manner, more earthy and convivial than theoretical or spiritual, Hardy was like most English union leaders I'd met. When I saw him four years later in London, he was secretary of the National Minority Movement, communist-influenced left wing of British trade unionism . . . succeeding Harry Pollitt of the Boilermakers, who became Communist party leader. NMM president was Tom Mann, to whom Hardy introduced me.

Mann was thin, aging, ailing, but still alert. A leader of the 1889 London dock strike and first president of the Dockers union, Mann promoted the New Unionism that then swept England . . . and with which the later CIO sweep in the United States was often compared . . . a unionism for all the workers, as against the exclusive craftism of the old unionism.

Like many early IWW leaders, Mann was "political" as well as industrial. (As late as 1924, I saw LaFollette buttons worn around Wobbly headquarters.) He was secretary of the Independent Labor party in 1894. In 1910 he led a syndicalist movement in British unions that stressed industrial unionism and strike militancy and rebelled against the pale pink reformism of the Labor party. In 1913 William Z. Foster brought Mann to the United States to help turn IWWers toward working in the major unions. Mann became a founder of the Red International of Labor Unions.

Hardy, like Mann and William D. (Big Bill) Haywood, not to mention Foster, was not anarcho-syndicalistic like many later IWW leaders. The Wobblies I knew best were of the Haywood-Hardy school, that fed into the communist movement.

Hardy's speech, as I recall, combined porkchops with class struggle as union organizers commonly did: The bosses are robbing us. We work our guts out; they get the gravy and push us around. For more money and better conditions, we must organize, stick together, show the bosses we'll fight them if we have to. The radical organizer carried this logic further: We're up against a setup. The bosses have the big money. They own the factories, press, politicians, police, and some labor leaders. We need unions that unite not divide the workers, fighting unions, democratically run by the rank and file. And—ultimate aim—this country would be much better off if run by and for the working people, instead of by and for the lousy rich.

From Chicago on, I was in an American mainstream. Plenty of company on the freights. Plenty of empty boxcars deadheading back west for grain. Nobody hid. Trainmen chatted with us. Bulls, outnumbered, kept out of our hair.

We pulled into LaCrosse, Wisconsin, after midnight. It had been raining. The yards shone clean and chill in wet-reflected lights. We drew back into the relative warmth of our cars, till we heard a cheerful voice outside: "Hiya, boys! End of the line. All out!"

We piled out, a hundred or more. Raincoated men shepherded us jovially through the yards. Railroad bulls! Said one:

"How's things been? Boxcars is hard on the bones, what? Company should put in cushions." One Ye-eah, two spits. Hobos are like that—no sense of humor. Another tack: "Guess you could go for some coffee. There's a diner down track, open all night for the rails. But make it snappy——" One "Who's payin'?" No other word, no break from the ranks.

Bull points to freight with engine and caboose, ready to pull out. "That there's loaded. Ride outside and you'll likely break your ass." A harder tone: "You just keep off that one!" The good fellow again: "I'm taking you to one that's all nice empties. It'll pull out in an hour."

We chose our cars. The bull stood around chatting. When the engine bumped on, he shouted a cheery "Aa-a-all ab-oard!"

Early morning arrival in a farm town beyond Minneapolis. After a hard, cold, dirty night, all was bright and clean as the sun rose to cheer us. We jumped out to stretch our legs, found perches to sun ourselves. We saw the sheriff coming with a small posse. One or two hid behind cars, most stood our ground.

Burly and stout, the sheriff strode proudly toward us with shining badge. We waited for him to make the first move. Passing a few stragglers, he took his stand before the first sizable group.

"Good morning, boys, good morning." He beamed. "It's a

beau-u-tiful day, ain't it? Just had to come down to welcome you." To his deputies: "Go down the train and see if any of the men need anything."

Grinning, the hobos responded in kind. "What, no brass band, sheriff?" "How's about coffee? Last town give us quite a spread." Winking, some held out hands, which the sheriff duly began to shake.

One American at Oxford had told me: "We have no classes. The laboring man is highly respected——" "——when labor is in demand," broke in another.

Not everything was so peachy. The harvest army had camp followers.

With a score maybe to a boxcar, we were often body to body. Stretched on the floor in the dark, I didn't mind bodies rolled against mine by the jolting. I didn't like stealthy fingers. It was all right if the fingers felt my head . . . some guy feeling around for room to lie down. When they began at my feet, and felt on up into my overalls and shirt, it wasn't so good. I'd jerk up and swear . . . to see a shadowy form creeping away.

Sometimes I slept so exhausted I didn't feel the stealthy fingers. I might wake to find my shoes off . . . though I kept nothing in this obvious hiding place; nor in my pockets, which I might find pulled inside out. Once I awoke, after a crawly nightmare, to find my fly-buttons undone and my private parts exposed to public view.

Then there was hunger. Not inadequate diet, no diet at all. Once a man came back to our boxcar with a loaf of bread . . . so proud we all made wisecracks. Before eating any, he passed it around with a pocketknife. Each took no more than the man before; some refused, saying they'd eaten. We left a big chunk for the loaf's owner.

A can of beans was an occasion. Two guys came by one somehow. (Nobody ever admitted buying anything.) As they wolfed it with their fingers, they saw me watching. I said I wasn't hungry. They made me finish it.

I visited the "jungles." In these woodsy gathering places near the tracks, I might learn where to find corn or fruit. I never saw "slum gullion." A can of beans perhaps, or of hot coffee, might be shared.

The comfortable and arrogant equated "hobo" with bum or beggar. We knew better. I never saw a hobo begging. Talk a line about it—sure:

"I ain't a-goin' hungry, bud, not me. I'll swipe first, or hit up a farmhouse for a meal."

"Whaddya say we hit the stem, guys? 'Give us a handout, mister—I'm clean outa hootch and me poor kids is starvin'.' I tell you, I'll sooner do that than pray for my soup at some suckin' mission."

"Look at that Shorty pickin' his teeth. Bet he's hit every back door in town. Gravy on his shirt too. How d'you do it, Shorty? Take me along next time."

Only beggars I saw were Momma's boys running away, or mission stiffs.

Before I got my first harvest job, I hadn't eaten for several days. I had two cents I clung to. I had to hike on a hot day to the little North Dakota town of Cavalier. I was empty, queasy, uncontrollably thirsty. At the first lunchroom, I plunked my two cents on the counter and asked for water and some stale bread. The waitress gave me an already filled glass of lukewarm water. I didn't look at it—just poured the water down my parched throat. Halfway my glance caught something black in the glass. It was a dead fly. I didn't, couldn't stop.

Near the North Dakota border, the freight stopped at a water tank. Some got out to walk and sun. I stayed in my boxcar with a short man around 30 and two youngsters. Chuck, one of the younger, got out to "nose around." He came back on the run, so furtive that Shorty exclaimed: "So you seen a dick! So what?"

Chuck came close and hissed: "The Wobblies is coming. Let's beat it."

"Why?" I asked.

"Doncha know?" he whispered. "They'll throw us off if we don't join!"

"What's wrong with joining?" I said.

"Ain't nothing wrong . . . but who's got the dough?" This from Shorty, who now took charge. "You, Chuck, slip out again.

If the coast's clear, rap on the wall and beat it to the other side of the train. We'll follow."

No rap came. No more sign of Chuck. Peeking out, we saw a dozen men.

Incongruously I thought of the sheriff and his posse. The man striding ahead—tall, weather-brown, overalled—was clearly the leader. "We're all leaders," the Wobblies boasted, but some always stuck their necks out further than the rest. The others deferred to this man, who spoke with authority:

"Morning, fellows, heading for the harvest?" I nodded; my partners kept still and silent. "Guess you know you can't ride no harvest-bound freights without you join the IWW." To his group: "That right, fellows?"

"Sure thing." "We ain't carrying no scabs . . . nor scissorbills." "You tell 'em, Slim!"

Slim took some papers from his pocket and turned to us. "I ain't shittin' you guys. I'm an IWW delegate. Want to see my credentials?" We didn't, we were convinced. "Case you don't know the IWW, you sure heard of the Wobblies." We all nodded.

"Well, Wobblies is just an ignorant name for Industrial Workers of the World. We organize the working man everywhere . . . or aim to. Take this harvest. If we're organized, we don't have to work for no lousy three or four bucks a day, like some in Minnesota. In Dakota, we don't work for less than six bucks, and some parts we got it up to more. If we don't like the grub, we don't get sick on it. We ask Farmer John real polite to do better. If he says to go suck ourselves, we just say: "Okay, we won't work . . . and you won't get a man from the jungles or the freights. They're all carrying Red Cards like us."

He stopped and said abruptly: "All right, you guys going to join up, or get out and walk? I ain't got much time. Got a lot more to talk to."

"How much is it?"

"One dollar. Red Card's good for a year. You can ride on it anywhere."

I said I wanted to join but was down to a few nickels. Shorty said he hadn't a red cent. The IWW delegate sized us up with shrewd eyes.

"Likely you got nothin' in your stomachs but gas," he said, "yet you suckers think you can beat the system without organizing.

"Okay, fellows," he turned to his companions, "do we put them off?"

They whispered together. Then the delegate dismissed us. "They say you could be flat, at that. I know how it is. Here, take this." He handed us a copy of *Industrial Solidarity*. "Read it and get wise. We'll let you ride this time. But first pay you get, you look up a Wobbly delegate and join. How about it?" We swore we'd do just that.

After the Wobblies left, Shorty breathed deep with relief, grinned, and slapped me on the back. "Well, we got away with it," he said.

Shorty glanced at the IWW paper, then set it down. His partner looked through it at the pictures and spread it out to lie on. I asked for it. "What do you guys think of all this?" I said.

"Of all what?" said Shorty.

"What the Wobbly guy said, and what's in this paper."

"A lotta shit, ain't it?" said Shorty's sidekick, more asking than asserting. Shorty took the paper and glanced at it again.

"Don't know as I'd say that. It ain't all crap. Take this paper, it's for the workin' man." He seemed to lose interest. I asked him:

"You gonna join, like you said?"

Shorty squinted at me. We were moving again, but the Wobblies could have stayed with the train. "Could be. Why not? How's about you?"

"Sure, first chance. We'd oughta stick together, right?"

Shorty relaxed . . . I was too green a sucker to be a spy.

"Go to it," he said. "But watch yourself. The Wobblies ain't so strong as they make out. Don't let the cops catch you with a Red Card. Even the guys you work with, don't let on till you're real sure. I know. I been a union man. What they done to us when we went on strike was a shame."

"What about the stuff they say in this paper?"

Shorty squinted at me again. "Kinda nosy, aintcha?" He turned away to his partner. But he looked at the paper again, then said to me:

"Wanta know what I think? They got the right idea about all being in one union—not one union scabbing on another, like where I was."

Shorty glanced from the Kid to me. "And I don't care who knows what I think!" Having dared this much, Shorty dared some more: "And they ain't so wrong about what we could do if we stuck together. We could tie up any job tighter'n a cow's ass in flytime . . . tie up the whole works."

Shorty paused, aware he was making an impression. Then he lay back and yawned. "But I tell you what. That ain't never gonna happen. You know why? Because workin' men just won't stick together. Nossir, they never done it, and they never will."

I hired out through the county agent at Cavalier. The work was called shocking (in Canada, stooking)—setting bundles of cut wheat on end in separate shocks (stooks), to await coming of a threshing machine.

On my farm I was the only hired hand. I slept and ate in the house, and worked as long as there was light each day. At time to pay off, the farmer, a big tough guy, wouldn't pay me the rate he hired me for. He said I was too slow and offered a small lump sum. We stood by the barn arguing for an hour. Several times he threatened to beat me up. I wished the Wobbly delegate and some fellow workers were around. It became a haggle. I settled for twice the farmer's first offer, but less than the hiring rate.

After that, I worked with a crew that went with threshing machine from farm to farm. Pitchfork work—pitching bundles from shocks into horsedrawn wagons, then from the wagons into the thresher. All was regulated now. Ten hours work a day. An hour for lunch. $6 a day, and no chiseling. We slept in the hay-lofts of big barns . . . good sleeping. My crew were mostly Scandinavian. They stuck together. "Cliquish, them squareheads," said the Americans. Farmers and thresher-owners treated them with caution and respect.

The work was hard, and uninterrupted. No toilet breaks; you relieved yourself where you were . . . if modest, behind the wagon. The Swedes set the pace, a fast one. After three hours

I'd begin to wilt, and the last two—before noon or day's end—were endless. But my system took it and throve.

We rolled out of the hay to the premature crowing of roosters. The horses snuffled, snorted, bumped their partitions. A drowsy barnyard was not yet astir. The harvest moon lingered through the coming of pale daylight, as the stars vanished. Grumbling we shook the chaff from our overalls. From the warm barn we stepped into the crisp chill of a North Dakota morning. The air cut cleanly through caked nostrils and dried mouths. We took a pail of water from the well and spilled it into tin basins. Icily it tingled our sunburned, wind-chapped faces.

Our minds were on the hot, lamplit kitchen. Women's voices. Sizzle and spit of frying. When the door opened, steam and smoke poured into the frosty air, with the smells of bacon, coffee, and body sweat. We followed loaded platters to the eating shack, hurrying to "come and get it."

Yellow popeyed eggs joined in the frying. Fried potatoes in reach all down the long table. Ham, bacon, or country sausage. Hot cakes stacked high, syrup thick as molasses. Prunes, canned fruit, apple sauce. Sliced tomatoes with sugar. Dessert for breakfast! Pie and cake with every meal.

A gourmet might have detected some monotony, some inelegance. I did not. So the same fried potatoes were reheated for each meal. So cake and pie stayed days on the table until finished. So porkchops were main dish for lunch, supper . . . often breakfast too. So what? I was in gastronomical heaven.

Sears and "Monkey-Ward" catalogs in outhouses were our only reading. None shaved till threshing was done. We worked Sundays too. The Swedes talked Swedish; the rest talked little. One threshing done, we moved to the next farm.

Once, as my muscles hardened, I had energy left after supper to walk out onto the prairie. The stars sparkled bright, the air was crisply clean. The vast flatness stirred me. I found myself on a railroad track. Ahead glittered town lights. They drew me to them. I walked the ties for miles before I gave up. The beckoning lights had grown no nearer. The next morning I was told: "Why, that town's some 20-30 miles away."

Then the harvest, and all my labor, came sharply to an end. We had our harvest stakes . . . mine less than $100; others who'd followed the harvest further had more. But the goose that laid the silver dollars had died a natural death. No more jobs within hundreds of miles. The others were heading back to Duluth, Twin Cities, Chicago. I alone was heading on.

Every year thousands followed the harvest from the Texas Panhandle to North Dakota. Then all turned back. Why? The harvest went on in western Canada into October. Why not keep following?

"They won't let you in."

"The Canadians keep them jobs for themselves."

"I heard you can't beat your way on the Canadian 'roads."

Nobody thought much of my idea. But I wanted to see Canada. It had a working class too, I was an internationalist. I bought a ticket and rode the cushions to Winnipeg.

Winnipeg was labor-conscious . . . not long emerged from a general strike . . . with labor and radical papers on its newsstands. To keep my pledge to the Wobbly delegate, I searched for the IWW but could find no trace. Nothing like Chicago's West Madison Street . . . all homeguard on poorer streets . . . no floating population of migrants.

I visited labor haunts and halls. I talked with workers in restaurants which served English fish-'n'-chips, kippers, real tea. Most were very British. Latest immigrants had bypassed eastern Canada, heading for homestead chances in the west. Many carried old-country union cards. All had been made union-conscious by the general strike.

There was no IWW in Winnipeg, they said, but "something like it" or "just as good." It was the One Big Union—born of revulsion against craft separatism during the solidarity of the general strike. The OBU hadn't made much headway, it was said, but was still in business.

OBU headquarters was on an upper floor of an office building . . . no Wobbly-type haunt for workers coming and going. The official I met—Russell, I believe—was youngish, energetic, in business suit. "Yes," he said, "we're like the IWW in organizing all workers, and no union scabbing on another. But we're not so syndicalistic."

Russell was vague about organizing agricultural workers. He signed me up and gave me a card as red as that of the IWW. In a copy of the *OBU Bulletin,* he marked a list of OBU offices further west. He suggested the Saskatoon area for wheat-harvest jobs. "That's a long way off," he said. "How d'you plan to get there? Fare's pretty steep."

"I thought of beating my way like I did in the States."

"O-o-oh?" said Russell.

I couldn't penetrate his reserve. "Well," I said, a little piqued, "how do the rest get to the harvest?"

There was some government plan for low-rate harvest fares . . . which I didn't pursue. Even if I could qualify, I didn't want to blow my stake.

Without guide in a new country, I kept away from the Winnipeg yards. I headed for Portage La Prairie, next town west, to join the harvest-bound.

The wind of the western prairie greeted me as I approached this town at nightfall. It spoke distinctly in the frosty silence—as may the ocean on a stormy night. Coming from none knew where with nothing in its way, it spoke of the endless and the everywhere. One can hear the same wind, I've heard it, blowing from the icy north over the wastelands of Newfoundland; or reaching even to the cropped and rolling hills of Wyoming. It cares nothing for humanity. From far far away the wind blew— over land without bounds, from a round horizon that was no boundary either.

Before me in this wilderness lay a rough settlement of man —rough like the forces of nature it was built to resist. Afraid to spread out, the houses clung to each side of one long, long main street.

Westbound freights passed through Portage La Prairie one after another each serpent-long. The open doors of empty boxcars—scores and scores of them—gaped greedily for the grain of the west.

I ate at the rougher end of a frontier town—in a converted saloon with high stools up against a long counter made for the standing. Its operators were Chinese. I saw none of my kind who might be heading my way. I spoke with men hanging around bars and billiard rooms. None knew what I talked about.

Nothing linked them with my chain of thought. I was a stranger
leading a strange life, and hinting darkly at strange things.

Daunted I was, but not diverted. I walked alone to the
stalled freights on the edge of the prairie. Nobody hailed me.
Nobody stopped me. I saw nobody. I heard nobody. I climbed
into a boxcar in the center of a long train. I spread out a newspaper and rolled my coat into a pillow. The train started, and I
fell asleep. Only passing some country depot did I see signs of
humankind. At the first water stop, I walked up and down looking vainly for a fellow hobo. After that I gave up.

To be all alone amid endless empties . . . of this might a
hobo dream, after dodging dicks and hobo crowds and finding
never a boxcar to rest in.

Then one night, about dawn. . . . The train had stopped
far out in houseless prairie. Stiff with cold, I walked, jumped,
flapped my arms. Passing one car, I heard a faint shuffle. I stood
still and listened. No sound. I stepped back and stood still
again. A faint breathing sound. I looked in the boxcar door. A
man leaped back as from a ghost.

"Nothing to worry about, bud," I said. "I'm on the bum too."

Backed into a corner like a trapped animal, he was breathing deeply. He wore a tweed jacket and soiled pants, not overalls. His mustache predated a few days' growth of beard. I
waited for him to calm down. I'd met one crazy guy on the road;
that was enough. I gave him a cigarette.

As he relaxed, he would talk only of himself and his plight.
He gave his full name and asked mine . . . which I'd never
known a hobo do. He told of his job hunt from Toronto west; of
vanishing savings that left him not enough for fare; of his contacts and plans in Saskatoon. In the States, a hobo had a "line,"
or several lines about himself, pat and brief, and then clammed
up. To cap the contrast, this Canadian slapped his pocket and
said the two dollars in it was all he had left.

Saskatoon was a surprise. I'd expected a bleak farm-frontier
town. I found a snug modern city with all conveniences. Picking
up the harvest money I'd mailed ahead, I enjoyed good food,
movies, a nice room. Only trouble was the weather. It had been
raining, and was still raining. A government employment office
welcomed me and said harvest hands were urgently needed, but

. . . There might be a long wait for the rain to stop and the grain to dry up. Meanwhile, they'd get me a stopgap job.

I went to work as a laborer on the Canadian National Railways. It was hard labor, handling ties and rails, sorting lumber, digging, shoveling. But it was good to have income through the long wait for the harvest.

My Saskatchewan farmer had been a machinist in England. His food was English too. Black-strong tea five times a day, soggy cooking, fried eggs and potatoes at every meal. The hours were 12 a day—starting out before daylight, getting back after dark. After the rain's delays, there wasn't a minute to lose. The 12 hours lagged less for me than the 10 hours in Dakota. Instead of five hours without a break, we had a break every three hours . . . morning and afternoon tea with sandwiches dividing each six-hour stint.

When the harvest was done, I could feel the breath of northern winter down my neck and I headed south to the United States.

On my first Montana freight, a brakey came down the train looking in the cars for hobos. I was alone in my boxcar.

"You a union man?" he asked.

"Why . . . ye-e-es," I said, surprised.

"That's good. We're strong for union here. Don't like no-bills, and sure won't carry no scabs. Let's see your card."

I hesitated, he mightn't call mine a real union card. "Mine's not your kind of union. I joined in Canada . . . only one I could."

"All right, all right, quit stalling. What's its name?"

"It's the One Big Union——" I stopped, to observe the impact.

"So you're a fellow worker! That's what you call yourselves." The brakey's grin was as wide as the west. "To look at you, I wouldn't have thought you was a Wobbly. Why, that's just fine. If you ask me, IWW's better than the old American Separation of Labor. Bet you can ride on your Red Card anywhere in the northwest. Let's see it, bud."

I explained I'd wanted to join the IWW, but couldn't find a branch in Canada and had been told the OBU was much the same.

"Well, I swan," exclaimed the brakey, examining my card. "I never seen one of these before. Guess it's like the Wobblies— all for one and one for all. You can ride on it. Good luck," he said moving on, then turned and grinned "fellow worker!"

On another Montana freight, another trainman asked to see my union card. He too was well impressed, saying the one-big-union idea was much better than "all these craft unions." He invited me to the caboose to show the crew my OBU card. We drank coffee together, and they gave me some of their lunch. I talked union with men to whom the word meant solidarity. Kiddingly they took me up as their "fellow worker" by letting me help with their way-freight unloading, as I offered to do.

After some unintended backtracking across Montana, I joined the main-line stream of westbound hobos at Harlowton. The cold of a Montana fall seemed to enrage these men. They were unlike any I'd hoboed with before.

These were not the furtive runners-away of the east, not the more vigorous harvestbound workers. They were harder, more bitter. They cursed explosively as the frosty night stiffened them. They lit bonfires . . . some on boxcar floors. Veterans (of World War I) talked much of violence, wished they'd kept their guns. "We'd show the cocksuckers!"

Whom did they mean by this vague oft-used obscenity? One heard mention of the "rich bastards" . . . but rarely. These men were not like the Wobblies or the union railroadmen. The Wobblies' enemy was "the system"—the capitalist system, the employing class; their outlet to agitate, organize, educate to change it. The western "rails" turned their hostility against "the companies" or "Wall Street." My new fellow hobos were individualists . . . "100% Americans" (a term then much promoted for antiradical and antiunion purposes). Their hostility took no clear or consistent direction. They had no idea of organizing.

One beckoned me to his boxcar corner. Drawing me close,

he pulled out a gun to show me. "This says I ain't gonna freeze!" he rasped, shivering. "This says I ain't gonna starve." He hadn't eaten all day.

"What will you do with it?" I asked. "Get into jail?"

"Sucker!" Gloomily he shook his head. "They's one born every minute."

Wedged between mountainous cliffs was a small Idaho town. I walked from the freight with two hobos, both veterans, both with growths of bristly beard. They drew aside to whisper, then turned to me: "We're gonna pull a holdup . . . need you for a lookout. Okay, kid?"

Startled, I looked for an out. Back on the track a car-to-car bumping ran through the train . . . from a second locomotive attached for the steep pull. I turned and started running for the train.

"Hey, you!" yelled one of the men.

"A-aw, let him go." The other shouted after me, "We was kiddin', get that."

The hostility of these men was scattergun . . . its target, vague powers responsible for their plight. No handy personal symbol, like Herbert Hoover during the Great Depression. The men were not political. With equal venom they turned on each other, or on more fortunate workers.

"Look at that fat hogger sittin' up in the cab. Thinks we're dirt, the lousy stinkin' son of a bitch!"

"Them rails got it so soft . . . the suckin' bastards!"

"Hear where plumbers is gettin' twelve bucks a day . . . but just you try to get into their suckin' union!"

Maybe a Hitler could have organized these men against Jews, communists, Wobblies, unions. I doubt it. These were men looking for an American frontier closed to them . . . men of individual enterprise in an increasingly monopolized society. They weren't ready for concerted action.

I stopped over at Butte, Montana—a name of labor lore. City of the Western Federation of Miners and early IWW. City of Big Bill Haywood. Battleground against the copper barons. Armed patrols of union copper miners once guarded its daily labor paper, the red *Butte Daily Bulletin*, edited by Bill (Wm.

F.) Dunne, the coming communist leader. A city of the lusty, brawling West that was also a lusty, labor city.

It was around three in the morning. Our fire of sticks and paper was dying down, too weak to burn into the boxcar floor. We were high in the mountains and numb with cold. The train began a long, slow, corkscrew descent. Far below, through the clear, cold air, we saw the sparkling lights of the magic city of Butte. With each curve we came closer . . . till the fairy lights became plainly electric, their welcome chill and drab. Enchanting approach to a grim and grimy city.

I was a stranger, without contacts. My stay was short. I saw no signs of the fighting solidarity of former years. In Winnipeg, and later in Seattle, you heard labor talk on all sides. They were cities of recent general strikes. Butte—in some union doldrums —was not.

I was hurrying to get to the milder climate of Seattle before I froze. But I still kept away from loaded freights or passenger blinds (the cutoff corridor nook where first car meets engine tender). The men I was with were in more of a hurry. We were nearing the coast. Across the Hump was the warm, wet country. My partners wanted to ride the blinds the rest of the way. I pointed to empty boxcars on a freight.

"Hell," said one, "we'd grow whiskers. I'm going to nose around." He came back elated. "A fast freight's comin' through . . . makes as good time as a passenger, maybe better." This freight pulled in on schedule. Every car was loaded and locked.

"Where we gonna ride?" I asked.

"On top, of course. Lay in each other's legs."

"How's that?"

"If we don't, we'll roll off . . . case we go to sleep."

The fast freight stopped barely long enough for us to climb on top of a car. We lay on the gangplank face down, each man's head and shoulders cradled in the legs of the man ahead. The train was soon up to a dizzy speed. I became aware of some bumping and squealing below us. "What they carrying?" I called to the man between my legs.

Hogs," he yelled back, "ho-o-ogs. Can't you smell 'em?"

The ride was both precarious and dizzy and I yearned for

some slowdown. It cured me for life of rollercoaster or "wild mouse" rides. That hog train carried us right through to Seattle with hardly a slowdown or stop.

Two years after its 1919 general strike, Seattle was still in some labor and radical ferment. It had a labor daily, the *Union Record*. I met Harvey O'Connor, then city editor. I liked his style —radical but not sectarian, principled but practical, a good craftsman, a labor organization man. The IWW, still strong in northwest logging camps, published its western organ here, the *Industrial Worker*. Its young editor, Harold Haines, was educated but down-to-earth, an idealist with a twinkle. Here I met Vern Smith, later to be my IWW editor boss in Chicago. A tall, ruddy westerner, he combined book knowledge with much labor experience.

I felt drawn to such people as these, as I couldn't to most intellectuals. They too could theorize, but not just from books. Perforce, or by choice, they'd known working-class life, and unions, strikes, reds, as part of it.

Then there were the Litchmans. Mark was a lawyer with a cause—many causes, in fact—a dynamo of purpose, effort, and fight. He and his hospitable wife, Sophie, held open house one night each week. There, in comfort and with refreshment, I shared with others, also excited, my excitement about the new world a-borning. I met labor and radical speakers I'd heard at some of the city's many meetings.

At work, in that Seattle winter, I got a worm's-eye view of life, labor, and the coming revolution. In those bright evening hours at the Litchmans, I was introduced as some kind of interesting "whatisit." When cold dawn routed me off my hard cot, I was just a punk again, as on the road. Not that I didn't try to better myself.

Washed, white-shirted, and with what was left of my Oxford accent, I presented myself to the YMCA as available for a position. Mr. Caldwell was impressed, nay enthusiastic . . . sure I could build a fine career in Seattle. He appraised me as "clean-cut," an Americanism which I took to mean white, washed, white-shirted, and with enough charm to make women feel motherly and employers reach eagerly for my services.

Mr. Caldwell sent me off at once with a letter to the personnel manager of a large firm . . . who didn't share his enthusiasm. "What's the matter with that character?" he grumbled. "I ask for an office boy, and he sends me you—with a letter no less!"

After more unsuccessful forays, Mr. Caldwell tried the church route. He bade me join a certain Episcopal church. "Attend services regularly," he said. "Volunteer for activities. Some of the businessmen are bound to notice you. I'll put in a word with the minister."

As I turned to leave, Mr. Caldwell called me back. "Sit down," he said gruffly. "I have something personal to say." I sat down tense on the edge of a chair. "Relax!" he ordered. Then suddenly he rapped on his desk and said: "Smile!" There he had me; I was the despair of photographers. Mr. Caldwell laughed—but briefly.

"You know why you don't get hired? You're too serious. Next time I send you out, I want you to smile, be easy, confident. Sell yourself, my friend. Employers like a man who's cheerful. God's in his heaven, all's right with the world. Be a booster . . . not a sourpuss."

I tried . . . even practiced before mirrors. My best-rehearsed smiles must have failed to give employers the reassurance they craved. I went to the church . . . on the heights, in a suburb of fine homes. I was living downtown, on Skid Road—the fare nearly busted me. I saw worshipers who looked like big businessmen—their cars were that big. None of them saw me.

Finally I let Mr. Caldwell down by showing up in a blue workshirt. True, my one white shirt was dirty. But there was deliberation in my defiance. He glimpsed me through his door, but didn't greet me. I told his secretary I was flat and would do anything. My Seattle oddjobs career began.

I washed windows and cleaned up in private homes. I lived in as man-of-all-work, in a well-to-do home . . . of the head of a "100% American" antiunion league, it turned out. I became potboy in an expensive boardinghouse. I served as busboy in a top businessmen's club. I worked in a Woolworth basement and, for a toothsome spell, as night watchman in a candy factory. The jobs kept me in food and cot, but they carried no kudos.

Job snobbery, be it admitted, prevails also in labor and radical circles. In the AFL, the skilled crafstmen—the "pompous trades and proud mechanics," as a British Chartist once called them—were tops. The left saw them as rather middle class; it lionized the worker in heavy industry, or larger plants. Unionized workers in lighter, consumer, or service trades were lower in the social scale. As to the unorganized millions who dug and wheeled, who hewed and carried, who scoured pots, mopped floors, and ministered to the sanitation and comfort of both working and employing classes, well . . . job status was usually skipped in introductions.

From my "100% American" boss, and from the bosses whose club dishes I bussed, I learned employers could be more class-conscious than workers.

Mr. R.W. Blue ran one of the outfits cashing in on the racket pioneered by Mayor Ole Hanson, who claimed to have smashed the general strike and saved America from red revolution. They courted employer groups with recipes for breaking unions, stopping communism, assuring high profits.

I had no idea of Blue's connection when I took the job in his home. Nor did he suspect me of low-percentage Americanism, until he discovered me in my basement cubicle reading the Seattle *Union Record.*

"Why d'you read that rag?" he demanded.

"Just picked it up on a streetcar." I was on guard. "Anything wrong?"

"It's a red rag, a labor paper, communistic. . . ."

"Isn't it the AFL union paper?" I asked.

Mr. Blue stared at me suspiciously. "AFL, IWW, socialists, communists, anarchists . . . they're all the same when you get down to it. Some of the worst strike agitators claim to be good Americans, even antired . . ."

He broke off to tell an anecdote about "one of our people" who, after a successful meeting, was buttonholed by an innocent-looking man asking questions. People gathered around, and before he was through, the questioner had "made a fool of our man." Mr. Blue looked straight at me. He ran his fingers under his collar. There was warning in his tone.

"When anyone questions me, I get hot under the collar. I know he's not with us. Chances are he's a red. I tell our people, 'Never argue with one of them. The reds always get the best of it in an argument.' "

The clubmen were more relaxed. I got some earfuls. Waiters they recognized, either trusting them or lowering their voices; a busboy was just a self-moving part of the furniture. To the clubmen it was all a matter of money, like everything in business; they didn't speak of "Americanism." Labor was out to get all the money it could . . . from them. Unlike Blue, they didn't lump all labor together, they drew distinctions.

With some AFL unions, you could do business, even buy you a leader. One way or another though, it cost you money . . . the bastards! The socialists (referring more to liberal Democrats than to a dwindling Socialist party) would take your money for social legislation. A crazy bunch like the IWW could wreck your business. The communists (including all the left) wanted to take most of your money now for the workers, and all of it in the end, as in Russia. So you were against labor, in the very nature of things, just as labor was against you. The bastards!

Of course, you couldn't talk that way in public. Public relations called for buying ads in labor papers on Labor Day, showing capital and labor arm in arm, united for Americanism, against communism. You had to pay guys like Blue (out for your money, like everyone else) to holler that every strike was a red plot. Maybe it was. Who could tell? Leeches like Blue cost a lot and were pretty stupid. But they just could be right. If the reds had any sense, what couldn't they do? Why take chances?

To the other side of the tracks I went when I could . . . to meetings, lectures, debates. Anyone who had visited revolutionary Russia could draw a big crowd. Thousands turned out for Lincoln Steffens, he who said: "I have been over into the future, and it works."

Factional squabbles were chiefly below surface. At one IWW business meeting, attended by hundreds, debate raged for an hour on the loan of an IWW typewriter for a campaign enlisting Wobbly sympathy but not IWW-sponsored. Bored stiff, I thought this was rank-and-file democracy gone crazy. Later I learned the campaign was supposedly communist-inspired. The division was between procommunist Wobblies and a syndicalistic old guard. A united Communist party had been launched in June 1921, but "underground." Anticommunist Wobs privately talked of it as foreign, middle-class, bohemian, Jewish—much as did the "100%" brothers of the AFL.

But if all the reputed communists in Seattle had been laid end to end, they'd have made some long "bridges" in many directions. They included many AFL local officers and members. The symptoms? They advocated amalgamating craft unions into industrial unions; organizing the unorganized; inner-union democracy; independent labor political action; no racial discrimination; recognition of Soviet Russia. The reputed communists included many Wobblies; college profs and students allegedly conning Marxian classics on the sly; and folks who turned out, and dragooned others to turn out, for the Soviet-sympathizing meetings.

Communists were identified not only by what they advocated, but by the way they went about things. I gathered that Brother X of the AFL, Comrade Y of the Socialist party, Fellow Worker Z of the IWW had been happy, each in his own way, until the communists snuck up behind the scenes.

Brother X wanted to unite the crafts into industrial unions. He had a good speech about it, that everyone liked . . . you could slip out for a quick beer, knowing how long it would last. Comrade Y thought the United States should recognize Soviet Russia—a pretty big red splotch on the map, and "socialist . . . or . . . oh well, let's not get into an argument." Nobody did. Fellow Worker Z wanted to organize all the workers. He didn't care who knew it. Nobody else cared . . . unless some organizing got under way.

Come the communists. . . . Soon Brother X finds some members missing a beer to stay and applaud . . . speak, too.

They offer a resolution that has to be voted on, and makes the business agent mad. Brother X can't make his speech any more without being called a communist. Comrade Y is pushed into a committee for Soviet recognition, and to speak at a mass meeting. After that, everyone argues with him. Fellow Worker Z is put on the spot. People get after him (communists no doubt) about a bunch of workers the AFL doesn't want—asking the IWW to organize them.

And the women! Never were much of a problem in AFL or IWW. Now the boys can't sit around a spittoon philosophizing without some dame comes in with a petition . . . for Negro rights, say . . . and hisses "white chauvinist" if anyone drops the word "nigger." Next thing there's a girl works in the office and gives you an argument—not about sex but politics! Sneakiest thing about the communists, you can never be quite sure they are communists.

After my Seattle winter, I realized communists were a problem to a lot of people. Others must wrestle with it. I had a problem of my own.

On my potboy job I got ptomaine poisoning. I lost appetite and interest in life. I wanted to get away. I shipped out as "flunky" in a sawmill logging camp. If not a rest cure, it was a cure.

Within yards of cookshack and mill, you could be alone in icy stillness amid tall evergreens. They might sough in the wind and drop snow on you; otherwise there was a cathedral quiet. The stars sparkled through the treetops with breathless brilliance. In this church of nature, one couldn't kneel without slushing through the snow's crust. One could stand erect, as the trees themselves, without servility.

Here one could reflect or let feeling rule . . . till dirt and hate and nervousness, the pots, the pans, the Blues, all dwindled into insignificance. My irritations vanished. I developed a terrific appetite.

For appetite the place was perfect. I helped the cook-commissaryman feed scores of ravenous lumber workers. I hus-

tled firewood for the huge range . . . cutlery for the long tables
. . . big pitchers of coffee . . . steaming platters of food. When
the men stomped out into the snow again, the hectic pace relaxed. Cleaning up the debris. Washing the dishes. Sweeping the
floor. Then solid comfort by the stove, with coffee, with choice
morsels enjoyed at leisure—and with Bud Morgan.

Bud was a big man, big-bellied as a cook should be, but not
soft. A tower of heartiness, with a bell of a voice. When he
roared out "Roses are shining in Picardy" with sentiment, or
"Sailing down the coast of Tripoli, sweetheart you and I," the
tall trees nodded. His language was lusty and colorful, earthy
and ribald. A trencherman himself, Bud wanted everyone to eat
well. Instead of chiseling himself some profit, he ordered more
and better food than he had to.

Women and children had no place in western camps. Bud
never talked about family. Between jobs, his rooms in Seattle,
Portland, Sacramento, seemed to have been lonely places, with
only a landlady to kid with. Bud lavished his warmth on the people he fed . . . on anyone who showed up at his cookshack. If a
luckless drifter poked in his head, he found luck. Bud fed him all
he could eat, then chewed the rag and tried to help.

One night a seedy little guy showed up. Bud, as usual,
cooked and waited on him. They were still talking when I hit
the hay.

The next morning Bud fired me. "Shorty needs the job
more than you do," he explained. "He's in trouble." Lest I think
him soft, Bud added: "Shorty owes me near a hundred bucks.
This is the only way I can get some back. You don't mind, do
you?"

As it happened, I didn't. I was fattened up. I had a nice
stake. It was spring. I was raring to go.

It was late at night and raining, when I reached Portland,
Oregon. I'd blown my stake traipsing up to Vancouver and visiting in Seattle, and had sent ahead the few bucks left to San
Francisco. We were cold, wet and empty. My partner was
steering me through the yards to lights and people.

"What's the matter?" I asked. "D'you want to get picked up?"

"Why not?" said he. "It's better'n trying to flop in these yards."

I got his point. We made ourselves conspicuous. No one was interested. We headed for town. Now we wanted cops, we could find none. Only after a long wet hike through deserted streets did we see one.

We walked slowly by him on the other side of the street. He didn't hail us. We crossed and walked back toward him. He still wasn't interested. We took the initiative. "Say, officer, hows about vaggin' us? We're flat and no place to flop."

He looked us over. "I got other things to do. You can vag yourselves." He told us the way to the jail—another long rainy walk. A yawning sergeant entered our names on the blotter. We were shown to our cells.

As the cell door clanged shut, I tried to imagine myself a class-war prisoner. Radicals and strikers were always going to jail in the Twenties. The Wobblies had packed the jails in their free-speech fights. I couldn't get the feel . . . for thinking how warm and dry my cell after the boxcars.

When daylight woke me, I examined scratches on the wall. Few obscenities. Some IWW slogans. "Agitate! Educate! Organize!" Lines from Joe Hill songs. Some real class-war prisoners had been here.

After breakfast of coffee and dry bread, we were taken before a judge. A score of vagrants, we were handled wholesale. The roll was called. The bored judge told us to "get out of town, be gone by nightfall." How did he think we should travel without money? He didn't say. He didn't say to take the next freight out, as smalltowners did.

I didn't take a freight, but a passenger—as blind baggage. All went fine until my train stopped unexpectedly at a small depot high in the hills near the Oregon-California border. I stuck out my sooty cindered head, and found myself staring into the eyes of a railroad bull.

He frisked me so expertly he found a $2 bill I'd artfully hidden on me. He handed it back without a word. "Okay, come

along," he ordered . . . to jail, I thought. He didn't explain. He
steered me into the depot and told the drowsy clerk: "This
man's buying a ticket for $2—for as far as it'll take him."

The bull waited till I got my ticket. Then he left. The clerk
dozed off. For the rest of the night I was alone in the little
wooden waiting room. High in the mountains. Cold and the fra-
grant pines outside; inside, a small smoky stove. Without a cent,
but with a ticket. A passenger waiting for the next train. "The
roads" were up two bucks on me. But I was still ahead.

Deprived of my emergency fund, I was extra hungry and disheveled when at last I gaped on the glories of San Francisco. A
soaring, gleaming cosmopolis rising sheer from ocean and bay
. . . often mysteriously shrouded in sea fog. It had an Arabian
Nights quality—as witness what happened to me.

A dirty, penniless tramp, dodging cops and sickly empty inside, within hours I was eating my fill of fine food, leaning
against drink-laden bars, lolling in armchairs, chatting in
comfortable homes with princely company—princely, that is, in
wit, good will, and character. It happened easily, naturally. This
was San Francisco.

After claiming my suitcase, I had just enough to get a room
and clean up. I wanted also to eat and was looking for a dish-
washing job, when I recalled Vern Smith had said he'd write
about me to two friends here. I called one of them, Max Stern, a
reporter on the Scripps paper.

"Come right over," he said heartily. "We'll grab a bite at the
Press Club. I want you to meet some of the guys."

Meet them I did, in some numbers. I don't remember
names, except Stern and George P. West. I do recall how the
food and drink stroked my insides till they purred . . . and what
good guys they were. They were easy and friendly as old pals.
"Wobblies" and "reds" weren't bad words to them. They could
say "communist" without snarling and baring their teeth . . . or
without looking over the shoulder and lowering the voice. They
were, like the IWW preamble, for the millions who suffer hunger
and want, and against the exploiting few who enjoy all the good
things of life.

These newsmen had a living patron saint. "You must meet Fremont Older," they said. Some promised to take me to him. They made a date.

Refreshed and emboldened by this San Francisco debut, I called Smith's other friend—Roy Danforth, city editor of the *Oakland Tribune*. He too accepted me sight unseen, inviting me to dinner at his Berkeley home. There I enjoyed home warmth and familyness. Enchanted by the view over the bay to San Francisco, brimming with good food, friendship, and understanding, I lay back in an armchair and wondered.

What manner of people were these?

It was more than western hospitality. They showed me fellow-feeling. On Seattle's labor papers, this didn't surprise me. But these men all worked for the capitalist press—the "kept press," the "millionaire press," the "yellow press." I inquired of Danforth.

"Radicals, all radicals," he said expansively. "No matter who owns the papers, the working newspapermen around here—from city editor down, but not up—are all radicals of some kind . . . socialists, communists, anarchists, singletaxers, syndicalists. They get around and see how things are run. Their sympathies are with the working people, the underdogs."

Fremont Older was on the up side of city editor. He was editor of the San Francisco *Call-Bulletin*, a Hearst paper. The Hearst press, which started as friend of the working people, had already come to smell in labor and radical nostrils. "But Older is still okay—and how!" I was told.

My visit to Older was almost ceremonial. Three reporters I'd met at the Press Club escorted me. They stood admiring "the old man" and drinking in his words. Older was craggy in build, jutting features, character. His stormy crusades had washed away silt and overgrowth. The granite stood out. Still independent, a battler, at a time when smart editors bowed to the moneybags with servile conformity. Older read us an editorial he'd written in defense of prostitutes—humane enough to be daring, a bit shocking to prudes and the business office . . . pure Older.

Older sent me off elated. "Young fellow," he said, "I want to congratulate you. You've got the right idea. You're starting out the right way. You're going to have a very interesting life."

From the Older heights in San Francisco, I had to come down again to a rutty road. Hard jobs, dirty jobs, easiest to get because lowest paid. California's beauties entranced me, as I worked my way down the coast. In old age, I promised myself, I'd retire there to enjoy its sun and flowers, its mountains that roll down to the sea. Until then, there was more doing in the uglier world of class struggle in the industrial east. I was on my way back.

Los Angeles was but a stopover. From Skid Row, from Pershing Square, it looked grim and gray like an eastern city . . . with a trace of the queer. I worked there just long enough for a stake to carry me back to the harvest . . . meaning to start in the Texas Panhandle and follow it up to North Dakota. I rode the Southern Pacific freights to New Orleans.

Through southern California, Arizona, New Mexico, Texas, the SP crossed hundreds of miles of desert . . . with scores of miles between settlements. In shadeless desert a man could die of thirst and exposure to the sun. Once I got stranded miles from the nearest community. By the time I'd hiked there, my lips, mouth, throat, were parched numb. My sweat drained me of all vitality. I felt sick and dizzy. The sun beat down unbearably—continuously—without an instant of relief.

I'd read of the Bisbee, Arizona, "deportations"—when vigilantes ran striking metal miners and their families out of town . . . "deported" them to the desert. I had to feel the desert myself to measure this atrocity and to understand why talk of being "put off in the desert" held such grim fascination for the hobos. Then I saw it done.

We were far out in the desert when our freight stopped. It had quite a load of hobos, most white, but also a few blacks and more Mexicans. It was dusk. Three men with clubs and flashlights came down the side of the train.

"Any greasers here?" One flashed his light into our boxcar.

No one answered. The man ran his beam around the car. In a corner huddled two Mexicans. Their brown eyes were timid and scared as the light hit them. "All right, unload!" He waved the Mexicans out.

Thinking it a general order, a black and a white hobo also got up to jump out. "Not you," said the man. "Just greasers. We don't carry them."

"What they gonna do, out here in the desert?" protested a white hobo.

"You wanna get off too, and find out?" answered the man. The hobo shut up. "Don't worry. They ain't human."

In the northwest a man could ride on his union card. Here —and in the Deep South—a man rode on his skin color. I felt ashamed for mine.

The one "radical" I met on this trip was also a racist. We were passing through Texas. He was a big man, with wide mouth and face baked brown to red. He could flush redder when he swore in anger. He hated the bosses and Wall Street. He beefed bitterly about the worker's lot. I felt emboldened to talk about the IWW. Red—so tagged for complexion, not politics— was delighted. He knew about the Wobblies, was all for them. Soon as he got a job, it seemed, he'd be all set for a general strike.

When I made some crack about the Ku Klux Klan, Red stopped me short. "What's wrong with the Klan?" He glared at me glassy-eyed. I spluttered.

"I like it," said Red. "It's a good radical outfit, like the IWW."

"How can you compare them?" I gasped.

"Well, the IWW's radical for the working man and against the bosses. The Klan's radical against the nigger, to keep him in his place."

At New Orleans I tried to wash in the muddy Mississippi and reached town double-dirty. I had cop trouble and had to dodge into a Salvation Army mission and rebelliously to sing and pray for my soup. When I rented a room, rumpled bedding and used condoms soon told me my landlady was getting more rent than mine from it.

Disgusting me most were my first encounters with the overt racism of a southern city. The freight on which I fled it stalled in Louisiana swamplands, and for a whole long night I was under continuous attack from monster mosquitoes. My hobo life was getting worse and worse.

It was now late for harvesting in the Texas Panhandle, and I headed for Kansas. Moving through the south, I overheard some puzzling snatches of talk: "It's four bits a division now." "Always was a quarter." "It ain't now. It's fifty cents . . . or off." "If they's enough of us, and we stuck together——" "I seen it done . . . they had to back off." Before long I was to find the pieces of this puzzle put together.

From Louisiana into Mississippi and on to Arkansas, I saw poverty compounded by racism that made skid rows and hungry hobos seem privileged by comparison. I'd lived only in white slums, and only guessed how much worse the black slums must be. From slow-moving freights, I now saw tumbledown, flyridden shacks, swarming with half-naked children and lacking the barest necessities. Poor blacks and poor whites shared the poverty. The whites had similar shacks and were similarly underclad. Undernourishment even showed more in the bony angularity of the whites than in the more rounded forms of the blacks.

Irony more glaring than I'd felt as a child in Belfast, where slum Protestants fought slum Catholics instead of both joining to fight for themselves. Poor whites raised to hate and separate themselves from poor blacks under conditions crying to heaven for common struggle.

Our freight stopped at an out-of-the-way spot. It carried a score or two of hobos, black and white. Marching down from the front of the train came several white trainmen (blacks were barred from such jobs). Each carried a club. They shouted: "All shines get off." "End of the line for coons." "Come on, unload!"

The men went methodically from car to car. Brandishing their clubs, they hunted out hidden black hobos and made all get off. A white hobo in our car laughed. Another growled, "Don't kid yourself, our turn's coming."

Once they had put off all the blacks and driven them from the tracks, the trainmen stopped and regrouped at the caboose. Then they started marching back. This time they were more genial but just as methodical. They didn't brandish their clubs so fiercely, but they kept them handy.

"Okay, you guys," they said, "you're white, you can ride. But you gotta pay. It'll cost you four bits—fifty cents, one half dollar. That'll take you to the next division." Those who could, paid. Those who couldn't—fifty cents was blood money to a hobo—were thrown off. They followed the disconsolate blacks away from the tracks—but separately.

Outside Kansas City, Kansas, there was a spot well known to hobos, where westbound freights stopped. The tracks were at the foot of a wide, bare slope, topped by a fringe of thick woods. In these woods was a "jungle," now thronged with harvestbound men. As from a theater balcony, we could view the freights and their crews below. We could pick our train and car, and time our descent. The trouble was lack of cover on the way down. In daylight, hobos heading for the freights could be clearly seen, and they could not disguise their purpose.

Arriving around noon, I kept watch on the scene below. I expected to see freights loaded with harvestbound hobos. Instead the men were staying in the woods. Freight after freight pulled out, with no sign of riders in the empty boxcars. I asked, how come?

"They's gettin' tough."

"There's been shootin'. I'd wait till dark if I was you."

Toward dusk I saw the first dash for the freights. Three men went down the hill—but not with the unhurried stroll of last year's harvesters. They ran crouched like soldiers risking a coverless run before enemy guns. They disappeared behind a train. Then I heard a couple of shots—sharp cracks in the peaceful evening. Surely not fired at these men! Maybe at some thieves. Maybe warning shots in the air, to scare off hobos. But why? The Kansas wheatfields needed thousands of harvesthands. I was taking no chances, nor were most of the others. We waited for dark.

It got dark. No more light than the stars above and the locomotive headlights below. I thought to make a run for a likely freight. As I stepped into the open, I saw the flash and heard the crack of a gunshot below. I turned back, to wait some more. Through the night, there was sporadic shooting. A quiet hour maybe—as if to put us off guard. Some of the more daring might chance a run; then a crackle of gunfire.

Whatever the intent, the effect was obvious. I'd read of vendettas between farmers and the hated railroads. Were they deliberately blocking the farmers' labor supply? Or was it a hint our labor was now in less demand?

Maybe it was the gunfire, the contour of the battlefield, the contrast between these dwindling, defeated harvesthands and last year's advancing army. As I lay sleepless, my mind kept turning over a French poem on the battle of Waterloo, and the phrase "fin de siècle." That's my only claim to premonition then of what hindsight now clearly reveals. New machinery for harvesting with fewer hands, the combine, bulldozers, and the like, were ending a way of life for many Americans. It was the end of an epoch for casual migratory labor.

In a quiet hour just before dawn—when the most active night gives up exhausted—I slipped down the hill and hid in a westbound boxcar. I ran into no further interference with the harvestbound. Our numbers were sharply reduced. Farmers came to jungles and freight stops hunting for help. Hearing $8 a day was being paid in western Kansas, I kept pushing west until I got it.

The work was different from that in North Dakota and Canada. No shocking of bundles. After the reaper had done its work, we pitched the long loose wheat into horsedrawn wagons; then from them right into the threshing machine. It was harder work with less respite, but at $8 a day I made a fair stake. My enthusiasm for the harvest was waning, however. After the Kansas City experience, I foresaw hazards as well as hardships on the long trek north.

In a jungle, as I headed back eastward, I ran into a bunch of Wobblies, first I'd met this year, with bundles of IWW literature. One I'd seen in Chicago and knew by name. He was to become a leading academic authority on labor, an apologist for the AFL bureaucracy. Seeing him many years later at a Washington party, I reminded him of that Kansas jungle encounter. He looked blank and responded not at all . . . whether forgetful or embarrassed, I still don't know.

The group looked rather forlorn, offering their propaganda to returning harvesthands. The Wobblies I first met, the year before, were organizing the harvestbound for job action, for porkchops.

Porkchops—commonest meat on western migratory jobs —was the Wobbly word for wage-and-condition demands, the workers' bread-and-butter interests. Its use reflected lack of contact with Jewish workers in the cities. Once I showed some Wobblies a cartoon of an IWW soapboxing on New York's east side: "What you want is porkchops—and more porkchops." They could see no humor in the puzzled expressions of the Jewish audience.

In that jungle, I again got that vague end-of-an-epoch feeling. If it is a living organism, an organization takes on the characteristics of the people who compose it. It grows and changes with them. It may die with them, unless new generations join and adapt it to themselves.

The IWW was born in western mining camps, from the rape of an independent, frontier working class by ruthless employers. The Western Federation of Miners was its base, the miners' Big Bill Haywood its leader. As a stripling, the IWW boldly challenged the American Federation of Labor, offering industrial unions for all workers, instead of craft unions for a favored few. The AFL kowtowed to capitalist rule; the IWW proposed to overthrow it.

The AFL had a corner on union business in the industrial east. It left lower-paid factory workers out in the cold. The IWW made sorties into the east—as in the big Lawrence (Massachusetts) textile strike, also in Akron and other centers that later became CIO strongholds. A remarkable flying squad of strike agitators like Joe Ettor, Arturo Giovanitti, Elizabeth Gurley Flynn, led these sorties. The IWW's more lasting base was in the camp life of the west.

In the Socialist party, chief radical outlet for city workers, the revolutionary appeal of the IWW did more to counter reformism than to furnish guidelines for union organization, though it diverted some from work in AFL unions. Election politics meant little to footloose western Wobblies—on reason, perhaps, why they sometimes appealed to a link with the voteless, immigrant factory workers. A frontier tradition of direct action suited them more than the "sewer-socialism" (preoccupation with municipal ownership) of the SP or AFL-type collective bargaining.

These traits, including an accentuated distrust of politicians, attracted to the IWW the theoreticians of a professedly apolitical or antipolitical syndicalism. This syndicalism produced little in lasting organization, but indirectly had far-reaching influence on American labor attitudes.

In the Sixties, the New Left rediscovered the IWW—attracted by its distinctively American roots, the verve of its free-swinging activists, its revolutionary stance, its participatory democracy, and an individualism that detracted from its organizational success.

When I first met the IWW, in 1921, it had already changed in many ways. The western metal miners had long since left, to practice a more conventional unionism. The IWW was no longer capable of the eastern sorties that once brought it fame. Some thought was given to organizing in industries like steel and packinghouse, and in 1923 I was to work in them and write promotion to this end. But it was more thought than organizing. That job had finally to wait for the CIO.

Ideologically, the IWW was losing its revolutionary appeal. A desiccated syndicalism did not excite the postwar radicals. It could not match the inspiration of the Russian revolution, or offer fields of activity comparable to those of the rising communist movement. Communists were picking up red banners once flaunted by the IWW. They were to carry them into the unorganized industries and into the AFL itself.

In the early Twenties, the IWW still had some base in western harvest fields, logging camps, general construction, maritime —all migratory occupations. In maritime, a communist-inclined left was eventually to forge ahead. The lumber industry was becoming more homeguard. Heavy equipment was taking over in basic construction. As to the harvest fields, I'd already had a foretaste of what was in store.

I mailed my harvest stake ahead and beat my way to Chicago. Arriving at nightfall dirty and hungry, I headed for West Madison Street. In a quick-and-dirty not far from the Northwestern station, I saw a sign "Dishwasher Wanted." The coincidence of need and opportunity was too much. Without thinking, I walked right in and was put to work.

My gorge began to rise at the grease, the filth, the stench, the sweat, the piling pressure. I felt like smashing the dishes and going berserk. I worked until it was time to eat. Somehow I didn't mind eating the greasy stuff. But once full, I took off my apron, threw it down in a corner, and walked out onto West Madison Street.

The proprietor ran after me. Anger flared on his puffy pallid face. Unmindful of the passersby, he stood on the sidewalk in shirtsleeves and soiled apron shouting at me to come back. He shook his fist and cursed me as I hurried away.

That was my personal end-of-an-epoch. I wanted to get away, never to see West Madison Street again. I wanted no more of the kind of experience I'd sought when I first came to Chicago. I'd had it.

Chapter Three

THE UNORGANIZED WORKERS

*Radicals kept alive the hope of organizing
the mass of industrial workers. Eugene
Debs, Big Bill Haywood, William Z.
Foster helped prepare the road John L.
Lewis was to travel.*

There was something abrasive about Chicago. . . .

The workers I had identified with so far were grossly exploited and capable of radical action. But by the nature of their lives and work they were unstable, disorganized, individualistic . . . and their role in the American economy was declining fast. Here in Chicago, in giant factories, mills, and plants of every kind, was a working class wonderfully organized to work together for production. If it organized for its own advantage—and Chicago labor had shown some ambition along these lines—what mightn't it do to better its lot and to transform society? To strike the roots I sought, I should have stayed on in Chicago. But . . .

Chicago was the center, the hard core of the United States. Around it my labor life was to revolve, and in it I worked long and repeatedly. Never did I quite live down my first boxcar impression that Chicago was some kind of hell. New York had its superstructural graces. In San Francisco, a pleasant sea fog might cloud one's head, but on a clear day one could view mankind from the heights of high purpose. Other cities had their special, even romantic appeals; one could live as well as work in them. Chicago was just a hasslehole to earn or swindle money and slug it out in the struggle for existence.

My Chicago life—as hobo, factory worker, reporter, editor, printer—was to take me from West Madison Street to drab rooms in westside worker neighborhoods, to courtship in northside apartments, to a home on a street half-black, half-white in the south side's battleground between the races. I put up at all the big Loop hotels that I once envied, even drove up Michigan Avenue once in a city limousine, with cigar too, to be introduced to the mayor. I ended up in Chicago blacklisted as a red (courtesy the *Chicago Tribune*), kicked from job to job, and shadowed by the FBI. Earlier I'd seen Chicago's Red Squad bullyboy its way around the IWW; I'd paid the graft extorted by its traffic cops and inspectors; I'd seen Chicago police beat and kick helpless drunks with jovial sadism. I learned of graft and gangsterism, involving bosses and politicians, too hot for its detectors to dare to publicize.

In other cities, CIO was to be a great crusade with flying banners. Chicago took it in its down-to-earth stride. It was real business, real class struggle—Chicago knew all about that, whatever it called it. When cops killed a dozen unarmed Republic Steel strikers in 1937—most shot in the back—Chicago suffered no emotional cataclysm. That was routine life-and-death in Chicago. Mayor Kelley, the killer-cops' commander, made it up to the labor boys in other ways.

Mayor Daley's police reception for dissidents during the 1968 Democratic convention may have surprised some of the younger generation who came from other cities. It could not have surprised an old Chicagoan.

Having long had the feel of Chicago, I came to understand why various radical labor projects, thriving in the sophisticated, cosmopolitan hothouse of New York, should shift to Chicago as more central to American working-class life and struggle, only to die of attrition there, if they didn't flee back. To survive in this hard core of the United States, a red had to be pretty hard-core himself. I invited one to my house for a party.

"Why?" he asked.

"We're just having in some friends for a social evening," I said.

"Yes, yes," he said testily, "I understand. But what's the purpose?"

"Wh-y-y . . . just sociability . . . I guess." I had a new-found sense of guilt.

"M-m-mn, sociability?" For a moment he considered this frivolous notion. He didn't show up.

In Chicago life was real and life was earnest. As an earnest young man with a purpose, I should have stayed there. But my young-man fancy turned to San Francisco's foggy heights, Seattle comradeship, Los Angeles sunshine, and now even to the kackle-klatsches of New York. Torn between dire duty in Chicago and possible pleasure in New York, I compromised. I went to Detroit.

Detroit was different—a one-industry town, concentrated. Chicago's factory-fortresses reeked grimly of the masters' feudal might, the workers' past defeats. Detroit's auto plants shone mighty, bright and modern, looking ahead. Looking to the future too were youngsters in these plants, some to come into my ken again, 15 years later, as CIO leaders.

Where did these youngsters get the push, the thought, the vision, that started them on this road? Not from YMCA or churches. Not from schools or colleges. Certainly not from the AFL. In a dozen grimy halls in poor districts, a dozen kinds of red revolutionists kindled the spark—Marxian educational groups, communist trunklines and offshoots, leftwing socialists, Proletarian partyites, all drawing inspiration from you-know-where, you-know-what, and you-know-whom.

Granpa Marx and Papa Lenin had lots of American kids in Detroit. Bright kids, working-class kids. But for these forebears, they might have had but one American dream—to climb over their fellows, to go into business and make money, to push and higgle-haggle their way to personal success. The Russian revolution gave them another dream, and started them reading Marx. No more for them the climber's shame in being a worker, but pride in being of the working class—the class that should lead the world to a future free from poverty, exploitation, war.

To these youngsters, the auto plants were no longer prisons where they must serve time until, leaving their mates in durance, they went out for the big money, for success. In the red glow of their youth, they saw the plants as future bastions of the workers' might which some day might belong to and serve all the people. All knew the first step must be union organization. The redder the kids, the more dedicated they were to this goal. When CIO came—more out of than to Detroit—when it captured the auto plants, young people from the plants and oldtime radicals took the lead, not big-bellied organizers smoking cigars and slapping backs in hotel lobbies.

When they stirred the stirring workers with their words and their example, were these new leaders calculating the per capita that might come their way? Was their goal a piecard and promotion to union big shot? Did they dream of swivel chairs and pretty secretaries in plushy modern offices? Did they vision a brave new world with Wall Street and General Motors forever on top, and union leaders cut in on the gravy and the government recognition?

Yes, some of them. Those I knew best, and who did the most stirring, had other visions. Somewhere inside them lurked precepts handed down from Marx and Lenin through older radicals in dingy little halls. They saw the union struggle as part of a longtime working-class struggle for power to change the world.

I got glimpses of Detroit's radical circles, but found no free-and-easy admittance as in the more Wobblyfied west. I headed for New York, stopping off to visit Powers Hapgood in the western Pennsylvania coalfields.

To reach the coalfields, one had to leave cities and main highways and head for the hills, following tortuous byways until one found—dug into the side of a craggy peak, or nestled in green countryside—a close-packed, coaldusty little town that might have been cut out of some city slum. I hunted till I found some mining towns. I didn't find the miners or Hapgood. A long strike had closed the mines; the miners were gone from their homes.

Their homes? The houses they lived in didn't belong to the miners, any more than the mines, the stores, the townships, built on their labor. The companies owned the mines, the miners' jobs, the houses they lived in, the authorities who made the rules, the police who enforced them. I finally found the miners and their families in the woods and the fields, living in tents. They were short of food, clothes, everything. In his union duties, Hapgood faced countless human problems. One I did not anticipate.

Bourgeois theorists maintain that radical thoughts are pumped into workers' minds by outside agitators influenced by disaffected intellectuals. Yet outside agitator Hapgood, a Harvard socialist, found it hard to convince the miners that American capitalism allowed workers any rights at all. State police were picking up and jailing strikers on any, every, or no pretext. When out of jail himself, Hapgood shuttled from courtroom to jail on dozens of these cases. I went along on some. Most of the miners were foreign-born. Language handicapped them, but even more their assumption that police, courts, judges, laws, were all devised to keep them down and to break their strikes and their union. Hapgood had constantly to argue that they had some legal rights and should use them.

If the miners had studied the histories of early American strikes, they might have scored many points in their arguments with Hapgood.

Back in New York, the positive Frank Anderson took charge of my uncertainties. He had me stay with him to write up my experiences; and when he gleaned I still wanted to serve the movement as a worker, yet have some fun, he talked my way into a place where both were possible: Brookwood Labor College. For the next few years I worked in basic industries, in great factories and on the ships at sea, relating my work to union needs. Let the work be hard, conditions grim, I could always look forward or back to days of comradeship, study, flirtation at Brookwood.

A.J. Muste was the man who ran Brookwood, residential labor college of the Twenties. We could not then have imagined his later career as militant activist in radical and pacifist causes— until in his eighties he matched the youth as man of action against the Vietnam war. To us young Brookwooders, A.J. was essentially the moderate. We respected his counsels of caution, practicality, a relative labor conformism. But our favorite crack was that he always looked for the center with his "On the one hand . . . But on the other hand. . . ." I would have expected him to progress ever rightward, a typical social-democrat. Youthful impatients, we didn't suspect that fires like our own might burn beneath the diplomatic calm of this lean and eager man.

The International Ladies Garment Workers, the Amalgamated Clothing Workers, and some second-string leaders of other unions, aided Muste in his Brookwood project, if without great vigor. But for all its early efforts to conform, Brookwood was soon redbaited by the AFL executive council under the educational guidance of Matthew Woll—chief sniffer-out of dangerous thoughts before there was a House Un-American Activities Committee.

Labor idealists liked Brookwood. To the romantic, it had aspects of a quasi-Utopian colony. To the more practical, if optimistic, it was a step toward advancing labor from the rear end to the vanguard of progress. To me, at my age and in my state of mind, it was altogether enchanting.

Brookwood was beautiful—if not beyond compare, certainly by compare. To the miner, Brookwood was green, clean, all above ground—no coaldust, no cricks in the back. To the machinist, Brookwood was greaseless days far from the grinding roar of metal against metal. To makers of suits, dresses, hats, Brookwood was fairytale country to which they were wand-wafted from the square, treeless hills, the trash-strewn cement valleys of Manhattan or Chicago. To those who had known poverty, Brookwood offered ease, security, the fresh-air pleasures of the well-to-do.

Physically, Brookwood was a George Washington country mansion, white and wooden-grand with high pillars and wide portico. It looked out over the wooded hills and valleys of a large estate near Katonah, New York. Nestled in surrounding greenery were cabins and cottages for faculty and students. A new, red-brick women's dormitory rose behind the main building.

In fall, the Brookwood air was clear and crisp; the sun shone radiant. Rains greened the country till the woods yielded to many-colored shrivel and decay. Fruit and vegetables were stored away. Evenings became welcomely warm indoors, and most sociable. Appetites grew with outside work and the coming of frost. In winter, we snugged in under the snow, digging out a road for the little Ford station wagon to bounce to the village for groceries and mail. Ice-firm ponds reddened the cheeks, chapped the lips, nipped the noses of city-pale skaters. Sled runners replaced wheels. Young people bundled for warmth and affection on night rides behind snorting steaming bell-tinkling horses. Indoors a winter doldrum set in. Confinement took its toll of earlier sociabilities.

Spring was a real busting-out all over. Magician-like Brookwood cast off its snow mantle to reveal spectacular glitter and glamor. Amid fat, bursting buds, sun-dimpled rivulets, babygreen grass, murmuring trees, young men and women slipped off arm and arm to tread through daisies of dalliance, to lie and linger on bewitching hilltops. As to the Brookwood summer, we knew it not. It was back to the working class for us.

Economically, Brookwood was months of freedom from want. We all knew where the next meal was coming from. In turns and by squads, we gathered its ingredients, cooked and served them. The food was good, plentiful, even balanced by a dietician. Shelter? In cabins and dormitories we had strong cots and lots of blankets. If fires went out and we got cold, it was our own fault. There was coal to fetch and stoke; and wood all around for the chopping. Clothing? With khaki pants from Army Surplus and a couple of workshirts, a man could get by; and for fancier dates, love would find a way. Socially, Brookwood was coeducation at close quarters. Faculty families hovered around but didn't interfere.

Spiritually, Brookwood was a labor movement in microcosm —without bureaucrats or racketeers—with emphasis on youth, aspiration, ideals.

Classes covered sociology, economics, labor history, the practice of collective bargaining, but not Marxist theory. The teachers were experts, contributing the extra effort and devotion of persons addicted more to causes than careers. Most students returned to their industries and unions—as they were supposed to do—better equipped to handle day-to-day union problems and to assume leadership, as many of them did.

Into this little labor paradise, I bounded like a colt first let loose in a green paddock; I kicked up my heels.

She swept me onto the dance floor—and onto her feet—the first social night. I couldn't dance, but I had fun. All I knew in my daze was that she was a redhead and exciting. I'd had no inoculation against the infectious female.

Early boarding schools kept me from girls and two-sex stuff. Bees-and-flowers talk left me cold. At teenage Harrow, seductive females were excluded. A few sisters might infiltrate, briefly and under close guard, for a cricket match. They looked, acted, and were treated like sisters. Illegality remained. Before leaving, a true Harrovian had to take out at least one "chorus girl" or "town girl." Without money or nerve for a London chorus girl, I dutifully and grimly set out to date a town girl. Aside from the stealth involved, I recall only long silences, uncompleted advances and awkward retreats, dangling fingers, hot flushes to the face, and another face expressionless, determined not to recognize that anything was afoot.

In the British army, I suffered a handicap. In officer-training for the Royal Field Artillery, we were gunners in rank, pay, and uniform but wore white bands around our caps. The Australians with us didn't. Wherever we were stationed, the Aussies got the pick of the women while we were avoided. It was their higher pay, we thought until we learned the Aussies passed the word that white capbands meant venereal disease.

At Oxford, it was back to a womanless world, or nearly. There was, I believe, a women's college on the outskirts, whose chaperoned inmates one might rarely see but not touch. Somehow they suggested Blue Stocking rather than Woman or Sex to me. Whether or not long, dark blue cotton or woolen stockings were required, I forget. In my English labor and radical activities, I recall few women, and had no woman comrade. In the United States I again fell into a womanless world, that of migratory labor. Then, of a sudden, coeducation, my first taste at Brookwood, with Tess!

No sun ever shone with such glory as when Tess arose. No birds ever chirped so blithely as when Tess stepped out. All Brookwood, all nature, became suffused with her charms. I mooned around bemused, bewitched, in a cloud of rapturous confusion. Then—first inkling of my infidelity—I cast side glances at Tess's girl friends, also adept at the game of love— girls who could speak before spoken to, even kid around in my rather abstract areas of conversation.

With Tess and her friends, I made trips to Greenwich Village—where Floyd Dell then held sway. I recall much emphasis on Love and Sex; on Art, a secondary conversation piece; on Rebellion against the mores and beliefs of middle-class, midwestern America, whence most Villagers sprang.

I compared things with London's Chelsea, where Love and Art were equally in vogue, and Rebellion against Victorian moralities belatedly continued. A teenage visitor to my brother's pad, I'd been more struck by its black sheets and pillowslips than by the conventional unconventionalities of London's polite bohemia. Love and marriage mixed little, I'd noted, monogamy was out, reproduction but an accidental byproduct of sex. Religion, if at all, was exotic; politics a bit square.

Greenwich Village didn't then hold it square to be a political radical. A cynical nihilism was not in vogue, as with beatniks of the Fifties. A few dashes of bolshevism were as much a part of a Village cocktail as a drop or two of atheism and a couple of jiggers of free love. To do much about being a red was perhaps square, but anyone reaching that point had grown out of the Village anyhow. About free love, on the other hand, one was expected to do more than I, for one, believed physically possible. In Greenwich Village a hobo Wobbly wasn't an outcast or freak. On the contrary. Into this social set I could slip, and fit too easily.

At the moment I didn't care. I was discovering so much. The touch of a woman's hand. The mating look in her eye. The feel of body to body. The electricity of chance contact. Hair that tingled alive. Arms softly round and firm in embrace. Breasts beckoning back to babyhood. Bodies fresh and awkward as a baby colt, or sinuous like a lazy cat. Teasing, taunting moments that to me brought not itch but ecstasy.

By late train from Grand Central we'd return to Katonah. Our laughter, our capers, how they might strike belated pedestrians on New York's sidewalks or echo in the vaulted catacombs of Grand Central, we heeded not—absorbed in ourselves, intoxicated with youth and sex. Our conversation—sophisticated, witty, emancipated, radical, and daringly naturalistic—it seemed. Now when I hear a bright, coeducated 15-year-old regaling girlish company with risqué jokes and flights of fancy wit, I sometimes wonder and blush for my retarded youth.

Hiking from Katonah to Brookwood in the small hours, we dinned deserted roads and silent fields with "Rolling home, by the light of the silvery moon"; "Three o'clock in the morning . . ."; "Margie"; "K-K-K-Katy"; "Come landlord, fill the flowing bowl . . ."; and Wobbly songs.

I was but dimly aware that Brookwood frowned on such antics. Everyone was kind and considerate. If any hissed maledictions like "Greenwich Village playboy" or "petty-bourgeois intellectual," they were shielded from my ears. Tactful efforts were made to reform me.

For the first time in my life, I faced the charge of being frivolous. Dealing the shock was a sweetfaced, demure young lady with roundly bobbed and fluffed-out hair, and a slightly oriental lift to her wideset eyes. I'd noticed her out of the corner of my eyes. She made me think of a French writer's description of the Muses: "Tant nettes, tant honnêtes, tant pudiques . . ." and so constantly occupied with their arts that "even Cupid put down his bow and arrow . . . and did not dare to shoot." She spoke kindly but firmly, saying undeniable things. But I winced when she said I was doubtless doomed by background to be a dilettante. After that I kept out of her way.

Only later in life did I learn that some Brookwood girls had taken pity on my infatuation and projected a rescue mission. Their idea was that a rich man's daughter was trifling with the affections of a simple-minded poor boy. At any moment, her whim might be to cast me off—to who knows what despair. The trifler was drawing me into flighty fickle company, to the detriment of my studies and my usefulness to society. They consulted my nemesis of the Muselike image. She refused to go along, because (1) she was too busy with her studies; (2) it would do no good; (3) I had it coming. As a concession to social conscience, she gave me her brief lecture. After that, finish— she'd have no more to do with me.

As for me, trifle was my favorite New Zealand dessert. I loved the trifling. The rescue was neat too; all innocently, I enjoyed its attentions.

Tess and friends were related to Brookwood's early benefactors. They weren't in the groove of a strictly trade-union college —into which Muste was purposefully pushing Brookwood.

When they left, I gave all attention to fellow students who came from the unions. I became aware of a whole new body of critical opinion, standards, ethics, attitudes.

The students were a fair sample of active American trade unionists.

Joe was a cooper. His trade had its heyday when sleek dray-horses drew bellying barrels of beer through the streets. It was on the decline, as was his Coopers' union. Like it, he clung to pride of craft, and stubbornly took the conservative side in labor arguments.

Buck was an Irish-American electrician from Boston. He could sense a slur at the drop of a syllable, and rise in his wrath to defend the Irish, the Catholics, the AFL—with equal vigor and vituperation. Though Buck's mental reservations didn't surface in the stress of battle, he was serious and studious and curious about contrasting attitudes at Brookwood. His union, International Brotherhood of Electrical Workers, was due to expand greatly with the New Deal, in competition with the CIO, and Buck became one of the more forward-looking leaders in IBEW headquarters.

Julius looked impressive—a softer, plumper, vegetarian John L. Lewis. His bulk, his brows, his resonant voice, his authoritative manner, made him a natural for leadership. In his International Ladies Garment Workers, his social-democratic views fitted him into a union machine veering ever rightward from socialism; and he was proving reliable in its fight against a strong communistic left wing. He was to rise high officially.

Jack was a machinist, a nut-splitter. As a boomer-machinist, he had rough-and-tumbled through many strikes. The International Association of Machinists, led by William Johnston, was then one of the more radical AFL unions. Socialist influence had been strong; the IWW had made some impact. The IAM subscribed verbally to the class struggle. It favored all-inclusive organizing of workers and the labor-party idea. Jack was radical to similar extent. But the Russian revolution and left-right fights had created an annoying interruption to his train of thought. He was coming to look with equal jaundice at red upstarts to his left and old fogeys to his right. Jack later became a district director of the CIO Steel Workers Organizing Committee.

Muf, a railway clerk, stood for what was then hailed as "practical labor idealism." Between the hidebound right and the wild left, he tried to steer a left-of-center course. A Brookwood product and disciple of Muste, he looked for progressive policies that might avoid collision with the union officialdom. Later he worked for the short-lived Musteite movement (Conference Committee for Progressive Labor Action). Phil E. Ziegler, editor and finally general secretary of the Brotherhood of Railway Clerks, eventually hired Muf as his assistant.

Ziegler was one of the union sponsors of Brookwood. Others included Clinton S. Golden (then IAM, but later Philip Murray's sidekick in the CIO steel drive); John Brophy, then a district president of the United Mine Workers; and a number of needle-trades union officials.

The coal miners at Brookwood were roughly left-of-center. Broad-shouldered, slowspoken Tony, a Yugoslav, good-naturedly argued a social-democratic line against the left. Mike, more of a hothead, was a Musteite who later did collide with union officialdom. Young Joe was an Americanized second-generation immigrant who sniffed at old-country attitudes.

Spike and I upheld the honor of hobodom. Of the proletariat, he liked to affect a stance to its lumpen side. How I got into Brookwood was more of a puzzle . . . possibly passed off on benefactors opposed to AFL exclusivism as representing "the IWW element." A.J.'s wife, Anne Muste, had a simpler explanation. Pressing my case, Frank Anderson had talked and talked far into the night till A.J. was limp, while I said nothing. "We figured," said she, "that anyone who could stay silent under so much talk might add something new to Brookwood—and could at least survive here."

Spike was a huge man, clumsy, bearlike amid the chinaware of Brookwood refinement, or so it pleased his humor to appear. Like Jack, he was from the IAM and had been a boomer-machinist. Like most hobos, he was secretive about his past, merely hinting at not-to-be-admitted activities. Jack, his buddy, had tales to tell. Spike had been an inside-man in organizing and strikes. An all-around machinist, he could apply for any job. His "open-shop face" and simpleton affectations endeared him to the bosses. But the job Spike did was not for them, it was for the union.

Before proceeding further left, I must define "left" as I use the word.

The American communist movement was "underground" at the time. That is, it had always to look out for cops. It was just exercising rights legal under the Constitution—freedom of speech to express communist ideas, freedom of press to print and propagate them, peaceful assembly to promote its movement. On the other hand: In January, 1920, Attorney-General A. Mitchell Palmer, aided by J. Edgar Hoover, had some ten thousand persons arrested in 70 cities on suspicion of being communists, anarchists, socialists, syndicalists. Leaders of the (then two) communist parties were jailed. Some 500 were deported forthwith. The Labor Department ruled that members of the United States communist movement were deportable as such.

In continuing their legal activities therefore, the communists had to guard against illegal clouts. To be openly communist was to wear a "Kick Me" sign. The communists soon came up for air with an overground Workers party, but not until 1925 did they add "Communist" to it.

There was perhaps some compensation for the red. It was less common then, than later, to fire a suspected communist from his job, expel him from his union, blacklist him, abrogate his civil rights, break up his family, expose him to scorn and hatred as potential spy or traitor, drive him to suicide, or make him victim of some murderous screwball. Penalties for the communist were severe enough. But, after all, you couldn't be a communist—it wasn't legal.

The word "left" was protectively applied to those, including communists, who shared certain beliefs but who might or might not be communists in the punishable sense. The beliefs were along these lines:

Socialism—with the means of production owned and run by the people for the benefit of all instead of the profits of a few—

was a good thing. It could advance into a communism under which the state as an instrument of class rule would wither away; all would get what they needed, according to their need; motives for imperialist war would disappear; and mankind might look forward to true freedom, fraternity, and equality.

The ruling capitalist class would not without a struggle give up its pelf and power to socialism. The working people had most to gain from a social transformation that would put them on top. They should struggle for socialism and could win it, if led by a party based on the working class and true to its needs and mission.

Such party must be international in outlook, supporting all liberation efforts, defending those who won power for socialism in whatever country. Given the stress of real struggle for socialism, it must be a disciplined party of action, capable of changing tactics and still acting as a unit, like an army in the field. It must prove itself and mobilize the workers by day-to-day devoted service to their immediate needs.

A number of Brookwood students leaned to this body of beliefs and were politely classified as of "the left." In their turn, they called those aiding their current campaigns "progressive"; and those opposing, "rightwing" or "reactionary." The "right" or more conservative were less finicky about definition. They called all who criticized them from the left—particularly in union elections—"lousy communists" or "communist stooges."

On the left were Art and Bob, both IAM Machinists, and George

Art was a veteran of many union battles. Short and stocky, he was a sociable joker, full of the rough humor of the shops. Politically, he'd take no dirt from anyone. He was sure, stubborn, forthright. He called the working class the working class, spurning the then-fashionable concessions to bourgeois terminology. I thought of him, in New Deal days, when I heard Harry Bridges at a Washington party lifting liberal eyebrows with his talk of "the working class." Art doughtily defended the Russian revolution. He had no use for social-democratic reformism, though strong for immediate demands. On union issues, he was a militant.

Bob was young, slim, handsome, with dark, curly hair. Of Italian parentage, he sang "Bandiera Rossa," the Internationale, and other radical songs in Italian, usually changing their "socialismo" into "comunismo." With his guitar, with love songs as well as labor songs, and with his radiant good humor, Bob could turn even social-democratic heads—if feminine.

Art brought out the working-class roots of revolution; Bob, its romantic aspects. George made many think of the caricature commissar.

George was consistently serious. He *could* smile; I saw it happen. It was the faint, indulgent, shamefaced smile my father might be betrayed into by some errant babe who did not yet know right from wrong. George had attended classes in Marxian economics on Manhattan's east side. I looked in on them. A stern-visaged pedagogue mystified his pupils with heavy accent, long words, and mathematical abracadabra, verbally caning them into confusion upon confusion. I felt lucky to escape without a trauma from such a Dotheboys Hall of mental misery and spiritual starvation. Perhaps George was less fortunate.

George was logical; he spoke from an informed, thought-out position. He was reasonable, conceding points that had validity. He was listened to with respect—if also with a little irritation. Somehow, reasonable as he was, George could impress others as a bit rigid and doctrinaire. Maybe it was the way he closely hewed to a party line that was generally if seldom accurately known, but that George had studied down to the last comma in the last issue of *Inprecorr*.

George had a calm, bedside, or father-confessor, manner for the politically uncertain or troubled. He knew how to listen, draw out, understand, then give comfort and guidance with the assurance of one who has long plotted and plodded the road to everlasting grace. But George's calmness stopped at his own emotions. After marital complications with a high-strung wife, he came to find a calmer one. Somehow the intervening emotional storms swept George's old convictions down the drain, till he came to look on them as so much sewage.

George's classmates predicted he'd become an editor of the

Daily Worker. Actually, in a few years, he became an antired organizer for a union fighting the left full-time on every front, at
home and abroad.

The women students—from the fewer unions that then had
many women—also ranged from right to left. Those from little-
organized industries were more hopefully than actually unionists. YWCA-ish, they wanted to do right but were little versed in
union struggle, still less in labor politics. The young women
from the needle trades more than made up. Unionism was their
daily life, their bread and butter, their inspiration, their struggle
center. Most were steeped in both radical and union politics.

Right and left were fighting it out in the needle unions. In
milder form, the conflict was ideological, involving extra-union
politics in the Jewish and other immigrant communities. At its
most acute, it was an all-out struggle for union control. In the
Amalgamated Clothing Workers, Sidney Hillman and a left responsive to his leftward gestures kept the conflict within
bounds. Hillman tried to steer a left of center course of appeal
to all but the far-right. He preferred to buy off rather than batter
down potential opposition; if carrot failed, he used the club. In
the Ladies Garment Workers, right-left conflict approached civil
war. The left wing won elections in local after local, until it
posed an actual threat to rightwing control of the international
union.

Brookwood had some women students of "leadership
caliber"—that is, of matronly composure and stable build, loyal
to union leaders who sponsored them. It also had centrists who
didn't enjoy factional hair-pulling and being bitter against the
left, but for whom the left was too far out for respectability. But
the leftics fascinated me most.

These were among the younger and prettier girls—not a vi-
rago among them. They were lively, enthusiastic, emotional—
shedding many a tear when Lenin died. Some inspiration they
drew from old-world revolutionists, but more was American. Of
Russian-Jewish extraction mostly, these young women were born
in the United States or brought here as children. They learned
about socialism from Eugene Debs, about labor from working in

American shops, about class struggle from the turmoil and strikes of unionization.

Here, I marveled, were young women who could stand up to any man in labor or political argument. They had spunk—had shown it on picket lines and in organizing nonunion shops. Practical and down-to-earth, they had wide horizons. They read books—social science as well as poetry and novels. Politically active, they were inspired by humanistic aims and a world-ranging revolutionary philosophy. And they were feminine.

Caroline—she who had made me think of the Muses—seemed quieter and more studious than most, but she was not untypical. Brought in childhood from Bessarabia, she worked in American factories from her earliest teens, often as main support of her family. She educated herself through night classes, correspondence courses, much reading. She was a pioneer of the Amalgamated Clothing Workers in Milwaukee and worked for the union in a big Philadelphia strike. Politically, Caroline had been active in the Young Peoples Socialist League and in socialist campaigns for Congressman Victor Berger and Mayor Daniel Hoan. With other Milwaukee socialists, she opposed the First World War. With the younger and more enthusiastic, she was swept leftward by the Russian revolution and its impact on the American radical movement.

At 23, Caroline was an all-around labor activist—well-grounded in public speaking; in influencing others; in all forms of organizational work; in understanding union and political issues. If she seemed quiet, it was not for being retiring, but because she was recovering from serious illness, and because she wanted to profit from her first educational break.

Before I left Brookwood, I was drawn to Caroline by an osmosis that was gradual, inevitable, final. She had brains, practicality, labor experience, organizational sense. She had social vision and purpose . . . was in fact the most social person I ever knew, toward every individual within her reach as well as in the generality. Quite a deal—and all wrapped up in one trim, sweet, pretty package.

We left Brookwood together, hand in hand, to hitchhike to Chicago. I was on my way back to factory work; she to work for her union in its pioneering of unemployment insurance. We had no more property than we could carry on our backs, and no interest in acquiring any. What had that to do with "the movement"?

The thick copper wire came out of a machine. When there was enough for a coil, the man at the machine cut the wire. I took the coil, tied it, and stacked it for loading onto a handtruck. This I did eight hours a day, six days a week, month after month. Where the wire came from or went, what the machine did, nobody told me. The middle-aged man at the machine knew what it did and took pride in mastering its quirks. But he spoke little English, and I'd learned not to be curious about another man's job, lest I be suspect of wanting to steal it. The machine was one of a hundred or so, its operator one of a hundred, and I one of a hundred young men taking, tying, stacking. In all, I believe, this Western Electric plant in Chicago employed some 20,000 workers.

This was a good job. At $26 a week—less $4 for a room, $12 for meals and such, and nothing for dependents—I could save. After work and travel time, and an hour to wash the copper green off body and clothes, there wasn't much time or energy left for riotous living. The job was steady. The machines shook the floor, but never shook ahead the leaden hands of the moon-faced clock I watched eight hours a day, six days a week. At last I dared to ask for a Saturday off, for an out-of-town trip to Caroline, who had gone home sick. The foreman laughed.

"Why sure, kid," he said. "I know how you feel. Take your Saturday as well as your Sunday. You won't even have to come back Monday. This is a steady job. They only want steady men."

I was told when I was hired that this was a good and steady job, a job with a future for a clean-cut, ambitious young American like me. It was my first encounter with modern progressive personnel policies.

Earlier hirings had gone like this. First you waited hours in a bare dingy hall or shack. You sat on a hard backless bench, if there was room, or stood leaning against the wall. The only other furniture was spittoons. If the office counter was open, you spat in one or swallowed your gob. If closed, you spat on the floor—with symbolic gusto. At last a heavy-set character would amble out, with pencil behind ear and dead chewed-up cigar. Silently he'd stare at us, one by one and up and down. I don't recall one ever opening my mouth to look at my teeth, feeling my muscles, grabbing a fetlock to raise a hoof, or slapping my rump but one felt like that. Then he'd point at some with his cigar.

"Hey you, I thought I told you not to come back."

"Ain't nothing for you, Jack. Come back tomorrow."

"Things is slack. You'd oughta know better than waste your time—and mine."

Among those left, the hiring boss would pass over the colored, foreign, older, and point to some young whites. "Hey, you . . . and you . . . and you!"

We snapped to attention.

"Ever work here before, kid?"

"No, sir."

"Ever do this kind of work? No matter, you'll learn. Go to Room 3 down the alley. Ask for Hank. He'll tell you what to do."

But at Western Electric, what progress, what politeness! I waited in a nice reception room. A cute receptionist helped me fill out an application, then ushered me into the personnel man's office. He bade me sit across the desk from him, glanced at my application, then gazed earnestly at me.

"Leonard," he said, "I think you've come to the right place. Western Electric is looking for young men like you." I fingered back my hair to look more clean-cut, and straightened the collar of my blue workshirt, wishing I'd thought to wear a white shirt and tie.

"We have a place for you in our big family," the personnel man went on. "W-E spells we, you know. It's more than a job, it's an opportunity. You'll start at the bottom, of course. But we pay well and believe in promotion. Where you'll be, there are young fellows earning $2 more a week for easier work. . . ." He trailed off, then recovered his style.

"Look, Leonard, that isn't all. We just promoted a young man near your age and not long here. Made him foreman over a whole bunch of young girls. Now whaddya say to that!" He grinned and winked, then dismissed me, chuckling. "Take a look into that department down the corridor. All girls—and some real purty. How'd you like to be their boss?"

I couldn't miss the young men getting $2 more. One or two were always hovering around. They promoted company games and affairs, and tried to talk real chummy. What productive work they did, if any, I couldn't learn. Off the job, in a bar, I asked a machine operator. "Them?" he said. "Them's office snoopers . . . stooges . . . spies. Watch out for them."

If any had ears cocked for whispers of union agitation, I doubt they heard any. At work, in washrooms, at lunch, none dared say a word that mightn't sit well with the company. There seemed no union even remotely interested in organizing Western Electric. I scouted around. The AFL referred me to the International Brotherhood of Electrical Workers, but its Loop office closed before I could get there after work.

One evening I found the union's office open later than usual, and buttonholed an important-looking man who was just about to leave. Was it Umbrella Mike Boyle himself, I wondered with trepidation.

"We got members at Western Electric," he said gruffly. "What's it to you?"

As I tried to explain, the man paused long enough to look at me quizzically. He asked what kind of work I did. I told him. "That ain't no trade," he said. "Ever do any electrical work?"

"No."

"This is an electrician's union. Our apprentice lists are closed for now. Ain't a thing we can do for you."

He brushed by me as I murmured something about "organizing."

The sea had been my first choice. It had movement, variety, some unionism. My first job was on a ship tied up to a wharf on Staten Island. Cockroaches made my bunk as black as my brother's blacksheeted bed. They fled when I turned on the light; I learned to live with them. The AFL International Seamen's Union sent me to its Cooks & Stewards union. Deck, engine, and stewards sections functioned like separate unions.

It was a two-room business office in an office building, with no seamen around. The agent looked bored enough to welcome anyone. For a $5 initiation, he signed me up at once. Plumply soft, with white manicured hands, he wore a neat business suit, white shirt, and tie with jeweled stickpin. After issuing my union book, he wanted to shoot the breeze.

"You know, friend," he said, sitting me down and offering a smoke, "we're happy to get a good American like you in the union."

My Limey accent was still obvious. I'd given him the facts as to my birth, nationality, noncitizenship. I demurred faintly.

"No matter," said he. "You said you'd taken out first papers or was going to, didn't you? The point is they got so many foreigners and coloreds and Chinks going to sea these days—and on American ships—it's a shame. We've got an American union and we want to keep it American."

I asked if the union agent could help me ship out to sea.

"Sure can," he said. "Stick around and I'll give you a letter."

The letter was on union stationery and signed by the agent in his official capacity. "Just go to Pan-American Petroleum," he told me, "and hand this to the man in the hiring hall. He'll look after you."

"Why," I said surprised, "do you have a union contract?" I knew the ISU, strong in the war years, was by now an almost memberless shell.

"No," the agent replied. "No contracts any more. They pretty much busted us with the open-shop drive after the war."

"But won't this letter give me away as a union man?" I objected.

"Now look here," the agent said. "Just do like I said and don't ask so many questions." He wasn't huffy. He explained: "You see, with so many foreigners and such going to sea like I said, some companies get men from us if they can. They know they'll get good Americans who know the trade—not sea-lawyers or troublemakers or IWWs or reds or riffraff."

"Good American," I was learning, had little to do with nationality. It had a lot to do with skin color, race, rebelliousness. It didn't include Asians, Africans, Afro-Americans, Jews, Mexicans, even if born in the United States. The British or Scandinavian immigrant could be a "good American" on arrival. The idea, predating Hitler, seemed to be that the light-complected were clean, decent, aboveboard; the dark-skinned (including light-skinned Jews—for anti-Semitism was part of the package) dirty, sneaky, foreign. In labor struggles then, the "good American"—or "100% American"—was the strikebreaker, the Legionnaire, or other rowdies who wrecked union halls and castrated and lynched agitators. The IWW, the communist, the militant unionist, might be scion of the Pilgrim Fathers, fair as a viking, devoted to American constitutional principles of which his would-be lynchers knew nothing, but he could never be a "good American" like the stooges or goons of the open-shop bosses. The Cold War made "good American" the antonym to "communist."

The union agent's letter did the trick. At the hiring office of Pan-American Petroleum, I walked past all the waiting seamen, handed the letter to the hiring boss, and was at once signed up as a messman—at $40 a month—on the oil tanker *Edward L. Doheny III.*

At sea I found relief from tensions, as in the Washington woods, and a sea-breeze appetite. Pan-American was one of the best feeders in the tanker business. Caribbean nights and days were gorgeous. I lay on the deck all I could, to sun, to look out over the endless surge and swell or up into star-sparkling skies. The Panama Canal brought shore leaves; the fascination of lock-changing; sullen heat and relaxing tropical evenings; the lush greenery of the jungle; passionate torrents of rain that exhausted and purified the atmosphere.

At San Pedro I signed off the *Edward L. Doheny III.* I wanted some time in Los Angeles. Then too, the going wage from the west coast was $10 higher, and I wanted to ship next in the deck department.

Not long before, there had been an IWW strike on the San Pedro waterfront. Besides my blue union book in the ISU I carried, duly concealed, the red card of IWW Marine Transport Workers 510. (Alas for my trusting port agent! But I bore no outward signs of the beast—no hooked nose, no devilish dark complexion, no thick foreign accent . . . a Limey accent didn't count. How was he to know I wasn't a "good American"?) I didn't learn of the strike till I'd left ship. My fellow seamen hadn't heard of it. There had been mass actions, arrests, free-speech fights. But it had been more demonstration than strike. Embers of discontent had been fanned into a blaze, which had burned itself out.

When next I shipped out, I was one of a bunch recruited for an oil tanker of the Atlantic Gulf & Refinery Company. We looked like a press-gang's haul, most boozily surprised to see what a ship was like. The mate looked us over. "Any of youse been to sea before?" he asked.

Only two besides me raised hands. One had once been a cook in the Navy; the other, a passenger steward.

"We need two ABs for this trip," the mate said. "You," he pointed at the ex-cook, "you're AB." He hesitated between the ex-steward and me, and my heart thumped at thought of such instant promotion to skilled Able-Bodied sailor. But the mate's finger settled on the other. "You too," he said, "you're AB. The rest's ordinary seamen, deckhands."

The LaFollette Seamen's Act was on the books, hailed by ISU and AFL as a labor victory. It required so many ABs on each ship—with specified experience and qualifications. But without a strong union, it was little enforced.

The voyage back east was very different from my westward trip. The food was miserable, of poor quality, poorly cooked, some rancid or maggoty. The crew's quarters were overcrowded and filthy. The mate was a regular Captain Bligh. He kept us deckhands working every minute, at largely made work—swabbing decks already clean; soogee-moogee over cabin paintwork; repolishing brass knobs; shifting lines and tackle that could have stayed put; chipping off paint, painting all over, then chipping off to paint again. The mate carried no cat-o'-nine-tails—just gave that impression. Big, bulky, red-faced, with nail-grating voice, he seemed always standing over us—on gangplank, bridge, tanktop, any elevation—wherever we worked. He'd yell at us whenever we slackened. We hated his guts.

Still, I got to like working at sea better than other jobs. Besides travel, outdoor life, the ocean, there was a special intimacy in living with those you worked with. At first I'd been warned:

"Never put yourself where you can't get away from the men

you work with—like in a camp or, least of all, a ship." When I asked why: "Look, you're . . . sorta . . . shy. The men on those jobs are tough, regular brutes, and they hate Limeys. They'd make life so miserable you'd want to die. You'd have to fight to make them lay off, and you don't look like a scrapper."

They were right about me; as a likely loser, I'd learned from childhood to avoid scraps. They were wrong about the men. Some were tough enough. There could be drunken brawls, rough horseplay. But I found no such petty, mean, sadistic bullying as made life miserable for a "rabbit" or a "groise" at Harrow. If things went too far someone—usually a tough guy—would call a halt. One could count on more human decency and fairplay, I found, than in the middle-class world.

On a ship you got to know each other. Sometimes in a crowded fo'c'sle in rough weather, you knew the other fellow too well; he got on your nerves. Mostly you thought you knew all about him—only to find much still held back, to be drawn out little by little as friendship developed. Then, too, on a job like the Atlantic tanker where all felt put upon, solidarity against common grievances was stronger and more intimate for living together. We had no union and dared not "mutiny," but we could work out little ways of kicking against the pricks.

On this tanker, one crew member wasn't drawn into these intimate little job actions. Claude was a college boy from Virginia. He seemed standoffish to the others. "Summer sailor" they called him, or "that college punk." They didn't pick on him, but treated him with reserve. He didn't know how to join in their talk and came to have no one to talk with.

I talked IWW with Claude. He was interested, as a student might be. He was even sympathetic. The rough-and-ready Wobblies sometimes fascinated nonradical Americans, much as did the legendary "bad men" of the West. In a way too, Wobbly aversion to government and politicians was sister-under-the-skin to romantic notions of pioneer free enterprise. I became Claude's only confidant, until at last he thought to ask:

"How about the Nigras? Where does the IWW stand on them?"

I told him it believed in full equality for all workers, regardless of race, color, nationality. I added my own emphasis, when he made some crack I didn't like. In the ensuing argument, Claude went white-faced with fury. He wouldn't talk to me again for the rest of the trip.

As I walked away from the ship at Philadelphia, one of the seamen ran after me. "Did you sign off?" he asked, breathless.

"Sure," I said.

"Good," said he. "And don't go back. That prick college punk told me he was going to the police to have them arrest you as a red."

After working at sea, I decided to give the Great Lakes a shot. Having already transferred from the ISU Stewards to its east coast Sailors' union, I now had to transfer to its Great Lakes union. MTW 510 of the IWW required no transfers. All the ISU seemed to have was some small offices with a payroller in each, paid perhaps from such treasury as survived the union's collapse. I ran into no union members on the ships, nor around the offices where I made transfers and paid dues.

The Lake Carriers Association, creature of the U.S. Steel Corporation, controlled hiring on the Lakes. It had a blacklisting system. Every seaman had to carry a "discharge book"—popularly called the "fink card." This gave the whole record of his employment on Lake boats, including reasons for discharge, if fired, and other employer comments.

A 12-hour day was still the rule on U.S. Steel's ore-carrying boats. It was 4 hours on, 4 hours off, around the clock; and what with eating and such, about 3 hours sleep at a time. The continuous on-and-off regime had a treadmill effect—though I liked not working too long at a stretch, and hobo life had trained me to sleep on and off quite readily. There were no long periods on open water as at sea. It was tying up and untying at port after port—all United States ports, looking much alike—at all hours of the day and night. With the long working hours, a grueling deal.

I was therefore disposed to take up Vern Smith on a proposition he made when I landed in Chicago and paid him a visit. Vern was then editor of the IWW weekly paper *Industrial Solidarity*. He felt the IWW should do more about organizing in the big unorganized industries, and that it might help to expose their working conditions. He wanted me to write up Great Lakes shipping, and then go on with a series of articles on a different industry each week. That was okay for industries where I'd worked, I agreed, but how about those where I hadn't?

"Just go to work in them," said Vern patiently. "Work on as many jobs in each as you can. You'll have a few articles ahead on those you know. We can wait till you get the dope on those you don't."

Packing was my first new industry—in the Chicago stockyards. I was hired by Armour's to handle hams. Sometimes I trundled them around in a wheelbarrow. The cement floors were uneven, broken, with pools of water. If I spilled my load of unwrapped hams, I picked them up and wiped off the dirtiest with my apron. Nobody seemed to care.

This job took me around, so I stayed with it a while. I could talk little with the other workers, however. They were either foreign-speaking or afraid to talk, or both. It was that way in all the open shops. The foreman might hear or be told what you said. The man working next to you might be a company stool pigeon. It wasn't only talk of union—everyone knew you'd get fired for that. Talk of your work might sound like complaint, and the company didn't want dissatisfied workers. Even the weather wasn't quite safe. If you grumbled too much you'd seem like a sorehead. Safest was to smile and say nothing; if you didn't smile, you'd look like a sourpuss, and the company liked cheerful workers.

After quitting Armour's, I was down bright and early the next morning at the Swift hiring hall. I was put to work at once, in the soap department. When I quit that job, I hired out the following day at Wilson's. Finally I put in a stint at Cudahy's. Why was I hired so soon and so often, while others waited hopelessly in the hiring halls? I was young, white, "American"—ostensibly a "good American"—and willing to do anything. I had no record; each time I claimed no previous employment in the Yards. Black workers were coming in, not yet in great numbers. The all-white bosses resented it, and showed their resentment. Most of the workers were immigrants from eastern Europe.

As in all unorganized industries, I saw whipcracking regimentation and rotten conditions. I saw workers used like machinery—hundreds of women sitting as if chained to each other and their benches, as hour after hour their nimble fingers at incredible speed repeated the same small mechanical movements. Most of all I remember the fear in the eyes of hard-driven workers—fear of bosses and spies fed by the greater fear of hunger and want in the slums, if they lost one job without getting another.

Steel was another industry I worked in. At the Chicago mills of Carnegie-Illinois, I lined up with scores of Afro-Americans, Mexicans, and European immigrants. I was singled out for a soft job—greasing cranes. Black and Mexican workers got the heavy labor jobs; I saw no white faces in those gangs.

The companies brought in Mexicans by the trainload, much as British colonialists imported indentured servants to do their labor. At this Chicago mill, Mexican workers were housed in a big barracks building inside the plant walls. The company controlled their coming and going through guarded plant gates. Outside, Mexican families lived in shacks huddled close to the mill—within reach of the company police.

Language and segregation separated Mexicans from Afro-Americans. Preferred status, as well as segregation, separated whites from both. Among the whites, language and job favoritism separated the American-speaking from more recent immigrants. The divisions were made to order—or ordered to be made—for unchallenged company rule over a serflike labor force.

Later I worked at the Gary mills of U.S. Steel. My job was closer to the blast furnaces; I saw more of the basic operations. But my most indelible impressions were formed on the way to and from work. The glow in the sky at night, the sky-reaching flames, outlined a mighty fortress with turrets and battlements of smokestacks and sentried walls. At change of shifts, lost among thousands going in or out of the gates, I thought less of the power of the industry and the few who owned it than of the potential power of the men who built and worked it.

These workers didn't all materialize from separate cars in parking lots, or scatter to them when they left. For some time and distance, they were marching armies. They carried no flags. No battle songs were on their lips. Their workclothes were their uniforms. Their faces were tired or set. There was little greeting or joshing. They had no common purpose—except to get to work, or get to hell away from it.

These thousands of all nations and races, men of brains, skill, and strength to make a country's steel, were all for the moment doing the same thing at the same time. What mightn't they do, I dreamed, if ever they tired of being industry's servants and resolved to become its masters?

The industries I worked in were all nonunion, antiunion, open shop . . . with no sign of union. If there was talk of organizing, it was far from the shops. The Chicago Federation of Labor in militant days had tried to organize. By now in the Twenties it had withdrawn to its limited base in the crafts. If there were union craftsmen in some pockets of major industry, this meant nothing to the mass of workers. The IWW talked industrial unionism without men or money—or even ambition by now—to do more than talk.

There were "old socialists" all around Chicago, some leaders of craft unions. Some had settled into swivel chairs and revolved only in them. Some talked of organizing, but cynically. Some hated the communists for prodding them; others aided the left in pressing for organization.

The communists were the liveliest labor influence. No longer in the good graces of the CFL leadership, they still had enough delegates to raise an issue, if not to pass a resolution. Their push to amalgamate crafts into industrial unions was popular, notably on the railroads. Thousands of locals, scores of central bodies, some internationals, adopted amalgamation resolutions promoted by the leftist Trade Union Educational League.

In 1917-19, the Chicago "militants," led by William Z. Foster, had instigated big union drives in packinghouse and steel. Their radical initiative and spirit won backing from old-line money and muscle, in a combination such as produced CIO success in the Thirties. Foster, a lifelong radical, was for years a voice crying for industrial organization. During the war, he and his leftwing militants became a power in the Chicago labor federation, and its leaders John Fitzpatrick and Ed Nockels worked well with them. Besides pushing organization, the CFL promoted a labor political party, hailed the Russian revolution and demanded Soviet recognition, and took other stands that bore a radical stamp.

The CFL got a dozen crafts to combine for a drive in meatpacking, with Fitzpatrick as chairman, and Foster, Jack Johnstone, and other lefts in leading posts. A national strike won wage increases and an 8-hour day. In steel, Foster, as CFL delegate to the 1918 AFL convention, won action for an organizing campaign of 23 unions. Foster led the drive, with AFL President Samuel Gompers its titular chairman. It enlisted hundreds of thousands of steelworkers, and the 1919 national strike, though broken, ended the 12-hour day and 7-day week.

In my Chicago days, little was left of all this union ambition. In 1923, the CFL leaders broke with the militants, now known as communists, and the CFL relapsed into typical AFL somnolence. Nationally, the AFL had launched a campaign of redbaiting, charter-lifting, and expulsions against the communists and all their ideas for labor advance. It reached a peak at the 1923 AFL concention in Portland, Oregon, when William F. Dunne, an elected delegate, was unseated for being a communist.

It was an emotional convention, marked by a passionate ovation for George Berry, Pressmen's president, who had broken a strike of his own members in New York by importing union scabs. Besides banning Dunne, the AFL leaders denounced labor-party proposals, Soviet recognition, Brookwood-type workers education, Federated Press (labor news service), and all else their redbaiting specialists suspected of radical taint.

Having burned its witches and driven the communists out of its stockade into the wilderness, a purged, purified, sanctified AFL bundled up for a 12-year sleep, not to be seriously disturbed again until the CIO in 1935 took up where the earlier communists had been forced to leave off.

By ironical coincidence, the CIO in 1948 chose the same city of Portland, Oregon, to stage an emotional redbaiting performance very like that of the AFL in 1923. The same Philip

Murray who had made the AFL motion to unseat Dunne in 1948 conducted the oratorical extravaganza against CIO's radicals.

The name of William Z. Foster held magic for me. It was nothing personal. I first met the rather dour Foster much later on the creaky wooden staircase of a Cleveland communist office. He was a tall man in black raincoat, with collar turned up. The wide brim of his dark felt hat was down. The hat was big, as was his head. The way he was covered up—it must have been raining —and the dim staircase made me think of the conspirator. The thought was momentary and incongruous. Whatever he might have had to do "underground," Foster could never *look* as conspiratorial as did his communist archfoe Jay Lovestone.

On introduction, Foster didn't clasp my hand and smile politician-style. A cold fish, I thought. Told I worked for a railroad brotherhood, Foster made a crack about brotherhood leaders that seemed a bit spiteful though I couldn't dispute it. As speaker and writer, Foster informed and edified but didn't excite me. It wasn't so much the man as his lifelong record. He personalized the working class for me. A worker himself, of wide and varied experience, Foster devoted his whole life to the workers' movement, not to one trade or group but to the class.

I often heard lib-labs deplore that such a promising union leader as Foster should have got "mixed up with" the communists. For want of a better term, I use "lib-labs" not in its original British sense, but to tag a group in the Twenties of American college people, professionals, ministers, social workers, inspired more by the British Labor party than by the Russian revolution. They rendered many professional services in labor struggles, and like the British Fabians but with less success, tried to mold labor's thinking to their own liberal or social-democratic design. Such lib-labs argued that if Foster had "kept his nose clean" of the communist mucus, he could have exerted much influence in top labor ranks as an outstanding and indispensable organizer for future drives.

As things were to turn out, however, no matter how far out of character Foster might have gone in watching his step, the next steel drive at most might have given him a job comparable to that of Clinton S. Golden—and probably a shorter-lived one. John L. Lewis was to be no Sam Gompers, forced into steel organizing and letting a red-hot like Foster stick out his neck and take the rap. Philip Murray was no John Fitzpatrick, buddy of militants, willing to take titular lead while they did the actual leading. CIO's trinity, Lewis, Murray, and Sidney Hillman, had this in common, that if in front and signing the checks, they wanted no doubts at all as to who was boss. Foster would have been the lib-labs' biggest prize, but he eluded them. They had to settle for Golden and John Brophy, who served early CIO with distinction. But so too, without title, did Foster and his communists—and more strenuously.

Oddly perhaps, I bracketed Foster with John L. Lewis and Eugene V. Debs as the three greatest working-class leaders in the United States in my time. When I heard Debs speak, he seemed a bit confused by the complications of the post-Russian-revolution world he was soon to leave. I was moved more by what I read about Debs and heard from youngsters like Caroline whom he inspired and led—also from oldsters, including rail brotherhood men. As working man, union agitator, organizer, labor leader, Debs was as true to the working class throughout his life as he knew how to be. Like Foster, he was not narrowly "economist" but embraced what he believed to be the most possible revolutionary working-class politics.

Lewis was quite different. Conservative, often reactionary, through most of his career, Lewis opposed the radicalism of both Debs and Foster. But when he started and led CIO (1935-40), Lewis found himself cast in the role of working-class champion. Practical, power-conscious, and little ideological as he was, Lewis instinctively rose to the role. Strategist of union struggle, he now led not one or two unions, nor unions alone, but a widespread working-class upsurge, and he led it in that class spirit, though not with the others' consciousness of class purpose.

My stint at Western Electric ended when I took a job with the IWW, first on *Industrial Solidarity*, then in the printshop. I got $27 a week, tops for officers and all employees except printers. This maximum, like the one-year limit for elective office, was to discourage "piecard artists." I enjoyed being where labor and radical issues were under discussion, and not being too tired, after work, for meetings and radical socializing.

In 1921 the migratory workers of harvest, railroad, logging, and construction camps had set the tone on West Madison Street. By 1925 their numbers were much reduced; mission stiffs and cockroach business were taking over. The IWW, itself declining, still held the fort at 1001. By now, a few blocks away on West Washington Street, there was a later fort, held by the Workers party and its *Daily Worker*.

IWW minds kept turning in this direction, but visiting was rare. Some oldtimers felt rivalry, and pro-communist Wobblies guarded their tongues. Some officials were hostile. George Williams, my printshop boss, had been IWW observer at a convention of the Red International of Labor Unions in Moscow. His adverse report led the IWW to decline to affiliate. Vern Smith was pro-communist and later went with the party.

After work, Wobblies and communists mingled more. Besides meetings, I recall parties around "Bughouse Square," the Greenwich Village of Chicago. I found the communists I met at them a bit too arty, emotional, unstable, for my taste. I preferred the communists from the shops and the unions. Through Caroline I met young needle-trades lefts. They worked full shifts in the shops, but also had the stamina to spend their nights in caucuses, union meetings, rallies of all kinds, and then pass out leaflets at factory gates in the bleak early morning. In other unions too, leftwingers were active in TUEL efforts for inner-union democracy, amalgamation, a labor party, and sometimes elected leftwing slates.

In England, such labor activists were known as "ginger groups." Even Ramsay MacDonald once defended them. He called them intemperate in language, rash in action, often a nuisance—their proposals ill-timed, ill-conceived, if not hare-brained. But, said he, the movement needed the impatience of youth, and the resulting irritations gave it impetus. MacDonald was then in a mellow mood, thinking of the gingering-up done to union leaders, not himself. When later some ginger got down his own throat, he was less mellow. He called his critics "easy-oozie asses."

In the United States, the vigor of the communist-led left at first took union officials by surprise. Its ideas had knocked around before, without stirring up much dust. When the lefts made them into urgent demands for union reform, democracy, militancy, some minor officials swum along with the tide. Most top shots at once sensed a threat and said "No."

When any members "start something," a union leader's first thought is: "Are they going to buck my machine, maybe run candidates against it?" As TUEL promotions spread and gained ground, this fear became epidemic. Unions that hadn't held a convention within memory found something calling itself "the rank and file" demanding that one be called. Half the unions (the other half didn't hold real elections) were faced, for the first time in ages, with slates of candidates dubbed "independent," "rank-and-file," "progressive," even "leftwing." Small wonder the AFL leadership soon acted with surgical sharpness to "cut out the cancer of communism."

Most communists I met at this time were Foster followers engaged in union activities. American-speaking, usually American-born, they had radical roots (predating the Russian revolution) in the Socialist party, IWW, Socialist Labor party, and other American precursors of the communist movement. I couldn't think of the movement as a foreign importation, as anticommunist historians so strenuously aver. Yet in the sense the American working class was itself a foreign importation, there was a point.

The Socialist party's foreign-language federations played much part in generating an American communist party. Their members were largely employed in the unorganized basic industries where I had detected but little union-mindedness. Too bad I hadn't contact then with such foreign-language workers' groups. Some were quite strong—with social, welfare, political activities, clubhouses, an extensive press, including daily papers.

The language barrier isolated these immigrant workers, who made up most of the labor force in major industries. It also helped protect them through the dark ages of the antiunion open shop. Most bosses had little idea of the union and radical thoughts expressed in the incomprehensible lingos of the "hunkies," "bohunks," "wops," "polacks," they treated with easy contempt.

The CIO leaders, when they launched their drives in these industries, soon contacted the communists, to get organizers who knew the industry and had done some union spadework, and to establish relations with foreign-language groups influential among the workers.

Receiving word that my father had died and my mother wanted me back in England, I got Federated Press credentials as a foreign correspondent and left.

Federated Press was the wire and mail service of the labor press—a miniature Associated Press, started when there were many labor and radical daily papers. These included the *Seattle Union Record, Butte Daily Bulletin, Milwaukee Leader, Oklahoma Daily Leader, New York Call* (later *Leader*); quite a few foreign-language socialist and communist dailies; an IWW daily, the Finnish *Industrialisti* in Duluth, Minnesota.

The postwar depression and open-shop drive, press trustification, declining labor fervor under Harding Normalcy and Coolidge Prosperity, factional fighting, the drying up of European immigration, all took their toll of this daily press. But FP also served many local weekly labor papers and union organs. Its executive board, representative of subscribing publications, included all shades of labor opinion.

During its 30-year life, FP reflected the personality of Carl Haessler, its managing editor. A former Rhodes scholar at Oxford, philosophy professor at an American university, Fort Leavenworth prisoner for opposing United States entry into the First World War, Haessler brought to his work for labor a keen mind, the sharp nose of a debunker, and a personal, professional, and labor integrity that was absolute. Haessler kept FP factual, honest, and enlisted on the side of the working and common people—just as he (I, too) believed the capitalist press to be enlisted on the profiteers' side. With it all, Carl was a salty, genial redhead, with a sardonic sense of humor—quite a devil at deflating stuffed-shirts.

Federated Press had full-time reporters for its daily news service from bureaus in Chicago, New York, Washington, D.C. It also had a network of string correspondents throughout the United States and the world. Some worked almost full-time—for love rather than money—and were designated "bureaus." Others were occasional correspondents getting occasional small string-checks. All big labor struggles found "FP's Special Correspondent" on the job—the byline often a well-known name of liberal, labor, or capitalist press.

Not a few "bigs" in bigtime daily newspaper work served an eye-opening apprenticeship with FP. Some continued to work for it on the side. FP inspired remarkable devotion. In a book borrowed from Haessler, I noticed the author had penned: "To Carl Haessler—from an old admirer and devoted follower of Federated Press." Signing was a top editor or a leading New York daily. I wondered if AP or UPI treasured any tributes like that.

The British unions were swinging left when I covered events in 1925. The employers were on a wage-cutting offensive and the workers, disillusioned by the 1924 Labor government, were not to be pacified by Labor politicians. Leading the Trades Union Congress were militants like Chairman A.B. Swales; Vice-Chairman A. A. Purcell, also president of the International Federation of Trade Unions, who was plugging for a Soviet-including world labor unity; George Hicks, head of a committee of major unions preparing for a general strike to back the miners; A.J. Cook, red leader of the miners' union.

I met these leaders at affairs of the London Labor College and the National Council of Labor Colleges—the left wing of workers education, outgrowth of a worker-student revolt. In 1899, American philanthropists started Ruskin College to bring workers to Oxford, and it linked up with the university extension work of the Workers Education Association. But in 1909, Ruskin's worker-students, restive under "capitalist paternalism," went on strike against dismissal of their principal. As rivals to Ruskin and the WEA, they started the Central Labor College and the NCLC, to promote strictly working-class education. The Labor College was the first school I'd found where Marxism was not taboo. (Even at Brookwood, student lefts met privately in each other's rooms to study the Marxian classics.) George Hicks and A. J. Cook were both graduates of the Labor College.

In the ranks, the leftwing National Minority Movement was promoting shop committees, shop-steward activity, amalgamation of craft unions, international trade union unity, councils of action (uniting unions locally for joint action). In this period —as in 1920—councils of action sprang up to meet crises and dwindled when tension declined. In the May 1926 general strike they were widely formed to meet the emergency.

The 1925 Trades Union Congress at Scarborough reflected the leftward swing. It backed its leftist General Council; called on unions to "struggle for the overthrow of capitalism"; urged shop committees as a weapon "to force the capitalists to relinquish their grip on industry"; favored unity with the Soviet trade unions. The TUC defied Labor party leaders with an anti-imperialist resolution passed 3,082,000 to 79,000 over the opposition of J. H. Thomas, Colonial Secretary in the 1924 Labor government. It denounced the American Dawes Plan and accused the British empire of capitalist exploitation of colonial peoples, asserting their right to choose "complete separation from the empire."

While in London, I joined the Communist Party of Great Britain. Since it was the most moving force behind most labor moves I favored, this seemed the obvious thing to do. But Scotland Yard evidently took a dim view. On my next visit to England, seven years later, secret police detained my wife and me, searched our persons, bags, and papers, and grilled us about our "political activities." More than 35 years later, vacationing in the British colony of Fiji, I was shadowed by agents of its Counter-Intelligence Department and learned the imperial sleuths had passed on to the United States resident authorities their desiccated tidbits of information about me.

I found the party very working-class, and so British that, as a fervent internationalist, I had forebodings of polycentrism to come due to the native roots and engrained national predilections of most communist parties. The British commonists, never underground, had no conspiratorial style to fascinate or repel. They looked, dressed, behaved, like any other British working people. The most un-British thing about my branch was the little beer drunk; we made up with gallons of black-strong tea.

Cold War recanters made much hay—and more mazuma—

out of bibulous, amorous, and soul-rending exploits while in the party. I seem to have missed the fun. My comrades frowned on alcoholic indulgence and included no women. We met in the branch secretary's home, and neither he nor his wife were of a kind to seek, inspire, or tolerate infidelity. There was little emotionalism. Our branch was of the working class, all wageworking except myself. If there was some dive where artier comrades met to make love, drink, and rend their souls, I missed it.

We concentrated on factory agitation and activities in unions and other worker organizations, notably the Labor party. Unlike early new-lefts of the Sixties in the United States, we didn't write off the labor movement because of reactionary leaders and passive ranks. Rather we saw this as the big challenge we must meet to bring the working class into action. Labor party leaders, intent on changing an all-inclusive class party where rival tendencies might contend, into a doctrinally social-democratic party, were trying to ban communist influence. But in the unions, the CP was too deeply rooted to be dislodged. Communists taking the floor at any meeting would typically begin, "Speaking as a communist . . ."

From England I went to Germany, to teach at a Berlitz language school in Berlin, and continued to correspond for Federated Press. After the relative well-being of London, I found Berlin in this 1925-26 winter a capital with the shakes—shrunken into a misery you could feel.

Fellow correspondents were helpful contacts. Louis Lochner of Associated Press and Frederick Kuh of United Press had both been FP correspondents themselves. Most hospitable were Margaret Goldsmith of the *Philadelphia Inquirer* and her husband, Fritz Voigt of the *Manchester Guardian*.

At the Voigt-Goldsmith apartment, I met Reichstag deputies (usually social democrats), journalists, lawyers, often Jewish. Liberal, brainy, perceptive, they were also a rather complacent crowd. With middle-class security and scope for their talents, they were among the more fortunate citizens of the Weimar Republic. They saw and deplored the misery around them. They feared the hate and frustration in the hearts of a defeated people. They tried to alleviate misery and promote reform.

Social democrats in power had averted a revolution that might have joined Germany with Russia in building socialism. I felt outraged when I heard of Soviet troubles with a heritage of feudal backwardness. If only Germany had combined her modern industrialism, her skilled and organized working class, her limited democratic experience, with the huge land area and resources, the rugged people, the revolutionary zeal of the USSR. . . . In Germany now, it was as if a Kerensky had won, leaving his country at the mercy of greedy imperialists, without social revolution, economically devastated, bitter at betrayal, with little hope for the future.

These German liberals, I'm sure, felt differently. They were happy to have been saved from "barbarous Russian bolshevism." They saw no writing on the wall in the spoutings of Mussolini or the antics of Hitler's beerhall rowdies. Germany was a highly civilized, cultured, modern, democratic nation. How could it fall prey to such a barbarity as fascism? Meanwhile the German ruling class—its financial and industrial overlords, not the embittered Junkers and generals—was hedging its bets between the traditional conservative parties and the social democrats. Few chanced much money yet on such a long shot as the Nazis.

From Berlin, Carl Haessler called me back to the states, with a letter saying that Oscar Ameringer had a job for me as assistant editor of the *Illinois Miner*, weekly paper of the Illinois district of the United Mine Workers.

Chapter Four

THE UNIONS—A MIXED BAG

*There had long been unions, industrial
and militant like the Mine Workers, or
craftist and affluent like the Locomotive
Engineers. The labor movement was
always quite a mixed bag.*

He'd surprise me when I was working late in my *Illinois Miner* office, the only one open in the Mine Workers' Springfield building. A coal miner stranded in town, or immobilized for lack of another drink, might be expected; the miners paid me and were entitled to an occasional kickback. But this man—tousled too, from day coach travel—was more apologetic than the miners. He didn't start, "Look, bud. . . ." He took off his coat and paced about, running his hand over thinning hair.

"Len, I'm in trouble. It's bad. I don'd know what to write."

Soothingly I praised him as the best boss I ever had, because I seldom saw him and I hated bosses. Head cocked birdlike, he looked pleased. "I neffer bother you, do I, Len. Now, do I? So now you gotta help me."

I offered pencil and paper. He sat down, elbows on desk, and chewed the pencil, looking at me from the corner of his eyes. Then he burst out: "Look, I can't type. I can't spell. I don'd know no grammar. Dammit, why'd I always haff to be an editor and write columns?"

The first time, I wracked my head for ideas. After that, I'd be ready with notes and clippings. The next morning I always found some pages of penciled scrawl and no more boss for maybe weeks. I just had to type the stuff, correct some spelling or detail, slug it "Adam Coaldigger," and add it to the copy.

Like others who register in public life, Oscar Ameringer was quite an actor—a humorist, sometimes a comedian, never a clown. His German accent was from birth. He could make it thick or thin, or disappear. Writing so the average guy could understand, Oscar was a popular socialist pamphleteer. At his best, he was a first-rate columnist—of the Will Rogers style, people's humor with a punch. Anyhow Moe Annenberg and Arthur Brisbane thought so when they tried (but failed) to buy him for the Hearst press.

Oscar was also a good editor. Not the executive type, for which I was thankful. Not the copyreading type, for sure. Not the reporter-in-chief kind. Not the pundit of the editorial page. In fact, Oscar wasn't any kind of editor, except his own. Yet for some half century, this working musician, artist, humorist, union organizer, socialist agitator, was titled "Editor." If the quality of his publications was the test, he was a very good editor.

Oscar was a promoter. He called himself "a salesman of ideas." He was an extraordinary money-raiser. He was at his best on the platform, speaking directly to people, humanly and with humor. With other public figures I knew, there was a clear line between public image and the private man; in Oscar's case, the two tended to merge. When I knew him in 1926, I found him in private more humanly engaging than in his public act.

Ameringer survives his autobiography, *If You Don't Weaken*, to emerge as a real man . . . a *mensch*. But he does weaken a bit—diluted doubtless by his collaborative ghost, McAlister Coleman, some of whose quirks also emerge. There is even a trace of shirt-stuffing—for which Mac should not be blamed—as notably in two photo-portraits.

The Oscar I knew stuffed his shirt with no more than his own rather plump person. He didn't conceal from me the commoner characteristics of our common humanity. When he put on an act with me, I assumed ulterior motives, as with a child. In the moan-and-groan act I've recorded, I guessed he was trying to con me into writing his column for him. If I had, he wouldn't have been like the many VIPs under whose bylines I was later to write. When Coleman obliged, Oscar liked gleefully to brag of what he had gotten away with.

Oscar was about 60 when I knew him. But his bespectacled eyes missed few of the better-stacked women. Neither prude nor braggart, he told stories about himself that were candid as well as funny. His light touch skirted few human areas as untouchable. When all was said, if not always done—I had my fingers crossed on that—Oscar stood out all human. He couldn't be blackmailed. He told me of one attempt.

"They threatened to have the picture printed in the papers," he said. "I told them to go ahead and see if I cared."

"Well, what happened?" I asked.

"They never did it."

"You mean it was just a bluff?"

"No, they had the picture all right."

"How did they manage to frame you?"

"Frame me?" Oscar's eyes twinkled. "They didn't have to. They just happened to catch me."

The Oscar I knew in 1926 was hard to tag politically. He wasn't a tagger himself. He was political. Oscar was known as an "old socialist," a "reformist socialist." At times he called himself a "revisionist," when it came to Marxism. He was a pal of early socialists whose red faded to a pretty pale pink. But Oscar was not a "yellow socialist."

In his prime, Oscar was a Debs kind of socialist, a fighter for the poor and oppressed. As early unionist, as later socialist organizer of poverty-stricken Oklahoma farmers, he fought for reforms and preached socialism. Debs appealed to the heart; Oscar tapped the funny bone. Oscar explained Marxian economics with an original finger act. I forget what each pudgy finger stood for, and how they joined to make his points. There was always a laugh—and what he said made sense.

Old friends told me Ameringer was always to the left of his buddy Victor Berger, the socialist congressman, who once defined socialism as "anything that's right." Anyhow both Berger and he, unlike European counterparts, opposed World War I and gave socialist grounds for so doing.

I was familiar with social democrats. In British lands, the woods were full of them. They were more parliamentary than socialist, for social reform rather than social revolution. The closer their reform politics took them to office, the further socialism receded from their thinking. Then, since the Russian revolution, there were social democrats who lived only in hope of reversing it; social democrats in government who turned their guns against workers' uprisings; rightwing socialists in all lands so hating the Soviets and the communist left that they'd lead the attack on any workers' struggle they deemed to be "red" or "communistic."

If Oscar had some affinities with the first group, he had little use for the second. When I knew him, he was a Soviet sympathizer, and tolerant even of domestic communists. He tried to keep out of right-left fights. Radical factionalism seemed to bore him—a not unhuman reaction, incidentally. There was the generation gap, of course. Oscar was a pre-Russian-revolution socialist. He could feel for post-RR radicals, including communists now bearing most of the brunt. He couldn't quite understand them and resented their slurs and their sharpness.

Oscar could talk money out of a stone. Not that the miners' locals were so stony when they lapped up his humor and voted him funds—until John L. Lewis took over in the Illinois and Oklahoma coalfields. In the heat of the Illinois miners' rebellion against Lewis, Ameringer lampooned him with biting humor. When Lewis enlisted other old foes in his CIO drive, Oscar wanted in on Lewis's side. John Brophy told me he went to Lewis on Ameringer's behalf. Lewis ruminated. Then he rumbled:

"I hold nothing against the man for the foul names he called me. Let bygones be bygones. But how can I let him loose on the miners again? It wouldn't be right to expose them again to his financial appeals."

In his own way, Oscar always tried to be on the side of the angels. If heaven there be, he must be there, tootling his clarinet, making the angels dance to his tunes. If he's still Oscar, he'll be concocting schemes to wheedle treasure from the heavenly hosts to elevate the lowlier angels' lot and to end the ghetto of hell. While he sprouts cherubic wings and tootles his way through everlasting bliss, it won't be Oscar if he forgets the poor devils cast into outer darkness. To them his eyes must twinkle: "I'm really one of you boys—just look at me now!"

While Oscar Ameringer was my boss, Frank Farrington was the bigger boss, as president of the Illinois District of the UMW which paid for the *Illinois Miner*. Farrington was a big bull of a man—big fore and aft and up and down. He could bellow like a bull. Wave a red flag before him, he'd have made a bull-like charge at it.

It took a bulky and commanding presence to stay on top in the rough-and-tumble of UMW politics. Lewis had it, with extra flourishes—and Farrington was big enough to trade blows with him. The Illinois District's 60,000 members and relatively good contract added much to his stature. In the battle between the two UMW giants, Farrington regarded the *Illinois Miner* as a weapon. If its editor happened to be a socialist and gave the paper a progressive line, that was coincidental. Like Lewis, Farrington personally was a conservative Republican.

While I worked under him, Farrington was not in battle array, but his presence registered. He was the brusque, tough-minded executive. He could growl at a visitor, "I'm too busy to see you"; or relenting, check his watch and say, "All right, I'll give you just three minutes."

Farrington hated reporters—wouldn't talk to them if he could help it. In the Twenties unions usually figured the press was out to do a job on them. It wasn't only radicals who spoke of the "kept press," "lying press," "yellow press," and advised, "Never believe anything you read in the papers." The miners were so lied about when they struck they hardly cared any more what the papers said. AP and UP legmen would come from Farrington to me to wail. I couldn't buck his tell-the-bastards-nothing policy, but I came to think of low-paid, hard-pressed reporters as workers too.

I wasn't around during Farrington's bigger battles with Lewis, but I was there at the kill. The build-up was full of mystery. First the rumors. Lewis spies had long kept hidden in this hostile territory. Now, it was said, some Lewis man had openly and boldly breezed into town. Was it just bravado? Did he carry a gat? What was his game? To provoke something? Just to be seen and skedaddle? But no, he remained.

Then a confirmed report. A well-known UMW international organizer—Lewis man, of course—had arrived from Indianapolis. The nerve! No concealment. His hotel, room number, his comings and goings, his visitors, all were breathlessly reported. Nothing happened. Interest sagged. But the Lewis rep didn't leave. Still mystery enough to intrigue the curious.

Suddenly a master hand jerked the dangling strings. A dozen Lewis men slipped into Springfield—some said a score, some a hundred. They came separately, inconspicuously. Lewis must have said to "avoid individual controversy"—his term for fistfights, gunplay. There were no brawls. The Lewis boys seemed to spread all over. It was uncanny. You had a feeling they were closing in. Something was definitely cooking . . . something big. Rumors were a dime a dozen around the District building.

The Big Boy upstairs must have known. Farrington would never let Lewis catch him by surprise. Why hadn't he let out a roar to scare the "Lewis goons" away? Why hadn't he ordered his own troops into battle against the invaders? Before he traipsed off to Europe, to some international miners' affair, Farrington must have felt sure all was under control. But was it? The suspense was terrific.

The climax, when it came, was a blockbuster. Lewis produced a letter, duly signed, dated and all, showing that Farrington, while UMW district president, had made a three-year contract to serve the Peabody Coal Company as its "labor representative" for $25,000 a year. Farrington was finished. The Illinois board hastily replaced him with Vice President Harry Fishwick—a smaller man whose tenor bleat couldn't match the Big Boy's now silenced roar. I served but briefly under Fishwick before moving on.

I had no more contact with the UMW anti-Lewis rebellion in Illinois, and didn't study its complex causes. I just got the unanalytical impression that, without Farrington, it was like a chicken with its head cut off. It kept going spasmodically, in circles, ever-weakening, until Lewis made a meal of it.

In those days I saw Lewis as through a glass, darkly—the glass darkened by the execration of his foes, including Illinois miners; socialists once strong in UMW; a communist left (which he swatted unmercifully) fighting Lewis all over the coalfields and the whole of the outside liberal and radical community. To lib-labs Lewis was a byword for hard-shell labor reaction. In 1926 liberals and radicals were rooting for John Brophy, running against Lewis for UMW president, and Lewis made much hay out of their "interference" in the union's affairs.

The counts against Lewis were plenty. Reactionary. Red-baiting (he—or his editor—used redscare stuff too crude for even the Hearst press). Autocratic. Brutal. Lacking in vision and labor statesmanship—this from the liberals. To the attack Ameringer added ridicule. To most opponents, Lewis was a tiger, a formidable one. They feared him. Ridicule pictured him as vain, egotistic, pompous, a Mrs. Malaprop in misuse of fancy language. Subtly, it suggested he might be but a paper tiger.

After observing Lewis dispatch Farrington, I had my doubts. True, Farrington laid himself wide open, and Lewis doubtless had help. But the tigerlike stealth and deliberation with which Lewis stalked his prey, the tactical finesse of his pounce, did not suggest papier-mâché to me. Later, I came to doubt that Lewis was ever a Mrs. Malaprop. Flowery he might be, with flowers run wild from the Bible and Shakespeare. But Lewis could also use words with acute precision. And sometimes he produced surprising and graphic verbal effects, with a distinctly creative flair.

The early Lewis may well have been as sinister as his foes made out; I wasn't close enough to know for myself. Certainly he went all out for personal, dictatorial, centralized control over his union—and did so ruthlessly. Rebellion against him was always rife until his machine control became absolute. After he died the chickens hatched by such absolutism came home to roost. Under the lesser men who succeeded Lewis, the machine he left became a byword for corruption and collusion, and by the end of the Sixties rank-and-file revulsion had reached mass proportions. But between the Twenties and the Thirties, Lewis acquired a new public image, as seen from the left. His onetime detractors said he was a changed man. Letting bygones be bygones, Lewis said little, though he might have been excused for noting some changes in others, too.

My first major assignment on the *Illinois Miner* was to cover the British general strike. The stories appeared under my byline, with London dateline. The device, if misleading, was better than a Springfield dateline, and my curious name lent mystery, if not authority. It had its uses . . . for others at times.

In the early Thirties, I was a not-too-active member of the Washington (D.C.) Newspaper Guild. Robert M. Buck, a former Chicago alderman, was bull o' the woods. A young calf, Eddy Gilmore, had the nerve to run against him for local Guild president. That was too much! The old bull snorted and r'ared and tore up the ground.

I was in my office minding my own business when a snotty young reporter walked in on me. "What's your name?" he asked.

"Len De Caux."

He laughed. "How d'you spell it?"

I spelled it, and he laughed again. "I don't believe it."

"All right, don't! What's so funny?"

"There couldn't be such a name. I was sure he invented it."

"Who?"

"Why, Bob Buck. Didn't you know you're the guy in the background pulling the strings of a communist plot to unseat him?"

"I didn't. Do tell. It sounds interesting."

"Bob's done it before; it makes an impression. A sinister sort of foreign name, you know. Yours has been going over big. Nobody can pronounce it—that helps too. Bob's an artist, but I thought he'd overreached himself making up a name like yours."

For helping me cover the British general strike, I must give belated credit to the *New York Times*. Wherever I was in the United States, I got it. Somewhere between it and my other steady favorite, the *Daily Worker*, I looked for truth. There was something reassuring about the *Times*. Not that it was impeccable, but so many thought it was. If caught with your sources showing, it was no calamity to admit you saw it in the good gray *Times*. But once . . .

I was working on the *Locomotive Engineers Journal* when the Grand Chief Engineer called me on the carpet. With him were several Assistant Grand Chief Engineers. I was asked why

I had printed a certain item. Was it true? Where did I get it? I said I'd rewritten information appearing in the *New York Times,* assuming it to be true because of that source. I felt safe, expecting the paper's name to make an impression.

It did. At least a minute of silence followed, judging from the ticking of half a dozen big railroad watches. The Grand Chief waited for one of the AGCEs to say something. The AGCEs waited for him to speak. Finally he did. "The *New York Times?*" he said. "Is that a reputable paper?"

Before leaving the *Times,* a story John L. Lewis once told me:

It was long before CIO. The Mine Workers had trouble with the operators, big business, press, government—a perennial problem. A Wall Street club invited Lewis to speak. He felt ill at ease. His hosts were coldly polite, but clearly a hostile audience. He was in the camp of the corporate enemy. Lewis scanned the stony faces, looking for any that might be responsive. He had to settle for one man whose skeptical expression at least suggested some possible interest.

"I decided," Lewis related, "to devote all my eloquence to convincing that one man at least. I watched his every reaction. If I seemed not to reach him, I changed my approach. The man paid close attention, and at last I felt I was affecting him. I added argument to argument, until I actually had him nodding his head."

After the speech, the man came up to introduce himself. "I'm Adolph Ochs, publisher of the *New York Times,*" he said. "Congratulations on your address. I came with my mind made up, against you and your union's stand. You've changed my mind, convinced me, moved me. Now I'm on your side."

After that Lewis was walking on air. He'd made a dent in a solidly hostile press. The *Times,* in particular, had been printing scathing indictments of the miners one after another. Maybe from this opening. . . . Lewis studied the *Times* every day looking for signs of a change. He hoped especially for an editorial reflecting the publisher's change of heart. At last an editorial on the miners did appear. Lewis dwelt on every word. It was another scathing indictment.

As for myself, on the *Illinois Miner* I had arrived. With $35 paid on the dot each week, I could pick and choose at a nice cafeteria. On occasion, in business suit, white shirt, and tie, I might stroll self-consciously through the lobby of Springfield's Waldorf-Astoria, the Abraham Lincon Hotel, and eat in its coffeeshop. I slept in a bed so clean no bedbug dared risk encounter with my landlady. My mattress, if not exactly cloudlike, was at least softer than a boxcar floor.

As I lay abed, I'd listen to the distant rumble and wail of departing freight trains. They called to me; they almost enticed me. I resisted the call, most comfortably. Even now in California —electrification, aviation, trucking, and all—I still hear the blamed things in the still of the night. Now they hoot at me.

The work was pleasant. I made my own hours—late come, late go. For a labor paper, the *Miner* was good—trying to interest as well as exhort. I wrote much as I pleased, and it pleased me to write. Copy went to Oklahoma City for makeup and printing, so after each copy deadline, I was free for long weekends—some with my still-sick Caroline in Madison, Wisconsin.

I was aware all this was affecting me. With an appeased stomach, a regular salary, and work that is pleasant and socially useful, one doesn't sweat it so much. A lot of things can wait— including the revolution. I still wanted it, but with less subjective urgency maybe.

Meanwhile, down in the mines . . .

There's a gulf between working worker and official worker— between Joe Blow on the job and Mr. Joseph Q. Blow in his union office. It can make the membership seem quite remote. There was the young lady from the Virginia garden-party set, hired as clerk by CIO, who complained to a sister deb: "Gee, I've worked there two weeks, and nobody's told me yet what they sell." Then there was the ex-engineer driving a swivel chair in Locomotive Engineers' headquarters. Climbing socially into a suburban country club, he couldn't reveal he worked for a union. "They wouldn't have understood," said he. He told clubmen he "worked for a big New York banker." (Grand Chief Stone ran labor banks in New York and elsewhere.)

I went hunting for the miners . . . in my spare time. Union papers aren't encouraged to have inquiring reporters probe the members' minds. My successor's inquiring mind led him too close to the opposition. He lasted just long enough for word to get back to district headquarters.

The Springfield subdistrict had been quite left, and working miners I met included communists. They couldn't so call themselves; the UMW got sticky on that. At some early stage, communists were added to a grab-bag clause listing those barred from membership. The list, reflecting pet peeves of the moment, included at one time or another IWW's Ku Kluxers, members of the National Civic Federation, Working Class Union, One Big Union, and Boy Scout leaders. The leftist miners I met, however, read communist papers, argued like communists, and didn't hide their sympathies.

A point of contact was the Taylorville project run by Tom Tippett, a miner who was with Federated Press before becoming a labor educator. He brought speakers and classes to the miners in their homes and union halls.

Actually I came closer to the miners after I left the *Illinois Miner*. I made a reporting trip for FP through the Hocking Valley and southeastern minefields of Ohio to the West Virginia Panhandle. Illinois was prosperous by comparison. The competition of nonunion southern fields with northern union mines was rocking, almost wrecking, the UMW. Supposedly union operators brazenly undercut union wage scales and conditions. Unemployment and misery were rampant. Each night I slept in a miner's home. I saw children kept from school for lack of shoes, for shame over ragged clothes. I saw actual hunger. I saw pigs and chickens better cared for than people; they could be eaten, the people couldn't.

The miners in these fields were more outspoken, militant, radical, than most I met in Illinois. The communists were strong in spots, and some subdistrict union officials were angling for their support. In southeastern Ohio, the miners were largely foreign-born. Many read communist papers and belonged to left-led, foreign-language groups.

The miners, in the United States as in Britain, were a remarkable union phenomenon. Isolated in much of their work and in small, often remote, communities, they were not isolated in union thinking, organization, struggle. In both countries, the miners were among the first to organize, to strike, to respond to the teachings of Karl Marx. Even in the United States, the Socialist party once claimed a third of the miners in its ranks.

The miners were missionaries spreading the union gospel. In mining communities they took under their unionizing wing carpenters, barbers, busdrivers, hotel and store clerks. The metal miners, in isolated western towns, were like that too. Neither coal nor metal miners were exclusive in their unionism; what was good for them was good for all workers. So it was to be that the UMW founded, financed, and led CIO to unionize the major industries. Thirty years earlier, Haywood's metal miners—more impetuously, less practically, with much less money—had similar ideas for the IWW.

Many miners were union missionaries after they ceased to be miners. In the later Twenties hundreds of thousands of coal miners became dispersed. Breakdown of union conditions, labor-displacing machinery, mine closings, unemployment— starting long before the Great Depression and continuing through it—drove from the coalfields the younger, the single, the restless. They scattered all over the United States seeking jobs. Few could get jobs covered by the exclusive craft unions. Most gravitated to the big unorganized industries like steel, auto, rubber, electrical, where labor was in demand and you learned skills as you worked. In such industries, miners were among those few —including the communists, whose ranks many ex-miners joined —who kept candles of unionism burning all through the feudal darkness of the antiunion, company-union, open shop.

When the CIO bugles blew, ex-miners were among the first to enlist. They remembered the union lingo. They knew about *Robert's Rules of Order*. They hadn't forgotten that a union has to fight for what it gets.

I've mentioned hunger, misery, unemployment, in the coalfields in 1926-27. I saw it. I felt it—less acutely because vicariously. Myself I was doing all right. The English adage, "I'm all right, Jack," could have been the American national motto in those years up to 1929, as again in the Fifties and Sixties. Americans put the idea less pithily:

This time prosperity's permanent. We're going to get more and more affluent. No one need go hungry. Everyone can become rich. Maybe some depressed areas, a sick industry or two, some pockets of unemployment. If Uncle Sam's pockets are large, it's because he's so big and has so much money. Who cares anyhow? Eat, drink, and be merry; spend, spend, spend, for tomorrow will bring ever more things to buy.

The workers? The labor movement? Don't make us laugh. We don't have workers, or classes, any more in the United States of America. The workers are middle class—incipient capitalists. Along with their cars (soon two in each garage), they're buying stock in the companies that employ them. Who's going to strike against himself? The unions are big business. Look at their labor banks. They're capitalist outfits more than unions. Isn't one of them operating coal mines in West Virginia? Nonunion, at that! Even communists spoke of "bourgeoisification" of American workers. Jay Lovestone, Workers (Communist) party secretary—not yet AFL International Affairs Director—was expounding American "exceptionalism."

A premature Old Left perhaps, I balked at ditching the labor movement and joining the laughs at poor saps who'd thought there was a working class with a historic mission. I was even going to work for the most capitalistic of unions—and the one with the nonunion coal mines at that!

A ghost, some zombies, and Peter Pan presided over the little wonder world I entered in the fall of 1926. It was all rather improbable.

The ghost was that of Warren S. Stone. His big handsome head with cropped mustache graced office walls at Brotherhood of Locomotive Engineers headquarters in Cleveland. He'd been dead more than a year, but his spirit was omnipresent. The zombies were holdovers from the Stone regime. President W.B. Prenter was grayly aged, sicklied over with disgust at life and not far from the grave. The others were robust gentlemen. It strained metaphor to compare them with haunts from the cemetery of a dead past. Peter Pan lived on ageless after Stone, chasing the fairy Tinker Bell with innocent abandon, unburdened by guilt, unmoved by contumely.

For me, this world partook of pleasures and palaces I'd once glimpsed longingly through the slit of a boxcar door . . . when I first saw Cleveland in 1921 and feared to venture into its opulent bustle.

The BLE Bank Building was the high spot of Cleveland's skyline, its tallest skyscraper. (The BLE also claimed a "world's largest," through controlling interest in New York's Equitable Trust office building.) The railroad companies hadn't yet reasserted a supremacy never relinquished, by building their soaring Terminal Tower over a new Union Terminal on Cleveland's Public Square. The BLE Building, across the street from the newer Bank Building, was substantial enough, if not so tall.

From either Brotherhood building, one could look down on a squat and aging Chamber of Commerce building and much of Cleveland's trade and industry. To look down on the common people from lordlier heights, one could head out Euclid Avenue toward wooded hills and rent an apartment for $1,000 a month, say, at the BLE-owned Park Lane Villa.

All this in an age when old-fashioned unions operated from Dombey-and-Sons dumps, with rolltop desks and maybe high bookkeepers' stools—when the more ambitious rented a floor or two in an office building or owned an unpretentious building far from big-business structures it didn't presume to ape. Not till many years later did labor skates compete with modernistic, beglassed, bemarbled headquarters for their greater glory. True, even then some of the labor fraternity owned stately Gold Coast pleasure domes and country estates. But these were the personal property of the more acquisitive, who needed little more office space than the rims of their fedoras to keep tab on their more profitable transactions.

What was improbable about the substantial world of BLE financial success? Weren't its livewire executives in tune with the times?

"We set out with only one theory," said President Prenter

in a magazine article. "That is the theory that in America there is no such thing as a working class as distinguished from a capitalist class. . . . It is the Brotherhood's aim in its financial enterprises to show its members and workers generally how they can become capitalists as well as workers."

That was exactly the tune of the times. "Only one theory" . . . one ism only: capitalism.

"Labor has become capital" was the strange device on the banners of these Brotherhood crusaders for the Fatherhood of Free Enterprise. "Labor banking," said Prenter, rubbing it in, "has demonstrated labor's complete answer to the theories of Marx and Lenin."

The BLE had a dozen complete answers to Marx and Lenin —a dozen labor banks. It had almost as many holding companies, and a score of investment, mortgage, and industrial companies. Besides office and apartment buildings, and other enterprises of all kinds, it operated coal mines and held 50,000 acres of Florida real estate. On the graves of poor Marx and Lenin it was piling some $100,000,000 in paydirt—mostly originating from the paychecks of the locomotive engineers.

To prove labor fit to become capital, the labor capitalists showed themselves as adept as capitalist capitalists in sucking money from the working stiffs. They showed a similar tendency to be autocratic, antiunion, nepotic, graftish, and to be swallowed up by bigger capitalists.

What made this Stone age seem dated, when I reached Cleveland, was that it had come to an end. The Stone empire—like the British empire later, but with American tempo—had been in liquidation, mostly forced, even before Stone died. Prenter kept waving the flag after the sun had set on it. At the 1927 BLE convention, the ruins were displayed. Instead of ruling a $100,000,000 empire, the engineers found themselves decapitalized and in hock to capitalist capitalists for some $19,000,000.

The labor capitalists were pioneers both coming and going. Their ventures collapsed several years before the general collapse of the Great Depression. Like coal and other sick industries—and a few million folks in "pockets"—they managed to go bust right in the midst of the Coolidge boom.

Come boom or bust, all was order and propriety on the 11th floor of the BLE Building. The corner office suite with best Lake view was for the Big Shot. Then, one after another, in descending order of protocol, came the slightly less grand offices of the slightly less grand officers.

When I came, the maximum leaders were a President and some Vice Presidents. Below them, to tend the lowly labor end, came the Grand Chief Engineer and the Assistant Grand Chief Engineers. Noting this distinction, the 1927 convention abolished the Presidential and Vice-Presidential offices, and Grand Chief Alvanley Johnston—asserting "I'm a labor man not a banker"—then took over with his assistant grand chiefs in tow.

Everything on the 11th floor was proper, probable, and as you would expect. The First Assistant Grand Chief kept his eye on the Grand Chief next door in his slightly grander office. The Second Assistant Grand Chief, in a slightly less grand office on the other side, kept his eye on the First Assistant Grand Chief. The Third AGCE kept his eye on the second AGCE . . . the Fourth on the Third . . . the Fifth on the Fourth . . . and so on. If the Third got a bigger mahogany desk, he gloated, and the Fourth ground his teeth. Swivel and armchairs were exactly appraised and compared. If a prior number got a thicker carpet, the other ordinal numbers wanted as much, or more. If the executive eye ever closed, the secretarial eye was ever open.

The only improbable thing on the 11th floor was the popping in and out of Peter Pan. He didn't belong there. You had to be fast to trail him. He ran as much as he walked. He didn't dally or linger. Down down from the upper-floor Lakeview suites —back back from the daylight-drenched front offices—his trail led, behind the eighth floor elevators, to the dim dingy office of the *Locomotive Engineers Journal*, Albert F. Coyle, Editor.

This was the realm of Peter Pan. His spirit ruled, though Coyle P. Pan was often absent. Here all things were possible. If there was a rug (I hadn't time to notice), it was worn threadbare. The furniture was Early Thrift Shop, or Late Salvation Army. Albert himself had a battered rolltop desk. We all liked that desk. When Albert popped out—after popping in to skim the cream off his correspondence, dictate pronunciamentos, and stir up problems by long-distance phone—we could roll down the top over mounting piles of unfinished business. This made us feel better, and protected against open windows, fans, or prying strangers.

Albert had a lively young secretary. Betty's black eyes were alert, as quick as a bird's. But they had a blind spot. They couldn't see or compare the size and sheen of office desks, the depth of nap of office carpets. All Betty looked for was to save the world—and keep up with Albert.

She'd wait all hours for Albert to arrive on the run—"no time to wait for a taxi"—from the old Union Depot. Her eyes sparkled as he editorially blasted United States imperialism in Nicaragua, the Philippines; defended Sacco and Vanzetti; whooped it up for labor, consumers' cooperation, and Florida real estate. Betty didn't flag or fail when Albert took her with him to continue dictation in cab or streetcar; or on the Night Flyer East, to leave him at Ashtabula and return; or on the Night Flyer West, to debark at Sandusky. Betty managed to keep up with Albert. The railroads never quite did. Soon after, they quietly yielded to air travel for the Alberts.

Into Albert's whirlpool I was thrown—a poor substitute for my predecessor, Harvey O'Connor, who must have known how to make the waters stand still, or at least behave. The massive *Journal* somehow got to press each month. A weekly cooperative news service got written, mimeographed, mailed. A hundred Coyle projects got some attention. Albert didn't complain, though at times his eyes asked, "Why did God make the tortoise?"

The ghost of Warren Stone was a bit from Jekyll-and-Hyde.

On the one hand, an American success story. Starting as a humble hogger, Stone left the cab to rise and rise to pinnacles of bankerdom. He could soon scorn his $25,000 BLE salary as peanuts and point to a $50,000 offer from a New York bank. He came to rule a $100 million financial and industrial empire.

Thrift was one key to his success. He bade office secretaries economize in stationery, and checked their wastebaskets after hours, they claimed. The thrift of the working hoggers helped most; though Stone husbanded his own money too. While misfortune befell his corporations, he was said to be worth some half million when he died. Stone was virtuous. To discourage ogling and necking, he forbade female employees to wear short skirts or bob their hair. Affectionate and generous, he cast his bread on the waters; it came back in unexpected claimants to his estate.

Tenacity was another key to Stone's success. He held on to what he had. Critics called him despotic. Fellow officers, after he died, said he'd been autocrat of their meal tickets, dictator of their directorates. "Warren Stone was a Czar," Grand Chief Johnston told the 1927 convention. "He told us what companies we should be directors of. He said, 'You will be a director of this, you will be a vice president of this.'"

This arbitrary beneficence with sinecures was less criticized while Stone lived. In convention, delegates noted how firm was his presiding hand and did not complain—on the floor, anyhow. One told the 1927 convention that Stone had "ruled by an iron hand and strong arm." A man couldn't "express himself as he wanted to," said he, "because he was sat down so hard that he would scrounge in his seat and was afraid to get up."

Stone could be a rugged individualist. When union pickets walked before his barbershop, he brushed past them. No "two-by-four" union, said he, was going to "bully" him. The United Mine Workers was more than two-by-four in dimensions. But employer Stone insisted on running his business his own way. The Coal River Collieries, bought with BLE money, operated union mines in West Virginia, nonunion in Kentucky. When the UMW balked at a wage cut, the company, John L. Lewis charged, shut down its West Virginia mines, imported strikebreakers, and evicted union miners from their homes. The UMW leader said Stone and company had acted just like any of the "coldblooded, hard-boiled, nonunion coal companies."

There you had Dr. Jekyll Stone, a paragon of all the capitalist virtues. To welcome such a labor prodigal, Wall Street was happy, if not to kill the fatted calf, at least to shear the plump lambs of BLE.

But there was also a Mr. Hyde. . . .

When the good Dr. Stone retired, after ministering to free

enterprise and scattering the Brotherhood's bounty, from his quarters might emerge a Mr. Hyde, out to undermine the very foundations of capitalism. A decade before "that man in the White House" was "untrue to his class," creepingly socialistic eggheads hailed this Hyde-Stone as their man. He had a New-Dealish brain trust headed by a noted liberal, Dr. Frederic C. Howe, and including my boss, Albert F. Coyle. He was willing to promote any new, even radical, idea if he took a fancy.

The Plumb Plan for railroad nationalization was one of Stone's babies. He didn't tremble or retreat when it was called socialistic. He was a leading founder of the weekly paper *Labor*, which mobilized rail labor to pressure Congress for many progressive purposes. A leader in the Conference for Progressive Political Action—and interested in the labor-party idea—Stone was top labor backer of Robert M. LaFollette, Progressive third-party candidate for President in 1924—when Lewis was for Coolidge, and Gompers only belatedly and reluctantly fell into line. Stone was strong for cooperatives—both Rochdale consumers and producers' coops. This got him into trouble again with Lewis, who frowned on cooperative miners in Ohio paying themselves less than UMW made the operators pay.

Politically, Stone was a George W. Norris progressive—though he could sprawl around in endorsements. He favored public ownership and social-welfare legislation. He was even openminded on the Russian revolution and authorized Coyle to promote a sympathetic labor delegation to the Soviet Union.

Not all agreed which was the Jekyll and which the Hyde side of Warren Stone. But contradictions between the two were evident—at least to those who found something contradictory in labor becoming capital in one and the same person. Coyle had liked Stone and been loyal to him. To Coyle, Stone was all Dr. Jekyll—a great and shining progressive. Albert was Jekylly like that himself.

Albert Coyle was charming and disarming. He was small and slim—the faster to move. Behind round, rimmed glasses, his eyes beamed blessing. He was youthfully eager and earnest—outgoing in every way, even to stepping out of his office to greet the visitor. He couldn't wait for his approach, couldn't sit still, anyhow. He'd cock his head, glow with fond affection, clasp your hand in both of his, and so draw you into his sanctum.

At work Albert was a wonder. He'd take a deep drink of water, say "A-a-ah, that steams me up," beam all around, summon his secretary, and seat himself on his rickety swivel chair, wound up to toppling height. So poised, Albert could dictate articles, editorials, statements, one after another—without notes, without clippings, and without stopping. At speaking Albert was equally fluent. Billed by his lecture agency as a popular speaker on many subjects, he traveled much on lecture circuits.

Like a miniature tornado, Albert blew through the stuffinesses of railroad brotherhood life. Among the stuffiest were the official journals. When Albert took over that of the BLE, he added color, artwork, pictures, modeling makeup and style on the popular news magazines. He made the magazine political, with articles by progressive Senators, coverage of Congress, a department titled "The Road to Political Power." Other departments covered labor, railroad, foreign affairs, book reviews, etc. He sought letters from the engineers, and tales of railroad life and adventure. The Coyle tornado swept far beyond journalism. He blew in and out of Washington, from union to union. I could visualize his reception.

Locomotive engineers were solid citizens, men of weight and cautious responsibility. Like their engines, they preferred to stick to the rails. I'd watch their faces when Albert held forth in his office on civil liberties, political action, international affairs. Lower lips tended to sag. Eyes glanced uneasily toward the door or popped with hypnotic fascination, fixed on Albert's glimmering glasses and his dancing lips. When they left, Albert would say: "Well, they didn't disagree, did they? All I've got to do now is prod them into some action."

It was hard to discourage Albert. Before I came, he ran for Congress against Theodore Burton, an entrenched reactionary Republican. Albert buzzed all around, challenging Burton to debate. Burton ignored him completely and won by two-to-one or more. Albert demanded a recount.

When at his "base of operations" (the *Journal* office), Coyle had visitors of all kinds. For every good cause—and newcomers kept adding to his list—he had his beaming blessing. I heard only two hot arguments . . . one with A. O. Wharton, new president of the International Association of Machinists; the other with Nathan Fine, historian of labor parties.

Wharton was less restrained than the engineers. He had some Indian blood, boiling to battle invaders. When Lewis knocked out Big Bill Hutcheson at the 1935 AFL convention, Wharton had to be held back from leaping into the fray to "kill the bastard" (Big John, not Big Bill).

Immune to Coyle's eloquence, Wharton argued back. Expletives aside (not from Albert, who didn't swear, smoke, drink—except water—or make passes at women), it was quite a debate on the "new unionism." Wharton's latest style was reminiscent of what was once called pure-and-simple unionism. Albert wasn't going to let Wharton make him look like the Prince of his name on the tobacco can. His new unionism, he insisted, was the very latest and still-coming style.

Since Warren Stone ordained him, Coyle had preached a wide-ranging new unionism. It included a modern business approach to the investment of union funds, to serve labor and humanity. This Albert (bless his bounding heart) really seemed to believe, though I doubt the thought occurred to most get-rich-quick labor-become-capitalists. Anyhow, Albert by now was retcent on this. The Brotherhood's investment troubles were leaking out. The glint in many members' eyes didn't encourage volubility.

On other aspects of his new unionism, Albert had much to say. A modern union, he held, was part of a labor movement, the American people, the world. It must concern itself not only with its own immediate interests, but with those of all working people, all humanity. Unions should lead in progressive political action, striking out independently of Wall Street's two old parties. They should promote cooperatives, civil liberties, democratic rights. They should lead the fight against poverty, for social justice, against imperialism, for international peace.

Wharton retorted that Coyle sounded just like Bill (William H.) Johnston, his predecessor as IAM president. Bill

Johnston, once a Salvation Army captain, preached a broad labor evangelism; with Stone, he had supported the Plumb Plan, CPPA, the LaFollette movement. Coyle was flattered. Wharton made clear he intended no compliment.

Wharton said Coyle's new unionism was dead as a stinking mackerel. Like BLE, the Machinists had learned not to spread out too far. They weren't going to organize all the workers. Industrial unionism was as dead as the IWW, and as said mackerel. His new unionism, said Wharton, was a skilled-worker unionism, a stick-to-your-knitting unionism. His union was going to look after the skilled machinists, and to hell with the ragtag-and-bobtail of unskilled workers—who couldn't be organized anyhow. The skilled were the key men; a good tight union could get a good price for them. A lot of riffraff didn't strengthen, just weakened a union. As for all Albert's fancy ideas to save the world . . . Nuts!

Coyle seemed to be pursuing rather than escorting Nathan Fine on his way out. Both men were small, Fine the plumper; a clash would have been no more than a sideswipe between sparrows. But both were agitated. Fine had come to Coyle as a sympathizer with the labor-party idea and been shocked to find him little on guard against communists.

Some socialist and union leaders had given the idea a spin, without much result. Communists and the TUEL had gone to the grass roots, producing a big crop of labor-party resolutions from local unions. The anticommunist left ("pinkos" as against "reds") was much concerned that it, not the reds, should be on the inside of any possible mass labor party.

I knew the attitude. Some years before, I'd visited the office of *Labor Age*, a magazine promoting the line of A.J. Muste (then head of Brookwood Labor College) later embodied in the Conference for Progressive Labor Action. The editor, a small, sallow-faced man, was elated. He was chuckling and chortling. Knowing me only as a Brookwooder, he tried to bring me in on his glee. "Just great, isn't it?" he said. "We're in, they're out."

"They?" I asked.

"Why, the party, the communists, of course. They're so

boxed in with their farmer-labor party they can't support LaFollette, and he won't have them. The unions are for LaFollette. So
the comrades are out, out, out, and we're in."

I was surprised later when this editor—Louis F. Budenz—
switched to the communists and the *Daily Worker*. I was less
surprised, when the Cold War put the communists "out," to
find this same Budenz becoming informer-in-chief, top namer of
names, in the persecution of the left.

I didn't expect Coyle to be so indignant. He was no communist. In a rare moment of self-analysis, he called himself a
"Jeffersonian democrat." He could have been torn to pieces in
any polemic. No doubt this incident added to his repute as an
"innocent," subject to communist seduction.

If innocent Albert might be in some ways, in this instance
he was like more realistic leaders who did manage to launch
mass movements. In starting CIO, John L. Lewis set his face
against factionalists of right, center, or left whose chief concern
was to keep out the communists. He figured he needed all the
horse, foot, and dragoons he could get, and was not inclined to
fight off would-be supporters. Franklin D. Roosevelt also welcomed left support when he could get it. The British Labor
party—the pinkos' model—was not started as a factional fight
against the reds, but built by the most redbaited of the times.
There was also that stirrer-up of the people who attached no exclusion clause to his, "Come unto me all ye that are weary and
heavy-laden."

Anyhow Coyle deplored factional fighting on his side. He
also had some fellow feeling for those who stick out their necks
without thought of getting their snouts in the trough. At the
time he was boosting the idea that officeholders in a labor or
people's movement should kick back much of their salaries to
the movement. Albert wanted to start a move among United
States labor leaders for this kind of kickback. That I would call
innocence!

Coyle worked hard and long to organize an American labor
delegation to the Soviet Union. Nobody without his bounceback
could have succeeded. Few union leaders of rank dared defy

Granny AFL and the powers to which she bowed; and most, even of these, were egotistic, thin-skinned, and given to sharp chills in the feet. Albert bounced over every setback. The prima donnas retired to their dressing rooms, in high or low dudgeon, with or without bouquets. More durable troupers replaced them.

Besides Coyle, those making the trip included: James H. Maurer, president, Pennsylvania Federation of Labor; John Brophy, United Mine Workers; Lillian Herstein, Chicago Teachers; Silas B. Axtell, counsel for Seamen's and Longshoremen's unions; Frank L. Palmer, ex-editor, *Colorado Labor Advocate*; James W. Fitzpatrick, president, Actors & Artistes Federation. Also braintrusters Stuart Chase, author; Rexford G. Tugwell, Columbia University; Jerome Davis, Yale; Paul Douglas (later Senator), University of Chicago.

During preliminaries, an unobtrusive visitor might slip in and out of our office—always discreet. But discretion was small part of Albert's valor. He freely introduced him as "Mr. Jay Lovestone, of the Workers (Communist) party."

Lovestone, then the party's executive secretary, had been underground. Coyle never had; with none of the attributes of the mole, he'd have suffocated. In appearance, Albert could have modeled for a cherub; the pale hawk-nosed Jay, for a devilkin. Albert was so open as to lay himself wide open. Jay was close and secretive. Impulsive, Albert rushed into the midday sun. Jay preferred the shady side of the street; he liked to move incognito, under different names.

To anticommunists, a man like Jay was the archetype of the communist—conspiratorial, devious, bitter, factional, chockful of ulterior motives. Alas for the stereotype! Communists of the Lovestone type didn't last in the movement; most, as did he, became its bitterest enemies.

My dictionary describes a jay as "pugnacious and destructive of the eggs and young of other birds." Jay was pugnacious enough in communist in-fighting and interested in the eggs and young of others. Bounced from the Communist party, Jay took over—amid much anticommunist squawking and wingbeating— the egg-laying Homer Martin, first UAW president, and devoted much attention to his young.

During Lovestone's Cleveland visits, I had occasion to meet

and eat with him at the Olmsted Hotel. He surprised me with his easy manners, his plausibility, even some sense of humor. He surprised me even more with some of the things he said, in inviting me to join the party.

Politely I told Lovestone that he and his faction were my main reason for not wanting to join. William Z. Foster and his TUEL followers were at least at home in the working class. With the Lovestone crowd apparently on top in the factional fight tearing the party apart, I was inclined to sit things out. Lovestone showed no offense. He argued my views were closer to his group's than to Foster's. It was easy to talk with Lovestone; a good listener, he readily understood what one had in mind. In the process, I got a clearer idea of what was on my mind.

American communists, as I'd seen them, were devoted, if not fanatical. In union organizing, they were out front, taking the rap, first to get fired in often hopeless causes; in strikes, first to get bashed or jailed. Within unions, they fought so bitterly for reform that the piecards felt threatened enough to gun them down, expel them, run them off their jobs. Yet hated, rejected, driven from pillar to post, the communists fought on for the poor and oppressed wherever they saw them. They grabbed every wildcat by the tail, or at least spat back in its face.

The communists were taking on the most deep and devilish of American oppressions, that of the black people, as earlier radicals hadn't thought or dared to do. They saw it as a national question, and they fought for full equality in every sphere, 40 years before the black people forced "civil rights" into practical politics. They also fought "white chauvinism" among white workers, and particularly in their own ranks.

In addition to everything else, the communists took on the burden of defending the Soviet Union in its efforts to build socialism; and of supporting liberation struggles against imperialism everywhere.

In such uneven and many-fronted battles, I didn't expect the communists to be saints. I knew of excesses of discipline, factionalism, dogmatism, intolerance; of unbalanced, malicious types hanging around.

My chief kick was that the American communists always

seemed to bite off more than they could chew, take on everyone at once, attempt the impossible. Why not try caution, seek allies, practice the art of the possible?

As to my personal motives . . . When I joined the party in Britain, I was unemployed. Now I had more to lose—a job that I liked and that paid $200 a month. General strikes were once demanded for each May Day. What if I had to strike my job and carry a red flag onto Public Square? That gesture might stir the gallant Albert, but would the 11th floor understand? Such thoughts I put differently, even to myself, arguing that the British communists were practical working folks, not so wild and up in the air.

When I complained of American communists being extremist, romantic, impossibilist, Lovestone agreed. He took my words —though some must have been both ignorant and unfair—and made them stronger. If I urged a little caution, moderation, possibilism, he called for far more than I had in mind. Lovestone was then on his "American exceptionalism" binge, theorizing that American capitalism differed from other capitalisms and was just going up and up. This was two years before the Great Depression.

When we talked, I thought Lovestone was getting carried away. In effect, he annulled the class struggle, sidetracked socialism, deplored nearly everything the American communists did. At last, I said:

"The way you put it, there's hardly any point to having an American Communist party."

"Maybe there isn't," said he.

By the time Caroline, convalescent, agreed to come to Cleveland, Coyle was no longer with us. Moved to the 11th floor, I had to adjust to it and restrict myself to editing the *Journal*—an interesting job, but less exciting and far-ranging than keeping up with Albert.

To find lodging for us, I had to advertise. But how to describe our relationship? I'd long held marriage a bourgeois institution—wrongly, I later realized, since it predated capitalism and persisted under socialism. To be with Caroline, I'd gladly have committed matrimony, but her attitude was the hitch. She too took a dim view of marriage, but more important, wasn't too sure that I was the one guy she'd want to be stuck with.

My first thought was to say what I meant: "Two young lovers want room and board together in nice home." Then remembering the Waipawa Vicarage, I realized that—without some suggestion of wedlock—this might set tongues a-wagging. In at least indirect deference to the institution, I changed the wording to, "Young man and fiancée. . . ."

I knew I was taking a chance with Caroline, who had never conceded we were betrothed. I anticipated problems with landladies. But, so help me, I didn't think I was involving the Brotherhood of Locomotive Engineers.

Soon, however, the switchboard operator reported inquiries about me and "my financier." Anything financial was in a sensitive area for the BLE. My finances became a subject of curiosity around the 11th floor. I gave thought to them myself. I decided to hit up the Grand Chief for a raise.

I was jittery, and the boss was a reluctant dragon. When I asked an appointment, he dodged and stalled. When at last I bearded the solidly packed Alvanley Johnston in his den, his mien was grim, his manner was brusque, his voice was gruff. I blurted out my mission. Then a surprise.

The Grand Chief took off his reading glasses. He leaned back in his chair. All the lines of his grimness relaxed. He became jovial. Gradually a light dawned. I'd forgotten I worked for a labor union . . . don't think that isn't easy. Now I had that union's chief negotiator on his home grounds. People who don't seem to care about money make no sense to a union leader— they annoy him. Instead of presenting him with a problem, I'd given him a chance to play. He made it a baby bargaining session. He probed me, and I got to know him better. As our talk got personal, the Chief confided he'd once voted for Eugene Debs.

Johnston came from the Great Northern or Northern Pacific—roads where, in 1921, trainmen asked freight-riders to show their union cards, and where my One Big Union card made a hit. The strike of Debs' American Railway Union in the

1890s had much support on them. Now rated a conservative, Johnston was for Herbert Hoover in 1928.

Leader of a labor aristocracy corrupted by capitalism; class collaborationist; bourgeoisified by high income, investments, business associations—radicals could say this of Johnston. There was more to say.

Some wrote off locomotive engineers' unions as hardly unions at all, claiming the fascists didn't have to smash, just to incorporate them. On the other hand, in England in 1925, I found the Associated Society of Locomotive Firemen & Enginemen a militant radical union; its chief, John Bromley, a leading left. In the United States, Debs came from the BLE's twin and rival, the Brotherhood of Locomotive Firemen & Enginemen. As secretary and editor, he was of its establishment, until he broke to form the ARU as an industrial union. The BLE, under Warren Stone, took more progressive stands on many issues than most less aristocratic unions.

The Republicans had some union roots. In the Midwest, progressive Republicans like Senators George W. Norris and Robert M. LaFollette were more liberal, if not radical, than most Democrats. Republican states in this area had the better labor laws. Labor, particularly rail labor and farmers, were basic supporters of these progressive Republicans. But there was another reason, in 1928, for some rail labor leaders to be for Hoover. The Democrat running against him was a Roman Catholic, Alfred E. Smith.

The BLE establishment was Masonic and Protestant. My second editor boss, Carl Rudolph, an engineer of German Catholic background, made the elective grade by becoming a Protestant and joining the Masons. The internal conflict in BLE was between the ruling Masons and a small but rebellious Knights of Columbus minority.

Seniority was BLE's rock of ages. If on a railroad payroll long enough—the first 40 years were the hardest—one might rise to a good run and good money for old age and one's heirs. The low men—on extra board for occasional yard or switch-engine work—hardly had a job; they could but dream of seniors quitting or dying. In between, jobs and pay were just middling, considering the skill, long service, and responsibility.

Like rock strata recording the ages, BLE seniority lists told much about United States immigration. At the top, English, Scottish, Welsh names. Lower, German and Scandinavian names. Then cheeky upstart Irish names to put a Celtic curse on Saxon and Teutonic seniors. At extra-board level, maybe some Italian names. I recall no other Mediterranean or eastern European names. Mexican names were as absent as those of Jews.

Jews seemed as far-out to the hoggers I met as black people. The southerners reacted to blacks in southern style; the northern politicians played on these prejudices, and shared them. Most didn't know a Jew when they saw one. Betty, who was Jewish, was a puzzle to engineer visitors. They knew she wasn't WASP—could she be so far-out alien as Irish or Italian? Ignorance of Jews fed anti-Semitism. In the small towns from which most engineers came, "Jew" meant huckster, shyster, trickiness with money.

Some of BLE's labor-capitalists, when called to account, tried to hide behind this prejudice. They'd been tricked by Jewish financiers, they wailed, and "the kikes around here are trying to get us all the time." Yet most bankers and businessmen playing ducks and drakes with BLE money were as WASP as the BLE officers and probably picked on that account.

Caroline came to Cleveland pale, weak, and shaky. She went to bed at once, in the big bed in the big room with windows on two sides and trees, birds, grass outside—the best I could find or afford. A widow lady and her maiden sister welcomed us—with reservations, I fear. They installed me in a separate room. Then they retreated, to keep watch from downstairs. They had a nice home, kept clean and cheerful. They fed us well. But never before had they rented to a "young man and his fiancée."

It was the spring of the year. Fresh icebreaking winds from Lake Erie drove Cleveland's smoke back on itself. Daffodils began to pop out. Little children, too. From work I now bounded home with dreamlike strides. My soaring spirits couldn't fit into a crowded bus, I chose to walk. The people seemed to part before me, as I wove my way westward.

Over the big bridge I sped. To my right the lake. Under me and far to my left, the smoke, the soot, the scum, the silt of the Cuyahoga River . . . the warehouses, factories, mills, that clung to its sides. Beyond, smoke-wrapped, frame shacks and dingy streets where the black and foreign swarmed.

At the end of the bridge, grassy slopes and children's playgrounds. The little people waved, and laughed at the sucker who walked so fast when he might have stood belly-and-bottom bumping in a bounding bus, or sprawled in private indignation through the bumper-bumping ritual of the rush-hour crawl. I swung my arms. I played monkey-squares, leaping over names in the cement. I tried not to break my mother's back by treading on the cracks. I whistled. I sang—when out of earshot. My goal was Caroline—so dear and dainty in her negligee—the pearl within that oyster shell of widow lady and maiden sister.

Caroline got well enough to take short walks. Hand in hand, we strolled along the cliff above the lake. The spring air became milder. The lake waters lapped more softly. The trees grew leaves to murmur with. The grassy earth got moistly warm. A broad-based tree hid us from the windows of our wardens. There we held each other close, in a community of feeling that all of nature understood.

Meanwhile the widow lady and her maiden sister kept unrelenting watch. They placed no creaking padlock on the turret door behind which my love lay languishing, but dragonlike they lay in wait. And finally they spoke: "We think you should get married."

Caroline and I considered. The widow lady and her maiden sister were immune to social criticism of the marriage institution, even to jokes about it. Should we let them push us around? I held it would be inverted truckling to the institution to defy it to our disadvantage. Caroline objected that, whereas she liked me very much, she didn't love me—a position she held to all through our 35 years together. It boiled down to whether we liked our lodgings well enough to yield an abstract point. We concluded it'd be too much trouble to move.

Caroline had to know one thing. Must she take my name? Was that equality? We consulted a woman lawyer, who said that, for certain legal purposes, Caroline would become Mrs. De

Caux. Caroline was indignant. It looked as if the deal was off. As a way out, the lawyer suggested I might take Caroline's name, if we preferred. Thinking of becoming Mr. Abrams, I realized that (1) there was no genuine and effective equality between the sexes here; and (2) there was genuinely effective anti-Semitism.

Besides equality, Caroline was concerned with separate identity. Why, she asked, must two lovers give up their freedom, independence, often their love, to a common name, a common abode, and the irritations of too-close confinement? Children could complicate things, but that was a contingency we didn't contemplate, given Caroline's precarious health.

I scouted around City Hall and got a Justice of the Peace to come out to the house. We used no ring, symbol of bondage as much as a ball-and-chain. Caroline got up and put on her walking-out attire. There, by the side of her bed, the JP recited some mumbo jumbo, and we were legally hitched. The widow lady and her maiden sister grimly watched to make sure there was no slip-up. They signed as witnesses, with emphasis. The JP pocketed his fee and left. That was that.

Or almost that. As soon as the others left, Caroline had me call the lawyer to learn how and when we could get a divorce. After all, how long did one have to be hogtied to a man one didn't love and a name one didn't want, just to satisfy a widow lady and her maiden sister?

Having established we could stay on, we soon decided to leave anyhow. We moved in with a woman teacher in Rocky River near those lake-front houses into whose lighted windows I once looked with envy—from the outside. In the winter we were lucky to get for nominal rent while the owners were in Florida a fine furnished house in middle-class Lakewood, with housekeeper service included. When Caroline was strong enough to do a little housekeeping, we rented a modern furnished apartment in Lakewood. By the summer of 1929, we were renting a nice, fully furnished house in Rocky River, while the owners were away.

I was "working for the movment," I argued with myself—at least trying to make *Journal* readers feel part of a labor movement. Caroline and I read and talked much about the movement. We had labor and radical visitors and contacts. But Hoover had recently taken office. On top of Coolidge Prosperity, Hoover Prosperity was raising capitalism's success psychosis to its dizziest height. As we looked out from our comfortable middle-class way of life, active radicalism did seem a bit far out.

We were the same two who, hand in hand, had set out from Brookwood in the spring of 1924 to change the world. The world had changed. Or was it we who had changed the more?

The latter thought occurred to me when, at the end of that 1929 summer, the Trade Union Unity League held its founding convention in Cleveland. One of the delegates—from the New York needle trades left wing—was a young woman friend of ours at Brookwood. We put her up at our Rocky River home. "What a bourgeois life!" she remarked.

It set me thinking. I made a mental note to do something about it. I might have spared myself the trouble.

Chapter Five

DEPRESSION'S NEW DEAL

The Great Depression ignited the workers'
discontent. Washington but dimly
reflected the mood. The New Deal bogged
down, the AFL doddered. CIO's time
had come.

Hardly had the TUUL convention adjourned than
the stock market crashed. Far from Wall Street, I saw no leaps
from high office buildings. But all around my little world I heard
sounds like the multitudinous bleatings of wool-stripped herds
at shearing time in New Zealand. Radical thinking had kept me
from the crowds surging into the stock market—buying and selling like crazy along this easy road to La Dolce Vita. It was the
only time I was money ahead for being red. I pitied the wailing
herds—but not unsmugly, as I patted my bank passbook.

Cold winds of caution blew on us too. That winter we
moved to a cheaper apartment—out St. Clair Avenue on the
east side. In Lakewood we paid $65. Here it was $55 for a room-
ier furnished apartment looking out on a parklike ravine, a $10
class differential for a worker neighborhood presumably. This
eastside apartment we kept for four depression years—or left to
find it still vacant awaiting our return. At any thought—ours or
his—of our moving, the landlord cut our rent—to as low as
$27.50 before we left Cleveland. Other tenants kept getting out
of work and deeper in debt. With most of his apartments vacant
or rented for promises, the landlord loved anyone who paid anything in cash.

Across the ravine was a big plant, White Motors. A few
blocks away, the Slovenian Workers Hall—in frequent use all
through the depression for radical meetings and affairs. To our

west, east, south, other working-class neighborhoods. We'd moved closer to the human heart of the depression.

Factory after factory went on short time, laid off, or closed down. There was no unemployment insurance. Public relief was meager and doled out under humiliating conditions. The jobless couldn't pay rent or meet mortgage payments. Furniture and appliances with unpaid installments were repossessed, and the rest set out on the sidewalk. Evictees perched forlornly on the pitiful remnants of their possessions. Breadlines and souplines grew longer. Thousands of homeless found shelter in rolling boxcars. The homeguard homeless raided dumps for metal and packing crates to build shelters in the mushrooming Hoovervilles.

The unemployed were told to be patient. There had been too much inflation of wages and prices, so now there had to be deflation to get inflation started again. It was a time for faith, hope, and charity—faith in our system, hope for the future, charity for the present. There were still personal problems, and in facing them folks heard other, even communist, ideas.

You know you shouldn't listen to them reds—commoonists, they are.

Who's listening to any com—any reds? I don't know none.

What about them guys come shoutin' to the neighbors to put your furniture back?

Who says they was com-myew-nists? Why, I known old Charley for years. He'd be in the American Legion if he could afford it.

But they was an agitator stirring them up, and doing most of the hollerin'. Now wasn't there?

I didn't notice.

You sure enough noticed when the cops arrested that red.

Was that what he was? With them sheriff's men putting out the furniture soon as we got it in, I wasn't payin' much attention.

Who won anyhow?

Guess the sheriff did. He got it out more times than we got it in. Whe-e-ee! all the stink that was raised! My old woman was real embarrassed . . . though you shoulda seen her use the broom on that sheriff's man. Anyhow, we got took in by some folks we never known before. And now they're starting a march to City Hall to raise hell.

Who's they? Them commoonists?

There you go! I told you I don't know no communists. Why, old Charley . . .

You ain't kiddin' me. Why, you even talk like a red now yourself.

S-o-o? Maybe they got a point. You know what that red said, that started it all . . .

The most fully employed persons I met during the depression were the communists. They worked 10 or 12 hours a day— maybe 16, if you counted yakking time. Most got no pay. A few full-timers had theoretical salaries, more theory than salary. The money was contingent—if some came in, you might get some. Most worked for love, or spite, if you prefer.

Work they did. They were in on every protest I saw or heard of. If they didn't start things themselves, they were Johnnies-on-the-spot. The anti-eviction fights were their babies, or adopted babies. They brought demanding crowds to the relief offices. They organized block committees, mass meetings, demonstrations. The communist-led Unemployed Councils later took over this work. Cleveland played full part in all national actions, each Hunger March on Washington, the "Bonus March."

Marching columns of unemployed became a familiar sight. Public Square saw demonstrations running into tens of thousands. The communists brought misery out of hiding in the workers' neighborhoods. They paraded it with angry demands through the main streets to the Public Square, and on to City Hall. They raised particular hell.

What the jobless might have done without the communists, who shall say? They wouldn't have starved silently. Their actions might have been more individualistic, less purposeful until, through trial and error, they developed leaders and organization much like the communists provided from the start—in their plight, the only kind that made sense.

The communists made immediate demands. More relief, in cash and jobs. Public works at union wages. Hot lunches for school children. An end to evictions. They exposed and fought racist discriminations against black Americans—worst sufferers from the depression. They demanded jobless and social security. They fought in the way most open to the dispossessed—by raising hell to force concessions from the rulers.

In doing this, the communists didn't fail to emphasize that capitalism was proving a lousy system, and should be replaced. It might surprise their grandchildren to know how many Americans agreed during the Great Depression. The communists also pointed out that in the Soviet Union there was no unemployment, no boom-to-bust cycle. In Pullman smokerooms, on long train trips, I found even salesmen getting this message.

If the communists were as nasty, cantankerous, conspiratorial, and subversive as charged, that scared the ruling class of people all the more and forced more concessions. Somehow the communists didn't scare the unemployed. In hundreds of jobless meetings, I heard no objections to the points the communists made, and much applause for them. Sometimes I'd hear a communist speaker say something so bitter and extreme I'd feel embarrassed. Then I'd look around at the unemployed audience—shabby clothes, expressions worried and sour. Faces would start to glow, heads to nod, hands to clap. They liked that stuff best of all.

He strode to the center of the milling intersection . . . tall, bare-headed, with unkempt hair. His grease-stained topcoat, unbuttoned, flapped in the icy wind. Unshaven bristles darkened his face. His thin body didn't fill out his suit. He took command, and order emerged. He signaled the crowd to clear the street. Men with red armbands helped carry out the order. Then, imperiously, he waved to the traffic to proceed. His long arms motioned furiously to speed its movement. With clear semaphore signals, he controlled its turns. He had no whistle. His upthrust arm was enough to stop the traffic, his gestures to move it on. The man looked wild, but his eyes were calm, his moves were sure.

This street-scene is etched in my memory. It was in the heart of working-class Cleveland, during a communist-led demonstration. Police had attacked an earlier demonstration. In the street battle, several unemployed had been injured, and one had since died. In the same neighborhood, the Unemployed Councils had called a mass protest, a solemn occasion that brought out thousands. The authorities, under criticism and on the defensive, withdrew every cop from the area, many blocks wide. If police were near, they were hidden; not even a traffic cop in sight. In the bitter mood of the people, a police uniform would have been a provocation.

The crowds surged through the streets. I wondered if some incident mightn't turn them into an unruly mob. Then I noticed men with red armbands—stewards from the Unemployed Councils—moving quietly among the people, preventing congestion, directing circulation. Traffic was trying to get through. Streetcars, trucks, cars, were held up. Then, at an intersection where I could hardly move on foot, this man had stepped out to take charge.

Another time, I'm standing on the outskirts of a Public Square demonstration, listening to the speakers, absorbed in the mood of the crowd.

It was as unexpected as if a wall had moved and hit me broadside. I was thrown off balance. As I tried to recover, I was hit again. Globules of indignation coursed through my system. Before my mind could tell me what had happened, my fists were clenched, my dukes were up.

The broad rump of a big horse had batted me. It swung around, battering and scattering the people near me. Then the cop on the horse turned its head toward the platform and rode it right into the crowd. The people were peaceably assembled around the statue of free-speech, once-Mayor Tom Johnson, to petition the government for a redress of grievances, though "petition" was too humble a word for their mood. The mounted police moved in. The cop who hit me didn't use his club; he let his horse do the work. But I saw other cops with clubs coming down on the people.

It was routine. The press reported no injured demonstrators

in hospital. Ordered to disperse the crowd, the police had done their job efficiently. It was routine all over the country during the depression. At first it was less routine if heads were bashed, women and children trampled, many reds and jobless arrested. Then that got to be routine too.

A young French student joined me after one of the demonstrations. I asked what he thought of them. "Not bad," he said. "The masses are on the move. But why no bombs?"

"Because the communists are on the job to guard against such stuff."

"Why should they?" he asked.

I explained that provocateurs had often planted bombs to furnish pretext for the most vicious crackdowns. The party had also to combat an American tendency, in the pioneer tradition, to turn to individual violence. "What point would there be to the bomb anyhow?" I concluded.

He shrugged. "To scare the bourgeoisie."

The communists I knew, in Britain and the United States, contrasted strikingly with the early scare-image of bearded bolshy with knife in teeth and bomb in hand. They were socially responsible to an unusually high degree. Some individualistic American recruits might at first tend to "go off half-cocked." The communist influence was toward organized action, more rational than emotional. In American left-right union fights, there were irresponsibles on both sides; and the fights were all-out to an extent I found un-British. (British kids were told to "play the game"; American kids, to "go out to win.") Each side accused the other of wrecking the union. But the dyed-in-the-wool communists I knew—as distinct from opportunists traipsing in and out of the left—were solid unionists, sincerely anxious to strengthen the union.

I asked one American-born, lifelong red why he was a communist—his personal angle, not a stock answer. "I've thought about it," he replied. "I was always a very orderly person. When I was a kid, a mess really upset me. I guess I got upset about the disorder of capitalism, its waste, its poverty, its unnecessary suffering, its wars, its depressions. I couldn't see how things could be set in order without socialism. Some revolutionary disorder might be inevitable in bringing it about, I knew. Even in that, I've always looked for the socially constructive——"

I've written as if only the communists were doing anything for the unemployed at the start of the Great Depression. How about government, AFL, churches, liberals, socialists? Weren't they doing anything? From where I saw things in Cleveland up to 1933, all I can say is: Not that I noticed.

President Hoover, it seemed to me among many, was just waiting for the storm to blow over. He refused federal funds for the jobless. The Reconstruction Finance Corporation doled out a couple of billions to banks and corporations, supposed somehow to trickle down to the unemployed. I couldn't understand how. I wasn't good at economics. Neither was the government, as it turned out.

The churches increased their charitable activities. But, apart from a few black ministers, I saw no church leaders or liberal respectables leading eviction fights and hunger marches, exposing their heads to be bashed and themselves to arrest. Some gave verbal support to watered-down versions of the communist demands. They didn't get loud and troublesome in demanding an end to misery in a country glutted with overproduction.

Unemployment insurance was already the rule in other developed countries. In the United States, there was no government unemployment insurance, nor social security. With one out of four workers thrown off the job, and mostly penniless, did Republicans, Democrats, and other respectables start an uproar for a comprehensive system of unemployment insurance?

No.

The socialists were on record for unemployment insurance. Their voice was weak and less heard than that of the communists. They tried to steer clear of movements in which communists took a leading part.

The AFL didn't lead the march for unemployment insurance. It opposed it as a "dole," as "subsidizing idleness." President Hoover himself congratulated the AFL leaders for this, at their 1930 convention.

The communists put unemployment insurance in the forefront of jobless demands—in hunger marches, picketings, demonstrations. They didn't leave it at testimony on the rabble roster of some Congressional hearing. They got mean and nasty. They harangued and they hollered. They were extreme and unreasonable. They got results, even from the AFL. After more than two years of organized left-wing agitation for unemployment insurance, reaching into thousands of AFL locals, the AFL executive council in its belated wisdom came around to endorsing the idea in July 1932.

The Mr. Communist I best recall in Cleveland was Israel Amter. He was a tall, gaunt man, or seemed tall because he was gaunt. His features were Lincolnesque, to those who saw purpose pushing up from the plain people. To those who didn't, they were the features of a "goddam kike communist." Amter was District Organizer of the Workers (Communist) party—renamed Communist party in 1930. He presided over creaky-floored offices up the creaky stairs of a creaky old building in the downtown area. Most of the time he was out and about.

Sometimes I saw Amter passing out leaflets or lugging around literature. "Pitches in on what he asks others to do," I once commented to a more bureaucratic comrade. The other sniffed—he may have had a cold—and said it didn't bespeak executive efficiency. Be that as it may, Amter stimulated folks to efforts almost as great as his own.

I've called Amter "Mr. Communist," not that anyone else did, but because he suggests in a way the man who came to be known as "Mr. Republican." Senator Robert A. Taft was held a man of principle—conservative principle. Amter, to me, was more ruggedly principled. He had been a musician, a composer. He was also creative in communist composition. He inspired confidence; he was a leader. His wife, Sadie Van Veen, added the human touch. She was down-to-earth—a rousing, cheerful, organizing sort. Amter moved on to New York, and to jail for leading the unemployed.

Among district organizers who followed, I think of Herbert Benjamin—later a national organizer of the Unemployed Councils. Benjamin was small, pale, rather frail, but with staying power. He had wit and sophistication. He was reasonable and readily grasped situations—a good organizer. Johnny Williamson was a DO who left a deep mark, both personally and organizationally. I must have left Cleveland around the time he came, since I think of him chiefly in other and later connections.

The communists of DO or comparable level whom I knew during depression and CIO years tended to become typed. As was said in my religious childhood, they had "left all" for the movement. They couldn't count on the normal satisfactions of lives they'd left, rising income, family security, respectable standing. Outlaws of the system, they faced its constant hostility. In this sense the party full-timers became declassed. Yet in commitment to a class, they were more classed than most—more than the worker trying to save and buy his, or his children's, way out of the working class—more than union leaders with middle-class income and standards.

The communists tried to concentrate on the working class, to relate the needs of each workers' group to the needs of the class. If they didn't always succeed, if at times their theory or practice was faulty, if often they were a corporal's guard trying to act like an army, there were also times, as in the unemployed agitation of the Great Depression and in the organization of CIO, when they achieved remarkable results.

Along with the DO, in a center like Cleveland, there were other full-timers or much-timers—section organizers from key areas—functionaries of party-inspired "mass" organizations. There were also volunteers in orbit, some apprentices for more full-time work. A mixed group, the volunteers—and unusual, since most people won't take the risks they took for a cause.

There was always the fabled Jimmy Higgins, the saint of the movement, seeming rather literal and rigid to many, as most saints do, and devoted to something more than himself. He was no simpleton. He had thought, and often read, a lot. He had observed life closely and pulled much wool from his eyes. He had drawn conclusions and stuck to them.

Simpletons there were around the movement. Usually with emotional problems, they misunderstood what they heard and didn't think for themselves. They wanted the party to wipe their noses like Mom did, to boss them like an all-wise Pop. They expected others to be more selfless than they were. They went gaga over guff. These were the bound-to-be-disillusioned, whose disillusions swamped the Cold War market.

There was also the planted spy and informer—the stool pigeon—less effective then than in the Cold War because of the mass proportions of the discontent. Some of us thought we could smell him. The stool pigeon knew his job stank to most people. At first he might excuse it by some twisted personal standards, by the capitalist maxim that any money is good money, by swallowing some of the bunk about the communist menace. But once intimately involved in union or communist activity, the stool pigeon not only defied the decency-standards of others, he must also have suffered some collapse of his own. He had to realize that, in a peculiarly personal way, he was betraying decent people, usually poor and persecuted, who sincerely believed in what they were doing. The resulting rot in his moral fiber caused the "smell" some thought we could detect.

A communist headquarters showed little of a movement whose roots were elsewhere. Not likely to be seen at Cleveland's creaky old party office were communist leaders often more influential than the party full-timers—activists in local unions, black and foreign-born organizations, Unemployed Councils, and other workers' groups. In the more demonstrative fields and left groups, some might be open communists. Elsewhere, particularly in AFL unions and unorganized plants, they were likely to be under cover, though liberally tagged as reds for their opinions and activities. The party membership came largely from these activists, plus a sprinkling of professional, intellectual, small-business elements.

These were the communist communists—convinced and courageous enough to belong to the party or work closely with it. A handful—running to hundreds, even thousands at some times and places, but still a handful compared to the million-masses and their mass movements. Yet this handful had a widely radiating influence during the depression. Many around them echoed their ideas and their slogans. Then, as since, rightists called all active rebels "communists." They had this much excuse, that millions were talking much as the communists talked and doing as they urged without even knowing what communism was.

The rebellious included embattled farmers fighting foreclosures with "penny sales" and sometimes with arms; embattled and near-starving sharecroppers; up to 17 million unemployed—also employed workers who faced wage cut after wage cut and shivered to see the jobless throngs at factory gates. Also veterans marching for their "bonus"; small-business people going bankrupt by tens of thousands; squeezed professionals, salesmen, churchmen; even some children of the rich who rebelled against privilege and plenty in the midst of hunger and want.

Among employed workers, communist activities were less conspicuous than among the unemployed. The AFL was down to a miserable minimum of membership, the more skilled and job-fortunate as a rule. Its unions mostly washed their hands of unemployed members on the grounds that, once jobless and unable to pay dues, they ceased to be members. Conservative unions did little to resist wage cuts, opposing strikes as ill-advised with so many unemployed around. Rail brotherhood leaders claimed credit for initiating, negotiating, and enforcing a "voluntary" 10% wage cut.

The left had the field of union militancy to itself. It was in poor shape to occupy it. Many unions had thoroughly purged their "communists." Coolidge Prosperity had sedated militant moods in all but the "sick" industries. The remaining lefts in rightwing unions—their ranks depleted, their once vigorous TUEL caucuses disorganized, themselves cautiously dodging expulsion—couldn't counter the policies of retreat and surrender.

One comeback to the expulsions and AFL shrinkage was the Trade Union Unity League. Largely communist-led, it combined efforts to rally left forces in the old unions with new industrial unions in unorganized sectors. It had short-lived unions in coal mining, steel and metal, needle trades, agriculture, food, shoe, furniture, marine, textile, auto, lumber. TUUL unions led most of the few strikes and organizing drives of 1930-33. I recall best the National Miners Union strike in Harlan County, Kentucky, because of aid-seeking miners who stayed in my Cleveland apartment.

TUUL's public efforts in Cleveland didn't impress me. Its headquarters was in a flatiron building, whose big windows at the narrow end kept away workers risking their jobs by any interest in union. It was curiously run by a man who inspired much mistrust and who, in later years, became a government witness against the communists. In other cities, however, I heard of TUUL building some substantial union nuclei . . . merged by 1935 into the AFL and independent unions forming the base of CIO's new industrial unions.

More significant, in Cleveland, were hints I heard of union stirrings in unorganized steel, auto, electrical, and other big plants. This stuff was hush-hush—the most underground of communist activities. Company stool pigeons were everywhere listening for union talk, and trying to worm into any potential union nucleus. Union hopefuls had to be as careful as communist shop groups which were sometimes the only union hopefuls there were.

In nearby Akron, some rubber workers were plotting for union organization, with left assistance. One device was to form little social clubs with fancy and oft-changing names like "Excelsior" or "Ameliorative Club."

The AFL had some skilled members among the maintenance crafts. For the production workers it had federal local unions which it directly chartered and controlled. All might join, pending craft claims to parcel them out. AFL officials kept them under thumb and tried to avoid "trouble."

Where company unions existed, they could offer scope for union agitation by putting the bosses on the spot with criticisms and demands.

In these 1929-32 years, the communists worked through any and every kind of union organization they could find or start in the unorganized industries. They were often the only moving force for unionism. Prospects were too grim, pickings too slim, to attract piecard artists.

Many noncommunist workers wanted a union, and some raised occasional hell. These "troublemakers" found little interest, much suspicion, and no help if they approached some porky AFL official in his downtown office. On the other hand, if there were communists in his plant, the troublemaker would find sympathy, help, guidance. He might be glad to associate with a group, however small, that was at least trying to do something.

In early depression years, black power won little recognition. The black vote, nonexistent in the south, tempted few northern politicians. The white press ignored or maligned black people—too poor, it held, to attract advertisers. No television revealed to whites that blacks too felt pain, want, desire, anger. No mass civil rights movement pricked the conscience of white churchmen and students. The black people just weren't raising enough hell to scare the ruling whites.

In the labor movement many craft unions, arrogantly racist, excluded black workers. The more industrial of AFL unions enrolled black members but didn't assure them equal rights. The more progressive leaders held that blacks should have equal job and union rights; that economic gains would gradually bring more political rights; but that talk of social equality was provocative, upsetting to deep-seated southern prejudices.

Liberals echoed the complacent clichés of white imperialism —that force or laws can't uproot prejudice; that backward peoples must be *gradually* prepared for equality; that it's all a slow educative process.

Meanwhile black workers—last to be hired, first to be laid off, with least savings from lowest wages, and discriminated against in relief as everywhere else—were the first and worst sufferers from the depression.

They were also among the first to get the message when communists spread among the jobless urging them to demonstrate, march, picket, sit down, sit in, fight back. Black unemployed joined with white in all communist-led actions I saw. "Black and White, Unite and Fight!" was the slogan. "Jim Crow Must Go!" was given pointed applications.

Besides black protests, in which whites usually joined, against all forms of discrimination, I recall restaurant sit-ins like those of the late Fifties. Young people organized the restaurant actions, on the initiative of the Young Communist League. Black and white, arm in arm, they'd walk into some coffeeshop. All would order the same thing—usually coffee and doughnuts. If whites were served and blacks were not, the whites wouldn't eat or pay till the blacks were served. It could become an endurance contest, until some scuffle might give the police an excuse to move in. Some restaurants yielded and began serving blacks. The young reds, revisiting to check up, could get pretty full of coffee.

I don't recall the communists pulling their punches on any aspect of black rights. Unlike earlier socialists and Wobblies, they didn't soft-pedal "the Negro question" as but part of the whole labor struggle. They fought for black social, civil, political, as well as job rights. They wrestled with "the Negro question" as a "national question."

Many white liberals and radicals attacked and ridiculed the communists when they called for self-determination in the Black Belt. Black people found the idea less outlandish. They didn't have to be indoctrinated with Marxism-Leninism to know they were exploited not only as workers but also as blacks; that they were not only oppressed workers but also an oppressed people. Looking around the world, they could compare their subjection with that of any colonial people under the thumb of imperialism. To follow a Marcus Garvey back to Africa might not appeal to many black people born and raised in the United States. But what was wrong with national liberation here, with running things at least where they were a majority?

Three little girls stood outside a garage on our Cleveland street. They wore the red scarves of Young Pioneers. The youngest was in tears. The older were scolding her. As I came by, they all appealed to me.

"She did say it," said an older one. "She's no Pioneer."

"I did not," sobbed the youngest.

The eldest hushed them. "We'll let Comrade De Caux decide."

"All right," said I, "let's hear what's up."

"We were walking down this street on the way to the rally,"

the eldest began importantly. "Connie here pointed into the garage and said, 'Look at the dirty——' "

"I didn't use the bad word," Connie burst in. "I didn't, I didn't, I didn't. I never do. I said Nee-gro."

"That right?" I asked. The others nodded. But the prosecutor went on:

"Connie knows enough not to say the bad word. But she did say he was a dirty Negro. That was awful. It would have hurt his feelings if he'd heard it."

"But he didn't," Connie protested. "And I didn't *mean* anything."

Just then a black mechanic crawled out from under a car in the back of the garage. His overalls were smeared with oil and grease. He wiped his hands on a rag and grinned as he waved to the children.

Connie took my hand. "He *is* dirty, isn't he?" she appealed plaintively. "Now isn't he?"

Everyone in or near the movement, from Connie up and down and all around, got involved in the Communist party's campaign against "white chauvinism." It was as intense, at times as extreme, as any party campaign.

White members went around in a tizzy. They had to check every figure of speech they used; the American language, especially slang, abounds in racist allusions, often hidden by long usage. They had to reexamine all the conventional attitudes of white life. Many became acutely self-conscious with black people. The bashful became tonguetied, semiparalyzed. The extroverted flushed and blushed with extreme politeness and camaraderie. The blacks were embarrassed too. The more kindly gave the white comrades credit for trying to bridge an almost unbridgeable gap. The rest laughed to cover their winces, noted all slips, and hated white people as whites all the more.

The "bad word" itself told a story. The communists wouldn't even let us write it in a quote from some racist; we had to put "N——," or use asterisks or some circumlocution. I'd known the word from babyhood as part of the vernacular of British imperialism. The British used it for the dark-skinned worldwide whom they set out to conquer, rule, exploit, and convert to Christianity. The Americans used the word with extra venom and derogation, because the days and locale of slavery were closer to them and they felt guilt and fear more intimately.

In the Sixties, I tried to check use of the word by many little white kids I knew in my California neighborhood. Whether from northern or southern states, all used it as part of their basic vocabulary. When I objected and explained why, they tried to avoid it, though usually protesting it was the word their parents used. Only in deference to their tender age, could one say the kids used the word innocently. They used it as an insulting word, a disparaging word, or a "humorous" word. My shopmates in the Sixties used the word as commonly, and were surprised to hear objection.

Yet four decades earlier, not a tot joined the communist Young Pioneers without learning the word was bad, and why. Jobless and unionizing workers reached by the communists—as later those in areas of left influence in CIO—learned the word was racist and tried to avoid it.

The communist movement, as I saw it in Cleveland until I moved late in 1933, was flanked by many organizations of special appeal.

The left-led Workers Ex-Servicemen's League interested me. I'd seen British veterans of World War I, of whom I was one, in the forefront of labor and radical activity, ardent red-flag wavers. It had seemed only natural; that war made me a red. Yet in the United States, wealthy rightist reaction corraled most organized veterans into the opposite camp—that of war-breeding jingoism and anti-radicalism.

After World War II, I asked a CIO organizer, a wounded veteran who had served in the thick of combat, how veterans got suckered like this. "Most veterans want another war," he said bluntly. "That's because most were never in combat. They lived well, were treated well. They felt important. Only a small number took all the hell of the last war."

In the early depression years, however, the WESL and the communists had some influence among veterans. Unemployed vets, sporting service caps, medals, war mementos, were prominent in jobless demonstrations. The ragged hungry veteran, displaying some war emblem, was a common sight on breadlines or selling apples on the street.

The WESL pushed demands for relief, including speedy payment of adjusted service pay. It was one of the movers in the 1932 "Bonus March," which brought tens of thousands of veterans to Washington. They camped in the Anacostia flats, until President Hoover drove them out, with General Douglas MacArthur and Dwight Eisenhower enforcing the order. Bayonets and tear gas were turned against the veterans, two of whom were killed and many wounded. Roosevelt's New Deal later granted their "bonus."

Another important group was a Small Home Owners organization, working with the Unemployed Councils in the fight against evictions. It grew to some 20,000 members in Cleveland.

The Young Pioneers were a small but colorful element at communist rallies. The Young Communist League appealed to the youth who wanted action. There was also the International Labor Defense and women's, fraternal, sports, and other organizations of many kinds.

The foreign-language organizations included many mass-production workers, more representative of them than was the craftist AFL. Under left-leaning leadership often, they had their own halls, clubs, welfare and social activities, their own press—including in Cleveland a daily communist paper in Hungarian, *Uj Elore*. At communist affairs, the massive choirs, the dramatic and cultural groups of the foreign-born organizations furnished most of the entertainment.

The movement also reached out to the white-collared and professional. It attracted social workers close to the depression-desperate poor; teachers who taught their children; newspapermen who reported the workers' discontent; lawyers who defended arrested demonstrators; doctors who tended their bashed heads; little business people with customers too poor to pay; socially sensitive artists, writers, intellectuals.

Helping to shake confidence in the capitalist system were the spreading bank failures. My savings were in the Standard Trust Bank, the reorganized BLE bank, and the first local bank to crash. I next chose the Cleveland Trust, a byword for stability. I got my money into it just before its massive doors clanged

shut. Three different about-to-crash banks I tried—before concluding any old sock was safer than a bank.

Most of those drawn to the movement by the Great Depression contracted radicalism like a child its first measles or
mumps. Turned 30 by then, I'd already had 'em. Calluses of
generalization covered the sensitivities of my youth, protecting
me from the more generous, romantic, emotional appeals. I was
cautious, practical, inclined to watch my step.

But I did feel the movement was at last on the move. For
ten years I'd wanted most to identify with the working class.
The communists' line and their fighting spirit had much appeal.
I'd still had to be sure that, in the United States, they weren't
talking to themselves while the working class marched by un-
heeding. Judging from British experience, I had assumed the
American workers would move in some pink-socialistic direction
like the British Labor party, leaving the communists far outfield
on the left. That wasn't happening. The dwindling socialists,
the lukewarm liberals, the middle-of-the-roaders were as high and
dry as Hoover from the workers' discontent. The communists
were really zipping into things.

I saw no bandwagon rush to the communist movement.
The joiners weren't so many as to be conspicuous. I certainly
couldn't see socialism just around the corner. What I saw ahead
was a chopping block to which I preferred not to volunteer my
head. I wanted to be red but not dead. I went to the national
office in New York, to see if I could serve and still keep my head
from the chopper. Clarence Hathaway, with whom I met, had a
soothing voice and manner. A stringy Swede from Minnesota, he
had a Foster-like working-class and union background. I felt
more confidence in him than in a Lovestone. He indicated that
a member-at-large need not suffer too much tanning from over-
exposure.

The movement breathed new life into both Caroline and
myself, as many others. The neuroses of which so many moderns
complain had small chance to develop when every spare moment
was in demand for activity outside of personal concerns, on behalf
of people who urgently needed help, in a social cause inspiring

hope and enthusiasm. If a sleepless moment gave a neurosis a chance to nag, there was always some ponderous theoretical document to demand prior attention, and to induce slumber.

Who could become introspective while being talked deaf and having to yak back in self-defense? Who could indulge in melancholia with cheerful bustlers all around, with young people popping in at all odd times to tell of their battles today and their dreams for tomorrow?

Yes, but—it has since been asked—didn't we know we were stooging for Stalin and the Soviets? I for one did not—I thought we were doing what we were doing, and a pretty good job at that. If the Soviets and Stalin got more bang than did Hoover out of this American working-class activity, more power to them.

True, ideas generated by the Russian revolution were spilling over into other countries as French and American revolutionary ideas had once done. They packed a wallop for and against American radicals. Caroline and I decided to go see for ourselves the source of all this inspiration for our side—and of many nasty cracks by the other side.

In London, I interview Harry Pollitt, top red, for the American *Daily Worker*. Communist headquarters is on King Street, over a bookshop. Anyone can walk in and on upstairs. No harness bulls, or comrade guards. Free and easy, good old England of the never-shall-be-slaves. But—I still glance around as I go in. And as I go out.

My collar feels tight as I walk away, and I look over my shoulder. Why? I just went into a bookshop. This is England where one can join a union without getting fired, even join the Communist party and be open about it. Must be a drafty little gust made my neck twitch.

Heading for Paris, we detrain at Dover to catch the Channel boat for Calais. The usual formalities—passports, baggage inspection, currency.

"This way please, sir."

We're standing in line. "We're not through here yet," I protest. The man's not in uniform. What business is it of his? Another man is saying to Caroline: "You too, if you please." Both men are inconspicuous—medium height, medium build, medium age, medium voices, medium manners.

"What's up?" I ask. "We haven't cleared our bags and papers."

"We've got your papers and your luggage."

They steer us into a small room with no sign on the door—bare but for a table and some wooden chairs. Our bags are there, opened up. One man starts frisking me—for personal papers he takes from my pockets and spreads on the table. A matron searches Caroline's person and purse.

The dicks take all the papers from my briefcase too. By trade and from habit, I have quite a few. They go through them one by one, lingering over personal letters, mostly of the bon-voyage kind. One letter stops them. It's from a United States friend—not a red—introducing us to a girl friend in Berlin, who's doing clerical work for—hah!—International Press Correspondence, the communist documentary periodical usually called *Inprecorr*. This letter both men read. They make notes too.

"Why are you going to see this person?" asks one.

"Just a possible contact. We may not even look her up."

They aren't interested in my answers. Cynics. But now they're getting hot. In my wallet they find a torn folded yellowing scrap of paper. On it are written two long numbers, the first preceded by "NYL"; the second by "Prud." The men gaze at the numbers. Both copy them down. They turn to me. "What are these numbers? What do they mean?"

I happen to have two life insurance policies. I wrote their numbers on a scratch pad, for handy reference, I laugh as I explain. The men are not amused. They stare at me stonily, skeptically. When at last they are through with my papers, each one, alternately, questions:

"What have you been doing in England?"

"Why did you come?"

"Who have you seen?"

"What meetings have you addressed?"

"What meetings have you attended?"

"With whom have you met?"

"Have you engaged in any propaganda?"

"Or any political activity?"

The men pay little attention to my answers. I don't drop names or details. They aren't friendly, nor very hostile, just medium. Then they escort us to the Channel boat. One carries Caroline's bag. The other helps with mine. They ease our way quickly through all barriers. I start to thank them—then realize they're giving us the bum's rush.

In Berlin—depressed in 1932 as when I lived there in 1925-26—a young comrade of the Rote Front Kaempfer Bund takes us in charge. He has one of the motorcycles on which young Red Front Fighters career around the city, with satisfaction to themselves and annoyance to the Nazis. Caroline and I manage to squeeze into its sidecar.

It's a weekend. The River Spree is gay with the white canvases of little yachts, yawls, skiffs, sailboats of all kinds. Red flags line the docks and river banks. Comrade Hans tosses it off lightly. "It's just a regatta we're having."

"Who's we?"

"The boating section of our Red Sports organization, natürlich."

We try to imagine a Red Regatta on the Hudson or the Thames.

A national election is due. Party emblems and flags festoon the streets. Hans rides us all over Berlin, proudly pointing to the Communist party (KPD) decorations, drapes, emblems. Decoratively, the KPD predominates. In the elections, it would draw the largest vote of any party in Berlin.

In middle- and upper-class Charlottenburg, the KPD lags in drapery and window signs. The bourgeoisie evidently prefer bourgeois parties—this year the Nazis most. Along with the traditional conservative parties, the Nazis also make a splurge in the downtown business sections.

In working-class neighborhoods, the KPD is far ahead. Each party has an election ballot number which it advertises widely. The KPD number hangs out of most tenement windows, with the number of the Social Democratic party (SPD) in lesser evidence. Along the little-business streets of working-class sections, however, the SPD predominates.

Hans has to hunt to show us Nazi signs in working-class areas. Finally he locates a few in one of the worst slums. To get this much display, he claims, the Nazis have to pay 10 marks apiece to lumpen-proletarians who have lost all self-respect. The Nazis are on the streets, however.

When he sees their brown uniforms, Hans gives a whoop. Right toward each group he rides. Shooting by as close as he can, he shakes his fist, giving the communist crooked-arm salute. "Die Nazis haben Angst," he shouts. "Sie haben Angst . . . haben Angst . . . Nazis haben Angst von den Kommunisten!"

It makes Caroline and me nervous. But Hans is having a good time, and later we can console ourselves we did nothing to dampen defiance of the Nazis. His use of "Angst" (fear) puzzles us at first, directed at the fear-casting Nazis. Then we note the Nazis do look rather scared. They stick close together, in bands of a score or so. Pastyfaced and youthful, they look high-school age. They don't venture into working-class residential areas, but hang around business streets on their outskirts.

From Stettin we take a Soviet ship to Leningrad. Not much of a tub, but for us first sign of liberation from capitalism. The red flag on her stern. Red Corner amidships. Radical-minded passengers. Easily friendly crew. Russian-speaking Caroline is gabbing away at once. I see her arm around a woman crew-member—another first, seawomen, and not just in the stewards department.

After depression-embittered class struggle in the United States, after the English thought-police, after the skulking Nazi threat in Berlin, we relax with relief on the Soviet ship. Comrades and friends all around. Compared with American ships I've worked on, I find more on-the-job democracy. I like the ship's Red Corner—notices, slogans, reading matter, the inevitable chess board. An officer and seaman chatting together. Caroline listens, and joins in.

Caroline has relatives living in Moscow. The mother's like

most Jewish working-class mothers I've known in the United States—in sentiment, housekeeping, gumption. Her daughter, our age, works in a factory, is active in the party. Self-assured, well-informed, the organizing type. Two sons One away with the Red Army in Siberia. The other, with OGPU!

I stiffen—can't quite live down my American feelings about dicks, from my years on the road. I keep a close eye on this young man. He's not plainclothes, wears some kind of OGPU uniform, acts a bit stiff and self-conscious in it, and blushes when kidded. Once he tries to take advantage of his uniform, to get us to the head of a line at a railroad station. A country-woman gives him a dressing down; others in line glare or join in. Flushing scarlet, he meekly withdraws to the end of the line.

Caroline is delighted. She remembers Czarist days in Russia, when peasants and workers had to kowtow to uniforms, especially those of the police. She loves the way pedestrians argue with traffic cops, the way people handle pushy passengers in streetcars, talk to them about how to behave on social, if not socialist, grounds. Caroline gloats over the "nash" (our) that crops up in casual remarks about the people's property, the people's affairs. Not "they," "them," "their," as under capitalism, but "we," "us," "our."

We like the factory visits and have leeway in choosing them. The railroad union hosts me fraternally, once it learns I work for the BLE. Caroline can manage without an interpreter. We sit in on workers' shop meetings. Nothing like this in American plants where I worked—not until CIO came along. Discussions are about "our" factory, "our" products, "our" affairs. The CIO sit-downers were never to get as far as "our," though Italian workers did, briefly, when they sat down in 1920. As some management or union official takes us through the shops, he gets comments or complaints when we stop to talk with the workers. If he doesn't agree, the beefer—particularly if a woman—may appeal to Caroline: "Now is this the way we should be running things in our factory?"

The Soviet Railway Workers union took us to Kharkov and helped us compare it with American rail unions. One industrial union, instead of many craft unions as in the United States.

What about the charge it wasn't a real union, just an arm of the government? "Arm" was not the word. The union was part of the body and mind, the bones and sinews, of what the Soviets held to be a workers' government, out to boost production, to build socialism.

Not independent, said American critics. Independence of company control is vital to bonafide trade unionism. There were no private employers in the USSR. Its unions weren't independent of a socialist system of which they were a basic part. How independent were American unions?

The rail brotherhoods were not company unions. They could, and did at times, act against the companies. But they depended on them in many ways. The companies owned the railroads, controlled the workers' jobs, took the profits, made all major decisions. They ruled the roost. Their influence, at closeup, seemed all-pervasive.

Independent of government? American rail unions operated under special laws made and enforced by government. Only theoretically were they free to strike—their strike votes a required preliminary to going through the long delaying procedures of the Railway Labor act. At the end of that road, government would act against any big rail strike as against a near-revolution, and Congress get ready to pass another law. Other unions were subject to ever more comprehensive and binding laws, and to direct government intervention in large-scale labor disputes.

Union membership was not compulsory in the USSR. The BLE in the United States bragged of close to full membership without a closed or union shop. Benefits and social pressure did the trick; the non-member was a despised "no-bill," and BLE pensions depended on keeping up dues. In the USSR, the unions ran social security, housing, clubhouses, vacation resorts. It paid to belong.

In my plant experience, on-the-job protection—worth the price of admission to any good union—made the big difference between union and nonunion conditions. With all the labor laws and union contracts, you needed the shop steward, chapel chairman, shop committee, union rep, a live local, to enforce them. In the USSR, there were also on-the-job beefs for the unions to handle. The grievance procedure gave final say to the union.

In the planned economy of the USSR, the relation of wages and hours to prices and production were subject to overall determination by government and unions . . . with no capitalists to cut in on most of the pie. In the United States wage-hour issues also tended to be determined at top level, through pattern-setting deals involving companies, unions, and government. The man in the shop could say what he wanted, not what he would get. But once the pattern was set, the deal went back to the shops—with plenty left for local interpretation and application. In both countries.

All comparisons broke down, however, before the basic differences between a capitalist and a socialist economy. Under capitalism, the unions had to fight the owners of industry for real concessions. Under socialism, the workers were part of the common ownership, with a major stake in producing for their own and the common benefit.

After our visit to the Soviet Union, I returned to my job with the BLE in Cleveland. I resumed my side activities in the lively leftwing movement of a depression-ridden industrial city. The activities were fine. The job was okay, as jobs go, but seven years of it made a rut. So when Carl Haessler offered me the Washington Bureau of Federated Press, I gladly accepted.

I wasn't one of the bliss-was-it-in-that-dawn boys who flocked to Washington to remake the world. Looking at the New Deal, I had styes rather than stars in my eyes. In 1932 I'd voted for William Z. Foster, not Franklin D. Roosevelt, for President; for James Ford, a black man, for Vice President, not John Nance Garner, FDR's sop to the south. I came as one might leave the battlefront for some diplomatic powwow. The battle for America, I felt, was being fought by the unemployed on the streets, the stirring black people, veterans on the march, workers risking their jobs for union—and by the reds trying to give purpose to the struggle.

Roosevelt won fame for bringing a New Deal of social welfare to the common people, as did Lincoln for abolishing slavery. Neither started with such prime purpose. FDR's 1932 campaign talk of a "new deal" was vaguely rhetorical. He was elected to do something about the depression, to get rid of Do-Nothing Hoover.

Roosevelt did something—to the delight of all, including big business, groaning as if its end were near. He set government to rescuing the capitalist economy. He did something about the banks, stock market, farm "overproduction," sinking prices, subsidies to business. He remembered the forgotten man to the extent of checking evictions and mortgage foreclosures, starting some public works, getting some relief to the jobless.

The National Industrial Recovery Act crowned the New Deal's first phase. It aimed at "fair competition" through industrial price and labor codes, granting labor consultative representation in NRA code-making machinery which business effectively controlled. It included a Section 7(a) conceding that workers had the "right to organize and bargain collectively through representatives of their own choosing . . . free from the interference, restraint, or coercion of employers." The NIRA was not a socialistic but a capitalistic program, with overtones suggestive of the "corporative state." Big business, labor leaders, nearly everyone except the reds, hailed it at first with hysterical unanimity.

Meanwhile the mass upsurge was growing in the shops, on the streets, in jimcrow ghettos, on the farm, even in studios and studios. John L. Lewis had pulled a fast one. In 1933, taking advantage of the hope and confusion around NIRA's Section 7(a), he put everything into a coal organizing campaign, with the slogan—summons almost—"The President wants you to join the union." The drive was a phenomenal success.

In other industries, millions of workers were going on thousands of strikes. A general strike tied up the whole San Francisco Bay area. There was a ferment of union organizing. The unemployed too were on the march. "Panacea" movements multiplied —Technocracy, Utopian, Townsend, End-Poverty-in-California (EPIC), "Ham-and-Eggs." Father Coughlin and Huey Long sought followers with fascistic answers to the discontent.

When I came to Washington in 1934, the New Deal honeymoon was waning. People squawked back at NRA's Blue Eagle.

Worker delegations shook fists, demanding delivery on labor rights and representation. Big business started to say nuts to the whole deal it once hailed. That was when the devil was sick . . . The devil got well, the devil a New Dealer was he. Corporations that operated at a loss in 1932 were again making profits by the end of 1933. Industrial production increased in 1934 over 1933. Prices rose.

Still Wall Street was disappointed. Government regulation became irksome as profits rose. The masses, unsatisfied with sops, were on the march demanding more. Radical and socialistic ideas were spreading. Strikes and unions grew among workers unappeased by the company unions that mushroomed under NRA. As 1934 wore on, a big part of big business declared war on FDR. For a brief honeymoon, Roosevelt had been hero to both Wall Street and the masses. Caught now in the conflict between the two, he moved over "a little to the left of center," and increased his Congressional support in the 1934 fall elections.

The Supreme Court didn't read the election results that way. Early in 1935, to Wall Street applause, it declared unconstitutional the NIRA, the Railroad Retirement act, the Frazier-Lemke act (to relieve mortgaged farms), the Agricultural Adjustment act. Roosevelt fought back, with his so-called court-packing, and some concessions to win him workers' support.

These included the Works Progress Administration (WPA), jobs for the jobless; Wagner act (National Labor Relations act), which labor pried from FDR to back up the right to organize; the Social Security act, bringing the United States belatedly into line with other advanced industrial countries.

For such social-welfare measures, working people most honored and remembered Roosevelt, affirming the mystique of his identification with the common man that won him repeated re-election. Essentially this welfare New Deal was wrested from government by popular rebellion against intolerable depression conditions. In the case of the Wagner act, it took the further CIO uprising to make of it more than a declaration of good intentions. Roosevelt had the political gumption to yield to some of the needs of the times and the political savvy to take the credit.

Coming from Cleveland to Washington was like leaving the modern world for a period masquerade. White-collar snobbery . . . old-fashioned traditionalism . . . meaningless bombast . . . southern atmosphere . . .

In a Cleveland summer, you hung up coat, took off tie, opened collar, rolled up sleeves for the day's work—might even leave coat and tie at home. In the sultry humid heat of Washington, before air-conditioning, there seemed to be a daylong coats-and-ties rule everywhere. It was a white-collar city, with little industrial working class. The social-climbing clerk set its tone.

I hated the southern stuff. The low-paid white clerk with barely paid black maid. The housewife, who scrubbed her own floors in the north, sipping a mint julep and wailing: "Oh, my deah, the girl (twice her age) came late, and I had to——" Every hard, menial, flunky job done by black people. The junior executive thinking like a plantation owner on the back porch of his Georgetown diggings. Luxuriating in "gracious southern living" while a "Mammy," with kids of her own on slum streets, coos over white brats she should be walloping.

Washington's black slums, so close to the Capitol, and stretching far and wide. The great home of George Washington across the river in old Virginny—what about his slaves? Even the White House reeks of the south. The dated southern architecture of older office buildings. The heat . . . shutters for every window . . . wheezy old ceiling fans . . . like slavery days, or British sahibs fanned by skinny Indian servants. That roomy, moldy, old-fashioned feel and smell.

Southern congressmen felt at home in Washington. That said it. Rep. Howard W. Smith (D., Va.), hater and blocker of everything good for the working people. Wing-collared and old-style in garb and manners with a sly, beady eye to serve the northern capitalist. Southern congressmen who rode the Roosevelt bandwagon, now slipping off. Hangovers from slave days, sponsored by the slaveowners' heirs and by northern sweatshop capital invested in the south. "Elected" on platforms of white supremacy, racism, redbaiting, by small power cliques. "Elected" by barring blacks from the polls with trickery, firings, KKK tar-and-feathers, clubs, whips, lynchings. "Elected" by keeping poor

whites too from the polls with poll taxes, and offering them jimcrow to eat when they're hungry.

The American Federation of Labor has its wing-collar-
wearer to match Rep. Smith—Vice President Matthew Woll.
Leading light of the National Civic Federation, designed to
mate labor leaders with big business, Woll could have modeled
for Daniel DeLeon's "labor lieutenant of capitalism." He misses
few tricks in its defense, opposing most welfare measures as "socialistic," including unemployment insurance at first. He's the
bantamweight champion redbaiter. Woll's AFL influence goes
far beyond his own small union. He was heir-apparent to Sam
Gompers, but got lost in the shuffle after Gompers died. John
L. Lewis helped him get lost, and neither has forgotten this.

AFL headquarters is on my beat. It has little news, but FP
is a labor news service and owes this deference. The AFL's aging
building is roomily oldtime, sedate—no rush of people in and
out. I head upstairs to see President William Green, though
knowing he won't see me, if he sees me first.

Back in 1923, a Woll committee investigated Federated
Press, and cluck-clucked. Along with all other labor shades, FP
included communists and Wobblies on its board. Like Associated Press, it gave representation to member papers. Such things
Green does not forget. In any case, he doesn't care for reporters.
They try to trip him up. He must guess they make fun of him
behind his back.

"Mr. Green's too busy to see you," says his motherly secretary, looking less worried than her boss who putters, pink-faced
and fretful, in the background. "If there's any news, you can always get it from Mr. Roberts."

Mr. Roberts is an oldtimer, small and wizened. He snoozes
in a cluttered little office that looks like a stockroom, with bulg-
ing shelves of mimeographed stuff. He's in charge of handing
out press releases—usually texts of speeches. The New Deal is
busting at the seams with press agents, information directors,
publicity men, public relations experts. They waylay reporters,
cozy up, buy drinks. They grind out releases to shower on all in
ceaseless profusion. The AFL, in 1934-35, has Mr. Roberts. He is

peace-loving, unhurried, undisturbed. All he knows, he says, is what's in the handout. His modest title is "legislative representative."

Others besides Mr. Roberts will see me, if Mr. Green won't. John P. Frey welcomes me. Mr. Frey wears no wing collar; his high stiff collars and conservative suits create the tintype effect. Gossips claim he wears nightcap and nightgown when he checks under his bed each night for reds.

Mr. Frey is a scholarly person. He has read and written books and articles—written them himself, to judge from the internal evidence. Along with the more worldly Woll, Frey is rated the brains of AFL craft unionism—figuratively, as Big Bill Hutcheson is rated its beef.

Mr. Frey knows all about FP; he remembers every AFL convention. Yet he doesn't close his door, or refer me to Mr. Roberts. He is courteous and makes no disparaging remarks. He likes to talk—to anyone. Through the history of craft unionism Mr. Frey takes me, from the days of Belshazzar to the guilds of the middle ages, then further up-to-date with AFL craft victories over the Knights of Labor. It's fascinating—the first time.

Only when its executive council meets, is there much doing at the AFL. Mr. Green sees us all after sessions. While they're on, we can hear through closed doors the ranting and roaring of the Teamsters' Daniel Tobin (you learn to make your voice carry on a truck), the growls and grunts of others, and Mr. Green's plaintive "Gentlemen! Gentlemen . . ." We can buttonhole the more vociferous members when they make sorties out of sheer indignation; the sly, quiet ones when they head for the toilet.

Once I really got on the inside of the AFL council. But that was a few years later, when I was no longer with FP but with the CIO. The council chanced to meet in the Hamilton Hotel—behind doors too stout for even the Tobin voice to penetrate. Reporters waited in a pressroom on the floor above. Restless, some went prowling off. One friend returned, to draw me mysteriously after him. He led me to a bathroom, where some reporters stood on toilet and stools with ears toward an air duct. Joining them,

I found myself listening in on the deliberations of the AFL council.

This might seem a doubtful privilege. After sitting in at many closely guarded executive sessions myself, I got to feel they could keep the curious away in droves by no more than opening their doors. On this occasion, however, the AFL council was deliberating punishment for its CIO rebels. I was curious about David Dubinsky with one foot in each camp, as a CIO man who hadn't followed Lewis in resigning from the AFL council. I soon recognized Dubinsky's voice and heard his words distinctly.

Across the street from the Hamilton was the Tower Building, where the Mine Workers still had their headquarters. I dropped in to see Lewis. As I left the building, I saw Dubinsky bustling toward it.

The next time I ran into Lewis, he told me deadpan: "Dubinsky was very surprised when he visited me after the AFL council meeting. He started to tell me what a fight he put up there for CIO. I stopped him and said, 'David, this is what you said.' I gave him back his exact words."

The executive council was the power-center of the AFL. There tussled its proud rulers, then left their orders for Mr. Green to carry out. When the tumult and the shouting died, the captains and the kings departed, all of AFL that still stood in Washington was its ancient covenant and the contrite heart of Mr. Green. (It was Mr. Green himself who once called the AFL the "Ark of the Covenant.")

I have accorded to Mr. Green a "Mr." denied to most others. He deserved it. One couldn't think of him, nor he of himself, as a naked Green. He was above all a respectable person; a happier fate might have made him a reverend one. Mr. Green had a fine pulpit presence. He dressed and behaved with sober dignity and decorum. He meant well—when he meant anything. Sometimes he was satisfied with resonance of phrase.

John L. Lewis wasn't fair to Mr. Green when—urged once to meet him face to face to "explore each other's minds"—he protested: "I have done a lot of exploring in Bill's mind—and I give you my word there is nothing there." Mr. Green had a well-stocked mind, full of the wordy wisdom of many wordy generations.

A congregation that found comfort in sonorous diction might have acclaimed Mr. Green's talents. He was eloquent in echoing the familiar phrase, in honoring the time-honored sentiment. His talents were esteemed by the comfortable when he reassured them that labor was God-fearing, patriotic, employer-loving, red-spurning. They kept things going through dull spots of an AFL convention, when the boys wanted time for a drink, a caucus, a poker game. They were otherwise wasted on the crotchety old curmudgeons of the AFL executive council.

They were also wasted on millions of unorganized workers who wanted to know what use AFL was if it couldn't help them get organized.

The chief source of labor news was the administration. NRA's General Hugh Johnson was bellowing about his tough cavalry backside; many workers were bellowing back. So many agencies got in on labor stuff they almost pushed out the Labor Department. "But Madame Secretary," objected a new reporter to Frances Perkins's "no comment" on a strike, "you're Secretary of Labor. Shouldn't you do something? It's your job to keep labor down." Lots of others thought it their job. Trudging from agency to agency, delegations of undowned workers cursed the Washington runaround.

Congress was less of a source, more discussive than decisive, though committee hearings could be revealing. Besides southern congressmen, House types included Tammany-type machine men from northern cities, and the equally pig-eyed, but more straitlaced, smalltown Republicans. A handful of newcomers, products of the popular revulsion, provided contrast.

These newcomers brought some fresh air into Congress, soon stifled by an ancient apparatus that balked their initiative, muffled their voices, frustrated their plans. Most didn't last. It took a near-revolution to inject even these few. Why such meager results from so much rebellion?

Basically because of the imbalance of power between rich and poor. Most black people and immigrant workers couldn't vote. Poll taxes disenfranchised many native poor whites. Rural voters got more representation than the city millions. But reform all such things, and capitalist power was still supreme. It controlled the economy and people's jobs; the channels of information and opinion-creation; the old parties and their political machines.

Consider a congressional district. In all but smallest towns, factories by the tracks. Nearby the lowly shacks of black people, Mexicans, the lowest paid. Further off, the trimmer but still lowly dwellings of white working people, merging into those of better paid workers and little business people. Still further out and stretching far and wide, homes of the well-to-do—business, professional, executive. In far wooded outskirts, estates of the wealthy.

Who counted most? Not the idle rich—except for shakedowns—but the active rich and well-to-do. Owners and managers of industries, banks, newspapers, radio stations, big stores; leaders of more prosperous businesses and occupations. These rulers were not a unit, except on basic class interest. They were not the political machine, but they could control it; to them it must turn for money, promotion, pull, to win elections. The machine—city hall, party bosses, jobholders—reached widely through aspiring henchmen into business, unions, churches, fraternal organizations.

If class lines showed as I saw them in pre-Hitler Berlin, lower paid worker and colored sections might have been communist; higher paid worker and small-business sections social democratic; well-to-do sections capitalist liberal to conservative or fascist. But the American two-party system obscured class lines it followed in its own peculiar ways. It was a machine to control elections—a machine with a spare tire—a one-party machine, with one party in control or two alternating for similar purposes.

What happened when popular revulsion brought demand for change, as in the depression? The machine tried to control results as usual. If its grip slipped, some new-type congressman might get elected. It might try to take him over, become a "liberal" machine—still run by much the same bosses and sponsors. Or it might declare war on the new-typer, call him communistic, redbait him to defeat.

The redbaiting campaign was a triumph of American technique. It owed its wallop to a nationwide thought-control apparatus that could sell bunkum like it sold soap; and to supine victims who didn't challenge gross lies about communism but lent them credence by protesting their innocence of this devilishism and trying themselves to redbait. The communist bogey was thus left to suggest treason to the patriotic, church-burning to the religious, looting mobs to the businessman, assassination to the idiot, bombs to the noise-shy, disorder to the orderly, war to the peaceful, an enemy to the warmonger, even loss of freedom to the wage slave. Everything the politically unsophisticated might fear or hate could be whipped into the mix of red paint. The machine had but to dip in its brushes and shake them at the new-typer, then goodby, Mr. Congressman.

Washington newspapermen were divided into two classes, an upper and a lower—in income, that is. The upper were men of wrinkling brow and serious mien. (There were also a few women, defensively aggressive under the prevailing male chauvinism, and usually with a male correspondent for mate.) Each had an upper-class home in Georgetown, Montgomery county, or Virginia, membership in the National Press Club, and a judicious disposition from weighing his publisher's whims and wishes against his own. All, except hardshell reactionaries and flaming radicals, took pride in being independent, objective, impartial. "I have to be impartial," one told me, "my publisher's a Republican, my editor a Democrat."

The lower class newsmen didn't belong to the National Press Club. In my time, an unpretentious booze-and-steak joint, the Washington Newspapermen's Club, catered to them. Mostly they just grabbed a bite on the run. These were the working newsmen on the Washington dailies, like reporters and deskmen anywhere.

Not so the UC trained seals. Interpreting national politics was their be-all and end-all. Their bylines were blazoned like banners at a time when there was no TV, and even the new-coming radio was slighted. (The little news-filching I did for radio was the most despised and least paid of my activities.) Some cultivated—as helpful for salary and tenure—a ponderous deportment, a supposedly thoughtful expression, pipe-in-mouth photoportraits, some society airs ("He gets around with important people"). But babbitts aside, Washington correspondents were interesting folk.

The London *Times* correspondent Sir Willmott Lewis attracts the attention of young newcomers as the witty, worldly-wise, English aristocrat. Started as a lowly untitled legman, I believe; but titles are hot stuff in America. Sir Willmott is liberal, hep, and mostly on the side of the angels. He has a twinkle that says he knows how he's typed, and finds it fun.

Tom Stokes, of Scripps-Howard, deserves pointing out. A liberal and a gentleman. Not an English gentleman; more like a nice, shy, lanky American smalltown boy. Modest, mild, sensitive, he can lay on like a good liberal with his typewriter. Not too radical though . . . lucky for him.

Bustling Fred Perkins—also out of Scripps-Howard, from the other side of the bed. A good fellow for conviviality and for saying the kind and conventional thing—did it for me when I fell from grace. No radical, but a business believer. Gets to cover labor. Not so sure about unions. A straight reporter, he hopes—without introspection. He's lucky too.

At the Press Club we're bound to run into Charley Stewart. The club has news-tickers, releases, members who've been all around, newsworthy visitors, a typewriter-room, telephones, a bar. What more does a feature man need whose feet started hurting long ago? Charley's in those relaxed years around 70—doesn't dream of marrying the boss's daughter—views all careers with detachment. Figuring me for a red, he tells me he's boxed the compass—single-tax, socialism, syndicalism, communism, anarchism—and pushing ever left now finds himself on the right. A younger Charley could have been one of those radicals who welcomed me to the San Francisco Press Club in 1922, a Wobbly on the bum. Most by now doubtless called themselves "liberals" not "radicals." But Fremont Older was there then; he didn't care what he was called.

Rodney Dutcher is less likely to be at the club, but he'll be around. Plump and kindly. A liberal liberal—tolerant even of those to the New Deal's left. For the underdog. Plain nice about everything; not a mean streak. He had to die too young.

Somewhere I must include Paul W. Ward of the Baltimore *Sun*—for a personal reason that may be revealing. Paul looked more legman than byline big. No wrinkling brow, no pipe, just the long inquisitive nose of a good reporter. His skepticism of the New Deal could have made him a conservative attuned to his paper, or a radical needling the deal from the left. I didn't think of him as either—just Paul Ward, who liked to dig through the bunk for the dope. Guess I must have been sentimental about reporting, about a craft pride unrelated to the owners' purposes, about the legman's romance with his work which only in a radically different society could produce real babies.

Ray Brandt and Marquis Childs of the St. Louis *Post-Dispatch*. Liberal in style and thought. A mite highbrow for the roughnecks, but doing distinguished progressive reporting. In later CIO days, I visited their paper in St. Louis and lunched with staff members. Reminded me of Oxford—not so tweedy, but pipe-ish, deliberative, determined-to-be-thoughtful.

What about such people and papers when the Cold War turned the press to screaming lunacy? Did they murmur their alarm at "communism" with restrained madness? Or did some stand up and fight? I ask for information, not rhetorically. By then I had my own troubles, and didn't notice.

About Paul Y. Anderson of the same paper I don't have to ask. He died in the mid-Thirties. He was impulsive, tempestuous, disturbed. He fell for John L. Lewis like a ton of bricks, while I was falling like sand through a time-glass. He also fell for the anticommunist virus—contracting it during some silly little infighting in the Washington Newspaper Guild.

Ken Crawford too—of New York *Post* and Philadelphia *Record*, long before *Newsweek*. So passionate a liberal then, he liked to be thought a radical. Soon to start along a Newspaper Guild road to passionate anticommunism. Bullet-headed Robert Allen—more like a bombshell—was another. So aggressive we used to think of him as Drew Pearson's left wing. He too later contracted quite a dose of anticommunism.

As to the hidebound conservatives—to quote Caroline, "I spare myself." An avid reader of a wide range of political opinion, Caroline would buy papers just for their columns. Once I asked if she'd read a certain column by George Sokolsky. "Sokolsky?" she said. "I spare myself."

To defend their loot against "creeping socialism" at home and real socialism abroad, the ruling class needed slicker mouthpieces than their old-boys. There were new-boy liberals offering better service. The old men of Washington press reaction were a joke, even then. They had the entree and top billing. But who read them, except dowagers, aging clubmen, and politicians whose axes they ground? As to the smaller fry of press reaction, they were like any business rank and file. They made their money by suiting their commodity, news, and comment, to those who paid them.

There were a few tablefuls of liberals then (1934-35) at the National Press Club. There were pioneer enthusiasts for the Newspaper Guild, when this meant sticking out one's neck. There were some doughty good guys. But I missed the freshness of the 1922 San Francisco reporters who hooted at the capitalist topdog and hoped the working-class underdog would lick him, a Jack London class-struggle approach. These Washington liberals saw no continuing class struggle. They were remote from the fight in the shops for union, in the streets for jobless relief; from the growing strikes and mass movements. Washington's confused reflection of the struggle seemed more real to them than the struggle itself.

The proportion of liberals was unduly small. The country was floundering out of the trough of a depression that had caused near-revolutionary reactions among millions. The swell that had raised Roosevelt to power was rocking the boat, threatening to swamp it. Yet in the capital's press corps you could count the radicals on one hand, and needed no abacus to calculate the number of liberals. It was almost as bad as in Congress.

I reported Washington during a honeymoon period for the left. Hitler, Mussolini, Hirohito, were scaring the world. The U.S.S.R.'s Maxim Litvinov was calling for collective security against fascist aggression. In France, the communists were part of a forming popular front. In the United States, the communists had gained some following in the depression and more indirect influence. They had irritated liberals by criticizing the New Deal from the left. They had enraged AFL officialdom by challenging its leadership and agitating among unorganized and newly organizing workers. New Dealers mostly saw the communists as an embarrassing looney fringe, extreme, cantankerous, but to be taken into account insofar as it stirred up the people.

The *Daily Worker* was in on things with the bigtime press. It had a bureau in the National Press building and two correspondents, Seymour Waldman and Marguerite Young, man and wife. Marguerite was lively, good-looking, an experienced reporter. Seymour too rated his status. They attracted much attention in the press corps—and not all hostile—being kidded a lot, but usually accepted as a tonic or a necessary evil.

To Bob Buck, bossy old ex-Chicago alderman who ran the Washington Newspaper Guild, they were a convenience. When criticized or opposed, he could point to the communist menace, as publicly personified by Seymour and Marguerite. Some of the local legmen might yawn after a while. But some big-shot Press Club liberals took alarm lest their support of a union for less fortunate brothers might expose them to the red smear.

Their publishers were relatively liberal and found distinction in having a liberal Washington correspondent. With misgivings, their big advertisers tolerated a liberal treatment of That Man Roosevelt, even if whispered to be a Kerensky. But if beyond him a Lenin seemed to loom . . . !

What was the liberal correspondent to do when suspected of sympathico loft of the New Deal? If a quiet, controlled type, he might possibly continue on his quiet way—letting the evidence accumulate that he was just the pinko liberal he was. If a passionate type, emotionally conditioned to think himself in mortal combat with reaction, he could be needled. Marguerite, for instance, was a needler. The passionate one hated to seem flabby or chicken—particularly to the kind of girl before whom he'd like to spread a peacock-tail of bold and brilliant radicalism.

Before the communists spread around with their which-side-are-you-on stuff, one could turn a ruddy cheek to friends and a paler cheek to one's publisher. Not any more. The passionate liberal often came to direct most of his passion against the communists, for making things hard for him.

The liberal with less pent-up emotion tried to draw a meticulous boundary between his liberalism and the Communist party line. That was hard to do. In its popular-front endeavors, the party supported nearly everything he'd stood for. He had to dodge all over the lot avoiding causes he'd once embraced. It made him bitter—against the communists. I recall the relief expressed by then liberal Ernest K. Lindley, in a speech right after the German-Soviet nonaggression pact. Now at last, said he, a clear line could be drawn between communists and liberals.

These were the early years of the American Newspaper Guild. A trade union for newspapermen! What a radical idea it was held to be! Imagine a union bullying Mark Sullivan and Westbrook Pegler! Infringing the press freedom of Roy Howard and William Randolph Hearst! And those boldface fulminations against the red riot and rebellion of strikes—what if their writers shared union affiliation with John L. Lewis and Harry Bridges! The Guild had to point out there were also less conspicuous newspapermen who did the most work and got the least pay, "the working newspapermen."

The Guild was a clear-cut union effort—for collective bargaining on wages, hours, conditions. Given the nature of the trade and its product, it also stirred members to wider thinking about ethics, standards, social function. Ideas as well as wage-beefs were bandied around.

In Heywood Broun, the Guild had a magnificent leader, hero, and punching bag. With the gin on his hip, his disheveled deportment, his blunderful good humor, Broun upheld the right to be human—about all that united the early discordants. Broun was firm on the bread-and-butter union purposes. He'd have no truck with professionalists or company unionists. He also knew that a union crusade calls for a crusading spirit, and that ideas and ideals rate high with union pioneers.

Broun was a famous columnist at a time when columns still gasped some fresh air into a suffocating press. Ancients may recall a time when people spoke of "a fighting editor," battling "the interests." That was before the monopoly stage of newspaper capitalism—before a millionaire handful cornered the press, with their nationwide chains, syndicated mass products, hired-hand editors, and their thought-control. I don't know that I ever heard of "a fighting columnist," but columnists supposedly had some leeway to express personal and divergent opinions.

Before long, even this much freedom of expression wore thin. The rightwing columnist or radio commentator had to make up with shrill style for the lack of individuality in his corporation-patterned opinions. His liberal counterpart became ever more pallid in docile submission to red-scare restrictions. The radical wasn't allotted a syndicated column or good radio time in the first place. Heywood Broun, however, belonged to the heyday of the columnist and helped usher it in. He had easygoing wit and humor, a liberal tolerance, and some capacity for indignation. He could appeal to both the simple and the sophisticated.

After *The CIO News* was started in 1937, I got Broun to write a weekly column for it—for a slim couple of bucks. We started the paper on a shoestring, and Heywood said he'd be "happy to grow up with it." I hoped he would apply his special touch to CIO and labor issues, and was curious how he might try to do it. Oscar Ameringer, with homier and less disciplined style, had done the sort of thing I had in mind. But he was a specialist in humorizing labor and socialist propaganda.

When the Broun columns began arriving, I was disappointed. This wasn't Broun, I thought. The columns were serious, with but a rare flash of the Broun wit. Only later did he even try to approach weighty labor issues in a lighter vein.

Later I realized I was wrong. This was Broun. He wrote a light column for a living; he wasn't light himself. He maintained a playboy image for his public; he wasn't playing about the Guild and CIO. Broun was serious about the labor movement. Maybe too serious. He had a strong sense of humor, on the surface. Had it gone deeper, it might have served him better, even in his search for a serious purpose. It might have spared him that deathbed conversion by Monsignor Fulton Sheen.

The Washington political scene was not the center of attraction for me. There must have been some unregenerate Wobblyism in the secondary importance I attached to its politicians and their doings, as compared with the class struggle at the point of production. I was happy when Federated Press sent me to cover the 1935 convention of the American Federation of Labor in Atlantic City. After that I returned to the Washington FP spot, until offered my CIO job. But for me, as for it, the CIO really began at that AFL convention.

2   MOVEMENT

Chapter Six

IMPETUS—JOHN L. LEWIS PLANS A COUP

John L. Lewis, an unlikely Lochinvar,
delighted the young and rebellious by
rescuing their cause from the AFL
dungeon. He planned and timed his coup.

"Where'd all them reds come from this year?"

Two men of girth were sounding off as they brushed by me into the Hotel Chelsea bar, on the eve of the AFL's 1935 convention in Atlantic City.

"From the Je-e-ew De-e-al, I guess."

"They got no business here. Some's even delegates."

"We'll fix 'em next year." A chortle. "Hold the convention in Florida. They ain't got the money to go that far."

I thought I knew or could recognize most of the reds at the convention. There weren't so many. I looked around some more and checked the delegate roster. There wasn't much menace, but I could feel a mood.

The Old Guard had the votes to overwhelm any conceivable opposition. The setup was as it had long been, and still is, for that matter. Each international-union boss appointed (in effect or in fact) his associate delegates, a tight-knit top officer group that voted as a unit. At this convention, the 275 international union delegates had 29,205 out of a total of 29,746 votes. The same men had headed these delegations for years. The name of each told you how his union would vote. The names of a score of bigger-union bosses told you how the convention would vote.

Of the few votes left, some hundred delegates from Federal Labor Unions had no more than 411 votes between them. Among these were the newcomers—the "reds" of whom I'd heard complaint—from the little organized auto, rubber, steel, radio, and other mass-production industries. There were some communists among them, but most had no observable political coloration. It was their rebellious mood that made the Old Guard see "red." I'll call them the Youngsters, regardless of age.

So why should William Green look even more fretful than usual? Why did Matthew Woll, white-chested under black bow-tie, look less penguin-proud as he skirted the lobby so warily that a wisp of hair kept falling over his high forehead? Why did dour and dignified John P. Frey argue so vehemently with lobby groups? And why did the near-voteless Youngsters act so cocky? They had no chance to have their way. They had little chance even to be heard—unless the Old Guard split apart.

Woll was chairman, Frey secretary, of the top-policy resolutions committee. Controlling few votes, they were, like Green, only the clerks or mouthpieces of the Old Guard top command. The big bosses were men like William L. (Big Bill) Hutcheson, ponderous autocrat of the Carpenters, the Teamsters' volatile Daniel J. Tobin, and the poker-pals with whom they made their deals.

Tobin was a loud and lively orator, a Democrat. He once called the newly organizing less-skilled "rubbish . . . riffraff or good-for-nothings." Other craft bosses used less printable terms —in private. Typically, Tobin did his name-calling in public and was too stiff-necked to retract. Hutcheson could grunt and pound with more effect than he could orate. His per capita carried more weight than his arguments. For his Carpenters union, Hutcheson claimed all workers who touched wood—just as Tobin claimed for his Teamsters all who moved. Big Bill was a Harding-Coolidge-Hoover Republican; he liked to run his own business his own way.

Earnest, irascible Arthur O. Wharton, of the Machinists, carried some voting weight. I cited him earlier as out for the skilled and to hell with the rest. But with the New Deal, he saw a new light and joined the scramble for all the dues payers he could get—with an eye particularly on auto parts.

Add to these three, the heads of the Electrical Workers, Bricklayers, Plumbers, Railway Clerks, Musicians, Streetcarmen,

Letter Carriers, and you had 10 men with enough votes together to control the convention. Along with like-minded Old Guardsmen from the Painters, Hodcarriers, Longshoremen, United Garment, and lesser building and metal craft bosses, they held the overwhelming majority of convention votes.

Biggest union boss was actually John L. Lewis, longtime pillar of the Old Guard command. After Gompers died in 1924, Lewis had been strong and shrewd enough to put his man, William Green, into the AFL presidency, and had been a top arbiter of policy ever since. Lewis paid the AFL per capita on 3-400,000 regardless of ups and downs in Mine Workers membership.

David Dubinsky was new to AFL top ranks. A deceptively jolly-looking rolypoly, he had a deep mean streak against communists. A onetime socialist, Dubinsky expanded his Ladies Garment Workers with the New Deal and was at last admitted to that Politburo of the AFL, its executive council. Some liberals lifted their eyes in hope. But anticommunism had become more important to Dubinsky than socialism—as for his once-socialist cronies who formed a caucus around the Jewish *Daily Forward*; his machine had barely wrested victory from a communistically inclined leftwing. This brought about the seeming anomaly that Matthew Woll, the AFL's top conservative, became sponsor of Dubinsky and his crowd, their go-between with the rest of the Old Guard.

Anomalous in another way was the position of Charles P. Howard, head of the steady, influential Typographical craft union, who became a leading advocate of industrial unionism for the mass-production industries. Tall, black-haired, sallow, intense, he tried to chart a way for it through the AFL maze, with a printer's painstaking parliamentary exactitude.

Latest comer to the AFL hierarchy was Sidney Hillman, sharp of mind and sharp of feature. His Amalgamated Clothing Workers had but recently been admitted to the AFL. It was a substantial union. Hillman had an "in" with the Roosevelt administration. His voice and vote counted.

Others who counted included the Hotel Workers Edward Flore and the Pressmen's George L. Berry. Ex officio, I must add William Green and gentle, kindly Frank Morrison, AFL secretary-treasurer. They had a voice at least, if little more.

There was the AFL from on top in 1935—a score or so of big union bosses, half a dozen of whom might decide most issues.

Among themselves the labor bosses seldom used union names. Each knew the name of his own union and liked to roll it off his tongue. He found the names of other unions too long or tricky to use and often got them wrong if he tried. In any case, he thought of the man who ran each union, not of such an abstraction as the union itself.

Abbreviations like Miners, Carpenters, Teamsters, Amalgamated, ILG, might sometimes be used. It wasn't good form to say Lewis's union, Hutch's union, etc. It was common to speak of Lewis, Hutcheson, Tobin, Hillman, Dubinsky—or more cozily, of John, Hutch, Dan, Sidney, Dave—as if each union president were the personal embodiment of his union. Each usually thought of himself that way, with a certain justification.

Like other American businesses, unions were run from on top. There was a boss and his subordinates. The boss might answer to a board of directors, but he set things up for the board to approve. He wouldn't be boss for long if he couldn't handle his board, and most union bosses were dug in for a long, long time. The boss, with his sub-bosses, set things up for conventions too—held so a good time might be had by all. The votes were calculated in advance, to avoid mistakes.

As in first-generation control of more commercial businesses, the typical union boss was a tough, grasping, old buzzard, with a strongly proprietary attitude toward "his" business. A few were once union pioneers, even radicals, but in office lived down such juvenile delinquency. The once-radical were expert at sniffing and driving out the now-radical. Successors followed the customary business route: apple-polishing to get co-opted, then lying in wait to doublecross the old boss or be next in line when he died. One big boss per union was the rule—an absolute monarch under thin constitutional guise, or a manipulator of rival barons who ruled absolutely in their respective fiefs. With age and experience, the big boss became more secure—and ever more autocratic.

From facing early challenges, the union boss had learned never to give a potential opponent an even break and to classify all opposition as the work of some satanic enemy. Latest challenges had come from oppositions inspired by Foster's Trade Union Educational League. Having used anticommunist bans to drive out or silence such opponents, the union bosses continued indefinitely thereafter to dub all inner-union critics as communists or in league with communists. So from the Twenties on, the AFL passed anticommunist resolutions with repetitious uniformity, supposedly to register American labor's abhorrence of communism. The union bosses who nodded them through weren't students of communism; they identified it with their opponents. Unanimously they abhorred opposition.

There were other angles to this anticommunist syndrome. The ad salesman's, for instance. Soliciting corporation ads for labor publications, he found anticommunism to be a much more sure-fire pitch than labor-paper cartoons showing Capital and Labor arm in arm. Employers thought it fine to buy some influence with unions by spending money on a favorite cause. Union bosses saw in anticommunism a common ground for winning favor from employers who otherwise hated the unions' guts. They carried over the anticommunist pitch into their speeches and public relations. It was of the essence of the National Civic Federation effort to get labor leaders and antiunion corporations into bed together.

The union boss looked at things from the top down. The man on the job saw things differently, from the bottom up. To him, the union was the conditions under which he worked. If the union was any good, it meant higher wages, shorter hours, job rights, fringe benefits. In the shop, the member knew the union well. Outside he tended to lose sight of it. He had a right to go to union meetings. Mostly he did not. It cut into his free time, and when he'd gone, said he, he'd seen that things were "run by a clique."

So they were. The clique was those few who enjoyed meetings, taking the floor, arguing, points of order, committee work, voting—and hoping to be elected, or caring who was elected. Then there was the clique within the clique that really ran things. The clique decided who should be delegates to the union convention, usually repeaters. Few but the delegates and the clique knew or cared what happened at the convention—unless, of course, there were some sharp shop issue.

The gulf between the union boss in his top office and the average man in the shop was so great they were hardly within shouting distance. Neither was much interested in the other. The union boss didn't have to concern himself with the working member, except in a general way during negotiations. He ran the union through sub-bosses, organizers, and such, who in turn manipulated the inner cliques that ran the local unions.

That was the AFL picture, at its most democratic—omitting extreme autocracies and outright rackets—when CIO stepped on the stage in 1935.

Atlantic City in the fall wasn't a bad setting for a convention that, for once, had the elements of drama. A real issue. A challenge by new to old. Conflict and suspense. A dominant and unpredictable protagonist.

You walked out of a stuffy, smoky auditorium into a lobbyful of gossips. Eyes popped for the bigs who elbowed through or paused to chat. Ears were cocked for their chance remarks. You moved on outside. At once a cold wind from the Atlantic beat about your head and cleared your mind. You were on the boardwalk. The salt air syringed the smoke from your nostrils. The breeze buffeted you into animation.

Around you the luxe of big hotels—not like the flophouse stalls, the boxcar floors, the coffee-an' at greasy spoons, of lowlier living. Ocean views from upper suites. Fresh white linen. Fancy coffeeshops and bars, and fancier dining rooms. You got the feel of a posh vacation—and for free, on an expense account.

I got the feel vicariously. My FP budget allowed for no luxe, even under "Misc." Caroline and I put up at a roominghouse blocks back from the boardwalk. We ate moderately, with close attention to the right-hand column of the menu. I saw many Youngsters doing likewise. There wasn't much luxe in the early stages of union organization. In their later stages, the Old Guard and their hangers-on were living it up.

Not for a long time had the AFL moguls faced challenge.

Once socialists had opposed the Gompers Old Guard. There had been policy debates, real contests for office. After the socialists died out or succumbed, a few progressive might raise their voices—but only until the Old Guard perfected its red-scare technique at the 1923 convention. The pyrotechnics around the unseating of William F. Dunne as a communist were designed to scare off all further opposition. Those rockets' red glare lit up every progressive cause in communistic light.

From 1923 to 1935 the Old Guard was in unchallenged control. Radicals were barred. Liberals feared to raise their voices, except in the anticommunist anthems. If any rebel Youngsters showed up, they might as well have stayed home. In 1934, it is true, Lewis seriously raised the question of industrial organization. He didn't upset the applecart. A compromise was reached to issue a few industrial-union charters without infringing craft claims. The Old Guard remained in full control.

This year you could feel the challenge—in the mood of the Youngsters particularly. On boardwalk, in lobbies, in lower-priced restaurants, you could hear them laugh and kid—making jokes about the Old Guard. A treasonous mood.

Among the more lively I recall rampageous Emil Costello, from a big furniture FLU; perky boyish James B. Carey, radio; and adroit Thomas F. Burns, rubber, a future political sidekick to Sidney Hillman. Spunky, aggressive, and quite unawed by the everlasting big shots, Costello was not afraid to stand out as a leader on the left. Carey, normally respectful to elders, was like the cheeky kid who saw the Emperor was unclothed.

On the serious side were Wyndham Mortimer and young, dark George Addes, leaders of the new United Auto Workers; and Sherman H. Dalrymple (later United Rubber Workers president), a steady man of southern background. Mortimer, ex-miner and longtime auto worker, sober and intense in his working-class radicalism, was middle-aged and not flamboyant. Yet he was perhaps the most impressive of the Youngsters in his thoughtfulness and strength of purpose. Others I recall included Russell J. Merrill, Carl J. Shipley, John North, from auto FLUs; and W.W. Thompson, a rubber worker whose speech was to provoke a famous encounter.

Coming from the unorganized, mass-production industries,

and ranging politically from communist to conservative, the rebel crowd shared a common belief—that, with or without AFL assent, their industries must be organized in industrial unions free from craft claims and raids.

A small minority with few votes, they could expect to be ignored or squelched—except for one thing. This year the Old Guard was divided. Its biggest shot was going to champion the Youngsters, and, said rumor, he was ready to fight.

Everyone was guessing about John L. Lewis when I arrived in Atlantic City. The rumors flying up and down the boardwalk had a source. It was the President Hotel, remote from AFL headquarters at the Chelsea. There Lewis had established himself, with much entourage.

The Old Guard craftists heard the rumors. They were disturbed but not upset. They expected Lewis to rear up; he was feeling his oats. But after all, he was one of them, had always stood with them against the "reds," even led the fight. They expected Lewis to shoot off, but he just hadn't the votes. He'd have to compromise, and they could bury the rebellion in a whoopadoop of anticommunism.

Some of the Youngsters didn't expect much of Lewis either. They knew of his Old Guard record—a Coolidge-Hoover Republican, a redbaiting reactionary, in fact one of the flashiest of red-scare showmen.

Lewis once called opposition to himself within the UMW "the first step in the realization of a thoroughly organized program of the agencies and forces behind the Communist International at Moscow for the conquest of the American continent." At another time he said that "three times the Bolshevik leaders have attempted armed insurrection and revolt in the United States . . . during the steel strike of 1919, in the 'outlaw' switchmen's strike of 1920, and in the railroad and coal strikes of 1922."

In the UMW, it was true, the communists had given Lewis a run for his money. When George Voyzey, a little known rank-and-file miner and reputed communist, ran against Lewis for UMW president on a TUEL program in 1924, the Lewis vote-counting apparatus had to credit him with 66,000 votes—to 136,000 for Lewis. This was more than the 60,661 votes credited to the better known John Brophy in 1926—to 173,323 for Lewis. In the early Twenties, communist miners helped elect many anti-Lewis local and district officers; and the Nova Scotia UMW district even voted to affiliate with the Red International of Labor Unions.

In conventions, Lewis used to roar his redbaiting at opposition leaders like Alex Howat. He might single out some inconspicuous communists from the assembly for excoriation, and subsequent ejection. If he found no delegate handy, Lewis might single out a visitor. At the 1926 AFL convention in Detroit, he pointed dramatically from the platform to William Z. Foster in the visitors' balcony, denouncing him as "the Archprince of communism in the United States."

In the excitement and confusion ensuing from his personalization of the communist menace, Lewis would move fast to push through some measures he had more on his mind than the menace.

This technique—after he had long abandoned it—was turned against Lewis himself at the 1940 UMW convention in Columbus, Ohio. While he was speaking on the stage, some local rightists had a red flag, with crude hammer and sickle, lowered above him. Lewis didn't brush off the trick with an ad lib, as he was good at doing. His face was grim. It was the only time I saw him look nonplused in public. He hated to be victim of the kind of ploy he'd once used so often against others. While big Ray Edmundson shooed back an onrush of emotional delegates, Lewis felt forced to voice one of the anticommunist clichés he'd been shunning in his CIO years.

In 1935, however, there had long been talk in Washington of a "new Lewis." I'd had my doubts. Head of a shattered union in a declining industry, Lewis had been rated a know-nothing, do-nothing conservative. Yet after the Presidential election of a man he opposed, Lewis had plucked New Deal first-fruits while barely in the bud. Overnight he rebuilt his union and his own reputation. Given any kind of chance, the miners would have rebuilt their union anyhow. Lewis saw they got a good chance, and right away. Quick on his toes, he moved fast. You had to hand it to him. But what would he do with his new power? Just sit on it, like other labor leaders?

The Washington angle was of course political. The Hooverish Lewis was now a New Dealish Lewis—behind most New Deal labor moves. So too was Hillman, Roosevelt's labor lieutenant. But Lewis was no FDR lieutenant, and he carried more weight with labor. Lewis was pushing, hustling, embarrassing, Roosevelt, it was said, for his own labor purposes. With NIRA's Section 7(a), the Wagner act, and other labor laws; the Guffey act for coal, Lewis's repute grew in politics, as in union organizing.

Lewis moved fast in the coalfields. He moved fast in Washington. In such a molasses pot as the AFL, he couldn't move fast. At the 1934 convention he'd done what he could, but he didn't have the votes. Before the 1935 convention, I'd shared a common left attitude on Lewis: A big wistful, wishful "if only," trailing off into a resigned "but of course——" If only Lewis would act and fight like he talked . . . If only he'd start things from on top, to speed the movement below in the shops. . . . But of course the AFL bureaucracy was too encrusted. But of course the great antiunion corporations were too strong. But of course Lewis himself—how much could you really expect from a man like him?

Typically, every reflection on Lewis seemed to end with a question mark. Lewis had begun to plan it that way.

My first tipoff on a really new Lewis came from the Youngsters who went to the President Hotel to see him. To them he was making himself readily available, and they came away glowing.

The man was impressive. Big, bulky, bushy-black of hair and brow, imperious. Deliberately impressive, no doubt. But the impression registered. He exuded power and confidence.

Most Youngsters were used to fighting their way—to being shut out, pushed in the face by those in power. Yet here was a man of power who welcomed them, asked their problems, offered his help. Lewis gave seasoned advice and practical tips. He made them feel power was on their side. He set out to create that feeling, some recognized—and felt all the better. The sea heard some yippees, as they charged back along the boardwalk to tell the gang.

A most significant angle to the Youngsters' reports: Lewis seemed not to care if they were right or left, or red or pink, or whatsoever color.

Not so David Dubinsky. He, too, was for industrial organization. But he was finicky about the Youngsters he'd talk to. He wasn't going to open his door to any red.

One of Dubinsky's organizers, Rose Pesotta, introduced me to him on the boardwalk. "He's here for Federated Press," she said.

"That's communist," said Dubinsky and turned away.

Redbaiting was the first resort of the anti-industrial Old Guard, as of the antiunion corporation. For a fact, many communists were influential in the union beginnings. To start out with antired discrimination and division was to play the enemy's divide-and-conquer game, and to court failure. Lewis's reported attitude was a tipoff he meant business.

After the convention opened, Lewis tipped his hand again, and with deliberation. He threw into the hopper two resolutions of little more than a dozen words apiece—in place of the many-paragraphed resolutions traditionally offered in advance by progressives, to be duly printed in the proceedings and sentenced to death in committee.

Lewis had carefully picked these seemingly minor items months before, Brophy told me, as capable of passage and for their significance. One barred AFL leaders from holding office in the National Civic Federation—of which Matthew Woll was then the acting president. The other ordered the *American Federationist*, AFL's official magazine, to stop taking ads from anti-union corporations.

As soon as he learned of the Lewis move, Woll conceded. He told the convention he was resigning from the NCF—not failing to point out that Lewis's man Ellis Searles had but recently withdrawn from it. Both UMW motions were side-tracked to convention close, then passed without objection.

Lewis had gauged the impact these two moves would have One pointed directly at the great antiunion corporations as the main enemy, and poured scorn on the AFL's submission to them. The other, on NCF, did so indirectly and—besides publicly embarrassing Woll—made clear that Lewis himself, formerly linked with NCF through Searles, was indeed a new Lewis.

Watching Lewis throughout this convention, I could see a man who seemed eminently sure of himself, with every move, word, and gesture calculated to have the effect they usually produced. Only later, when I came to work with him directly, did I realize how long, carefully—and often secretively—he had thought out and worked out the strategy for launching the big CIO drive.

The high spot of the convention, its big show, was supposed to be the main debate on industrial organization. It arose over a minority report signed by Howard, Lewis, Dubinsky, and three others. This called for organizing the unorganized, mass-production industries into unions with unrestricted, industrial-union charters.

Lewis and his top associates made the case for industrial organization with vigor and eloquence. The other side also brought all its big guns into action, arguing back ably and often with emotion. The debate was unusually high-level and urgent for a labor convention where speeches were mostly formalized foregone conclusions. In this case, too, almost anyone could have calculated in advance the final vote. It was 10,933 to 18,024 against the minority report.

It was misleading to call the issue craft-versus-industrial unionism.

Only on paper could one provide for unions that did not overlap. DeLeon made industrial outlines, but the workers did not fill them in. A priest drew up a pie-chart for the IWW. The Wobblies called it "Father Hagerty's Wheel of Fortune" and paid it little attention. Most American unions "just growed" out of the needs of particular groups of workers. As they grew, the AFL tried to delineate jurisdictions. Most were unions of craftsmen, based on trade rather than plant or industry. But some were industrial unions—as of miners, brewery, garment workers. Trying vainly to adjudicate dividing lines so one union might not poach on another, the AFL was in never-ending turmoil over "jurisdictional disputes." They couldn't be settled on principle. The strong prevailed, the weak got raped.

When, with the New Deal, doors began to open for unionizing the mass-production workers, the AFL could no longer muddle through. Most of them were composite mechanics, semi-skilled, or unskilled workers. Even craftists recognized that few could be classified along craft lines predating mass production. The more arrogant at first talked of ignoring such "riffraff" as unorganizable anyhow; the more ambitious, of putting them in Class B locals, with rights inferior to those of Class A craftsmen. The "riffraff" had other ideas. The company unions and independent unions that sprouted under NRA put all workers in a given plant into the same organization. That alone made sense to mass-production workers.

The AFL compromise was Federal Labor Unions, directly chartered and controlled by the AFL national office. These took all workers in a plant into one FLU, but subject to later craft-union claims for some. The 1934 convention conceded industrial-union charters in a few industries, as auto and rubber, but so hedged as to protect craft-union claims.

The technical issue at the 1935 convention was the demand for unrestricted, industrial-union charters in mass-production industries. Only to that extent was craft-versus-industrial unionism the issue. The industrial unionists did not challenge the craft unions in their traditional jurisdictions. The craft unionists realized that restricted industrial unions might have to be formed in some mass-production industries.

The real issue—more important than any technicalities—was the actual intent and ambition to unionize unorganized millions.

In steel there was technically no issue. The old Amalgamated Association of Iron, Steel & Tin Workers had long held an AFL industrial charter it could call unrestricted—though a score of craft unions infringed it. Had it been as strong as the Mine Workers, it could have asserted its industrial jurisdiction. But the AA was a joke—with but a few thousand members, wide open to craft raids, and headed by aged fuddy-duds who resisted all progress or ambition as "communistic." AFL resolutions to organize steel meant little or nothing, if things were left to the AA and the craft unions. The Old Guard craftists didn't care. They didn't believe steel could be organized. They were as skeptical, and unambitious, about most other unorganized mass industries.

There were rumors of "gentlemen's agreements" under which some big corporations would tolerate certain crafts if their leaders discouraged organization of production employees. There was also no doubt some AFL moguls feared an influx of newly organized industrial unionists would undermine their present power in a more limited setup. Nor were the Old Guard craftists alone in their lack of faith. The great antiunion monopolies—backbone of Wall Street—had always managed to bar or break union organization. Few believed they could be forced to yield now. Lewis and the Youngsters were ahead of their times.

There lay the real issue—the will to organize. If the AFL had had it, if it had mounted at once the strongest possible organizing campaign, with all the money and organizers necessary, it could have adjusted or subordinated differences over organizational form. In fact, after CIO showed what could be done, some AFL craft unions were quick to follow suit. The Machinists, Electrical Workers, Teamsters, shedding sterile craft attitudes, went out to organize big plants the only way it could be done, with all the workers in one union. At the 1935 AFL convention, however, the Old Guard was acting dog-in-the-manger over members nobody had.

The conflict reached deep into labor ranks, and personal feelings. Least emotional were the big industrial-union bosses—with increased power under the New Deal and reaching for more. More shook up were the craft bosses, passionately resenting the challenge to their long rule. Strongest were the feelings of the battered union pioneers in nonunion industries. Lewis went all-out to inject their sense of urgency into the convention.

The conflict involved impatient youth against bossy old age, radicals against standpat conservatives, class struggle breaking through class collaboration, poor kicking against rich, the downtrodden determined not to be doormats. The young, the rebels, the reds were on one side; the old, conformist, conservative, on the other. Some of Lewis's big-shot associates were embarrassed at times to find which side they were on.

After defeat of the industrial-organization resolution, most Old Guarders thought the battle over. For Lewis and the Youngsters it had just begun. Lewis now had several big-treasuried union leaders committed to promote industrial organization within the AFL. They were soon to call themselves the Committee for Industrial Organization. The Youngsters were still to be heard from. Their champions had spoken, not they themselves.

Ordinarily, they would have got short shrift. It was near the end of a second convention week. There had already been a long night session. Normally the platform would have pushed toward adjournment, referring most remaining business to the executive council. But this year, Lewis was using all his power and wits to make sure the Youngsters were heard.

First were the Mine, Mill & Smelter Workers, complaining of craft agreements scabbing on their metal miners' strike. Delegates Paul Peterson, Reid Robinson, Alex Cashin, had beefs about the crafts like those of other Youngsters. Issues of the earlier debate were reopened, with more delegates joining in. The vote was almost identical. Then auto, rubber, radio Youngsters in turn voiced similar complaints—about craft raids, restricted charters, imposition of unwanted leaders, Class B memberships.

It got too much for the craft Old Guard, who felt it was rehashing an already settled question. They were tired of night sessions. They wanted to close shop and go home. Normally Green would have failed to recognize the Youngsters; points of order would have been "well taken"; tabling, referral, debate-closing, motions passed. But this year Green had to keep his eye on Lewis, who also knew a trick or two. Seeing Wyndham Mortimer vainly trying to get recognized, for instance, Lewis sent for him. He advised him to go to the platform, stand by the microphone near Green, and from there start talking. "I know Bill," Lewis said, "he won't dare to shut you up."

In this kind of atmosphere—while W.W. Thompson was

giving the rubber workers' case for an unrestricted charter—Big Bill Hutcheson rose to make a point of order that the question had been already settled.

I was at the press table when Lewis rose to object to Hutcheson's objection. It was "pretty small potatoes," he said, to try to silence minor delegates this way. Big Bill said he was raised on small potatoes and that's why he was so big (6 feet 3 inches, I believe, and some 300 pounds).

Lewis walked over to Hutcheson. They had words. I saw Lewis's fist shoot out to Hutcheson's head. The convention stampeded in shouting confusion. Reaching its center, I saw Hutcheson sprawled among overturned chairs. Lewis was brushing himself off like an unconcerned victor.

The incident itself may have been small potatoes. But even a little flashbulb can light up a scene to make a lasting and meaningful picture. The Youngsters chuckling their delight. The Whartons wanting in on the fray. The reporters really excited. Removed from it all in a washroom, Lewis's sidekick Tom Kennedy innocently asking the bloodied Big Bill as he entered, "What happened, Hutch?"

Forlorn and alone on the rostrum, poor Mr. Green. Appalled at the fight between two masters both of whom he can no longer serve. His gavel-pounding appeals for order unheard through the din and disorder.

"You shouldn't have done that, John," said he, as Lewis passed.

"He called me a foul name," growled Lewis.

"Oh, I didn't know that," said Green.

The flash lit up the battling Lewis as a John L. Sullivan of industrial organization. For millions, it gave meaning to those polysyllabic words they might never try to pronounce. They did follow sporting events.

With this blow, Lewis hammered home one of the main points he had come to the AFL convention to make—that AFL fakers were blocking a real union drive, and that he was ready to lead the workers in shoving them aside and getting down to the job. His was a calculated strategy, long thought out and much subtler than some of his bold crudities made it appear.

Lewis had long wanted to organize steel—to protect the flanks of his own union, and as basic to the future of the whole labor movement. It could be done, he believed, in a period of general organizing ferment. His 1933 coal drive told him the time was ripe, and that he was the man for the job.

At first, Lewis tried to get the AFL to act. The 1934 convention called for a steel campaign, and some restricted industrial-union charters. The AFL had done nothing in steel. It issued craft-hedged charters in auto and rubber so autocratically as to demoralize organization.

Lewis knew the AFL well enough not to need the 1934 lesson—maybe even then was going through motions to convince others he was giving the AFL every chance. By 1935, he knew just where he was going and what he must do. He was going to the AFL convention in October, to be sure. But he was going with no illusions to show what was holding back union organization, to offer himself as leader of a real drive, to show that the AFL couldn't be made to move or even to permit movement.

The last point was the hardest to get across to his own associates. In 1935, most of the leaders whose help Lewis needed bowed to labor-unity-in-AFL as to a fetish. It was no fetish to Lewis, an irreverent pragmatist, convinced the AFL would try to block any real and immediate industrial organizing. It was no fetish to most of the Youngsters—still less to the workers they came from, who wanted effective unions and cared little what they were called or how affiliated.

But Dubinsky . . . Once buffeted as immigrant socialists and Jews, he and his *Daily Forward* cronies had found shelter in AFL respectability. Dualism to them was almost as bad as communism—and they pointed with reminiscent horror to the short-lived Needle Trades Workers Industrial Union of the TUUL.

But Hillman . . . His Amalgamated had been a "dual union" breakaway from a corrupt and ineffective AFL union. It had flourished in outer darkness, but had long wanted in. When it won AFL affiliation, Hillman gained status with the New Deal as an "in" labor leader, not an outcast dual unionist.

But Charles P. Howard . . . President of a skilled craft, he liked to say the Typos began as an industrial union, but tolerantly let other crafts split off. Independent, the ITU said it started the AFL, not the AFL it; and in or out of affiliation, printers usually kept their many jobs with AFL central bodies. Howard could never persuade them to leave their cronies for a dual-union wilderness. What would that do to the Allied Printing Trades label?

But the left . . . Radicals had tried all kinds of union approach: DeLeon's purist—and memberless—industrial unionism; IWW turbulence; socialist challenge, then submission, to AFL conservatism; TUEL work within major unions; TUUL independent unions. In 1934-35, the left was liquidating dual efforts, to inject its red blood into AFL's anemic veins. In the midst of its anathemas against dualist sectarianism, for Lewis even to hint at a new breakaway—no, John, no, John, no!

Even Lewis's own Mine Workers . . . He was in firm control. The union would do as he said. But it wasn't wise to push things. Lewis's henchmen were AFL-minded—Old Guardist; they'd have to be gentled along. The members would want to see other unions, too, opening their treasuries.

While CIO was in its first form—a committee of AFL union leaders—Lewis often lost patience at the slowness of his associates to reach conclusions long obvious to him. At every step they had to be shown. Meanwhile time was a-wasting.

One lone, Harvard-accented voice haunts memory. Before adjournment, A. Philip Randolph spoke up for the black workers, as he did at every AFL convention. About the only black delegate granted the floor, anyhow.

America's most exploited workers were little represented in this "parliament of labor." Many crafts barred or discriminated against "non-Caucasians." Industrial unions offered a welcome, but not equality. CIO, when it started, tried to do better. No labor leaders—except the communists to come—gave black workers urgent first-rank attention.

It took a quarter century more for the black people to shout and fight their way to "the floor" of national attention.

After I returned to Washington, the London *Daily Herald,* an FP client, asked me for an exclusive interview with Lewis. He readily agreed.

Sitting beside Lewis at his desk was Charles P. Howard. I soon suspected the show was more for his benefit than for mine. The Committee for Industrial Organization had not yet been formally launched, with Howard as secretary. Lewis stressed to him the interest of a waiting world. Howard seemed impressed— chiefly perhaps by Lewis's august style.

When I rose to go, Lewis became pleasantly personal. "I didn't realize," he said, "that the *Herald* had a bureau in Washington."

"It doesn't," said I. "I just represent the paper on assignment. My job is with Federated Press."

"O-o-oh," rumbled Lewis, and his jaw clamped.

We both glanced toward Howard. Fortunately he still seemed a bit dizzied by the Lewis spell and was not paying attention.

Some weeks later, the Committee for Industrial Organization opened its office in the Rust Building. I was surprised when its director, John Brophy, called me in and offered me the job of handling its publicity. I was sure it wasn't Lewis's idea. I was right.

When Brophy asked Lewis's approval, he told me it went like this:

"Who is this man?"

"He's Washington correspondent of the Federated Press."

"O-o-oh." (I could still hear the echo of that earlier O-o-oh.) "Federated Press has always been against me. Oh well . . . what's his background?"

"He was assistant editor of the *Locomotive Engineers Journal.*"

"You mean to say he worked for that man Coyle!" (Lewis hadn't forgotten an intercepted letter written by Albert F. Coyle in support of the 1926 campaign of Brophy for UMW president against John L. Lewis. He used this letter to denounce Coyle as a master of "red intrigue," at the same AFL convention where he pointed his finger at "Archprince of communism" William Z. Foster. "Mr. Coyle," Lewis had orated, "is the editor of a scab-herding, strikebreaking organization, to wit, the Brotherhood of Locomotive Engineers, and he is boring from within to break up the United Mine Workers.")

"Yes," murmured Brophy—as self-effacingly as possible.

Lewis grumbled and snorted. Finally, he opined we are all subject to change, and went on: "All right. Before Coyle, what did he do?"

"Before that, he was assistant editor of the *Illinois Miner*."

At this point, Lewis almost blew up. He shook his head. "Look, if you'd gone out hunting for my worst enemy, you could hardly have found a man with a more consistent record of working against me and for my opponents. What is this?"

Then Lewis leaned back and laughed, still shaking his head. He must have been thinking of all the "enemies"—including Brophy—that he was himself drawing into the CIO. "You can't think of anyone else?" he asked.

Brophy said he couldn't.

"All right then," said Lewis. "This man has always been against me. Is he now for what we're trying to do?"

Brophy assured him I was.

"Okay, then," Lewis concluded.

A footnote to my CIO debut. Brophy was wrong in the belated suspicion expressed in his autobiography, that I asked a little time to consider the job in order "to consult with" my "friends in the Communist party." I knew all my friends, communist or not, would be pleased and had no cause to consult them. But I thought my partner Caroline should have a say.

Brophy was also forgetful, or singularly inattentive at the time, if he "had no idea then that De Caux worked closely with the communists." When he sounded me out for the job, I told him frankly that I had close sympathies with the communists, had many friends among them, and associated myself with them in a number of ways, though not organizationally.

If Brophy discounted my own protestations, he should have listened to a real authority. Hardly had I started work than I noticed a familiar face and figure in the anteroom, waiting to see Brophy.

"Why, hello, Jay," I said, "what brings you here?"

The man smirked sourly, but didn't answer. While he was with Brophy I happened, in speaking to Brophy's secretary, to refer to him as Jay Lovestone (expelled from the Communist party some years earlier, Lovestone was now operating a "Communist Party [Opposition]" of his own).

"That's not the name he's registered under at the Ambassador Hotel," she said.

"That's Jay for you!" said I.

After Lovestone had left, I went out to lunch with Brophy. "What did Lovestone have to say?" I asked.

"He warned me against you," said Brophy.

We laughed.

Chapter Seven

UNDER WAY—THE CIO UPRISING

*An idea's time had come. The workers were
on the move—or sitting down. They looked
to Lewis, and he did his best to see they
did. There were also other kinds of labor
leaders.*

After I went with CIO, Washington became more
than a white-collar capital to which the people sent stuffy ambassadors. I met the people coming themselves. They breezed
into town like men from the shops making downtown calls.
They shunned fancy spots for drugstore counters and lunchrooms. If hot, they took off coats and ties, and opened collars.

These were not like worker delegations of the early New
Deal—lost in governmental warrens, small under the Capitol
dome, gaping at the White House. Little interested in government and politicians, they were here to do things for themselves. They had a place of their own to go to—a person, rather.
The place wasn't the office of the Committee for Industrial Organization in the Rust Building, not at first. The name was a
mouthful, its initials not yet widely known.

These men had been told to "go see John L. Lewis and get
some action." At the Union Station they'd pile into a taxi and
tell the driver to take them to John L. Lewis. Washington taxi-
men were used to that sort of thing. This Lewis they knew.
They'd drive to the Tower Building, where the United Mine
Workers had its headquarters and Lewis, his office.

Later the UMW bought the University Club Building, and
Lewis got a big office there. The CIO kept moving to ever larger

headquarters. If asked to drive to the CIO, the average taxi driver would say: "CIO? Sure, that's John L. Lewis, ain't it?" He'd likely drive to the UMW Building.

Lewis didn't see many delegations at first. His office referred most to CIO Director John Brophy in the Rust Building. After trying to see such a big man, they found such a small man (physically anyhow) as Brophy a letdown. But he gave them service and was in close touch with Lewis.

I can't here call Brophy John—the way I thought of him— lest he be confused with Lewis whom few called John and none thought of that way. Yet none who knew the two would be confused. They were opposites. Brophy was short, and middle age had added little flesh to the slimness of his youth. Unassuming, he looked mousy next to the leonine Lewis. A prominent nose belied the mousiness, betraying an inquisitive and stubborn streak.

Small stature made some touchy, bumptious, disposed to strut like Napoleon, their secret paragon. Brophy was too smart for that. He capitalized on lack of grandeur—a homey man of the people, like any Tom, Dick, or Harry—though not cocky like Harry Truman, say. He didn't try to bull his way. Least of all did Brophy strut. Lewis could strut sitting down.

For all their prior conflict, Brophy and Lewis got along well at start of CIO. Brophy appreciated that, unlike others, Lewis hadn't underrated him or pulled his punches. He was also of a type to fit with Lewis.

Lewis tended to shrink his associates—inevitably more than deliberately. I recall how it felt to sit on the back seat of an auto with Lewis. The spread of the man was enormous. I didn't really have to shrink to fit in. I just felt shrunken. Brophy came to his CIO job pre-shrunk.

Fierce as he often seemed to be, Lewis relaxed with the mild and retiring. When W. Jett Lauck, the economist, paid a rare visit, Lewis's face lit up with pleased affection. He was also fond of Walter Smethurst, his CIO assistant; J. Raymond Bell, a brother-in-law, who became CIO Comptroller; and Cecil Owen, a newspaperman hired for Labor's Non-Partisan League who later became UMW editor. These men were kindly and rather shy.

Lewis knew Brophy was only outwardly mild, and he never quite let down his guard. Brophy feared Lewis less than did most. He'd taken punishment from Lewis—which he didn't want repeated; but he'd lived to tell the tale. Brophy knew Lewis's intelligence, his power, his fighting trim—and his own subordination in the CIO setup. For all these reasons, he was loyal to Lewis at start of CIO. They worked hand in glove. The hand was Lewis's, but the glove prettied it for some who'd seen it bare and clenched.

There was another reason—a common commitment. When Lewis asked if I was "for what we're trying to do," I'd taken it as a formality. I soon realized that Lewis's generosity to former foes was starting off CIO with a genuine feeling that "what we're trying to do" was more important than recriminations. Brophy felt it. So did I and many others.

Lewis made many fear him. How and why?

The undesigning had no cause to fear. With them, Lewis was usually sensitive and considerate. To those who would thwart him, he offered all the reasons for fear that he could devise. Such an autocrat as Lewis in the UMW bred loyal and/ or servile henchmen. If some were rather doglike, there were also many who genuinely admired the Old Man, The Boss, and followed him along strange paths more out of faith than from fear.

In CIO, I was to see many turn against Lewis. Those who had been closest to him found the peace of their subordination shattered by their first thought of defection. The rebel-in-thought-only affected fighting poses and was ready to box every shadow. If Lewis frowned, he turned and ran. Before a blow was struck, the defector was weaving around punch-drunk. After the bout, he could think and talk of little else. The lesser fry who turned against Lewis showed their fear in the exhibitionism of their defiances, the shrillness of their abuse.

Why all this fear? Lewis was no ogre, no wizard. He held no

life-and-death powers. He had a formidable scowl, wits quick as his fists, and a powerful determination to have his own way. Most of his other fearsome qualities were in the minds of his victims.

In the 1937 Chrysler negotiations, relates Saul Alinsky in his Lewis biography, the corporation's counsel, Nicholas Kelley, was so hostile and insulting that Lewis tried to cut him down to size. His words scorched Kelley so much that he jumped up and cried, "Stop it, stop it, Mr. Lewis!" and finally shouted: "Mr. Lewis, I want you to know, Mr. Lewis, that I-I-I am not afraid of your eyebrows."

Lewis had a sense of humor about the monster-image he presented to some. His dramatics were not unconscious revelations of a colossal ego, obvious enough without them. He designed them to create certain practical effects.

Lewis's sublimity might totter on the edge of the ridiculous. Many, from Ameringer on, tried to push it over. They never quite succeeded. Lewis didn't seem to care. The man posing on a high place who looks anxiously down may be due for a fall. The daring trapeze man who soars boldly aloft may break his back if he falls, but he isn't the butt of laughter.

Once, after CIO's victory over General Motors, I arrived with Lewis at a big Flint stadium. The crowd surged about him as he entered the spacious corridor around it. Instead of going to the platform, Lewis headed off in another direction. I decided to stick as close to him as I could. Hundreds of others were trying to do the same thing. At the head of this moving mass retinue, Lewis forged slowly ahead. When the procession came to a halt, I elbowed my way to an open entrance through which the head of Lewis had disappeared. There I reached the front row of the crowd, now standing back from him at a respectful distance.

They were watching solemnly—as the historic occasion demanded—while the great man relieved himself at a urinal. No one cracked a smile or a jest. Least of all Lewis. He zipped up his pants and washed his hands. Then he headed into the ranks of his admirers, which parted to let him lead the way in all majesty out of the men's room. The procession closed around Lewis again, as he forged back around the corridor to the platform.

Brophy helped Lewis unfurl the banners for the CIO crusade. Lewis was the mighty general to lead the hosts of labor against the bastions of Wall Street, dauntless and resolute. Less obviously, he was also the statesman, designing the policies he grandiloquently proclaimed. Brophy worked out organizational accommodations with a certain finesse. It helped that he seemed retiring, almost tentative. The militancy (sometimes radicalism) of the newly organizing workers needed to be given its head. Brophy was not of a mind or character to stand in its way. Lewis was of a mood to glory in it and to lead it right on.

The other top CIO leaders were less involved at first. Men of power and connections, they had ties with the AFL and the Roosevelt administration. They were wary of a possible fiasco. They wanted to be sure of success before plunging in with their men and their money. Lewis, too, held back, not to find himself alone. In its first half-year, the CIO as such was a modest operation, its organizers paid by the unions that loaned them. The first big splurge was the launching of the steel drive in June, 1936.

The workers were waiting for CIO, pounding on its doors long before CIO was ready for them. I heard the pounding as soon as I started work with CIO late in 1935—in delegations, on the phone, in the mail, in the news. It came from within the AFL, and from all the unorganized industries. From AFL locals and central bodies—beleaguered outposts of unionism—came sighs of relief and anticipation that reinforcements were on the way. In little-organized industries, union pioneers hailed CIO's advent and called for help. We heard from auto and rubber workers, seamen; from radio, electrical, shipyard, furniture, textile, steel, lumber, workers; from gas, coke, glass, and quarry workers, from sharecroppers, newspapermen. . . . All said, "CIO, let's go!"

The auto workers included veterans of struggles like the Toledo Autolite strike who had been in pitched battles against attacking troops. At UAW's second convention (South Bend, early in 1936), I saw it dump AFL controls and ready itself for CIO advance.

On the west coast, the Maritime Federation of the Pacific tried to keep alive the solidarity of the San Francisco general strike; and unionism was marching inland. East coast seamen laid the keel of the National Maritime Union, following the much-publicized "mutiny" on the S.S. *California* which brought pugnacious young Joe Curran to the fore.

Electrical and radio workers formed their new industrial union, the UE. It combined AFL radio locals with the independent Electrical & Radio Workers Union. Denied a charter by the AFL, it looked to CIO.

Rubber workers were giving a most significant come-on signal. They were sitting down—without waiting for CIO or caring if it approved.

The sitdown was the stratagem of the man on the job.

CIO strategists were once scratching their heads about one aspect of a plan of action, when Lewis chuckled: "Leave that to the men on the job. They'll find a way—they're ingenious about things like that." They were ingenious enough to initiate the tactic without which CIO might hardly have broken through and to add to it more wrinkles than the smartest swivel-chair leader could think up.

To the man on the conveyor line, the thing to do in a showdown was to pull the switch. All on that power line would have to stop working. If united on the beef, they'd stay stopped until it was settled. Meanwhile, in the nature of line production, a stoppage in one department would soon stop others—and the boss would be tearing his hair.

If the men just walked out, the boss could have his goons turn on the switch and guard it, and get foremen or scabs to keep things going.

If the men stayed in and sat down, couldn't the boss have his goons throw them out? Yes . . . and no. It's human to resent being thrown out, from your job, your livelihood. The stay-ins might resist. Now bosses don't always mind some resistance —outside their plants. "Teach 'em a lesson," you know. Only strikers and goons would get damaged. But think of a fight in the midst of all their delicate expensive machinery!

The workers, too, were concerned for the boss's machinery. In the many sitdowns of 1936-37, damage to plant equipment was negligible—caused less by the sit-downers than by actions against them. The sit-downers usually took disciplined precautions to guard against damage—on their own initiative, since sit-downs were the most rank-and-file of union actions.

In the 1920 sitdowns I saw in Italy, the workers ran up red flags, claimed the plants for the people, and tried to keep them running. The American sitdowners claimed the jobs were theirs, but not the plants. Significantly perhaps, they often acted as if the plants were also theirs.

Unauthorized and unexpected sitdowns by rank-and-file or unorganized rubber workers led up to the first big strike involving CIO, the five-week walkout of 14,000 workers at Goodyear's Akron plant. In subzero weather, the strikers patrolled 11 miles of fences and gates, with 68 improvised shanties to serve the longest picket line in labor history. They kept the plant closed and prevented serious violence. When so-called Law-and-Order mobsters threatened attack, the Akron Central Labor Union voted to counter with a general strike.

The settlement was enough of a victory to give the United Rubber Workers a big spurt. It was a good kickoff for CIO, which was quick to claim credit. Lewis had made his first major CIO speech in Akron. CIO contributed five experienced organizers and a few thousand dollars. Lewis pressured company chiefs behind the scenes. CIO deserved some credit.

But, as in the auto sitdowns and other job actions that got CIO rolling, the initial impetus came from the men on the job. Union pioneers, often radicals, long active among them, sparked the actions. Theirs was the idea whose time had come. CIO helped give it expression.

I was not in the shops where these winds were blowing. I was but a visitor to picket lines and occupied plants. Most of my duties were with union officers, delegations, meetings, conventions. But as I went out into the field, I got the feel. How to describe it?

Once on a sea voyage I met a young Arab seaman. He was a man of few—but well-chosen—words. He'd lived in Egypt. I asked how it was.

"Under the British and fat King Farouk," he said, "it was dark."

"Was it better after the revolution?" I asked.

"Oh, yes." His teeth flashed white. "Then it became light."

I asked what he meant. All he would say was:

"You could tell anyone off."

1936 and 1937 were years of liberation for American industrial workers. They felt as zestful as any newly liberated people.

I remembered how dark were the open shops of the Twenties—the factories, ships, steel mills, packinghouses, labor camps, I worked in. The worker could "tell anyone off" only if not overheard. He could argue his rights, but not on the job— there he had no rights. He could beef . . . and be told, "If you don't like it here, you know what you can do . . ." Now he could do other things besides quit.

Then, too, the worker could walk off the job—but alone and without hope of return. He could ask for more pay—and get his last paycheck. He could join a union—if no one found out. He could whisper about union into some conspiratorial ear— likely that of a company spy.

Still there were men and women brave enough to try to organize. They were the rebels, the reds. They were hounded, red-baited, fired, sometimes shot down. They became heartsick when fellow workers turned chicken, or turned on each other, or turned out to be provocateurs. Almost they came to believe that "workingmen will never stick together."

Now, in these very same plants where I had worked . . .

Once a man had to slink into the men's room to voice a beef—and flush the toilet lest his voice be heard. Now he and his buddies might wear union buttons right on the assembly line and stewards vie to fight for their beefs. Stop-work meetings might be held in the shop. If things got too bad, there might be a sitdown on the job, or a walkout from the job, with good prospects of walking in again. All this, and more money, too—higher wages, shorter hours, paid vacations and holidays, fringe benefits. All won because working people had learned to stick together.

Along with all this light, new light on the word "union."

To many workers, it had only meant potbellied grafters with diamond stickpins—little cliques of gravy-train snobs with a corner on cushy jobs—high initiation fees, long apprentice-ships, rituals, all sorts of tricks to avoid sharing the goodies. Or highbinders in Washington or New York making deals with government and companies for a dues kickback from workers' wages in return for keeping labor down.

A strong CIO point was to disclaim responsibility for what AFL unions had been or done, to proclaim that a CIO union was different. It wasn't always so. But where new unions grew from the bottom up, as could happen now, their leaders were close to the ranks from which they sprang. The workers might have a union they could call their own.

There was light after darkness in the youth of the move-ment—youth that was direct and bold in action, not sluggish and sly from long compromise with the old and the rotten. There was light in the hopeful future seen by the red and rebel-lious, now playing their full part in what they held to be a great working-class advance against the capitalist class. There was light, and a heady happy feeling, in the solidarity of common struggle in a splendid common cause.

Here a paradox, not without parallel in newly liberated lands. The man who symbolized all this light breaking through darkness was a bigbellied, oldtime labor leader in his late fifties. An autocrat, per capita counter, egotist, power seeker, with none of the altruistic evangelism of a Gene Debs. He was a man who had bowed the knee to capitalism, who had been merciless against the red and rebellious.

There's more to be said about this John L. Lewis.

Relations with the AFL were a nuisance at first. AFL for-malities delayed much organizing. To appease his top CIO asso-ciates, Lewis had to go through tiresome, frustrating gestures to unity. It was a break for him and CIO, when in the fall of 1936, the AFL executive council suspended the CIO unions. But still unity maneuvers had to continue.

In launching CIO, Lewis had kindled hope in the shops for a real organizing drive. Each sign of CIO and AFL getting to-gether brought slump and discouragement. Some independent industrial unions, as in electrical and shipyard, couldn't get into AFL and couldn't join CIO while it toed the AFL line. Many newly organizing workers didn't want into AFL at any price—or wanted out for more freedom, if temporarily in.

The AFL got a poor image during the early New Deal organizing ferment. It was identified with the paunchy lounge-lizard "organizer" who redbaited union militants, exposed the union to craft raids, forebade or broke strikes, denounced sit-downs, counseled timid submission.

Lewis had to tread a tightrope—a strange simile for one then usually likened to a bull in a china shop. On the one hand, to pacify treasuried associates like Dubinsky, insistent on keeping within AFL limits, he had to make gestures toward reuniting with AFL. On the other hand—and more important to him—Lewis had to guard against discouraging the newly organizing. He had to convey to them that CIO was going ahead with its drive, regardless of "unity" hocus-pocus.

Lewis was actually subtle in his crudities, his abrupt and rough defiances of the AFL, his insolences, as when he offered to make Green CIO chairman at the same "honorarium" as he got from the AFL. Once, criticized by Dubinsky, Lewis burst out that his associates had wanted him not for a diplomat but as a "man with a meat-ax." They did and they didn't. His axlike swings often appalled them. But they also had some carnivorous interest in the products of his meat-cleaving.

In his publicity, Lewis favored the kind of one-two punch he gave Big Bill. Few Madison Avenue firms would have counseled such verbal fisticuffs as good public relations. But their specialty was soft-soaping the public for big corporations. Lewis was on the other side of the class struggle. His technique suited his fighting image. It helped him speak, over the heads of timorous colleagues and reeling AFL leaders, directly to the workers he wanted to lead into battle.

With Washington liberals, it could be hard to defend Lewis's thrusts. When I went out among working people, I learned that (1) they'd read or heard what he said—as they wouldn't have, had he been "diplomatic"; (2) his words had meaning for them; (3) they usually chuckled or applauded. After one set-to with Washington bellyachers, I took the train to Philadelphia and grabbed a taxi. The driver, unaware of my connection, said:

"You see what John L. Lewis said?"

"No," I lied, "what was it?"

He recited the piece of truculence that had so upset the eggheads. He did so with relish, personalizing it even more than Lewis had done. I asked what he thought of it.

"Me?" said he. "I should give a damn. That Lewis got some good ideas. But I don't take sides."

The driver turned to me, and while I winced at the traffic hazards, he bubbled: "You know this Lewis fight against the AFn'L . . . it's the best break the workin' man's had. Nobody give a damn for us before. Now we got two outfits bustin' a gut for us."

Brophy and I hit it off. We ate together, traveled together, sought each other out to compare notes. I helped in his troubleshooting, in forming and affiliating new union groups. When he couldn't be in two places, he'd send me to one. It got so that Brophy once wanted to formalize my position as his organizational assistant.

Perhaps I was wrong in thinking Brophy so closely akin to myself during the first two years of CIO. A dozen years later, I took my leave of a CIO becoming as flat as stale beer from a Cold War banquet. I dropped in to say goodby to Brophy. We had long drifted apart, but I hoped in parting to revive memories of the zip and effervescence of CIO's big bubble-up.

"Those were great days, John, weren't they?" I said.

"These are still great days for CIO," he replied.

I shut up.

Brophy was 16 years older than I. Maybe I credited him with too much of my own relatively youthful enthusiasm. But we were closely attuned. Reading his posthumous autobiography, I hardly recognized the man I knew.

His account of childhood and youth in the coalfields rang true. A serious inquiring youngster reaching out for a broad labor program—trade union, labor party, and more. But in his leadership life, he takes pains to dissociate himself from socialists to whom he was close, saying he always eschewed "Marxist materialism," and that the Papal *Rerum Novarum* was his lodestar. He makes retroactive the anticommunism of his later years; and continuous, an anti-Lewisism markedly absent at start of CIO.

Brophy was a devout Catholic, but one who bolstered my belief that religious differences need not divide the workers. When his church leaders mixed into CIO politics, he resented it, he told me. Naturally he was pleased, as was I, when some aided the workers' cause, though this happened seldom enough considering how many CIO members were Catholics.

With or without mental reservations—he expressed none to me—Brophy promoted the left-to-right unity of CIO's first years. He opposed the redbaiting factionalists who tried to divide it. He resisted many pressures to sift out communists and fellow-traveling militants.

In CIO's formation, Brophy and I met with scores of delegations representing new union groupings. It was his job to assess their character and potential, and to advise Lewis if they should get the CIO nod. Frequently the leaders of these applicant unions included communists, alleged communists, or lefts said to play along with the communists. If Brophy didn't know this already, he was soon warned by shrill telephone calls or by factional counter-delegations.

This was more rule than exception. If top officers were obviously not leftwing, there were usually signs, or claims, that lesser officers or subsections were under communist influence. There were few areas of new organization where lefts didn't exert some influence by being among the first, most active, and most militant in union organizing.

Brophy was not personally procommunist, nor was he then anticommunist—that came later. He was a fair judge of character and integrity, and of union strength, sentiment, potential. Lewis had used him for such appraisals, around mining, before giving him the CIO job. The choices Brophy had to make were not hard for a practical trade unionist. A closely knit group of able responsible militants would present itself, representing some actual organization and labeled leftwing. Contesting their claims might be a motley faction of ex-communists, rightwing socialists, and the like with little to offer but a consuming hatred of communists.

Brophy gave his nod—as Lewis would likely have done anyhow—to those who could contribute most to CIO strength. He discounted the redbaiting charges, partly because he didn't believe them; partly because he didn't care; partly because he opposed the divisive factionalism they reflected.

In our intimate evaluations, Brophy and I nearly always agreed. He held it no shame for a union leader to be called a communist. I deemed it a compliment, suggesting a unionist in principle with a broader labor loyalty than the company-loving conservative or the shifty opportunist. To some of the maligned lefts, I doubtless gave too much credit—judging from some of the subsequent somersaults from left to right.

I recall but one disagreement—over the rival claims of Harry Lundeberg and Harry Bridges on the west coast. I favored Bridges; Brophy did not, arguing that Bridges was too AFL-minded at the time. When Lewis threw his weight to Bridges, Brophy claimed it was because Lundeberg misplayed his hand— threatening to go AFL if Lewis didn't accept his terms. Lewis was not of a mood to bow to such an ultimatum.

CIO rightwingers blamed Brophy for the many leftwing union affiliations. They didn't dare criticize Lewis, whose name and repute were still sacrosanct in CIO. A close associate of Sidney Hillman asked me to lunch in New York to pump me, I felt sure, for his boss. While consulting other leaders on broad issues, Lewis kept CIO administration in his own hands, with Brophy his factotum on detail. Hillman was curious on some of the detail. His man complained that Brophy leaned too far to the left, and quoted his chief: "I can understand having to use communists to reach some union groups, but Brophy goes out *looking* for communists!"

By the time of CIO's first national conference—at Atlantic City in the fall of 1937—Hillman had mellowed. The leftwing unions had made substantial gains; the maligned lefts had proved capable organizers and leaders. Hillman now tried to sort the sheep from the goats. Joe Curran—often cantankerous in his leftism—was then held "one of the worst of the communists." Hillman had a private session with him and reported enthusiastically: "Joe is a good boy, a real good boy. He has to act red in his setup. But he's all right. We can handle Joe."

Rough in his public pose, Curran was smooth in personal relations with CIO's top leaders. So were some other lefts. But I don't recall anyone ever saying Harry Bridges could be handled —any more than Lewis.

In his book of afterthoughts, Brophy said he was much influenced by Cardinal Newman's *Apologia Pro Vita Sua*. I liked the title's suggestion of apologizing for one's life. Most of us should; we could have done better. But we don't have to do it like a prisoner conducting his own defense.

A decade after he left CIO, and five years after I did, I heard Lewis make a long speech to a UMW convention, ranging over his career. I got an uncomfortable feeling this was an "apology" for his life before the court of current opinion. Lewis omitted or played down the parts I liked best. I felt like rising from the press table to object. Tom Kennedy in the chair, a long-ago socialist, may have had like thoughts. He grinned and waved to me, an unexpected gesture to an unredeemed red like me, then in that outer darkness intended for weeping and wailing and gnashing of teeth. I wanted to object to the court that prisoner's words should not be used in evidence against him; more qualified counsel should plead his case.

Similarly with Brophy's Apologia . . . Brophy ended his life in a period when anticommunism was in vogue—nay, compulsory. Knowing he must soon vanish into the mists, alone, he clung to the hand of Mother Church. He had his reasons, his rights—the right to change his mind. But how about the rights of that John Brophy whom I knew intimately, respected highly, and liked most warmly in 1936-37?

I know how it is. There may come a sore that eats and festers into a vital part of us. It has to be cut out. The skin must be joined again—the before in time with the after. At the once healthy spot, all that shows is a scar. Both Lewis and Brophy carried scars.

CIO was often compared with the British New Unionism that broke away from a Trades Union Congress Old Guard as craftist and conservative as the AFL. In 1888, strikes of match and gas workers led up to the Great Dock Strike that paralyzed the port of London, and in the next year 200,000 unskilled workers—deemed unorganizable by the Old Guard—joined the new union ranks. Union revivalism led to independent labor political action.

Leaders of the New Unionism were the reds of the day—socialists like John Burns, Tom Mann, Ben Tillett, Keir Hardie, Karl Marx's daughter, Eleanor Marx, and her husband, Edward Aveling. Their broad working-class appeal aroused workers unreached by a narrow craft business approach.

In America's new-unionism sweep, it was similarly natural that communists should be to the fore. Rather than Lewis, a man like Eugene Debs, William Z. Foster, Big Bill Haywood, might have been expected to lead. Debs did, in fact, lead industrial organizing and big strikes in the United States at the time of the British New Unionism. Haywood was the most militant working-class leader of his time. Foster's big 1917-19 packing and steel drives were the most immediate precursors of the CIO campaign. But Lewis was ostensibly no more than a pragmatic business unionist.

Few now challenged the business-union concept that a union's job was to get what it could for the workers under capitalism as against the IWW idea of continuous conflict with bosses until capitalism was overthrown. The workers wanted results here and now. If they also wanted to change society, they were more likely to look to political action than to their union. This business unionism was based, in effect, on class submission. It didn't challenge the capitalists' control of industry. It struck to win from them an agreement.

In periods of acute capitalist crisis, doubts might arise. Failure to challenge capitalist control might lead to taking lower wages, for instance, for the sake of capitalist stability. Then more far-reaching class struggle to win power for labor might make sense to many. But CIO was launched in a period of relative recovery from an acute crisis. There was little real challenge to capitalist control. Business unionism was the order of the day. There were different kinds of business unionists, however.

The narrow one-craft kind was declining, as new methods of

production made it ever harder to define a pure craft. But the ideology and practices persisted among leaders who ran their unions like business associations, job trusts, based on limitation of membership, and often with a reactionary business mentality. Yet the member craftsman was not a businessman, but a wage worker who'd had to fight the employers for most of his benefits, and radical sentiment was sometimes strong in the ranks.

The Hutcheson-Tobin kind of union leader headed a multi-craft union. The hundred thousands enrolled in Carpenters or Teamsters didn't all drive nails or teams. Seeking ever more per capita and power, these leaders went after all the dues payers they could get. More political than the one-craft kind, they traded their influence—Hutcheson to the Republicans, Tobin to the Democrats.

The industrial unionists represented workers of all kinds in a given industry. They had to mobilize them as workers, with appeal to labor solidarity, rather than by trade or occupation. Leading more of a mass movement than the crafts, they came up more against government and legislation and were the most political segment.

Union-leader types—as seen in CIO, though most could also be found in AFL—broke down into the "pure-and-simple" kind; the Murray kind; the Hillman-Dubinsky kind; the "communist" kind.

The pure-and-simple claimed to be practical business unionists without ideological or political commitment. The claim didn't stand up. All union leaders were in politics of one kind or another up to their necks. All were influenced by current ideologies. The pure-and-simple leader in effect disclaimed interest in distinctively labor ideologies, preferring those prevalent in a capitalist society. He might react less as a labor man than as a Catholic, Protestant, Jew; a Democrat or Republican, a white or male chauvinist, a patrioteer, a Mason or a K of C.

With emotion, Philip Murray once told me he hated ideologies and had no ideology himself. He meant radical ideologies, of course. Actually he was so committed to one labor ideology I here name it for him.

Though spending most of his life in the shadow of Lewis, Murray had his own distinctly different style. In the Steelworkers and as CIO president, he hewed predictably to the line of a labor philosophy that was broadly social-reformist in character, though shying away from socialistic implications. It called for reforms within the capitalist structure, without challenging capitalism itself. As a devout and disciplined Catholic, Murray based his philosophy on church doctrine, as he understood it. Murray's wartime Industry Council Plan—for tripartite government-employer-labor councils in each industry—was designed to fit in with Papal perspectives of reconciling labor and capital under more orderly and humane capitalist conditions.

Sidney Hillman and David Dubinsky were rivals with many differences. Yet they may be bracketed as social-democratic or social-reformist leaders, who started at least with certain working-class premises looking eventually to change "the system." Deemed social sophisticates, the Hillman-Dubinsky school were unblushingly class collaborative in their business unionism, but plugged hard for labor political action. Many supported the Socialist party until it disappeared from practical politics, then turned to various labor, farmer-labor, LaFollette-type, third-party projects. Roosevelt and his New Deal so enraptured them that they came to rest at last, for most practical purposes, on the broad bosom of the Democratic party.

Such social reformists followed a coherent course. At first they pushed reforms as steps toward socialism, then made reforms an end in themselves, seeking capitalist support for them. Finally, they became integrated into the capitalist establishment, as its labor experts, and dropped the socialist goal altogether.

The Murray group called the Hillman group "pinkos"; and were called "conservatives" in their turn. In practice, they became little different. Murray (when Lewis wasn't looking) and Hillman reacted similarly on major issues. In CIO, the Murray kind were mostly Catholic, the Hillman-Dubinsky kind, often Jewish. The religious angle was coincidental. Many non-Catholic leaders shared Murray's labor philosophy without knowing or caring if it had Catholic origins. Still less was the Hillman-Dubinsky social reformism Jewish. In England, most labor leaders were social reformists of this kind, as were the social democrats of western

Europe, and German immigrants carried the idea to the United States.

I use quotes for the "communist" kind of union leaders, not that there weren't real communists among them, but to include those who were not and who still were driven out of CIO because so tagged. I would also dodge argument as to what might or might not have been a correct communist line.

In day-to-day conduct of union affairs, the "communists" practiced much the same business unionism as other union leaders—trying, that is, to win maximum benefits for their members under the conditions and within the limitations of the capitalist system.

Quizzing Murray privately about communists in CIO before a radio interview in 1946, Martin Agronsky pinned him down to Ben Gold, of the Fur & Leather Workers, the one CIO union president who was an acknowledged member of the Communist party. "Mr. Gold is an estimable gentleman," Murray replied. "He runs an excellent union along sound trade union lines. He is highly regarded by the employers of his industry." Murray, critical of the ethics of some non-left unions, could have said as much of most CIO "communist-led" unions—with variables no doubt in respect to the employers' regard.

Under a constant searchlight of redbaiting hostility from press, employers, and opposing union factions, the "communists" had to meet higher standards than most union leaders in respect to honesty, democracy, businesslike operation, militancy, and results. Because they proclaimed higher principles, their lapses were more harshly judged.

Inner-union democracy was not one of CIO's Ten Commandments. Lewis, who had fought long and hard to centralize control over his own union, cautioned new unions against rank-and-filism. Murray, in Steel, ran things from the top down. Hillman tried to do the same in Textile. The tumultuous democracy of the early Auto Workers horrified CIO's big shots. They'd have liked a top-controlled Organizing Committee, as in Steel and Textile. The boisterous auto workers jumped the gun on them.

The "communists," the left, did most to push rank-and-file

democracy, and made many newly organizing workers think it one of CIO's cardinal principles. The CIO bigs found it unwise to repudiate the thought. They were in the fix that Lewis put Roosevelt in in 1933, when his UMW organizers proclaimed, "The Presdient wants you to join the union." What could FDR do—say he didn't want them to join? He kept his mouth shut. So did the CIO bigs. The idea made a hit. It helped "communists" to get elected, and in office they were sharply watched for any breaches of this "CIO principle."

In regard to switches of line due to outside influence—a common charge against the "communists"—this did not greatly differentiate them from other union leaders. Most CIO leaders were highly political and made their unions switch line at the behest of the Washington administration, to adjust to changes in national and foreign policy, and, in some cases, just to be sure they were on the opposite side to the communist line.

The "communists," in fact, shared many common procedures with other union leaders. The left-led unions distinguished themselves chiefly insofar as they were less corrupt, more democratic, more principled about their members' and general labor interests. On the rights and opportunities of black workers, for instance, the "communists" were usually far ahead of the rest of the labor movement.

The distinctions were often a matter of degree. Was there a more categorical difference? Considering the Currans, Quills, and their like who switched from reds to redbaiters at the call of the Cold War, one might argue there was not. They fitted into the social-reformist category, where such transition was the rule, though usually not quite so abrupt. But there were less opportunistic lefts, with a distinct philosophy.

These held essentially to the concept of a working class capable of transforming society. While usually scrupulous about the immediate concerns of their members, these "communists" tried to relate union policies to the interests of the working class. Other leaders related union policies to wider interests—to those of AFL or CIO, for instance, to national, Democratic party, New Deal, or more special interests. The "communists" stressed a national and worldwide working-class interest.

In following, paralleling or approximating the line of the

Communist party on broad policy issues, the "communists" were not alone. They joined with—and some themselves were—mild progressives, even conservatives, since the CP tried to formulate a line of widest appeal. They were also union leaders, with a primary responsibility to their own members and limited to policies they would adopt, or at least tolerate. They adapted the line to their union's concerns. If the two conflicted, the line had to bulge or yield.

John L. Lewis didn't fall into any of the categories listed. In the AFL, he had gone along with the Hutcheson-Tobin group, accepting the formulations Woll and Frey drafted for it. When he made his CIO turn, he dumped them as unceremoniously as his other ties with the AFL Old Guard. He didn't adopt any of the social-reformist, radical, religious, capitalistic philosophies current in the labor movement.

Lewis became a puzzle to the eggheads. After CIO hit the jackpot, deep-thinking journalists came seeking to learn his philosophy. Some consulted me before or after interviews. Lewis charmed and excited them. He cleared their minds of preconceptions, but offered little in their place. In the afterglow of the Lewis presence, some thrilled to a rolling Lewisism. When they wrote it down, somehow only the rhythm remained.

Only negatively was I sure of Lewis. As CIO leader, he no longer expressed—except possibly in some private grumbles—any of the antediluvian Coolidge-Hooverisms of his early battles against the socialists. He was too complex and unrestricted to be a pure-and-simple unionist. He was not a Hillman-Dubinsky nor a Murray social reformist; not a communist, nor yet a "communist." He carried a minimum of ideological baggage.

Religion preoccupied Lewis (unlike Murray) so little that I had worked long with him before I even became curious. Then a reporter started it, by asking questions I couldn't answer about Lewis and religion. I went to Lewis. "Tell him nothing," he said. "He's on a fishing expedition."

In all the writings about Lewis, I recall only one religious reference—in the gossipy little C.L. Sulzberger book, *Sit Down with John L. Lewis*. It asserted that Lewis's mother was a member of the Reformed Mormon Church; that he was "reared in piety and went to Sunday School"; that "later he became an agnostic." That was all.

As to liberal and radical schools of thought, Lewis liked to give the impression he was well read. If so, his readings were not decisive. Lewis was intelligent and discerning. But his mind ran to practical politics, personal psychology, conclusions from his own experience and observations, rather than to theories absorbed from books.

In the fighting which was Lewis's political way of life, his lack of philosophical baggage gave him an advantage. He could move fast in any direction, and his enemies were seldom sure which it would be.

Philosophically, in that moment of history, Lewis might have been likened to a horn waiting to be blown. A blast of air from CIO's new millions filled the horn, and it tooted loud and strong. In bidding CIO organizers go forth boldly, Lewis liked to use the saying, "He who tooteth not his own horn, the same shall not be tooted." Himself he single-mindedly identified his own horn with that of UMW or CIO. He tooted.

Man matched movement. Lewis responded to the mood of millions fighting for union; they responded to him. They wanted the benefits business unionism could bring, but couldn't win them through the narrow business separatism of AFL crafts. The industrial form was not in itself enough; it had to be filled out by fight. They were up against billion-dollar corporations, an embattled capitalist class. They fought for union in a class spirit.

In the General Motors sitdown strike of the 1936-37 winter, steelworkers, coal miners, rubber and glass workers, swept into Flint from afar to aid the auto workers. In major CIO struggles, as in a general strike, the workers reacted as members of a working class in combat. Unorganized workers of all kinds tried to get into the nearest CIO union, regardless of name or industry. They just wanted to "join the CIO." It was a mass movement with a message, revivalistic in fervor, militant in mood, joined together by class solidarity.

As it gained momentum, this movement brought with it new political attitudes—toward the corporations, toward police and troops, toward local, state, national, government. Now we're a movement, many workers asked, why can't we move on to more and more? Today we've forced almighty General Motors to terms by sitting down and defying all the powers at its command, why can't we go on tomorrow, with our numbers, our solidarity, our determination, to transform city and state, the Washington government itself? Why can't we go on to create a new society with the workers on top, to end age-old injustices, to banish poverty and war?

Many started on this line of thinking; not many followed it through. Few dared to go so far, so far ahead. Those few in CIO's first years were respected as prophets (as once was Debs) rather than hounded as crackpot reds. For they were among the pioneers of union initiative within the plants. They were the sparks that helped light the fire of struggle. Without them, CIO would have had fewer flames to feed with its oil, and later to douse with its lukewarm water.

Powers Hapgood had felt the back of Lewis's hand. Lewis goons had beaten him up in earlier UMW days. Lewis enlisted him in the CIO drive. When Lewis and Murray split, Hapgood stayed with Murray's CIO. Before he died, Hapgood said to Saul Alinsky of Lewis: "He is a great leader. The other so-called labor leaders I have worked under are like children compared to John. He can set you afire, he is the greatest of them all."

No other leaders at hand could have led the CIO uprising of 1936-37 as did Lewis; they couldn't have "set you afire." Craftism aside, no Woll, Green, Hutcheson, had any fire to impart. Hillman had a certain subdued fire; Murray a few well-controlled embers. They and their social-reformist colleagues would have temporized with the AFL to start with. They'd have lacked Lewis's ax-like will to cut through all restraints.

The social-reformist tended to be even duller and less scrappy than the more earthy pure-and-simple unionist. He had rationalized his accommodations into a philosophy of gradualism and piecemeal reform. A compromiser, an adjuster, he typically counseled moderation. A disorderly challenge to the existing order upset his concept of progress. In turbulent times, he became agitated and shaky, if not chicken. Lewis was no philosophical social reformist. He was not chicken.

Philip Murray was a high type of conventional labor leader —intelligent, experienced, with some vision. After he became CIO president, I tried dutifully to give his speeches the kind of play I'd given to Lewis's. But Murray's speeches seldom made news, and they lacked the fire of the old maestro. A Lewis CIO speech might be windy, but it always blew battle. It could suggest goals "over the hills and far away." Lewis didn't spell them out. Maybe his unlimited style, and his lack of limit-setting to the workers, caused the listener to create his own goals. Murray depicted the workers' advance to "carpets on the floor, pictures on the wall, and music in the home"—but not much further. He kept his goals carefully within the confines of the existing social system. He opened prospects comforting to men of moderation and good will, but . . . ho-hmnh!

Charisma depends for its impact upon people looking for its kind of spell. For his CIO time and crowd, Lewis had that charisma. Once CIO won all that capitalism would allow it—an assigned subordinate place in the capitalist scheme of things—less charismatic leaders took over. Sitdowns and mass struggle gave way to union administration, dues collection, labor-board briefs, detailed negotiation. The swivel-chair tribe began its own long-lasting sitdown in union office. This tribe rode to office on the broad shoulders of Lewis and the backs of the agitators, the militants, the reds. Once arrived they turned—dutifully, patriotically, devoutly—to kick in the face those on whom and over whom they had scrambled up.

The CIO uprising shook up conservative labor theorists, but after 1937 they recomposed themselves. In a first breakthrough to unionism, they held, it was hard to avoid some disorderly struggle and some radical guff. But once the law and the employers accepted collective bargaining, order reasserted itself. Union leaders could consolidate their machines, discipline their members, and collaborate in orderly bargaining procedures. The class struggle, if such it had been, was at an end.

Into this complacency, a little doubt may retrospectively intrude. How much might the workers have fought for and won, if

they'd heard only wheedling voices: "Now, now, boys . . .
Don't, don't, don't . . . Watch out for reds . . . Respect authority, trust the Governor, the President . . . Capitalism's okay,
let's make it work . . . Don't be mean to the boss, we want to
work with him . . . Don't try to change things too much . . .
Thus far, boys, but no further." In short, how might things have
gone without the reds in the ranks and a John L. Lewis blowing
off his big bazoo?

Lewis surprised everyone by the way he adjusted to the class
militancy of the radicals. It suited the mood of insurgent workers, to which mood Lewis instinctively attuned himself. The
Murrays, Hillmans, even some AFL leaders, weren't dumb about
radicals. In organizing, they used them where necessary. The
needle unions had used revolutionaries, socialists, anarchists,
poets even, to get things started—for the bureaucrats to take
over. The trouble in the Thirties was that radicals meant communists—horrors! Other CIO top leaders were scared stiff,
scared silly, of the communists rallying to CIO, until Lewis bade
them be brave.

History books are full of hypocrisy, evasions, and lies about
the communists in CIO and elsewhere. The lies are from union
factions that fought the left for their piecards. The evasions are
to cover the past of reds who became antireds and sometimes to
protect the communists. The hypocrisy is to shield the respectables who played footsy with the communists. Everyone in labor
or progressive politics played footsy with the communists at
some time or in some way. A rule of the game was that the communist player should not proclaim his communism. That way
the respectable, if caught at it, could say with shocked innocence, "Good gracious, we never knew he was a communist!"

Workers repeatedly elected communists to union office. Not
that many were communists themselves, they just liked the reds
as union leaders. In Britain, the union candidate who was a
communist usually proclaimed the fact; it often helped him get
elected. In the United States, few could indulge in such frank-
ness. It wasn't a matter of putting something over. Lefts who admitted to being communists usually won along with the rest of

the slate, if the slate won; those who didn't were so redbaited anyhow by the opposition, it might have made little difference if they had. American legal and extralegal penalties on communists imposed the reticence. Some camouflage was necessary as communists moved into battle for progressive causes. It was expected, if not demanded, by the allies they battled alongside.

Not only liberals played footsy, conservatives might try it, too, to reach people over whom the reds had influence. The politician who wouldn't touch communists with a ten-foot pole looked for other-length poles. The old-line AFL leaders got mad at the communists for playing hotfoot instead of footsy. They too welcomed communist aid when they needed or could get it. In the spillover from the CIO upsurge, communists helped build up some AFL as well as CIO unions. All the CIO leaders worked, or played, with communists at some time or in some way.

Dubinsky might seem an exception. He drew the line at Communist-party communists and sympathizers. To substitute, he succored and cherished other brands of alleged communists, especially ex-communists. Even he coexisted for a time with orthodox communists, in the American Labor party.

Murray used the help of communists extensively in the steel drive. He played ball with them all through the Second World War. He turned against them decisively only when Cold War was declared.

Hillman was on-again, off-again, on-again with the communists . . . depending in the Twenties on whether they were for or against himself; in the Thirties and Forties, on how they stood on the Roosevelt policies.

Lewis had the most consistent anticommunist record—until he launched CIO. Then, as any sensible leader would have done, he accepted the proffered help of an influential element in his new field. Lewis distinguished himself not by doing this, but in the way he did it.

Had the Hillmans and Murrays called the tune, they would have haggled for maximum help at minimum price, applied heresy tests to the help, conspired with anticommunist factions sprouting wherever the lefts gained influence. Publicly preaching anticommunism, they would have given private pats to communists who helped for nothing, or whom they hoped to buy off. In Steel, Textile, and other areas under the Murray-Hillman kind of control, such anticommunist intrigue was common—under cover at first. When Murray and Hillman were delegated CIO authority to reconcile UAW differences, they injected this approach into Auto too. Lewis did not instigate it. The broad sweep of his initial leadership discouraged it, and for some time kept would-be redbaiters under cover, if not under control.

Lewis threw out his arms to welcome all who could or would help CIO. He gave credit, where due, on the basis of performance. He wasn't finicky about a man's shade of pink or red, if he was a fighter in the ranks. Opposing redbaiting division, Lewis emphasized all that united the movement and gave it a crusading spirit. In this first outbreak of the CIO uprising at least, he tried to arouse the ambition of the working class, not to curb it.

Chapter Eight

OVER THE TOP—
THE GM SITDOWN STRIKE

*The General Motors sitdown strike put
CIO across. It shed light on extraordinary
ferment in a remarkable union . . .
during the period of CIO's greatest
struggle and glory.*

"A month," said the man from Wall Street.

"Six months," said John L. Lewis. Jaw clamped, he rolled over in bed.

The man from Wall Street could study a mountainous back in striped flannel pajamas, a tousled mane on the pillows. What else could he do? How bargain with a man on his sickbed who has turned away? Try to make him roll back? Go around the bed and say, "Look here——"? Sympathize, "There, there"? John Thomas Smith must have thought it a most unfair labor practice for Lewis to get sick at a time like this.

Lewis knew what one could do. Three years later, Franklin D. Roosevelt received him in bed at the White House for their last meeting. They couldn't agree. The President turned his head away. Lewis put out his hand. Roosevelt shook it, but kept his head averted. "Goodby, Mr. President," said Lewis, and walked out.

But Smith didn't want to say, "Goodby, Mr. Lewis," and walk out. He'd come to Lewis's bedside in the Detroit Statler Hotel to end the 1936-37 General Motors strike. The Du Ponts had sent him, as GM general counsel, to supersede the too-human William Knudsen. He had his orders from Wall Street.

At first Smith had been coldly upstage, impersonal, as became a soulless corporation. Lewis set out to break him down. He cleared his throat, glared at Smith, glanced down between their chairs. "What's the matter?" asked Smith. "Move your chair closer," said Lewis, "so I can tell my grandchildren how close I once sat to one and a half billion dollars."

Now this one and a half billion was leaning right over Lewis's bed. But Lewis had turned his back; it'd have to come closer yet. It did. It settled the strike with a six-month, not one-month, sole bargaining agreement.

Earlier, Roosevelt, with Hillman at his side, had telephoned Lewis urging a one-month agreement, which GM might concede. Lewis brought Wyndham Mortimer, UAW leader, in on the call. Mortimer had checked with the men sitting down in the plants. He and they knew the union needed at least six months to consolidate itself. Mortimer could clamp his jaw like Lewis. It clamped—after he reported the men would sit till hell froze rather than settle for less than six months. "One thing I like about you fellows," said Lewis, "you sure know what you want." Lewis did too.

I was in Lewis's suite that night, among UAW men sprawled all over a bedroom. The day had started in a drafty old courthouse. The GM men wouldn't take off their overcoats, said they were leaving. Governor Frank Murphy barely averted a breakup. When they got down to business, Knudsen nudged Mortimer and kidded: "This is a hell of a committee—three lawyers, a coal miner, and only us two auto workers." Besides Smith, the lawyers were G. Donaldson Brown, a son-in-law of the duPonts; and Lee Pressman, Lewis's CIO sidekick. When Lewis, pleading sick, left for his hotel, it was agreed to settle things there. Knudsen and Mortimer were to agree on plants to be covered; Brown and Pressman settle legal issues; Lewis and Smith decide the key question of contract duration.

To us who waited, it was as if Wall Street had come to Lewis's bedside to surrender. Far from unconditionally, of course; it still ruled the land. But its wealthiest corporation had conceded defeat on union recognition. Ordinary working stiffs had beaten it. They just sat down and would not be moved. If at this strongpoint, CIO had breached Wall Street's antiunion walls, might not all of them soon come tumbling down? It was a night of extraordinary triumph.

Lewis had rubbed it in to Smith as to a cartoonist's silk-hatted, big-bellied Wall Streeter with dollar sign on hat and vest. Smith had protested he'd "worked his way up." "Started as a newsboy, no doubt," quipped Lewis. "Yes, and worked my way through college," said Smith. Once the deal was made Smith, to show he had the common touch, came to hobnob with the roughneck auto workers who lay in wait. Tall, slim, aristocratic G. Donaldson Brown couldn't unbend so easily. Unlike Smith, he got his start by marrying the boss's daughter. He waved and withdrew. The stockier Smith lingered, and got stuck.

The man who stuck him was John Brophy. Smith risked a pleasantry as he entered our room. It reminded Brophy of an anecdote—with a beginning, an elastic middle, and no apparent end. We didn't mind. Everybody talked about Wall Street. Only rarely was it personalized—as when J.P. Morgan found a midget on his lap at a congressional hearing. Wall Street had come to Detroit in the cold impersonality of a Brown and a Smith. Now we could study this Mr. Wall Street in person, at closeup. It was a rare confrontation. We didn't care how long it lasted.

During most of the strike Brophy had his hands full, carrying the ball for CIO. On February 3, 1937, Lewis came. He took the ball and began kicking it all over the lot. Brophy now had time to tell anecdotes.

I was with Brophy from the start of the strike in December, 1936. We shuttled to and fro between Detroit and Flint. Brophy's duties were with the UAW strategy committee and the negotiations Governor Murphy got started in Detroit and Lansing. My duties were to assist him. Meanwhile Lewis was in Washington, confronting the White House and Wall Street, and giving long-distance guidance. Brophy called him daily, or more often, to report and consult. I was at his side and drafted the policy stuff suggested.

In transmitting Lewis's guidance to UAW leaders, Brophy had his troubles. Not that the auto workers didn't welcome Lewis's leadership; he was tops with them. The problem was in passing the CIO ball from Lewis to a butterfingers like President Homer Martin, the union's titular head.

As soon as I arrived, I was told the score, in the world's

most score-conscious union, where the score kept changing and everyone added it up differently. Within hours, I was briefed by an intimate of Walter Reuther, by a lawyer (Larry Davidow) close to Martin's ear who had me home to dinner, by two organizers, and by office employees who made none-too-cryptic remarks at the water cooler or in the men's room. Politically I was briefed by members of the "Progressive" and "Unity" caucuses, by right and left socialists, Lovestonites, Trotskyites, and by one guy who didn't like anyone. The "communists" seemed more warned against than warning. They spoke to me only as union officers about union affairs.

The Reuther sidekick gave sound advice. Walter wasn't yet an international officer, but he was on the executive board and lined up with the left in the Unity caucus. His friend told me to be careful of Martin, who was a kook; and to check with Mortimer, the solid guy. This score I hardly had to be told. I could count—certainly up to two, when the two were Martin and Mortimer.

Homer Martin had the charm of a popular preacher or successful salesman. He was boyish. Like the outgoing Albert Coyle, he sprang from his desk to greet me, clasping my hand in both of his. "The leaping parson of Leeds," some called him. Young and handsome, Homer was also athletic. He had been national hop-skip-and-jump champion, as well as Baptist preacher. He could make an eloquent stir-em-up speech. Picked by AFL's Francis J. Dillon as his next in command, Martin jumped to the CIO side before Dillon got dumped. With his running start and his personality, Homer might have gone far in CIO. He had little labor grounding and less sense, but he could have got by if he hadn't been a sucker who couldn't stay put.

The smart sucker—there were such—let himself be suckered by those who ran things and carried him on their backs. They might develop a vested interest in keeping him on top. But the sucker who wiggled so much he was bound to fall, and who could be double-suckered into suspecting his carriers of plotting his fall —well, Homer was that kind.

The chief trouble at the moment seemed to be that nothing

stayed long in Homer's mind. Consider a typical Brophy-Martin day:

10 A.M. Brophy tells Martin why Lewis wants him to hang tough with the federal mediator. Martin beams, punches fist in palm. "By gosh, he's right," says he. "I sure will."

11 A.M. Martin meets mediator and agrees on softer stand.

12 noon. Martin reports to UAW strategy committee. Looks injured when charged with weakening. Soon his innocent face lights up. "You fellows are dead right," he chuckles. "We've sure got to hang tough."

1 P.M. Someone joins Martin at lunch—maybe a man of the cloth, a politician, one of the butters-in—known or mysterious—who hang around.

3 P.M. A frantic call comes to UAW headquarters. Martin has met with an alleged intermediary for the company. He's now announcing all our troubles are over—the union has just got to give a little on—

4 P.M. Martin returns to UAW, little put out by the grim looks that greet him. He readily agrees he may have been overenthusiastic.

4:30 to 6:30 P.M. Strategy committee plans for evening session with Governor Murphy in Book-Cadillac Hotel. Martin orates on importance of hanging tough. Brophy warns the governor is quite a wheedler. Two guys are tipped off to guard Homer at dinner, lest someone else get to him.

9 to 10 P.M. Governor Murphy is at his best. He has dignity of office, personal charm, democratic condescension. God, Country, Humanity, are on his side, and he on theirs. He understands the problems of the rebellious auto workers, their feelings, wants them to win all they constructively can. But arbitrary stands are inimical to industrial peace, and he must warn—

10 P.M. The governor pauses for breath. Aware that Martin has been nodding agreement, a couple of UAWers rise to beat him to the floor.

10:15 P.M. The governor raises his hand in benediction, also to interrupt. His voice shakes with emotion. Some think they see tears. He forgives the men who just spoke. He is suffering political martyrdom rather than use force against the sit-downers. But the situation is dangerous. How little he asks, and only in the workers' best interests.

11 P.M. Homer wipes the mist from his glasses. He chokes back a sob, or possibly phlegm. He speaks with warm sympathy for the governor. Never will labor let him down. His counsel is that of our best friend . . .

11:30 P.M. By some miracle, or trick, Martin is stopped just short of making a commitment. He is hustled off to his hotel in a cab. His hustlers are ready to hammer away at him all night. It isn't necessary. Homer agrees at once the governor's tears should not deflect us from our hang-tough policy. "Bless you fellows," he says fervently as he bids them goodnight. "You can count on me."

Mortimer was no match for Homer at the hop, the skip, and the jump. He was one to keep his feet on the ground—and to stay put. Martin had skipped from the pulpit into the labor movement, and felt uncertain and ill at ease in it. Mortimer was born, grew up, and spent his life in the movement.

Son of a coal miner, a local leader of the Knights of Labor in Pennsylvania, Mort became a miner himself at the age of 12. The miners' missionary unionism was in his genes. From mining, Mort went to work in other heavy industries. He was a steelworker for years, an auto worker for two decades before being elected UAW vice president. Mortimer never worked on a job he didn't try to organize. He was pioneer leader in Cleveland of the AFL federal unions of auto workers that formed the UAW.

In this GM strike, Mortimer had really earned his leadership. He was the UAW organizer who, alone at first, had come to Flint to mold the kind of union that was the key to victory in this key strike center. He knew the people sitting down and what was on their minds. As national leader now, he could speak with certainty for them, and he kept checking with them to make sure he was sure. No wonder Lewis sent Martin packing— on a speaking tour—so he could have Mortimer at his side in settling the strike.

To me the most consistent thing about the consistent Mortimer was his working-class philosophy. Brophy had a mining background similiar to Mortimer's and developed some of the worker attitudes that went with it. But Brophy, according to his posthumous testimony, rejected the working-class conclusions that could follow. Like Phil Murray, he preferred the social philosophy promoted among workers by his church. Lewis, also with mining background, had little working-class philosophy, though in early CIO he showed a shrewd appreciation of class instinct and interest. Mortimer translated his working-class experience into a consistent attitude toward life, labor, and politics. He read and studied much, to think out his position. He grew into and stayed with a radical working-class philosophy about which he was forthright and sincerely convinced.

The General Motors sitdown strike of 1936-37 was a make-or-break showdown for UAW, maybe for all CIO. Its defeat could have been as demoralizing as the AFL's muffed chances at the start of the New Deal. When it was won, the UAW was made. The doors of success opened for all CIO.

Lewis knew this strike was crucial. He gave it all he had. He took on the Wall Street powers behind GM. He took on Washington, including the President. He guarded against weak leaders who might settle for less than victory. Like the sit-downers, he knew their determination to stay in was what would win. A fighting leader, he matched their fighting spirit.

In transmitting Lewis's hard line, Brophy had trouble with more than Martin. An absent Lewis couldn't be specific. Sometimes, in applying the Lewis line without attribution, Brophy had to buck CIO organizers like Allan Haywood and Adolph Germer. The redbaited Brophy was suspect at times of being under left influence because of counsel I knew came from Lewis.

The continued occupation of GM plants week after week scared many responsible people, who saw far-reaching and dangerous implications. Roosevelt was scared, Murphy still more; they wanted off this hot spot, before it burned a hole in their pants. General Motors and part of Wall Street were scared—for their plants, their profits, the system that had kept them rolling in blissful billions. Some labor leaders were scared too.

Facing danger, the old-line labor leader looked for a face-saving "out"—the specialty of politicians. To get the sit-downers out of the plants, Roosevelt and Murphy would have offered CIO almost anything—except victory, which wasn't theirs to give. No Murray or Hillman would have held out like Lewis; they'd have leaned on their White House friend. But they had nothing to say—though FDR kept Hillman close to say it. Lewis was in charge.

Germer and Haywood were up against something new in their long labor experience. Experience makes for caution. They were disposed to advise these rash rookies to go slow, watch their step, listen to friends in public office. Germer, long a rightwing socialist fighting the left, got gloomy when masses were on the move. He had grave misgivings that communists were moving them. He counseled moderation, compromise, unless Lewis specifically ordered otherwise. He found it hard to distinguish between the Lewis strategy and a deeply suspected "commy line."

My mind went back to the 1920 sitdowns in Italy. I was in Siena at the start, and the workers in my neighborhood occupied a big garage. Folks chuckled when the owner had to argue with rich customers that it wasn't he who raised the red flag over it. The workers argued, too, on how to run the garage under socialism. In big industrial centers, the factories were liberated fortresses festooned with bunting and red flags. The workers looked chipper with bright hopeful slogans, gags, and songs.

The higher-ups didn't chuckle or sing. The rightwing socialist and union leaders were scared stiff. They wanted an out, just as did government and employers. Premier Giolitti, "the Fox," made a package of promises. The workers came out and no one gave a hoot for them any more.

The GM strike had militant workers occupying the plants—with bright slogans, gags, and songs. It had friends of labor in the governor's mansion and White House. It had its scared and weak-kneed leaders. Two extras helped tip the scale for victory: Lewis and the left.

UAW's real leader in the strike was not the harebrained Homer Martin, but the resolute Wyndham Mortimer. In key

Flint, the key leader and strategist was Robert Travis, also of the left. Travis had followed Mortimer in charge of organization in Flint and prepared the ground for the epic struggle. He led it resourcefully, zestfully. Younger and more exuberant than the sober Mortimer, Travis too knew which class side he was on.

Lewis's closest aide was a smart, aggressive, young lawyer, Lee Pressman, whose counsels ranged beyond his legal work. Pressman worked in close sympathy with Maurice Sugar, the UAW counsel—a longtime radical who was thoughtful and broad-gauged, as well as alert and practical.

It is invidious to stop at a few names. All up and down in UAW there were leftwingers—among its leaders, functionaries, organizers, activists, and rank and file. The lefts worked well with many who were not themselves of the left but who shared its response to the times.

Were these lefts communists? Some were, some weren't. American communists had to dodge so many penalties, and were so lied about, that specific answers could long cause individuals to be hurt. Perhaps future historians—after anticommunism has been factually dammed even at its American source—may delve into the role of actual communists in the great 1936-37 upsurge and cite many names, not to "expose" but to honor.

The communists and lefts who came to the front in the Great Depression and the rise of CIO filled a need for leaders from the workers' ranks who could think and act in class terms, not shrink back confused from collision with the capitalist class. When Lewis urged a hang-tough policy against GM and its spies and goons, against police and troops, against Wall Street and Washington, even against Roosevelt and Murphy, it shocked liberals and old-line laborites, including some of his CIO associates. It didn't shock the communists and lefts, but sounded exactly right to them.

It didn't shock Mortimer and the leaders close to him. It didn't shock Bob Travis and the organizers and activists working with him out of Pengelly Hall in Flint. They were 'way ahead of Lewis, had started on this kind of struggle long before, against all the capitalist forces arrayed against them. Least of all did it shock the rank and file of men and women who bore the brunt of

battle—in occupied plants, on picket lines, and wherever else it
raged.

The lefts were but a part—a numerically small, if a key part
—of the UAW dynamics. To stress their role is to restore some
of the credit stolen from them, not to detract from the credit
due others. Names crowd in on memory. George Addes, Ed
Hall, the Reuther brothers—scores more.

Addes was young, dark, serious, modest. Rose Pesotta—an
ILGWU organizer and one of Dubinsky's best gifts to CIO—
first talked up Addes to me at the 1936 UAW convention in
South Bend. Addes wasn't up front like Martin and Mortimer.
He lacked the flash and push of a Walter Reuther or Dick Frank-
ensteen. Rose was pushing him for UAW Secretary-Treasurer.

Addes had been a leader in the 1935 Toledo Autolite
strike, which gave the union one of its first bases. Rose stressed
chiefly his character—sincere, practical, honest, steady. The emphasis was on the steady; UAW needed that. Addes handled the
union's business with enviable efficiency, and exerted a
steadying influence, through all the years of his top leadership—
and he lasted longer than most. In the heat of the factional
fights, he showed a sense of fairness that reflected integrity.

Second. Vice President Ed Hall was solid—in physique, too.
Earthy and decisive, he couldn't take much of Homer Martin's
flighty foolishness without exploding. He was for horse sense—
and some horseplay, in rollicking contrast to the serious Mortimer and Addes. Ed wasn't the only joker when auto workers
got together, the least inhibited roughnecks that ever set Wall
Street back on its heels. Their kind of humor was hard on
solemn subservience to tradition and the powers-that-be.

Hall had Adolph Germer's number. Full of dark foreboding,
Germer counseled conservatism with the special intensity of the
once-radical. If mistakenly thought to "represent Lewis," he
could have been taken too seriously. But not while Hall was
around. With his eye on Adolph, Ed would start some militant
bluster. Adolph would be on him at once, towering over him and
shaking a finger, "Now wait a minute, Ed!" Fat little Ed would

stand right up to the tall, gloomy, graying figure of the once-
famous socialist who in earlier days strode down the aisle at
UMW conventions to challenge the mighty Lewis. Ed would
shake his finger back at Adolph, impudently defending his bluster. With grave emphasis, Adolph would make his points until
he finally relaxed under the good-natured needling.

The Reuther brothers . . .

The "Rover Boys," they were dubbed. Knock off a few
years, and you could picture them throwing teen-age legs over
bikes and dashing off eager-eyed from their Wheeling home—to
discover the world and make it theirs. Walter, Victor, Roy, each
had a lot on the ball, and they stuck together.

In the Illinois mine town where the career of John L. Lewis
became a family project, if you fought one of the Lewis boys, it
was said, you had to lick all five. John L. came to stick up so
high he put his brothers in the shade. I knew only one, A.D.
(Denny) Lewis. He was warm and unaffected. Facially, and in
shaggy brow, he faintly resembled John L. He had some feel for
personal politics, a roughly cordial union boss. About there the
resemblance ended. Denny called his brother "The Boss." Loyalty to him came first, and he liked to stress an almost carbon-
copy subordination.

Walter Reuther's brothers were less in his shade. Sometimes
I wondered what, if anything, he had more of, aside from being
older. Drive was perhaps the word, not to call it push. All
three boys had the same first interest—the labor movement.
Two worked their way around the world together; all three set
out to change it. They had good heads and spunk. Roy, least the
politician, struck me as a Powers Hapgood type of organizer—a
compliment. Victor inclined to theory. In Germany he might
have stuck out more than Walter, as a social-democratic or union
leader.

At Flint, I observed the brothers in action, creditably, in
the GM strike. Roy worked out of Pengelly Hall on some critical
assignments. I heard Victor's voice from a sound truck in some
tense mass moments. Walter kept turning up and making his

voice heard. Not a top officer then, he was a board member and local president on Detroit's west side.

On the victory day, Brophy and I were invited to Fisher One plant for the triumphal march-out. Inside the plant, we saw how the sit-downers had lived through those six weeks and how strangely neat they'd kept things. We left the plant when they did—bearded faces ready for the victory shave, lugging their gear, flaunting their gags, waving to the cheering crowd.

Walter was there. His quick eyes noted Brophy and the CIOers. "Trust CIO to show up at the head of the procession when there's a victory parade," he quipped, as he passed on to a place still further ahead. In ways like that, Walter was perceptive. He worked hard. He fought well. He deserved much credit —and he saw that he got it.

Lest any detect, in my comments on Walter Reuther, a trace of the green and the sour—as from the grape—I hasten to call it to attention. Such reactions are a tribute to success, if one of its minor penalties. Walter became by all odds the most successful new leader thrown up by CIO. My tribute is belated. Lewis and Murray recognized Walter's drive very early in the game and paid their tribute. It irritated them. Lewis once observed that the heights are cold. But the occupants didn't want their lonely chill disturbed by warmblooded youngsters scrambling up.

Lewis knew all the publicity angles. Walter was an eager student and fast learner. Once I was trailing Lewis as he left the train at St. Louis for the 1940 UAW convention and press and welcomers surged toward him. It took me by surprise when Lewis's big hand reached back and drew me to his side, as the flash bulbs popped. Thrust outward by the maneuver was Walter Reuther. The result, as both knew, was that St. Louis papers couldn't show convention delegates how close was Walter to the great John L.

Walter's rise was rocketlike, ejecting in flight the booster apparatus that got him started. His career followed a typically social-reformist trajectory—from socialism, through reformism, to capitalism. There's much more to say about Walter Reuther. Now I refer only to his early image.

The so-called Reuther Plan—for producing war planes in

auto plants—was an early publicity triumph. Whatever his part in framing it, it brought Walter great repute. Washington liberals went gaga over it, or rather over Reuther. After its unveiling late in 1940, Reuther spoke on it to the National Press Club. He stood out fine as the brainy up-and-coming young labor leader of the New Deal, in its current war phase, and his admirers drooled with delight.

"Why, Walter," I observed tritely, "I didn't know what your middle initial stood for; now I know it stands for Plan."

"Some people say it stands for Phony," he replied.

Walter shouldn't have looked at me when he said that. I was not one of those. I wasn't a Walter admirer at the time. But, far from thinking him phony, I found him genuine with a rare consistency—the most single-minded, sincere, and dedicated Reutherite I ever knew.

At the time of the 1936-37 GM strike, the Reuther brothers were to the left, if not of it. In those days, only company stooges or spies asked precise questions about political affiliation. The rest of us controlled our curiosity. Like children seeing a western, however, we had to know who was on which side. We asked as they do: "Is he a good guy?"

The good guys were on the working-class side; the bad guys on the capitalist side. The good guys ranged from class-conscious radicals, through all shades of sincere pink and humanitarian fervor, to stodgy conservatives who really wanted the workers to win.

If you asked a communist the good-guy question, "He's 100%" might mean a real communist; "He's okay," some other kind of leftwinger; "Okay, I guess," a not-too-guaranteed united-front attitude. These guesses could be wrong. Many communists enthused most over union builders who showed their stuff in action, rather than by words or affiliation.

Among younger brighter union pioneers, some kind of radical affiliation was the vogue. The Communist party had the widest influence and prestige. "The party" or "party line" invariably referred to it. There were also right and left socialists (more of the left than the stuffy right), Proletarian party, Love-stonites, several brands of Trotskyites.

At first there was a united front. The struggle was so broad it swept along the small radical factions willy-nilly side by side. After the battle, the contention of radical factions sneaked into union affairs. Socialist party members began to caucus more against than with communists. Proletarian partyites split hairs to separate themselves from the CP. Lovestonites encircled Homer Martin with tales of communist plotters, offering to finger them. The Trotskyites agreed on one thing only, that Stalin's hand was behind everything.

As to the communists . . . Cold War historians—using victorious anticommunist factions as their source—have recorded their actual or alleged shenanigans voluminously, ascribing to them all disruptive initiative. My impression was that the communists were often so "in" they didn't want to start anything. They could deplore factionalism as responsible unionists; while the outs had to gang up on them to get in.

Curious as it will seem only to the uninitiated, other avowed radical factions started most of the anticommunist red-baiting in UAW—including factions that called themselves "communists" when talking to themselves. To avoid confusion, I have stuck to the traditional practice of applying the words "communist," "red," and—by extension—"left" to those of Communist-party persuasion or association, rather than to others making less accepted claim to the distinction.

During the GM strike, I started to work more closely with Lewis. While Brophy represented CIO on the scene, my duties were with him. When Lewis came, he didn't have to take over; everything betook itself to him.

Lewis liked room around him and freedom to move. He shucked off detail. I didn't expect specific assignments. I stuck around and when things I could do needed doing, I did them. Lewis usually had many people walking in or out or sticking around, apparently of their own volition. As time went on, I felt free to walk in whenever Lewis was on CIO business, using my judgment when to come or go. Only once did he dispute that judgment.

At St. Louis for the 1940 UAW convention, I stuck around in Lewis's hotel suite while UAWers came to greet him. Walter Reuther arrived, a bit breathless as usual. He glanced meaningfully in my direction, and I rose to go. Lewis noted the glance. "Stick around, Len," he said. It cramped Walter's style, as he tried to explain his loyalty to both Lewis and Roosevelt. At the moment, Lewis wasn't in the market for dual allegiance.

Back in Washington after the GM strike, I worked more with Lewis than with Brophy. CIO was shooting up fast. The original committee of absentee union leaders was becoming a big labor movement. Taking personal charge, Lewis began departmentalizing the headquarters setup, and as a department head, I dealt with him directly.

Coming closer to Lewis meant coming closer to Lee Pressman.

Lee Pressman looked like an alert, ambitious well-turned-out product of Harvard Law School. He was. He came to Washington with the New Deal, one of "Felix Frankfurter's Happy Hot Dogs"—all young, smart, of the legal elite, and keener on policy and politics than on moneymaking.

It was fortunate that Lewis and Pressman came together at this CIO moment in history. Without Pressman, Lewis's grand design might have been less grand, even smeary in spots. Quick and flexible like his boss, Pressman readily adapted to Lewis's pragmatic power politics. Lewis was the policy designer, but Pressman was more than his instrument. With a thought-out attitude, Pressman filled in blank spaces, smoothed rough edges, and thus influenced trends in Lewis's act-fight program.

In the Lewis-left alliance that triggered CIO's initial success, Pressman was Lewis's most intimate coadjutor. Lewis's general strategy required this alliance. But without Pressman to understand its detailed implications, it might have been less effective, even bungled at times.

Brophy disliked Pressman, and said lawyers shouldn't butt into union policy. With me, Brophy (1) conceded Lee was smart and worked well in the leftward direction that both Brophy (then) and I favored; (2) implied Lee was an ambitious lawyer left-leaning only because he found it to his advantage; (3) predicted—less dolefully than seemed warranted—that he'd turn rightward when that offered greater advantage. I defended Pressman. He was obviously a good guy. As to predictions—one could only wait and see. As it turned out, when our leftward-sailing bark hit storms, Brophy abandoned it 10 years before Lee.

Brophy's aversion to Pressman was not political—not then. Pressman had nothing against Brophy, personally or politically. He just seemed to have nothing, either for or against. It would have been un-Christian for Brophy to hate Lee, but nothing in faith or doctrine said he couldn't boil inside when Lee looked right over his head. Pressman could give that impression.

A triumvirate ruled CIO—Lewis on top, Hillman and Murray at its triangular bases. Below these three much empty space. Dubinsky, while briefly with CIO, involved himself little. Visiting heads of out-of-town unions might rate some red carpet. But Brophy, Jim Carey, Dave McDonald, and other CIO officials were just part of the help. If anyone from the CIO office might rarely lunch, or otherwise hobnob, with one of The Three, he drew many jealous glances. Then to have Pressman arrive, and at once hobnob regularly with Lewis, Murray, or Hillman, sometimes all three!

Some friends asked if I could do something about Pressman. Lee was an okay guy, they said, and doing fine work. But his seeming arrogance annoyed some CIOers. Could I get him to fraternize with the common people? There wasn't much I could do; Lee got hep without me. But in studying his problem I got to like him. I found him an okay guy.

Posture, profile, manner, contributed to the impression of arrogance. Lee just couldn't slope modestly. He was so uncompromisingly erect as to create a well-tailored effect. From some camera angles, Lee's profile looked surly. He had an abrupt manner, which some took personally.

Caroline helped me understand Pressman. When I told how he overawed the help at CIO, she laughed. "The big show-off! I've known dozens of Jewish boys like him. He isn't kidding me." Caroline grew up in once-socialist Milwaukee with many young fellows in her Yipsel and Marxian circles. All began poor. All were quick and smart—to smart-alecky. All made out to be radical, cynical, sophisticated. None intended to be small cogs. All were show-offs. They were for the "cause," but also looking for the main chance. One found it as a New Deal architect of Social Security. Another, from rich women. One became secretary to a big city mayor. Another went from communism to Wall Street. Yet another wrote speeches for a head of the U.S. Chamber of Commerce, while still a maverick radical himself. A few stayed with the movement, as union lefts, as communists. Others became artists, doctors, businessmen.

With these examples in mind, I realized all bright young men were not gentile-born into the exclusive clubs of the corporate or political elite. Some had to have gall and guts, and to know to trick a two, to make it and still retain sympathies formed on the other side of the tracks.

Lee knew his trade tricks. An uncluttered desk—in his case a table-type without even drawers—created an aggressive executive impression, all cleared and polished for action. His mannerisms on phone and with business visitors—abrupt, always and at once to the point—an organized response, with a 1 and a 2 and a 3. No stuffed shirt, Lee like Lewis could also laugh at the devices he used. Living for years across the same suburban street from the Pressmans, Caroline and I came to know and enjoy Lee and his family. Jim Carey called us "the Bethesda Set" which might have been more apt, if we hadn't depised the then-famous Cliveden Set; if two families could make a Set; and if our street hadn't happened to be in Chevy Chase, not Bethesda.

A passing tip of the hat to labor lawyers. I didn't agree with Brophy that lawyers should stick to their lawbooks. It couldn't be. The lawyer was the universal fix-it man, in labor as elsewhere. But like other laborites, I was suspicious of the breed— out for their fat fees, middle-class, slick, slippery—until I got to know many lawyers who worked for and with CIO in its upsurge. I found lawyers who compared well with the best militants in ardor, and added extra brains and skill.

During the rout of CIO progressivism—the so-called purge

of the communists—I made a mournful auto trip around the country, to assess the havoc. In many cities CIO activities had fallen to the level of an ingrown timorous chamber of commerce. Most who had carried the torch were sadly disgruntled, looking for any old stick to beat the wolf from the door, leaving the labor movement to look out for itself. Almost as bad as the renegades were those of little faith—and that lost—who were taking it out on old comrades. Among the still stalwart were the best lawyers. Few had become turncoats. Most took their beating—in loss of clients and prospects—without discarding the principles they championed in building CIO.

Before leaving the GM strike, I must pay my respects to Governor Frank Murphy of Michigan. Accompanying union leaders who conferred and negotiated under Murphy's ever-present insistence, I whiled away much time studying his big Irish head, listening to his rich, soft voice, and reflecting on his style. The man was Lewis-like in eyebrows but in little else. No blow-for-blow fighter, he was a puzzle and challenge for Lewis.

Some writers depicted Lewis as a brute who twisted the arms of softer, more scrupulous men. To me, this was a poor likeness of one who enjoyed a rough fight with the biggest bruisers, and it did not depict the Lewis-Murphy confrontation. Lewis did like to take on the big ones, of any kind. He sized up Murphy as a humanitarian and noted his Irish revolutionary forebears.

Murphy was pressing to get the sit-downers out of the plants with less than victory. He had the power to use troops to shoot them out. This he threatened to do, and nearly did, showing Lewis his signed order. To shame Murphy for his legalistic arguments, Lewis reminded him of his Fenian forebears, one of whom was hanged by the British. He said that Murphy would be responsible for certain bloodshed; and that he Lewis would go into a plant himself, to be first to bare his breast to the bullets.

To Murphy's credit, he stopped short. Lewis could be proud he did all he could to influence Murphy, and apparently applied the right psychology. Lewis was no more a brute than was Murphy a softy.

In the long sessions I attended, Murphy looked to me more like a brooding man with a conscience than the politician he had to be. As a politician, he was certainly on the spot. Elected in popular upsurge that overthrew Michigan's entrenched Republican rule, Murphy owed a lot to labor. He also owed something to the Democratic party and the man in the White House, at the other end of a pulsating telephone line. Catch-cries about "illegal seizure of property," "mob rule," sounded like shrieks of doom to his party's big-money bosses.

Could Murphy afford to be the "weak New Deal governor" who yielded to the mob and abetted the seizure of private property? On the other hand, could he afford to be the "strike-breaking governor" who used troops to shoot down unarmed strikers? As a politician, Murphy had to use his wits to get the men out of the plants by any means short of shooting.

As the kind of man he was, Murphy also faced a crisis of conscience. He wanted to get off the spot, but also to acquit himself with credit, not only in the eyes of his party and labor but also before God, country, humanity—his own conscience today, and history tomorrow.

That's a lot to deduce from watching a big Irish face and listening to a modulated voice. But in those tense weeks, Murphy put a lot into his expression, his tone of voice, and his words. At times he invited an irreverent comparison. Imploring and pleading, he looked like a man of sorrows acquainted with grief. The beads of sweat on his brow, the tears that welled to his eyes—one thought of the crown of thorns. In those smoke-filled rooms, the airy wisp over his head, could it be no more than a smoke ring?

Murphy was devout in his Catholicism—concerned with matters of soul and conscience. He was thoughtful, philosophical to the point of introversion. He was a humanitarian, an idealist. Murphy was also a bachelor. He had no wife to prick the bubble of self-dramatization. Women who sought the attention of this handsome Hamlet-like personage weren't going to make the mistake of bringing high tragedy down to lowly earth, as might a wife.

From early youth I was immunized against the wiles and wheedlings of the soul-snatching profession and suspicious of laymen who greased their political wheels with spiritual unction. I didn't fall under Murphy's spell. Less concerned with his problems than with victory for the auto workers and CIO, I resented his efforts to soften our hard strategy.

Looking back, however, and comparing with other public figures, I came to think Murphy did well by his own political lights, and those of his time. I also concluded—without being an authority on such inner workings—that Frank Murphy must have won the battle of his own conscience.

This working-class struggle took on the proportions of a people's struggle and won the help of a public service—from the U.S. Senate no less. The Senate Committee on Education and Labor set up a subcommittee to counteract illegal interference with the workers' civil rights through espionage, provocation, organized violence. Chaired by Senator Robert M. LaFollette, Jr., of Wisconsin, it became known as the LaFollette committee.

Company spies, employed directly by the corporations or through agencies like Railway Audit and the Pinkertons, were a serious bar to the right to organize. Through investigations and public hearings, the committee exposed this spy system, also company gunmen, private armies linked to public authorities, and police violations of the workers' rights.

At Flint, company spies honeycombed the first local unions. Henry Kraus, in *The Many and the Few*, tells how Mortimer and Travis had constantly to combat them. In UAW headquarters, a group photo of early union delegates was spotted all over with white circles, marking individuals later proved by the LaFollette committee to be company spies.

During the General Motors strike, the presence of Senate investigators did much to restrain police, sheriffs, and National Guard. In the 1937 Little Steel strike, the restraint was less apparent. After the Chicago Memorial Day massacre, the LaFollette committee did remarkable work in publicly demonstrating the responsibility of the police.

All through early CIO years, all over the field, I ran into men from the LaFollette committee doing their brave, shrewd, and conscientious work. Testy Senator LaFollette had a staff of unusual character· and ability. Confused and misguided before his suicide in 1953, La Follette turned around and redbaited it in Cold War style. He couldn't take from it, nor from his earlier self, the credit for a great service to the people's freedom.

Heber Blankenhorn's record spanned the long gap between the 1919 steel strike and the 1937 Little Steel strike. In 1919, for the Inter-church World Movement, he exposed the same kind of antilabor spying and violence as he prodded LaFollette into probing from 1936 on. A brilliant trial lawyer John Abt, who later became Sidney Hillman's counsel and aide, was the committee's secretary and prepared its cases. Charles Kramer, chief investigator in Flint, also grilled the police after the Memorial Day massacre. Other names spring to mind, Bob Wohlforth, Ben Allen, Bob Lamb, Allen Sayler, Jack Burke, Dave Lloyd, Charles Flato, Luke Wilson, Ralph Wilson, Ralph Winstead (who later met a mysterious death, possibly at the hands of public enemies whose path he crossed).

The men from the LaFollette committee were good guys with the same kind of flame in their hearts, the same kind of song (sotto voce) on their lips, as all the other youngsters (and oldsters) daring and fighting for the workers' freedom on a hundred fronts in those glory days.

A prospective question haunts me as I pay tributes, "Why did you leave out——?" I see one omission now. My own fellow galley slaves.

The galleys we toiled at were from the printers. Many wielded the whips—any reader could give us a flick. Ameringer said a labor editor's job was like "feeding melting butter on the end of a hot awl to an infuriated wild cat." It could be worse, if the editor was expected to trowel out lard no cat would sniff at.

With CIO, I was lucky. I made my own job from the start, with an expanding movement. Lewis didn't interfere; and if I was attacked, he made my fight his own. Murray didn't interfere either. Before critics, he would wash his hands—which were pretty clean anyhow—saying he never told me how to edit *The CIO News* or run the publicity department.

The young man on the make seldom sought a labor editor's

job. Denny Lewis once averred you couldn't get a good man for less than $5,000 a year—then quite a high salary. At start of CIO, its scores of news editors and publicists got much less. Yet they were well-qualified people, and many kept applying to "work for CIO" regardless of salary.

After *The CIO News* was started in 1937, much of its circulation—approaching a million at one time—was in union and local editions, each with its own outside pages, but with the national edition in the center pages. Through placing editors for these editions and for other CIO publicity jobs, and through close contact with the rest of the CIO writing fraternity, I got to know hundreds in this field. Nearly all were genuine CIO enthusiasts, closely akin to all other union pioneers and activists.

I recall only one who applied as for a conventional job, concerned about salary and prospects. I was curious about his motives. "CIO's such a success," he explained, "I think it's going places and want to get on the bandwagon." This man went other places and did well, with top billing and salary. He wouldn't have wanted to push the CIO bandwagon anyhow.

Those who went places with CIO . . . The places they went were rough to travel. They worked hard for little or nothing. Their rewards were those of other union pioneers—joy of battle, love of comrades, pride of achievement, but mostly blows. Most, in the end, were forced out, redbaited out, to make place for men with bigger bottoms to hold down swivelchairs. While they fought, they were good, stirred themselves as they wrote the stuff that stirred the workers. Sneak up on one, you might catch him trying to sing, in shamefaced cacophony, the songs on the lips of the marching millions.

In the GM strike, I think of UAW editors Henry Kraus and Carl Haessler. That curious blond mop of fuzzy hair on top of Henry, showing up in thick of struggle. Henry who wrote the history he helped to make in a book that made those moments live on. The red head of the incomparable Carl Haessler. Restrained next to the romantic fuzz of the bubbling Henry, but fiery too. Applying his talents in the center of things in Flint. Imparting, as was Carl's wont, a subtle essence of principle to all around.

I think of the typewriter-pecking word-warriors in Toledo, Cleveland, Milwaukee, Chicago, San Francisco—in smaller industrial centers too; in mining, steel, rubber, textile, oil, auto towns; in electrical plants, in ports, on ships, in factories and fields. And whom have I not left out?

Do I romanticize the days of my youth? I did that for the Teens and Twenties. By now I was 37. Those generous juices of my youth calculation had chilled to below room temperature. Now with a job I might have made for myself—and largely did— for a movement advancing beyond all expectation, I counted myself the most fortunate of persons. Such good fortune could swell the jowls to restrict the vision. But I could still see around me and recognize in others the generous impulse, the daring deed, the flame of passion, and the singing heart.

So what became of the flame and the song?

The ancient Greeks had a torch event. One runner started with a torch which, when he tired, he passed on to another waiting runner, and so on. Something like the Pony Express, with torch instead of mailbag. You weren't supposed to forget torch or mailbag. Politically, Americans played it differently.

A runner started out with blazing torch, with eager eyes, and with the gait of a gazelle. There was some applause. When he began to weaken, no other runner waited for him—just a big goon with a gat. The goon knocked down the runner, kicked the shape out of him, and trampled the torch in the muck. The crowd in the bleachers pelted the runner with pop bottles and gave him the bronx cheer, as he limped from the field. Then the band played "God Bless America" and other entertainment was provided. The runner might end up handling the peanuts and popcorn concession.

All was forgotten until, much later, another runner suddenly appeared—from nowhere? He looked surprised to find a torch in the muck. He raised it and—surely the old embers were dead!—it burst into flame. By now, nobody knew where the torch came from—except the popcorn man. He might wave a sendoff. But the new runner didn't wave back; he wasn't interested in peanuts and popcorn.

Off went the new runner with blazing torch, with eager eyes, and with the gait of a gazelle. There was some applause.

When he began to weaken, there waited for him the same kind of a goon with a gat. The popcorn man might have liked to get into the race again, but by now he had fallen arches and the gait of a grounded gorilla.

Maybe some torch embers survived between the CIO sitdowns of the Thirties and the civil rights, black power, antiwar, and student sit-ins of the Sixties. But what a long intermission! Though doubtless good for popcorn sales.

As to the song . . .

I started with "The Red Flag." Even saw Ramsay MacDonald's lips once move to it, though he could have been substituting the words of "Tannenbaum" or "Maryland, My Maryland."

As an immigrant in the United States, I learned to substitute the words of "My Country, 'tis of Thee" for "God Save Our Gracious King." But it was the same pompety-pompous tune. I preferred "The Internationale." Even Morris Hillquit sang it then. And David Dubinsky! Though he had an out. His International Ladies Garment Workers was known internally as "The International." Knock off an "e," say "Union" instead of "Party," and David could sing himself to the head of "the human race."

But these long intermissions!

After many years of patriotism-first, I was moved to nostalgic tears when the strains of "The Internationale" somehow sneaked into a Chicago movie house. The song—and the thought—still kick around, it's said.

The song on the lips of the American people, when I arrived, was "Yes, We Have No Bananas." Then, for me, came Wobbly songs. I didn't go much for "Hallelujah, I'm a Bum." I was a working—or workless—hobo, never a bum. We sang it for the defiance that matched our radical mood.

Came "East Side, West Side" of the Al Smith campaign. Then the Depression brought "Who's Afraid of the Big Bad Wolf?"—and finally that apocalyptic paean of New Deal euphoria, "Happy Days Are Here Again."

As CIO got under way, from a million throats burst a great song of the workers' struggle and triumph, "Solidarity Forever! For the Union Makes Us Strong." CIO didn't say where its song came from; to most it was a CIO special. They might have shrugged blankly if told it was born of the IWW 20 years before but never died. ("IWW? Never heard of it.")

From still further back—echoing from the voices of black slaves whose spirits were fighting free—came other "CIO songs." The one I most often heard and best remember was, "Just Like a Tree That's Standing by the Water, We Shall Not Be Moved." Nor do I forget the snotty rank-and-file version, before CIO union leaders became fixtures: "So-and-So's a Horsethief—He Shall Be Removed."

("CIO? Isn't that the same as AFL?" "Yes, kid, but once it wasn't.")

From CIO days, there echoed more recently a song of striking black workers, and some whites too, which civil righters of the Sixties revived: "We Shall Overcome."

It's odd that many new lefts of the Sixties at first disregarded the working class—in their thinking, anyhow. This at a time when the number of wage or salary earners divorced from ownership of the means of production was rising from 85 to 89% of the gainfully employed.

Yet, as in the Thirties, the discontent that fired the torchrunners and song-singers of the Sixties, came from working people—from the black, the brown, and the poor, the most exploited American workers; from young people taken from work or school for imperialist war; from students in training to serve capitalist profit purposes they despised.

In CIO's Thirties too, there were students. I vividly recall speaking for CIO at Vassar and the dimpled knees below rolled-up jeans around the three-sided gallery. There were also other less memorable college occasions. There were alert and radical students, if less rambunctious than today's. There were leftwing student organizations and the American Youth Congress, politically hep and leaderish. But often it went like this:

His young eyes are eager, if rather abstracted by thought. His shoulders have bookworm's hunch. He sidles up in lobby or backstage, on any CIO occasion. He wants to help CIO, to get in on the workers' struggle. I ask his occupation. He is truckdriver, busboy, office worker, factory worker. The question may stump him, but he recovers. His father—uncle, grandfather, maybe—is a union man, member of Local 1234, International Union of These, Those, & Them. He's suspiciously accurate about the union's name. It's the mark of the—don't say the word "student." His credentials are of the working class.

In the Sixties, it went the other way. Half the students had union parents but wouldn't let on. Many, working their way, joined unions; that was coincidental. The blacks were working class. Another coincidence?

During the radically barren Cold War years, many erstwhile working-class enthusiasts moved as individuals into the middle class, and failed to transmit their erstwhile attitudes to the new radicals of the Sixties. Unions raised the living standards of millions, but didn't change their class status as workers who must sell their labor power to employers.

The working-class idea hit a peak in the United States not so much in the Depression as in the rise of CIO. Before CIO, many radicals held the old AFL in as much contempt as the New Left felt for the AFL-CIO. The working class became a concept to conjure with when newly organizing millions seemed to promise a movement capable of transforming society. The Cold War purge and domestication of CIO disappointed many great expectations. It led many to write off the "labor movement" as a factor for social change.

How much, the New Left rightly asked, was "labor" doing to aid black liberation, to oppose American imperialism and its war in Vietnam? How much, memory asks, did the AFL leaders do to promote the working-class upsurge of the Thirties? How far would CIO's top leaders have gone, unless pushed? The drive came from below—from the more disadvantaged workers, both black and white; from radicals, rebels, reds. Students, teachers, intellectuals, helped to give it verve and direction.

The AFL-CIO split was between relatively privileged craftsmen and the hard-driven, underpaid, mass-production workers. The AFL-CIO merger of 1955 combined newly organized industrial workers with the older crafts, both groups now enjoying benefits and protections that set them apart from millions of unorganized, little organized, or misorganized black, Puerto

Rican, Mexican, also white, workers at the bottom of the wage and security scale.

The Sixties repeated the CIO pattern of the Thirties insofar as challenge came less from within the official labor movement than from unfortunates outside it.

In the early Sixties, after long absence in the west, I witnessed a Labor Day parade in New York. The needle trades marchers from dress and millinery filled me with nostalgia. In the Twenties, radical young Jewish women sparked these unions. Caroline was one such, from another city and union.

Women in their fifties marched by, row after row. Time hadn't taken from their figures, but added to them. Less gay and perky, with less light a stride, they marched with the old determination. I still thought, as once, that if I were a boss I'd hesitate to tangle with these union women.

Then my heart gave a jump. What if some might be the very same women I once had known?

It couldn't be. The girls I'd known were reds . . . their hero the fiery communist Ben Gold, fighting rightwing union reaction and corruption. They wept when Lenin died. They read and read—communist as well as romantic literature. Then—twenty years before the Cold War and Joe McCarthy—rightwing victory in union civil war drove them out or tamed them.

No, those I knew must long since have gone. Smart as well as pretty, they must have grasped American opportunity—to marry business or professional men, to make money themselves. Now they'd be bragging about homes, cars, families—sunk deep in the boredom of middle-class life. Like others I'd known. ("The working class? Oh, yes, I remember.")

On a crazy impulse, I looked in the phone books for a name that still could thrill. I found it. I phoned. I heard the well-remembered voice. She remembered too.

Doing? Why, she was still at the trade, in the same union. Why not? It was her trade, her union. In the thirty-five years since last we met, someone else had come into her life. She was full of him and very proud. Her son was getting his Ph.D. at the University of——

I heard her husband's voice. "Who's that?" and her telling him. Still jealous? after all these years. I didn't look her up. There was another reason. Was her son a "good guy"? He was at a university of big sit-ins, teach-ins. She was proud of him. I didn't want to risk a disappointment about him or her.

This way I could dream of one torch that wasn't dropped, of one song that lived on.

Chapter Nine

THE OTHER SIDE

There was also the official top-down side to CIO—in steel and textile, for instance. CIO survived the Girdler counteroffensive— successful, lively, a new kind of labor movement.

While the Auto Workers were making history with their General Motors sitdown, their headquarters were in a seedy old office building on the fringe of downtown Detroit. On its ground floor was a little drugstore coffeeshop. There UAW President Homer Martin, breaking under the strain, once hysterically told his troubles to astonished customers, until rescued by a federal conciliator.

Meanwhile the Steel Workers Organizing Committee was occupying the whole 36th floor of Pittsburgh's tallest, swankiest skyscraper. Chairman Philip Murray was no more likely to be telling his troubles to drugstore customers than his equally dignified counterpart, Chairman Myron Taylor of the United States Steel Corporation.

With a different start, both John L. Lewis and Murray might have become big-business executives. Lewis could have slugged it out with the roughest of "robber barons." Murray might have made it by another route. With his good looks, poise, diplomacy, he might have charmed his superiors into co-opting him all the way up to the top. Placed next to the jutting Lewis, Murray seemed to bite his lip with painful modesty—adjusting instinctively to the exaggerated Lewis pose. On top by himself, Murray had all the presence of the executive portrait.

SWOC was something new—a union planned and started from on top, with a half million bucks in the kitty to make it big business from scratch. In Murray it had a smooth, distinguished chairman; in David J. McDonald a handsome, elocution-trained secretary, who might have made it to Hollywood and almost did. The psychology was from Madison Avenue. Spend money to make money. Nothing succeeds like success. Tell the world you've got it made.

For contrast, look at those crazy auto workers. No dough. No discipline. Always in a fight. With leaders just thrown up from the ranks—some kooks, and half of them reds. It was clear the auto workers needed a top AWOC—with a top Chosen One to tell them what to do, to hire and fire the help, to hold the members in line.

But first things first. Steel was the basic industry—backbone of Wall Street's antiunionism. After Steel the rest would follow. Steel also meant most to the Mine Workers who put up the most money. Steel and Coal were linked, Steel itself a big mine employer. So the auto workers would have to wait their turn. They'd have to hold their horses.

The auto workers didn't have horses; they had jalopies. Into them they jumped and off they went. They got where they were going while the SWOC Cadillac was still purring its warm-up.

The Auto Workers won the first key battle for CIO. But CIO's massive intent in Steel also helped. And these two were but part of the story.

Before the General Motors showdown, the Rubber Workers had fought for and won much union recognition. The United Electrical & Radio Workers (UE) had won an election at General Electric's big Schenectady works, after winning a strike at Camden RCA. Other unions were similarly advancing under the CIO banner, with advice, encouragement, and some limited aid from CIO, but otherwise pretty much on their own.

CIO's big guns were trained on Steel where advance was slow. SWOC signed up many workers, without initiation fees or dues. It broke through the antiunion terror of some closed company towns. It made inroads into company unions. But up to the time of the GM sitdown, SWOC had won no major strikes, elections, or agreements.

The GM strike victory made its impact on all fronts. The UAW knocked off Chrysler, and hundreds of thousands joined its ranks. Workers everywhere—AFL, CIO, and unorganized—began sitting down. Early in 1937, sitdowns were pulled by hosiery, shoe, hotel, restaurant, steel, transport, tobacco workers; by seamen, shipbuilders, clerks, printers, pressmen, janitors, electricians; by Woolworth store girls, rug weavers, watchmakers, garbage collectors; by Postal and Western Union messengers, farm hands, bedmakers, food packers, movie operators, gravediggers.

Biggest beneficiary of the GM victory was SWOC. Myron Taylor began secret talks with John L. Lewis during the GM sitdown. The outcome of these talks strongly influenced Wall Street strategists then consulting on overall policy toward unionism. Once GM had accorded union recognition in mid-February, U.S. Steel followed, on February 28; and on March 2, 1937, it signed an agreement with SWOC.

This opened still wider the union floodgates opened by the GM strike. Hundreds of thousands more workers joined CIO's now million-man ranks, and employers everywhere started signing up. The U.S. Supreme Court caught the spirit, and in April 1937, upheld the Wagner Labor Relations act.

Many AFL and independent unions—prompted by their lefts—began swinging into CIO. National Maritime Union; AFL Fur Workers; Transport Workers (from Machinists to CIO); also machine workers (from Machinists to UE), hosiery, leather, boot-shoe, office, optical workers, technicians, retail clerks, inland boatmen. West coast longshoremen and woodworkers were also on the way.

Then, late in May 1937, when it seemed nothing could stop the CIO, a mighty capitalist counteroffensive was mounted—not against the militant leftish rank-and-file unions, but against CIO's richest, most respectable, most from-on-top, most collaborating of new unions, the SWOC.

Steel had a background of labor struggle unmatched by the infant auto industry—from Homestead to the 1919 national strike led by William Z. Foster. But in drafting some of the first declarations of CIO's steel drive—before SWOC's own setup took over—I found 1919 was out of bounds.

There were a number of reasons. That drive had failed to establish a permanent union; SWOC was to be a Success Story. AFL craft leaders had divided and betrayed the last campaign; this one was CIO—all together in one industrial union. The earlier drive had led to a national strike; SWOC hoped to organize without strikes—and did in fact sign U.S. Steel without one. The 1919 effort had been a regular class struggle with Wall Street, Washington, state, and city governments using armed force, police, press, scabs, goons. SWOC frowned on the class struggle idea. Were not labor's friends in power? Franklin D. Roosevelt in the White House, his pal Mayor Kelly in Chicago City Hall, New Deal governors and mayors all around.

SWOC leaders particularly wanted to liquidate the memory of the last drive's leader, William Z. Foster. He was now at the head of the Communist party, which some of his ablest steel organizers had also joined. Communists had kept alive some union activity. They had influence among foreign-born steelworkers, some following among the black. They had promoted a short-lived Steel & Metal Workers Industrial Union and been active in 1933-35 efforts to organize through the AFL.

The SWOC leaders, coming mostly from coal, had little background and few contacts in steel. They found the ready help of the communists invaluable. Foster, who should know, wrote later that 60 of the first organizers hired by SWOC were members of the Communist party. Bill Gebert, a party leader, was liaison man and in charge of mobilizing foreign-born groups.

Rallying all their supporters and contacts, the communists threw themselves into the campaign more unconditionally and self-effacingly than is usual in politics. SWOC used their help and, rather underhandedly, tried to rub out their faces completely. It put communist steelworkers on the payroll, if needed, but each one was a marked man, closely watched at all times and dispensed with as soon as possible. Any move he might seem to make to win personal following would be countered quickly by undercover redbaiting or slander, by transfer to other territory, or by firing.

Any noncommunist steelworker active enough to acquire some following might get the same treatment. Pats on the back while needed, then a sharp reminder to toe the "SWOC line" or keep his mouth shut. If he still showed the often rebellious initiative of leaders pushing up from the ranks, he too might be slandered or redbaited or put on the payroll and transferred elsewhere.

From the top down, SWOC was as totalitarian as any big business. The "Committee" was a purely nominal board of directors. The Mine Workers supplied most money and so dominated, with a little token representation for the lesser contributions of the Amalgamated Clothing Workers and International Ladies Garment Workers. The members, besides Murray and McDonald, were second-stringers from UMW, ACW, ILGWU, the old Amalgamated Association, and CIO Director Brophy. After a little rubber-stamping, it faded away.

Murray was SWOC, even more than Lewis was UMW, Hillman ACW, and Dubinsky ILGWU. True, Lewis was the power behind Murray's throne, so long as UMW supplied the money and Murray was his UMW subordinate. But Lewis, trying like a good executive to delegate authority, let Murray run SWOC to an extent he later regretted. Murray built his own SWOC machine—a network of subordinates subject to his personal power to hire or fire, promote or demote. It was a Murray machine, not a Lewis machine, though at first its key men, like Murray himself, were on the UMW payroll. When the Murray-Lewis split developed, Van A. Bittner was one of the few Steel big shots from UMW who hesitated even momentarily. Most automatically stuck to the piecards which Murray now dispensed from an independent Steel treasury.

Murray got his key men from UMW, and around them built his SWOC (later United Steelworkers) machine. They knew all about machine loyalty and control. They in turn picked their subordinates, as steelworkers, too, had to be drawn into the machine. They didn't favor the pushy kind.

After SWOC got a permanent staff, I visited its Pittsburgh headquarters only occasionally. The staff quickly jelled into a setup—a Catholic setup. I may have felt this the more because

SWOC's publicist Vin Sweeney was so eminently devout. In national CIO and most other new unions, religion didn't stick out as it did in SWOC. Perhaps it wasn't this that turned me off, since I was not aware of having any particular religious prejudices. Perhaps cliquishness was too strong a word. Maybe most top-down setups are stuffy and rigid. Some got that feel at UMW headquarters. I didn't. There, if okay by Lewis, you were in.

Visit Auto in early years, or other new bottom-up CIO unions. If from CIO, you were at once among enthusiastic friends—with enthusiastic factional enemies lying in wait. People bubbled over with "the score." They wanted to talk, eat with you, invite you home, socialize. At Pittsburgh, it was bleak. Other CIOers who made more frequent official visits told me of lonely hotel nights and moviegoing. They took along books to read.

Non-Catholics had minority representation in SWOC headquarters. Harold J. Ruttenberg, able research director, and Clinton S. Golden, eastern district director, were of the social-reformist rather than Catholic school of unionism. The left was conspicuously unrepresented.

Golden since the Twenties had been hero and hope of those I've called lib-labs—liberal intellectuals flirting with labor and social reformism. Coming from the Locomotive Firemen, and having organized for the Machinists and Hillman's Amalgamated, Golden had the union background which lib-labs lacked, but he could speak their language. He was a big man with a booming voice—an asset for the organizer before sound equipment. I first met him at Brookwood Labor College where he was manager and field rep.

Lib-labs had talked up Golden to head the steel drive Lewis planned. They didn't know their Lewis. Still less did they know their Murray—after he got the spot and made Golden his sidekick. They gossiped that Murray would be front man, and Golden the works. Murray was both front man and the works. Golden adjusted at once to being a Murray lieutenant and did good work. He didn't become really integrated into the Murray machine, however, and after some years he moved on elsewhere.

Some months after the steel drive started, I decided to make a field trip to report its progress. I had to observe protocol, but I didn't feel like starting through the chilly top SWOC setup, nor through Golden's office there. I picked Van A. Bittner's western (Chicago) district.

Bittner operated more independently than Golden because he had, as it was said, a "direct line" to Lewis. Not that he'd have used it against Murray, to be sure. "Loyalty" was the big word to Bittner, as to Murray and Lewis, the basic code of the UMW machine. Its breach, when Lewis and Murray split, was to both sides the ultimate in moral collapse.

In his own district, however—subject to the overall SWOC machine—Bittner could largely run his own show, and he had a style all his own. As dictatorial as Lewis and a step-watcher like Murray, Bittner shared neither Lewis's Olympian detachment nor Murray's religiosity.

Van was peculiarly quicksilvery in playing with the left. Within hours he could make a riproaring "Americanism" speech, consult communists on hiring some lefts, and publicly deny there were communists in CIO. Dan Tobin of the Teamsters, similarly, could in one breath damn "communist control" of a local, in the next deny the Teamsters had any communists.

In the Twenties I heard AFL leader Jim Wilson, of the Metal Polishers, demand union exclusion of all communists. A reporter reminded him one of his own local union officials was a well-known Canadian communist leader. Wilson looked mildly reflective. "Oh, him!" he said. "He's all right. He's a good man." To Bittner, a "good man" he could use was just not a communist. Why not? Because "communist" was a bad word, and he was a good man.

Van once told me he was going to redbait the *Chicago Tribune* right back for its redbaiting of CIO. He could show, said he, that the *Tribune* was part of a communist conspiracy against Americanism, because the "millionaire socialist" William Bross Lloyd had been a big stockholder.

From Bittner's office, I went down the chain of command of regional, subregional, local, directors. Mostly from UMW, they were solid men, loyal subjects of Lewis, Murray, Bittner.

They'd better be. If some lacked imagination or initiative, all understood discipline and handling men.

I was getting a line on a well-oiled union machine, but not much on the steelworkers. I didn't contact lefty organizers doing much of the spadework, lest they suffer for "going around" their superiors. But I did ask about steelworkers I'd read about as company-union leaders who had gone CIO, as fired union men who became Wagner act cases, or as witnesses before congressional committees. I got this kind of answer:

"Oh, him! Yes, I know Whosis. He's around. Why d'you ask?"

"Thought I might look him up, get an angle, you know, on how the men feel in his mill."

"O-o-oh." A longish pause. "Why don't you see John Doe? He's subdirector—knows what's happening there."

"But Whosis is on your staff, a local officer too, isn't he?"

"Yes."

"He's okay, isn't he?"

"I guess so."

Finally I took bit in teeth, and looked up some of these steelworkers in their homes, avoiding any known as lefts. Coming from national CIO through the SWOC hierarchy, I was treated, as in SWOC offices, to formal cordiality, official information, and for the rest, a clam-up.

In later years, I tried to check on what happened to some of these union pioneers. Some had drifted away. A few had toed the SWOC line enough to rate some minor staff or local office. Those I met seemed integrated into the machine—cautious, clammy, cliquish.

What, I wondered, might have happened to those who fought and blustered their way to Auto leadership, if they'd had to learn the minuet of union politics under the strict eyes of duennas appointed, paid, and controlled by some Auto Workers Organizing Committee?

As I returned from the field, I ran into some of the SWOC chain of command. I didn't mention the names of steelworkers I had visited. They were mentioned to me, usually with some disparaging remark.

The Textile Workers Organizing Committee, launched shortly after SWOC got its U.S. Steel agreement, was conceived like a twin to SWOC. Sidney Hillman was the Murray of TWOC (also its Lewis). Lewis loaned me to Hillman, to help get things started. In drafting statements, I found it hard to avoid echoes of those I had done for SWOC. In planning, financing, direction, Hillman deliberately followed the SWOC pattern. TWOC, like SWOC, was to be run from on top—by Hillman. His ACW—like UMW in SWOC—would supply most of the money, leaders, key organizers.

Just as SWOC swallowed the decrepit Amalgamated Association, so Hillman had in mind swallowing the old United Textile Workers, under a similarly devised agreement. It proved a less chewable mouthful. Like Steel, Textile had some union background TWOC would as soon forget—including an unsuccessful national strike in 1934.

Unlike Steel, the textile industry was chaotic, competitive, balkanized. It had been marked by much antiunion violence, notably in the south; by union corruption and division in some northern pockets; and by flareups of radicalism, as in the IWW-led Lawrence, Mass., strike and the later communist-led Passaic, N.J., and Gastonia, N.C., strikes. Hillman's keynote was to be middle-of-the-road moderation and union responsibility—looking to organize the industry as well as the workers.

Going into the field for TWOC, I found Hillman's key ACW men running things much as did Murray's UMW men in SWOC. They had hundreds of organizers—often young people from outside the industry willing to work for little. A few lefts might slip in without too much screening, but the policy was to avoid them. Hillman's lieutenants in TWOC were sophisticated about radicals. Those once socialistic themselves believed they could sift the pale pink from the actual reds. Of the reds they wanted no part, except for some limited or emergency purpose.

Unlike Murray, who wasn't interested in such dessert, Hillman would have liked to have his inspirational cake as well as eat it. Both did without the extra daring and dedication an uninhibited left contributed to other new CIO unions. Murray dropped his hired lefts as soon as he could, without regrets. He made deals with communists when he had to, but he regarded radicalism as "ideological" (a bad word to him) or plain "filthy." Hillman liked some flame in the hearts of his organizers, if controlled and constructive, and some songs on their lips, if not IWW or communist songs. Some radical inspiration once helped his own ACW get going.

But practical politics came first. For TWOC, Hillman could count on communist support without any quid pro quo, and any quids might come back to curse him. Lewis might wash his hands and say the employers hired communists and CIO just organized them along with all the other workers. From Hillman's TWOC that wouldn't have sounded quite right. TWOC was out to sell itself as a responsible, efficiency-geared, disciplined union with power from on top to enforce sound policy on everything.

A byproduct of Hillman's policy-engineering was a Frankenstein like Emil Rieve. Hillman was creatively complex, Rieve rather mechanical.

In later years, Rieve and his Textile associate George Baldanzi competed in dogging me. If Baldanzi might make an open pounce, Rieve preferred a typewriter approach. Murray, when CIO president, would pass on Rieve letters defaming me. They were lengthy, but only one point still stays with me. Rieve reported that the editor of a local edition of *The CIO News* had been seen on the street talking to a salesman of the *Daily Worker*. That point I pondered long, and still ponder. It must have had some hidden significance.

Rieve looked more like the movie comedian Hugh Herbert than like Frankenstein, but he wasn't so amiably vague. An experienced, energetic union leader, Rieve headed the Hosiery Workers federation and brought it to TWOC. He was the logical successor to Hillman as Textile leader.

Baldanzi, both eloquent and able, also came to TWOC from an organized sector, the Dyers Federation. When Rieve became president of the CIO Textile Workers Union, Baldanzi was made executive vice president. Two steering wheels on one machine! Their rivalry didn't help me. Instead of sometimes veering in different directions, each tried fiercely to steer more to the right than the other.

Compared with subtle, sagacious Hillman, sophisticated Lewis, brooding Murray, reflective Brophy, Rieve was a trifle crude. At one time socialistic, it was said, Rieve had tried to be noncommunist progressive in a period when some social reformists flirted with the communists. I doubt Rieve did. He was not flirtatious, politically anyhow. His hatred of the left was deep-seated and abiding.

In a semicircular European chamber of deputies, Rieve might have taken his seat in center-to-left. In CIO, he was to the extreme right.

For a fascistic extreme right—antidemocratic, antiworking-class, racist, xenophobic, as well as anticommunist—there was no place in a labor movement like CIO. At one time some professed to see fascist possibilities in Lewis—*fuehrer* or *duce* traits. They noted his domineering character; his mass appeal; his lack of traditional social philosophy (though Mussolini had one); his political flexibility; what they called his demagogy. It was sheer fantasy. Lewis's base was in the unions, the miners, CIO. Labor, the workers, made him strong, and he knew it. Even for a right of owner-class conservatism, CIO had no place. But within itself, CIO had its own degrees of rightism, as of center and left. Its extreme right made anticommunism its chief concern.

Rieve was a CIO delegate to the Soviet Union in 1945, following the Paris founding of the World Federation of Trade Unions. President Roosevelt approved the trip, State Department and Armed Forces aided it, Sidney Hillman promoted it, Philip Murray blessed it. Those to the left of the delegation, Joe Curran, Reid Robinson, Albert Fitzgerald, Lee Pressman, and myself, were enthusiastic about its fraternal purpose. The center, Allan Haywood and John Green, duly approved it as CIO policy. Rightwingers Rieve, James B. Carey, Vin Sweeney, had varied reactions.

Delayed in London on our way back, I shared hotel room and reflections with religiously anticommunist Sweeney, Murray's Steel editor. Vin was disturbed by his Soviet experience. We'd seen devastated Leningrad—the war wounded—crippled women and children gave us flowers. The Russians we met were cordial and kind, treating us not only like fellow workers and allies, but like personal friends. Vin thought and prayed a lot. He consulted Catholic churchmen. Scorning Marxist materialism, he looked for answers to his Jesuit training. One of his conclusions: "Those Russian communists are pretty swell. Guess you can't blame them for what the American communists do. It's just the American communists I can't stand."

Anticommunist Jim Carey was on the spot. As CIO secretary-treasurer, he wanted to assert himself as head of the delegation—an initially disputed point. He had to hew to CIO policy, which then called for friendship with our Soviet ally, with the workers' unions as special good-will ambassadors. He hailed the Soviets, their war effort, their unions, their social welfare activities. Rieve and Sweeney kept warning against the Russian reds putting something over. Carey worried more lest CIO lefts put something over by finding him deviate rightward from CIO policy.

As to Rieve . . . I could detect not a wobble in his undeviating anticommunism. In the U.S.S.R. he observed limited diplomatic courtesies, but restrained his private sneers chiefly on account of big, belligerent, fist-handy Joe Curran. Then at the peak of his leftism, Joe enjoyed making things hard for Carey, Rieve, and Sweeney all through the trip. When we recrossed the Soviet border, Rieve threw out his arms, breathed deep with assumed relief, and said: "Thank God, we're back in civilization." He winced as Curran turned fiercely on him. Luckily for Emil, Joe's counterblow was only verbal. Rieve alone refused to sign our friendly report. Carey had to put it out in his own name, with benediction from Murray.

Rieve kept his anticommunism pure and undefiled, unyielding to leftward temptation, even from Lewis, Murray, Hillman, Carey, or CIO's adopted policies. Maybe Big-Brother Baldanzi was watching to pounce on the least flutter of softness on communism. Yet when I put all CIO vice presidents, successively, on national radio hookups, only Rieve was really redbaited. Not the then leftist Curran and Robinson, but Rieve, drew the rightist bouquets: "Go back to Russia, you stinking Red"; "Filthy Communist, Watch Out!" and the like. These postcard tributes puzzled me, as I rechecked the text of Rieve's mild speech. The only reason I could guess at—if kook rightists had to have a reason—was that Rieve, born abroad, still retained some foreign accent.

Ironically, TWOC—like SWOC in the Little Steel strike—was more damagingly redbaited than the quite-red (at first) UAW and CIO's left-led unions.

In its first six months, TWOC won union agreements covering 200,000 workers. After that, it met setbacks as economic recession began late in 1937. Its successes were chiefly in the middle Atlantic and New England states. In the south it made little progress. Considering the millions spent, size of staff, and the top-drawer attention it got, TWOC proved one of the most disappointing of CIO drives.

There were many reasons. The textile industry was not concentrated and trustified—like steel, auto, rubber, electrical—so that if you knocked off a few big companies the rest might follow. It was moving more and more to the nonunion, race-divided south—the toughest area for any union campaign. Leftism was not one of the reasons for TWOC weakness. Nor was any too-daring defiance of white racism.

In the deep south TWOC was led by A. Steve Nance, long an AFL leader who knew how to adjust his unionism to white supremacist mores. He was born in Georgia, from generations of Georgians, and his father and grandfather had fought in the Confederate army. He picked his staff in such a way as to be able to say: "One thing they cannot charge against us is that we are foreigners, reds, outside agitators, or damn Yankees."

Lest I be included in such categories, I kept away from CIO's southern campaigns. I didn't escape all criticism. A CIO southern publicist, Allen Swim (who got my job when I was dumped in 1947) said pictures of black and white fraternizing in northern CIO publications had hurt southern organizing.

With a correct southerner like himself, Nance thought southern employers would sit down and try to agree. He died, after about a year, a disillusioned man. Southern as they were, his organizers got the full treatment. Franz Daniel of TWOC told the 1939 Textile convention southern newspapers kept repeating that "all of us were communists, and that we were foreign agitators'; employer-hired evangelists preached that TWOC organizers were "agents of the devil"; and the Ku Klux Klan joined the fight against TWOC in full force.

In 1937, while TWOC took its drubbings in the south and SWOC faced worse in Little Steel, other CIO unions were doing fine. The rampaging Auto Workers were knocking off all the big ones—except Ford, which they came to later. The UE followed its GE Schenectady victory with certification at the East Pittsburgh works of Westinghouse. Before the year was out, UE was in or headed for national negotiations with General Electric, Westinghouse, General Motors, and had won a series of strikes.

The Rubber Workers won a 59-day Firestone strike and elections in Goodrich and Goodyear at Akron; and recognition in seven U.S. Rubber plants. Meatpacking was swinging toward CIO, and a Packinghouse Workers Organizing Committee was planned. In New York, the CIO Transport Workers swept the field of urban transportation in subways, elevated, buses.

On the west coast, CIO won the solidly organized Longshoremen, who resumed their march inland, after defeating the efforts of Teamsters' David Beck to stop them. The Woodworkers were beating the Carpenters in lumber and adding their numbers to CIO. On the east coast, the National Maritime Union made CIO dominant among seamen by winning many elections. To white-collar workers, CIO was bringing modern unionism through the Newspaper Guild, Office & Professional Workers, Retail Employees, Architects-Engineers, State-County-Municipal and Federal Workers.

In all these new CIO unions, as in Communications, Shoe, Cannery, and others, and the older Fur and Mine-Mill unions, there was much leftwing influence. Many leaders were communists or close to the left. CIO gave none the financial and organizing help it lavished on SWOC and TWOC. None could claim as much conservative and anticommunist respectability. But during the big CIO upsurge, they did well on their own. Their unexcluded, sometimes uninhibited, radicals seemed to help more than hurt.

Certainly the leftish image of most did not expose them to

such massive, violent redbaiting attack as was launched against SWOC in 1937, on the pretext of the Little Steel strike.

I was not as close to the Little Steel strike as to the GM sitdown. This was a SWOC deal; I was from national CIO and wasn't invited. Lewis, rather huffily, wouldn't butt into "Murray's show." Later Lewis said Murray acted without consulting him "for the first time in Murray's life."

The strike was spread over the mills of Republic, Youngstown, Inland, and Bethlehem steel companies. It had no clear center. Its direction was also diffused. Murray fell ill, and McDonald was hardly a substitute. Regional, subregional, local, directors had charge, while rank-and-filers and leftwing or otherwise subordinated organizers bore the brunt at mill level.

My national CIO job kept my hands full. For the capitalist offensive based on Little Steel hit CIO broadside in its public relations, as well as elsewhere. Just a reminder then, of the kind of strike it was:

• In the Memorial Day massacre at Chicago Republic Steel, police attacked a peaceful picketing parade, killing 10 workers (shot in the back and clubbed as they fled) and injuring scores more for life.

• Striking steelworkers were gassed, clubbed, shot in Youngstown, Massillon, Cleveland, and elsewhere—bringing the total killed to 18 (all on the strikers' side), with hundreds gravely wounded.

• The loud, goonish Tom Girdler, Republic Steel president, tried to rally all capitalist forces, in and beyond steel, to "stop CIO."

• Governors, mayors, sheriffs, police, were suborned against CIO, sometimes with hard cash, as the LaFollette committee later revealed.

• The Mohawk Valley Formula was widely applied, with its "citizens' committees," back-to-work movements, and other strike-breaking techniques.

• Alleged friends of labor in public office betrayed it widely. Ohio strikers at first hailed Governor Martin Davey for sending in the National Guard, but soon found it used to break the strike by armed force.

The GM strike was a far-reaching class struggle, with the workers on the offensive and a minimum of violence. In the Little Steel strike, the capitalists took the offensive and made of it a murderous class war.

The anti-CIO public relations offensive was highly organized and extravagantly financed. Millions were spent on every device to guide opinion formation. Local business and civic leaders were bribed or bullied into "citizens' committees." The press didn't need to be bribed; it let down the dams of all restraint. Anti-CIO propaganda flooded the land. Liberals began to fret or faint, and laborites to get cold feet.

From professional experience, I knew how wealthy owners could use the mass media like faucets to turn "public opinion" on or off, to keep it under quiet control, or to make it a surging torrent for class or imperialist war. But never had I seen so sharp and sudden a switch of "public opinion" as that on CIO in the late spring and summer of 1937.

The year started well for us. After the GM strike victory and the U.S. Steel agreement, CIO was riding high. A big part of Wall Street had okayed CIO recognition, and its press and pundits nodded approving heads. Spreading sitdowns upset the Nervous Nellies, but their nerves calmed when they saw CIO agreements working to keep them under control. Nothing appeased the more reactionary rightists, of course, but the "more responsible organs of public opinion"—controlled by union-accepting capital—gave CIO a lot of credit.

For a spell it became the vogue to picture CIO as a bandwagon of small aggressive upcomers who might even make John L. Lewis first labor president of the United States. CIO's public relations were called "excellent," sometimes "brilliant." Business and liberal outfits invited me to their confabs to explain the secret of CIO public relations success.

Then, late in May, the Little Steel strike got under way. The Memorial Day massacre occurred. Some billions of dollars of Wall Street saw a chance to stop CIO, and Girdler expanded his offensive to the cultural front. All at once CIO's public image was defaced. The shots that killed the steel strikers were a signal to press, radio, politicians, to make "violence" their major charge against CIO. Redness came next with the pious Murray and the babbittarian McDonald fronting for a communist conspiracy, and Lewis looming ominously as a red dictator. For the more sophisticated, "irresponsible" became the word for CIO. (To sign up U.S. Steel without a strike was "responsible trade unionism"—which employers were said to love. If the Little Steel companies showed less than love, SWOC must have become irresponsible.)

The public relations offensive was as brazen and fictional as it was sudden and all-embracing; and once the strike was broken without CIO being stopped, it was called off as suddenly as it was started. But while it was at its height, only Lewis and the left seemed to retain any composure or sense of proportion. Hillman and other CIO leaders were wringing their hands, and the rout of labor's liberal friends was almost complete. President Roosevelt, who should have been in a position to distinguish fact from fiction, called down "a plague on both your houses"— a political ineptitude that laid him wide open to Lewis.

What, oh what, had happened to CIO's public relations, callers kept asking me, and what were we going to do? Heywood Broun, genuinely distressed, wanted CIO to spend money to match the capitalist propaganda drive. Lewis resisted, pointing out that the other side could always outspend us; and through control of the media, could buy more public opinion with its dollars than we could with ours. If money was available, Lewis was always inclined to spend it on building the organized strength that commanded acclaim—rather than to buy acclaim that would vanish unless based on strength.

On one Broun point, I was all on Lewis's side. Broun wanted Lewis to improve his and CIO's image by smiling when photographed. This Lewis always balked at doing. His smile was engaging enough, in relaxed moments. It might have softened some middle-class hearts, as it did when Lewis turned on some private charm with individual capitalists. But a John L. Lewis smirking for the cameras like a movie-starish Homer Martin or

Dave McDonald, or even like the toothy crowd-charming FDR —it wouldn't have seemed right. Not worth risking disillusioned murmurs from a battling rank and file, "That just ain't John L."

I had watched Lewis fight through to success in the GM strike. Now I saw his head unbowed under bouncing brickbats, and my respect increased. He reacted like a working-class leader who knew the class struggle was not a kissing game, and who didn't kid himself about the "alignment of class forces," as Marxists might put it, though he wouldn't. Nor was Lewis of any idea-first school of thought, holding that in the beginning was the word. The words and ideas of the great anti-CIO propaganda offensive didn't fluster him.

Lewis knew the other side controlled the organs of opinion formation and a big store of propaganda gases. When the workers advanced and the wind blew with them, the gases served little. But when the bosses' offensive forced a labor retreat, as in Little Steel, they'd use their gases to the full. Labor shouldn't breathe them in, but don its masks and rally to fight back.

I liked liberals, a bit wishy-washy, but usually well-meaning. I preferred folks who wished labor well to those who wished to clobber it. But at the moment I was disgusted. "The liberal," Broun said, "is the man who heads for the cloakroom when the fight starts." The fight was on. The Girdlers were out to trounce CIO. Let the liberals head for the cloakroom then, but not add their own little stink bombs to the attack.

The Girdler-hacks said CIO had gone too far. It was violent, communistic, irresponsible. Not caring for the public, it had enraged public opinion. Plaintively, liberal press and radio pundits echoed this tune. Why, they asked, hadn't the once-nice CIO stopped before going too far? Why did it use violence? Why didn't it drive out the communists? Even more exasperating were leaders in CIO itself who parroted the liberals; who fainted at the sound of distant guns and urged retreat.

With all these people in mind, but prudently unnamed, I wrote a column headed, "Fair-Weather Friends." It was widely quoted in the press as another Lewis slap at Roosevelt. Anyone could put on the shoe if it fitted. But looking in on Lewis that

day, I felt I was getting more credit than my due. He was reading the newspaper stories and studying my column. He congratulated me. I admitted Roosevelt wasn't foremost in my mind
when I wrote it. For this candor Lewis repaid me with the much
reduced enthusiasm of a "H-m-m-mph!"

I didn't share Lewis's growing Roosevelt-hetz. To me Roosevelt was a capitalist politician running a capitalist government.
He depended on workers' votes and union support, and should
be made to pay for them. In upheavals like the GM and Little
Steel strikes, U.S. governments had traditionally used all their
powers against labor, whereas Roosevelt had been more neutral.
I couldn't feel as betrayed as did Lewis when Roosevelt let CIO
down by failing to step out of his capitalist role to champion the
workers.

This was 1937. Roosevelt had been reelected with aggressive
and wholehearted CIO support. Most still saw Lewis's blows as
those of a rather punchy sparring partner of The Champ in the
White House. In this instance, Lewis saw more clearly than I
that Roosevelt was the prototype fair-weather friend, the model
for the delinquent liberals.

Speaking of the Lewis-Roosevelt split, already foreshadowed, Lewis's subjective style made things seem more personal
than they were. Both men were practiced enough to subordinate
the personal to the political when they chose. In his Lewis biography, Saul Alinsky repeatedly speaks of the two "hating" each
other. To me the word doesn't ring quite right.

Lewis liked to strike his foes in hot blood. He worked up a
good mad—spicing the preliminaries with verbal malice—then
put all he had into his blows. He wasn't so personally malevo-
lent and vengeful as "hatred" suggests. As a fighter, Lewis was a
pro; and a professional soldier can fight his foe to the death
without necessarily hating him. He may also nurse his wounds
and gripe, as could Lewis, until they healed.

In the years leading up to the open break, I sometimes ran
into Lewis as he was returning from visits to Roosevelt in the
White House. His quips were in the mood of a fencer who felt
he'd done pretty well in a bout with a well-matched opponent.

Lewis loved to take on the big ones. In Roosevelt he took
on the biggest, one who held himself champ in the same sport.

Both liked the battle of wits, I'm sure, up to a point. That point was when either felt outsmarted, outbluffed, or betrayed politically. Then anger followed.

Mrs. Roosevelt once ascribed the Lewis-Roosevelt antagonism to their different class backgrounds. I doubt it, in the sense she intended. Lewis might ridicule the patrician and try to take him down a peg. But he was intrigued by the different specimen and would have tangled more readily with a rival upstart. And Roosevelt's lofty lack of understanding of labor didn't annoy Lewis; it gave him an advantage he relished.

In a sense more political and Marxian than social, however, there was a class gulf between the two. Roosevelt may not have thought of himself as the liberally inclined head of a capitalist government; nor Lewis of himself as momentary leader of an insurgent working class. But that is how they behaved to each other in the early years of CIO.

Nice liberal people who are on top want to do all they can for those who are not. They try, too. One thing they can't do is understand them; they aren't in their shoes. Listen to a nice white housewife discussing her black maid, or to liberal commentators and politicians discussing "race riots." In the Thirties, they discussed sitdowns that way.

President Roosevelt was a nice man. He wanted to be good to the working people—and was, in many ways. They did a lot for themselves, too, under his administration. He was kind to labor leaders, especially those like Hillman and Murray, who did what he wanted. He'd have been nicer still to Lewis—who carried more weight—if Lewis had let him. But Lewis acted cocky —downright cheeky at times. No matter how much Roosevelt did for the workers, Lewis demanded more. He showed no gratitude, nor did he bid his followers be grateful—just put on the squeeze all the harder. Roosevelt was a tolerant man—even when workers acted outrageously in sitdown and Little Steel strikes. Did Lewis show appreciation and try to make things easier? Damn that Lewis!

As 1937 went on, the gunfire died down. The shot strikers were buried. Little Steel mills resumed work, with only Inland even recognizing the union. Roosevelt relaxed. He blessed the houses on which he once called down a plague. Lewis filed away his complaints—for future reference. The debris of hot class war was cleared away. Fresh air dissipated propaganda gases. "Public opinion" was allowed to calm down.

With fair weather, CIO's friends returned, all sunny smiles. Before yearend, I was invited to reveal to a Madison Avenue luncheon the secret of CIO's once-more-good public relations. I didn't divulge our trade secret. Now it can be told, in one word: success.

Lewis didn't have to smile into any cameras. He didn't have to add to CIO's beggarly public relations budget. The Girdler-backers cut down on theirs, and not just because of its size. The purpose had been to stop CIO. CIO hadn't stopped. During and after the strike, as before it, most CIO unions advanced spectacularly. Even SWOC was signing up other companies. In a few years, it brought Little Steel, too, into line.

A million more workers joined CIO unions. They won strikes, plant elections, union recognition, better wages and conditions. Good public relations for CIO!

Euphoria. That was the word for CIO's Atlantic City conference in October 1937. For me, for many others, for a whole movement.

It was a celebration. CIO's success—its tempo and extent —surprised and exhilarated all, from right to left. There was credit aplenty to go around. Congratulations were bandied to and fro. Never before, nor after, was there such togetherness organizationally, socially. Even politically, the factions were lulled into momentary truce.

It was a show, with Atlantic City picked by a showman's hand.

On this very spot, ladies and gentlemen, in this same month of October two years ago, in 1935—in this very auditorium of this same Chelsea Hotel—the renowned John L. Lewis, the redoubtable champion of labor, knocked out that man-monster Big Bill Hutcheson, and flabbergasted the A F of L.

Now look around, ladies and gentlemen. It is but two years

later. Mr. Lewis is back again in the center of the same stage where once a certain Mr. Green did Big Bill's bidding. Here today, Mr. Lewis has gathered together leaders of a brand new labor movement, the CIO, which already rivals in numbers the ancient AFL and far exceeds it in esteem.

Lewis repeatedly picked Atlantic City in the fall. Here he staged his dramatic retirement as CIO leader in 1940. He liked the brisk, restoring walk up the boardwalk, from the center of turmoil to his quarters in the President Hotel. There, a bit remote but close enough, he could brood, make plans—available to those who came to him, not he to them.

To this same President Hotel Lewis repaired in October 1941, when he felt the final showdown with Murray approaching. Against the familiar pasteboard backdrop of Atlantic City's hotel skyline in the fall, the two had their last words, and Lewis was through with CIO.

October 1935, October 1937, November 1940, October 1941, each time in Atlantic City—the beginning, the middle, the end, of John L. Lewis, of CIO. An anticlimax: In the fall of 1946—long after Lewis—CIO returned to Atlantic City to prepare its Cold War surrender. 1935, bugle call to action. 1937, victory celebration. 1940, end of one CIO, start of another. 1941, Lewis fadeout from CIO. 1946, a whimper.

Looking back from the 1937 CIO conference to the 1935 AFL convention, I relished the fillip Lewis intended. Promise made, promise fulfilled. Some of the same delegates in the same auditorium—with strange additions. The same seaview hotel rooms filled with smoke, but fewer poker games. Lobbies crowded as two years before, but cigar sales off. A host of reporters, and gossips. Big shots elbowing through lobbies, or lingering to chat. Sidling eavesdroppers eying, and being eyed. Knowing and known persons all jumbled together in resort style. Outside, bracing fall winds. Across the gray sands, the bridling waves in never-ending comment on the piffling concerns of all conventioneers.

Missing was the craftiest Old Guard. But Lewis, Murray, Hillman, Dubinsky, were here again—with much the same entourage. So were the same few Youngsters who, in 1935, defied Granma AFL in her boudoir. Just two years older, but

some already aping the cigar-poker dignity of Granma's potbellied beaux. Along with the oldsters and maturing Youngsters,
many newcomers—and how new their style!

Labor bureaucracy had closed the door to the young in
spirit, the questioning, the rebellious. It co-opted dull schemers,
who did as they were told and watched their step—so domesticated that some of the now toothless old tigers who raised them
from cubs could blush for them.

CIO upset this closed-door pattern. It "opened the door to
the communists"—as John P. Frey put it. Not in older line
unions like UMW, ACW, ILGWU, nor in their SWOC and
TWOC. But in newcomer unions—more on their own—new-
type leaders were everywhere on top.

Those of UE were typical. Young men like brainy Julius
Emspak; nervous, restless, organizing Jim Matles; lively, showy
Jimmy Carey. UAW's Homer Martin was more oddball than
new-type—a Fidgety Phil who couldn't sit still. But Wyndham
Mortimer was of the new type. So too, in different ways, darkly
shy George Addes and that great big, new-boy Dick Frankensteen. Walter Reuther, a new-typer too, then leftish like Carey,
was not yet on top—though on his way.

From the west, and from the left, a handsome Harry and a
hardnosed one: Harold Pritchett of Woodworkers, Harry Bridges
of Longshoremen. Big Joe Curran of Maritime was another lefty
—red-rough to the eye, slick-smooth to the right touch. More
colorfast, sailor Blacky (Ferdinand N.) Myers, eager, alert, all-
outer.

"Red Mike" Quill of Transport personalized redness to the
crowd. More so than soft-spoken Ben Gold of Fur, the most advertised communist. Quill featured Irish wit and blarney, with a
blackthorn cane for shillelagh. His fiery retorts to redbaiters delighted the left. "I'd rather be a red to the rats," said he, "than a
rat to the reds." Flanking Quill and also on the left, solid Austin
Hogan and fluid John Santo—the latter with Irish-American
brogue imposed on native Hungarian accent.

New-typers too, and on the left, were Don Henderson of
Cannery, Mervyn Rathborne and Joe Selly of Communications,

Reid Robinson of Mine-Mill. Soon to come from Organizing Committees were Grant Oakes, Joe Weber, Gerald Fielde, of Farm Equipment; Don Harris and Henry Johnson (one of CIO's rare black leaders) from Packinghouse.

The white-collar leaders differed little from the blue collars. Some college was now more common for all, and the mental strife of leftism did more than formal education to sharpen wits and broaden horizons. Big, bearlike Broun of the Newspaper Guild was different from anyone anywhere, but not his slim sidekick Jonathan Eddy. Jake Baker, of Federal Workers, was a bit tweedy, but Eleanor Nelson (rare woman CIO leader), Art Stein, Henry Rhine, of Federal, were typical new-unionists. So too Abe Flaxer and Henry Wenning, of State-County-Municipal; Lewis Alan Berne, of Architects-Engineers; Napoleonic little Lewis Merrill, of the Office Workers—in some ways a ringer for less officy Arthur Osman, head of Retail's wholesale empire in New York.

Up to Osman, I've listed only international or national union leaders who were, or might have been, at CIO's 1937 conference. There were hundreds of other new-typers and leftists on other levels—heads of state or local movements, or of parts of all but CIO's most old-line unions.

Many of these new-typers were trained in the communist movement as I knew it—a movement, that is, of militant unemployed; of union pioneers before New Deal permitted or CIO paid salaries; of rebels against corrupt inaction or reaction in AFL unions. Like many new radicals of the Sixties, they were young-minded persons coming out of their shells and relating to the whole world around.

Not all the new-typers were communists, or sympathetic, though many were. Not all were leftist enough to work with the communists, though most did. Some were in-again-out-again, on-again-off-again, some factionally hostile. All were close enough to the left to know the score.

Put a bunch like this cheek-by-jowl in the same hotel with old-line labor leaders and their still older line henchmen, and what did you get? Clash, conflict? No. This 1937 confab was a picnic, a love-in.

Lewis was in his element, right on top. The unchallenged champ. He absorbed adulation with distinctive poise and grace. Beside his chief, Murray was all modesty as usual, or more than usual, after Little Steel.

Hillman's tensions dissolved in smiles. During the anti-CIO offensive he had been ground unmercifully between the upper and nether millstones of Roosevelt and Lewis. Now he congratulated all, including the lefts.

Dubinsky became almost as convivial as he looked. His union had done well in the CIO upsurge. Its last convention had resounded to chants of "CIO . . . CIO . . . CIO" as the delegates hailed Lewis with emotion.

All the hangers-on tried dutifully to get into the mood of their chiefs.

Everyone watched everyone else, of course. The new-typers studied the old. They responded to good treatment with respect, figuring they could learn from men with decades of union-leading behind them. Collectively, the new-typers disturbed the big shots, but didn't upset them too much. They were hardly invited in such numbers, but they got here just the same, and must be accepted. Sizing them up individually, the big shots felt more at home. They'd handled many a cocky youngster in their time.

Homer Martin arrived late and barely showed himself. The big shots discussed him as house psychiatrists might a new patient. After Homer cracked up, who then? Mortimer? Logical, but too experienced and red-set for easy handling. Addes, not enough drive. Frankensteen—seemed to have the stuff—could be handled too. Reuther, coming from outside but pushy enough to be a pain.

Everyone knew Jimmy Carey. He'd made himself known, in the nicest way, to every top shot, to second-stringers too, and the office help. Everyone liked Jimmy, and called him that. He said "yes, sir" to male elders, "yes, ma'am" to female elders—the mark of the parochial school, said Brophy. The big shots didn't take him too seriously. He was in and out of Washington so much, they wondered who ran his union.

The other UEers were as unfamiliar as Jimmy was familiar. What of Emspak? Must be smart to get and hold his job with so little push and politician about him. Matles, too—skinny, accent and all, on top of a job usually held down by at least 200 lbs. of brawn and blarney.

Joe Curran and Mike Quill were easier to understand. Dangerous? Surely their leftism couldn't be the coming thing! Joe . . . likely a good boy at heart, as Hillman said, just going along with his crowd until he could get on top of it. As to Mike . . . there was a real politician, likable too, for all his redness.

Ben Gold might be dangerous, head of a solid union. He was eyed curiously and handled with care. But butter wouldn't melt in Ben's mouth. The communists were going along; Gold would, too. You knew where he stood.

Chief conversation piece was Harry Bridges. He was delayed, and curiosity grew. Bridges was a west-coaster, known chiefly in the east for his work in the San Francisco general strike. The big shots were unsure how to handle him. Angular and edgy as his nose and profile, he didn't fit readily into their pigeonholes. With his Australian accent and abrupt manners, he might have drawn some ridicule, but didn't. Somehow that wouldn't have worked with Harry. How deal with a man like him? With outright attack—which wasn't then on the CIO agenda.

Bridges' maiden speech to national CIO was as long as long-awaited. It drew the crack that "Two-Gun" Smith, the stringy-bearded old miner always on hand at Lewis shows, had been clean-shaven when Harry started. The Bridges speech sounded awkward to the Washington-tuned ears of CIO leaders. It included radical phrases such as even the reds avoided. It was full of rank-and-filisms that didn't jibe with Lewis-Murray-Hillman ideas of running things with discipline from on top. It drew platform rebuke for plugging class solidarity more than contractual sanctity. Still, along with all the rest, Bridges got his full share of brotherly backslapping. Never again in CIO were things to be quite like that.

Beyond this advanced position of success and good-fellowship, it was hard for CIO to push ahead. A new depression had begun. On some sectors, CIO momentum might still carry it forward. But old heads warned that, with growing unemployment, dropping dues income, and victories harder to win, CIO would do well to hold the line against counterattack.

The no-man's-land before it was mined with booby traps.

Chapter Ten

BOOBY TRAP

As CIO's momentum declined, it faced the trap of internal dissension set by the red-hunters.

CIO started as a new kind of labor movement—a challenge to the old AFL and the status quo it complacently guarded. It was new in its youth and fervor, new in the broad sector of the working class it brought into action, new in the way it accepted and integrated its radicals, new in its relative independence of corporate and government control, new in many social and political attitudes.

All this was evident in the militant upsurge of 1936-37, which carried CIO beyond the initial intent of its old-line founders. But already in 1938—even before CIO was constituted as a Congress of Industrial Organizations—old influences were bidding for control.

As economic recession checked more sweeping advance, the new unions turned to consolidation—trying to make their new agreements work, to assure steady dues income and union discipline. They lost some of their fighting fervor, and employer and government pressures increased.

But the new movement—thanks largely to its radicals—did not at once surrender its working-class independence. For years CIO continued to distinguish itself from the AFL in labor militancy, in fighting for black workers, in welcoming radicals, in political action, in foreign policy. It was definitely—if decreasingly—to the left of the AFL.

In 1938, anti-CIO forces in press and Congress began an intensive campaign to divide CIO with the catch-cries and intrigues of anticommunism. They provided the smokescreen for future retreats from CIO's early advanced position and a decade later the pretext—monstrously ballooned by the Cold War—for CIO finally to squat side by side with AFL as another complacent custodian of the status quo.

A sallow, sickly little man hovered around the fringes of early CIO. He avoided me, and I learned only later that he was Benjamin Stolberg—a liberal journalist with a sharp and sometimes lively style.

Early in 1938 a friend sent me galley proofs, with references to myself, from a series of articles written by Stolberg for the Scripps-Howard newspaper chain. The references were redbaiting and slanderous. I threatened suit, and in final printing they were toned down. Other CIOers were less lucky. Stolberg's "Inside CIO" series attacked all he called leftwing, close to the left, or tolerant of it. He pictured CIO as rent from top to bottom by strife between communists and anticommunists.

It was a first of its kind, and started a trend. Before that, rightists had redbaited CIO, like the New Deal, in blunderbuss style. They called both "communist" (their favorite hate word) for seeming to back the have-nots against the haves. If they could point out actual communists, that was fine—but not important. To them, Lewis and Roosevelt were worse than communists. Stolberg attempted precision redbaiting—to name alleged communists or lefts rather than damn the movement as such. He drew his allegations from Lovestonite sources and made the incredible Homer Martin his hero. Like Lovestone, Stolberg was later hired by David Dubinsky.

CIO's rightwingers didn't hail Stolberg as they might later have done. His timing was too close to the CIO-baiting of the Tom Girdler crowd; Girdler in fact said the Stolberg series confirmed his own charges. Stolberg also spread his shots too widely. He was especially malicious against persons like John Brophy and Heywood Broun whom he lumped with the communists. He spared no CIO top shot he thought too soft on the left. CIO speakers regularly denounced Stolberg, and Brophy dubbed him "Stoolberg." No CIO leader would openly defend him.

CIO unity was still too strong, and most members liked it that way. It took years of hammering away on anticommunism —mostly from outside—before it could be widely used to proscribe the left. In some unions, of course, rights and lefts contended from the start. But organizing success and the need for union unity tended to reduce such factional conflict to little more than the contention of "ins" and "outs" for union office.

Only in UAW was there a dangerous split. It was not between right and left. Responsible CIO and UAW leaders knew that Lovestone, the Ford company, and the AFL were taking advantage of Homer Martin's personality problem for their respective purposes. The anti-Martin forces that finally prevailed included all political shades, from right to left.

National CIO opposed redbaiting as an enemy tactic—an estimate confirmed by the experience of every CIO union. If further confirmation were needed, the Dies "un-American" committee soon supplied it.

The House Un-American Activities Committee was set up in June 1938, with Rep. Martin Dies (D., Tex.) as chairman. It was supposedly directed against both fascists and communists, but quickly forgot about the fascists. Dominated by reactionary southern Democrats and northern Republicans gunning for Roosevelt, it was an anti-New Deal, anti-CIO committee.

HUAC picked on CIO unions when negotiating or striking; on New Deal agencies with appropriations before Congress; on New Deal Democrats like Michigan Governor Frank Murphy in election campaigns. Its first lists of CIO "communists" included the dead, the nonexistent, communists unconnected with CIO, excommunists, noncommunists, and anticommunists.

CIO stood up well and enhanced its prestige in the 1938 depression.

In the Great Depression, the AFL's record had been miserable. Jobless members who couldn't pay dues were usually deserted. The AFL pushed no real remedies and still opposed unemployment insurance as late as 1931. Its unions retreated before wholesale wage-cutting, holding it folly to strike when so many were jobless.

CIO in 1938 did much better. With dues income off and fewer chances to organize, CIO slowed the pace of its drive. It did not halt it. New packinghouse and farm-equipment campaigns were pushed. UE won its first national contract with General Electric. Mine-Mill organized brass workers in Connecticut. CIO unions fought efforts to cut wages and revoke gains. Rejecting the old bugaboo that strikes can't be won in a depression, they called many strikes that at least held the line. The Fur Workers, after a 15-week lockout in New York, even won substantial wage increases.

The new CIO unions didn't abandon their unemployed members. They tried to hold them with token dues, or none at all. They helped them get relief. The largely left-led Industrial Union Councils in major cities promoted demonstrations for more relief and jobs, and remedial programs of every kind. Nationally, CIO lobbied energetically for more WPA and PWA funds and projects; for public housing, increased jobless benefits, expanded social security; for a law to shorten working hours and place a floor under wages. Besides helping pass the Wage-Hour law and various relief measures, CIO warded off many antiunion bills and repulsed the first attacks on the Wagner labor relations act.

A united CIO fought unemployment. Lewis gave militant and broad-gauge leadership, as he had done in organizing. He continued allied with the left which did much to formulate and promote the CIO program. Hillman and his followers also made notable legislative contributions.

On the armor of CIO's unity, the new redbaiting at first made little dent. Into the softer brain tissues of newspapermen, it penetrated deeply.

In 1938, a faction called the Mariners' Club sought control of the National Maritime Union by redbaiting the leftwing administration of Joseph Curran. It elected its candidate, Jerome King, as national secretary—though he was later expelled on fourteen counts of antiunion disruption, including taking money from the Standard Oil Company. A New York labor reporter, Edward Levinson, press-agented this faction so obviously that

NMU officially protested when he was later appointed UAW publicity chief.

In 1937, this same Levinson wrote the book, "*Labor on the March*," published early in 1938. It was a good journalistic account of the rise of CIO, which didn't divide CIOers into "communists" and "anticommunists." Only toward the end did Levinson grind a factional ax against the left and disparage the communists' part in CIO. The book read as if written in the unity spirit of CIO's first two years, with a last-minute bow to the Stolberg line first publicized in January, 1938.

Rereading books on early CIO, I found some still stood up well, though written in the heat of reporting those times, as notably *Labor's New Millions* by Mary Heaton Vorse, *The Many and the Few* by Henry Kraus, and most of Levinson's book. Then I turned to Stolberg's book, *The Story of the CIO*—a reprint or rehash of his Scripps-Howard series. Though most attuned to current Cold War anticommunism, it had about it the mold of a dead and disfigured past. Subsequent events had contradicted many of his lopsided accounts of factional fights and made anticommunist "heroes" of many of his "communist" villains.

Levinson and Victor Riesel were of the same labor journalistic school as Stolberg. Both got a start on the *New Leader*—which became like an English-language supplement to the Jewish *Daily Forward*, retailing the *Forward's* brand of anticommunism in a then indifferent gentile market. The *New Leader* was supposedly a rightwing socialist paper. Its socialism evaporated in time with the attrition in rightwing socialist ranks. A rightist availability for any form of anticommunism remained

Once I found Lewis relaxing in his hotel room after a session with Sidney Hillman, who had been bellyaching about the reds. "You know," Lewis mused, "I believe Sidney is really scared of them (the communists)." Then, over a gap I could fill in, Lewis went on to ask why, with all the anti-Semitism let loose by Hitler, the *Forward* kept on attacking a fellow Jew like Lee Pressman.

Riesel wrote a labor column for the *New Leader* when CIO was young. In it he fingered Pressman and me as evil red counselors to the innocent Lewis. It was like the earlier ploy of blaming

Tom Corcoran and Ben Cohen for Roosevelt's misdeeds. The person of Lewis, like Roosevelt at first, was then sacrosanct. To save himself legwork, Riesel studied my CIO publicity. I had to read his column to learn how devilishly I followed the party line.

After Stolberg made the big time, Riesel too went all out for the big dailies, the big dough, with a similar line. Less obsessed than Stolberg, he wrote for hire, it was a job. A Stolberg might avoid me. Not a Riesel.

During World War II, I was on a radio network panel with Riesel; Phil Pearl, AFL publicist; and a Hearst antired specialist, a renegade communist whose name I forget. Off the air, Riesel made out to be on my side. I guessed he did the same with Pearl; Phil and I should have compared our sympathizer lists. Riesel took my arm chummily, as we walked away together. He said the Hearst man did "too much redbaiting, keeps at it all the time." I reminded Riesel how he used to redbait me in the *New Leader*. "Why, Len——" he began, then stopped, pained by my tactlessness.

I knew Levinson well when he reported the CIO upsurge for the *New York Post*. He was an able reporter, persistent, but rather plaintive. What fretted Eddie, I was never quite sure. He was on our side and things were going our way, still he seemed unhappy. I concluded he wasn't the kind to join in dancing in the streets. Levinson didn't redbait in his early coverage of CIO. His paper was pro-CIO, and so was he. But in 1938, he made the switch to redbaiting the NMU. By the time he was officially injected into UAW's troubled politics in 1939, he was widely known for his antileft intrigues.

Many other reporters made a similar switch in 1938—mostly to meet the press demand for more of the Stolberg stuff. Big dailies hired redbait specialists just for the labor beat—usually renegade communists, red-hating "socialists," or former fellow travelers who claimed to have been seduced by the communists. A developing factional fight in the Newspaper Guild against the Broun-left administration added to candidates for these jobs.

The antired specialists for antilabor papers found little favor at the time in CIO. They prowled around the outskirts of CIO events. If they showed at the press table, they were typically brazen or shamefaced. Mostly they met their CIO contacts in dim cocktail bars, behind the potted palms in hotel lobbies, in secret opposition caucuses. They were considered in a class with Dies committee informers, a role some played.

There were also reporters of integrity and high repute who began in their own way to make the prevailing switch. I think of Louis Stark, of the *New York Times*.

Longest on an exclusively labor beat, for a paper of much prestige, Louis Stark was already unchallenged "dean of labor reporters" when I was a Federated Press reporter. He was deanlike in his dignity; serious, thoughtful, thoroughly informed. Sensitive and reserved though he was, Lou would go out of his way to help less knowledgeable reporters.

When CIO was started, from acquaintances we became friends. Stark was as enthusiastic as I was. As top labor story, CIO must have been a sweet revenge for years spent covering that dull and backward bureaucracy, the old AFL—and one that accorded with his own ideals. Beyond the call of duty that threw us together anyhow, Stark liked to join Brophy and me to gloat over great events. He threw in his own ideas too—once even a draft of some answer he thought CIO should make.

As mutual confidence grew, Lou would call me up at times on a Sunday morning. We'd meet at the Shoreham or Wardman Park hotel and walk along the park slopes, or I might go to his apartment. Lou usually had something on his mind he wanted to talk out. At first it might be some aspect of CIO policy. Soon it became personal problems.

Stark worried about his CIO sympathies showing and was deeply upset when AFL President Green complained about him to his publisher. When he covered the AFL's 1936 doings in Florida, I thought he overcompensated and sometimes wrote as if there were no CIO side to the case. I didn't blame him—just wondered which was better to have, a friend compelled to dissemble his feelings or a foe impelled to make amends.

In our next talk, other things were on Lou's mind. He felt the *Times* had restricted his beat in the 1937 General Motors strike by assigning Russell Porter to cover the employers' side, and limiting him to the labor side. I told him the deal was too big for one man, but Lou was not to be comforted. Already charged by the AFL with being pro-CIO, he said, he was now suspect of being too prolabor, and this was a broad hint, a warning.

Stark and I had no further intimate talks for some time. When next he gave me a Sunday call, he had a curious new worry. Someone close to him had been involved in some kind of radical association. I forget the details. Lou was a liberal social idealist, but nothing about him or what he told me, I thought, could lay him open to red smear on such a sophisticated paper as the *New York Times*. When he persisted in worrying, I put him down as a compulsive worrywart.

The *Times* had not yet descended to the redbaiting level of the Stolbergs and Riesels. It preferred to be factual rather than factional, I assumed. If it assigned Stark to assess right-left differences in CIO, I thought he would try to do this judiciously, quoting each faction's claims.

I was therefore surprised when the *Times* in 1938 ran a series of articles from Detroit by Louis Stark "exposing" rather than reporting communist influences in UAW. Stark did his fingering with circular motions rather than the stubby directness of a Stolberg. But he did a similar job on Wyndham Mortimer and other UAWers, some far from leftwing, whose union policies Homer Martin, Jay Lovestone—and soon Reuther—opposed as following the Communist party line. As to the CP line, that was treated as ipso facto bad, and disruptive of unions the communists did much to build.

From Stark I had expected more than a parroting of one faction's propaganda. At least he might have quoted the other side's claims, I thought, if only to knock them down. As to the communists, couldn't even a Stark dare to be fair enough to give them as much as a quote?

On Stark's return to Washington, I set out to confront him. He avoided me. At last I cornered him in a dim and deserted alcove of the Willard Hotel. He'd have had to push by me to escape. Mildly I asked his grounds for some distortions I saw in his stories. Louis didn't answer. His sullen silence told me our friendship was at an end. When I appealed to his reporting standards, he showed more spirit.

Had he interviewed anyone on the other side, I asked, Mortimer for instance? Or perhaps checked the Lovestone version of the CP line with Will Weinstone, the party leader in Detroit?

"Don't be naive!" Louis shot back. For one so mild, it was a flareup.

I wasn't being naive about things in general. Other reporters were doing worse than Stark, and I hardly lifted an eyebrow. I was just being naive about Louis. With no one else would I have argued as I did, knowing I laid myself wide open to the red smear.

Later, Stark wrote another series from Detroit redbaiting the lefts in UAW and CIO. This time, he included me. It was a guarded reference to my being "close to Mortimer." Before long, he spelled it out.

The next time I saw Stark, at some convention, I pursued him. He had left an itch I had to scratch. My kidding had a pricker for him.

"Nothing personal, Len," said Louis and hurried away.

Parenthetically, family tiffs—over such things as divorce and child-raising—played a part in many of the political switches.

• A domineering, once-radical Dad divorced the Mom of his teens-to-twenties kids, to marry a doll. The kids sided with Mom. They became communists. Dad turned passionately to anticommunist politics in his union. Neither Mom nor doll was very political.

• A socialistic newsman divorced a lefter-leaning wife, claiming in court she was making communists of his kids. To justify himself, he became deeply emotional thereafter in antileft union intrigues.

• A passionate redhead loved a handsome black-haired communist, and both loved the movement. The redhead's love turned passionately to another. She told the judge she wanted her freedom because her husband was a communist and she hated communists, then started hating them for real.

• Two labor men, in different cities, had son or nephew seduced leftward by the Young Communist League. One youngster kept liking the YCL—which so embarrassed the union leader that he had to "take steps." The other got disgruntled; and protectively his old man gruntled too. Both labor leaders took out their feelings on CIO's left wing.

If Fulton Lewis, Jr., comes up next, it's for a change of pace. He suffered no crisis of conscience, I'm sure. He had no switch to make.

When I was a Washington correspondent, Fulton seemed one of the best-adjusted trained seals performing for the Hearst organization. In CIO days, he broadcast for the National Association of Manufacturers. CIO didn't buddy-buddy with the NAM, so I didn't run into him.

After CIO got regular radio time on the major networks, Fulton Lewis surprised me. He came to my office and said he might like to broadcast for CIO. We were thinking, as one project, of sponsoring a news commentator, but I'd hardly thought anyone of Fulton's bent would offer himself or imagine he'd be acceptable. I tried to find out what was on his mind.

Fulton Lewis said he'd been "a prostitute" for Hearst so long it had hardened a resolve to be independent, if he got a chance. As radio commentator, he didn't want to tie himself to one sponsor or kind of sponsor. Having broadcast for the NAM, he now thought to balance things by broadcasting for CIO.

When Fulton Lewis called himself "a prostitute," I didn't take it for confession. Newsmen often used the word kiddingly in self-description.

In my 12 years as CIO publicity director, I got to know hundreds of newspaper and radio men covering labor. CIO put labor news on the front page and multiplied specialized labor reporters. Many others covered CIO occasionally—editors, columnists, magazine, and even sports writers like Paul Gallico, whose fresh and vivid reactions to the CIO drama I well recall.

The labor reporters were reporting class struggle from our side and most wanted to tell it like it was. But they were also working for a capitalist press, for publishers who were big employers themselves, bound by a hundred ties to the rest of the employing class. The rare liberal or professedly pro-labor publishers were sometimes more acutely class-conscious in antiradicalism than the hard-shell reactionaries.

A few reporters were hacks or heels who brazenly served antilabor purposes—some claiming to believe their stuff, some doing a lot of devil-may-care drinking, some shrugging it off as what they were paid to do. But most were decent, intelligent persons who could understand and sympathize with the workers' cause. They devised paddings for their sensitivities.

Associated Press men took comfort in AP's supposedly factual and objective reporting standards—claiming to be impartial between capital and labor in serving the news interests of a wholly capitalist press.

United Press labor reporters tended to be breezily extroverted, taking the world as they found it. Two UP youngsters found in CIO a launching pad for their careers: Cyrus L. Sulzberger, who stuck close to Lewis personally; and William Lawrence, who covered Flint in the GM strike.

Cy Sulzberger, perky fresh and with the seeming innocence of a spoiled nice-kid, had the advantage of an august newspaper name, with corresponding connections. He could pester Lewis at any odd hour, without Lewis objecting. Cy assumed that everyone, like himself, was out to make good.

Bill Lawrence gave UAW a break and got one for himself. He checked with strike leader Bob Travis a statement suggesting a General Motors-Flint Alliance doublecross, and UAW was able just in time to stop a premature evacuation of the plants. Lawrence thus got a break on a big story. A top labor reporter there after, Bill was good company and quite a joker.

International News Service men were less staid than AP men, less breezy than UPers. They had Hearst to serve. Averse to much thought or introspection, they often liked to drink and might shoot off at curious tangents.

The labor reporter typically denied he was partisan, but his sympathies or prejudices showed. Very few confessed to any leftism, even privately. If any did, I suspected innocence or design. If innocent, they'd soon quit, be fired, or change their views. If designing, they just wanted to edge up to CIO lefts who could be useful. In any case, if any leftism crept into their reporting, it wouldn't get by their copy desks.

Yet there were many left-inclined newsmen in those days who made themselves felt in the Newspaper Guild. Only in rare cases of short-lived catering to left-led local labor might they rate the labor beat. Social reformists with animus against the left soon became a common choice.

When the 1936-37 CIO uprising began, most labor reporters were uncommitted persons out to cover a new kind of front-page story. They didn't have to take sides between AFL and CIO; there was little AFL side to take. CIO was where the action was. If the newsmen flocked to us and gave us much space, it wasn't due to CIO sympathies, as the AFL darkly suspected, but because they were newsmen. Between capital and labor, the publishers did the side-taking. They blasted CIO in screaming headlines and turgid editorials, and through columnists like Westbrook Pegler. But someone had to tell what the yelling was all about, and that was the labor reporter.

By 1938, the tumult of mass action was dying down. The labor reporters had a chance to rest their legs and think things over. Their copy was seldom front page any more, unless John L. Lewis took a notion to make it so. They saw the Stolberg clan cutting in on their space—with little more effort than contacting Lovestone's boys or the Dies committee. The publishers loved, and demanded, this labor redbaiting. So did employers generally. AFL leaders liked it and so did a few CIO bigwigs, sub rosa.

If a reporter treated the fingering and factionalism with some sense of proportion, if he tried to report the left as fairly as the right, he became suspect. He, too, might be smeared, or be held too dumb to know the score.

On this point, the more sincere and thoughtful labor reporters must have felt in their intestines the conflicting tugs of the class struggle. Some quietly moved to other fields. Most took the clearly indicated course. If good reporters, they felt bad to turn from reporting to propaganda. They felt better when they could take sides wholeheartedly, by learning to hate as well as bait the reds.

What were the communists up to in 1938 that they hadn't been up to before? Did some change in party line cause the switch in press treatment, the emergence of HUAC? From time to time, the communists made policy switches—as did others. When liberals who tolerated began to execrate, when once-reds became antireds, they usually blamed some communist switch. In 1938, this was less plausible.

During the rise of CIO, American communists followed the general policy of the Seventh World Congress (July-August, 1935) of the Communist International. The 65 parties represented, including that of the United States, agreed that fascism and the war it threatened were the main danger. They urged unity of all antifascists in a broad united or popular front. As applied to the labor movement, the policy was to build and strengthen trade unions, as a major bulwark against fascism. In place of the "united front from below" directed against "social-fascist" leaders of labor, the communists were now eager to work with nonred leaders for working-class solidarity.

"We advocate and consistently uphold the right of the trade unions to decide their policies for themselves," said George Dimitrov, the Comintern leader. "We are even prepared to forego the creation of communist groups in the trade unions if that is necessary in the interests of trade union unity." United States communists tried to follow this line in CIO—to the point in 1939 of liquidating their system of union factions and shop papers.

None of this stopped the right wing from making communist "interference from outside" a major point against the left. There was this to be said: Outside politicians, from Roosevelt down, repeatedly interfered in CIO affairs to serve their purposes. Neither they nor the communists could "dictate." They could urge a certain course on their followers, and punish them in some political way if they didn't comply. The union followers had to operate through union rules to secure adoption of the course. Democrats, Republicans, Socialists, Catholics (through the ACTU), and other outside groups all worked hard to influence unions along their lines.

Like these others, communist members of unions might

meet with comrades from outside to confer on general policies. But as communists gained in union influence and office, they tended to keep within the bounds of their own union in respect to its affair.

In my own CIO experience, I could verify only two major communist interventions—both in UAW and both dictated by concern for union unity.

The first was in 1938, when UAW was endangered by factionalism which Homer Martin was riding hard in all directions. Outside friends, including CIO leaders, Democratic politicians, church and other public figures, expressed concern and made suggestions. So did national Communist party leaders, who suggested an end to the union's caucus system.

UAW was divided between a "Unity Caucus"—including communists, socialists, Reutherites, and more progressive elements generally—and a more conservative, Martin-Frankensteen-Thomas "Progressive Caucus." Urging a united union without regard to political and caucus divisions, the communist leaders tried to impress on UAW leaders Martin, Walter Reuther, and Richard Frankensteen the advantages of taking the lead for union unity.

Both Martin and Reuther preferred to continue fighting it out along the old lines. Frankensteen came out for setting union loyalty and unity ahead of the old caucus loyalties. He got much support from unity-minded UAWers of all kinds, including the lefts. Martin at once punished Frankensteen, demoting him from his job as assistant president and from direction of the Ford drive. Reuther took the opportunity to break completely for the first time with his leftwing allies.

The other instance was at UAW's March 1939 convention in Cleveland, after Homer Martin had split away the part of the union he was to take into the AFL. The Addes-Frankensteen forces and their leftwing allies were now in the majority, opposed by a minority antired faction led by Reuther. With this support, and on their union leadership records, Wyndham Mortimer and George Addes were first in line for top union offices.

In maneuvering to prevent the Addes-Mortimer-Frankensteen majority from registering its advantage by convention vote, Reuther had powerful allies in Sidney Hillman and Philip Murray —whom Lewis appointed in 1938 to represent CIO when UAW asked aid in settling its internal problems. As Roosevelt's chief lieutenant in CIO, Hillman was concerned to counter Lewis's swing away from the administration, and Murray was cautiously going along with him. Neither wanted UAW to align itself with the left or Lewis-led forces in CIO.

Lewis was beginning to sense what was afoot, and Hillman and Murray were careful to get his sometimes reluctant okay on major moves. Neither side wanted an open breach, so friction went little beyond suspicion and irritation. Meanwhile UAWers heeded the two as speaking for Lewis.

Operating thus delicately, Hillman and Murray found in anticommunism a handy cover for their moves—though here too they were cautious. In private dealings with the left, they disclaimed anitleft animus. They avoided open redbaiting. But through Reutherites like Eddie Levinson, whose appointment they secured, they managed to redbait without attribution.

Murray and Hillman were grooming the good-natured and inoffensive R.J. Thomas for UAW president. When Martin defected, Thomas had succeeded him as acting president. Since Thomas had been with the Martin faction, this had helped hold some of it in the CIO column. By now, however, Thomas was less clearly in line for the UAW top spot. Left to themselves, the delegates would likely have chosen a Mortimer-Addes slate.

In this situation, some national communist leaders urged the left to set UAW unity, and wider CIO unity, ahead of personal and factional advantage and yield to Hillman and Murray. The UAW lefts reluctantly agreed—though some broke with the party over this issue.

Hillman and Murray pushed their advantage beyond the naming of Thomas to abolish the vice-presidential offices held by Frankensteen, Mortimer, and Ed Hall. These three were even denied election to the executive board as members at large, when Reuther objected.

At no point in his rise was Reuther himself guilty of such unfactional softness as the lefts were induced to display at this convention. The very idea of setting unity ahead of personal ambition or factional advantage was virtually unheard of in UAW, until the communists suggested it.

Elections to the UAW executive board showed that the relative strength of delegate groupings could have produced different results. Out of some score of board members, the Reuther faction could elect only four.

At this point, my own communist associations may come into question—as indeed they did, in the Fifties, before two congressional committees.

During my twelve CIO years (1935-47), I often met, ate, drank, conferred, in the course of my CIO duties, with fellow CIOers I believed to be communists or close sympathizers. We met in our CIO capacities and talked in union terms. I recall few contacts with outside communists.

One was in the earliest days. I was invited to meet Jack Stachel, then labor secretary of the Communist party. We met in a New York hotel room and discussed labor unity. The party was strong for a united trade union movement. Both CIO and AFL leaders then professed concern for labor unity. Stachel worried that national CIO showed signs of being careless about it. I explained the reasons, as I saw them.

On another occasion, some years later, I visited the home of a fellow CIOer and found him entertaining a man who functioned as legislative representative of the Communist party. We had a drink and discussed legislative matters with full agreement. The CIO program was close to that of the party, which wanted broad unity behind aggressive immediate demands.

At another time, when open communists were becoming a trifle more acceptable socially—though not in CIO headquarters —I was in my CIO office when my secretary yelled through the door that there was a personal call for me. I picked up the phone and asked, "Who's calling?"

"This is Earl," a voice replied.

"Earl who?" I asked, not having the foggiest.

"Earl Browder," the voice said. "I'd like to have a chat."

"Fine," said I. "So would I. Where shall we meet?"

"Why don't you come over to Marguerite's office?"

At the *Daily Worker* office of Marguerite Young, in the National Press Buiding, I chatted inconsequentially with Earl Browder, then CP chief, about current CIO and national affairs.

Shortly after my severance from CIO in 1947, I was in a New York lunchroom when a friend passing my table said: "Johnny Williamson would like to see you." Williamson was then labor secretary of the Communist party.

I first saw Johnny during my 1921-22 winter in Seattle. At the many labor and radical mass meetings of the time, he kept popping up from the audience to ask questions reflecting a Socialist Labor party viewpoint. I liked Johnny's looks—he was bursting with sincerity and had an inquiring mind. Later I heard much about him as the Communist party leader he became, from friends in Cleveland where he was district secretary, and on account of his help to CIO in organizing Ohio auto, rubber, and steel workers. He was able and practical as well as devoted; and his friendly workingman's style made him a natural for union work.

"I heard you were feeling bad," said Williamson, when we met at a bar, "and felt we had let you down." I didn't deny feeling bad; I was down in the mouth about CIO. But it never occurred to me to feel let down by the left. Johnny must have assumed I shared an attitude common in the job-conscious tradeunion movement. A porkchopper serving some leader or faction counted on lasting job support in return. Union machines were built and run that way. Leftwing porkchoppers were not immune.

It is true the voluminous records of "Un-American" committees murkily hint at more communist connivings than I here report. The first time I was up on this rap—before the Senate Internal Security subcommittee in 1952—my lawyer checked back through transcripts of HUAC hearings. I was surprised. The Dies committee stuff was typically wild, but later informers were relatively guarded. Not so Louis Budenz—the man I briefly met when he was editor of *Labor Age*, in his first anticommunist incarnation.

Budenz lied to HUAC that he was once present with Lee Pressman and me, and Roy Hudson of the CP, when we were "going over" the draft of a speech Philip Murray was to deliver.

I never joined in any such consultation at any time; it was the sort of thing that just couldn't happen. I ran into Budenz when he reported CIO gatherings for the *Daily Worker* but limited myself to press table courtesies. The closest I came to private encounter was when once, during the 1940 UMW convention in Columbus, Budenz without invitation took an empty chair at my lunch table—with UMW Editor Ellis Searles sitting at the next one. Roy Hudson I never met. His friends called him "Horseface," I was told. If I ever saw him, I didn't recognize him from the description.

So much ado as was made about so little! And who cared if informers lied, as under congressional immunity they typically did? When Murray purged, when liberals avoided, when employers blacklisted, it was enough that HUAC had had one in its pillory.

When the first constitutional convention of the Congress of Industrial Organizations was held at Pittsburgh in November 1938, CIO was already on the downside of the peak it scaled in 1937.

Opposing formation of a permanent rival to the AFL, David Dubinsky withdrew his Ladies Garment Workers and Max Zaritsky his Cloth Hat & Cap Workers before the convention. These defections removed a potential source of friction, and the convention was remarkably united.

Differences were adjusted in advance or off the floor, and the delegates adopted all major policy unanimously. This pattern of unanimity was to be followed at later conventions. It meant expressing objections in private and swallowing compromises in public. At Pittsburgh, few off-floor differences disturbed the surface unity.

Homer Martin was threatening a ruckus. Murray and Hillman managed to gentle him, at least for the convention's duration. As part of the blackmail they paid, they asked the UAW executive board to rescind its vote to publish the union's paper as an edition of *The CIO News*. The Mine Workers had joined a dozen international unions in subscribing to *The CIO News* for their membership. With UAW added, its circulation would have risen well into the second million, making it possible to become a bigtime and popular offset to the employers' press. But Homer had to be humored.

Of some long-range significance was a difference over three words for CIO's new constitution. To the ban on discrimination, on account of "race, creed, color, or nationality," Harry Bridges wanted to add "or political belief"—as did the more progressive unions. CIO's top leaders didn't agree. Hillman in the chair squelched a floor effort to recommit the clause. The point at issue does not appear in the printed proceedings.

It probably didn't trouble Lewis too much that the amendment would have put the United Mine Workers' anticommunist clause at variance with the CIO constitution, since international unions traditionally held that their own constitutions took precedence over those of bodies they affiliated with. Lewis wanted, I think, to warn the left against taking too much for granted—reserving the right to clobber any allies who might later turn against him—and to make an easy concession to the pressure of Murray and Hillman for a firmer stand against the left.

The UMW anticommunist clause had come into question earlier in 1938, at a convention which failed to rescind it. At a time when they were fighting Lewis, communists had been included in a hodgepodge clause which, from time to time, had barred from UMW membership saloonkeepers, Ku Kluxers, IWW's, leaders of the Boy Scouts, and members of the National Civic Federation. The ban was a club held in reserve for oppositionists who might become troublesome, rather than an ideological heresy test.

After Lewis started CIO, a contradiction arose. On the one hand, the clause warned that Lewis would still brook no opposition in UMW, and was a pat answer to redbaiters who smeared even him. On the other hand, it mildly embarrassed a new Lewis who welcomed all in CIO and got effective support from the communists. Lewis, however, lost little sleep over inconsistencies.

By 1938, the Lewis-left alliance had worked so well, and Lewis had so long abstained from redbaiting, that I was curious what he might do at the UMW convention. I made a point to be present when the clause came up.

There was a floor move to strike out the reference to communists. If Lewis had approved, this would have been done like all else he favored. His nod was hardly to be expected. He would have lost an inner UMW and public relations convenience, and his enemies would have had further evidence for their charge that he was "going communist."

Lewis glossed things over. After letting a couple of delegates speak against the ban, he put readoption to a vote as routinely as other constitutional clauses. The whole matter drew little attention at the time.

One person would be paying close attention, Lewis knew—George Morris, the *Daily Worker* reporter, who sat at my end of the long press table. Lewis was pacing up and down the platform, as he often did when presiding. Right after the clause had been readopted, his pacing brought him to our end of the platform. He paused and gave a friendly little wave and grin to George.

Another issue that didn't reach the floor of CIO's 1938 convention was the choice of a Secretary. Chairman Lewis and Vice Chairmen Murray and Hillman of the preceding Committee were clearly slated for President and Vice Presidents of the new Congress. Charles P. Howard, the Committee's Secretary, had died a few months before the convention.

As a stopgap, Director Brophy was named acting secretary to prepare for the convention. But few imagined he was thereby placed in line for the elective job. When CIO grew from a promotional committee into a big labor organization and Lewis directly assumed administration, Brophy's influence was sharply curtailed. At Pittsburgh, Brophy, with no union base of his own, drew support chiefly from leftwingers who held back, however, so as not to embarrass, and let men like Dick Frankensteen take the lead. Lobbying was addressed not so much to fellow delegates as to Lewis, Murray, and Hillman. These three would decide. Brophy later claimed Murray and Hillman were willing to settle for him. If so, it was lest worse befall.

In CIO's new office-making, its elder statesmen saw a chance to arrange things as they'd long wished they could. Each believed a union boss like himself should be boss without restraint from fellow officers. Secretaries of unions, though supposedly a meekly bookkeeping breed, had sometimes caused trouble. Now, thought the old union bosses, if I had my way. . . .

Murray gave the tipoff. When he had his way in SWOC, he chose for Secretary-Treasurer, not some potential critic or rival, but his own office clerk and personal secretary, young Dave McDonald. Lewis would have liked his own daughter and office assistant, Kathryn Lewis, for Secretary of CIO.

Now Hillman might have sympathized. He'd had his own troubles with a socialist, Joseph Schlossberg, as Secretary of ACW. He had understood Murray perfectly and been pleased with the trend he started. As to Murray, how could he object to Lewis following his pioneering example? But . . .

Some people found young Kathryn hard to take. They gagged at one dose of John L., they balked at a double dose. I got along well with Kathryn, who knew I was all for her old man, and was okay by him. I also found some appeal in their feelings for each other.

Lewis wore his public self like a mask. Through a mask one can sometimes see the eyes—a contrast. During long CIO sessions, I might study Lewis's eyes. When they turned inward, they were mild, bland, almost soft—seemingly untroubled by inner conflict. In public life, Lewis could register much emotion—for a purpose, it often seemed. Into his private life, he allowed no sobsisters to mush.

Its outlines were in the public domain. A family man with never-broken home. A retiring, loyal, and guiding wife—a former teacher who taught her husband much. A son in college studying medicine—remote from the hurly-burly of his father's life. And Kathryn . . .

Lewis could keep all his family life to himself—all except Kathryn. Wife and son were his opposites. Kathryn took after him. It was intriguing to see the masculine Lewis reproduced in feminine form. The political boss in embryo, with an egotism that reflected and magnified his. Even the bigness of Kathryn was in keeping. And through it all, the young woman.

In furthering Kathryn's ambition to become a labor leader, Lewis was less male-chauvinist than most. He was as nepotic as most persons who can get away with it. He came from a family that stuck together. He never apologized for sticking by his kin or for trying to give his Katey a break.

But Kathryn could do things like this:

When Lewis made his surprise endorsement of Wendell Willkie in 1940—after keeping his intentions a complete secret— I was one of those with him when he broadcast his speech, from his UMW office. Disgruntled with Roosevelt, I was not for Willkie. I expected no Roosevelt endorsement, no matter how qualified. I cherished a faint hope that Lewis might throw back at Roosevelt his "plague on both your houses," in a way to further the cause of independent labor political action. When Lewis finished, most of us looked down self-consciously. There was little chatter, no enthusiasm. Kathryn had come with a concealed supply of Willkie buttons. Now she went around the room pinning them on all lapels.

I was embarrassed—for her, for Lewis, for myself. I wished she might skip me. She didn't. I took off the button as I left. But later I cooled off. Kathryn wasn't sensitive about things like this; nor was her old man. She hadn't favored the course Lewis took, I was later told. At this point, all her loyalty just surged up.

Not many Lewis henchmen followed him as far as Willkie. Those that did were called stooges scared for their jobs. Not all of them were. There was another motive. Take John O'Leary, seemingly as typical a UMW machine man as ever served Lewis, and the man who got the UMW vice-president spot when Lewis dumped Murray. I once remarked to O'Leary that he was one of a pretty select few to follow Lewis on this. He grinned and nudged me like a fellow conspirator. Out of the corner of his mouth he muttered: "I just couldn't let the Old Man down."

Reverting to 1938, Lewis soon realized he couldn't with impunity put over Kathryn as CIO Secretary. Hillman blanched, and even Murray balked. CIO was already so overwhelmed by the Lewis presence, it could take no more. James B. Carey got the spot. He was supposedly Kathryn's choice, as a bow to youth and the new unions. Nobody had anything against Jimmy then. CIO's triumvirate liked his respectful manners. To Lewis, Carey must have looked as good as any young secretary he could hire on the open market.

Growing up in a period of gathering Nazi, Fascist, and Japanese aggression, CIO was relatively little divided on foreign policy until 1939.

The left called for antifascist unity and collective security against aggression, and Lewis and Hillman agreed for the most part. Murray demurred at resisting fascism in Spain. To avoid offense to American Catholics, supposedly pro-Franco, Lewis stopped national CIO from aiding the loyalists—a stand which he later said he regretted. Otherwise, CIO's policy was vigorously antifascist. Lewis spoke out strongly, both in the United States and at an international antifascist congress in the summer of 1938 at Mexico City where he warned the United States might have to fight if Hitler extended his aggressions to the western hemisphere. Few then advocated involvement short of that.

CIO rights and lefts divided chiefly over the left's aggressive demands—to lift Roosevelt's embargo on arms for Republican Spain; for collective security measures; for job actions such as those of the CIO longshoremen who stopped shipment of American scrap metal to Japan. The rights attacked the lefts for injecting outside issues into union affairs. After 1939, the rights injected most foreign policy to embarrass the lefts.

In September 1938 Britain and France capped their appeasement of Hitler with the Munich agreement which sold out Czechoslovakia, wrecked Soviet hopes for collective security —and undermined CIO unity. The Soviets saw Munich as designed to divert Nazi aggression away from the west and toward the USSR. So did some rightwing CIO factions, and thought it fine. The lefts feared Roosevelt might go along with the plot.

Lewis was already suspicious of Roosevelt, if for other reasons. He feared that Roosevelt's increasingly overt alliance with Britain and France was heading the United States into another European war. Lewis had gone along with Samuel Gompers' policies in the First World War. By now he saw them as having stopped labor from taking advantage of its war opportunities. Several times I heard him privately deplore labor's mistakes in World War I, and say they must not be repeated. Lewis shared a fairly common American attitude toward war: Fight only if attacked. Resist involvement in other people's wars. Keep out as long as possible. If war still comes, support your country patriotically. But don't let the war profiteers sucker you, to increase their blood money at your expense. Keep your end up.

The nonaggression pact of August 1939 between the USSR and Germany took many by surprise, including CIO lefts. It wasn't shocking to those like myself who saw it as a quick move by the Soviets to avoid being patsy for a gang-up. When the sit-down or "phony" war on the western front followed Hitler's invasion of Poland, we suspected he was still angling for western cooperation, or at least toleration, for a drive to the east.

At this stage the war was too much like the imperialist First World War for most American radicals to want to jump in on the side of Britain and France. If, by another route, they had in the fall of 1939 reached the same conclusion as Lewis, when he said, "Labor in America wants no war nor any part of war," a position which that year's CIO convention endorsed.

Ostensibly it was the common attitude. Sidney Hillman, at the Hosiery Workers convention, had recently said: "American labor will resolutely oppose American participation in war or any action which might lead to war, except only as a last measure to preserve our people and our institutions against foreign domination." Emil Rieve, his right bower, said that "the natural American abhorrence for the methods of fascism should not provide the springboard to throw this country into a European war." Roosevelt in 1940 was still promising that American boys "are not going to be sent into any foreign wars."

But under the surface there were seething differences on the war, and much else, when CIO convened in San Francisco in October 1939. Under White House and Catholic pressure, Hillman and Murray wanted anticommunist action. The Catholic hierarchy, which had been complacent about fascist aggression and opposed to aid for Republican Spain, made communism the main enemy; and from 1937 on, the Association of Catholic

Trade Unionists had been boring from within CIO unions with anticommunist factions. All rightwing factions now saw a chance to clobber the left on war issues and support for Roosevelt. Their ploy was to lump communists and fascists together for common denunciation.

Roosevelt loomed large behind the CIO scene. To Lewis, he seemed to be moving in to take over. Roosevelt was mobilizing aid for Britain and France, and feeling his way to a third term. He needed labor support which Lewis threatened to withhold. FDR had the support of Murray privately, Hillman openly, and CIO's right wing generally. On Lewis's side were the UMW and other machines he could control and CIO's leftwing unions.

Since Murray was an uncertain element, still subject to Lewis in many ways, Hillman stood out as the main challenger of Lewis. He was Roosevelt's chief labor lieutenant, his chosen spokesman in CIO. At this point he deserves a closer look.

Chapter Eleven

HILLMAN

*Sidney Hillman, a social reformist wedded
to Roosevelt and his New Deal, was bound
to clash with John L. Lewis.*

Sidney Hillman was the labor man most closely
linked to Franklin D. Roosevelt, in his New Deal and World
War II. The rightist opposition redbaited, Jew-baited, alien-
baited him, made him its chief bugaboo. The other big labor
name linked with Roosevelt—but in reverse and soon to clash
with Hillman—was John L. Lewis. No stooges, like most other
union leaders in politics, these two were outstanding protago-
nists on the national stage. They were cofounders of CIO—itself an ambitious break from AFL stooging—and it is through
CIO eyes I now look at Hillman.

Trim and neat, sharp of mind and feature, Hillman looked
like an up-to-date professor or rabbi. He was emotional—
highstrung and nervous at times, a hand-wringer under reverses,
but mostly eager and enthusiastic. Hillman could be brusque
when sure of himself—impatient with the fuzzy-minded. He was
not arrogant. He could show modesty—partly genuine, if also
political—toward persons like Lewis and Roosevelt. In ordinary
human relations he was sensitive, if abstracted. At times uncertain, more often purposeful, always trying to be practical, Hillman felt acutely the pulls of conflicting impulses. All in all, he
registered pleasingly as a man of thought and feeling deeply
involved in the people's affairs.

I couldn't feel so warmly toward Hillman as I did toward
Lewis. I was with him less, in opposition more, and we didn't
feel at ease together—except briefly in Paris in 1945, the year before he died.

In depicting public personalities, one's partisanship is bound to show. It's the gentlemanly, broad-visioned Roosevelt against the truculent oaf Lewis; or labor's fearless champion Lewis against the tricky, capricious Roosevelt. It's the patient, gentle Murray against the brutal, dictatorial Lewis; or manly, forthright Lewis against the weak and hypocritical Murray. I was for Lewis, not Hillman, in their earlier differences. Against my heroic image of the leader of the CIO uprising, the moderate and essentially social-reformist Hillman didn't measure up. During his years of government activity, I saw Hillman little. I respected him as leader of CIO's Political Action Committee, still more as founder of the World Federation of Trade Unions. He never quite set me afire.

Yet looking back and measuring him against most other labor leaders, I'd say Hillman was more than man-size.

Knowing Caroline helped me appreciate Hillman—though she was no more a Hillmanite than I. Both came from Czarist lands where, like black Americans, their people suffered double oppression; they were poor and they were Jews. Caroline had childhood memories of the pogroms. Pale and distant they seemed in the glare of American atrocities against the black. Twelve years older than Caroline, Hillman came earlier to the United States and was older when he came. He had been a teenage revolutionist—the Czarist regime held union activity to be revolutionary, and Hillman was jailed for it.

Arriving in 1907, Hillman found himself among those sweated workers, the latest immigrants from eastern Europe. He was a leader in strikes of some radical fervor. In place of the Czar, Hillman now faced employer-controlled government. American freedom was not for workers who rebelled. His friend John Williams said Hillman told him that "the police of Chicago were more brutal than those of Russia; that its prisons were more loathsome; that the treatment of prisoners was more barbarous. And he knows whereof he speaks, for he has been inside of both."

However, some freedoms won by workers' struggles did offer openings of which Hillman was quick to take advantage. The union he helped found, and led for the rest of his life, was the

Amalgamated Clothing Workers of America. Caroline was a pioneer member when in her teens she worked in Milwaukee clothing shops. She went through a long Amalgamated strike in Philadelphia. She worked for the union in Chicago, when it pioneered in unemployment insurance in the Twenties.

Through Caroline, I was close to the Amalgamated. I found poignancy and romance in its growth. I admired the intellectual and spiritual contributions of Jewish immigrants to the labor movement.

But unions grow older.

The 1940 Amalgamated convention was too emotional for my taste. The emotion was whipped up to sweep already swept people onto Roosevelt's third-term and war-policies bandwagon. A prodigal effort was made to banish opposition that was neither visible nor audible.

I could take the one-way flood of oratory; I was used to that. I expected patriotic music, dramatic devices, ovations. One little thing threw me. At every chance, with or without pretext, the band struck up "God Bless America," and all joined in singing it. The delegates rose as for the national anthem. They paraded to it in their snake dances. I got hoarse, and bored, and decided to sit things out at the press table.

The delegates were parading in the umpteenth ovation for FDR or Hillman. They started "God Bless America" on their own, and the band had to take it up. I saw no trace of dwindling enthusiasm. I looked at the faces of the singing women. (In the ACW, the leaders were men, but most of the workers were women. Women got to be delegates to conventions.) They sang fervently, and with relish, sucking in deeply the sweetness of the repeated "God Bless America, my home sweet home!"

I got the message.

Like Hillman and Caroline, these were mostly long-Americanized Jewish immigrants. They had çome from countries of anti-Semitism, feudal backwardness, political despotism. They had fought despotic American bosses and won through to freer lives and higher living standards. Hitler was now belching forth old-world hatreds and multiplying old-world oppressions. Their

America was defended by Roosevelt in the White House, with Hillman at his side. Their emotions overflowed in this song.

The song was also smug, as was the attitude. These immigrant revolutionists, once battered and battling, were rising in the world. They were preparing their children for professions or business. They were staking some claims in the establishment. The lower-paid jobs were being taken by Afro-Americans, Mexicans, Puerto Ricans, and white American women from the hidden hill settlements of the south.

Themselves, they weren't doing too badly.

Union leaders, too, grow older. Those of the Amalgamated did so more gracefully than most. The Hillman machine was a coterie, a clan, of like-minded persons who founded the union and collectively led it for the rest of their lives. Year after year, for half a century, the same men met as ACW executives or convention leaders, as the union's spokesmen in CIO, in political action, in all other Amalgamated endeavors.

Other unions offered the same leaders year after year, if with more turnover and less continuity from the union's birth. But the Hillman clan were more sprightly than most. They were alert and intelligent men of Hillman's generation, and like him in makeup and background. They stuck to their union jobs, not so much as the best and softest they could get, but because Hillman made life interesting. Some were well equipped for business or politics and might have been tempted away otherwise.

In Chicago, where things started around 1910, lanky Frank Rosenblum was one of the restless, rambunctious young men in the shops who founded the union. An outstanding leader, he was the most independent of the clan—about the only one, said Caroline, who continued to "talk back to Hillman" as time went on and Hillman's prestige ballooned.

From Chicago too, small Sam Levin, who looked mild and sensitive, and big Sidney Rissman, who looked like a butcher—appearances that could mislead. Also reedy A.D. Marimpietri; lively Bessie Abramowitz, who became Mrs. Hillman; Jacob ("Jack") Potofsky, most faithful Hillmanite in a union of faithful Hillmanites, and famous in a beardless era for his goatee.

From Milwaukee, eloquent Leo Krzycki, not so much part of the ACW machine as one of its oratorical effects. If speaking could organize—and it certainly helped—Leo was one of the "greats" as organizer for ACW and CIO. He could sway the hard-to-sway Poles and stir things up in English too.

Cincinnati was Jack Kroll, agreeably smooth, calm, confidence-inspiring, whose personality contributed much to the CIO Political Action Committee. Charles Weinstein of Philadelphia was a rougher diamond, with whom I essayed no intimacy. Nor had I much contact with Joseph Schlossberg, ACW Secretary until he retired in 1940. An old socialist, idealistic, inspirational, older, he seemed lost in the realistic opportunistic world of Sidney Hillman—who didn't try too hard to make him feel at home.

Joe Salerno of Boston was a later comer, who plunged duck-like into the waters of CIO politics. He was not typical of the close-knit, rather exclusive ACW machine. Among New Yorkers, fatherly, kind Abe Miller; round-faced executive-type Louis Hollander; small, smooth, smart Murray Weinstein; August and Dorothy Bellanca, whom I barely knew. From Rochester, dapper little Abe Chatman, with darting eyes, who was exceptional as an assimilated rebel. . . most others were born to the clan with the birth of the union.

Toward Hyman Blumberg I had a special feeling. He came to pick on me, as a Lewisite and left, and I still liked him. Blumberg was one of the shrewdest and most resourceful organizers in Hillman's able stable. Tough, he was also humorous and urbane, with sentiment under the surface.

The ACW machine was made up of capable men like these. As a group they reflected Hillman, or he was a composite of them. They respected Hillman's judgment as strategist, and he didn't have to dragoon them. If there was challenge, it was within the family. To the world, ACW presented a solid Hillman front.

The Amalgamated fought its way to success through touch-and-go strikes and organizing drives; against police and gangster violence; redbaiting; all kinds of employer, AFL, and political opposition. Not till the Thirties was it so accepted by employers as to become impregnable. Then it got so ACW could "run itself," as it was said. But still Hillman kept things too lively for his longtime cronies to grow old complacently. With restless energy—often beyond his physical strength—he kept starting things, and throwing his machine as well as himself into them.

From the Twenties on, unemployment insurance, the Russian-American Industrial Corporation, labor banks, cooperative housing, were among many activities Hillman initiated beyond the routines of union administration. Then came CIO, in which Hillman involved his whole clan; American Labor Party; Labor's Non-Partisan League; many governmental prewar and war activities; CIO Political Action Committee; the World Federation of Trade Unions.

After Hillman died, much of the life went out of his clan. Potofsky, Rosenblum, and Blumberg carried on. They and the others held together and held things together. They didn't start much new. Cold War engulfed most Hillman causes. Rosenblum stood up and talked back at times. But the Hillman clan was growing old—a fate Hillman himself avoided by dying.

What might have happened to another clan, CIO's leftwing leaders, if the Cold War hadn't cut short their labor lives? Hillman's group began forming around 1910. The "communist" clan got started in the early Thirties, became a recognizable entity in CIO in 1936-37, and continued as a cohesive group for a decade thereafter. The lefts were young people who came out of the shops under the common conditions of their time. They came forward through initiative, daring and tenacity in organizing, strikes and other struggles. They became leaders of successful unions.

Like Hillman's associates, the lefts were able and ambitious. They were inspired by a common philosophy. They could work together programmatically—as did Hillman's men. They had no chance to settle sluggishly into swivel chairs. Believing the working class should lead the social struggle, they fought on many fronts. Hillman's group lived out their lives as ACW leaders. The CIO lefts were cut down in their forties.

Few leaders can keep on top or ahead of events all through their lives. Hillman's clan made a stab at it, up to the middle Forties, when they fell behind. The CIO lefts might have done better. They were about a generation younger, and associated with a continuing radical movement. If they could have survived through the Fifties without loss of union following, they might have proved the missing link between the old left and the new left of the Sixties.

That isn't the way it was. The rout of CIO's left was sweeping. Most of the many lefts I'd known ceased to be union leaders. In the early Fifties I visited one to philosophize. Such an able group could not be rubbed out just like that, I argued. The old cliché that agitators give place to administrators didn't apply. Many lefts had proved able administrators, too, just as Hillman's men had performed both roles. Certainly conditions had changed. The warm political climate in which the lefts emerged was freezing into a new ice age. But the working people were still here. "Surely," I said, "a time will come again——"

"Of course," said my friend. "When it does, new leaders will be thrown up, as we were. Our generation has shot its wad." Coming from a man in his forties, that was pretty bleak. It proved not too far from the mark, as the Cold War deepened its chasm between two radical generations.

One thing couldn't be charged against CIO's lefts—that they fastened onto and fattened in jobs newcomers might better have filled. Rather they vacated space (involuntarily) that no comparable claimants showed up to fill. Like Hillman, they didn't grow old on the job.

Thomas F. Burns of the Rubber Workers, a Hillman lieutenant, once said of CIO that "Hillman wrote the lines of the play and Lewis acted them."

Must have been some other play than I saw. In the big CIO show I attended, Lewis produced, directed, and acted the lead. He didn't write the play, but neither did Hillman. Millions of workers provided the plot and acted it out. The writers were many, from far back. Lewis, big ham that he was, wrote or rewrote many of his own particular lines.

Some Hillman admirers claimed he chose second place because Lewis was vain and had more mass appeal. If so, Hillman chose wisely to bow to necessity. He didn't have to step back to let Lewis take the center stage. Lewis was already there and had planned it that way.

Hillman was no second-stringer, however. He was an ally of Lewis, never a lieutenant. In many fields Hillman was an initiator, policy-creator, goal-setter—self-willed, too, as his ACW followers knew. But Hillman was also self-controlled and a realist in his attitude toward Lewis, as toward Roosevelt. He knew Roosevelt was President of the United States. He knew Lewis was founder and topkick of CIO—and no bones about that either. Hillman also knew Lewis was entitled to the CIO top spot, not only in drive and mass appeal and as head of the key union furnishing most support, but also as planner and strategist who gave the movement its direction, a direction not always pleasing to Hillman.

But, said some, Hillman was more the theoretician of CIO than was Lewis. Lewis was no theoretician. How much was Hillman?

Few labor leaders were theoretical. Most were practical politicians concerned with power and immediate results. Their articles or utterances with theoretical content were usually supplied by ghostwriters or elicited by theoretical interviewers. If confident that ghost or interviewer would make a presentation helpful to their purposes, they inclined to express or accept thoughts the writer needed to fit his pattern.

Hillman was more productive than Lewis of the kind of articles, interviews, speeches, that theorists and historians turn to. He had more brain trusters, was more receptive to their attentions, and was acute and alert in assessing their ideas. But first of all he was a practical politician. And insofar as he was a theoretician—a role he frequently disclaimed—how much was he the theoretician of CIO?

Both Hillman and Lewis grasped eagerly at the opportunities presented by NRA. Both did so as practical politicians and got practical results. Hillman was much the more enchanted with the long-range possibilities of the deal—its theoretical angles, so to say. He glorified its corporative aspects—the integration of labor, employers, and government into a corporate capitalism. He preached that industrial unions fitted into the design much better than the old AFL crafts. From this it might have been argued that Hillman was the wise man who read the times aright, who saw that big business and government needed modern efficiency-geared industrial unions for the corporative setup envisaged by NRA, and that Hillman therefore wrote the CIO play in which Lewis was to star.

That is stretching and squeezing things to fit a quip. It is of a piece with another legend, that the New Deal created CIO, rather than being one favorable circumstance of the times that gave American industrial workers a chance to start something for themselves.

Much less enamored of the New Deal than Hillman, Lewis was early disenchanted. The way he started CIO was not the least Hillmanesque. It was direct, forceful, urgent. It often left Hillman lagging behind. Lewis didn't seek the good will of government and big business by offering CIO as a partner in the emerging design of state monopoly capitalism. He went directly to the workers—or they came to him—defying big business and government both, if they stood in the way of the workers' will to organize. A play like Lewis acted, Hillman would not have written.

The corporative aspects of the New Deal took root, if not in their NRA form. In fact, the idea of closer industry-labor-government cohesion had been kicking around for some time, cropping up particularly in times of war or economic stress. Philip Murray's tripartite Industry Council Plan of the early Forties was an example. In the expanding American imperialism of the Cold War, the idea became implemented in practice, less formalized and with a much humbler place for the labor partner than Hillman or Murray might have hoped.

Lewis didn't much go for the idea. In one sense he might have been called an old-fashioned free-enterpriser; in another sense, a radical. He favored labor independence from government control.

Hillman's background distinctively fitted him for his New Deal role.

In building his own union from the ground up, Hillman was drawn into many battles. But he early showed that realism was his forte—his critics called it opportunism. To secure the union against destruction, Hillman set out to enlist the support of employers. He became a great salesman of unionism to employers—a soft-sell salesman. In his industry, this got results, particularly when coupled at first with some hard-sell strikes. The Amalgamated did much to regulate a disorderly industry. It offered the bosses production experts, bank loans, a disciplined work force. It reduced cutthroat competition by stabilizing labor costs. It helped the manufacturers themselves to organize.

This approach worked less well when Hillman tried to apply it to the textile industry—also disorganized and competitive, but larger scale and more sprawling. In the south, the employers wouldn't buy it. In most other industries CIO set out to organize, this Hillman technique probably wouldn't have worked at all. Their big corporations couldn't be talked into letting a union help them run things. The class-struggle approach of Lewis and the left compelled them to do what they didn't want to do.

Hillman was not single-track, however. He had another approach, through government. In Washington, he became a topnotch labor-industry-government politician. The New Deal gave Hillman his big chance. It was made for him, and he for it. Through his own union, Hillman had pioneered in planning, industry-regulation, capital-labor adjustment, social welfare of the very kind the New Deal had in mind. A brain trust? Hillman had his professors, economists, social workers, long before the New Deal. He even had a bevy of cooperating employers. He furnished a readymade model for the whole New Deal.

Roosevelt recognized Hillman's familiarity with the ground. He wanted him more for his practical initiative in planning than for his influence over the labor movement, which was not great. Hillman became a Roosevelt pet and won backing for some of his labor and social welfare plans.

Lewis approached things differently. The battle came first, the soft-soap later. Aroused workers storming the open-shop citadels and threatening Washington itself were more important to his calculations than the political interests of dubious friends in public office.

Hillman was well equipped and well placed to importune

and influence Roosevelt, to promote plans of potential help to labor, and try to have them fairly administered. All this was important to CIO. But without the militant workers pounding on the doors, it might have availed little. Hillman's mind might tell him this, but his heart misgave him. He got the heeby-jeebies when he saw how roughly Lewis and his left allies aroused the masses, and how Lewis pounded at the delicate nerves of FDR himself.

It was said that Lewis the Fighter and Hillman the Fox deliberately divided the field. That was true in a way at the start. But irritations soon developed, and after 1939 the two were consciously at odds. Objectively, no doubt, when they didn't cancel each other, the outside threat of Lewis and Hillman's inside wirepulling at first combined to good effect.

If you didn't like Sidney Hillman's politics, it wasn't hard to do a job on him. And I don't refer to the crude redbaiting anti-Semitic job attempted by rightists in the 1944 elections, when they claimed Roosevelt's alleged remark, "Clear it with Sidney," meant he was under the thumb of a foreign Jew-communist. That whole line was as ridiculous as it was ugly.

After they split, Lewis liked to imply that Hillman was dazzled by White House glamor and the Washington fourflush; was stooge and toady to FDR; was ready to sell out labor for a mess of liberal pottage. That came closer but was still off the mark.

Power impressed Hillman, as a political realist—the power of Lewis, in fact, and still more that of Roosevelt. The White House was a maximum power center, and Hillman was doubtless tickled to have the key to its back door (the right of admission as an off-the-record visitor). The White House impressed Lewis, too.

Hillman did stooge for Roosevelt in CIO (was his lieutenant, to put it politely), but he was not a toady. Hillman always tried to enlist influential individuals for his causes. FDR was his biggest catch, a long step toward his goal of making government serve the cause of social welfare.

Like other union leaders, Hillman was often accused of selling out. The charge had nothing to do with money for himself—in which he was not interested. In union parlance, a sellout is to settle for less than one might have won by fighting harder and compromising less. When Hillman did this, he deliberately intended to subordinate immediate gain to more long-range advantage. In respect to FDR and the New Deal, Hillman was more anxious to maintain an "in" with the Chief Executive than to extort momentary gains by fist-shaking. This was not the Lewis technique, but it could be held to be a technique rather than a sellout.

The job that could more fairly be done on Hillman was the basic critique of the social reformist.

"Certainly I believe in collaborating with employers," Hillman told the writer Joseph Gollomb. "That is what a union is for. I even believe in helping an employer function more productively, for then we have a claim to higher wages, shorter hours, and greater participation in the benefits of a smooth industrial machine." That is a common enough union-leader attitude. It is not the only possible attitude. It is a far cry from the IWW preamble: "The working class and the employing class have nothing in common. There can be no peace so long as hunger and want are found among millions of working people and the few, who make up the employing class, have all the good things of life."

The Hillman doctrine was not more American than the IWW preamble. In American labor, the class struggle idea had the deeper roots—in the manifest conflict when workers began to organize and strike on any scale, and found not only their employers but the whole capitalist class, government, police, press, aligned against them.

The American Federation of Labor, like its predecessors, recognized the class struggle in its preamble, as at first did the Machinists and ACW—until Hillman had such language eliminated. In this, he was less radical than the old AFL, which right up to its merger with CIO in 1955 continued to start its preamble: "Whereas, A struggle is going on in all the nations of the civilized world between the oppressors and the oppressed of all countries, a struggle between the capitalist and the laborer, which grows in intensity from year to year——"

Hillman preached what most union leaders just practiced, collaborating with their employers in countless ways. Class struggle—so obvious in earlier labor days, and in the CIO uprising, for that matter—became less evident with union recognition and legalized collective bargaining. Labor leaders piously renounced it, but they couldn't banish the idea from workers' minds—still less, those of the employers. Industrial conflict did not disappear but tended to increase, assume new forms, and spread to new groups of workers.

The union leader who daily buddied with the bosses usually tried to appear to his members as a fighter against the bosses. If he talked collaboration, he found it well to balance it with some militant talk. Otherwise too much buddy-buddy with the bosses might land him in trouble with the rank and file, such as defeated Steelworkers' President David J. McDonald in 1965. A deep-seated feeling persisted in the ranks that unions were organized *against* employers, to force from them better wages and conditions than they would otherwise grant.

Hillman had his share of critics who said he was more concerned with employer acceptance than with wage results. They cited the relatively low wages in clothing as compared with other unionized industries. ACW had its seemingly neglected low-wage sectors, but it could also be said for Hillman that he pioneered in fringe benefits sometimes as important as wages. But on the whole Hillman got away with his emphasis on collaboration, because his union stabilized a once-chaotic industry and stayed strong through many vicissitudes; and because he was an outstanding leader who raised the members' spirits by the vision of goals he set, and by many beneficial projects.

Beyond his union, Hillman expanded his union-employer doctrine into a philosophy of class collaboration for social reform. He had won over many clothing employers with his integrity, his realism, his practical business sense. With the New Deal, he directed his winning ways at a capitalist President and his administration and at the captains of American industrial monopoly, seeking their cooperation for labor and social welfare.

A John L. Lewis might storm at the capitalists—though he, too, had his winning ways for the right private moment. He might stir up the workers to demand more and more. A Sidney Hillman shook his head. Such dramatics might be all right for early organizing, if not carried too far. But in the long run my way is better. The President can do more for us than we can do for ourselves. He can be wheedled, maybe pressured, but gently please or we may lose him.

History may accord Lewis the greater credit for CIO's initial success. Without Hillman to "keep labor in line," as Roosevelt expressed it—the relationship worked that way, too—the President would not have lacked for smoothies to see that labor got the necessary concessions. But without the storming workers— and a Lewis and his left (or objectively left) allies stirring up the storm—the concessions would have been much smaller.

A sincere social reformist, Hillman sought to serve the immediate needs of working people without regard to any theory of ultimate aims. Because this was a capitalist society, he worked through capitalist channels to serve those needs, and sought the agreement of the class in power. Along this traditional American labor route there lay some pitfalls.

One was that in trying to serve one section of workers, one might ignore or do disservice to others. Hillman didn't fall into this trap. He was an industrial not a craft unionist, a promoter of general unionism and social reform.

Another pitfall was that in trying to win the employers' good will for reform, one might do more to offer them service than to fight for the workers. Hillman was sometimes charged with falling into this one.

Still another pitfall was that in promoting class collaboration, one might cross the line from lobbying the capitalist class into becoming its instrument, or that of its government, to hold down the workers when they might gain more by rising up. Hillman tottered on this brink at times.

A true case against Hillman would have to be the very opposite of that attempted by the rightists in his heyday. Hillman was not a foreign Jew-communist intent on "red riot and rebellion," slyly worming his way through government and seeking socialistically to subvert free enterprise. Quite the contrary. Temperamentally, and by conviction, Hillman strongly opposed "red riot and rebellion." Even if it seemed to offer immediate advantage, he deplored it as wrong and damaging in the long run. As to free enterprise (read capitalism), Hillman should go down in history, along with Roosevelt, as a savior of this system in its years of crisis.

Hillman was a mitigator and adjuster of class struggle. He was the best friend of the good capitalist—and of bad ones, too, if they chose to get wise. He set out to show them that, by giving the workers a little here and there and by organizing their labor relations wisely, they could stay in the saddle indefinitely, riding a relatively docile working class.

If I wanted to do a job on Hillman, it would be along the preceding lines. But I don't. He stacked up better than most American union leaders, especially his fellow social reformists.

Unlike his European counterparts, Hillman didn't twist socialist professions into the service of capitalism and imperialism. Whatever his adolescent attitudes under Czarism, he was not a revolutionist in the United States. He was drawn to the more practical aspects of trade unionism, with little interest in socialist theory. Hillman imbibed the concepts of the immigrant in a politically liberating but economically wage-slave society, and of the social workers and liberals who aided him. His developing outlook drew upon his experience as a special kind of union leader, and the wide vistas opened by association with Roosevelt and the New Deal.

Hillman boasted of being pragmatically impervious to abstract theory. In earlier years he had many socialists around him. He respected some, found others fuzzy, and disregarded all who tried to push him along any socialist line. He liked to tell them he was doing more for the workers than all their windy theories. If something seemed good to him, he didn't care if it was called socialistic or not. His purpose was reform, not socialism.

"Labor" was one of Hillman's abiding concepts. It was not as narrow as the AFL idea of an official trade-union movement, nor yet as broad and precise as the Marxian concept of "working class." Early in 1918, when ripples from the Russian revolution were reaching labor on this continent, Hillman wrote an unusually romantic letter to his daughter (quoted by Matthew Josephson in his Hillman biography). He called the workers he had addressed at a Montreal mass meeting "perhaps the masters of tomorrow—still the slaves of today." "Labor," said Hillman, was "the new champion . . . irresistible . . . this new Messiah— messenger of love, freedom and plenty to all." "Labor will rule," he wrote, "and the World will be free."

Hillman was a strong proponent of labor political action, but "Labor will rule" became gradually more remote from his realistic appraisal of the American scene. His labor politics tended to merge with the bourgeois-liberal ideology of the Roosevelt New Deal.

Unlike rightwing socialist union leaders around him, Hillman did not turn on the Russian revolution with Menshevik fury and counterrevolutionary intent. He never became a Dubinsky—plotting endlessly and far afield, through ex- and anticommunists of all kinds, against left-oriented unions and socialist revolution everywhere. Hillman's attitude was friendly and humanitarian. In 1921, he visited the Soviet Union. He raised substantial funds for famine relief. To "help the Russians help themselves," he established the Russian-American Industrial Corporation to aid the Soviet clothing industry.

In his own union, Hillman brooked no opposition from communists or anyone else. The American union boss was like that; he tolerated dissent only so long as it didn't organize to threaten his machine's control. Steering a left-of-center course, Hillman faced less leftwing opposition than arose in the Ladies Garment Workers. When there was opposition, he suppressed it. In his other operations, Hillman was ever on guard against communist influence. He made his alliances with the left from time to time, as did other CIO leaders, but paid as little as possible for its help. Lewis's more generous enlistment of the left in CIO disturbed Hillman from the first and was a source of friction between the two.

Hillman made his sharpest right turn in the 1939-41 fight against Lewis and the left, when the right wing kept claiming that communists and Nazis were alike and allied. Hillman knew better, but didn't let on. He was well informed and sophisticated, and he had personal reasons for distinguishing between the two opposites. His own family was in Kovno, Lithuania, and Hillman tried frantically to get them out of reach of the Nazis and to safety with the communists. His younger brother, Mordecai, was saved by getting to Moscow and staying there. But his mother, two sisters and their families, Hillman learned in 1945, were all killed in October 1941, by the Nazis in their merciless genocide against the Jews.

Yet Hillman did not repudiate the anticommunist tactics of his henchmen and even joined in the kind of redbaiting from which he had once held himself fastidiously apart. In fact, to avoid hitting the powerful Lewis himself, Hillman directed most of his fire at Lewis's left allies.

To compensate for the outrage I then felt, I may be over-fair now if I say that perhaps Hillman's heart wasn't altogether in the redbaiting, witchburning orgies his crowd so much enjoyed. At any rate, I'm sure Hillman was relieved when 1941 brought the antifascist and national unity of a people's war; and he could follow Roosevelt in being liberal, if not always generous, to his former factional foes of the left.

There was greater glory ahead for Hillman, in his leadership of CIO's Political Action Committee, and in the noble vision of world labor unity, when he helped found the World Federation of Trade Unions. But at the moment it's 1939. Fighter Lewis and Foxy Hillman are in the CIO ring, squaring off.

Chapter Twelve

COLLISION COURSE

As Roosevelt headed toward a third term
and war, Lewis tried to break his spell over
CIO and chart an independent course.

Hotel lobbies can tell tales. The Hotel Whitcomb lobby in San Francisco, for instance, just before the 1939 CIO convention.

Samuel Wolchok of Retail buttonholes me. "This is the year for resolutions against communists and fascists," he says portentously. I don't rise to the bait. Harry Bridges pops in and is soon surrounded. He's on his home grounds, a host to the convention. A man of provocative angles—facially, in posture, politically. Phil Murray passes through. With flushed face, he looks tense and disturbed. He moves with softly catlike circumspection, not pausing for more than a nod or a wave.

The lobby fills and refills. Delegates from here, there, and everywhere. But no sign of Sidney Hillman or any of his clan. Hillman has set himself up at a hotel some distance from convention headquarters. Is he sulking in his suite? If so, it's getting brinkish.

I observe John L. Lewis as I go in and out of his rooms. He shows no tension. Once as I leave, he says casually as if the thought had just occurred: "Say, if you happen to run into Sidney, why don't you ask him to drop in for a chat."

I make it happen. I take a cab to Hillman's hotel and go to his room. Hillman doesn't hide his tension—nor his eagerness. The two have their chat. They make their deal.

On Hillman's side is the President of the United States with all the powers at his command. Hillman has recently spent a day at Hyde Park, touring the grounds with its Squire to admire the trees. Lewis still has most of CIO, and himself—more than a match, he feels, for the President and all his forces, with Hillman thrown in. Lewis gets the long end of the deal.

Speaking for Roosevelt, Hillman wanted the convention to be a whoopadoop for FDR—his war policies, his push for AFL-CIO unity, his third-term ambitions—all put over with "anti-communazi" resolutions to pull the teeth of CIO's left wing. Speaking for himself, Lewis wanted the convention to tell Roosevelt to go to hell—asserting independence of all powers and potentates except Lewis—and to adopt a strong antiwar stand. He wanted to show who was boss of CIO, not FDR but JLL.

The outcome: No endorsement of Roosevelt or his policies, except his professed neutrality; no whoopadoop, but no attack either. A strong antiwar resolution. A brush off for Roosevelt's AFL-CIO unity plea. No public "anti-communazi" redbaiting or right-left division. A private assurance by Lewis that he wasn't going to let the reds run away with CIO.

Murray was carrying water on both shoulders. Lewis had to put over the deal on him as well as Hillman. He waved the wand of a threat to resign. A threat it seemed to both in 1939—not a promise as it was to become, for Hillman at least, in 1940. Lewis was not bluffing. He was willing, even wanted, to step out of the CIO presidency in 1939. He had a hunch this was the time, and later regretted he hadn't followed it.

In 1939, Lewis could have stepped aside while still undisputed boss of CIO, before Roosevelt had seriously sapped his mass support, and before CIO split wide open on right-left and foreign policy issues. He could have made Murray nominal president, while still in control himself. Lewis could thus have forced Murray and Hillman into the open. While public responsibility for CIO imposed restraints on them, Lewis would have been freer to push his own line more vigorously and independently.

If these prospects appealed to Lewis, they appalled Murray and Hillman. Murray, in a ticklish but at least concealed position, shrank from becoming either public puppet or open rebel.

Hillman didn't want to report to Roosevelt that he couldn't deliver a CIO which had become a donnybrook of dissension, and whose real leader was sitting things out.

Outside of the deal, Lewis pulled a minor fast one that made his side chuckle and the other side fume. The Hillman crowd counted on one moment when a demonstration for Roosevelt could hardly be avoided—when his message was read to the convention. The message this year was long and followed up a White House initiative to bring CIO and AFL together—ostensibly to facilitate war production, but also to subordinate Lewis and the left in a whole more manageable than CIO by itself. Lewis had retorted by proposing an all-embracing American Congress of Labor, including AFL, CIO, and railroad brotherhoods.

Now San Francisco was a hospitable convention city, no place for early-to-bed-and-early-to-rise. But at the break of each convention day, Lewis rapped the gavel right on time. First order was the reading of stacks of greetings—small stimulus for early-birds in search of meaty worms. One morning, a handful of bleary yawning delegates were holding their aching heads, while Secretary Carey droned through the usual pile of messages. At the end of one was the name of Franklin D. Roosevelt, and some doubtless clapped. I wasn't on deck myself, but when I arrived later in a slowly filling hall, I saw no signs and heard no echoes of any ovation.

If the Roosevelt message drew little attention, the same could not be said of Lewis's first post-convention move—when he handed Hillman and Murray the antired lollipop promised if they'd be good boys at the convention.

It was a session of the CIO executive board to mop up organizational litter left by the convention. San Francisco liquor and late hours enhanced its hangover mood. Most looked droopy and drowsy until Lewis began speaking and jolted us all. Lewis sat at a table, leaning forward. Neither smiling nor frowning, he spoke softly but seriously. And what was he saying?

For the first time since CIO began, Lewis was giving an anticommunist talk. It was no redbaiting rant of the old Lewis. It was anticommunist, nonetheless. Coming from him, in the touchy state of CIO's internal politics, it could mean much. The rightwing board members glanced meaningfully at each other. Nervous Hillman and Murray looked unusually smug. The lefts stared straight ahead, trying to betray no reaction. Lewis looked at no one. He spoke as if in general, or to a remote audience.

Lewis couched his talk as a warning to the communists. They'd never take over CIO, he said; they'd better stop trying. Things had reached a point where some young men were told that to get ahead in CIO, they'd have to join the Communist party. That wasn't so, would never be so. CIO would tolerate no outside interference.

Heard coolly, Lewis's words were not exceptionable. No outside interference was standard union doctrine. The communists subscribed to it—objecting particularly to antileft government, political, religious, and employer interferences rampant in CIO. When they themselves, as union members or officers, expressed their viewpoint within their unions, they didn't call this outside interference. But for Lewis to single out the communists, in the politics of the moment, made his little homily reverberate widely. He further stimulated speculation by announcing some administrative changes.

The office of Director of CIO, held by John Brophy, was to be abolished, said Lewis, and Brophy would get some other "place of distinction." It proved to be "Director of Local Industrial Unions," which Brophy called "nearer a place of extinction than distinction." Lewis appointed Allan S. Haywood to the newly created post of Director of Organization. It was a roundabout way of demoting Brophy and elevating Haywood in his place.

Lewis also curtailed to California the jurisdiction of West Coast CIO Director Harry Bridges. Hillman's crowd had long objected to Bridges' wide CIO powers. The right wing also wanted Bridges out of its hair in Oregon and Washington, where a right-left fight was raging in the Woodworkers.

The action on Bridges, so timed, was clearly a concession to Hillman and the right. The case of Brophy was less clear.

Brophy sought me out that evening—in a secluded recess of the Whitcomb Hotel where I was trying to relax and absorb the implications of the day's events. He was obviously distraught. If he hadn't been a teetotaler, I'd have thought he'd been trying to drown his troubles. He walked up arms swinging, chin up, as if spoiling for a fight. "Well, you see!" he burst out. "Now Lee [Pressman] and you will be next. What are you going to do?"

When Brophy and I were close, at start of CIO, we used to philosophize about Lewis's amazing switch. Brophy held that when Lewis changed course, he recognized all the implications and would follow them to their logical conclusion. Lewis would be equally logical, Brophy predicted, if and when he decided to switch back to the right. To Brophy, I now concluded, this must seem such a turning point. I wasn't sure myself. As to the angry triumph of his head-chopping predictions, I ascribed it to misery's love of company. Yet I also heard the echo of an earlier puzzle about Brophy.

A month before, Brophy had written to the Dies Committee on Un-American Activities trying to clear himself of red-smear charges. This in itself was not noteworthy—except that Brophy hadn't bothered with such stuff before. I was surprised when Brophy came to my office about it.

"Well, you saw what I wrote to the Dies committee!" he had begun.

"Yes," I said, "I ran it in the paper——"

"What are you going to do?" Brophy had interrupted.

I shrugged, not sure what he was driving at.

"You, too, should clear yourself with the Dies committee," he said.

"Why?" I began argumentatively. But Brophy hadn't come for a chat. He stood as if delivering a warning, an ultimatum almost, then turned and left.

I had no intention of following Brophy's advice. I was more vulnerable to radical charges than he and would just have invited new smears. I also felt it demeaning to yield in any way to the committee's postulate that it was bad or wrong to be a communist. In any case, our CIO policy had been not to make itemized denials that might dignify or channel the redbaiting, but rather to defy the Dies committee as a tool of CIO's worst enemies.

Whether or not the two incidents were connected, the fact was that after San Francisco Brophy cast his lot with CIO's rightwing in all its anticommunist maneuvers. I came to conclude he had misjudged the timing of his rightward leap. Lewis did not follow through on the antileftism suggested by his off-the-record talk, and Brophy's new rightism did not rehabilitate him. It must have fed his animus against the left to continue demoted while unrepentant lefts suffered no comparable penalty for a long time.

In Brophy's posthumous autobiography, he relates a circumstance that, he says, "no doubt helped to bring on my demotion." After the outbreak of war in Europe in 1939, Brophy made a Labor Day address in Des Moines taking a position he calls the opposite of Lewis's anti-involvement speech on the same day. Brophy argued his position with Pressman, who he assumed reported it to Lewis. By then I was no longer so intimate with Brophy as to know his thinking. It would be understandable that the overwhelming anticommunist propaganda following the German-Soviet nonaggression pact might have caused his switch, as many others. That doesn't appear to be his claim. Rather his autobiography tries to reconstruct a record of consistent antileftism—which makes it hard for me to recognize the Brophy I knew.

Whatever Brophy's motivations, from that moment in San Francisco our ways parted. For the next eight years, though my offices in CIO were next to his, we had little to do with each other. To me Brophy seemed to have become listless in his laborism—buoyed chiefly by a revived aversion to Lewis and a newfound aversion to his onetime friends of the left.

At the moment I didn't ponder Brophy's personal problems too deeply. I anticipated problems of my own. Early the next morning, Caroline and I left with Lee Pressman and his wife for Los Angeles. Louis Goldblatt of the Longshoremen & Warehousemen drove us in his car along the beautiful coast route. His clear, sharp mind made him congenial company. We talked little of what was most on our minds. On critical matters, Louis and

Lee were both close-mouthed unless they had something to say and a reason to say it. Also we were taking a vacation break we didn't want to spoil.

From Los Angeles, we four easterners went on by train, stopping at Albuquerque for an excursion to Santa Fe. Only then did we pick up copies of the *New York Times* and other eastern papers full of repercussions to Lewis's antired remarks. Rightwingers had at once leaked their version to pet redbaiting reporters, but western stories had been vague. Those we now read—emanating from Detroit—spelled out rightwing interpretations in great detail. Their consensus was that Lewis had turned right and would purge CIO's left. Lee and I would be among the first to go, they said, and many individuals and unions were added to the list.

Lee and I shrugged and kidded. We had expected such stories. There was nothing to do, and little to say, until we could talk to Lewis himself. For our vacation's sake, I was glad Lee was more brusque than bellyacher.

Once back in Washington, I was one of several "purgees"— including Pressman and Brophy—who made our separate ways to Lewis in succession. With me Lewis was friendly, conciliatory, concerned. He declared he had had to do something in San Francisco, because the Dies committee was more of a menace than I probably realized; it was threatening to subpoena CIO files. He assured me he intended no witch hunts or purges.

Lewis expressed indignation at the kind of newspaper stories of which I complained, and we agreed that Edward Levinson was most likely the "authoritative CIO sources in Detroit" to which they made attribution. Since Jay Lovestone had delayed leaving the sinking ship of Homer Martin, he and his henchmen were no longer a "CIO source." For finger jobs on CIO lefts, reporters now turned to Levinson. Without more ado, Lewis put through a long-distance call to Levinson and roughly bawled him out while I listened. When he hung up, Lewis said he had put Murray and Hillman in full charge of the Auto situation and had had nothing to do with the Levinson appointment.

"Why don't you talk to Murray and Hillman?" Lewis said, as I left.

I did. But not about Levinson, who had been their man. I

complained about the inner-CIO redbaiting originating in Detroit, and both understood me at once.

Sitting remote behind his desk, with windowlight from behind shading his face and shining on mine, Murray was cautious, controlled, ánd tense in manner, words, and tone. He either knew or suspected that I came from Lewis. Murray disclaimed any personal responsibility. He agreed it was bad for CIO to "foul its own nest." He said all I expected him to say.

Hillman was more interesting. I visited him when he was relaxing alone in his Carlton Hotel room. He received me with the courtesies due an emissary from Lewis. Things were touchy between CIO's Big Three.

With Lewis and Murray, I hadn't used the word "redbaiting." It was a catch-cry in union infighting. Those anywhere to the left were called "communists"; they retorted by calling the other side "redbaiters." Lewis didn't use such ideological tags. He thought, or at least spoke, in more personal terms. Murray, in his heart, was on the redbaiting side.

In this writing, I have used the word "redbaiting" reluctantly, because of its factional echoes and overtones. But it was the only word I found to hand for an ancient technique. Rulers have always "redbaited" anyone who stirred up the people. They have tried to identify him with some bogy word like sedition, treason, subversion, conspiracy, revolution, anarchism, syndicalism, socialism, and above all, communism. The technique was to popularize the word as one of horror or fear to the unthinking; then link your opponent with it—how accurately mattered not —in a way to include him in the emotional prejudice the word was intended to stir. Jew-baiting, Negro-baiting, the baiting of any scapegoat group, were always blood-brothers (and bloody brothers) to redbaiting. Hitler's anticommunism and his anti-Semitism were one in style and purpose.

In the labor movement, redbaiting was designed to divert attention from disputed union, labor, or political issues by so linking opponents with the bogy word "communism" as to turn against them the prejudice and hate of the unreasoning.

Rightwingers often argued it wasn't redbaiting to call a man a communist, if he was a communist. A valid point no doubt in a country where communists had equal rights and chances to be known and heard. Within capitalist limits, Britain, France, Italy, accorded communists some of these rights. The United States never did. Here prejudice against the word "communism" was one-sidedly mass-produced, and communists were rigorously silenced or suppressed. If therefore a communist led in a union or some other noncommunist movement, it might well be redbaiting to harp on the bogy word for him. For instance, all CIO leaders knew President Ben Gold of the Fur Workers was a communist, but until CIO split wide open, most dealt with him as a union leader without harping on his politics any more than they harped on the politics, race, or religion of other leaders.

When I went to see Hillman, I didn't mean to use the word "redbaiting" with him, any more than with Lewis or Murray. It slipped out. Hillman pounced on it. But not lifting his eyebrows in mockery, as CIO rightwingers then commonly did.

"Redbaiting is bad," he said. "It's bad business, thoroughly bad."

"Why, Sidney!" I murmured, amused to hear this from the leader of the crowd then doing most of the inner CIO redbaiting. Then I stopped. Hillman was evidently serious. He leaned forward, bringing his hand down on his knee. His manner was grave and earnest.

As I left, after hearing Hillman inveigh against redbaiting in ostensible agreement with me, I reflected that he was the only one of CIO's Big Three who had really suffered from redbaiting —he and his union and his people. Lewis and Murray had dished it out more than suffered from it; only with CIO did they get a taste of it themselves. Hillman must have let his mind slip back to when he was on the receiving end.

1940 was a year of conflict in CIO. War was under way in Europe, and American opinion, in CIO as elsewhere, was sharply divided between interventionists and isolationists, as the two sides called each other. Lewis was feuding with Roosevelt, behind whom CIO had united in 1936. An ascendant rightwing was using the year's sharpened anticommunist ax to strike at all leftwing necks that stuck out. Less noticed in all the brawls was the disputed long-range issue of working-class independence.

In its rise, CIO clearly expressed this independence, in the initiatives of the aroused workers and Lewis's response to them. The CIO was nobody's stooge. It took advantage of opportunities wrung from government but was not at all a government-directed movement. Through CIO, the workers revolted against company-union concepts of corporate paternalism and began to grope toward political independence. At the crest of the rising, there were many visions of what an independent working class could do.

Politically, however, CIO showed little of the breakaway imagination and initiative that marked its union organizing. Directed from on top, CIO politics tended to follow old and standard procedures. When Lewis and Hillman started Labor's Non-Partisan League in 1936, there was much talk of "independent labor political action." The action was chiefly to reelect President Roosevelt; the independence, to promote liberal candidates in Democratic primaries. Except in some language and new-found enthusiasm, LNPL departed little from the old AFL policy of rewarding friends and punishing enemies. It did, however, mobilize labor political forces more ambitiously than before, and in that sense was a step to greater independence.

Biggest block to CIO political independence was the fact that the bourgeois-liberal Roosevelt had preempted popular leadership from 1932 on. Lewis deeply resented Roosevelt's political sway over his own CIO followers.

By 1940, Lewis was driving hard for greater labor political independence. This was not the only element in his sometimes contradictory stands. But it was his strongest, if least understood, point.

Lewis's style was highly personal. He often fought like the hero (or villain, if you prefer) of a western movie—a source of much of his dramatic popular appeal. His philosophical vacuum drew in various extraneous elements. To piece together all of Lewis's political attitudes, tactics, declarations, alliances, conflicts, would make an intriguing jigsaw puzzle.

Lewis was more clear and consistent in the first phase of his CIO leadership than in its second (political) phase. By 1939,

CIO's first phase was over. Its unions had mostly won acceptance. But Lewis had more in mind. With CIO's sweeping initial successes, his ambitions grew for the movement he seemed to embody. He envisaged a labor movement using its union numbers and strength to struggle for greater political power.

In personal terms, this meant a challenge by Lewis to Roosevelt—whose outcome, in the temper of the times, was to be frustration and defeat.

It is hard to write of the 1939-40 period without having one's memories colored by what happened from 1941 on, after the U.S.S.R. and then the United States became involved in a war that dominated all considerations.

In 1939-40, the war loomed big in the background but was still far away. From Roosevelt down, the politicians were swearing not to involve the United States in foreign wars or send its boys to die in them. No CIO leaders openly opposed CIO's consistently antiwar and anti-involvement resolutions.

The struggle between "interventionists" and "isolationists" took more indirect forms. In CIO it provided much of the ammunition used in the Lewis-Roosevelt and left-right conflicts. The "interventionists" tried to attribute pro-German sympathies to all, like Lewis, who actively favored the United States neutrality. On account of Soviet neutrality, they similarly smeared CIO leftwingers.

In the case of Lewis and the lefts, the charge was libelous. In American big-business ranks, there were obvious Nazi-Fascist sympathizers. In CIO ranks, there were few, if any. Lewis had a stronger record of opposing Nazism and Fascism than had some of his critics. The lefts' record was even stronger.

The Lewis name became subject to association with big-business "isolationists" of pro-Nazi leanings when his daughter Kathryn joined the America First committee. Norman Thomas, as antiwar socialist, also spoke to America First audiences in the same period. It was to carry guilt-by-association rather far if all opponents of United States involvement were to be smeared as pro-Nazi because their names were bracketed at times with those of pro-Hitler isolationists.

Some claimed to see evidence of pro-German sympathies in Lewis's contacts with an international oil speculator, William Rhodes Davis, who helped the Mexican government break through a British-American boycott of its newly nationalized oil industry.

Lewis had long been interested in Mexico. Under President Lazaro Cardenas, a new and leftish confederation of labor (CTM) arose there parallel with CIO in the United States. CIO, under Lewis, had close relations with CTM, and with the Latin American Confederation of Workers (CTAL), in both of which Vicente Lombardo Toledano played a leading part. Lewis spoke at their antifascist and antiwar congresses. When Cardenas nationalized oil wells owned by United States and British companies, Mexican labor was delighted, but Wall Street and London were outraged. They started a boycott of Mexican oil, to strangle the industry and make Cardenas cry uncle.

It was in this setting that Lewis was alleged to have been involved in an attempt to break through the British-American boycott, when Rhodes arranged a deal for German purchase of Mexican oil. This was at a time when American big business was still trading with Germany in some volume.

In seeking some independence of the Roosevelt administration, Lewis had not so much tried to oppose as to mobilize more bargaining and pressure power. Whatever Labor's Non-Partisan League might have meant to Hillman, Lewis had more in mind than to make it a labor auxiliary to the Democratic party for reelecting Roosevelt and New Deal Democrats.

Along with LNPL, Lewis put much money and effort into reelecting Roosevelt in 1936—expecting something for labor in return. If returns were not adequate, as he later complained, he thought labor should reserve the right to look elsewhere. In 1938, Lewis welcomed Roosevelt's effort to purge the Democratic party of reactionaries, and gave it all-out support. This effort failed, and by 1939 Roosevelt was veering rightward again, as he sought business and conservative support for his increasingly interventionist policies.

Lewis's dream of bringing labor closer to the seats of power by forcing Roosevelt leftward now faded away. He was furious at Hillman and his kind for sacrificing CIO's bargaining power by offering FDR′ unconditional support. Lewis was determined, if he died politically in the attempt, not to let Roosevelt take labor for granted. But where else could labor go? All through 1940, Lewis looked for answers, and tried out some.

Lewis started the year by introducing Senator Burton K. Wheeler to the UMW convention in Columbus, Ohio, as a possible alternative to Roosevelt. The delegates heard Lewis assail Roosevelt and dutifully refrained from pro-FDR demonstrations, but they couldn't get excited over Wheeler. The Wheeler squib sputtered around a bit after that but never did more than fizz.

Lewis's next answer at least excited some youthful enthusiasm. It carried his ideas of labor political independence to their high-water mark.

Invited to address the American Youth Congress in Washington, Lewis responded impromptu to the occasion. The delegates had marched through the capital on a miserable wet February day, with wilted placards demanding "Jobs Not Guns" and charging the administration with reneging on aid to young people and the unemployed. Then they had stood on the White House lawn in drizzling rain, while Roosevelt lectured and scolded, pooh-poohing their stand on unemployment, calling their resolution against a Finnish loan "twaddle." When the 3,500 delegates gathered in an auditorium to hear their own invited speakers, they were a bit bedraggled.

The chance to hit back at Roosevelt gave Lewis the zip he needed, and he raised the delegates' spirits with a fighting speech. Lewis invited them to join with Labor's Non-Partisan League in a coalition independent of both Republican and Democratic parties. He told them the Mine Workers had also opposed the Finnish loan and going to war to suit "imperialistic world governments." He joined the Youth Congress in demanding action against unemployment. He championed the rights of black Americans and demanded an end to the poll tax.

Lewis returned to his office in a glowing mood, surprised by the fervor his speech aroused. It encouraged him along the course he followed in the next few months. When I congratulated him, he didn't respond as to a formal courtesy, but asked me to specify what I found good in the speech.

Addressing a big Mine Workers' rally in West Virginia, Lewis spelled out the coalition he had suggested to the Youth Congress. He said that if the Democratic party didn't advance a platform and candidate satisfactory to labor and the common people, he would—after the Democratic and Republican conventions—urge the assembling of a great delegate convention of CIO, Labor's Non-Partisan League, old-age, Negro, and farm organizations. Lewis said he made his demands chiefly on the Democratic party since "I don't expect anything from the Republican party because it is obvious that those who pay the fiddler call the tune."

On this popular coalition idea Lewis worked for some months, addressing the National Negro Congress, National Association for the Advancement of Colored People, Townsend old-age-pension movement, and other groups. He told the St. Louis UAW convention: "Some day in this country the people are going to lose confidence in the existing political parties to a degree they will form their own party."

In midyear a curious vestige of the old pre-CIO Lewis reappeared. Speaking to the NAACP at the time of the Republican convention in Philadelphia, Lewis defended Herbert Hoover's record in the Great Depression. Hoover should not be blamed, said Lewis, for a depression that "was laid on his doorstep when he came to the White House." Hoover's policies, he added, "had a powerful effect in the start at recovery in 1932"; whereas the New Dealers "did not fulfill their promises or complete their undertakings" but kept the country "in depression for seven more years."

The Lewis of 1940 was at a roadblock. He might try to push forward toward greater labor political independence, as the new Lewis of CIO had started to do; or—disturbing thought—he might turn back frustrated to some of the byways covered by the old Lewis.

The new Lewis had broken with his old Republicanism. At

the time of the Columbus UMW convention, he told the press: "The Republican party makes no claim of serving labor. It does not pretend to serve anyone but the financial interests who control it. In a major sense it is frankly hostile to labor." Before the 1940 Republican resolutions committee, Lewis voiced CIO demands upon a party which had "practically abandoned labor in the past eight or ten years" and had been abandoned by labor in its turn.

Still Lewis's defense of a Hoover whom most CIOers had never forgiven for their depression sufferings, was a tipoff he wanted to retain some links with old Republican cronies.

Around this time, like a ghost from Lewis's Republican past, K.C. Adams reappeared in his entourage. Adams didn't belong with the new Lewis of CIO, any more than did Ellis Searles, whose place Adams was to fill after Searles died. Aging and ailing, Searles had lingered on as Lewis's UMW editor, neither interfering with nor contributing to Lewis's new policies.

K.C. Adams was aggressive and opinionated. A jaunty, irreverent maverick type of political operator, he affected scorn for the New Deal and its "burrocrats." He doubtless found the CIO aberration just as outlandish, and could hardly have fitted into it himself. He didn't have to; he was engaged elsewhere. Not till Lewis fell out with much of CIO did Adams show up again; not till he broke with CIO did KC really come into his own.

Lewis seemed fond of Adams, enjoying his wisecracking company. He later permitted KC to express his atavistic attitudes in the UMW *Journal*—including know-nothing, lowest-common-denominator prejudices shocking to friends of the new Lewis. Shrugging off complaints that the *Journal* was taken to reflect his own thinking, Lewis disclaimed responsibility for KC's sentiments. He appeared tolerantly amused at KC as an interesting character—which in many ways he was.

The Lewis of 1940 could look forward to the future, with the Youth Congress. He could also sneak a look back at the old and departing age of Herbert Hoover and K.C. Adams.

Lewis's enemies in CIO were delighted to make Roosevelt the issue. If their positions on war and other issues might be weak or ambiguous, they felt on firm ground when it came to Roosevelt. Working people, in CIO as elsewhere, were overwhelmingly pro-Roosevelt. The social welfare glamor of the New Deal had not worn off. FDR's early class appeal for the common people to rally against the forces of reactionary wealth still echoed. If some became skeptical when Roosevelt courted and co-opted these same forces, the next spasm of wealthy reaction's assaults on him revived their loyalty.

FDR was tops with CIO's rank and file. But Lewis was, too. The difference, to Lewis's disadvantage in 1940, was that he was tops in union struggle for porkchops; in election politics, FDR was the champ.

An extension of the popular uprising that overthrew Hooverism in 1932, CIO had close links with the New Deal from the first, and Lewis himself threw CIO behind Roosevelt in 1936. Now he found no way to reverse the pro-FDR procession he helped to start.

Lewis's 1940 speeches for an independent, labor-led people's coalition were latecomer stuff. In 1937, at the crest of the CIO uprising, the idea might have struck root. If intensively cultivated, it might have grown into a challenge to the Democratic leadership—with much bargaining power and some promise of actual independence. Coming after Lewis's bargaining power had already been sapped, his speeches didn't mobilize support. Later in the year, Lewis dropped this whole approach as impractical.

The Roosevelt issue, a stout stick to belabor Lewis, was also a staff for up-climbing young CIO leaders. Walter Reuther grabbed it in UAW. With his slogan, "Lewis for CIO, FDR for the U.S.," he gauged the sentiments of UAW voters and gave aspiring porkchoppers of his bloc something to aspire with. Together they used it to clobber UAW's embarrassed left wing.

The 1940 UAW convention in St. Louis gave Lewis a record ovation—halted finally only because it was shaking the plaster from the ceilings. The pro-Lewis and leftwing delegates let themselves go for their hard-pressed and hard-battling champion. The Reuther faction tried to show it didn't love Lewis less for loving Roosevelt more. The two sides vied with each other to make the more noise and keep up the ovation longer.

Some writers later suggested such incidents might have led Lewis to overestimate his support. The inference is insulting. Lewis enjoyed acclaim, but he was not fatuous; he could appraise its source and its limits. In this case, I was with him and recall he had things well sized up.

In an atmosphere like the later Cold War hysteria, rights and lefts were fighting it out for office and influence in many sectors of CIO.

Hitler's Nazis and their fascist allies stank in the nostrils of all decent people, especially the workers. Like the United States, the USSR was at first neutral in the war. All the media campaigned to make Soviet neutrality appear an alliance, to link communism with fascism. Many CIO unions proscribed "Nazis, communists, and fascists," denying them union rights. These actions were directed solely against lefts in the unions; in no case were they used against Nazis, fascists, or other rightists. Rightwing factions seeking office promoted "anti-communazi" resolutions to embarrass leftwing administrations. Where the rights were in office, they used them to smear, threaten, or purge any radical opposition.

In state and city CIO councils, the conflict was at its sharpest. In New York City, the Amalgamated Clothing Workers refused to join the CIO council because leftwing unions were in the majority, with "reds" like Mike Quill and Joe Curran on top. In the New York state council, the ACW counted on control with the aid of its Textile and Retail allies. To make sure, it barred 99 delegates from leftwing unions—whereupon some 250 delegates walked out. The council was completely split, and national CIO had to step in to restore any semblance of unity. Similar splits developed elsewhere, and it began to look as if all CIO might split apart.

CIO's left wing was more vulnerable in 1940 than it, or others, seemed to realize. In this election and near-war year, the Roosevelt slogans were sweeping sentiment warward—with little objection from once jobless or underemployed workers now finding jobs with overtime in new and growing war industries. Hatred of Hitler . . . sympathy with Britain and France . . .

"national defense," with its patriotic and job-providing implications . . . the popularity of Roosevelt's New Deal . . . a
witches' brew of anticommunism mixed into the prevailing antifascism . . . all these ingredients were whipped together by the
most powerful job-controlling administration yet. Big business
threw in all its opinion-forming media. For all its occasional reservations on Roosevelt and his interventionism, it was increasingly interested in war profits and postwar expansion. The baiting of CIO lefts was one of the favorite outlets for its
anticommunism.

Within CIO, antileftism had strong promoters. The Roosevelt administration backed its propaganda with much "defense"
patronage. Ambitious upcomers like Reuther were out to ride
the antileft wave into power. The Catholic hierarchy concentrated on anticommunism, both through ACTU and through its
influence on Catholic union leaders.

But for the power and prestige of John L. Lewis as CIO
president, an incipient purge of the left in 1940 might have assumed proportions like the Cold War purge in 1947-49. The left
found protection in boasting it faithfully followed national CIO
policy which Lewis largely dictated.

Lewis and the left had freely chosen to work together in the
CIO uprising of 1936-37. In 1940 they came together willy-nilly
—not always or entirely to their mutual satisfaction. Both Lewis
and the left were anti-interventionist in 1940. But the left was
hostile to the big-business isolationists who courted Lewis
through America First. CIO lefts like Reid Robinson, Quill,
Curran, supported the more radical, working-class Emergency
Peace Mobilization—at which Lewis isolationists looked
askance.

Both Lewis and the left were anti-Roosevelt in 1940. But
the left was less obsessed and personal than Lewis, who was
working himself into an anything-rather-than-Roosevelt corner.
Left union leaders withheld endorsement of Roosevelt, coun-
tering pro-FDR sentiment with the no-blank-check argument.
They were uninterested in the Wheeler boomlet and averse to
any Lewis flirtation with old-guard Republicans, but pleased
when he tried to move toward a people's coalition independent
of both old parties.

Lewis needed allies, as did the left. In 1939 he had barely held CIO together behind a militant and independent program, antiwar, antiredbaiting, reserved on Roosevelt. In 1940 his influence was clearly not enough to swing CIO into any anti-Roosevelt camp. Having given up his first thought of stepping down in 1939, Lewis fought stubbornly through 1940 to be CIO leader in more than name. On whom could he count to follow him?

The ACW, Textile, and other Hillmanite unions were in the Roosevelt camp, outspokenly opposed to Lewis. Murray was personally for Roosevelt, though otherwise professedly loyal to Lewis. His Steel machine was out of sympathy with Lewis and the left. Centrist unions like Rubber and Oil were plugging for Roosevelt and passing "anti-communazi" resolutions. From his own Mine Workers Lewis could command only formal support. The ranks were pro-FDR; the leaders—his own machine—conservatively conformist.

The Auto Workers might have been one great CIO segment to follow Lewis, if with misgivings, on any militantly independent course. But Hillman and Murray had taken precautions in 1939 to keep its then dominant militants from assuming leadership. They had cleared the way for Reuther, whose increasingly powerful faction was bidding for control.

Lewis had payrollees in minor outfits such as Construction, District 50, Utility, among CIO regional directors (some already disaffected), and on his UMW staff. But these were usually more attached to Lewis's payroll than to the less understood causes he promoted. For his most active support, Lewis had to rely on CIO's leftwing unions.

The CIO left had more influence than might at first appear. It could throw behind Lewis not only the unions it directly controlled, but also many locals or sections of rightwing unions. It was dominant in many CIO state and city councils, and in various bodies linked with CIO.

On the other hand, the lefts were weaker than a union count might indicate. Out of 42 affiliates, about half were leftwing or went along with the left. A number of these, such as UE, Fur, Longshoremen, Maritime, Mine-Mill, Transport, Woodworkers, were substantial or influential. Others were smaller or struggling unions in a relatively dependent status. Only UE was in the 200,000-up group with UMW, UAW, Steel, Textile, ACW, which comprised the bulk of CIO membership.

Lewis's last-minute endorsement of Wendell Willkie was a confession of failure in his search for an alternative to Roosevelt. He admitted in effect that he had found no other place for labor to go except to the Republican candidate. His speech let down his followers with a thud. His opponents were stimulated by their outrage. His followers made a look-what-we-gotta-defend grimace.

By this time the Lewis camp was shockproof against his attacks on Roosevelt. Worried by the pro-FDR sentiment of their memberships, they took comfort from the quasi-syndicalist way American unionists, skeptical of politicians, will follow a fighting leader in a union scrap regardless of politics. A riproaring speech against Roosevelt might have left Lewis's followers chuckling, as they upheld his right to speak his mind. For Lewis to ask CIOers to vote for the Republican Willkie was pushing things.

In the Twenties, a union worker could talk and vote Republican in some parts without being called a company stooge. After the Great Depression, particularly in cities and industries where CIO organized, a class attitude developed. Whatever might be thought of the Democrats, the Republican party was generally held to be the party of Wall Street, big business, the employers, the millionaire press, in short, the bosses.

In the many congratulatory telegrams from CIO sources after the broadcast, I noted few good words for Willkie. Most praised Lewis for lambasting the administration's letdown of labor and for showing political independence, but were tactfully silent on Willkie. The mood was to leap to the side of an admired leader who had laid himself open to devastating attack.

On election eve, I was with Lewis in the Washington radio studio where he made his last broadcast for Willkie. Also speaking was Senator Hiram Johnson of California. As I studied that other old bull of the herd—much older than Lewis—and heard his conventional Republican speech, I got an uneasy feeling.

Johnson, too, had been a fighter in his time—a progressive

taking on monopoly capitalists. I recalled a cartoon of him as a great bull standing head down on the track before an oncoming Southern Pacific locomotive. That bull, long since, had purdently left the track, to live longer if less daringly. The monopolists now had the track to themselves. Their engines rolled on unimpeded, while the herds chewed their cuds to one side, awaiting tame bulls to lead them to the slaughterhouses of war or depression.

Now before me that old bull placidly chewed the over-chewed cud of a Republicanism that might have come from the grass roots in frontier days, but that was now a packaged mash sold by the very monopolists he once had challenged. I wondered if a John L. Lewis could ever end up like that.

After this election eve broadcast, Lewis and I went to a nearby Childs restaurant. It was late. The place was almost empty. Lewis was in no hurry to go home. We sat for some time, idly mulling things over. The campaign was ended. Nothing Lewis might now say or do could change things. He was relaxed like an unwound spring. In this not-that-it-matters-now mood, I tried to probe his motives. Lewis answered easily, as if casually putting things in order.

I felt closer to Lewis this year than I had ever done. His aloneness seemed to reduce the distance between us.

Three musketeers—Lewis, Hillman, Murray—had set out on the gallant and daring CIO adventure. No longer was it all-for-one and one-for-all. The swords of Hillman and Lewis were turned against each other. Murray's was in its scabbard when Lewis fought.

In his grandiose, theatrical way, Lewis had personified CIO. The role had become part of himself. Now a glamor-boy President had stolen his part as workers' champion, and flaunted his costume before the fickle crowd.

Had Lewis kidded himself about the loyalty of his erstwhile fans? I doubt it. He hadn't kidded himself about Hillman and Murray. He knew what was happening in Auto and Steel. He found something more lasting in his Mine Workers, but he also knew the means he'd used to get it.

Lewis's leftwing support, while voluntary and enthusiastic, emphasized his aloneness. It was not an unmixed boon. He knew that the anticommunism of the time could make it a millstone; and that it was conditioned by considerations other than his own. Lewis expected that, when push came to shove, the left union leaders would react like any other job- and power-conscious politicos. His trouble, come 1941, was that the shove was not his. It was an urge for self-preservation—coinciding with left principle—to get off the precarious antiwar spot they were on with a much-weakened Lewis.

In our late election eve chat, Lewis didn't dispute my judgment that Roosevelt would easily win. No doubt it was also his own. He looked at me quizzically, his eyes strangely mild under the shaggy brows of his often grim face. He philosophized as with a youngster (I was some 20 years younger).

"When I was a young fellow," Lewis said, "I just couldn't see how William Jennings Bryan could be licked. Everyone I knew was for him. The working people, the farmers, all the little people, seemed to want him. But Bryan was defeated."

The parallel was not a good one—for Lewis. To me it suggested that the powers of wealth and machine politics, counting for more than the people's wishes, might put Willkie in. Lewis threw out the thought idly, kiddingly, as if to indicate Willkie might have some odd sporting chance. The rest of our chat was based on the assumption Roosevelt would win.

I deplored Lewis's decision to quit as CIO head. CIO would never be the same without him, I said. Degenerating as it was into a sort of political company-unionism, it might go that way on the industrial field.

Lewis said he had done his main job when CIO was successfully organized. He had wanted to step down in 1939—both for personal reasons and because the Roosevelt administration and its eager agents in CIO were pulling the movement out from under him. He had no taste for being titular head of an organization that didn't follow his leadership. By now, November 1940, things had gone from bad to worse. Lewis said he was not again going to be talked out of a decision he'd had to make.

I found the prospect of a CIO without Lewis a desolating

one, and my feelings must have showed. Lewis grinned and tried to console me by saying, "I'll not be far away."

In announcing he'd retire as CIO president if the workers failed to vote for Willkie, Lewis was hardly expecting a Willkie victory. True, if Willkie had won—a long-shot chance of some appeal to him—Lewis would have felt vindicated enough to stay on as CIO head. He made the tie-in chiefly to insure and excuse his retirement, if FDR won; to show the strength of his peeve at CIO defection; and to emphasize a Willkie endorsement that might otherwise have seemed halfhearted.

Lewis's move seemed surprising at the time. But some kind of dramatic gesture was to be expected from a man like Lewis who was not disposed to slink away from defeat. "Never knows he's licked," is a common tribute to a battler. There are also those who know they're licked and still keep on fighting. In this spirit, Lewis girded himself for his last big CIO battle, at the 1940 convention.

Chapter Thirteen

FAREWELL TO LEWIS

*At a bitter, baiting convention, Lewis took
leave of a CIO that had left him.*

A lion lay wounded. At a safe distance, jackals sniffed
warily around. The more daring made little snarling forays . . .
Lewis was king no more. His royal mane was just a mane.
He could still roar, but he couldn't pounce as once. Their minds
full of past imagery, and past awe, many delegates to CIO's 1940
convention in Atlantic City could hardly realize that all they saw
was a shaggily leonine man about to step down from office.

The union leaders were wary and relatively restrained. Bitter as they were at Lewis, Hillman's Amalgamated associates
were aware of their chief's dignified and delicate position as National Defense Advisory Commissioner and Roosevelt's top
labor man. Emil Rieve and George Baldanzi of Textile were
vengeful, too, but more controlled than lesser rightwingers fresh
full of venom from recent local fights against leftists and Lewis-
ites. These together made up the overtly anti-Lewis right wing.

There was a considerable center, restrained in both pro-
Lewis and anti-Lewis manifestations. Murray men from Steel
and further afield. Reutherizers from UAW. From Rubber, Oil,
and like unions, men who were pro-Roosevelt and antileft, but
straddling the fence on Lewis. These duly applauded Lewis, but
without the enthusiasm of the left, from whom they took pains
to distinguish themselves.

From the camp followers more than the leaders came most of
the snarls.

A convention like this drew many hangers-on. The Handy
Andy type of "Organizer" used by a union boss for his personal
politicking. The would-be or sometime employees of unions, de-

pending on factional fortunes. Agents of outfits that sought to service unions or influence their policies. All these had to have sharp noses to sniff the factional winds.

Among employees of unions were many young men and women, often college-trained, attracted to CIO as a cause. They weren't content with humdrum technical chores. They had taken sides, and they soon found there were sides within sides to take. The unions, especially on the left, owed much to the fervor of their little-paid services. There were usually some of the kind on both sides of factional division.

From all these dedicated (if on your side) or factional (if on the other side) people, I must now try to separate a certain wriggly specimen.

He might have landed a CIO job in early days when all comers were welcome. He soon began to set himself furtively apart, to show unexplained aversion for some associates, to whisper in the ears of chosen union officers. If caught with weak alibis in conniving to discredit, in leaking slander, he pleaded he was victim of a "commy plot." After HUAC got going, his peculiarities became more obvious, and marketable. If fired by the union, some newspaper might hire him as antired fingerman. He might stay on with the union as pet of a rightwing faction.

Multiplying after 1939, this species swarmed around the 1940 CIO convention. No longer did potted palms conceal connivers. They strutted through the lobbies and lingered in the lavatories, reviling Lewis and all his works. They flung their taunts across bar counters, if no Lewis or left stalwart were observed at hand. Some black eyes came to mark the features of the less observant. Around lunch tables, they divided up the jobs of "reds" bound to go when Murray took over from the fallen Lewis.

As it turned out, this proliferating species didn't quite overrun CIO yet. But the future was theirs, if they could survive on slimmer pickings through the Second World War to enjoy the feast of the Great Cold War. Meanwhile the press and "Un-American" committees took care of many. Other congressional committees kept some around to whisper into ears and point the furtive finger. Behind every red scare, in and out of Congress, one had only to dig a bit to find one of this specialized species.

Some climbed high, designing the foreign policy of the AFL-CIO, serving in embassies and in CIA, conspiring with government funds to disrupt labor unity in other lands, as in their apprenticeship they disrupted it in CIO. Others became ensconced in union offices, conning credulous old labor leaders on the red menace, warning of the perils of disarmament if peace should break out in the Cold War, ever on guard lest their union bosses lend comfort to "the commies" by aiding any progressive cause.

The reporters at this convention merged into the camp followers. Snooper-informer antired specialists were among them in record numbers. The more bona fide labor reporters were also working for publishers now in bullfight mood—eager to see Lewis baited and bloodily dispatched and to celebrate with a redbaiting fiesta. And "CIO contacts" with anti-Lewis and antired "dope" hovered so close as almost to seem part of the press.

At each CIO convention I arranged a party for the press, with Lewis the main attraction. The reporters turned out for some shoulder-rubbing with Mr. Big, and I had to make sure he'd be present. Lewis showed up well on these occasions. His manners were pleasing and his wit sophisticated. Newsmen got tips from his calculated hints. They counted on his reliability and respected him personally. Lewis usually enjoyed reporters.

At this convention, Lewis was evasive when I tried to pin him down for the press party. When I persisted, he finally looked at me with that curious blandness of eye when his thoughts turned inward. "Go ahead without me," he said. "You'll have to excuse me. They're such bastards!"

This from Lewis, and the slow reflective way he said it! Since CIO began, he had almost written his own front-page headlines. Now he saw reporters who once ate from his hand as but part of a circling, snarling pack.

The anti-Lewis pack won their greatest victories in barroom gossip. When things got going, a lot of advance stories had to be amended. Lewis didn't lie waiting to be counted out. He got up and came back swinging. He made his set-to with Hillman quite newsworthy.

The elections had shown there was nothing phony about the Lewis-Roosevelt fracas. The two were sluggers, and there was interest in a post-election return bout, even if Hillman had to stand in for the champ. Hillman was top labor man in that overgrown military-industrial complex, the government's "defense" setup. FDR had groomed him to take on his *bête noire* with the beetling eyebrows. It could be a good grudge fight.

CIO fans were all keyed up. Superficial courtesies between CIO's two top leaders had fooled no one. Their followers had been fighting it out all through 1940, at every CIO event. Hillman nearly chickened out, pleading pressure of government business. Some baiting by Lewis and the pleas of Hillman's own seconds averted such a floperoo.

When the two men clinched, their perfervid fans got some emotional lift, but the actual performance in the ring was not so much. However, an after-the-fight manager for Hillman retold the story a dozen years later in such a way that no Lewis fan can withhold retort.

In his biography, *"Sidney Hillman: Statesman of American Labor,"* Matthew Josephson claims Lewis and his cohorts tried to create a Draft-Lewis fervor as pretext for Lewis to renege on his decision to retire; but by stoutly sitting on their hands, Hillman's supporters blocked the first day's effort to snake-dance Lewis back to power. Then Lewis tried to bait the Amalgamated into quitting CIO. To quote Josephson:

"His face livid with emotion, and pouring forth insult and injury, and even, by innuendo, race hatred, Lewis 'slammed the door on peace with the AFL and challenged the Amalgamated and other pro-Hillman unions to clear out of the CIO.' As he finished, a great roar of applause came from the crowd, which burst into a renewed 'draft parade' around the hall. The whole convention seemed on the verge of riot and bloodshed. The Amalgamated delegates sat 'grave, immobile, furious.' "

Hillman's aides persuaded him to leave Washington and rush to the rescue. To quote Josephson further: "Lewis had roared like a hungry lion. Hillman had moved in quietly and unobtrusively; he had, so to speak, walked into the arena to deal

with the lion before a crowd that was literally crying for blood."
Hillman dispatched the lion with one neat thrust—almost an
impromptu inspiration. After politely regretting that Lewis had
decided to retire, Hillman said it was his "considered judgment
that when John L. Lewis steps down there must be a demand
for Phil Murray." When Hillman ended there were cries of "We
want Murray," and an ovation for Murray followed. The Draft-
Lewis plot was foiled.

From where I sat, or rushed around, I saw little to correspond with this account attributed to sources in books, ACW,
and CIO records, and press stories—one a *New York Times* article printed six years afterwards.

The only evidence I saw of a Draft-Lewis "plot" was on
buttons worn by some enthusiastic pro-Lewis delegates. Among
the favors prepared for the first day's Lewis ovation were buttons
inscribed "For Lewis and CIO," "CIO for Lewis," "We Want
Lewis," and "Draft Lewis."

Some big CIO unions—including the Amalgamated and notably UAW—prepared for their ovations with trumpets, rattles,
special caps, flags, buttons, as at Democratic and Republican
party conventions. Their delegates paraded through the aisles on
the least provocation. National CIO was at first remiss. At its
1937 conference, Heywood Broun made us all feel self-conscious
when he lumbered to his feet and was followed by some limber
youth in a ragged procession down the aisle. At Pittsburgh in
1938, the ovations were little organized. San Francisco added
some western spirit in 1939. In 1940 there was clearly more
preparation than usual for the customary Lewis ovation.

It was hardly surprising. A leader like Lewis was not to
be let go without some effort to hold him. It was a love-
Lewis/hate-Lewis convention, and the Lewis-lovers didn't dissemble their love. I knew Lewis had made up his mind, and I
shared no innocent illusions that this convention could be stampeded into changing it. The least his devotees could do was try
to draft him—a testimonial which Lewis no doubt appreciated.

Lewis registered his decision at the time of his Willkie endorsement. Had he wished to continue as CIO president, he
need have made no vow to retire and could have been reelected
at Atlantic City with little question. But having made his deci-

sion, Lewis was not one to turn a meek departing back to his foes. He went out fighting, as he came in.

In his opening speech, Lewis was not provocative. He proclaimed his pride in CIO and defied its enemies and slanderers. He championed the 52 million "shrunken bellies," and the black people and poor whites disfranchised by the poll tax. Lewis took his leave in personal and sentimental terms. He deplored the disunity that had arisen and hoped the movement would show a more loyal unity behind its next president.

The next president had to be Philip Murray—the only man acceptable to all factions who could hold CIO together. It was well known that Murray was resisting Lewis's insistence that he take the job. He was reluctant to be put on top of a quarrel-torn movement while still subordinate in UMW to Lewis. "Jack [Lewis] is trying to set me on top of a dunghill," he once said. But Murray was clearly bargaining, and few believed he would resist Lewis to the point of refusing the job.

A long, noisy, snake-dancing ovation followed Lewis's opening speech. It was remarkable for the emotion of Lewis's loyal and largely leftwing supporters; for the contrasting reserve of more centrist delegates; and for the fact that, for the first time in CIO history, a bloc of delegates sat out an ovation for one of CIO's top leaders. By remaining seated, the Hillmanites gave conspicuous notice they were spoiling for a fight.

Lewis observed the unprecedented discourtesy but did not retaliate. The next morning his critics struck a second blow. Intended for him, the blow was directed at me, for printing Lewis's Willkie speech in *The CIO News*. Lewis replied defiantly but defensively; he did not counterattack.

When the Hillmanites struck their third blow, Lewis was ready to let them have what they were asking for. He'd been waiting for an issue on which he was on strong ground in CIO. ACW's Frank Rosenblum supplied it by reading an Amalgamated resolution demanding immediate resumption of negotiations with the AFL.

From the start Lewis had been badgered on unity with the AFL. His CIO associates had been reluctant to break with the

AFL. They had taken seriously the early unity negotiations, which Lewis saw chiefly as an obstacle to CIO's organizing drive. Of the eight founding fathers, David Dubinsky of the ILGW and Max Zaritsky of Hat-Cap withdrew from CIO when the split became permanent, and returned to the AFL. (Charles P. Howard's Typographical union did not defect; it was never in CIO as a union. Howard served as CIO Secretary as an individual until he died.) Hillman, despite some qualms, backed Lewis's position until 1939.

Initially Roosevelt had welcomed the break between a pro-New Deal left and the old-guard right of the AFL. It brought millions of newly organized workers behind his banners. When it led in 1938 to a permanent Congress of Industrial Organizations, Roosevelt merely expressed a pious hope that "every possible door to access to peace . . . be left open." In 1939, however, Lewis was becoming increasingly hostile and a number of CIO unions were left-led. Roosevelt feared that, instead of furnishing his labor muscle as in 1936, CIO might become an obstacle to his third-term and war policies. With Hillman's aid, he revived the labor-unity issue and tied it to national defense. In any "compromise" then conceivable, CIO's lesser left unions were bound to be sacrificed, and Lewis would carry less influence in the merged outfit than in a separate CIO.

Lewis's brusque style in dealing with CIO-AFL unity sometimes seemed unreasonable. His position was not. Negotiations had always been on the AFL's chosen grounds of determining which CIO unions it would admit as they were, and how the rest might merge or adjust jurisdictions with competing AFL unions. From this process new CIO unions had little to gain and much to lose. The only practical solution was to bring all unions under the umbrella of a united federation, and let them adjust differences thereafter within that body. This Lewis repeatedly proposed. It was the way in which AFL and CIO finally came together in 1955.

Each time Lewis made this proposal, the labor "peacemongers" dismissed it as the arrogant gesture of a man who didn't want unity. They pointed out that the AFL would not agree to such an approach and that Lewis knew it. Lewis stuck to his position. He offered unity on the basis of all CIO unions entering AFL or some new overall Congress of Labor, but resisted carve-up negotiations. Most of CIO was behind him on this.

Only big unions like the Mine Workers and Amalgamated, whose jurisdictions had been respected before in AFL, could feel as secure there as in CIO. All the new CIO unions—including giants like Auto and Steel—had reason to fear AFL encroachments. They were doing OK in CIO. They didn't want to negotiate on how much or how little they should be carved up.

By now Lewis had been subjected to so much heat on the unity issue that he was ready to boil over. His speech on the subject is the one Josephson so colorfully describes in the passage quoted. I noted no change in his complexion. It was always a rather ashy gray, which meets one dictionary definition of "livid." This is about the only point at which the quote approaches accuracy—except that the Amalgamated delegates were doubtless "furious," if not exactly "grave" and "immobile."

Lewis did excite the convention, though hardly to "the verge of riot and bloodshed." He did better that way five years before in the same hall. Then, with one blow, he made paunchy AFLers belly-bounce around for a few riotous minutes, and blood actually flowed from the nose of Big Bill Hutcheson.

"I am going to spare you a speech," Lewis began. "I merely want to make a few remarks on this subject." His speech turned out to be one of the longer, more famous, and most-quoted of Lewis's many long, famous, and oft-quoted speeches. Tracing the CIO-AFL split, Lewis deplored the defection of Dubinsky and Zaritsky, and added: "And now above all the clamor comes the piercing wail and the laments of the Amalgamated Clothing Workers. And they say, 'Peace, it is wonderful.' And there is no peace."

Some Lewis foes tried to find anti-Semitic innuendo in the fact that he coupled the names of CIO's two founder-defectors, Dubinsky and Zaritsky: "Dubinsky took the easy way. Zaritsky took the easy way. If there is anyone else in the CIO who wants to take the easy way, let them go on." This was not a very gracious invitation to the Amalgamated to get out if it didn't like CIO—in the heat of the dispute, a relatively mild taunt. To attribute anti-Semitic innuendo was far fetched.

In 30 years of working with leaders of AFL, railroad, and CIO, unions, I found Lewis one of the very few—outside of radicals and Jews—from whom I never heard an anti-Semitic remark. He was too intelligent to reflect the commoner prejudices, and he understood the sensitivities of Jewish unionists—many of whom were on his side, as well as in Hillman's camp.

Saul Alinsky, Lewis's biographer, relates that in the lobby after his speech Lewis overheard two miners making anti-Jewish remarks, and goes on: "He [Lewis] walked up to the two miners and in a voice seething with anger said, 'If I ever hear another word like that coming from either of you, I will personally see to it that you are expelled from the United Mine Workers of America.' He then wheeled and walked out of the hotel."

Lewis did not build up to any inciting climax. He made his more heated remarks in the middle of his speech, and then went on to speak of the baiting mood in which the press was covering the convention—a factor which historians who rely on press clippings might take more into account. He called a New York *World-Telegram* story "the most outstanding piece of distorted news that I ever read in my life."

After describing AFL attacks on CIO's auto and steel unions, and AFL collusion with employers on anti-CIO Wagner act amendments, Lewis insisted he had responded constructively to Roosevelt's labor-unity plea. He ended on the quiet, confident note that by building its own strength, CIO would "hasten the day, that happy day, when American labor can once more be unified."

The demonstration that followed was for Lewis, as man and as leader. His bluntness about his baiters made it the more spirited. I saw nothing riotous. In that respect, it contrasted with the earlier New York state CIO convention in Rochester, where the Amalgamated crowd held the platform; gestured their followers to rise or sit, applaud or boo; and whipped up mob hysteria against left or pro-Lewis delegates. To get into the hall, the latter had to run a gauntlet through lines of police and jeering catcalling rightwingers. Some 99 were barred, and 244 others finally walked out, leaving 300 Amalgamated, Textile, Retail, delegates in control . . . of themselves.

At Atlantic City, the "draft" theme was even less in evidence in this second ovation for Lewis than on the opening day. Right after the ovation, the pro-Lewis Committee on Officers' Reports concluded its report with an obituary on Lewis's presidency—paying tribute to his past services and for the future hoping only that "he will continue to work with us——"

Hillman's speech the next day was even longer than Lewis's —to that extent he was ahead. He denied the Amalgamated would bolt CIO, and then dwelt in detail on the problems of the National Defense Advisory Commission. It was exciting to see the nervous Hillman and the equally self-conscious Lewis confront each other. But it was a strain to concentrate on Hillman's words so as not to miss any expected snapbacks to Lewis. Only at the end did he cut the cackle on business and get down to controversy.

Hillman avoided assault on the royal person of Lewis, but soundly cuffed the whipping-boy. The communists, said he, are "elements who cannot participate in the democratic processes because they don't think; they take orders." He linked them by inference with Nazis and fascists. To eliminate the left from CIO's "democratic processes," the Amalgamated had proposed to amend the CIO constitution to bar communists, Nazis, and fascists from holding office. But Hillman chose rather to praise "a sound provision" in the constitution of Lewis's union "excluding communists from membership." "What is good enough for the United Mine Workers," said he, "is good enough for the CIO."

Into his anticommunist oratory, Hillman injected an anecdote purporting to show that communists don't mean what they say; and he said he could respect only people who did. Subsequent study and reflection might educe from this an indirect dig at the possibility Lewis might not have meant what he said about retiring. If so intended, the point was too subtle to regis-

ter with any I met. None had the faintest notion Lewis was
doing anything else but retiring. In fact, as one impatient anti-
Lewisite remarked, Lewis had been "doing it all week."

When Hillman named Murray two days ahead of schedule,
it seemed like the slip of a nominating speaker who lets out his
man's name before the end of his speech. Murray's known reluc-
tance had restrained others from referring to him as the next
president. When Hillman publicly named him, most took this to
mean that Murray, prodded by Hillman as well as Lewis, had
finally agreed to accept. Hence the demonstration.

After the Lewis-Hillman confrontation, the rest of the convention was relatively routine—except for one item.

The Amalgamated wasn't the only union pressing for an anticommunist stand. Lewis's 1939 antired homily in executive session had only momentarily diverted the pressure. Since then,
rightwing factions had been pushing ever harder everywhere,
splitting some unions and councils in half. So far, national CIO
(read Lewis) had stood above the melee.

At the 1940 convention, Lewis resisted rightwing pressure
until Murray tipped the scales of decision with his insistence. It
was important for Lewis's hopes of continuing influence that
Murray take the CIO presidency. He also knew what powerful
forces Murray represented in this.

Three or four Catholic priests formed a spiritual bodyguard
around Murray in his comings and goings at this convention.
Whether or not they gave him temporal as well as spiritual counsel, there was no doubt Murray was devout and his church most
influential in CIO—through its many faithful among officers
and members even more than through its ACTU factions.

Murray also represented the solid center of CIO's now
farflung bureaucracy. These were substantial citizens, Protestant
and Jewish as well as Catholic, who wanted no truck with reds
or other disreputables. Essentially conformist, they courted respectability by conforming to the standards of business-
dominated communities, employers, government. Until this
year, they had also conformed to the power and authority of
Lewis

Lewis looked for a formula that would satisfy this center (the Hillmanites could like it or lump it, the way he felt), without upsetting his allies on the left or splitting things wide open. He wanted to pass the miracle without violating CIO's longstanding convention principle of public unanimity.

There were practical reasons for CIO's incredible unanimity pose, aside from the Big Three's belief it was only right and proper CIO should appear as monolithic as were their respective unions under each of them. In CIO's early drives, it was often advisable to keep employers guessing about exact membership figures, such as rollcall votes were supposed to be based on. Even after CIO formally listed convention voting strength of its unions, some figures were more inspirational than exact, and rollcall votes were still avoided. Decisions by nose count of delegates weren't much favored either, since a bunch of peanut unions might thus conceivably outvote the big unions. Floor division was avoided by agreeing in advance, or in committee, on policies assured of adoption. Conventions acted by near-unanimous voice vote, with standing votes only to demonstrate foregone conclusions and no more than a handful standing opposed.

How then was Lewis to find a formula for convention unanimity on anticommunism, with reds and antireds diametrically opposed to each other? He found it in the weakness and/or opportunism of the left.

A curious conglomeration of words was concocted. To odorize the whole with Lewisonian incense, it included a quote from Lewis's opening speech. Of those who attributed CIO policies to "communist Philosophy, or Nazi philosophy, or fascist philosophy, or any other philosophy," he had said that "they lie in their beard, and they lie in their bowels."

Coming from Lewis, who conceived most CIO policies himself, these words were both apt and true—particularly "or any other philosophy." But the beard-bowels part—the most appreciated part when Lewis spoke—was now omitted. This made "they lie" sound weakly anticlimactic as Lewis's great rolling wave of a sentence was cut off in its crash.

The resolution then went on: "We neither accept or desire —and we firmly reject consideration of any policies emanating from totalitarianism, dictatorships, and foreign ideologies such as Nazism, communism, and fascism. They have no place in this great modern labor movement. The Congress of Industrial Organizations condemns the dictatorships and totalitarianism of Nazism, communism, and fascism as inimical to the welfare of labor, and destructive of our form of government."

To link communism with its capitalist extreme opposite under the jumble-word "totalitarianism" was just what the Hillman-Murray crowd and all rightists wanted. But how could the radical leaders of CIO's leftwing unions—some communists themselves and all aided by communists in building their unions —vote for this mishmash? The fact is that they did.

Tom Kennedy, resolutions committee chairman, moved at once to close a debate which, under a prearranged deal, did not even begin. The convention then passed the resolution by a standing vote with Murray, in the chair, announcing it was "adopted by what the chair believes to be the unanimous approval of this convention."

When Lee Pressman, as committee secretary, moved adoption of the resolution, I was at the side of the stage, ashamed to be seen at such a degrading moment. Though not seen, I could see. My glance fell on Pressman's profile. He stood sternly erect, like a Prussian guard both obeying and conveying command. Some saw arrogance in that profile. I saw something else.

I saw the face of a troubled man—troubled as I was sometimes to see it during the Henry Wallace campaign, after both of us were out of CIO. The man had a master and a mistress, who hadn't quarreled before . . . the master, a cause; the mistress, that bitchy dame Success. Success now had the whip hand. Lee didn't cringe. He "took his beating like a man," his bearing seemed to say—a beating to his intelligence and his cause-loyalty. "See, I don't shrink," said his expression. "This I must do. I do it!"

In that spirit perhaps, Pressman decided in 1950 to renounce his communist past. Success was sneering at him for a cause-doped sucker. Lee wouldn't slink away like other beaten radicals. He'd stand up to his beating. He'd go bare his breast—and as few others as possible—before the Un-American Activities committee. He'd join its Inquisitor Richard M. Nixon in sole service to Success.

In 1940, however, Pressman was but implementing a group decision, not personally recanting. It was a "smart" move to save the necks of the left.

Through solid union achievement, the reds had won influence in CIO that seemed imposing. Now they were slapped and didn't fight. "We just want to get along with you guys," they said—and the guys drew the worst conclusions. A union politician didn't mind swallowing a little verbal crow for a purpose, but the reds had principles. Old-line leaders cynically expected them to get into line with all other porkchoppers when the chow bell rang. Aside from some lurking regard for the principled exception or the gutsy fighter, they respected only the strength the left could command. In submitting like this, the lefts seemed to lack strength, principle, or guts. Uncharitably, the right assumed they lacked all three.

Many labor writers have embalmed the myth that the communists were a "disruptive element" in CIO. Actually the left leaned over backward for the sake of CIO unity—sometimes, as here, to the point of facing upside-downwise in the opposite direction. With some notable exceptions like the unsinkable Harry Bridges, left union leaders tended to be diplomatic and yielding to the point of softness with CIO's high command.

In the anticommunist year of 1940—almost as isolated and exposed as in the later Cold War years—CIO's lefts had much to lose from an open right-left fight in national CIO. In this instance, they acted as practical union politicians to preserve their influence in CIO and to protect the interests of their unions, as they saw them.

In the outcome, the rights hailed the resolution with much cockawhoop. They used this new "CIO policy" to justify further proscriptions and purges against the left. They took aggressive factional advantage.

On the other hand, the left avoided an ugly showdown at a

dangerous moment. Its submission helped preserve formal CIO unity for many progressive purposes. Its unions were to maintain respectable status for years to come—not, however, through such verbal accommodations, but thanks to the 1941 turn in the war.

On the evening after Murray was installed in Lewis's place, I took a long walk on Atlantic City's cold, dark, deserted beach and came to a decision.

The CIO that had become like an enveloping part of myself had changed. Its momentum had run down. The limits of its drive were clearly in sight. Its crusaders were becoming piecards, or being replaced by them. Treasury-full unions were interlocking with the personnel departments of monopolies that once fought them but now sought to use them. Snarling factionalists were out to purge any reds or rebels who might obstruct accommodations.

Philip Murray, the respectable conformist, had replaced John L. Lewis, the fighting "wild man." That, for me, pinpointed and personalized the change. Lewis might not feel as I did about CIO becoming a bureaucracy of achieved complacency. But he was independent, restless, demanding, in a way more suited to my notion that labor should not forever submit to its servitor status under capitalism.

Lewis had seen earlier than I—if not in the same terms—that CIO was becoming other than it started out to be. One last struggle he had made for CIO independence, politically. Misdirected, mistimed? Maybe . . . but it showed spirit, like the wild lunge of a great bull balking at the corral. The lunge had but marked Lewis as an outlaw. The herd had preferred secure subordination in the government's corral.

A new CIO would carry on under the old name. In Murray it had the kind of leader it wanted. In the mumbo jumbo of the anti-"totalitarianism" resolution it had signed its yellow-dog contract with capitalism. For this new CIO I could work, but after the old CIO, and Lewis . . .

From the beach I went straight to Murray—avoiding Caroline or any other who might try to change my mind—and tendered my resignation.

In his hotel room, Murray sat erect in a stiff-armed chair. He was not relaxed. A floorlamp cast shadows on his face. They didn't hide but rather emphasized his tension.

A year before, at Lewis's suggestion, I had gone to Murray to complain of intra-CIO redbaiting; windowlight from behind had shaded his face, and he was cautious, controlled, and tense. Then Murray was looking, not at me, but at an emissary from Lewis. Now, I guessed, he saw only Lewis, thought only of him. Seven years later, I was to sit across Murray's CIO desk, to hear him ask for the resignation I freely offered now. Lewis by then haunted him but dimly. New conflicts had arisen in this self-tormenting man. They found similar expression in his manner.

Now, in Atlantic City, Murray motioned me to a chair, and I announced my mission at once. Then I tried to level with him, speaking without restraint about my feelings toward Lewis and CIO. Murray listened coldly and wordlessly. I knew I was giving offense.

It wasn't like this the last time I'd talked to Murray about Lewis. During the 1940 Democratic convention in Chicago, I happened to be alone with Murray in a Morrison Hotel room. Some little emotional urge had made me say a good word about Lewis. Murray picked it up at once and tried to go me one better. "We all *love* John," said he.

Now, if he hadn't been controlling himself, Murray would have liked to snap back sharply, I'm sure. Once he almost did. Referring to the curious fascination Lewis sometimes exercised, my mind slipped to the misty mountaintops and grim valleys of Wales, and I used the expression "Welsh wizardry."

"I'm no mystic," Murray shot back.

It was a snub. It was also self-defense, perhaps unguarded. As I spoke, Murray must have been comparing his impact on people with the Lewis impact. Of the two, the introverted, religious Murray was more the mystic.

Murray heard me to the end without further interruption. Then he said that he did not wish to accept my resignation. He asked me to carry on with him in the same way as I had done with Lewis. As my emotions cooled, I was not too hard to persuade.

That night was when I really took my leave of Lewis and the CIO that was. Under Murray's administration, I looked in on Lewis at first from time to time. As friction increased between the two, it became embarrassing, and I discontinued my visits, lest they be misunderstood. One of our last encounters was in the Washington Union Station. Seeing Lewis, I plowed through the crowd, to show my personal feelings hadn't changed. "Aren't you afraid to be seen talking with me?" said Lewis bitterly.

After Hitler invaded the Soviet Union, I found myself, for the first time since CIO began, on the opposite side from Lewis.

The whole character of the war was changed for me. No longer could I compare it to the First World War, whose jingo imperialism made me a radical. When I was demobilized from the British army, I had resolved: No more war for me—on any pretext. Yet when Britain's rulers threatened the Russian revolution, I came to think of one war as worth fighting—a war to defend the workers' right to socialism against capitalist attack. I was responding to the wave of working-class sentiment that led in 1920 to union Councils of Action to defend the first socialist country against imperialist aggression. When the Nazis invaded the USSR in 1941, they made the war of international class concern to millions worldwide like myself.

I couldn't fathom Lewis's mind on international affairs. I didn't expect it to react like mine. I waited curiously to see how he might assess the far-reaching implications, in the United States as well as worldwide, of the great change in the war. It came as a cold shock when Lewis joined with Herbert Hoover, Alfred Landon, and tories of that ilk, in a statement that Soviet involvement should make the war even less our concern.

Lewis had taken many contradictory stands in his life—some outrageous to me, in pre-CIO days. I hoped circumstances might move him from this one. I couldn't turn on him as some CIO lefts at once did. Shrillest and most abusive were opportunists eager to get off the antiwar hotspot, and notably those who became redbaiting turncoats during the Cold War.

But events were moving fast. History was sweeping all CIO, including myself, onto one side and Lewis onto the other. Caroline soon resigned as research director of Labor's Non-Partisan

League, by now a Lewis instrumentality, on grounds it was embarrassing to work for Lewis while her husband worked for Murray in CIO. Lewis responded with gracious understanding.

Hillman once said he hated to be in disagreement with Lewis because he was "scared of his effectiveness." To me, however, it seemed that Lewis, mighty as the workers' champion, lost effectiveness in proportion as he led in a wrong direction. On the wrong side he became a Samson shorn of his hair.

After Lewis died, his years before and after CIO made many see him as just another of capitalism's labor lieutenants who after 1950 dropped his famous union militancy for banking collusion with the coal operators. The later Lewis himself glossed over the leftism of his five CIO years, 1935–40. But the Lewis of those years was the only one I knew. Defending his CIO leadership against its many defamers on the right has doubtless led me to softpedal his shortcomings.

Lewis *might* have led CIO toward real workingclass independence, I felt. But he did not. Indeed he had no clear idea of such a goal. At times responding instinctively to class feeling, he was not theoretically class conscious, not a radical or a Marxist. He was a *practical* business unionist, he believed, within the limits of the existing system. Power politics was the game he tried to play. If this drew him leftward in the CIO uprising, it also drove him back to the right when he saw CIO as Roosevelt's hopeless captive. The Willkie ploy was Lewis's device for bowing out. He might have preferred an exit to the left. Earlier in 1940, Lewis was working for a labor-led coalition outside the two old parties. He dropped the idea when it drew no support from the FDR-infatuated; it was not "practical politics"—though it might have been more practical had he espoused it in the early heyday of CIO.

Though Lewis fell short as the farsighted stick-to-it leader the first CIO deserved, I find it hard to dismiss him on a critical note. Having also seen glints of grandeur in the man, I close the shutter on the CIO Lewis I knew in a personal and sentimental mood.

I am not equipped to write about that Lewis who, as Mine

Workers' leader, defied the President and the armed forces at his command, Wall Street and the public opinion at its command, and all comers, by leading wartime strikes in an all-out fight for the miners. All I knew by then was what I read in the papers. Yet I discerned from afar the outlines of that same Lewis who once led CIO.

In 1946 I was in Mexico as a CIO representative at President Aleman's inauguration. In my halting Spanish I tried to explain CIO to my driver. I made little progress until I mentioned the name of Lewis.

"Ahi!" His eyes lit up. "Yonel Lewis! Un hombre mucho rebelde!"

Mexico had its Pancho Villa. Every country could boast its rebels. They were called bandits, traitors, communists . . . The Lewis who led the CIO uprising, who later bulked immovable before all the powers of the United States, was recognizable anywhere in this tradition. Right or wrong? He did it for his people, for the poor against the rich—so think the poor and the oppressed—they wink to themselves, and feel better.

The best pictures of Lewis showed him alone, unaware of the camera.

A broad, black-coated back. A black fedora atop a large head, made larger by back-bulging hair. A big and solid figure of a man walking slowly, black cane in hand. He looks neither to right nor to left; his gaze is cast down. The dark bulk of the man is sharply outlined against the pastel of a deserted Washington street. His aloneness is stark.

An inside shot. Lewis sitting alone, in a hotel lounge armchair. No sharp silhouette this time. A lighted window behind him makes his profile hazy. Untypically he is wearing his glasses; he is reading a newspaper. The big black fedora is on his big head, and his hair bulges back. Lewis is doubtless reading abuse of himself—the papers at the time printed little else. He is composed, thoughtful, and quite alone.

I saw and felt how alone Lewis was, most of all in 1940, when others fled from him—in ways he recognized, if not formally. In his period of wartime defiances Lewis must have felt all the more alone.

The man who identifies with the many must feel a special

aloneness. Lewis was great when he realized identity with the millions of workers he led to CIO. They filled him out. They made him big. They made him live life to the full. In his pride he said, "I am them, and they are me." Millions for the moment gloried, as did he, in the identification. The workaday world went back to its workaday ways. The millions awoke in the gray dawn of another workaday morn. They yawned and said, "John L. Lewis—yep, quite a guy! But what's it to us today?"

Then Lewis knew what he had known—that he was not they, and they were not he. He felt the air ooze out of his bigness. He was losing his identity. He was no longer John L. Lewis/CIO. He was just another labor leader trying to assert authority over followers who no longer followed him.

Lewis had fought with zest to impose himself on the United Mine Workers. He had beaten his union enemies. He had made the union into his machine. Quite a feat, with rebels like the miners—even if the union was near to wrecked. Lewis took pride in being John L. Lewis/UMW. This didn't make him very big until 1933. Then it made him big enough to become bigger. He became biggest of all as John L. Lewis/CIO. On this movement he didn't have to impose himself; he and its millions came together in the upsurge.

It couldn't last. Lewis fought vainly to preserve the image of John L. Lewis/CIO. This fight he couldn't win as he'd won the fight to impose his image on UMW. The CIO identification was too spontaneous, too diffused. John L. Lewis/CIO became divided into two—CIO on one side, John L. Lewis on the other. Vainly he tried to generate another CIO through District 50. Then he settled for being John L. Lewis/UMW. This identity no Hillman or Murray could take from him—and Roosevelt had better not try!

Lewis wanted a labor movement independent of government. For this he fought a rearguard action in CIO—when government and big business together were assimilating the new unions. In 1919, Lewis had told the miners, "We cannot fight our government." He wanted to live down the slur that this had been a craven attitude. He came to conclude that in the First World War labor had been too submissive; that in the next war it should seize all chances to better the workers' lot.

CIO had slithered out from under Lewis when he wanted it to play an independent role. The UMW was a less slippery base. The miners and Lewis were as one man when he led them in a fight. In their lonely mine patches, in the separation of their way of work and living, the miners didn't find it strange to be alone against the world. Lewis could choose to be alone.

John L. Lewis and the miners alone together—John L. Lewis/UMW—that for him may have been a closer identification of man with many than was John L. Lewis/CIO.

After 1941 I had no further contact with Lewis until 1952. I was then editing a leftwing union magazine, *March of Labor*, in Chicago. I went to Cincinnati to revive some old associations at the UMW convention. This was the occasion when I felt Lewis was trying to retell his labor life story without the best (CIO) parts. I was also annoyed at his brag of consistently opposing the Soviet-including World Federation of Trade Unions—presumably to redbait Murray(!), one of its founders.

To do him justice, Lewis didn't join, as did Murray, in the antired hysterics of the Cold War—disgruntled though he was with the CIO lefts for turning against him in 1941. He was trying to affirm, so far as I could gather, the consistency of his "Americanism." This was not seriously to be questioned, except in terms of the factitious counterposition of Americanism to communism. In those terms, Lewis had his "soft-on" periods, as did Hillman, Murray, Roosevelt, and many others when they fought side by side with communists in great common causes.

It was a poor time to revive any link with Lewis. I got the pitch around the hotel lobbies. It was not forgotten that I was with Murray, not Lewis, when they split. That I was no longer with Murray, but thrown out as a red, was a minor mitigating circumstance. Denny Lewis, Ray Thomason, and some other Lewis-foreverites were friendly. They remembered when I was on Lewis's side against Hillman. After Murray took over CIO, Denny once offered aid when rightwing anti-Lewisites were gunning for me. Maybe I looked like a prodigal son sniffing around for fatted calf, or one who might herd some labor stray lambs into District 50. More likely, they were just naturally friendly guys—when not in a fight.

For myself, I wanted nothing from Lewis and hesitated to approach him lest he misread my motives. In our encounter, he was neither hostile nor friendly. His manner was guarded and cool. He knew of my *March of Labor* connection, and that evidently caused his reserve. I interpreted his attitude as political and uninviting.

Not for seven more years did I again think of contacting Lewis. When Caroline died in 1959, my emotions turned to a past in which Lewis loomed big for both of us; and when Lewis retired from active labor leadership, I felt I could write without suspicion of ulterior motive. My letter was personal but also tried to assess his role, as against those of Eugene Debs and Franklin Roosevelt. Lewis's reply was personal and friendly. It ended with the great Lewis signature—2½ inches from top to bottom of the "J," and more than three inches across.

I recalled the end-of-day ritual in Lewis's office. On his desk the mail he had dictated. Space cleared all around it. Ora Gasaway standing beside him with blotter in hand, to absorb the copious ink before it spread. Then Lewis pulling up his sleeve and spreading his arm over the desk as, with circular motions, he executed that extraordinary self-portrait at the end of each letter.

The egotism and strength of the far-reaching lower loop of the "J," and of other loops and flourishes. The thick powerful downstrokes. The obviousness, the emphasis, the showing-off. Along with this, the intricate involutions—the backlooping, overlaying, and crossing of lines, until one despaired of tracing a way through the maze. That was Lewis—obvious to the point of crudity, but also subtle, complex, and hard to figure out.

One word stood out for me. Lewis said it was "generous" for me to write as I did. "Generous" was one of the words I most associated with the Lewis I knew.

It was not for Lewis to say, in his leavetaking at the 1940 CIO convention, that he was "something of a man." From him a brag, from anyone else it would have been plain statement of fact. Braggadocio was part of the public Lewis. So it was of other thick-thewed Paul Bunyans of early labor days with less to brag about. Compared with them, Lewis was refined and restrained—though he too could let himself go when the big winds blew.

Lewis had attributes the male claims as peculiarly masculine —aggressiveness, courage, fighting form—with an oversize physique to make them operative. He was well endowed with intelligence, cunning, strength of purpose. His skin was toughly resistant to the slings and arrows of outrageous fortune. If any Macduff laid on, it was not Lewis who first cried, "Hold, enough!" A formidable adversary and a mighty champion—with presence to betoken his prowess, and a powerful and eloquent voice to proclaim it.

There is another measure of a man. The man who lives for himself alone isn't much of a man. The man who lives for family and friends is more of a man. The man who lives for very many people—who at times may make their strivings his own—we call a great man.

Yet another side to being a man. The superman is a phony. The all-conquering, the all-wise, the ever-great leader is a figment of flight from reality. We recognize no one as a real man until we know his flaws and falls from grace. These make him human, we say.

By most standards, Lewis measured up as a man, standing tall among union leaders of his time. If you measured from the base of his faults and failings to his highest points, he could seem extra big.

Labor politics doubtless differs little from other kinds, insofar as the formula for survival and advancement is to do the obvious thing. Spit on your finger to feel which way the wind blows; never spit against the wind. Lewis usually knew which way the wind blew. He took account of the tides. He knew which was the safe and easy course. Yet sometimes he chose to chart a course against the wind, and to follow it stubbornly, come shipwreck or glory.

Only a fool, or a red, or a man like Lewis, does things like that.

Chapter Fourteen

MURRAY'S DILEMMA

CIO's new president is all but torn asunder.

A month or so after Murray became CIO president, I was leaving the National Press Club when I ran into Ernest K. Lindley of *Newsweek*.

"Why, hello, Len," he said. "What are you doing these days?"

"Still on the same old job with CIO."

"Really!" Lindley arched an eyebrow. "I thought you and Lee were out."

Whether subtle or uninformed, Lindley echoed the prediction of most Washington dopesters—that Murray's new broom would soon sweep CIO clean of Lewis's leftist remnants. They reckoned without two hosts, Lewis and Murray.

On the main floor of the Mine Workers Building, Lewis still occupied the commodious office of UMW president. On the floor above, Murray was assigned the less imposing office of UMW vice president. Neither spent much time at the ramshackle, crowded headquarters of CIO on Connecticut Avenue. Not till 1942 did Murray acquire a fittingly presidential office at CIO's new headquarters on Jackson Place, across from the White House. By then the UMW vice-presidential office was no longer his to use.

Visiting CIOers had long been wont to stop off at Lewis's UMW office to pay their respects. Lewis now referred them upstairs to Murray, so as not to interfere with Murray's CIO authority. Such scruples made it all the harder for the new CIO president to guess what was on The Boss's mind.

Murray was ostensibly free to devise his own CIO policy. But his own ideas ran counter to those of Lewis. He had to choose between "betraying" Lewis (a word both used for subsequent divergences) and being untrue to himself. To preserve a shaky equilibrium within CIO, Murray had to tolerate a symbolically rebuked but uncontrite leftwing, and to hold at bay a rampaging rightwing out to exterminate the left now "their man" was in office. Under mounting war pressures, Murray wanted to obey a government that demanded he check the workers' militancy—but to do so with minimum offense to an antiwar and anti-Roosevelt Lewis.

Keenly aware of the implications and repercussions of any step in any direction, Murray preferred, if possible, to take no steps.

I have agreed that Lewis was "something of a man." For Murray, I might quote Hamlet's reflection on his dead father: "He was a man, take him for all in all." It is a tribute such as Murray seemed to crave.

In accepting the CIO presidency, Murray noted that the press contrasted "this terrible man Lewis" with "this mild man Murray, this moderate, vacillating, weak individual." He concluded: ". . . I think I am a man. I think I have convictions. I think I have a soul and a heart and a mind. And I want to let you in on something there; with the exception, of course, of my soul, they all belong to me, every one of them."

Murray was a man of the right (to the right, that is, of a CIO that was itself to the left of center). He was of the right with more conviction and emotion than the less definable Lewis and the more opportunistic Hillman. Murray could make accommodations or alliances with the left in CIO, and even outside, in a brief and uneasy postwar flirtation with political progressives. These were tactical and superficial. More revealing was the way he could call radicalism "filthy," as if there were something unclean about challenging the authority, the order, the system, which God-in-His-Infinite-Wisdom had decreed for the conduct of human affairs.

Yet it was from the right, from his own camp, that the jeers came about Murray being weak or fearful, for postponing the break with Lewis, for not cracking down on the left. Actually

Murray showed much strength in his self-restraint, in restraining his own crowd, in sticking to his own policy despite charges of weakness that hurt but did not deflect him.

For all his lack of the Lewis charisma, Murray came to exercise in CIO an authority comparable to that of Lewis in his heyday.

To the CIO boys, Uncle Phil became a child's father image. Stern but kindly. Loath to use the strap, but capable of doing so. Older, more experienced, symbol of security, and definitely on top. To the left, after June, 1941, Murray was to become the father protector, instant replacement for Lewis as head of a progressive united front. To the non-Catholic, social-reformist right, Murray brought deep relief after a redoubtably antagonistic Lewis, and as next best to Hillman. With his own crowd, the Catholic right, Murray had possibly a little more than earthly authority.

In SWOC, power and preferment came from above. The Irish, Italian, and other mainly Catholic upcomers nosing out UMWers from outside steel looked to Murray as father-provider and mentor. Murray's crowd also extended far beyond his Steel machine. It included many other Catholic leaders of right, center, and—as time would show—some leftwing unions.

Catholic influence was always strong in American labor. British and Scandinavian immigrants might fill many skilled jobs, but immigrants from Catholic or largely Catholic countries made up most of the industrial working class. Of AFL members in 1900-1909, almost half were Catholics, according to estimates cited by historian Philip S. Foner. In CIO, the proportion of Catholic members was undoubtedly higher, and of Catholic leaders still higher again. Priests exerted much influence on their labor parishioners. There were also Catholic labor societies, including the early-century Militia of Christ and, in CIO times, the Association of Catholic Trade Unionists. In early AFL, this Catholic thrust was against socialism and Socialist party strength in the unions. Similarly, the ACTU devoted itself to combating communist influence, in CIO especially.

For his coreligionists leading in CIO unions, Murray had a

very special appeal. Some of the more devout might worry about their connection with such a rebellious and reputedly radical movement as CIO. They might tangle with local priests or draw frowns from Catholic hierarchs. They might become allies of CIO lefties opposed by ACTU. They could find reassurance in the near-saintly image of Brother Phil, opening his arms wide— after 1941 and for the war's duration anyhow—to all God's children, to his left as well as to his right.

In personality, Murray qualified for the father image he evoked and, judging from his biblical analogies, even recognized his quasi-spiritual aura. At the 1942 Boston convention, Murray said that Lewis, despite his 1940 pledge of support at Atlantic City, "denied me." Murray went on:

"You remember that ancient story where Peter, in the course of a conversation with Christ, said that he would never deny him, and Christ said that he would, he knew he would. And it is recorded in that incident that Peter not only denied Christ, but in his desperation to have the public know that Christ did not exist, he rushed to the home of a harlot and, standing in the midst of that den of iniquity, he denied the existence of Christ. And I told John Lewis in the wing of the stage in the Chelsea Hotel in Atlantic City that in all likelihood he would make me go through my Garden of Gethsemane."

In more down-to-earth moments, Murray was all a father should be. A handsome, kindly-looking man, he was also dignified. He exuded executive assurance, being skilled and experienced in handling people with understanding, diplomacy, and mostly integrity. When Murray presided over the CIO executive board, things were duller than under Lewis, but they were also under control and moved purposefully in a predetermined direction.

Once—it happened rarely—Murray turned over the chair to Secretary James B. Carey so he might step out for half an hour, and bade the board proceed with its routine business. Hardly had the door closed than suppressed ids started popping out. Board members bickered, traded personal insults, as uninhibited as children in their nastinesses. They disregarded Carey, except as part of the brawl. Then Murray returned. Teacher was back.

The boys took their seats, parked their gum, shut their mouths. Under his adult control, the meeting resumed its orderly course.

It was some time, however, before Murray could cash in on his many natural advantages as CIO leader. The first year of his presidency must have been the most miserable in his life. It almost killed him.

In Pittsburgh, Murray had his home and his cronies. From an office manned by his chosen henchmen, he presided over a union of his own devising and under his unchallenged control. This peace and security Murray left behind when he came to Washington on CIO presidential duties. In CIO, he inherited a staff of pro- and anti-Lewisites, of rights and lefts, with new rightwing intriguers now slipping in under Carey's auspices.

Throughout CIO, a right-left battle raged as ins and outs contended for the same union offices. Government pressures increased constantly for Murray to suppress labor struggle for the sake of "national defense." Of all the conflicting pulls and pushes that bedeviled him, hardest to bear no doubt were those building up to inevitable confrontation with Lewis.

Murray started by trying to absorb, rather than yield to, the conflicting pressures. He was everyone's man, it seemed, and nobody's man—not even his own. The rights claimed him. The lefts claimed him. Lewis claimed him. Hillman claimed him as Roosevelt's man.

Things had to go far for Murray to take action; and when he did, it was usually to take a firmer seat on the lid. Under it was what he regarded as an unholy mess. Murray wished neither to stir it up nor let it out.

1941 saw the last of CIO's major organizing successes and many prewar strikes. The victories over Ford and Bethlehem Steel—two biggest holdouts in CIO-organized industries—followed strikes marked by much worker initiative and militancy. But the times had changed, so that these events seemed more like delayed mop-ups than an extension of the 1936-37 sweep.

War preparations had made government and Wall Street partners in industrial control, and labor discipline was a prime government concern. In denying union bargaining rights, both Ford and Bethlehem had flouted the labor relations act, but the government still handed them juicy contracts. Due to labor outrage over this, the administration exerted some pressure on the companies, and the deals were concluded in Washington comings and goings amid much ballyhoo about National Defense.

Intervening now in all major labor disputes, the government differentiated between friends and enemies on the union side. Murray and the UAW leaders were being courted and taken into camp, so the Ford and Bethlehem strikes were almost condoned. But Lewis and the soft-coal miners were treated like "saboteurs of National Defense"—until they won a $1-a-day raise, forced the southern operators into line, and later extended the union shop to the steel companies' captive mines.

There were many other CIO strikes in this last prewar year, including a long Harvester strike, a 75-day lockout of Allis-Chalmers workers, and strikes of bus, electrical, auto, clothing, textile, store, aluminum, workers. Murray backed them with diminishing enthusiasm, as government pressure increased. When he finally turned against striking CIO lumber and aviation workers, it was in a Washington extravaganza of antired hysteria.

During the 1941 strikes of 20,000 CIO woodworkers in the northwest and 12,000 workers of the North American Aviation Corporation in Los Angeles, Murray was like a figure in a nightmare. At any rate, my memories are nightmarelike, of horror whose causes have become blurred and incredible. Murray seemed possessed by the demons he had been fighting off. His spongelike capacity for absorbing pressure was exhausted. Around him whirled a devilkins' dance of redbaiters acclaiming him their own. And what was it all about?

Lawyers and professional labor experts had taken over the chore of ending the class struggle. Assiduously they tended the government's antistrike machinery, spinning complicated arguments about the merits or demerits of labor disputes, about compliance or defiance of board decisions. Employers, workers, and government, could hardly have cared less about such niceties. Employers wanted to whip strikers back to work, with wages down and profits up. Workers rebelled against frozen wages while living costs and profits soared. The government wanted no strikes at all, expected labor leaders to prevent or break them, demanded exemplary punishment for rebellious unionists.

The administration had a rule of thumb much simpler than its experts' rationalizations. Murray and most top laborites were on its side, good boys at heart, so strikes they authorized were bad, but not really *too* bad. Lewis and the communists were antiwar; therefore strikes led by Lewis or leftwingers were punishable "sabotage of National Defense."

For punishment, Lewis would have been the perfect culprit. Alas, he and his miners were too tough to handle; moreover, Murray was still vice president of Lewis's UMW. The "commies" could be took—if you could just separate Murray from a left-led strike. To the clamor of big business, press, and CIO's right wing, the government added its inexorable demand that Murray disregard Lewis and "crack down on the communists." The lumber and aviation strikes were picked as most suitable for a showdown.

The CIO Woodworkers had decided not to return to work on terms dictated by the Mediation Board. It wasn't the first turndown of a government board by a striking union. But in this case the Woodworkers' leader, O. M. Orton, happened to be on the left side of a right-left struggle in his union; and Murray himself was with the board. Here was the long-sought chance to crack down on a "communist strike."

Part of the press hullabaloo over this was a gossip item that my CIO publicity department had aided Orton in getting out his turndown statement. Normally this would have been routine; we regularly helped visiting CIO union leaders. But in this case, Murray had sprung to the defense of the board, attacked the Woodworkers for rejecting its recommendations, accused Orton of "lying defamation," and demanded the union call off the strike. I thought I'd better check into things and speak to Murray.

Murray was in his UMW vice-presidential office—with Lewis, mum but never-to-be-forgotten, on the floor below. Murray was red-faced and so jittery in his movements I feared he might have a stroke. He said nothing as I told him I'd found no evidence in my department to support the gossip. So abstracted was he in his agitation I doubted he even absorbed what I said. After that, I resolved to keep in closer touch with what was going on around Murray in government quarters.

As I went in and out of government offices, or lingered in wait, I saw many "labor experts" I knew or knew of—graduates of CIO rightwing factions now on government payrolls. The remarks, the glances, the incidents, have long since faded; the nightmare mood remains: Redbaiting devilkins laughing and sneering. Darting up to stick out tongues, then retreating. This was IT, they chortled. Murray had surrendered. The commies were going to get IT. The devilkins' day had come. They were fanning fires to roast the CIO reds, might even get that great ox Lewis on the barbecue.

In and out of all this, now pale, now ruddy, stalked Murray, trying not to let loose his emotions in public, or to break down completely.

Having wet his feet in the bog of anticommunism and strikebreaking, Murray waded in deeper during the North American Aviation strike.

The UAW was organizing in the booming aircraft industry, and this strike followed a common pattern in union drives. It was directed against a company making high profits and paying as little as 50¢ an hour. The workers demanded a 10¢ wage increase and a minimum of 75¢ an hour. They had voted to strike, 5,834 to 210 by secret ballot, and had already postponed the strike once at the request of the National Defense Mediation Board.

Two days after the workers walked off the job, without union objection, they were amazed to hear UAW's Aviation Director Richard Frankensteen—who had been summoned to Washington and closeted with Murray—make a national radio broadcast denouncing the strike as "communist-inspired." The following day, Frankensteen addressed a strikers' meeting and ordered them to end the strike. He was loudly booed and overwhelmingly repudiated.

Thereupon President Roosevelt issued an executive order, with the approval of Associate OPM Director Sidney Hillman, instructing the army to take over the plant and open it. The strike was broken, at the point of the bayonets of 3,500 troops trained for "strike duty" at Camp Lewis.

Lewis was at the point of an open break. Murray, thrashing around in deep waters, nearly went over the falls of nervous collapse. He subsequently joined Lewis and the UAW in denouncing the use of troops to break strikes—thus sawing off the limb onto which Hillman had followed Roosevelt.

Washington in the first half of 1941 offered a foretaste of Cold War McCarthyism. Liberals and laborites might have taken warning of the fabrications and excesses of anticommunism, had not many of them been among its chief inciters.

To the standard outbursts of big business reaction and the Dies committee, liberal New Dealers, and rightwing CIOers now added their peculiarly emotional variations on the same theme. The liberals might be doing penance for past dalliance with the left. The porkchoppers fed their peeve on struggles for union control, hoping to feast on more sweets of office from a frenzied purge of the left. All fitted into the design of a "liberal" government deliberately using anticommunism to put the country on a war footing, to break strikes, and to discredit opposition.

Distorted accounts—then and since—of the period's labor events were one byproduct of this premature McCarthyism.

The labor upsurge in 1941 was not to be compared in character or extent with that of 1936-37, but there were some parallels. After the recession and unemployment starting in late 1937, United States war preparations and aid to allies were now creating new jobs and swelling profits. Increased job confidence, wages lagging behind mounting prices, knowledge that the bosses were raking it in, produced strikes and union advances that started with the coal, steel, and auto strikes and spread far beyond.

As in earlier CIO struggles, there was some communist influence over leftwing union leaders and activists. But in most labor disputes, the workers involved made the determinations, either directly through their strike votes or through union leaders who had to know their feelings if they were to continue to lead. Communist party influence was more general than specific. It was exerted on the side of union militancy in the rise of CIO and up to mid-1941. Thereafter, through the Second World War, it favored restraint, to increase war production without interruption.

The early 1941 strikes involved unions of all tendencies and were caused by obvious grievances and the chance to obtain redress. To single out allegedly leftist strikes as evidence of "red conspiracy" was a tactic that called for much exaggeration and misrepresentation.

The press was full of this kind of stuff, hashing and rehashing "exposures" of reds in CIO, giving columns of space to the most trivial gossip from its antired specialists. Its sources were not only the Dies committee, but also in the administration, in rightwing unions, and in CIO headquarters itself. When Murray turned against the Woodworkers and North American strikes, the press cockawhoop was strident and voluminous. Its "dope" now was that Murray had decisively broken with the left, and inferentially with Lewis, and was about to purge CIO in a massive redhunt.

In CIO headquarters there was a touch-and-go atmosphere. The rightist intriguers were elated, and trigger-happy with their redhunting popguns. All the rest of us were in a state of jitters— and notably Murray himself. He was avoiding reporters, and everyone else.

At last came a break. Lee Pressman asked me to draft a letter which Murray might send to all affiliates, repudiating the press stories about purges, splits, and redhunts in CIO. I went about the job with great relief, but without too much hope Murray would sign the letter. I made it as strong as possible, reaffirming traditional CIO policy against witch-hunting and appeals to intolerant prejudice to create factional dissension. Murray accepted the draft without change.

This Murray letter infuriated the rightwing pack, in government, press, and CIO. They held it a cowardly surrender to Lewis and the left, when Murray had just begun to fight. For Murray, however, it proved to be a wise and timely move. Shortly after, the Nazis invaded the USSR, and the United States government reversed the policies it had been trying to force on him.

When Hitler's legions crossed the Soviet borders on June 22, 1941, they caused many reversals of policy. Organized workers in many lands responded in sympathy and solidarity with the Soviets. Governments reversed their policies overnight. Winston Churchill and Franklin D. Roosevelt were as quick as the *Daily Worker* and CIO's left wing in reacting to the great change in the war. So was Sidney Hillman. Philip Murray wasn't far behind. No longer was anticommunism the smart way to involve the United States in the war. Churchill and Roosevelt hailed the Soviets as allies, who in fighting for themselves would help bring home the British and American bacon.

The anticommunist heat was turned off the chair on which Murray sat—a merciful reprieve from near electrocution. Now he could follow the government in treating unions as unions, without singling out some as "communist conspiracies." In the letdown after months of increasing strain, Murray had his delayed breakdown. He took off in hospital for a couple of months.

When Murray recovered, he still had ahead the inevitable break with Lewis, a prospect all the more painful while Lewis still had a foot in Murray's CIO, and Murray a foot in Lewis's UMW. Otherwise, by the fall of 1941, Murray had things made for his kind of labor statesmanship. He headed a CIO unified from right to left on the major issues of the war and Roosevelt; Lewis, the only discordant element was on the way out. Murray could now stand well with government, employers, and all CIO except Lewis. He rose to the occasion with unifying diplomacy and enhanced prestige.

For CIO's leftwing, the reprieve was as merciful as it was for Murray. Facing outright attack—with troops no less—and the purges and redhunts of all-out struggle within CIO, they had been saved by the turn in the war. Now from the protection of the once-mighty Lewis, CIO's lefts came under the protection of the less mighty Murray, and of the mightier forces of a whole nation girding for war. The Lewis-left alliance that built CIO was replaced by a Murray-left alliance that carried CIO all through the Second World War.

Not all CIOers, however, adjusted as quickly to the change in the war as did the heads of government and CIO. In some unions, the rightwing hated to give up the handy factional device of bracketing communists with Nazis and fascists, even after history had shown its absurdity.

As late as August 1941, while the Soviet Union was bearing the brunt of an antifascist war and communists everywhere had jumped to its forefront, the Reuther faction pushed through the UAW's Buffalo convention a sweeping ban on union officeholding by any member in any way "subservient" to "communist, Nazi, or fascist organizations."

In the fall, the CIO shipbuilding union similarly barred communists, Nazis, and fascists from election to union office. Redbaiting campaigns continued unchecked in the Newspaper Guild and the Woodworkers until rightwing officials were installed. In UE, CIO Secretary James B. Carey was still beating the dead horse of "communazism" when he was ousted as union president.

Chapter Fifteen

EPIGONI

Successors to CIO's Big Three.

"There were wonderful giants of old, you know . . ."
So began a school song whose concluding moral impressed my
boyish mind: "For all of we, whoever we be,/Come up to
the giants of old, you see." Applying the thought to labor's
big men, I had my doubts. William Green, Matthew Woll, and
other AFL top shots I knew, hardly came up to oldtime giants
like Gene Debs or Big Bill Haywood. Even little Sam Gompers
made them look small.

CIO revived some of my faith, with young labor leaders of
some daring, devotion, and intelligence, most of them to be cut
down before their prime. Moreover, CIO was started and
headed by men of recognizable stature like Lewis, Hillman, and
Murray. What of the succession to these three?

Walter P. Reuther was the only one to become CIO president, or to suggest comparison in other ways. But I must come
to him later. I'll start with James B. Carey, ward in national
CIO of all three presidents.

I felt a twinge of sympathy when Carey buttonholed me
right after his UE defeat in September 1941. The vote had just
been announced—635 for Albert J. Fitzgerald, 539 for Carey. It
was the first defeat for the first president of the United Electrical, Radio & Machine Workers. The delegates were streaming
out of the convention with something to gab about. As he
stepped from the platform, Carey looked lost—as if missing the
handshakes and backslaps that hail a winner. He drew me to one

side to blurt out some cover-up for his hurt, though he must have known I hated the policies that made it self-induced.

Ingenuous was the word for Jimmy Carey when young; he seemed boyishly to assume everyone liked him. The memory of this now caused my twinge.

For me, too, the world was young when I first knew him. He was one of the livelier Youngsters at the 1935 AFL convention in Atlantic City. At the start of CIO, he was a sunny Jim who set out to make friends and had few enemies. Into the design of CIO's founders, Carey fitted like the right jigsaw piece. Ah youth! . . . and on our side. Spunky and articulate—yet respectfully pliant to CIO's leaders; no communist, but politician enough to get on with the communists building CIO; projecting an Irish-Catholic image—what could be more American in union politics?

Without knowing the insides of UE, I thought of Carey, Julius Emspak, and James Matles as a youthful counterpart of CIO's Big Three Musketeers. From CIO's 1937 conference, I had a mental image of these three young fellows breezing down the boardwalk, arm in arm, joshing, full of the future.

Carey was innocent then, it was later said. If so, he wasn't a fool. He knew left from right. He knew a red when he heard one. Of his own choice, he was in the united front of CIO's 1936-37 uprising.

Our world grew older after 1938. The Dies committee blew the brassy trumpet of reaction. In CIO some softly echoed its call, to trade the Spirit of CIO for the Spirit of Anticommunism. Jim Carey grew older, and less innocent. He studied the knowledge of good and evil—for himself, politically.

By 1941, Carey had long looked at many UE builders through red rather than rose-colored glasses. Up to the UE convention—undeterred by the turn in the war—he sought to legitimize bans on "communists, Nazi, or fascists." Jimmy the "innocent" had become the calculating James B. who now excluded his old buddies from his calculations. In this instance, he miscalculated. In the dawn of a new CIO unity, his old-style, antired rant boomeranged. The convention decided to preserve the members' right to elect whom they chose. Fitzgerald, an Irish-

Catholic with much conservative support, saw his chance to win on the slogan that UE needed a full-time president.

Continuing as CIO Secretary, Carey had formally to subscribe to CIO war unity. But within UE he led a rightwing minority, which had few major successes until the Cold War enabled it to split the union and form a dual one.

During the war years, I had little to do with Carey. Murray ran the show. Few thought of Carey as second in command—if he was. There was but one command. ITU President Charles P. Howard, while CIO Secretary, assumed no administrative duties. When Carey succeeded him, he was still UE president, and Lewis continued to run things through department heads directly responsible to him. Murray added little to Carey's nominal functions, until Carey lost his UE job. Then Carey got a CIO department of his own, and other department heads as before reported directly to Murray.

Not until after Cold War had begun to follow the Second World War did I realize how Carey was trying to extend his authority through staff accretions, and find him making some moves in my direction.

He invited me to his office for some chats which were a curious exercise in confusion. I had to guess what was on Carey's mind, he didn't say it. His mood was emotional, to the point of temper tantrum, directed not at me, but seemingly inward. He paced his office, clenched his fists, contorted his face, until some kind of climax brought relief and even made him warm and friendly by the time I left.

The talks rambled, without coming to grips. The emotional outbursts were tangential. I must extract some remembered sentences, and compress and connect, to indicate what purport I could discover in them.

"Can't you see the way things are going, Len?"

"What things?"

"Oh, you know, the whole postwar trend."

"Yep."

A pause. Carey reddens, becomes agitated.

"Well, can't you see what's happening—the way things are going?"

"Yeah, I think so."

"They sure aren't going your way."

"My way?"

"You know what I mean—to the left."

"I'm sure you're right."

"We-e-ell?"

Another pause. Renewed signs of agitation. Then:

"If you see the way things are going, why don't you . . . uh . . . get wise?"

These warnings (or invitations) seemed to pain and annoy Carey internally. It was as if—through an irritating alter ego like me—he were confronting himself. At one point, I said Carey "had it in for me." He pounced on it: "But I don't, Len, I don't. That's just it. I like you."

One rambling chat did lead to something. In the ramble around, I gradually divined that Carey wanted more personalized attention to his personal publicity and if I wouldn't be his man, had someone in mind who would.

That someone proved to be Harry Read, a stringy, lethargic, middle-aged man who had been propagandist for the Association of Catholic Trade Unionists in its war against the left in UAW and other unions. I saw little of Harry after he came, and one more office conniver was hardly noticed among all the hopefuls standing in line for the decade-deferred purge of the lefts. (First promulgated by Benjamin Stolberg in early 1938, the purge didn't really start until 1947.)

I didn't move in Harry's social circles and was not privy to his amours—in fact had thought him too bony and desiccated to be in demand. But I began to get phone calls at home from a lady who said she had vital information she could confide only to me. When we met at a remote bus terminal, with secrecy precautions she insisted on, the lady told me that, to get even with Harry for his infidelity, she would reveal that he was plotting against me. I said I'd always assumed as much. Annoyed, the lady tried to startle me by telling the names he called me, the politics he ascribed to me, his plans to "expose" me, the candidates he was grooming to take my place.

As it turned out, I survived many plots I never heard of till later. When I was finally purged, none of the plotters could claim credit. As I anticipated, Murray made the decision—in his own good time and for his own less good reasons. When he acted, in mid-1947, Carey had been out of town for some time. He returned after the news was out and greeted me cordially. "Why, Len, I was surprised. I had no idea this was going to happen." I grunted something. "Really, Len," he went on, "I didn't even know about it till I got back."

"I believe you," I said. I did.

Carey followed the well-worn, social-reformist path from left to right. Though a Catholic, of increasing ACTU association, he was more in my Hillman than my Murray category. Yet it is hard to speak of him in the same breath with Hillman, a man who applied many creative impulses to his times. Carey was a product of times that brought out much in Lewis, Hillman, and Murray. He grew from youth to middle age as Secretary of CIO, and of the Industrial Union Department after CIO merged with AFL. After the IUE breakaway from UE, Carey again became head of a big union until ousted in the mid-Sixties. He had more scope than most labor leaders to show his mettle.

Though known chiefly for fratricidal strife against the left, Carey was social reformist enough to fancy himself to the left of Lewis and Murray, not to mention George Meany. When he first broke from CIO's united front, he imagined a "communist plot" to force him further to the right than he wanted to go— and so write him off as a reactionary. In later years, Carey made gestures designed to show him as both more anticommunist and to the left of Meany. If he could have pulled it off, that would have been quite a conjuring trick.

After measuring a Carey against a Hillman, it is no more unkind to measure a McDonald against a Murray.

David J. McDonald was more handsome than Jim Carey. He looked almost as young, though nine years older. He was less the ingenue than Jimmy, seemed more affected, had less appeal to the mother-father feeling. But both followed a similar route to power.

Like the Gilbert-Sullivan office boy to an attorney's firm who stuck to his desk till he became "Captain of the Queen's

Navee," these two watched their P's and Q's in office jobs until assigned their captaincies. For Carey, I refer to his rise in national CIO; I have less idea how he first rose in UE.

The office route to labor leadership was to become well-trodden in our increasingly white-collar age. Dave was a pioneer. He braved quips, sneers, slurs, from less successful union politicians. Yet a man's personal background in itself should not be held against him, if he does a needed job better than other available talent. There are other angles.

AFL President George Meany illustrated one, with his famous boast (to the National Association of Manufacturers in 1955): "I never went on strike in my life, never ran a strike in my life, never ordered anyone else to strike in my life, never had anything to do with a picket line." Starting as a presumably honest plumber, then business agent, Meany early acquired an AFL office; he followed the office route thereafter to the AFL presidency. His predecessor, William Green, more dependent on nods from above, polished the handle of the big front door most of his way to the top.

The union leader who fought his way to the front in rough struggles with employers, and rough union politics, developed certain characteristics. One used to be a kind of class consciousness—in early union days, as in the rise of CIO. Long after regenerate CIO leaders were smoothing off the last of their red roughnesses, some potbellied AFL oldtimers in their cups might still burp out long suppressed class feelings. The self-made union leader was also tough—at worst in self-seeking, at best in giving fiber to the labor struggle. In any case, the hard knocks champ was a different sort of person from the correspondence-school labor leader.

Carey owed his CIO position to a nod from Lewis. He continued as CIO Secretary under Murray's protection. He didn't have to fight to stay there; on the contrary, too much ambitious commotion would have led to his discharge. Murray, like Lewis, told him his place and saw that he kept it.

McDonald got his start as office assistant to Murray, who took him along with him to SWOC and there assigned him the title of Secretary-Treasurer. When Murray died, McDonald was next in line. To become Steel president, he had to be as artful as must any business executive out for the post next ahead of him, when it falls vacant.

Once in the Steel top spot, McDonald distinguished himself by being less the "labor man" than any known union leader. Murray was always the labor man. Having left the mines in his twenties for UMW office, Murray was no horny-handed son of toil, but he didn't manicure away all memories. Murray ran his union affairs as might any business executive, but he capitalized on his working-class origin, mixed at times with working miners, and insisted he was primarily a labor man. McDonald did not, or could not. He seemed to set out to be, think, and act like any corporation executive.

For all his long association with unions, no distinctively labor ideas seem to have rubbed off on McDonald. From Lewis, as he relates in his autobiography, *Union Man—The Life of a Labor Statesman*, McDonald picked up the expression "democratic capitalism"—a self-contradictory euphemism of National Civic Federation vintage that I never heard Lewis stoop to repeat in his CIO days. For himself, McDonald claims more credit for the concept of "mutual trusteeship"—managers and working force linked in mutual trusteeship to operate industry for the stockholders—which surely cannot have been absent from the pages of any business publication since capitalism began.

Amid such chamber-of-commerce Americanisms, however, McDonald did make room for unions, as offering a chance for the poor to better themselves and for union leaders to attain social equality with captains of industry. In hobnobbing with the latter, he says, he was "simply projecting the image of the labor leader to a social level of equality with the leaders of other elements of our society."

Making no claim to social-reformist, working-class, still less radical or socialistic attitudes, McDonald spoke with contempt of "pinkos" like Walter Reuther. There was quite a difference in the self-portraits of the two, if not so much in their union policies. Reuther fancied himself as liberal, progressive, social reformist, an advanced thinker. McDonald's ideology was that of the corporation boardroom and the Country Club. Walter could look at Dave and see himself as a flaming progressive. Dave could preen himself with big-business pals by making clear he was no such pinko as Walter.

My own limited impressions of McDonald were of a young man on the make, and making it—out for a good time, and to show off when he could. After he made it, a gaper at the Stork Club might have typed him as a well-set-up, banker-distinguished, but also playboy, business executive. If told the man had considered a Hollywood career, he'd have said that figured. He'd have gasped an incredulous "You're kidding," if told the man was head of a rough old labor union full of ordinary working people.

Allan S. Haywood was easier for me to understand. Having started his union life as a British miner, he stuck to an English labor pattern as closely as to his Yorkshire accent. Union leaders I knew in the old country had some barrel-bulge at the beltline, but their shirts were not otherwise stuffed. They affected a rough-tough manner, aggressive but also hail-fellow-well-met. If like a business agent of the United States building trades in some ways, they lacked the more mercenary traits of a get-rich-quick way of life. They were also class-conscious socially if not politically.

In the England of Allan's and my youth, clothes (along with a precious accent and a minimum of unearned do-re-mi) made "the gentleman." The upper-class man wore tailored suit, at times a derby or silk hat and spats. His shirt was white, with tie, and he carried a cane or rolled umbrella. Unless reduced to shabby-genteel, he dressed for dinner in tuxedo, stiff shirt, wing collar, black bow tie; and on formal occasions in all the glory of "tails." The English workingman, on the other hand, wore a cap, a shirt of any color, a scarf in place of collar and tie. He had other jobs for his hands than to carry a cane. He did not dress for dinner.

English union leaders rarely dress in upper-class style. When the press snapped J. H. Thomas of the Railwaymen in gray topper, morning coat, and spats trying to hobnob with the toffs at the Ascot races, it was a national sensation. I earlier mentioned reactions to Frank Hodges of the Miners addressing a meeting in "tails." These exceptions were seen as sellouts—a rank-and-file reaction not too far from the mark. Hodges, for instance, soon switched to the employers' side.

In the United States, I found fewer class angles on clothes —particularly after mass production hit its stride. Few labor leaders hesitated to dress and act like the rich. Lewis with his chauffeured Cadillac (George Meany adopted the same style) made no bones about "living well," on a level with employers and politicians he dealt with. When he mixed in Washington society—a reverse slumming he seemed to enjoy—Lewis dressed and behaved accordingly. Murray and smaller CIO fry were not lionized socially as was Lewis, but as occasion required, they dressed up, too.

Dave McDonald, a mold of fashion, rejoiced in conspicuous display. As Steel president, he beat both Lewis and Meany by having two Cadillacs with chauffeur and a $21,000-a-year Washington hotel suite awaiting his visits. One concession McDonald himself reports. When he and U.S. Steel head Ben Fairless went slumming together among the workers in the steel plants, at first they would drive up in limousines—then switched to a bus, on public relations advice.

Allan Haywood was not like that.

One New Year's Eve Caroline and I, on our way to an affair at the National Press Club, stopped off at Allan's modest apartment and asked him to come along. I felt stiff in the tuxedo required for the occasion, and Allan was stiff in manner as he grumpily begged off. He warmed to me, however, as I showed some effects of drinking he could handle better than I, and there came a moment of closeness. "Look here, Len," Allan explained, "it may be all right for you to dress up like that. Go ahead and have your fun. But I just couldn't. I never have and I never will."

Allan was a warm and friendly person with a homey back-slapping style. But in meaner stages of drinking, I heard, he could inveigh against "intellectuals" invading the down-to-earth movement in which he felt at home. When he went to New York as CIO regional director, Haywood must have dreaded the problems of the most hectic, intellectualized, radicalistic, and antiradicalistic sector of a movement more given to fancy ways in the first place than the old AFL.

By all accounts, Allan acquitted himself with distinction. Maybe even New Yorkers were human enough to respond to a man-to-man approach that set organizational regularity ahead of ideologies. Or maybe Haywood was a welcome contrast to his old buddy Adolph Germer. With his once-socialist, rigidly factional red-hating, Adolph was not for New York without rupture. In the wider open west, Germer was to continue fighting out his old battles with the left under less close observation.

In New York, Haywood learned to backslap with many brainy intruders on the labor movement. He came out of the ordeal with increased self-confidence. His confidence grew to the point that, after Murray died, he seriously challenged a sharpy like Walter Reuther for the CIO presidency.

By the time (1952) Allan Haywood mixed it with Walter Reuther for the CIO presidential title, I had no ringside seat. I doubt I missed much. Haywood was more the labor man, in a Murray sense, and a better backslapper. Reuther had everything else, except McDonald's support. I did see the earlier UAW series between Reuther and big bumbling R.J. Thomas; it was brutal, but not much more of a match.

Before Reuther took over UAW, its politics was a strenuous game played with great zest. If your side lost at one convention, there was always the next. After 1947, the game was over. If one could imagine Reuther playing any kind of game, he played only to win. When he won, he stopped playing.

Reuther quickly assured himself of total control. He wasted little time on healing the wounds of factional foes. Some he took captive and put to work for himself. Most he just threw to the wolves. If he had to bargain, he never gave something for nothing. "Walter always wants a piece of you," it was said.

My friends were among those who fell before Reuther, or from whom he carved out some pieces. I admit to some bias. But I also admit he was the only CIO successor to the Big Three who could be compared to them, both in the scope of his leadership and in some of its qualities.

Reuther was a leader, not just an officeholder. He read the changing times and. made his own adjustments, albeit without great flexibility. He captured and retained control of a big, rambunctious industrial union of modern mass-production workers —most typical product of the CIO uprising. He tried to be more than a one-union leader, to think of the whole labor movement.

In personality, Reuther had a problem. He signally lacked the charisma of a Lewis, a Debs, or other crowd-stirrers. Nothing could make him appear so lustily broad-gauged as Lewis, so seemingly loving-kind as Murray, so subtly—almost spiritually— appealing as Hillman to his own. Reuther registered as smart, to the point of intellectual, as able and determined, but otherwise as too self-centered and calculating to please.

Reuther's strength was in his concentration. Others might sometimes relax and say, "A-a-aw, what the hell!" Not Walter. He didn't drink, smoke, or dillydally in any way to distract him from giving his all to his purpose.

Like Lewis, Murray, and Hillman, Reuther periodically changed course. According to one's sympathies, one could see him as hero or heel by picking one period and ignoring others. The old Lewis of rightist reaction changed to the new Lewis of CIO progressivism. Hillman switched from prewar anticommunism to war and postwar united-frontism; Murray from war unity to Cold War purge and split. Reuther made comparable changes, with different timing.

Up to 1938, Reuther was a radical united-fronter, in the spirit of the CIO uprising. Then he grasped anticommunism as a grappling hook to climb to power in UAW; became prime mover for an antileftist purge and split in CIO, and for years one of the country's leading Cold Warriors. By the Sixties, Reuther found the Meany-Lovestone anticommunism excessive, refurbished his liberalism, and called for a labor revival.

Reuther was a man from whom much was expected.

Late in 1940, Philip Murray took to the White House a CIO plan for warplane production in auto plants, originating with the UAW Tool & Die Council in Detroit but credited chiefly to Walter Reuther. UAW sponsored the plan, and President R.J. Thomas launched it with a network broadcast. But the way press and radio trumpeted it, Murray might have been but a messenger boy, Thomas but a humble sidekick of Walter P. Reuther, and all others but his clerks or instruments. It was the Reuther Plan, with Reuther stressed far more than the Plan which was soon sidetracked.

Reuther himself was not sidetracked. Not yet in a top office in UAW or CIO, he became overnight the most ballyhooed labor leader in the land, singled out as "one union leader with brains and vision," darling of the Roosevelt administration, the "coming man." Murray had just announced his own Plan—for employer-labor-government Industry Councils. He barely hitched a ride on the publicity coattails of the Wonder Boy Reuther. He and other CIO leaders brought out plans for their respective industries. The media magnates were interested in none of the plans, only in Reuther personally.

It looked like a Madison Avenue miracle—a public image created to order. Yet there was little evidence of bought-and-paid-for public relations. The media mighty seemed to have made their own decision.

Long after the Reuther Plan was forgotten, big publishers continued to interest themselves in Reuther's fortunes. When he was moving in to take over UAW from R.J. Thomas, Henry Luce used his *Time-Life-Fortune* setup to promote Reuther. So obvious was Reuther's bigtime backing that Winthrop Aldrich of Chase National Bank reportedly phoned Thomas an offer of countersupport. But after Reuther reached the top in UAW, and then in CIO, his publisher backers seemed to lose interest. When CIO and AFL merged, with Reuther subordinated, he became just another labor leader—a category about which most media moguls could hardly care less.

The media liked to personalize events by singling out "stars," and a Henry Luce enjoyed playing kingmaker. But there may have been more to it.

The CIO uprising deeply impressed Wall Street. The Girdlers were given their fling in 1937, but couldn't stop CIO. After that, the assimilationists prevailed, their aim to tenderize and assimilate the new unions. Some favored adjustment in advance to the worst that might befall. During the great CIO sweep so much publicity centered on John L. Lewis that it was even predicted he might come to head some kind of labor government.

The extreme right had fascistic answers to this. There were also men of money who thought they could live with it, and some fancied the idea of becoming powers behind the throne of a great popular leader like Lewis.

It was all a pipe dream, as it turned out. With war coming, the government took over the unions, not vice versa. Under tamer leaders than Lewis, labor did not sweep on toward power but became subordinated to an expanding state capitalism. Still some plutocrats played with the idea that the workers' increased strength must lead to greater ambition for power; and thought to "join" more than "lick" the movement. They looked for the kind of labor leader who might lead it and who yet could be worked with.

To Henry Luce anyhow, Walter Reuther looked just right.

From the other side of the tracks also, some looked to Reuther with great expectations.

Seen from the right, CIO was at first a "menace"—clearly to the left of the old AFL, and determined to go places. Some of this aura clung to Reuther, evaporating slowly. Bircher rightists kept Reuther as a pet menace all through his most virulent anticommunist years. Meany, McDonald, and Lewis helped keep the myth alive. Lewis even called Reuther an "earnest Marxist." The others did not so desecrate the name of labor's prophet. More at a loss for words, they just kept on calling Reuther a pinko.

To the Soviets, he must have looked more white guard than pink. *Collier's* magazine, counting on United States atomic predominance, once published a special issue on colonizing the USSR after its anticipated surrender. It picked Reuther to adjust the Soviet workers to the "free world's" yoke. He obliged with a Plan, in article form, for their Americanization.

As a menace, Reuther was hardly convincing to any but the harried and retreating union lefties, whom he pursued with peculiar vindictiveness. If the communists were for anything, Reuther was against it. When they changed, he changed, too, to keep on the opposite side. From the time of his own early break with the left, no CIOer had a more consistent record of being antileft on all issues and at all times.

Some saw Reuther's undeviating anticommunism as less an

obsession than a cover-up or overcompensation for his errant youth—which included one never-to-be-forgotten indiscretion. While working in the Soviet Union, his brother Victor and he concluded a letter, "Yours for a Soviet America." This juvenile delinquency haunted Walter all through his rise in the capitalist world. He behaved as if he could never atone enough for it.

If the left could expect only blows for Reuther, some liberals had great hopes. When liberal ranks were split after the Second World War, and Americans for Democratic Action was formed as an anticommunist opposition to Progressive Citizens of America and the Henry Wallace forces, Reuther began a long-continuing association with the ADA, which looked to him as its major source of influence in the labor movement.

After Reuther in 1955 led a purged and domesticated CIO back to an AFL from which it no longer distinguished itself, there were still some on labor's side who looked to him with great, if diminishing, expectations. He was the only influential AFL-CIO leader who might buck Meany's reactionary rule. Reuther had the CIO tradition behind him—dead and damned as it now was in its more radical essence. He represented the new industrial unions of mass production rather than the more conservative craftists. He was personally ambitious, and in a windy way more liberal than Meany's crowd.

Reuther tried—if not too hard—to come up to the left of Meany. There was nowhere else he could come up—and coming up was important to Walter. In labor, there was no room to the right of Meany; if any appeared, Meany would damn himself for a leftist and hastily move over. The Meany-Lovestone foreign policy was such that Reuther had to express reservations or forfeit all liberal respect, though his distinctions at first showed little difference on the basic anticommunist issue. When his union got slightly less hawkish on Vietnam, Lyndon Johnson flicked his White House whip and Reuther came to heel.

Reuther was disappointing the expectations of his admirers. If he was playing it cool in hope of succeeding Meany, that wasn't working out either.

In 1967, Reuther stopped pussyfooting. He resigned from the AFL-CIO executive council in protest against the narrow conservatism of the Meany leadership. He issued a bill of particulars with his ideas for revitalizing the labor movement. Ousted from the AFL-CIO, the UAW joined with the Teamsters to form the more forward-looking Alliance for Labor Action.

Reuther was again trying to assume the key role in labor which others had expected him to play. There were two ways of looking at this role.

After the great CIO upsurge, Reuther came to look to the left—and possibly others—like the smart demagogic opportunist best qualified to lead the workers into accommodation with American capitalist expansionism.

In the later AFL-CIO context of class peace, imperialist war, and social stultification, Reuther could be seen as responding to new broadly progressive labor trends, and helping to open the door to them.

Leaders of Reuther's caliber, like CIO's Big Three, came to control their unions and largely chart their course. On immediate economic interests, as the members see them, a union leader cannot with impunity flout their wishes. But on broader and less understood issues, he has wide leeway to pick his own course among employer, government, political, and membership pressures. He does not just reflect the moods and wishes of the workers, but may in part determine or, within limits, disregard them.

The union in its embryonic form is politically amorphous. It is made up of workers of all kinds of opinions, drawn together only by common self-interest as against the employers. Insofar as it is democratic, therefore, it becomes a battleground of ideas— essentially, at this stage of history, between those who bow to the capitalists' rule and their profit system and those who seek working-class power to abolish it. The defenders naturally have the active support of all the ruling capitalist powers, which encourage and reward conservative union leaders who shield their unions from radical ideas. When I first met the American labor movement, in the early Twenties, leaders like that ran the AFL.

Radical ideas managed to spread anyhow. They arose out of labor struggles more intense than the guildlike adjustments favored by AFL craft leaders. They were spread by IWW, socialists, communists, and apolitical union militants. Flourishing in the mass discontent of the Great Depression, they helped to create the CIO uprising.

Alarmed at the new CIO unionism, with its open door in many cases for radical ideas, the capitalist powers turned to union leaders—in their sensitive and sometimes contradictory role as intermediaries between employers and workers—to close it. By encouraging the right kind of union leaders, and supplying them with much anticommunist hoopla against the radicals, they found they could bring the new movement into safe hands and live comfortably and profitably with it.

These considerations are my excuse for dwelling on the personalities of CIO leaders around whom—and sometimes in whom—raged the battle for control of the new mass unionism. They are also my excuse for a seemingly lopsided emphasis on right-left infighting in CIO. That was the battleground of a decade-long struggle to determine CIO's direction. Anticommunism was the smokescreen for capitalist advance to contain CIO within the limits of corporate liberalism and an American-Century foreign policy.

The virulence of the campaign against a relatively small radical minority suggests that an alternative course was not altogether foreclosed.

Starting as a revolt against AFL conservatism and the domination of the great corporations, CIO was well to the left of the AFL all through its first decade. But for the Cold War takeover, with its purge of the left and expulsion of leftwing unions, CIO might have continued as the more progressive wing of American labor, and in merger with the AFL, as a left wing within AFL-CIO.

Then, instead of being divorced from its natural allies in the working class, the new left of the Sixties might have found a large sector of the labor movement leading the fight for black liberation, against the Vietnam war, and for its other causes. Then the socialist countries and the liberation struggles of working and oppressed people everywhere might have counted on at least as much United States labor sympathy as CIO gave them in its first decade.

My next two CIO leaders built their careers on the other side of the fence from Walter Reuther. While Reuther quit the left in 1938, Joseph Curran and Michael J. Quill didn't turn against it till nearly ten years later.

In my early twenties, I sailed on freighters and oil tankers with some seamen like Joe Curran. If there was one, I counted myself lucky; the trip would be more interesting, and I might have some protection. If there were two, it wasn't so good; they'd probably fight, without benefit for the rest of us. They reminded me of some Wobblies I'd known in the camps—scrappers, strong physically; independent, not to say individualistic. A union scrap might attract them; so too, militant, even radical, talk.

With little union activity then, these seamen took out their pugnacity on each other; on bosun or mates if they could get away with it; in pushing around their fellows at times; and in much sorehead griping. Anyhow, this is the way I pictured Curran in the rank-and-file revolt that led to the National Maritime Union. I guessed he went along with the communists—the most radical activists then among the seamen—in much the way scrappier migratory workers once went along with the IWW.

These traits cast Curran in the role of arch communist to many CIO rightwingers. As late as 1945, he was the most cantankerously leftist of CIO delegates to the Soviet Union, and I recall earlier instances; during the war I chaired a CIO public relations committee (to improve CIO's image with the troops) that included Curran and Milton Murray, newly elected rightwing president of the American Newspaper Guild.

Milt Murray knew I'd opposed his campaign against the left and the remnants of the Heywood Broun tradition. He just laughed at me, when after his election, I proposed we work together on broad CIO and war issues. Joe Curran was less concerned about war unity. He raised hell against a proposal to add Irving Abramson, head of a CIO war relief outfit, to our committee. Abramson had been one of the nastiest redbaiters, and still was. But the left line, if not Joe's, called for working together. Furious at Curran, Milt Murray came to me, exploding: "This just shows you can never trust a communist. You can never work with one. It's taught me a lesson."

It was after midnight on Moscow's Red Square—the year, 1945. Joe Curran and Lee Pressman were headed, in high good humor, toward the Kremlin. Reid Robinson and I followed. We'd just had one of those huge Soviet late suppers, and it was hard to go to bed. So we stepped out for a walk.

The square was deserted. We four alone under a Moscow moon, the Kremlin walls ahead of us. Lee and Joe were goofing off. Reid and I didn't try to catch up. We caught snatches of red songs, slogans, quips. . . .

As we neared the Kremlin gate, Lee stopped and, in military style, saluted the Red Guard. The sentry solemnly responded by presenting arms. Lee was impressed, and sobered. It was one of those mood moments.

I was thinking more of Lee than of the scene. I'd been in Red Square before. This, I believe, was a first for him. Somehow I thought back to Lewis, too, a man of power, and impressed by power as was Lee. Here was the power center of an armed people who had defeated Hitler's once invincible legions. Here was the symbol center of the power of a working-class movement that had swept across the globe and into the recesses of all minds. Lee might well salute that power, and be sobered in the act.

What went through Curran's mind, I didn't speculate. More worldly-wise than Lee, Joe had known Russian, Chinese, and other ports as a seaman. Joe was also a sophisticate on communists. No student Marxist, no theoretician, he learned from life and action, from contact and clash—much as did Lewis. Joe knew his reds, or thought he did, at closer-up than Lewis. Curran was pretty sure of himself abroad, including the Soviet Union. Untypically, he wrote his own statements. He wanted them to say exactly what he wanted to say. He seemed to know what he was doing—and saying.

On this occasion, I had little chance to think my own thoughts about Curran. Robinson hadn't started out so jovial as Lee and Joe. He took my arm and into my ear he kept mumbling morosely about Curran: "He's a phony, that Joe, strictly a phony. You'll see. He'll show himself up as a phony!"

Reid Robinson, when president of Mine-Mill, was articulate and outfront as a leftwing CIO leader. He was one of two CIO vice presidents (Curran the other) elected to represent the left, when Emil Rieve and Frank Rosenblum represented the Hillman right, and R.J. Thomas and S.H. Dalrymple a rather dead center. Early CIO records are full of Robinson's speeches and statements. He was front man on many CIO and CIO-left occasions. He had a good platform presence, clear diction, and some eloquence.

Murray came to nurse a peeve against Robinson at the height of the Murray-left alliance, when he was handling other lefts with kid gloves. Murray could break protocol against Robinson and then, rather than make amends, pick on him the more as if to blame Reid rather than himself.

A big, bluff young man, Robinson came originally from Butte, Montana. He had a family background in the class struggle that associated him with the Big Bill Haywood tradition. He was personally sensitive.

On the night train from Leningrad to Moscow, during this same CIO visit, I found Robinson in tears in his compartment. Crippled Russian women, victims of the Nazi siege of Leningrad, had seen us off at the station with peace greetings and gifts of flowers. Over this Reid was sobbing. Call it a crying jag, if you must. He had been drinking, but these were the feelings it brought out.

At top levels, CIO was a sober movement. Drinkers were the exception. Lewis, Hillman, Murray, and others, at most toyed with an occasional glass to affect sociability. If younger CIOers strayed in any way from the straight-and-narrow, Old Man Lewis or Uncle Phil would lecture or discipline in a way to cockle-warm the sternest of oldtime hearts. At CIO headquarters, the breath of scandal reeked little of liquor or sex.

Years after both Robinson and I were very "out" of national CIO, I ran into him at a Los Angeles mass meeting. We were both in the gallery, and I could see Reid hated it—he who had spent most of his young life on the platform, in the chair, before microphones, in the center of the national labor stage.

To revert to Joe Curran, a much earlier incident comes to mind. I was entering the Mine Workers Building in Washington to see Lewis, when I saw Curran leaving and waved in passing. He turned and stopped me. "D'you know, Len," he said with a rather forced chuckle, "they're trying to make out that I'm a redbaiter! Me! Imagine that!" As bidden, I tried to imagine it. I just barely could.

Yet Curran was then one of CIO's most outspoken lefts—more so, in fact, than stricter party-liners who might mince words for the sake of CIO unity. At the United States embassy in Moscow in 1945—when Ambassador W. Averell Harriman was trying diplomatically to signal to us the coming American switch to anti-Sovietism and Cold War—Curran spoke up vigorously for continuing the United States-Soviet alliance and for $6 billion in credits to the USSR.

Curran's split with the left began toward the end of that same year of 1945. The pretexts were involved, and I doubt they were in themselves decisive. Curran could "see the way things were going," to use Carey's phrase. He liked to be with things rather than without them.

To me it seemed the NMU lefts underestimated Curran. With many communists among elected leaders and much following among the membership, and with a democratic constitution, the lefts felt they had Curran surrounded. He seemed to accept the situation, trying to stand out well to the left himself. Until the end of World War II and the switch to Cold War, Curran had no chance to rule as one big boss of his union. But his will and capacity to seize and wield power were not to be minimized.

Despite restraining associates and constitutions, the personal dictator has taken over in many lands. He has had to be ambitious, ruthless, politically shrewd and to have powerful backing. Curran had both the backing and the character. Back of him were government, employers, the armed forces (certainly the navy). The United States was out to expand its world power under slogans of preparing for an anti-Soviet war. In the strategic and subsidized merchant marine, a radically led union was not to be tolerated. It had to be taken over and purged of its reds. Curran was the man to do it.

Long before he took all power, I watched Curran run New York membership meetings, with thousands present. Unruly as they might become, he stayed on top. Forceful in presence and manner, he was shrewd and determined and knew how to use all his official powers. When—as happened during his subsequent purge of the left—Curran could add to these advantages the strong arms of hundreds of police, detectives, and "masters-at-arms" of his own selection, his control became indisputable.

Once in power, Curran repeatedly used the antired pretext to abrogate democratic procedures and to consolidate his total control over a union founded as a model of rank-and-file democracy to the point that in 1968 a federal court voided an NMU election on many grounds of lack of democratic rights for the members.

The National Maritime Union started as a new kind of union, rank-and-file, militant, democratic, and with radical leaders. It improved its members' conditions immeasurably and in short order. It fought race discrimination.

The old International Seamen's Union, when I was a member, catered to white Americans and was shot through with racism and jingoism. When it turned against the left, the Curran NMU machine reverted to this pattern with calls to "dump the aliens and kick out the reds."

Colored seamen were not conspicuous in other maritime unions. When hired, they were usually in one department, under white bosses. But on NMU ships, black and brown worked alongside whites. On one liner, I saw black, Puerto Rican, Filipino, and other colored waitresses working along with white waitresses with no kind of segregation.

NMU's record was due largely to communist influence. CIO verbally opposed discrimination. But only the left, and notably the communists, aggressively tried to right ancient wrongs and create genuine union and job equality. If some left-led unions fell down on this, it was usually due to communist influence being weaker than alleged. When others took action, it was often under left prodding, or to compete with the left.

In January 1948—after a dozen years of CIO—I visited a

number of CIO locals in the south, on a countrywide auto trip. My notes on some interviews with local oil union officials in Texas run like this:

"Your Negro members have equal rights?"

"Why, certainly. We don't discriminate; it's against the union constitution."

"How does it work out?"

"Just fine. We don't have no trouble at all with our Nigras."

"Do colored and white meet together?"

"Why, yes. The colored just naturally like to sit together. That's only natural."

(Another answer: "No reason why they can't. We got no rule against it. The colored boys just don't show up."

(Or again, in several cases there were still separate all-white and all-black locals.)

"I understand your black members are mostly on the lowest paid labor jobs. Do you have any on better paid and more skilled jobs?"

Some hesitation. Maybe a sideways glance at me. Am I trying to make trouble? Then a diplomatic answer.

"The union don't say they can't be. We just don't happen to have none in them kind of jobs. Don't have no trouble at all with our Nigras."

"But black members have the same seniority rights as whites, don't they? They're entitled to promotion on an equal basis, aren't they?"

"Why, bless you, of course they are." I can almost feel a wink coming—I'm white, too, after all. But I could be a Yankee troublemaker. No wink. "But they don't never bid in on white jobs. There just hasn't been one that's pushed hisself. We don't have no trouble a-tall——"

In the same Texas ports as these oil locals, there were also NMU locals—at the time still leftwing and resisting the Curran drive to take over. In the halls the *Daily Worker* was much in evidence. Port agents and members I met were militantly left. They were also militantly opposed to racist discrimination, and I saw no sign of it in hiring halls or meetings. Leaders of the black communities I interviewed testified that NMU lefties were in the forefront of all local struggles for black rights.

Only in Houston had the Curran rightwing made inroads. The left was still in the majority, but an aggressive redbaiting minority were at work, and I listened to their talk. It was so racist as well as jingoistic that I asked a ringleader why they picked on blacks as well as reds. "We figure every jig has a commie card," he answered, "and we treat them as such."

I can think of only one other CIO leader who had much of Lewis's crowd appeal. Murray at his most blowhard was rather dull. His charm was in his dignity, his kindly face, his decent respectability. You had to be a bit of an egghead to dig Hillman, if not one of his devoted Amalgamated followers. Others had to strain to get his points. As to the platform style of Carey, Brophy, McDonald, Haywood, Reuther—it didn't fascinate the crowd.

The man who had a little bit of something was Michael J. Quill. Something of the ham, for instance. He set out to capture attention, and to hold it with his wit and mannerisms. Quill aimed to personify the Irish politician—to most Americans an engaging image, as typed by the entertainment arts. To an exaggerated brogue, a direct and cheeky approach, and the usual blarney, Mike added an ever-present blackthorn cane—symbolic shillelagh—and the come-hither knack of an experienced actor. In just stepping to the mike, he could make his audience anticipate something humorous, or hopefully outrageous, to come.

Quill had more purpose then to entertain. He was always partisan. He used his humor shrewdly. Let others beat around the drooping bushes of slogans and clichés, Mike was direct. He aimed straight at some popular nerve. In a CIO debate, Mike could leave his side—the reds, in my time—in a state of chuckling euphoria. With his more powerful blows, Lewis could produce greater euphoria, but the chuckles were fewer. Yet Quill did not antagonize, as might more earnest and humorless reds. His pointed wit, like satire, could be taken as entertainment. He was personally popular.

Though Quill was closely linked with the communists, CIO leaders rated him an independently effective politician—elected and reelected as he was to the New York city council on the American Labor party ticket. They expected him to react more understandably to political pressure than a dyed-in-the-wool red.

When the Transport Workers first contacted CIO, John Brophy was surprised to note how well the leftwing pattern of collective leadership seemed to work. A committee of three or four would visit us—Quill, Austin Hogan, John Santo, Douglas MacMahon. They worked like a team of equals, not a union boss and his lieutenants. It was a novel idea, if un-American, in a country where one big boss is the rule from the Presidency down, in politics, business, unions. Insofar as it worked at first in the TWU, it may have led the left to underestimate the ambition and capability of Quill, as of Curran, to become the One Big Boss of his outfit.

With the initial advantage of top office, Quill had enough drive, cunning and acquired experience to make himself eventually the total boss of a firmly controlled union—in the approved American pattern. To complete the process, he had to break with his leftwing associates, and with the democratic inhibitions of an originally rank-and-file and radical union.

From my glimpses of Quill—in and out of his cups—he seemed a moody person, with some superstitious quirks. Brophy, Irish himself, used to talk of the "black Irish," referring not to color but to introverted gloom. Mike at first sight was the opposite—genial, humorous, extroverted. But he had his dark moods, and some moments of strangely hostile reaction.

Quill was a good Irish rebel in his youth—jailed for it, and all. His mind went back to rebel lore—to Irish patriots and renegades. He came from County Kerry, and visiting Eire once I found his name well remembered. With red rebels in the new world Mike successfully conspired to unionize the New York subways. After he turned on these reds, there were some moody moments, I heard, when Mike brooded darkly on renegades in his old country.

Quill broke openly with the left a little later than Curran. Many things may have figured—closeness to Earl Browder, to whom the Communist party gave the gate early in 1946; opposition to the Henry Wallace Progressive party campaign; differences over raising the New York subway fare. The left had many irons in the fire for Quill to pick from. His decision to switch was primary; timing and pretexts were secondary. Like Curran and many other CIOers, Quill yielded to pressure from Murray and the government—whose Cold War was directed against the left in the United States as well as worldwide. Murray, first to get the tipoff, proceeded with characteristic caution, but by 1946 was clearly maneuvering to line up CIO, and by 1947 was in the open. Quill, like Curran, had his orders by the end of 1945, but he obeyed more slowly.

The way things were going, it wasn't smart not to obey. On New York's municipal transit system, Quill played politics as they were—veering sharply rightward. When in January, 1966, his union tied up the whole city of New York, its public relations might have been stickier yet if Mike had still been Red Mike, and the strike he led dubbed a "communist plot."

On the other hand, left-led unions have sometimes managed to roll with the punches and survive. Practical diplomacy in the porkchops interests of their members has not necessarily meant sacrifice of all radical principle. When the Cold War orders were posted in the United States, however, it was clearly easier and safer for a union boss to obey than to buck them.

Religion may have played more part than I gave it credit. As head of a Catholic-conscious union, Quill had to stress his church affiliation, but I didn't put such a radical in a class with the Murray school of Catholic CIOers. Yet my Murray-Catholic friends didn't quite write him off—for all their quips about him as a skindeep Catholic, red under the skin.

Monsignor Charles Owen Rice was an intimate of Quill toward the end of his life. This was the same Father Rice who was ideologue of the ACTU in its war against the CIO left, and author of the pamphlet, "How to De-Control Your Union of Communists." He was also one of the priests close to Murray. By the Sixties, Monsignor Rice had turned away from his red-baiting past to win fame as a liberal priest, a united-fronter even, as in opposing the Vietnam war. The later Quill showed some parallel signs.

When Quill turned against his old buddies on the left, he

fought them with the requisite fury and all the anticommunist hoopla once used against himself. In Murray's CIO purge, Quill did the disagreeable jobs assigned to the renegade red. But the right's victory may have been too sweeping for his once-rebel conscience. He didn't seem too happy in his turncoat role. The Red Mike who once had "rather be a red to the rats than a rat to the reds," did his own ratting on the reds. Afterwards, he might still make some radical gesture, then nudge a passing red and say with a grin, "How was that now?"

Quill took some independent stands, as for a labor party and against the AFL-CIO merger. Then, shortly before he died, Quill spoke up clearly, sharply, angrily, against the Vietnam war, which the AFL-CIO condoned instead of condemned. Comparing "the revolutionary movement in Vietnam" with that of the Irish, Quill demanded an end to "this senseless war" and to United States "gunboat diplomacy" in Latin America. He predicted that "no matter how many men, women, and children are bombed from the air" in Vietnam, "these freedom fighters will eventually reach the greater part of their goal which is the right to live their lives in their own way."

There must have been solace for the once-rebel soul of Mike Quill in taking this then bold stand. It may have found solace too in the blaze of the great 12-day New York transit strike in which he died.

There is a strain of heroics in labor lore—even among conservative unionists. Union leaders compromise so much with employers that they are sensitive to the frequent rank-and-file charge of being chicken or selling out. The leader who seems to defy any and all powers in fighting for his union's demands, wins much kudos from his members—who exonerate him of almost any charge in such a fight. Lewis was this kind of leader. The same labor men who condemned his wartime strikes privately admired his fortitude in fighting for his group regardless of all else.

Quill had Lewis's strong help in the early struggles of the New York transport workers. When Curran and Quill turned against him in 1941, Lewis observed bitterly, and with some justice, that he had taught them all they knew. After the breach, Quill dramatically smashed a picture of Lewis from the wall.

But, like other union leaders, he must often have thought of Lewis and wondered how he measured up to him in daring, spunk, and . . . sometimes all-out fight regardless.

Mike Quill started as an all-out militant. He prided himself on fighting all-out for the transport workers. He ended his life in the maximum showdown fight of his career—and one that was in some ways reminiscent of Lewis.

Chapter Sixteen

WORLD WAR

War unity holds CIO together.

With briefcase, pressed suit, white shirt, clipped tie, shiny shoes, he might be any one of the hundreds of salesmen, lobbyists, politicians, union leaders, businessmen, besieging wartime Washington. I barely recognize him.

"Why, hello . . . Lefty," I say.

For a second he looks startled by the old nickname.

"What brings you here?"

He pats his briefcase, self-assured at once. "Got business with the labor board, manpower, and war production."

"How about grabbing a bite with me?"

"Sorry, I'm due at a luncheon of the joint labor-management."

"This evening?"

"Afraid not. Got to fly back to Milltown. CIO Council's got big doings tomorrow—with governor, mayor, AFL—even chamber of commerce!"

He grins at last, with a mischievous, oldtime glance.

Looks like my once-poor friend has "made it," in this land of opportunity for the bright, the white, the pushing, the lucky. Yes, but . . . Lefty is still a left.

Back home, the rights are gunning for him—ACTU grooming a candidate. Milltown's leftwing unions are active, vocal, the most win-the-war, but their votes fall short. They have allies, however, the Hillman crowd!

This is World War II. CIO's for winning it. The Amalgamated now has a key role for CIO unity, as once had Lewis's UMW. Its officials don't love the reds any more than did those of UMW. But CIO war unity is the line from FDR and Hillman, and the Amalgamated clan are disciplined. The lefts are whole hog for winning the war—as they were for building CIO. Lewis said, "Let them go to it!" So now says Hillman, about winning the war.

Lefty is a public personage, for the war's duration. When hot war turns to cold, he'll be hunted like a public enemy, with the Amalgamated in on the hunt. But as of now, Lefty never had it so good.

The first lefties I knew were Wobbly organizers. They traveled by freight and slept on boxcar floors, in camp-shack bunks, verminous flophouses or jail cells. They ate at Greasy Spoons. They wore overalls.

Foster's Trade Union Educational League introduced me to lefties who catered to the home guard and aped its customs. If they traveled by freight, they didn't brag of it. Mostly they hitchhiked, rode in jalopies, or by overnight daycoach if very flush. They borrowed a business suit to speak at union meetings. They ate and slept best when put up by comrades.

The Great Depression evened things a bit, by lowering many living standards to a level with Lefty's. It raised his status, to that of a recognized leader, recognized by the unemployed, and by police Red Squads.

When I knew Lefty then, his shoes lacked polish, his suit was unpressed, his shirt was blue. More nervous than now, he was aggressive in demonstrations, secretive elsewhere to avoid being fingered or fired. He was not like new lefts of the Sixties in hairdo or disarray. The party frowned on "petty-bourgeois bohemianism." If he fell short of his aim to look like a factory worker, he might have had no money for a haircut, no chance to shave.

With CIO, Lefty took a great leap, in his union organizing. He might get only partial expenses, or none at all. But he might hold a job longer than it took to check the blacklist, if the company feared CIO trouble for firing him. When a full-time organizer, Lefty drew regular pay and expenses—modest it from a left-wing union, but enough to change his manner of life.

Lefty now had assured status—with the workers, the

unions, and much of the public. But not with the bosses. In sit-downs and walkouts, he had to battle cops and company goons. He was in and out of jail. After the new unions were recognized, Lefty still faced redbaiting hostility, with threats of "exposure" by HUAC stool pigeons and rightwing factions.

The war made communists into allies instead of enemy, a snag in the Anticommunist Formula for busting unions and concealing foreign policy. For its duration, the government treated even leftwing unionists as quasi-respectable, in some ways a debilitating experience for Lefty.

The government drew union officials into all kinds of war-connected government-industry-labor activities, into commissions, committees, boards—on the periphery, not at the center of decision. It welcomed the war effort of leftwing unionists, but kept them from key posts or the payroll.

I saw little evidence the administration was "honeycombed with reds" during the Roosevelt-Truman "twenty years of treason." The few "reds" I knew on government jobs either didn't let on they were red, or were not, or first got reddish on the job. Antired pinkos hemmed them in, threatening to "expose" them if they changed one comma in any gobbledygook. I recall one pinko so full of venom that he'd pick 3 to 4 a.m. to telephone associates and hiss he was wise to them and would expose them as reds.

Within CIO, Murray and Hillman favored war unity, but intrigues continued. In their unions, neither Reuther nor Carey got into the unity spirit. At the 1943 UAW convention, Reuther rode redbaiting into battle against Richard Frankensteen and George Addes—the "Gruesome Twosome" his leafleteers called them. At UAW's 1944 convention, the lefts were attacked for too much devotion to war production, and the union's no-strike pledge got kicked around. In UE, Carey was less successful, and its 1943 convention voted 2211 to 780 against supporting his reelection as CIO secretary-treasurer.

John L. Lewis, having pulled out of CIO, drew fire for disrupting war labor unity—chiefly because of UMW District 50 raids on CIO unions. CIO leaders were cautious and restrained about his coal strikes.

District 50 was first set up for gas, coke, and coal byproducts, whose AFL federal locals turned to CIO. It also took in other workers who came under UMW's wing in mining areas. In 1940-41, restive in CIO, Lewis began to make District 50 still more of a catchall operation. When CIO Packinghouse and other unions purged pro-Lewisites and lefts, Lewis hired them as District 50 organizers in new fields. But after the Lewis-left break in 1941, Lewis fired all those lefts who didn't quit first.

In 1942, after the failure of his move for an AFL-CIO "accouplement," Lewis launched his much ridiculed drive to organize three million dairy farmers into District 50. He seemingly hoped, by a dramatic new drive and by raiding CIO and AFL unions, to build a big third-force movement.

If that was his aim, Lewis had no chance to repeat his CIO success. He could pay hundreds of District 50 organizers. But not for any money could he get the kind of organizers who battled to build CIO—reds, rebels, cause-addicts whom he set afire. The men Lewis now got were loyal only to his payroll. He no longer commanded the enthusiasm of radicals. The left was with CIO—and prodding AFL—for united effort to win the war.

Though no base for a new labor movement, District 50 could still serve to raid and harass and, after Lewis split with CIO, it looked particularly for weak spots in CIO unions. These raids caused most of the CIO flareups against Lewis during the war years. District 50 redbaited CIO as communistic and dwelt on Lewis's fame. Raided unions retorted by attacking Lewis as an appeaser of Hitler. The mudslinging rose little above mud level, but apparently added much to Lewis's bitterness.

The whole business was no great shakes. The raids were largely unsuccessful and gave Lewis no bargaining power with CIO. CIO raided and disrupted its own ranks more damagingly after the war, with an open season on leftwing unions even before they were driven out.

Based largely in the war industries, CIO unions grew rapidly to new status and security. With their wartime advantages, they could doubtless have been more aggressive on their members' behalf, as Lewis charged. Wages were frozen below levels attainable through free bargaining, while living costs broke through flimsy price controls, and war profiteering was scandalous. Others besides the miners struck during the war. AFL and CIO leaders deplored the strikes but didn't try too hard to stop them.

Communist and leftwing union leaders were more serious about labor's pledge to put victory first. They gave priority to the war's needs, trying on the homefront to match the commitment of the fighting forces on the battlefront. This was rather un-American, though not un-British, un-French, un-Russian. The Second World War merged battlefronts and homefronts elsewhere, but two world wars had left the United States unscathed. Had the CIO left been more "American," it would have joined the patriotic parade, as it did, but still played peacetime politics, as did most others. Instead it incurred much factional disadvantage by making its pledges with uncrossed fingers.

Before the war was over, however, the Communist party pendulum swung beyond all-out commitment to victory, to a Browderism that envisaged continuing class peace. Unable to make sense of the Browder line unaided, I consulted a smart associate who had fully accepted it. What about the goal of socialism—the one constant heretofore—I asked.

"We-e-ell——" It appeared we might have to sidetrack socialism.

"For how long?"

"Maybe for generations to come."

"What purposes are left for the Communist party to fulfill?"

"There doesn't even have to be a Communist party."

My mind went back to 1927, to the Olmsted dining room in Cleveland where I questioned Jay Lovestone, then a top party leader. The Lovestone line, based on the exceptional prosperity of the United States (up to 1929), was not quite the same as the Browder line of 1944, based on the American-Soviet war alliance. Both headed for a similar dead end. Socialism? "We-e-ell ——" In effect, forget it. Communist party? Doesn't have to be one.

The pendulum didn't stick at its Lovestone terminal. It swung back. Lovestone got bounced. When Browder swung it to his extreme, it didn't stick either. The swingback bounced Browder.

During the war, Lewis and the left had clearly defined—if opposite—viewpoints. Most other CIO leaders just went along for the ride, which wasn't too bad. Government recognized, employers tolerated, and they hardly had to organize. Membership swelled, and many new members knew unions only as an unquestioned working condition, whose officials looked to them much like any other strawbosses.

Below as well as on top, CIO was becoming transformed. Its unions began to look different from those the workers once had to fight for. Integrated into the government-industry setup, union leaders were sprinkled with honors—memberships on boards, commissions, committees galore, consultations, invitations, honorary degrees, titles, luncheons, junkets. But labor was not made a full partner.

Big business still ran the show. A military-industrial complex was in command, consulting labor only as needed to carry out orders. The workers were not in a real coalition to run the war. Their leaders got not even the token of a cabinet post. Hillman's jobs were the highest for labor in the administration, and he was ousted before too long.

Lewis raised hell about the service entrance assigned to labor. CIO and AFL leaders griped too, in a lower key. But really they expected little more than butler status over the help, in a capitalist society they saw as the end all of human progress.

Like Lefty, I too was socially uplifted. From the boxcar circuit of Wobbly days to the Washington cocktail circuit. From dodging men with guns to being entertained by Army brass. From the (No) Help Wanted halls of corporations to their paneled executive suites. From hiding my leftism to being introduced as a spokesman for progressive labor. It all added a trace of corpulence to a once-shrunken belly, led to some cigar-smoking to keep up with my company, and for the rest was a succession of conferences, lobbyings, receptions, briefings, junkets, committees, etc., etc.

One of my jobs was to get more radio time and fairer treatment for CIO by raising a fuss with the Federal Communications Commission, congressional committees, National Association of Broadcasters, and the radio networks. I capped the campaign by getting the three major network presidents together for a private lunch with Philip Murray. Making more money than they knew what to do with, they wanted to be nice to labor, as a public service. CIO got regular time on all networks, and I got pleasantly introduced to the entertainment world from which our radio talent came.

In liaison with the government's wartime public relations, I ran through a succession of information chiefs, from Archibald MacLeish to Elmer Davis; through brass of all kinds, from the patiently available War Secretary, Robert Patterson, and various generals, to the PRO colonels and majors so civilianly PR in their unwonted uniforms.

When I first came to Washington as a labor reporter covering the New Deal, it seemed remote from the class struggle in the shops and the streets. Now there was a fighting war on distant fronts, and the Washington reflection seemed all the more faded, fuzzy, and meaninglessly cluttered up.

One war byproduct excited me—the feelers put out toward world labor unity, toward "uniting all working people, of all nations, and tongues, and kindreds," as Abraham Lincoln put it, toward the goal of a working-class internationalism that should be the hope of the world.

This start was unromantic enough. The starters were British labor's sniff-nosed Sir Walter (later Lord) Citrine, a man little given to rosy dreams of world brotherhood; and Philip Murray, an even less ardent proletarian-internationalist. Sir Walter was a middleman between the socialist Soviets and the capitalist States. His Trades Union Congress was linked to the one through a British-Soviet trade union committee; to the other through the International Federation of Trade Unions, to which the AFL belonged.

Under pressure from his unions, and Allied sources, for a

closer win-the-war labor alliance, Sir Walter urged the AFL to join a British-Soviet-American committee along with CIO. This was to get around the division created by the IFTU, which excluded both USSR unions and CIO (the latter because IFTU admitted only one union center from each country). The AFL refused, wanting nothing to do with Soviets or CIO. This was Murray's cue to enter the act. From 1942 on, he denounced the AFL's dog-in-the-manger attitude to Allied labor unity, and demanded equal manger space for CIO.

As the war went on, pressures increased on Sir Walter. He stalled and maneuvered to cater to the AFL. It stubbornly refused to go along. Eventually the British called a conference of all national union bodies (from the United States, CIO, and railroad as well as AFL) to plan a World Federation of Trade Unions to absorb and supplant the old IFTU. Since the AFL would not attend, CIO got one up on it as the main United States participant. Of these doings, more later.

Another kind of international association during the war got me into belated trouble. I became a trustee of the Institute of Pacific Relations and attended some of its international conferences. My IPR activity was limited and did not continue after the war. But it was enough to win me a subpoena, in 1952, from the Senate Internal Security subcommittee which had harried Owen Lattimore. Of counts against me, I recall these snippets:

● I was alleged to have attended a Lenin memorial mass meeting in Los Angeles. I'd never heard of the meeting.

● I was alleged to have been "the power behind the Independent Progressive Party of Orange County," California. I wasn't. I was just a lazy member.

● In closed session, committee counsel Sourwine produced for the record a letter written by a lady I couldn't identify to an unidentified friend. She referred to a luncheon date with me and said she had found me "a good guy," or something equally vague and complimentary. At the risk of seeming ungallant, I couldn't recall either lady or date.

• A skeptical Senator asked if I really resigned my CIO job just to write a book—mightn't Murray have asked me to resign? I had to admit he did.

When I refused to answer the $64 question—was I now or had I·ever been a member of the Communist party or in any way affiliated with it—that apparently wrapped up the case.

What all this had to do with communist infiltration of the State Department, or whatever else they were supposed to be investigating, neither Senators nor counsel explained.

As to the many scholarly Far Eastern experts from government, industry, and universities whom I met at IPR conferences, their factual surveys and reasoned conclusions, considered in retrospect, showed they had a better idea of what was going on than penetrated to the higher reaches of the United States government. The delegations from Pacific and Asian countries were particularly interesting. The IPR conferences were informal forerunners of the more formal get-togethers held later under United Nations auspices. While some of the foreign delegations were governmental as well as expert, the private auspices permitted exchanges all the more valuable for their informality and relative freedom of expression.

It is typical of the depths of darkness in which the Cold War submerged all kinds of intelligent inquiry that the McCarthyites should have singled out the IPR for one of their most devastating attacks.

While in opposition at times on domestic issues involving the workers' interests, CIO hewed close to the government line on most war and foreign issues. On the matter of a second front, however, it showed some independence.

After Hitler occupied most of western Europe and turned on the USSR, a Soviet-Western war alliance was clearly in order. But its proclamation did not dispel suspicions dating back to Munich. Right in the Churchill and Roosevelt administrations there were saboteurs, and outside of government, strong capitalist voices urged Britain and the United States to hold back until Hitler could give the Soviets more of a drubbing.

In the United States, through all the delays in opening a

western front, AFL leaders said they were satisfied with government war decisions. CIO rightwingers equally protested they were unqualified to determine war strategy. In both groups there were those with tongues in cheek, who looked on the American left as the main enemy, the Soviets and world communism next, and Hitler's Nazis only third in the line of hostility. They suspected western strategy was to let Soviets and Nazis wear themselves out, and, unlike the lefts, they rather liked the idea.

Under these circumstances, the left wing exerted much influence on CIO's position. Throughout and around CIO, and reaching into lower AFL bodies, it mounted an extensive campaign for a second front. Murray did not have to yield to it. Vociferous as they were, the left unions were a minority in CIO, and Murray himself was no leftist. But the rightwing could not openly oppose a second front; and Murray doubtless felt Roosevelt might welcome some polite second-front pressure in his rumored differences with Churchill and with anti-Soviet elements in the United States.

Anyhow the CIO lefts were able to press their demand beyond their own immediate areas of influence. National CIO repeatedly, if moderately, exerted independent pressure for energetic Allied action in good faith. Shortly before the Teheran conference between Roosevelt, Churchill, and Stalin, CIO's 1943 convention stressed "coalition warfare" as the key to victory and called for "the decisive, full-scale invasion of Europe."

1943 found CIO engaging in political action more extensively, imaginatively, and independently than ever before. Passage of the antiunion Smith-Connally act was the springboard for the CIO Political Action Committee. The CIO executive board meeting called to cope with the act launched CIO-PAC and assigned Sidney Hillman to lead it.

Along with its antistrike features and other restrictions on unions, the act forbade them to contribute financially to candidates in federal elections. This speeded up CIO political activity which might otherwise have waited till the 1944 election year. The act couldn't prevent use of union money, in advance of elections, for political education; and by the time 1944 candidates were nominated, CIO-PAC substituted individual contributions for union funds. CIO was able to enter the 1944 campaign with an established political organization that had attracted many allies.

Technically, PAC was no more independent than Labor's Non-Partisan League. It was committed to Roosevelt. It entered old-party (chiefly Democratic) primaries to support the more prolabor candidates. Where PAC backed a Labor party, as in New York, it did so to increase support for Roosevelt and liberal Democrats more than to promote independent labor candidates —though this was possible in some cases. Thanks to PAC, CIO exerted much influence at the 1944 Democratic convention— though not enough to secure renomination of Vice President Henry Wallace, its favored candidate.

PAC revived on the political field some of the unity spirit of early CIO. It involved unions and members in registration drives, getting out the vote, and other activities so well that enthusiasm spread throughout and beyond the labor movement. Wealthy reaction, responding with frantic redbaiting and mudslinging, was not alone in seeing the possibility of a great popular movement that might sweep it into the discard.

Sidney Hillman was irrepressible. A year before he started PAC, he had thought he was at the end of his career. Roosevelt had shelved him, and Hillman took it hard. After two years as top labor man in the administration, including codirection (with William S. Knudsen) of the Office of Production Management, Hillman found himself demoted when the War Production Board replaced OPM. When manpower control—which might have gone with his WPB job—was vested in a new War Manpower Commission headed by Paul V. McNutt, Hillman knew he was shelved. In April 1942, he collapsed with a severe heart attack and was incapacitated for several months. Sadly he told his intimates he was "no good for anything any more."

When he recovered, Hillman resumed his duties as head of the Amalgamated Clothing Workers. But running a largely self-running union was not enough for him. PAC was the challenge he needed; ne rose to it with zest.

PAC, Hillman insisted: must be realistic, play practical politics, not follow any theoretical or third party will-o'-the-wisp. It must be well financed. He wanted $700,000 to start, from CIO's major unions.

But along with the practical politics—which humdrum labor politicians had always tried to play, with indifferent success—there had to be a spark to set people afire. Lewis had found one and fanned it into the flame of the CIO uprising. Roosevelt had found sparks he knew how to use. In CIO's 1943-44 PAC drive, Hillman found a spark and didn't douse it.

By spark I mean an emotional plus-factor conspicuous in mass movements, in revolutions, in wars deemed to be just—the exuberance of being one of many sweeping on united against the foe, through immediate gains, toward glowing if vague and distant goals. Idealists, romantics, cause-addicts, devotees, feed the flame. The practical politician who would exclude them risks demoralizing the movement or making it into something else.

In the popular movements of my times, the hardest and most devoted workers were the reds. Their zeal or narrowness might antagonize other enthusiasts, who not being communists themselves and knowing the movement was not communist, mightn't mind a little redbaiting. But it didn't stop at that. Antired leaders made rooting out the reds their first preoccupation, if not obsession. Then not only the rooted-out reds departed. With them vanished the nonred enthusiasts who joined the movement to pursue its progressive goals, not to take part in a retrograde, redhunting expedition.

Hillman was no more softened by red sympathies than was Lewis or Roosevelt. He had often fought the communists, and was a more close-in sniffer out of reds than the hell-and-brimstone Lewis in his unregenerate days, or the loftily indifferent Roosevelt. But now, Hillman hesitated no more than they to let the communists pitch in for a common purpose.

True, Hillman was handed his unity on a silver platter. PAC followed two years of a Murray-left alliance in CIO, sanctified by war unity and blessed by Roosevelt. It had the backing of all CIO, from right to left. Hillman grasped his opportunity with energy and finesse. He won the confidence of both wings in CIO to a surprising degree.

Hillman at once tested his united front in the New York American Labor Party. Calling a pox on right-left disunity—on the right side of which his own Amalgamated had played a big part—Hillman enlisted the leftwing unions dominant in the New York City CIO behind a plan to unite in the ALP all union forces—AFL, railroad, and both right and left CIO. Old-guard socialist leaders outside of CIO refused to go along. Hillman took the issue to the voters. In March 1944 the Hillman-left forces won a three-to-one primary election victory and dumped the Dubinsky-Rose-Counts leadership of the state ALP. Hillman was elected state chairman. The Dubinsky faction seceded from ALP to form their own American Liberal party.

Hillman's PAC formula was not particularly generous to the left, though acceptable to it. Top spots went to respectable poohbahs. CIO leftwing leaders were subordinated—even in ALP—to minimize redbaiting and to encourage more conservative unionists to rally to PAC. An expert and efficient staff, headed by C. B. (Beanie) Baldwin, directed the PAC campaign with pioneering initiative. Around the country, Hillman drew into leadership his own ACW lieutenants, who helped ease right-left friction.

In one respect, CIO's leftwingers were not restricted. They were free to pitch in, with energy and enthusiasm, in the volunteer door-to-door and other grassroots work on which PAC success depended. The left unions, with their rank-and-file origins, had more ideas on reaching and involving the many than would have occurred to those old-line union bosses whose politics ran mostly to the back door of City Hall.

During the war, a big, tousled farm-businessman remote from CIO's internal politics came to loom large in its orbit. Henry A. Wallace was CIO's 1944 choice for Vice President and potential successor to Roosevelt. At the war's end he was a leader of the liberal movement generated by CIO-PAC. And when CIO succumbed to the Cold War, its leaders turned with fury against him and his 1948 Presidential campaign.

CIO tried to distinguish itself from other Roosevelt supporters by a more advanced labor and social program. CIO-PAC and its liberal allies looked for new ideas on war and peace, imperialism, and world affairs that might justify the new political movement as a separate and progressive force. Wallace was the national leader who came closest to reflecting these gropings—including their fuzziness and lack of focus.

Wallace championed the rights of black people, whose denial mocked the Democratic party as a progressive force. His *Century of the Common Man* contrasted sharply with American-Century ideas of subordinating the common man to an aggressive postwar imperialism. Wallace early called for Allied postwar unity, to foil the plans of the "imperialistic freebooters." For these and similar utterances, usually to the left of his own Roosevelt administration, Wallace found in CIO and PAC a sympathetic hearing. Though too mixed-up for the sharp-minded left, he inspired the liberals, and the right accepted him as Roosevelt's Vice President.

Murray, Hillman, and other power-and-moneymen of PAC were not political philosophers. They counted themselves practical politicians, out for bread-and-butter legislation, out to elect candidates who would play ball with union leaders—concerned with today, perhaps tomorrow, but not the day after. Yet PAC had released popular forces that wanted to go places. Its top union leaders had no clear idea where those places should be. Henry Wallace was full of ideas—if none too clear either.

In his book *Gideon's Army*, Curtis D. MacDougall argues that Hillman had a chance to stop the dumping of Wallace at the 1944 Democratic convention—by calling Roosevelt long-distance at a critical moment—but didn't make the attempt. Hillman did help put Harry Truman in the line of Presidential succession. If he didn't try hard enough to do that for Wallace, it might seem quite a blot on Hillman's PAC record. On the other hand, none could then know that Truman's postwar foreign policies would diverge so sharply from those then advocated by Wallace and PAC.

At the Democratic convention, Murray was front man for the strong contingent of CIO and PAC delegates. But decisions were not to be made by generals like Murray; their maneuvers were for show. Staff strategists had fought things out on drawing boards, and the boys in the backroom now had the last word. From PAC, only Hillman had FDR's nod to get a look-in.

An amateur politician without background in City Hall,

State House, or Congress, Hillman like Harry Hopkins had enjoyed matching wits with the pros' in the capital's big time. He must have been fascinated to be consulted by the key political bosses at the moment of President-making. Hillman was also a longtime union leader—a specialist, that is, in compromise and accommodation, with a preference for accommodating politicians.

Henry Wallace was CIO's official choice. To its liberals and leftists—still to be reckoned with then—he was the candidate most likely to stand up to the southern Democrats and to continue Roosevelt's one-world foreign policies. James F. Byrnes was the menace—southern racist and reactionary, antilabor, jingo imperialistic. Harry S. Truman was in-between. A run-of-the-mill, machine-built politician he seemed to CIOers, but with a better record than Byrnes, a kind who might play ball.

Officially, CIO went out 100 percent for Henry Wallace. Murray made his nominating speech. He refused to consider any other candidate. CIO and PAC, in fact, were the only political machine plugging for a candidate so little the practical politician that he had no machine of his own.

The decision was not to be made on the convention floor, of course, but by Roosevelt himself and the big city Democratic bosses. The boys in the backroom had to take CIO into account, to be sure. But they took more account of the party's southern wing and of its big-money backers. How early Truman was picked is open to dispute. Roosevelt's last word apparently was the alleged "Clear it with Sidney," with or without which he indicated Hillman as the man to give labor clearance for Truman.

Hillman gave this clearance when he invited Truman to a private breakfast with him in his Ambassador East hotel suite. Pleased with his kingmaking role, Hillman regarded Truman as a good alternative to Wallace and was delighted that Byrnes had been "stopped." Murray was less pleased. Jealous by now of Hillman's political prominence and Roosevelt-assigned importance, Murray felt let down, even made a fool, when Hillman sawed off the limb on which he'd gone so far out for Wallace.

Had they foreseen how placing Truman instead of Wallace in line for the Presidency would change postwar foreign policy, Hillman might have been disturbed, but Murray would hardly have cared. Murray was to go along with Truman's Cold War policy as fast as he could relieve himself of CIO's past tieup with Wallace and get him and his followers off his neck.

Most labor leaders rode high during the war, and Hillman wasn't the only one who may have been affected by the altitude. Plain old porkchoppers, sitting atop swelling treasuries and enjoying fancy government favors, began to har-r-rumph like labor statesmen. CIOers who'd had to be tough to climb on top of their unions, or to build them, were softened by the treatment, more than those AFLers who had long been softly padded.

CIO leftwingers were less courted and favored. Those who didn't measure success by salary and personal prominence were correspondingly less corrupted. Those with a taste for loot found leftism a drawback and, with the Cold War, turned quickly to the redbaiting right.

The left was softened in a special sense. For the war's duration, leftwing unionists were less persecuted, and success came more easily to those who had once battled every inch of the way. They might lead large groups of workers with little radical or union background, a test of their mettle. If no more than lamebrain theoreticians, they wouldn't last long. If their radicalism guided them to practical policies of working-class appeal and benefit, they could distinguish themselves from the self-serving potbellies of union reaction. Many union-leading lefts became practical politicians—either in this good sense, or with the conventional opportunism of most American labor leaders.

On the whole, the war period caused the lefts to let down their guard, and to be taken by surprise when the Cold War launched its savage assault on them and all they stood for.

Chapter Seventeen

1945

*Turning point from world labor unity to
world division.*

It was like walking on air with impossibly long
dream-like strides. The war was ending. Fascism was vanquished.
Ahead lay peace and good will. I felt it the more since, in 1945,
I actually flew over much of the globe.

The year started with Roosevelt, Stalin, and Churchill planning a lasting world peace based on Big Three unity and the
United Nations. On this base, CIO joined with Allied workers
to forge world labor unity.

In the United States, AFL's William Green, CIO's Philip
Murray, and Eric Johnston of the Chamber of Commerce
dreamed of class peace, jointly proclaiming a lasting industrial
peace based on a "practical partnership . . . under a system of
private competitive capitalism."

1945 started with dreams of a world free from the hell of
war and reaching for heaven. It almost seemed possible that men
of good will might work together for peace, plenty, social progress, an end to ancient oppressions, that capitalism and socialism
might coexist in mutually beneficial competition, that colonial
peoples might freely proceed to freedom.

1945 ended with Truman shaking the atom bomb at the
USSR, and the Soviets retorting they'd have one, too. It ended
with world labor unity undermined; strikes of millions breaking
out all over the United States; and all realists scoffing at their
earlier dreams.

What happened during the year?

The war ended. A common enemy no longer united the
Allies. Roosevelt died, and with him his postwar dreams. At the

dedication of his monument, the United Nations, get-tough-with-Russia whispers were so loud one could hardly hear the FDR obituaries.

The United States atom-bombed Hiroshima and Nagasaki —to get the jump on the USSR in the Pacific, it was said. Right after V-J Day, Churchill tried out in Parliament the "Iron Curtain" slogan (taken from Goebbels) with which he was to wow the world (and a grinning Truman) at Fulton, Missouri, in March 1946.

Churchill, who once offered rebellious colonial blacks "a taste of the sjambok" (South African bullwhip), didn't intend to preside over the liquidation of the British empire. He left that to Labor and Tory successors, who refinanced the firm, under a new Commonwealth name, as a subsidiary of the American empire. Truman and Wall Street were in an expansive mood. They spread American bases, missiles, missions, investments, all over the world, right up to that Iron Curtain they hoped to roll back.

The spots showed proudly on Churchill's imperial leopard-skin. The dollar sign was waterfast in Truman's plebeian toga. Tiger Stalin hadn't changed his stripes.

The good words of Teheran and Yalta were not enough to stop capitalist imperialism from colliding with expanding social-ism and colonial liberation.

1945 was for CIO—and for me—the most international of years.

In January, at an Institute for Pacific Relations conference in Hot Springs, Virginia, I got inklings from Asian delegates of liberation conflicts to come.

In February, most of CIO's vice presidents attended an inter-national trade union conference in London to plan for world labor unity.

In March, on the CIO delegation's return, Murray and Hill-man joined Senator Claude Pepper, the Soviets' Andrei Gromyko, and others at New York's Madison Square Garden to acclaim world-labor and Big-Three unity (at Yalta).

In April, top union leaders from Britain, USSR, France, China, Latin America, and IFTU met in Washington; then moved their sessions to Oakland to keep an eye on United Nations founding in San Francisco.

In May, came V-E Day. The world labor leaders agreed on a draft constitution for the World Federation of Trade Unions —with CIO, Soviet, and other leaders making concessions for unity, only the British a bit sticky.

In June, Murray invited trade union delegations from the USSR, France, and Britain to visit the United States as CIO's guests.

In July, the Soviet delegation was received with cordiality and fraternity by CIO and its unions. From Potsdam, came rumors that get-tough-with-Russia Truman was getting tough.

In August, came V-J Day. I was in the Pacific on an Army-Navy junket for union editors, left as well as right. At Manila, General Douglas MacArthur gave us his ideas on world affairs, before leaving to run Japan.

In September, I flew back from Manila to the United States, then on to London and Paris for the founding of the WFTU. United States ambassadors and foreign dignitaries all gave us the glad hand for achieving labor unity.

In October, from Paris to Berlin with the CIO delegation. United States representative Robert Murphy, briefing us on steps being taken to straighten out the Germans, kept passing over de-Nazification. "And de-Nazification?" one of us would interpose. "And de-Nazification, of course," Murphy would say. It didn't seem uppermost in his mind.

From Berlin on to the Soviet Union, whose unions entertained our fraternal delegation. Ambassador W. Averell Harriman jarred the cordiality and fraternity but slightly with some discordant notes.

On the way back, I was among those held up in London by the postwar transportation jam. Phlegmatic Britishers didn't share our exuberance. Returning American officials, reporters, businessmen, were not optimistic about world unity. We could glimpse the gray rays of a Cold War dawn.

Back in the United States, a capital-labor showdown approaching. Tough little Harry Truman getting tough with labor. Gentle Phil Murray blasting back.

It didn't seem so dream-like at the time. Many Americans were still against chopping the world in two, between communists and anticommunists. Roosevelt, Wallace, Pepper, for instance, among the politicians; Hillman and Murray, speaking for CIO. On the opposite side, the Hearst press, *Chicago Tribune*, New York *Daily News*, and the interests behind them; AFL leaders, American Legion, Jay Lovestone, likewise. But as the war ended, the unity crowd were ostensibly on top. At Yalta, FDR had committed the United States to Big Three unity and the United Nations. Even Truman paid lip service to the testament of FDR.

It looked quite natural for Phil Murray and Vasili Kuznetsov to grab lunch together in a coffeeshop between committee sessions, more so perhaps than might similar chin-wagging between Murray and Harry Bridges, say. Kuznetsov was president of the All-Union Central Council of Trade Unions of the USSR, and led its delegations to the United States and the WFTU. Later he joined the Soviet diplomatic service and rose to be deputy foreign minister.

Kuznetsov knew more about the American steel industry than did Murray before SWOC. He had worked in the mills of Jones & Laughlin and U.S. Steel, and graduated from Carnegie Tech with a master's degree in metallurgy. He was fluent in English and well versed in United States labor affairs. As responsible labor leaders, diplomatic by nature and training, Kuznetsov and Murray could negotiate readily—reaching agreement, if that was their purpose, or giving and taking in reasonable disagreement.

Kuznetsov was a Soviet communist, Murray an anticommunist United States Catholic. They could still agree on world labor unity to preserve the peace, to keep down fascism, to better workers' conditions. They hit it off quite easily.

Other Soviet unionists were not unlike their United States counterparts in type—could take the floor and hold forth, handle beefs aggressively or diplomatically, closely follows a policy line. Americans followed their union-machine line like communists their party line; their jobs depended on it.

From other countries, the most conservative unionists

called themselves socialists, social democrats, syndicalists, some shade of pink, and held themselves to be to the left of American unionists who didn't even have a labor party. They reacted just like United States rightwingers to their (usually communist) opposition. The functionaries of IFTU and its trade secretariats, Walter Schevenels and J. H. Oldenbroek, could have fitted into Carey's CIO staff or that of Walter Reuther without anyone noticing.

Britishers Arthur Deakin and Ebby Edwards were doubly familiar, since many United States unionists were as British by birth and type as they. Sir Walter Citrine was distinctive—as persnickety sharp and policy-conscious as Hillman, with whom he was soon to match wits in London preliminaries to WFTU.

As for that old lion of French syndicalism, Léon Jouhaux, he could have stood in for John L. Lewis in portly, shaggy bulk —and, during his aging years of declining influence, a certain grumpiness.

Vicente Lombardo Toledano was in some ways unique. Under President Cardenas, Lombardo's CTM (Confederation of Mexican Workers) supplanted the AFLish CROM of Luis Morones, a leftward break comparable to CIO which established close relations with Lombardo and CTM. After later Mexican governments, more rightward and Yankee-minding, took over most of the unions—through subsidies, appointments, favors, crackdowns—Lombardo gave more attention to his other creation, the CTAL, a confederation of Latin American trade union movements.

Union leaders are traditionally supposed to come from the workers they represent. They may have come a long way from a brief or tenuous association, but are still classified with "workers" rather than "intellectuals." It was important for a craft leader to have practical knowledge of his craft. But in an industrial union covering many different occupations, the background of a leader in a particular occupation had less bearing—except as an election talking point—and professional qualifications came to count for more. Still, the leader was essentially the labor politician, with professionals or intellectuals in subordinate capacities. In less advanced countries, intellectuals might have an initial leadership advantage over the little-schooled worker. But as industry and unionism developed, less intellectual leaders rose from the ranks or were imposed from above. Many Mexican union leaders were now coming to compare with their Yankee counterparts. Vicente Lombardo Toledano did not.

Quiet and unassuming, Lombardo was an intellectual as well as a labor politician. With private income and a home full of books and art objects on the outskirts of Mexico, he had family ties with the Mexican power elite. Lombardo was also a professed Marxist and in his labor leadership tried to match theory with practice. He was attached to the labor and radical cause with a consistency rare in the get-rich-quick, turn-coat-quick setting of much Latin American politics.

From France came Benoit Frachon, head of the CGT (General Confederation of Labor), in plump build and well-rounded deportment a recognizable union-leader type. Frachon was quietly benign and congenial both socially and in the WFTU negotiations. In his big horn-rimmed reading glasses, he looked ruddily cherubic.

In the wine cellar of a small French restaurant in Oakland, I enjoyed a long evening relaxing with Frachon and his younger, harder-type associate Louis Saillant (later WFTU secretary). The proprietor was so pleased with his French guests that he kept treating us to samplings of his best imports. Both Frachon and Saillant had had grim experiences in the anti-Nazi underground. But now they just joked, gossiped, told anecdotes, and Frachon philosophized in homey, humorous vein about people and customs.

It was a very French evening. It reminded me of when I lived with French people in France, and we'd sit around sipping and chatting. No one got high, as over American cocktails. The wines created a sociable mood, loosening tongues for easy chitchat, kidding, cynical, a trifle malicious. The effect was light, brittle, and to my foreign ears, peculiarly French.

Giuseppe Di Vittorio, head of the Italian CGL (General Confederation of Labor), was a communist, as was Frachon. Otherwise he was a familiar enough type in the United States where Italian-American union leaders are almost as common as Irish-Americans. He and his wife would have passed unnoticed in any United States labor crowd.

So the French were French. The Italians were Italian. The Russians were Russian. The British were British. Union leaders from different lands had like characteristics. Put a bunch together, and if that was their purpose, they could get along famously. So what's new? What was new was the notion dinned into American labor for the next two decades, that Left was Left and Right was Right and never the twain should meet; that communism and trade unionism were incompatible. This in face of the fact that communists pioneered unionism in many countries—as in the American CIO—and when WFTU was formed, led many national labor movements, cooperating well with others in common labor undertakings.

For ten years of CIO, for that matter, communist and left-wing unionists managed to get along with the rightwingers. Differences might be sharper, nastier, more personal, because within the American family, and family squabbles are like that. There were also times—as in early CIO and the war years—when left and right not only met but got along well. The two wings, like those of bird or plane, made possible some high flying.

In the winter of 1945-46, industrial disputes began that brought two million on strike at one time in January, and had involved five million before 1946 was over. The biggest industries were hit—auto, steel, coal, electrical, packinghouse, oil, railroad, maritime.

What had happened to the industrial peace projected by Green, Murray, and Eric Johnston? For one thing, the National Association of Manufacturers wasn't in on it. Regretting their wartime concessions, most employers were now out to teach labor a lesson. Big business was denouncing big labor as a public menace; and the magnitude of the strikes reinforced its demand for a government crackdown on the unions.

Truman responded with maximum use of his war powers, though the war was long over. He commandeered railroads, seized coal mines, oil refineries, and other plants, and threatened to use troops as strikebreakers. He demanded of Congress the most rigorous anti-strike measures, including a draft of strikers into the armed forces. Congress preferred to devise its own antiunion measures. Truman, bitterly denounced by labor at the time, recovered labor support for his 1948 election only by opposing or vetoing congressional measures sometimes less drastic than his own proposals.

The government intervened in all major strikes. It made unions accept settlements largely government-devised. More gentle with employers, it tempted them to comply by price, contract, tax, and similar concessions. Higher profits uniformly followed the wage increases granted.

A formula emerged that—in a period of profitable United States expansion abroad, technological advance, and a growing domestic market—seemed to satisfy government, employers, and labor leaders alike. Big business benefited in rising profits from government planning, contracts, and labor discipline. Union leaders maintained standing with their members through regular wage increases and other improvements—relatively little resisted by employers who more than compensated by raising prices and cutting labor costs. If the formula depended on constant inflation, those who thought they were "getting theirs" didn't care; and the rest weren't organized enough to count.

Most of the labor officialdom became so integrated into this government-corporate setup as to go along almost automatically with the postwar neo-imperialism from which so many economic blessings seemed to flow. In CIO, however, the transition was not so easy.

In 1945, CIO was at first ostensibly united behind Roosevelt's declared policy of continuing war unity into the postwar. When it gradually became clear that Truman was embarking on the opposite course, Murray at first tried to soft-pedal things in CIO, to avoid dissension in the midst of brewing strike struggles, and possibly because of some lingering uncertainty. In the spring of 1946, after the Churchill-Truman declaration of Cold War at Fulton, Missouri, Murray began trying more openly to swing CIO into line.

What Hillman might have done, who knows? He died July 10, 1946, still on record for Big Three and world-labor unity, and against the growing American-Century imperialism. But the lines were not yet sharply drawn.

About Murray there was little doubt. At first cautious about antagonizing CIO's still influential leftwing, he was soon privately—even in my unsympathetic presence—referring to "those people" in disparaging, sometimes caustic terms. Long before the 1946 CIO convention, which officially registered CIO's switch, Murray could hardly hide his feelings. They were evident at Steel's May convention in Atlantic City. They burst out emotionally at the September Conference of Progressives in Chicago.

When the war with Japan ended, I was touring the Pacific front with a delegation of labor editors. We were briefed by generals and admirals in Washington, Hawaii, Guam, and by General Douglas MacArthur, who spent some hours with us at headquarters and at lunch in his Manila home. MacArthur spoke off-the-cuff, critically and competitively, about the Soviet Union, but so too about the British. With us, he tried to recast his labor image—that of a man of war abroad and reaction at home—by protesting a soldier's closeup hatred of war, and dwelling on his studies of American statesmanship. He said what he'd seen of the Australian Labor party convinced him United States labor was wise not to have started its own party.

Very different from the briefings of the brass was the scuttlebutt we heard from the troops, as different as the talk of Murray's CIO camp followers was soon to be from the measured platformalities of their chief.

From less inhibited junior officers we learned that, with Japan licked, "Russia" was fast replacing it as "the enemy." Our country's manifest destiny, its course of empire, lay further westward than Japan, it seemed; and peace might only come when the Reds too were licked, if then.

Among the GIs, there was a strong countercurrent of opinion. Their idea was that, with Japan and Germany defeated, the war job was done; they wanted to go home. Shortly after we left Manila, GIs demanding to be sent home began to demonstrate there and elsewhere. Active among them were CIOers who learned about demonstrative techniques during the rise of CIO —including Emil Mazey, who was later to become UAW secretary-treasurer.

CIOer GIs introduced us to Filipinos trying to form a labor movement, whose ideas also differed from those of our junior officer contacts. Like our GI friends, they didn't believe the United States must impose "freedom" by force of arms on liberated as well as conquered peoples right up to the Soviet borders, and beyond, if possible. These colonials wanted independence not only from Japan, but also from United States military, financial, and economic overlords.

Manila was more an occupied than a liberated city.

The boulevard auto traffic was endless, day and night. Like a big American city. And why not? It was all American traffic—army trucks, jeeps, cars for the brass. The Filipinos had ponycarts—kept off main streets, so as not to impede the American traffic. The ships crowding the harbor were nearly all American.

The center of the city was in ruins—from American bombardment more than Japanese demolition squads. If any government, apartment, office buildings survived or were rebuilt, United States authorities occupied them. The Americans had their own telephone system and electricity from power on American ships. The Filipinos did without. Filipino authorities still had the Presidential palace and found other offices in the slums.

Around Manila's outskirts the mansions of the wealthy stood undamaged, occupied by American officers for clubs and social facilities. Now the fighting was over, the owners were returning to claim some. They had owned plants that operated under the Japanese. They now made equally or more profitable arrangements with the American occupation.

Most Filipinos lived in misery that was bad enough before the war—seven to a room, according to one statistic. Unbombed houses were falling to pieces. Roadway gutters were open sewers. Streets and sidewalks were ruts, pools, and gaping holes. As we threaded our way between ruts and pools and jumped over holes, rats scurried for cover, and children swarmed out. One tot dragged a rat on a leash of string for his pet.

To these near-naked, hungry, scrawny kids, well-fed strangers in American uniforms meant only one thing. Even the tiniest greeted us, "Hi, Joe! Pom-pom?"—offering sisters or mothers in prostitution.

We made our own contacts through CIO friends in the forces, who sought us out when they heard labor editors were in town. We met Filipino trade unionists and radicals; Huks (members of the Hukbalahap, the People's Anti-Japanese Army); and some Americans who had fought with the Huks. We met them in little cafés, in slum homes, or remote cottages.

PRO guides took us on the official rounds. We met both Filipino Presidential candidates, Sergio Osmena and Manuel Roxas. We visited the block-long headquarters of the Chinese resistance fighters, who had motorcycle corps, dramatic groups, and many red trimmings. MacArthur still tolerated them, but the Counter-Intelligence Corps was beginning to move in, as it had already started to do with the Huks.

We met leaders of a burgeoning labor movement, the CLO (Committee on Labor Organization), inspired by the American CIO, some of whose members in the services were taking time out to help. Other "union leaders" to the right of CLO seemed mostly racketeers, labor contractors, or lawyers out for pesos or political squeeze.

Our Filipino friends seconded the go-home GI sentiments, but were skeptical about the United States promise of independence. The whole occupied country was in hock to the United States, which clearly would tolerate no policies counter to its military, economic, trade, investment, or foreign-policy interests.

Both Presidential candidates realistically accepted United States domination, as did wealthy Filipinos generally. Osmena was a big landowner. Roxas, who was to win the election, was favorite of the industrial and financial leaders who collaborated with the Japanese, and a big-money collaborator himself. Both, when we interviewed them, expressed much gratitude for past and prospective American favors.

Meanwhile the poorer people, peasants and workers, who did most to fight the Japanese, had the American CIC on their tail to see they carried resistance no further. Until a Philippine government could do the job of keeping down the Huks and other resistance fighters, and militant unions, the United States forces would attend to it.

The term "neocolonialism" was not yet in vogue. But if one country could be so subject to another in every essential aspect as the Philippines to the United States, and still become technically "independent," it might not be old-fashioned colonialism, but some hyphenate of the word had to be coined.

Manila was devastated. London was deeply damaged. Paris was the undamaged capital of a devastated people. Berlin was blasted to the humiliation of defeat. Leningrad was blasted too, but had pride of victory, as had Moscow. The Nazis strutted no more—in Berlin or anywhere else. In Leningrad and Moscow, they shuffled about prisoner tasks, at times under charge of a husky, be-rifled Russian woman (oh, Kinder, Kueche und Kirche!).

In the world capitals I visited in 1945, outside of the Soviet Union, it was Americans who strutted most—the best fed, best equipped, best cared for, richest, most technically advanced, least damaged, the most victorious-looking people ever to strut their stuff.

In London, less contrast between native population and prosperous American master-folk. But still contrast—and envy. Anti-American jokes in first place with music-hall comedians; the more malice the more they brought down the house. The war hit England hard, the United States not at all. Bombed-out gaps, as in a child's teeth, in London's once-solid blocks. The people short of food, clothing, the bare necessities, while the omnipresent Americans had everything. They modernized their quarters with every convenience, gratifying all whims with supplies from the United States. As they mingled with Londoners on the streets, their pockets bulged with money for luxuries most Londoners could only long for.

In Paris, Americans were still more conspicuously wealthy. The lowliest GI was a millionaire next to the average Parisian—in common comforts rather than money, though the dollar bought most. At an American PX, the GI could get things from soap, cigarettes, candy, up that were without price in French money. His trifles were riches to Parisians.

At the Grand Hotel where I stayed, there was no hot water

or heat, though American quarters had them. The Parisian's coal ration for winter would warm an American home but a few days. Meat was unavailable at my hotel, coffee made of some miserable cereal; even the Frenchman's wine was scarce, diluted, and prohibitively priced. The American-occupied hotel across the street—like other United States army hotels, messes, clubs—readily provided Americans with every food, comfort, luxury, the French lacked.

At a workers' mass meeting in Paris, the clothes vaguely puzzled me. The men wore Sunday suits, neat and clean if often threadbare. But they hung loosely, like ill-fitting hand-me-downs. Gone were the plump, jovial Frenchmen I remembered. Perhaps the suits had fitted when first they were bought.

Berlin, unlike the other cities, was capital of a conquered people. It was terribly devastated. But Manila was like that, too, and Warsaw and Leningrad had suffered longer. Few German young men on the streets. Old people and children roamed the once-proud Tiergarten, skirting around shellholes, searching among the charred stumps of trees for scraps of fuel.

Here, too, the Americans lived like lords. Their officers occupied the undamaged suburban mansions of the rich—supplied with all the comforts. To the victors the spoils? I felt more contrast in Allied cities.

In Manila and Paris, children were scrawny, ill-fed, sickly. In Berlin, most were rosily plump. The Nazis, I was reminded, had milked all Europe to feed themselves. Then, German enterprise was cozying up to American enterprise. It was but a few weeks after V-E Day, but already moneymaking Germans were fawning on capitalistically compatible Americans—as superior a people, they hinted, as the German master race itself.

Only in the Soviet Union, with few Americans to be seen, was the rich-poor contrast missing. Children didn't crowd around to beg or solicit; nor toadies, flunkies, con-men, pursue us for our wealth. Soviet discipline, no doubt, but also something more. The USSR had been invaded by the Nazis; it had not been invaded by its American allies, like the other countries. The Soviet people knew the Americans only from a distance—as allies and equals; not as prosperous, powerful strangers in their midst to be catered to, not as rich relations to be envied or hated.

A proud people welcomed our CIO delegation as guests. They didn't see Americans as "the enemy," as patronizing bene-factors or malefactors, as neocolonizers or business competitors. For that moment of time in 1945, Soviet citizens we met saw Americans as valued allies, as labor friends (through CIO), as prospective collaborators for peace and progress.

Americans, once stay-at-homes, covered the globe at the close of the Second World War. Travel had expansive effects.

The ancient Romans, traveling far and wide to build their empire, became convinced by their invincible legions they were superior to the barbarians in skill, cunning, culture, efficiency, politics, and way of life.

The British "shopkeepers"—traders, pirates, slavers, mission-aries, soldiers, and manufacturers and bankers back home—car-ried the Union Jack around the world, till the poor old sun couldn't set on it. Britannia ruled the waves, its navy invincible —as too its colored armies, if British-officered. The British de-voutly made it their mission to bring their way of life, their God, their moral code, their politics, to lesser breeds without the law.

The Yanks not only chased the sun around the globe, they beat it in their jet planes. They came out of the world war on top, of both enemy and allies. Their armed forces were the most intact and advanced, first with the atom and hydrogen bombs. In wealth, industry, technique, the United States was far ahead. The world, said Henry Luce, was in for an American century.

The U.S.A. had everything, the rest of the world little or nothing. Such good fortune, many Yanks concluded, must be de-served. Must be United States free enterprise, moral values, de-mocracy, or something, that made Americans so much richer, better fed, whiter, more clean-cut, more modern and efficient.

Even in western Europe, whence many American Joes came, no modern plumbing, no autos for all, no supermarkets, little to eat or wear, and money not worth a cent. Of course, the war and all that. The United States should help these people to their feet. But not their way, un-American, inefficient. They didn't like us anyhow. Help, sure, but don't let them sponge or make suckers of us.

To do things right, Americans must do them, or at least supervise them. All countries needed American money, equipment, know-how, and should pay for them, with a profit. With the atom bomb, Uncle Sam had the power to run things right all over this wretched, retarded, war-wrecked, old world.

But wait—maybe not quite all over. There was a big red splotch on the map where American power, bases, troops had not penetrated—maybe couldn't, without atom-bombing. A provocation—and the splotch was spreading!

The CIO delegates to WFTU and to the Soviet Union weren't like that. They represented the more advanced sector of United States labor—the vanguard of our working class, I liked to think. Begun as an uprising against employer-domination, CIO had departed from the capitalist norm.

CIO favored extending wartime unity into the postwar, and United Nations cooperation for peace and social progress and against fascism. It opposed imperialism and called for independence and self-determination for all countries. True, President Roosevelt proclaimed such policies. But, unlike AFL, CIO underwrote and promoted them with a vigorous lead for world labor unity. CIO had also opposed those forces in the United States that would negate these policies in favor of American-Century neo-imperialism and Cold War.

At Paris, the CIO delegates helped unite all major labor movements (except the AFL, for which a place was left open) in one World Federation of Trade Unions. The visit to the Soviet Union was a fitting followup to this unity of the labor of both capitalist and socialist countries.

By the time we gathered for dinner at the United States embassy in Moscow, most of us were enthusiastic about the Soviet people we'd met—their human, friendly warmth, their grit, their likenesses to United States unionists, the hope for the future they saw in CIO's attitude. After dinner, we had a long bull session with Ambassador W. Averell Harriman. We stressed our good impressions, and I heard no rightwinger dissent. Joe Curran, as noted, called for closer alliance and a $6 billion United States loan to expand trade.

Harriman listened, nodded, added his comments. He seemed to go along—at least I assumed he did, in line with proclaimed United States policy. When his comments were restrained or negative, I though he was just adding a realistic pinch of salt so we might not ignore practical difficulties.

Later that night a cold hotel room (no heat in Moscow before October 15) dissipated the warmth of good food, liquor, and cordiality. I woke and began to brood over Harriman's remarks and reactions. In delayed and sour reaction, I wondered if the ambassador had been trying, with diplomatic delicacy, to brief us on a new United States foreign policy, of the kind that was to go with Truman and the bomb. Harriman had given such briefings before—notably to a select group of American publishers at the United Nations Conference in San Francisco as early as April, a few weeks after Roosevelt's death.

By the time of the London World Trade Union Conference, February 6-17, 1945, Sidney Hillman had emerged as key man for world labor unity. He was delayed four days in arriving. Before he came, the conference stickled and bickered, due largely to left-right differences.

As in world power, so in labor, an American-Soviet-British Big Three predominated. While Roosevelt, Stalin, and Churchill met at Yalta, their labor counterparts in London were Hillman, Vasili Kuznetsov, and Sir Walter Citrine. Kuznetsov and his colleagues were eager for unity and not disposed to be difficult. But the Soviet trade unions, with 27 million members, loomed so large numerically, and leftwing influence was so strong in other labor movements, that Sir Walter and other rightwingers suspected communist designs in everything. The first dispute was over admitting the largely left-led unions of some liberated or ex-enemy countries.

After Hillman arrived and got busy, the atmosphere changed. His first speech was inspirational—not in rhetoric but in its urgent demand for unity and in its practical proposals to make unity possible. Behind the scenes too, Hillman worked to allay the fears of British and other rights; to make them understandable to the Soviets and the left; to get concessions from both sides, and to compromise or sidetrack sticky problems.

Hillman was in bad health, he needed rest in a warm climate; his family had urged him not to go to London. He insisted on going, though it might shorten his life, because of the importance he ascribed to this project. This spirit of his made itself felt in London and in Paris. Hillman gave the job all he had— brains, experience, prestige, realism, diplomacy, drive—most of all, heart.

Murray had started things and headed the negotiations and planning in the United States. He could well claim to have fathered WFTU. But when the infant was delivered, he wasn't around and had to let Hillman pass out the cigars. Murray didn't like Hillman running away with this show, as he'd done with PAC. He thought it all wrong when (and if) Roosevelt said "Clear it with Sidney" instead of "Clear it with Phil." But his base was in union leadership of Steel and CIO, and when their big struggles loomed, Murray wasn't going to head for foreign parts as Hillman was free to do. Murray tried to keep his hand on things through appointees. He named R.J. Thomas to head the CIO delegation to London; and eager beaver Jim Carey was ever ready to step in. But when Hillman showed up, there was just no one else in his class.

Murray's heart, however, was less in WFTU than was Hillman's. He was sensitive to jeers from the redbaiting right; and from the never-to-be-forgotten John L. Lewis—who summed up his attitude in a six-word cable: "Mineworkers will not participate—John Lewis." Murray was formally loyal to WFTU through its formation. But his first appointments—including the rigidly sectarian antileftist Adolph Germer and the latter-day anticommunist John Brophy—showed more suspicion of the left than unity spirit.

The conventions of Hillman's Amalgamated and Murray's Steelworkers in May 1946, at Atlantic City threw a sidelight on the two CIO leaders.

It was Hillman's last convention; he died two months later. Pale, weak, failing in health, he reminisced on his lifework. Ever the Roosevelt lieutenant, Hillman said his international labor policy had paralleled the governmental policy of FDR. It was a policy based on Big Three unity, but also "an independent American policy, neither pro-British nor pro-Russian."

With the defeat of Germany and Japan, Hillman explained, the United States, USSR, and Britain were the only nations with power to wage decisive modern warfare. For the sake of the United Nations and peace, Big Three unity was essential. "If today, a short year after the defeat of Hitler, it is possible for us even to contemplate war," he said, "it is because cracks have begun to appear in the war-born unity of the Big Three. And now is the time to stop these cracks from widening. We cannot afford to drift to a point where we have to take sides, because that would mean disaster. . . ."

With Hillman's words on my mind, I headed toward the Steelworkers' preconvention huddle. Harold J. Ruttenberg, Steel's research director, hailed me on the boardwalk. "You wouldn't like what's developing with us," he said. "You wouldn't like it at all. Things have changed a lot."

Harold didn't elaborate, and I didn't ask it. He was a Clinton Golden man in Steel—on the liberal side, as against the rightist Catholic command—but not so leftist as I. Anyhow I had an idea of what was cooking in Steel. It was an anticommunist mulligan, to feed the Cold Warriors. If that was what Harold meant, he was right—I didn't like it.

Golden resigned as Steel vice president shortly after the union's May 1946 convention. He gave reasons of health. Ruttenberg resigned soon after Golden. Whatever the underlying causes, redness was not at issue. Golden later worked on application of the Truman Doctrine in Greece. Ruttenberg became vice president of the Portsmouth Steel Corporation.

Hillman's "cracks" were appearing in CIO, right under Murray's nose. The "anticommunist" gases seeping from them didn't focus only on communists or communist sympathizers. Any wind might carry them far and wide, and even scrupulous antireds be among the first to choke on the fumes.

At WFTU's founding convention in Paris (September 25–October 8, 1945), the delegates divided in many ways—right and left, colonial and imperial, monied and moneyless, into geographical and political blocs.

Substantial and well-heeled were the American and British business-unionists—from unions with treasuries, contracts, steady dues income, accepted into the establishments of victorious and advanced countries. In the same club were delegates from Canada, Australia, New Zealand, other white-skinned British dominions. So, too, the Swedes and the Swiss, beneficiaries of their neutrality. Brother clubmen, if down in their luck due to Nazi invasion, were other Scandinavians and nordic Europeans —white, well-scrubbed, respectable, from normally ruling and prosperous countries.

French and Italians were more shaken up by the war, more radical, more communistic. The business-union men wondered how steady might be their per capita.

Momentarily the Soviet unionists—with millions of dues-paying members—stood well with the business-unionists. Their devastated country was a major victor, accepted by Churchill and Roosevelt as one of the Big Three.

Toward Poles, Hungarians, Rumanians, Bulgarians, Yugoslavs, Czechs, the Anglo-American outlook was more misty. They were reds in a less long-accepted fashion than the Soviets. The attitude was wait-and-see.

From colonial, semicolonial, and neocolonial countries, the delegates were dark-skinned, unprosperous, bitter. Expressing their anti-British sentiments with British accents were delegates from India, West Indies, British Guiana, Nigeria, Gold Coast, Cyprus, Gambia, Sierra Leone. They resented patronizing big brothers in the British Trades Union Congress.

The Latin Americans—from Brazil, Colombia, Cuba, Ecuador, Guatemala, Mexico, Panama, Puerto Rico, Uruguay—were anti-Yank, though distinguishing between the grossly imperialist AFL and a CIO which still showed good intentions.

The Chinese—with a union federation in newly liberated north China only in process of formation—were reserved. Polite, dapper, socially correct, they spoke English well, if they spoke to others at all. They were more tightlipped than the Soviet dele-

gates, who followed their line with discipline (being "organizational" or "loyal" we called it in American labor, and I was used
to it; the British too hewed to their line, if Sir Walter was watching) but who also spoke up for it and could be quite chatty, if
not so gossipy as some eastern European reds.

All told, there were around 350 delegates, alternates, and
observers, representing 66,760,000 union members in 56 countries. Only major absentees were the Germans and Japanese, not
yet rehabilitated in world labor esteem; and the AFL, invited
but unwilling to attend.

A British-Nordic bloc was the convention's rightwing. It
didn't include Britain's more independent white dominions or
her dark-skinned colonies, but did have the remnants of the
IFTU, of which Sir Walter was president and chief provider.
Once known as the Amsterdam International, the IFTU had
fought the European social-democratic battle against the Red
International of Labor Unions; it rallied the unions of Scandina-
via, Netherlands, Belgium, Switzerland, Austria, Luxemburg.
This was not a western European bloc in the later Cold War
sense of dividing west from east. The French and Italian trade
union movements were well to the left.

The left bloc of WFTU was Soviet-led no more
monolithically than the right bloc was British-led. Its strongest
contingent was the Soviet unions, with their eastern European
allies. But its most aggressive lefts were from capitalist countries
and the colonial world. Latin American, Asian, African, delegates usually aligned themselves with the WFTU left.

Between these two blocs CIO became the center, with ties to
each but tied to neither. Hillman was the honest broker, the
matchmaker, between east and west, between right and left—
and so the key man for unity.

In light of subsequent events, the so-called "colonial question" was gravely underestimated. The colonial delegates tried
to force it to the front with eloquence, venom, and much pre-
science. They were given their say with little rebuttal. One Dutch
union boss defended his imperial government on Indonesia, but
other empire-defenders were cagy. The convention applauded

the colonial delegates, passed some good resolutions, then got back to other business.

Some black delegates criticized Hillman for his handling of the colonial question. He doubtless played it too close to the British-Nordic (largely imperial) bloc, as he maneuvered to build a bridge between it and the Soviet-led bloc. This bridge-work Hillman made his main business. American rightwingers also had much in common with the British-Nordic bloc. The poor and struggling unions of colonial countries did not greatly impress the porkchopper who measured union importance by dependable dues income; and they were too "political" for his taste.

More attuned to the colonial liberation struggle were "the communists"—many of them communists, at that—who came down from the mountains, out of the forests, up from the underground of liberated countries in 1945. They were from the Resistance, people of pride and passion. They had been partisans, guerrillas, rebellious fighters against invading overlords—not just conscripts of their respective governments. The partisans of eastern Europe, the resisters of the west were akin to the Huks in the Philippines, the Japanese-fighting reds in China. They felt kinship with the forces of national liberation beginning to stir worldwide.

There were many of these people in and around the WFTU convention. They didn't want the postwar world to relapse into old ruts. Having driven out foreign oppressors, they wanted to settle accounts with domestic oppressors—with capitalists and collaborators now snuggling up to the Anglo-Americans as they'd done to the invaders. They were mostly—though not uniformly —of the left, enough for the quislings and their new dollar-pound sponsors to dub them collectively as "the communists."

Still, a bridge had to be built at Paris between labor's right and left banks for united world labor to march over. Hillman was its engineer. Leftwingers in the capitalistic west had to do much of the construction.

To Churchill, allied labor unity had been a war measure, and he soon lost interest. At the San Francisco U.N. meet, the British delegation—including Labor party but not union representation—joined with the United States to deny WFTU the advisory status favored by the USSR and France. The Clement Attlee Labor government, which followed Churchill in July 1945, was increasingly anti-Soviet and pro-United States; it didn't care for WFTU. Under it, the TUC later went along with Murray's turned-about CIO when it set out deliberately to wreck the whole project.

The British TUC initiated and promoted the WFTU plans under pressure from the ranks. Leftists led some big unions, and communist influence was stronger in the unions than at election polls. There was also a ground swell of sympathy for the Soviets. Soviet and British unions had long enjoyed fraternal relations, which the war made closer and warmer.

In the United States, Roosevelt was more enthusiastic than Churchill for closer ties between the Big Three. Hillman relied on this FDR attitude in promoting the WFTU. But he couldn't have done his job without a strong left wing in CIO. One third of the CIO delegation at both London and Paris were of the left. Just as Lewis had leftist Lee Pressman for close aide and adviser during the CIO uprising, so Hillman had a man of the left, John Abt, at his side throughout his leadership for world labor unity.

To me, the launching of WFTU was the highpoint of Sidney Hillman's high-soaring career. Its unity didn't last. The Cold War blasted this and more of humanity's highest hopes. But it offered lasting evidence of what world labor is capable of doing for peace.

Hillman boasted of being the follower of Roosevelt. At times he was ahead of a President who didn't understand labor, who had no concept of the role of the working class, and who might have been disturbed if he had.

Roosevelt died in a blaze of glory, not as commander of victorious forces in the world's biggest war, but as prophet with a vision of uniting mankind for peace. The blaze had died down, when Hillman too died the next year. While the embers still glowed, others doused them with cold water, but Hillman tried to fan them into flames. More than the fan of FDR, he started some fire of his own, within the working class.

I didn't particularly admire either Roosevelt or Hillman through most of their careers. Each in his way was a captive of class forces I opposed. Yet both, in critical times, contributed something distinctive beyond the requirements and restrictions of their overall policies. Both prided themselves on being practical politicians. At times, in practice more than words, each created visions that raised the sights of much of mankind.

As a person, Hillman seemed to have trouble making peace with himself. It wasn't a matter of conscience, I'm sure. As a clergyman's son, I know it is professionally possible, under all ordinary circumstances, to convince oneself of rectitude. Hillman could have been a rabbi.

Nor do I refer to the fact that Hillman was a worrywart, a bellyacher. He was highstrung; his chords ranged from high exhilaration to deep depression. He was nervous, tense, eager, restless, scheming, purposeful—best adjusted when grappling with matter-of-fact political problems.

Into this busy, practical person, into this active, resourceful mind, an alien element could intrude. Call it emotion. Idealism, vision, mysticism were evasive words applied to Hillman—the last with singular ineptitude. Whatever it was, it didn't fit into the computer-type innards of a practical labor politician.

Sometimes all Hillman's elements worked in unison. He could be "high"—exhilarated, intoxicated, not by the alcohol he didn't need but by some inner harmony. I saw moments like that in early CIO, again in PAC and at Paris. I doubt he had any when he led the redbaiting right in CIO against Lewis and the left. Then he looked disturbed, not at peace with himself.

Though Hillman rejected Marxism, some of his activities were hard to think of in other than class terms. This contradiction didn't worry Hillman. He was not theoretical, he said— finding this a convenient excuse for opportunism. Yet the concept of a working class with a historical role was not to be altogether excluded from a mind as subtle as Hillman's, given his background, his associations, and his lifework.

Hillman seemed most troubled when under criticism from the left for not being on the working-class side. But perhaps the

point is better made positively. Hillman seemed most exhilarated and self-confident when he was most clearly mobilizing and
uniting the workers for advance.

Paris was such an occasion. At high level, a world level, Hillman exerted his talents to the full for a great purpose in keeping
with his service to FDR, his social-welfare concepts, his labor
loyalty, his practical politics—and for a big step forward by the
world's working class.

I didn't get along too well with Hillman. He had reservations about my leftism—as I about his antileftism. Hillman was
also too nervous for my taste, inclined to be picky and irritable.
We didn't mix much socially. Yet the moment I chose for a
personal goodby was a social one.

The WFTU convention was about over. I stepped out of
the Grand Hotel one morning, to see Hillman across the street
waving to me. He asked me to join him for breakfast. His wave,
his greeting, his invitation were easy and relaxed. Unusual for
Hillman. For once I didn't wonder: what's his purpose, what's
his gripe, what does he have in mind?

There wasn't a thing on his mind. We just grabbed a bite
and chatted together. He had done his WFTU job, I thought.
He's relieved to have things tucked away. He's pleased with a
good job well done.

Then I stole a glance at the sharp eyes behind the glasses
and above the sharp nose. Sidney Hillman was at peace with
himself.

Chapter Eighteen

COLD WAR

Anticommunist formula for CIO vivisection.

When, in June 1947, Philip Murray asked me to resign as CIO editor and publicity chief, he would explain no
more than that he was "not satisfied." I became impatient and
asked why he didn't come right out and say I was too red for
him. "No, no, no," he said, shaking his head. "I'm not concerned
with a man's thoughts or beliefs."

Murray's words echoed his turning-point, antired edict at
the May 1946 Steel convention. "This union will not tolerate
efforts by outsiders—individuals, organizations, or groups—
whether they be communist, socialist, or any other group, to
infiltrate, dictate, or meddle in our affairs," it declared, and then
resoundingly averred: "As a democratic institution, we engage in
no purges, no witch hunts. We do not dictate a man's thoughts
or beliefs."

After March 1946, when Churchill and Truman (at Fulton) turned Big Three unity into a two-against-one, anti-Soviet
gang-up, and after Truman and Congress had shown in big
strikes they'd take no nonsense from labor, union leaders knew
the reins had been jerked and the whip had been cracked. It was
either pull hard as bidden, or kick over the traces.

For AFL leaders the choice was easy. Anticommunism had
long been their pet gimmick against rank-and-file revolt and
against CIO. Now it was national policy. It meant endless, job-
creating war preparations against the everlasting menace of communism.

For CIO leaders it was harder. They were committed to the
Roosevelt postwar policies and to world labor unity. To preserve
CIO unity, Murray, like Lewis before him, had tried to steer a

little to the left of center. In domestic affairs this worked well. It was easy to be to the left of the AFL; the workers applauded, and right as well as left unions benefited. But foreign policy was troublesome; it had been at the root of the Lewis split-away. With the obedient "patriotism" inculcated by schools and mass media, most CIOers followed government decision in foreign affairs. When the left diverged too sharply, it was in trouble, and unity came hard.

In the immediate postwar euphoria, CIO held together behind the Murray-Hillman line of Big Three unity, world labor unity, inner CIO unity. Murray now had to break it up. He wanted to do so gradually, without at once splitting CIO wide open. He found his formula from within his own Steelworkers.

Steel took after its founder. Lewis had to fight long to make over UMW in his image. Hillman and ACW grew together through its and his lifetime. Murray was handed SWOC like a platterful of modeling clay.

The Murray image was Catholic, conventional, conformist. So was his Steel setup, despite some early concessions to Lewis and minoritics. The Murray men were always the McDonalds, the Sweeneys, not the Goldens or Ruttenbergs, and still less the reds hired for initial organizing. Murray men—Catholic and conservative—held the key jobs and set the pattern, into which solid citizens of other faiths were also free to fit.

At the wheel of his machine, Murray could drive as he chose, provided he stuck to the road and didn't upset the machine. He could veer to right or left, or hug the center of the road. He could go into neutral and let his machine coast—as he did in the 1945-46 winter. Ostensibly unpowered by Murray, the Steel machine began getting locals to pass resolutions to deny communists the right to elective or appointive office, sometimes even to membership.

This campaign had a novel wrinkle; it was directed against "socialists," too. Most Murray men privately sneered at "pinkos" like Hillman and Reuther and their "socialist" followers, but there were other reasons. In CIO the communists, chief opponents of the Cold War line, still had influence which Murray recognized. With "socialists" added to the maledictions, it could be claimed they didn't damn communists as such, but as one example of "meddlers." There were also traces of a more subtle ploy.

In Auto, anticommunist redbaiting originated not only from the ACTU and an extreme right, but also from ex-socialists like Reuther and his associates—some still in the Socialist party. Some opportunists on the left, reluctant to defend communists as such, thought it smart to retort to communist-ban proposals: "Okay, let's also include socialists then; they interfere in the union as much as the communists." In UAW—before communists were denied elective rights under the 1940-41 "communazi" formula—this ploy might have deterred some pinkos who didn't want to proscribe themselves. In Steel, the Murray men were happy to include "socialists."

I said Murray let his machine coast, in deference to the fact that at Steel's 1946 convention he didn't favor adoption of the bans. But his machine had some guidance—from the Association of Catholic Trade Unionists.

After my severance from CIO, articles on ACTU machinations began to appear in the liberal press, and some people ascribed them to me. They were wrong. Though remote from ACTU's antired infighting all through the field, I had my own reasons to be aware of its promptings—as in the cited case of Harry Read, and in maneuvers from Pittsburgh to bypass me and send ACTU editors into areas of right-left conflict. But at the same time I had scruples on the subject.

By the all's-fair standard of American factional war, it might have seemed fair enough to retort to ACTU redbaiting of CIO's left with some comparable ACTU-baiting. ACTU claimed to copy the tactics of communists, the better to offset them; it too could be charged with "outside interference," if either group could. But the left had to fight ACTU with one hand tied behind its back. It didn't want, and couldn't afford, to antagonize a numerous Catholic rank and file. It avoided the you-too type of reply.

I knew enough about "the communists" in CIO to know how often the right was wrong in its charges. I knew far less about ACTU operations, and less again about how the many-faceted Catholic church related to a one-purpose outfit like ACTU. In CIO, most leftwingers were not communists, most Catholics were not ACTUers, and many lefts were practicing Catholics. I didn't want to Catholic-bait any more than to redbait.

However inspired, the antired resolutions were a suggestive gift for Murray when the Steelworkers gathered in Atlantic City in May 1946. He could point to the "growing demand" for a purge of the left; and in resisting it, stand out as champion of moderation and unity. To the CIO left, Murray could say: "I'm your friend, but the pressure is so great you must agree to——" To the right: "Look, boys, I'm with you. But take it easy and we'll take it. Easy does it."

Coming after press predictions of wholesale antired purges in Steel and CIO, the Murray statement adopted by the convention served to tranquilize the left. It was also a first step in Murray's gradualistic approach to a complete purge.

Stressing "no purges, no witch hunts," the left hailed Murray as champion of CIO unity. It slithered over the warning to communists and socialists, noting that it too opposed outside interference. The right needed no tranquilizer; it was close enough to Murray to know the score. It interpreted the key anti-communist-socialist sentence as declaring war on the CIO left. Declared or undeclared, the war was on anyhow.

Murray was a canny man, who tried to plan ahead. A case might be made, in hindsight, for his having schemed the step-by-step progression to CIO's finally complete about-face against its radicals. Yet characteristically Murray impressed me less as a schemer than as a torn man.

In September 1946, Murray's impulses betrayed him. At the Conference of Progressives in Chicago, he blurted out emotionally that labor "wants no damn communists meddling in our affairs," and disturbed his liberal friends by some of his foreign policy remarks. A few—including Henry Morgenthau, Jr., Senator Claude Pepper, Elmer Benson (then head of the CIO-allied National Citizens Political Action Committee)—met with Murray for breakfast at the Stevens Hotel. Curtis D. MacDougall, in his book *Gideon's Army*, says Benson took Murray aside alone in a bedroom, to express alarm at rumors he might resign as CIO president. To quote this account:

"Beating his breast and actually tearing at his clothing, Murray wailed, 'You don't know what I've gone through! My soul had just been torn apart!' And he kept repeating the same words, so that there was no use in continuing the conversation."

Murray was a good man, in most senses of the word. He was able, conscientious, well-meaning, devoted in service to his God, his church, his country, and through labor, to his fellow man. When these services coincided, and all held him in high esteem, Murray was at his best. He was a gentleman, a scholar, a leader poised, human, kindly, gracious.

When his loyalties conflicted and he could not seem good to all—when "foul and filthy," "diabolical," aspersions were cast on him—Murray couldn't take it. He was torn. He endured, but could hardly hide, an agonizing inner tug-o'-war. I saw him go through several of these ordeals.

Murray was now torn between the Roosevelt foreign program—still officially CIO policy—and a Truman government hell-bent for Cold War. He was torn between his church and one-world liberals and radicals supposedly soft on "atheistic communism." He was torn between the rights and lefts of CIO.

A Lewis would have decided brusquely and without qualms. A Hillman might have agonized till he worked out a policy, then worried only about its success. Only a Murray could have tried so long to be all things to all men.

Subjectively, by his own standards, Murray deserves the credit he craved. Under great strain, he tried to serve two opposite sides pulling further apart. He tried to hunt with the red-baiters and protect their prey. He tried to suppress his own feelings and be the unity man. He tried to perform a major operation in easy stages, to maim rather than kill the patient.

It was a long-protracted delaying action. Murray must have felt enormous relief when he finally let himself go—in whole-hearted, wholesale, and ritual excommunication of CIO's left wing.

The CIO convention in November 1946 at Atlantic City pointedly strengthened Murray's Steel formula. It declared: "We resent and reject efforts of the Communist party or other political parties and their adherents to interfere in the affairs of the CIO. This convention serves notice that we will not tolerate such interference." This time there was no assurance against purges and witch hunts; on the contrary, accompanying action foreshadowed them. The most Murray would say was that the declaration "should not be misconstrued to be a repressive measure," nor taken to mean "this organization is going to engage itself in diabolical pursuits."

To put teeth in the declaration, the executive board amended CIO rules governing Industrial Union Councils, to tighten control over these state and city bodies, requiring that they conform to "CIO policy" and not cooperate with "national organizations not recognized by the CIO."

A committee on which rights and lefts were equally represented took three days to work out the 1946 CIO declaration. The executive board and then the convention adopted it unanimously. As with the 1940 "antitotalitarian" resolution, rightwingers crowed at the spectacle of communists and leftwingers helping prepare and support an anticommunist declaration.

There was some method in the meekness of the lefts. They had to retreat under conditions that threatened a rout. To preserve the unity of a still relatively progressive CIO, they continued to make concessions as they had done since CIO began. They valued their CIO status for themselves and their unions. One thing was certain. The lefts didn't "start anything." All aggression came from the right. The lefts conceded, compromised, even turned around. To break up unity, the right had to do it.

The national CIO office at once began using the 1946 package to move in on left-led Councils. If it couldn't aid the rightwing faction to take over by ostensibly democratic means, it could overrule the majority, suspend the Council, have an administrator appointed.

In the matter of "national organizations not recognized by the CIO," the national office paralleled Attorney-General Tom

Clark's blacklist of allegedly "subversive" organizations promoting black and civil rights, opposing war and fascism, defending foreign-born and political prisoners. It made a small list of CIO-recognized organizations deemed pure of leftist taint—thus relegating all others to an unwritten blacklist.

This was shrewd strategy. The "anticommunist" campaign in which Murray now joined the Truman administration was directed against much more than the communists—against all opposition to the imperialist policy labeled Cold War, with its aggression abroad and its repression at home.

From the first CIO had cooperated with many united-front organizations—for black people, for youth and the unemployed, for libertarian purposes. It thus reached out beyond union limits and drew into cooperation with itself many other groups, inspiring and being in turn inspired by many fighters against oppression and reaction outside its ranks.

In making its Cold War switch, CIO now began to abandon these old associations on the pretext of avoiding communist contamination; and to confine itself to a narrow union regularity comparable to the old pure-and-simpledom of AFL. This forcibly imposed policy switch set the stage for the official labor insensitivity to issues like black liberation, the youth revolt, and the Vietnam war which so disgusted new lefts in the Sixties.

Murray opened his first antileft front in state and local Councils for several reasons. Councils dealt with broader political issues than might individual unions. Delegates elected to them were the more wide-awake and active unionists. Left influence was correspondingly great, and right-left conflict seldom absent. Moreover, national CIO had more authority to move in on Councils than unions, though it found pretexts to do this, too, in the case of Mine-Mill, Farm Equipment and, less directly, some other unions.

In my CIO offices was a United Press news ticker which attracted outsiders during sports events. On March 12, 1947, on my way out to lunch, I brushed by two teen-age office boys absorbed in an incoming news story.

"Gee!"

"Whaddya know! This is it!"

"Looks like the end for the lefties."

"Just ain't gonna be the same old CIO."

My reaction was delayed; I had other things on my mind. By the time I reached the elevator, the boys had gone. I turned back to see what excited them. The ticker was on an extra take of the same long news story. President Truman had decided to intervene in the Greek civil war, in place of the British. He was asking Congress for military, economic, and personnel aid to Greece and Turkey as an anticommunist measure. The Truman Doctrine, as it came to be known, following the Fulton Cold War declaration in 1946, spelled out the growing United States imperialist engagement worldwide.

I wasn't as quick as the boys to see the CIO connection. I had to think things over. To them, as to most Americans, a major government decision on war or peace meant that everything, including CIO, must fall into line. The United States and USSR had been allies. Soviet union leaders had been guests of CIO, had gone around arm-in-arm with Murray and Carey. Now the United States was shaking an armed fist at the commies in Greece, and Russia. So now Murray and Carey too would get brass-knuckled—with the CIO lefties. That, I figured, must have been the boys' reasoning. They were right.

Added to the Truman Doctrine, another new doctrine brought things even closer home to CIO. It took shape in the Taft-Hartley act, which was in effect a domestic counterpart to the new foreign policy.

Abrogating the Wagner act, which had aided labor's advance since the start of CIO, the Taft-Hartley act restricted unions in organizing, plant elections, strikes, political action. By requiring union representatives to sign noncommunist affidavits, it denied the workers' right to elect officers of their own choosing. Truman, who had proposed more drastic antiunion measures himself, had to veto the Taft-Hartley act to preserve any standing with labor leaders, but it was at once passed over his veto.

Among those who resigned in protest from the labor board

staff was Heber Blankenhorn, a pioneer champion of labor rights. A supporter of Taft-Hartley had said it would "instill in American unions a spirit of fidelity to America." Not the "spirit of fidelity," said Blankenhorn, but "the spirit of Fido, who must learn to lie down, roll over, and play dead, at the snap of a finger." After much yapping at this "slave labor act," most CIO and AFL leaders got the spirit; they lay down and rolled over.

Less given to coming to heel, John L. Lewis proposed to the AFL, with which he was for the moment accoupled, a course of legal defiance. If all union leaders refused to sign the noncommunist affidavits, he said, they could render the act inoperative. The 1947 AFL convention rejected the suggestion, and Lewis soon after uncoupled the UMW from the AFL.

To Lewis, communism was not the issue. He just seized on a weak spot in the act to resist it. Still there may have been more than irony in the way the "communist issue" haunted the career of America's most aggressive and original nonradical labor leader. Lewis used anticommunism to batter down opposition in UMW, then abandoned it when he started CIO. It was a major weapon of CIO's enemies. Within CIO, it supplied the chief catch-cries against Lewis and his supporters when he defied Roosevelt in the prewar years. When in 1941 the CIO left parted with Lewis over his negative attitude toward the Soviet alliance, he could again curse "communism," if rather tiredly by now. By 1947 Lewis must have been pretty sick of the subject from every angle. Yet it had to be a "communist issue" on which his good judgment picked for one of his last big labor fights.

Whether or not Lewis realized it, the noncommunist affidavits were more than a gimmick to snag the Taft-Hartley act. They were, in a broad sense, the key to labor's submission to the act. The seemingly stupid affidavit clause—later overridden in the Landrum-Griffin act—gave Taft-Hartley an anticommunist aura and betrayed its link with the Cold War foreign policy. It was also a useful tool for rightwing union factions.

Rightwing union leaders disliked many Taft-Hartley restrictions but learned to live with them. What they liked was the act's anticommunism. The affidavits helped them to squelch inner-union opposition and to raid leftwing unions—as they did increasingly even before these unions were ousted from CIO. In Textile, Auto, Wood, Utility, and other unions, ruling right-wingers used the noncommunist affidavits to dispose of remaining leftwing pockets. They secured a vote to comply with Taft-Hartley and sign the affidavits. Then—in conformity with union policy, they could now say—they removed from office those officers who could not, or would not, sign them.

The Mine Workers and the Typos (traditionally hard-nosed about their union's rights) stood out against Taft-Hartley, refusing to sign the affidavits. But CIO was no more willing than AFL to adopt the tactic advocated by Lewis. Murray, hating to be called chicken by Lewis, stood out for a while in Steel. The leftwing unions, chief victims, stood out as long as they could and then had to sign or be even worse ravished by raids. With the act's aid, CIO carried through its purge of the left. The spirit of Fido was to reign supreme over a reunited AFL-CIO.

Once Murray got down to business on his no-purge purge, it was natural I should be first of his immediate staff to go. There was a fetishism about the practice of anticommunism, itself a fetish. Lee Pressman and I were symbols of "communist influence" on Murray, as on Lewis before him.

At the start of CIO, Sidney Hillman's editor, J.B.S. Hardman, chuckled to me: "This is one movement they can't paint red. Why, with a leader like John L. Lewis, the paint just wouldn't stick." How wrong could one be! Long before fingering of communists in CIO became the vogue, the movement was called communist because of presumed association with "the communist New Deal" and "that communist in the White House"—and experts were judiciously red-painting Lewis himself.

Lewis himself seemed at first out of reach for Victor Riesel and his ilk. But listen here, said they, who should be at Lewis's side whispering leftism into his honest ears but Lee Pressman and Len De Caux! Once a gismo like that got started, it served a long time to bypass the doughty Lewis and the impeccable Murray in redbaiting CIO. This one served for twelve years, until

Murray symbolically disposed of it by removing the two symbolic conspirators from the proximity of his symbolically honest ears.

During the war, interest flagged in such minutiae. But by 1946, though not in my presence, reporters would pose the Pressman-De Caux question to Murray off the record like this, I heard:

"What are you going to do about the communists in CIO, Phil?"

"Now wait a moment, who says—"

"Aw, Phil . . . now look here. You know as well as I do . . . You yourself——"

"CIO won't stand for any communists meddling in its affairs. That's what I've said. But we're a democratic organization. We're setting our house in order in a democratic way."

"That's fine, Mr. Murray. But look here, Phil, you know what people are saying—that you listen to leftists or fellow travelers right in your own office."

"It's a filthy lie."

"Don't get hot, Phil. I didn't say it. I don't say I believe it. But you know what people say about Pressman and De Caux——"

I've mentioned how Martin Agronsky quizzed Murray about CIO communists in a cab, off the air, before the 1946 convention. By 1947, the heat was on Murray publicly, not just in cabs or off-the-record interviews. Once I escorted him to a Washington radio studio for an on-the-air interview by a panel of newsmen. They asked about communists in CIO. Murray was adroit under grilling and wasn't usually pursued when he evaded. But this time he was ill at ease and seemed particularly so when questioned on Pressman.

After the broadcast one of the newsmen, Blair Moody (later a United States senator), came up to Murray and apologized for pressing him on Pressman. He did it kiddingly, taking the arm of each of us in turn. "I had to do it, Phil," he said. "No offense intended. It's what everyone is saying anyhow. It livens things up. I really think a lot of Lee. For that matter, I could have questioned you about my friend Len here in the same way

——" He nudged me and winked in friendly fashion at us both.

Murray's face was like a thundercloud as we walked out. I was glad to escape without having to escort him back to his hotel.

Pressman was more obviously under fire than I. But Murray needed his wits, experience, and expertise to cope with new problems presented by the Taft-Hartley act. Murray also preferred a roundabout, gradualistic approach. Not till a half year later did Pressman follow me into exile.

Murray had his session with me right after final passage of the Taft-Hartley act—even postponed it until the result was known. Maybe he connected his decision to start purging with this event. He was a cautious man, could have had a lingering smidgeon of doubt which way the cat might finally jump. It was well over the right side of the fence. But cats are agile creatures. Conceivably it could turn around to the left side. After Congress voted to override the veto (331-83 in House, 68-25 in Senate), the cat had already jumped.

For me it was the end of the line. For thirty years I had been on a single track, with all my interests in the labor movement—my occupation, married life, social life, political life—and CIO the biggest part.

An unattached individual—still wobbly without the organizational crutches I'd become used to—I visited the 1947 CIO convention in Boston. Harry Bridges hailed me: "I don't blame you for getting out, Len. If anything, you should have done it earlier." The way CIO was going, I wouldn't have wanted to stay on. That was for sure. I couldn't even imagine the revival in my lifetime of the kind of movement it had been.

Of some subsequent loss of morale I must plead guilty. In painful years to come, myself-when-young would not have sought cover but might proudly have defied the Cold Warriors, "So I'm a communist—so make the most of it, you bastards!" Myself-when-middle-aged did not. In self-defense, I must offer personal testimony on the temper of times which in the relative freedom of the Sixties it is hard even to recall.

Elsewhere, persecution might drive reds to the hills to become guerrillas, or to the underground to join the resistance. In the United States, summer resorts drew folks to the hills, and there was then more retreat than resistance.

I joined in the retreat from Washington—the exodus of liberals and lefts that began in 1946, after Truman replaced a long-disemboweled New Deal with a Cold War administration. The Murray purge was little CIO brother to Truman's "loyalty" purge of federal employees. The company was not inspiring—people worrying about family future, political persecution, where the next paycheck was coming from, feeling they must look out for themselves. No joy of battle, no hope or plans for a comeback.

In my field of labor writing, the lines were sharply drawn between right and left. By now only leftwing unions would accept me, and some of these were still watching their step with Murray. In any case, I didn't want to compete with others needier than myself for the left's dwindling jobs.

I considered freelancing. From me, publications with money to pay wanted only redbaiting or other dirt on CIO, or demanded I "clear myself" in the current confessional style of I-was-a-red-but-the-reds-done-me-wrong. Some friends thought I might find semineutral ground in some fringe angles on labor. I could find none that, developed by me, would not be marketable chiefly for antilabor or antileft implications. Interest in union health and welfare plans, for instance, was chiefly to offset "socialized medicine."

I thought the *New Republic* might be hospitable, since Henry Wallace had become its editor after Truman fired him for opposing the Cold War. I had a pleasant wine-dine with an editorial factotum, who wanted to commission some articles and bade me come to his office in the morning. In the reception room, I ran into Publisher Michael Straight. We knew each other. While waiting, through the glass partitions I saw Straight sitting across the desk from my operating-editor and gesturing emphatically. What Mike said I didn't know. I did know he was leery of lefties. There was little more interest in articles from me.

Such little incidents—or imagined incidents—meant nothing in themselves. Their repetition produced a rather crushing cumulative effect. In the next ten years, there were more repetitions than I care to remember.

After the House Un-American Activities Committee "exposed" me in 1953, nothing was left to the imagination. I was fired and blacklisted like this:

Boss: "I've nothing against you myself. You do your job well and I'd like to keep you. But after this publicity, customers are calling in. The salesmen won't even let me wait till the big boss gets back. Sorry."

Employment Agent: "You've put me on a hell of a spot. When I sent you to that job, I'd no idea you were anything but a good American. But now——"

Another Boss: "Sorry, now this has come up, I can't hire you like I said I would. We could use you, all right. The big boss said okay, if the FBI would clear you. I called the FBI. They say they never confirm or deny such charges. But look here—maybe —I tell you what. If you can bring us written proof you're not a communist, we might still hire you."

All this was open enough. You could even put up an argument, for all the good that did. But you couldn't land a job— without leaving town, using a phony name, going somewhere you couldn't be checked on.

Of course, there were first-come labor jobs where one didn't expect to be screened for dangerous thoughts. One could be wrong, however. One bleak jobless winter in Chicago in the Fifties, I thought to make a few bucks handling mailbags during the Christmas rush. I was asked to fill out a form denying all conceivable radical associations. I didn't want to risk a perjury rap.

The open stuff could stimulate more than demoralize. So you were a red, you could be red-blooded about it. What got under the skin, to rot the fiber, was all the stuff that was nothing much, nothing you could pin down, nothing you had a right to kick about.

I look up an old friend and sympathizer, now in a Madison Avenue job. I make sure to phone him first. "Ye-e-ess, you can come up to my office." By the time I'm out of the elevator, he's out in the corridor waiting for me. Afraid to be seen with me in his office? Afraid we might be overheard? He doesn't ask me in.

Runs back for his hat. "Let's go out for a drink." Over drinks my friend expands. Now if I can wangle a recommendation from Phil Murray, or Walter Reuther. . . . No? Well, cover up somehow . . . maybe change my name . . . something can be done. But, good Lord, he'd have to keep out of it himself. My friend's a good guy. I don't blame him at all.

Another friend welcomes me into his office. He's frank he can't help me to a job. While talking, I drop the name of a man he once worked for. Not a red, not even very pink, but once had left support. My friend's eyes pop with alarm. He looks over his shoulder to see if anyone heard. As I sidle out, I feel like holding my hat over my face—to protect him.

A generation of good guys from my field, or surrounding meadows, on the run for their livelihoods or holed up where they hope the running-dogs of the right won't sniff them out.

A different group. Well-wishing liberals, less exposed, more influential. Their own bosses maybe. I avoid the Straight kind of antileft liberals. But So-and-So is "100 percent okay, even gave a job to——" So-and-So is cordial. Knows me by repute, sympathizes, agrees with me. I'd fit in well. Come back next week. . . . I come back. So-and-So is out of town. Said to look in when he returns. I look in. So-and-So's tied up, something came up—why don't I give him a buzz next week. I do. His secretary answers the next buzz, too—doesn't suggest a third. I get the message—or think I do.

So-and-So's a good guy. So is Such-and-Such. And Whosis, and—— Likely none can make a job—busy men, too, tied up like their secretaries say. But after the fourth runaround, one starts to get touchy. Not that one doubts they're good guys. Probably just getting by themselves, and don't want to rock a boat that's already listing too much to the left.

Whosis thinks of referring me to someone else, mentions Blowsis in his business club. Talks a progressive blue streak does Blowsis, but can you count on him? Doesn't know what he's talking about half the time. Whosis hesitates, mumbles a negative "Nnh-Nnh." By now one mindreads the "Nnh-Nnh" to mean, "And what would Blowsis think of Whosis for referring to him an identified—oh, well, an alleged—what's the difference?"

I've jumped ahead of myself. When I left CIO in 1947, I didn't have to latch onto another job at once. I had savings, severance, unemployment pay. I wandered off. Like a zombie, I showed up at conventions. At UE, the left kept its head above water, while a riptide sucked at its feet. At CIO, a supposed right-left compromise on foreign policy. "A fine resolution," quipped Resolutions Chairman Van A. Bittner, "no one knows what the hell it means." Once passed, Murray used it to club the left, claiming it endorsed the Marshall Plan and administration foreign policy. At UAW, Reuther mounted the driver's seat of a Cold-War steamroller, heading for total control of a once-uncontrolled union. I decided to wander further afield.

It was more than twenty years since I'd worked at the point of production—two decades of writing and talking about "labor," spent mostly with union officials. I was curious, as in youth, about the men and women embodied in the abstraction. How did work in a CIO-organized plant compare with before CIO? How did unionists think, feel, act, in their daily lives?

I also wanted to play truant. Once I'd hoboed 15,000 miles over the continent, coming close to the American people in middling and small towns, in camps and farms, on deserts, prairies, mountainsides. I'd had to pass up much I wanted to explore. In official labor service, I traveled the continent many times more—rushing from city to city by overnight Pullman, by plane, catching tantalizing glimpses I couldn't follow up.

Some day, I'd told myself, I'd start off in my car, with time to spare, to look into the nooks and crannies of America, to visit the American worker at home. That day had come. I had time, some money, no job, no boss. I started off.

AFTER ALL

Chapter Nineteen

FIELD TRIP

From the 1947 CIO convention at Boston, it was good to get away. 1937 at Atlantic City was the honeymoon of radical youth wed to still vigorous experience. 1947 at Boston was sour with approaching divorce. For a dozen years I had known the few score union leaders and their few hundred lieutenants who made up this convention. They had grown stouter, balder, grayer, but were still younger than an AFL convention— 30-40-50ish rather than 50-60-70ish. Business-union success, rather than age, had changed CIO. Some of the flaming young men of 1936-37 had become, or been pushed aside by, pallid administrators. Hardfaced labor politicians were forging to the front. A sign of new times was gangsterism, for the first time at a national CIO convention. It came from Steel.

Steel had once been as middle-of-the-road as Murray himself. By 1947 there had been some changes made. District leaders once lords in their fiefs by grant and grace of Good King Phil and Bonnie Prince David had learned to take care of themselves. Some hardfisted machine-men had risen in war on the left, and the Cold War now assured their rule. Mostly Catholics, they found in ACTU the doctrinal oil for their steely machines. At the Boston convention, the Steel delegates and their hangers-on were the shock troops of the right. Raucous and intolerant, they led the antileft demonstrations, whooping it up for Jimmy Carey, and really letting themselves go for Joe Curran—new hero of the antireds for his recent about-face.

There had been some rough stuff before at CIO doings, as when UE's Ernest De Maio was beaten up on the platform of the Illinois CIO convention, and goons, prostitutes, and liquor were freely used to "do a job on the reds." But it was a first of a kind when five Steel toughies went into public action at a national CIO convention. Reportedly led by William Hart, Steel director and ACTU chairman in the Pittsburgh district, they slugged Clifford Crozier, *Daily Worker* salesman, in front of the Bradford Hotel.

Crozier, a shipyard worker and former Canadian commando, was wearing a ring presented by President John Green of the Marine & Shipbuilding union to honor him as ace volunteer organizer for the union. Two of the Steel men pinned Crozier's arms behind him. Two others slugged him, then knocked him down and kicked him. The fifth tore up his papers. Murray had publicly to rap some knuckles he didn't publicly identify.

It was good to get away, to climb into my aging Buick and take to the road. I started by exploring some 30 industrial cities in New England, meeting workers in their homes and unions. New people in new places every day.

The fall foliage was gorgeous—with red not excluded from its many colors. The air had a sharp zip. The rocky coastline was grimly enchanting. Mountains, forests, lakes—New England had everything. Surprises too. To cross the White Mountains, the valleys, lakes, and meadows of tourist New Hampshire, and suddenly come upon a straight-up industrial city like Berlin, its streets thronged with shop workers from chemical, paper, and other plants. To find District 50, UMW—stepchild of John L. Lewis—the one big union in town. To visit lifelong residents who talked knowingly of the labor movement here and abroad. To learn that Berlin (N.H.) had a Labor party in the Depression that elected a mayor, four aldermen, state legislators, and ran a candidate for governor.

I must have enjoyed my explorations. I kept them up for months—after New England, starting out afresh from east to west with zigzags down the center. Yet after the trip I stashed away my notes until the Sixties, recalling only a mood that was bleak and sour. In this fall and winter of 1947-48, CIO's left wing was in retreat and might barely, if at all, survive. Hence my gloom. My emotions balked at what my mind told me must be. But there was still enough of the old CIO spirit to show how the movement had been, still was in parts, and might hopefully be again. And when I finally faced up to my notes, I found the hundreds of persons I talked with telling of some things more lasting than CIO's Cold-War politics.

After New England, I started out again late in November 1947 through upper New York state, Buffalo, Detroit, Chicago, backtracking through many cities of Ohio and Indiana to Cincinnati, Louisville, St. Louis—thence through Texas and on to Arizona. When recalled east in April 1948 for the Henry Wallace campaign, I circled back through California and over a northern route. By Arizona I had added another 70 cities to the 30 visited in New England, and had notes on some 400 persons interviewed.

More exciting than the big cities I largely knew were the middling cities that were new to me. In them—in homes, eating places, union offices, shops, clubs, meeting halls—I found an easier intimacy than in any big city. My CIO-known name was usually introduction enough, and I was often asked home to eat and stay overnight. I liked this best, because my hosts let themselves go at home, and I met their wives. Next best was socializing after union meetings or at union clubs; the "quick one" that loosened tongues; long lunches or suppers when a man relaxed over coffee and unburdened himself to a sympathetic stranger.

Visits to union offices were not necessarily stiff. Most CIOers accepted me as one of themselves. AFL people might be more formal, though some felt safer in talking progressive with me than with their local brothers.

I visited conservative as well as radical unionists, AFL and rail brotherhood as well as CIO, but found the conventional union types much duller than the battling lefts. The former were familiar from long before CIO and survived into the AFL-CIO of the Sixties. There was so much coverup about communists in the unions, for various pressing reasons, that I was particularly curious about open communists and how they fitted in.

It was still possible in many cities to look under "C" in the local phone book and find the Communist party. In this way I contacted a score of party functionaries. They were typically quiet, serious, rather intellectual, though stressing some worker background. In most places, however, local party leaders were not found in offices; they were union activists working in the plants. They might be union organizers dropped for being too red, or otherwise so "exposed" as to be pretty open. A few judicious inquiries would identify them, and when contacted at home, they were open about their party role.

It was hard even to recall old stereotypes of the "wild-eyed red." The red agitators of the Depression were now likely to be leaders in union or other mass work and to lead demonstrative activities as such; while the party functionary was being forced by the Cold War further and further back from the public eye. The communist leader who stood out before the workers as such was now relatively rare. I'll start with one.

Tom—well known as local communist leader—lived in a little frame house on the road between two textile mills outside a Massachusetts city. At change of shifts, workers from these mills regularly stopped off at his porch. They kept him better posted, he bragged, than were the union officials. Tom had worked in these plants himself while also "working part-time as spokesman for the Communist party."

With olive-black eyes, black hair, and prominent nose, Tom was of the Portuguese background common locally. Now in his middle thirties, he was born and raised in his city and had spent his working life in its mills. He was full of local pride. "Excuse me for talking so much about this place," he said, "but it's my home town." Tom had a typical worker's home—typical in the Forties. The family eked out a get-by living with the help of his wife's wages in a garment plant. Only picture on the living room walls was a full-page rotogravure of Franklin D. Roosevelt. There were books on the shelves, including solid books on labor subjects and the selections of the Book Find Club.

Tom's local pride was chiefly in his city's labor past. He spoke intimately of each strike and radical ruckus he'd taken part in; and almost as intimately of those his mother had told him about. Big Bill Haywood, Arturo Giovannitti, Elizabeth Gurley Flynn, were among his heroes.

When CIO launched its textile drive, Tom led in volunteer organizing locally, going from house to house to make converts and collect dues. The TWOC regional big shot came to his house to thank him. Their talk:

BIGSHOT: What do you do for a living?

TOM: I work part-time as a textile worker, and part-time as spokesman of the Communist party.

B: That's too bad.

T: You mean, that I work part-time?

B: That you're tied in with the party. Do you *have* to be a communist?

T: Yes, that's what I believe in. It's basic to my whole attitude——

B: Couldn't you keep quiet about it—not let people know you're a communist?

T: No.

Then, Tom said, he got after the union big shot himself. Why was he in the labor movement? For money? If he believed in it, what did he believe? That it was enough to sell workers collectively to the capitalists for a few more dollars and a few reforms? Why did he oppose those who wanted to abolish the whole system of wage exploitation?

B: I see we can't agree. But you're doing fine work for the union. Can we count on you to keep it up, and to cooperate with us?

T: That depends on you more than on me. It depends on what the workers want and if you serve their interests.

By now, ten years later, Tom was not disposed to cooperate with the Emil Rieve leadership of the CIO Textile Workers. He accused it of selling out, to wit: Increasing the workload in return for maintenance of membership; opposing wage-increase demands; accepting wage cuts in many guises; breaking or heading off strikes; not resisting speedup. It fought all rank-and-file militancy with redbaiting, he said. A recent example:

A local textile company increased the workload so as to lay off many workers. A departmental strike followed, which idled other departments. Rieve and his regional director backed up the company. They outlawed the strike, insisted on the speedup, disciplined all objectors, and had a number fired. With the workers in revolt, the TWU district leaders brought the Taft-Hartley law to bear. They sent special-delivery registered letters to every shop steward, local officer, executive, and joint-board member, demanding that each sign the noncommunist affidavit. Outraged at this use of the act, beyond its actual requirements, many said they wouldn't sign. A delegation of 40 went to Rieve to protest. He refused to see them. George Baldanzi, his fellow officer and rival, passed the buck back to Rieve.

Tom was a vigorous man of action and practical politics. Some 5,000 votes, when he ran for some local office, bore witness to his local influence. When I arrived at Tom's home, a delegation of local union leaders was leaving. "They're conservative union men, at the opposite pole from me," he said. "They told me they'd no use for my communism but agreed with me on labor matters."

What made workers communists? Some like Tom had a radical family tradition. Others dated their "conversion" to the Depression. Most I met cited more recent experiences in strikes and other union affairs.

Janet was chief steward in her department of a big Connecticut electrical plant, until a rightwing faction took control of her local union. She was then one of a score expelled as "communists" and for "rioting" (when rightwing rowdies and police broke up a petition meeting).

Janet had started with no radical ideas, when she worked in a garment shop as a member of David Dubinsky's Ladies Garment Workers. Her local was run by an appointed business agent and appointed officers. To get more democracy, Janet agreed to run for delegate to the international union convention.

The poll was to open at noon. Janet was at the head of a line of members stretching down the stairs and into the street. When she entered the union hall, she found some strange men sitting around the ballot box. Thinking all was on the up and up, she said kiddingly that as first voter she should be shown the box was empty. But the men were "mean and tough," she said, and told her: "You're only a member like anyone else. Drop in your ballot and get to hell out." Arguing that as a candidate she had a right to see the box wasn't stuffed, Janet reached for it and saw it was full. Three of the men grabbed her, roughed her up, and threw her on the floor, where one stuck his knee in her stomach. They told her to get out or they'd call the cops. "Go ahead," said Janet.

The police came and carried the little woman out, one on each side holding her so high her feet didn't touch the stairs One cop asked her what it was all about. She told him. "You better go home, miss," he said. "You haven't a chance. Those men in there are in with the bosses."

With a railroad coachful of her women supporters, Janet went to New York to protest to President Dubinsky. Barred from seeing him, they kept vigil in relays for six hours, till finally he let them in. Sitting with cigar in mouth and feet on desk, Dubinsky said: "What the hell business have you butting in? You're just a bunch of communists, and I'm not going to listen to you."

In the outcome, Janet was allowed to see the ballots, but without supporting witnesses. The stuffed ballots, in the same writing, she said, weren't even separate but folded in thick wads. The appointed business agent, running against her, was declared elected. Janet started to study up on becoming a communist.

How did nonradical workers react to union leaders who were open communists? Leather and fur workers had merged in the International Fur & Leather Workers Union, of which Ben Gold, CIO's most publicized communist, was president. I headed for Peabody, Massachusetts, a Leather stronghold.

It could hardly be said things had been slipped over on the conservative, largely Catholic New England tannery workers. At the union office, I was shown a scrapbook full of clippings, leaflets, pictures, that told a lurid story of the 1943 red-scare secession movement. As I went over it, Leather unionists gave me additional angles. "That whore Carey" (CIO secretary-treasurer), they said, encouraged the secessionists to expect a separate CIO charter. Outside politicians (Democratic, not Communist) got into the act. The secessionists started riots, gunplay, knifings, stonings, window-smashing. Redbaiting went wild. Companies backing the secession broke their contracts and caused strikes. Under Presidential orders, troops seized the strike-bound plants. The AFL chartered the secessionists. But the IFLWU won back most workers who went to the AFL and in Labor Board elections was victorious in all but three small plants.

Richard B. (Mike) O'Keefe, business manager, a wiry man of restless energy, was an IFLWU regular at the time—seemingly adjusted to running a conservative pocket in a leftwing union. But he was too much the extroverted politician to furnish reflections, and the others seemed in his shadow.

I found my philosopher later on—a local union president who worked full-time in a fair-sized New Hampshire tannery. I visited Mr. D. in his home. A bespectacled, middle-aged man of tall dignity, he talked freely of communism, communists, and the union. "They don't like communism in New Hampshire," said Mr. D. He related "a funny incident." The State CIO Council, dominated by Rieve's Textile Workers, denounced the Progressive Citizens of America as communist. Out of curiosity, Mr. D. went to a PCA meeting. He found it to be a liberal not a communist organization. Gradually, said Mr. D., he had come to conclude that "anyone or any organization that does anything for labor is likely to be attacked by some people as communistic." That had happened to CIO, he noted.

The IFLWU magazine, however, had printed some stuff that was too radical for some members. "I went to Boston," said Mr. D., "and told them a Republican or a communist will necessarily reflect his ideas in what he writes. Then the battle was on. They discussed it back and forth. I got my ears pinned back——" He stopped and grinned good-naturedly.

"Of course," he resumed, "our President Gold is a known communist." Mr. D. then related the praise of Gold which Philip Murray had expressed to Martin Agronsky in an Atlantic City cab, and which I had duly passed on.

The IFLWU was indeed "a well-run union," said Mr. D. Unlike the AFL union, with which the local workers had had bad experience, it was "meticulous and fussy about finances and organization." It had greatly improved wages and conditions, "giving us excellent service. It lives up to their assurance to us that it is run as a union, not a communist organization."

As to communists, Mr. D. knew there were many in the fur

end of the union, in the big cities. "But you won't find any in Leather here, in Peabody, or anywhere else in New England," he said. "It's all right to have communists in the union," he concluded, "if they don't force their ideas on other members. That goes for them or for any other political or religious group. Otherwise you won't have a union. Also you won't have a union if any members are thrown out for their beliefs."

"You've evidently found communists don't have horns," I said. Mr. D. paused, as if thinking over the trite remark. Then he broke into a hearty laugh. "Come to think of it," he said, "they're pretty much like other people, at that."

I knew many "alleged," "identified," "reported," communists in CIO. As an "acknowledged" one, William Sentner was a rarity in high union position. He was president of the UE district centered in St. Louis. A dark, stocky man, with prominent nose and strong face, Sentner showed no trace of the fanatic. Practical and extroverted, he was no pushover in union politics. I asked if it handicapped him to be known as an open communist.

"You can run into redbaiting under any circumstances, as you very well know," Bill replied. "But here, on account of me, I'll grant you it's a bit more pointed——" He grinned. "I didn't particularly choose to stand out this way," he went on. "It just happened I was well known here as section organizer of the Communist party when I went to work for CIO. I couldn't have hidden the fact I was a communist, if I'd wanted to."

Like radicals in many other centers, Sentner broke the first organizing ground for CIO. Assigned to Steel and Electrical, he also spread out to other industries. "We organized the warehouses," he said. "But Harry Bridges didn't come in, and the Retail union took over." The warehouse workers were restive under Retail rule. There was "a split between Trotskyites and social-democrats," said Sentner. They later seceded from CIO Retail to go to the AFL Teamsters and became the base from which Harold Gibbons rose to prominence in Teamster leadership.

Three big electrical suppliers, Wagner, Emerson, and Century, were held the key to organizing St. Louis. In organizing them, Sentner went to work full-time for UE and continued as its district leader from then on.

Despite the intensified redbaiting of the Cold War, Sentner had just been reelected district president. The election was close, however, and the rightwing Carey faction made gains. At the Emerson plant it won with a "machine-delivered vote," Sentner claimed, totaling "200 more votes than there were dues-paying members." Of the defectors from left to right, he said: "It's hard to undermine local leaders you yourself built up in organizing."

"The redbaiting as such doesn't go too deep," Sentner declared. "The members vote for me because I'm known as builder of the union, and because of my union services to them. The communist issue is just a complicating factor. I sometimes say it's as if the Catholic issue were concentrated on in a predominantly Protestant local."

In Evansville, Indiana, a UE stronghold half Catholic and half Protestant, I was told the majority for Sentner was overwhelming, despite organized Catholic opposition. "Quite a few Catholic members wouldn't vote at all," said one UE officer. "They said they wouldn't vote against Sentner, but if they voted for him they'd catch hell." This officer had got an invitation—evidently by mistake—to a private anti-Sentner meeting called by a priest.

Most lefts tended to deprecate or dodge anticommunism as a diversion from real union issues. In the Gulf ports, I found National Maritime Union lefts who didn't tack around it—or anything else—but sailed right in.

At the NMU hall in Port Arthur, Texas, a meeting was about to start when I arrived. With some 500 seamen present, it was standing room only. The meeting elected its chairman, and rank-and-file democracy was stressed throughout. The port agent was a tall, vigorous man with aquiline nose and reddish complexion, who wore an open blue workshirt and had a breezy seaman's style. He told me he'd been in Port Arthur since 1941 and "could lick anyone hands down for port agent," but didn't know if he'd run again.

Communications from ships' crews were read, most calling for unity in the union, opposing "redbaiting disruption" and hitting at President Joe Curran's part in it—which sentiments the meeting unanimously approved as reflecting its own. Pictures of leftwing union leaders were on the wall, notably Ferdinand (Blackie) Myers. He ought to run for union president, the agent told me—"even some of the phonies are for him."

Ex-Congressman Maury Maverick, when I talked with him in San Antonio where he'd also been mayor, said that only in the Port Arthur area had the Texas CIO-PAC been "fairly effective," having helped run Chairman Martin Dies of HUAC out of public life. NMU had spearheaded the local activities. But recently the state PAC had ousted the port agent as a communist. In four-letter words, he told me he didn't care. "I'll go to the grass roots—outside the refinery gates. That crowd don't do anything anyhow."

In Galveston, the port agent wore a business suit. He was plump, ruddy, kindly-faced, had been on the job nine years. He had recently shipped out to sea for two months and "never felt better, would like to ship out again, if I can get a good lad to run for port agent." Seamen—white, black, Spanish-speaking—crowded the hall. As I talked with the agent, they brought him their problems, which he readily settled.

One of NMU's biggest ports, Galveston was a leftwing stronghold. The *Daily Worker* was on sale in the union office, clippings from it on the bulletin board. Pictures of Blackie Myers and other lefts were on the walls. The agent said there had been "some trouble after the NMU convention, but the port is now solid. Only one member tried any redbaiting."

Here, as at other Texas ports, I was told on both sides that relations were good between the conservative Oil Workers and the leftwing NMU. "We organized them," explained the port agent. That story I often heard—of lefts organizing more plants than their own, for rightwing unions to cash in on their efforts. In this case, the Oil Workers still needed, and gratefully acknowledged, NMU cooperation in stopping oil shipments during strikes.

Relations were also good with the AFL (ILA) longshoremen. The NMU agent credited the black longshoremen, and

Wobblies in ILA ranks who insisted on rank-and-file democracy, for disobedience of President Joe Ryan's orders to work while NMU was on strike. The black longshoremen (in separate locals) outnumbered the white two to one, and were strong for solidarity.

On political action, the port agent said NMU had the best record for PAC collections and activity. It wouldn't deal with the "phony State PAC" that threw out the Port Arthur man, but worked well with other unions locally, where 400 NMU families lived. Along with other Texas NMU ports, Galveston had strongly endorsed Henry Wallace, with black members in the lead.

In Houston, the Curran right wing was moving in on a left-wing port. Operating from a whites-only hotel, chiefly its bar, it had plenty of money for liquor and like inducements, I was told, and made redbaiting its main thrust. The port agent told me—and apparently everyone else—that he was a communist, a common enough occurrence among the outspoken NMU lefts. He was a big man physically and had been reelected many times. Compared with most NMU fire-eaters, he was mild-mannered and reasonable.

"Big business and the government can't afford to have progressives in control of the NMU," he said. "Outside influences are behind the redbaiting campaign and putting up the money. But they can't win. If I thought they could, I wouldn't be beating my head against all this." This agent too spoke of IWW aid to good relations with ILA, and put me in touch with the Wobblies.

In Corpus Christi, the NMU atmosphere was more relaxed. In between reading off jobs and answering questions, the dispatcher was reading the *Daily Worker*. But from other members I heard more racy tales of the sea than union politics talk. When the union patrolman returned, he proved to be a serious young man in blue dungarees and workshirt, with an active interest in black and Spanish-speaking affairs. He said the port was progressive.

"We've got a good core of oldtimers, who've been through all the struggles," he told me. "They know the score and won't stand for any redbaiting. These, with the young fellows they influ-

ence, and the Mexican and black workers, furnish the chief support of the left. Curran and his crowd have only some rah-rah
patrioteering young whites. Some have been in the Navy, and
others are influenced by jingo flagwaving." Once he admired Joe
Curran, "but I've seen so many labor leaders go phony I'm not
surprised any more."

The patrolman said he used to spend 80% of his time on exclusively NMU business and 20% on general labor causes. Now
NMU matters had become so demanding, he had to spend 95%
of his time on them. After a long day, he was fixing to work till
midnight on NMU beefs. "It's a tough job," he said, "but we
get our influence because we're willing to work our heads off."

Having run into no IWW activity for some 20 years, I was
curious about the Wobblies of whom I heard NMUers talk.
They had headquarters on the outskirts of Houston, in a roomy
Mexican-style residence left them by an old Wobbly in his will.
Working Wobblies carried two cards—one in IWW Marine
Transport Workers 510, the other in AFL Longshoremen or
CIO's NMU.

Wobbly rank-and-filism and breezy radical talk were congenial to many NMU lefts, who saw them as a good influence
against Ryan in ILA and for solidarity with the seamen. Others
thought the Wobblies "all screwed up," resenting their uncertain
stand on Curran's redbaiting purge-takeover. At the time of my
visit, an MTW-IWW meeting with 15 members present had
come within a vote or two of supporting Curran.

The IWW house had a business office on one side of the entrance; on the other, a meeting hall with bookshelves, literature
table, stove, and a pool table in the rear. In the kitchen I sat
around for some hours drinking coffee with a handful of
Wobblies. The two with most to say were Mike, in charge while
the MTW delegate was out, and Manny, the theoretician.

Mike was a small, tense man, with wrinkling forehead, one
bunged-up eye, hooked nose, and a tight mouth. At first suspicious, he relaxed as we shot the breeze. A former member of the
west coast Marine Firemen, which flirted with CIO before following Harry Lundeberg into the AFL, Mike was curious about

"the inner sanctum" of CIO. "I've read most of your stuff," he told me. "I agreed with some, but there's a lot I didn't agree with."

Mike had practiced as well as preached "direct action"—organized action on the job. He related how he had been "raising the wages of Fijian and New Zealand seamen by direct action" at Vancouver, British Columbia, when the Canadian Mounties had moved in and arrested him. The seamen struck until he was released, but he was then deported from Canada.

Manny was a dark, somber man who had served time in San Quentin for "criminal syndicalism"—under a state law directed against IWW's organizing of migratory workers and its war resistance. He expounded a hard-shelled Wobbly philosophy of the anarcho-syndicalist kind.

On the right-left fight in CIO and NMU, Manny said, "a plague o' both your houses." Political action—he was against it. Russia—a revolution betrayed by commy politicians. One of my notes on Manny's sayings is, "Not a matter of power." I wish I had elaborated. It came to intrigue me when, in the Sixties, many ideas once current among Wobblies cropped up again, after a near half century, as new thoughts of a New Left.

My dozen years with CIO had interrupted my association with AFL and rail brotherhood people, and I now tried to revive it. AFLers I talked with ranged from local officials so openly racist and reactionary that in CIO I'd almost forgotten their kind existed, to some who could have doubled as CIO progressives, and in fact consorted with them. In between, many from liberal to conservative cautiously toeing the AFL line, and so conventionally respectable as to make "labor" look unutterably dull.

More colorful an occasional Teamster type.

Teamo used his big belly to bar me at the gate to his office. "If you're writing a book," he growled, "let me see a copy."

Just then Teamo was called to his phone. I sidled in and sat down across the desk from him. He was Teamsters chief and big wheel of the AFL in a Massachusetts city of some 200,000. One phone call followed another. Members kept dropping in. Teamo paid me no further attention except as an ear for his racy asides.

In his first long call, Teamo swore so much that his secretary, on the extension, hung up. I grinned at her. "What's the matter? Can't you take it?" She grinned back. "Him? That's nothing. You should hear the language from the other end." Teamo was arguing for the employers' right, under the contract, to put beer drivers on a fish haul to New York. He slammed down the phone and turned to me: "God-damned pigs! They kick when they're laid off or haven't enough work. But when the boss hasn't enough usual business and takes on some new hauls, they kick all the more."

Teamo was no more polite with the local members who kept dropping in. He made his asides about them too. His secretary was watching me quizzically. "They don't seem to like him, do they?" she said. "But you should see them turn out to vote for him."

It figured. Teamo was obviously a fighter—against all comers. It could be nice to have him on your side. I wasn't surprised to hear his reaction to John L. Lewis: "I voted with John L. against signing the anticommunist affidavits. He was right. He's got more god-damned sense and guts than all the rest put together."

"How come then," I needled, "you're having Teamster officers here sign the affidavits?"

Teamo became more official. He was no communist himself, he made clear, and the union needed labor-board services. "What we object to is class legislation that says only we have to sign them—employers don't, attorneys don't. Taft and Hartley are the real communists, as bad as Hitler, Mussolini, and Stalin. It's a communistic law."

This Teamo, burly and belligerent, could have been a composite of Teamster leaders I met. Before leaving town, I learned he had lately become wealthy through private business ventures. That fitted the picture too.

My seven years with the Brotherhood of Locomotive Engineers (1927-34) didn't lead me to expect any of CIO's flaming youth in railroad ranks. Since then we had all grown older. Age level in the brotherhoods was notably higher, due to declining employment and strict seniority.

Yet these elder citizens had recently been in a national strike turmoil. Running into me with Murray at the White House, my old boss, Grand Chief Engineer Alvanley Johnston, had greeted me like a fellow militant. Trainmen's A.F. Whitney had matched bluster and billingsgate with President Harry Truman and sworn he'd never support him. But by now that to-do was done with. Whitney, who had cozied up to CIO and even flirted with Henry Wallace, was now joining CIO in a prodigal's return to Truman's veal.

Early unionized, the men of the train crews were first to be dubbed "aristocrats of labor." The railroads levied toll on an opening-up America. Darlings of Wall Street, they played with governors and legislators like chessmen. But the brotherhoods were more public-minded than their bosses. They were main support of the LaFollette Progressive movement, of George W. Norris midwest progressive Republicanism—anti-Wall Street, pro-public ownership, anti-imperialist. During the Twenties, William Z. Foster (himself an old "rail") and his TUEL won much support from railroad workers. Hundreds of lodges joined the move to amalgamate craft into industrial unions. Shopmen and switchmen were foremost militants.

Since the Twenties, the "rails" had settled down. Of the LaFollette movement, their leaders said, "we won't repeat that mistake." They dropped the Plumb Plan for railroad public ownership. The labor-banking fiasco gave them a bad taste for all outside ventures. The Railway Labor Act and other laws gave rail labor an exclusive and highly regulated status. The brotherhoods drew back from the rest of labor, to mind their own business and to brood over their fading grandeur in an industry hemmed and jostled by the competition of trucks, buses, waterways, airlines.

As I went around on this 1947-48 trip, however, I found some relief in my brotherhood contacts. They were conservative, but in a dignified and sometimes progressive style that contrasted with the vulgar anticommunist hysterics of the CIO right wing and the Meany-Lovestone AFL. I found some Henry Wal lace sympathy, for·instance, and little shock at his opposition to United States Cold War imperialism. I recalled how many articles against United States imperialism we used to run in the *Locomotive Engineers Journal,* often by brotherhood-supported western Senators.

In Cincinnati, I paid a nostalgic visit to Phil E. Ziegler, grand secretary-treasurer of the AFL Brotherhood of Railway Clerks. He was a labor sponsor of Brookwood Labor College when I was there; had sympathized with some of Albert Coyle's progressive ideas, though appalled at his impetuous style; and an early sponsor of Federated Press, had had me write special articles for the *Railway Clerk* when I covered Washington for FP.

Like most liberals, Ziegler had adjusted himself to the Cold War by seeing American anticommunism as an inevitable reaction to "Russia's policies." As during the German-Soviet non-aggression pact, I sensed in liberals some personal relief that they could now clear themselves of redbaiting charges by pointing to the Soviet Union as chief enemy of their liberal principles.

Ziegler had no use for the Henry Wallace boom. He was reserved about the CIO purge of people like myself. "Maybe it's a good thing CIO is going to the right," he said. "It would be too exposed in the present state of public opinion in regard to Russia. It might be cracked down upon, torn up."

At the time, it was not the AFL people I met who stood out on labor's right wing so much as CIO leaders intent on stamping out all traces of the radicalism that once marked their movement. In New England, for instance, my labor contacts of all shades and affiliations pointed to CIO Textile as the ultimate in rightism. They blamed it for blocking any united labor action, and being aloof and uncooperative with other unions; for a deadening control over CIO Councils it dominated; and for being antimilitant to the point of company unionism. It was by all odds the most anticommunist of unions.

With my early CIO memories, I found it an odd reversal that the AFL textile union now leveled at CIO Textile the same charges CIO once made against AFL: company-union tendencies; lack of inner-union democracy; sweetheart agreements; wage and speedup sellouts; do-nothing conservatism.

There was something machinelike about the dominant rightist officials I saw, both in their methods of control and the predictability of their responses. They brooked no opposition, nor even disagreement, from within their ranks—seeming to defer more to the employers and their top union chiefs than to the membership. They were deeply involved in the politics (chiefly Democratic) of their areas, paying no more than lip service to CIO-PAC. Unlike early CIOers out to "stir up the people," these established executives and politicians were out to "keep 'em down." Any unrest below disturbed them; their power depended on being able to "deliver" their districts for top-decreed purposes. When criticized for lack of progressivism, these men typically blamed a "backward" membership, or resorted to red-baiting. If I asked about labor social, educational, political, community, activities, I might be told with a sneer that only "the commies" pushed such stuff.

Writing so much of "right" and "left," have I not neglected a large area in between? Actually, among union activists I found the area small. Most were either lefts, leftish, or playing with the left; or else rights or supporting or submitting to the right. The in-between progressive had not a happy lot.

In a New England industrial city, a former Brookwooder was business agent of a center-to-right CIO union. John had fine modern offices downtown. He had no kick on salary or expenses; his heart was full of other kicks.

A serious man with deep-set eyes and lingering Scottish accent, John was a socialist—in the old-country style of being more for socialism than against communism. After Brookwood, he had worked in a textile mill and helped organize it. He had held socialist meetings, bringing in Mayor Jasper McLevy of Bridgeport. John was fired and blacklisted. "The town was stirred up against me," he said. "But I gloried in it." Now after some years on his present union job, John was lonely and discouraged.

Reactionary Catholic influence hung like a pall over the

city, he said. The Bishop had even spoken against a five-day week. Louis Budenz had been brought in for unbridled redbaiting. Anitunionists picked on children of union members at school, ostracized CIO families. "There's no one to talk to," said John. "There are no liberals, except some Jewish people. But most of them are employers; I'd be suspect to the workers if I socialized with them. And the workers don't like union business agents." John tried joining the Unitarian church, but found it "thoroughly reactionary."

Now John was "wondering how much good I've done." He'd helped win wage increases and benefits, but "the workers say they'd have got them anyhow." He'd conducted educational work, "but the workers are very backward." As to other unions, CIO Textile dominated locally and discouraged joint activities. There wasn't a CIO council, "because Textile doesn't need it." The local Textile top shot "wants to drop the atomic bomb on Russia." The whole Textile setup "is reactionary and only sits on the lid. It needs a revolt."

John was no communist, but he saw how Cold War anticommunism was killing all radical labor spirit. A reactionary Republican machine dominated his district. "I'm tired of fighting it with no help from CIO," John said. "All CIO did was to send in someone interested only in sniffing out reds."

A progressive like John, working for a union that had joined the red-purge procession, was understandably discouraged, though not subject to purge himself. The purge was eliminating not only communists but most earlier labor idealisms. The reds bearing the brunt of the assault and their left allies seemed less discouraged.

Dick was neither lonely nor dejected. Some of his labor ideas, like John's, went back to British origins, but he had worked 30 years in the American town where I visited him. In his fifties, Dick was tall, slim, graying, a reader, a thinker. He lived modestly in the upper half of a small frame house with a plumply cheerful wife and grandchild.

Though not a full-time union official, Dick spoke with the confidence of a leader sure of his following; it was "we" all the time. He worked lobster shift in a chemical plant and devoted evenings and weekends to his unpaid union elective job and related labor and political activities.

Dick's local—in District 50, UMW—had nearly everything in town—all plants, busdrivers, machine shops, foundry, barbers. Even the bank clerks wanted in; and at the time the local was working on the store clerks. The local was a labor movement in miniature. It had sprouted from a union that became a locally successful labor party.

"We have a very live local," said Dick. "Attendance at regular local meetings runs 200 and more. We're also very independent." The independence showed in attitudes to higher union officials, who didn't run things from on top so easily as was common in Textile, for instance.

This was not a conventional leftwing setup. I didn't meet the local labor hero—the man who "really organized the local" and was called "tops" by all. He was not a left, I was told—just a man of great energy, independence, and devotion to the union. Dick had been asked to join the Communist party, he said, but on progressive advice had decided not to, lest he become labeled and impair his usefulness. Strongly opposed to the Cold War, Dick was enthusiastic for Henry Wallace's peace policies. Asked to start a local PCA, he had begged off only because "I have a hard job here and am kept very busy." But he passed out PCA stuff and "talked it up."

After seeing Steel's new role in national CIO, I was surprised to find on this 1947-48 trip many remnants of leftwing influence—in New York state, Youngstown, Lorain, Akron, Indiana Harbor, South Chicago, Gary.

One or two locals, I was told, were under "Trotskyite" leadership—a designation I took with reserve, as I did the "communist" charge. Both were used more to abuse than describe. They covered some strange bedfellows. Against the tougher anti-union companies, grievances accumulated, stewards had to be tough, job actions occurred, and a militant spirit prevailed, with corresponding left influence. During World War II, communist devotion to war production gave Trotskyites a chance to come

forward as the militants. Hence a certain seesaw in militant locals from "left" or "communist" to "Trotskyite" leadership, or
vice versa. In some less militant locals, left influences lingering
from early CIO were being systematically eliminated by emissar-
ies of the international union.

Two interviews may illustrate some of the old CIO spirit in
Steel.

He greeted me heartily at his door. "And what is the matter
with Phil? Letting you go, and putting that man in your place!
Why, the new *CIO News* stinks!" The burr could have been Phil
Murray's own. It came from Lanarkshire, Scotland, where the
speaker was born, not far from Murray's Blantyre birthplace.
Jack had deeper roots in steel than Murray. Born into a steelworker's family, he had been a steelworker all his life. He was
now top officer (unpaid) and grievance committee chairman of
a big Steel local.

A warm host, Jack lived in a rambling house with four children (two more were "grown and flown") and a jolly, capable,
decisive wife. In the creeping Cold War terror that was reducing
labor dissent to a whisper, it was refreshing to visit a man not
scared to speak his mind.

Jack's assessments of Steel's leaders were not flattering. He
joked about Dave McDonald's trip to Rome for a "Catholic
divorce." He said "Phil should send (Vice President) Thimmes
back to California." He thought "the Germano crowd" (Joe
Germano was Steel's big boss in Chicago and reputedly the
union's most powerful wirepuller) were out to make Murray a
figurehead. For John L. Lewis, Jack had respect: "He'd never
stand for the stuff that's going on in Steel." Jack also praised the
much redbaited Lee Pressman, still Steel and CIO counsel but
soon to resign. "He's the only man in the outfit worth a hoot,"
he said.

Jack said he'd been offered a job as Steel organizer but had
turned it down. "I knew it wouldn't last three months. I have a
mind of my own, I'm not a machine yes-man. I couldn't be one
of those international reps interested only in their PDs
(paydays)."

Jack was outraged and scornful at moves in his district for four-year terms of office, higher dues, and to bar communists from office. "Next thing, they'll want life terms," he said. "What's more, we wouldn't stand for what Emil Rieve's doing with the anticommunist affidavits. We'd split away first."

"It might be a good thing," he went on, "if they did use the Taft-Hartley law against us, and we had to hit the bricks. We'd do it, law or no law—learn to stand on our own legs, like the miners did."

Toward communists Jack showed only friendly feelings. A young steelworker I'd seen earlier in the Communist party office walked in while I was visiting, and the two discussed their union business with kidding intimacy. His own philosophy Jack capsuled like this: "One thing the workers understand is that the company is getting too much and they're not getting enough. That makes them mad. Why can't the company take less and let us have more, they want to know. That's Marxist. But if you called it that, they'd wonder if they were right."

In a Steel district far from Jack's, I visited the imposing headquarters of a big local union. It had clubrooms, large auditorium, more than the usual social facilities. In the business office I expected to see several stoutish white-shirted officers holding down swivel chairs in well-pressed pants.

The only person I saw was perched on the corner of a desk as if about to pounce. Slim and wiry, he wore a cap provocatively askew, khaki jacket, blue workshirt, soiled pants. As he sprang from the desk and came to me with freeswinging stride, it was as if some oldtime Wobbly had risen from the past to haunt the "labor fakers" of his scorn. Unlike socialists and communists who merged with the crowd, the Wobs were more proletarian than the proletariat. This man—"I'm Chuck," he said—was ostentatiously working-class in talk, clothes, manner, everything.

My name was enough for Chuck to welcome me. He'd read my stuff, was wise to CIO politics, was on my side. Chuck was not a full-time officer. He was a "griever" (grievance-committeeman), working in the mill and handling most grievances in his spare time—for $30 a month from the union.

The company, said Chuck, was one of "the most antilabor and toughest to deal with—always trying to get away with something. This keeps us constantly on our toes and makes the members militant."

Many members were black (15-20%), and as many Spanish-speaking (Mexican) and were "good militants," Chuck said, some "pretty progressive." Many, like himself, were for Henry Wallace. "Ours is the only leftwing local hereabouts," he declared. "We're always raising hell at conventions. The international hates us. We don't stand for Germano's strong-arm dictatorship."

Party communists didn't call the local "leftwing." They said it had been left-led, but a combination of Trotskyites and ACTU had defeated the left in the last election. They called Chuck a "good militant" but too easy to provoke, and with an itch to fight physically when provoked. He had been expelled from the party, they said, for "creating a factional situation," but "we can still work with him."

Wherever I went, one union in particular continued to exemplify earlier CIO attitudes that were disappearing with the Cold War change in the movement. That was the UE—the United Electrical, Radio, & Machine Workers.

The CIO uprising took on the class character of embracing all workers as workers, as against the traditional separatism of the AFL. From this followed certain conclusions about solidarity, democracy, social purpose.

One was a labor loyalty, or solidarity, not limited to one's own union but stressing joint activities, united action of all labor.

Another, arising from the participation of large numbers of workers in self-organization, was that workers should participate actively in running their unions rather than let union bosses run them.

A third conclusion was that a workers' movement should formulate its own worker goals, not take them from employers, government, or any other class; and that it should give a lead to other sections of the common people whose interests essentially coincided with labor's.

CIO Textile in New England, as noted, was often cited as aloof from other unions and opposed to joint activity; bureaucratically run from on top; exclusivist in its intense hostility to radicals; and committed to the government's Cold War without thought of an independent labor lead. UE was at the opposite pole. One of the strongest unions in most areas I visited, it exerted wide influence through joint labor and progressive activities; involved its membership to an unusual degree; and played a strong part in opposing the Cold War and its domestic repressions.

By the fall of 1947, UE was shaken by assaults from without and by rightwing subversion within. But it was still holding its own, despite some local rightwing takeovers. In most places one could count on UE to offer an oasis of labor liveliness in a spreading desert of rightist reaction.

Compared with rambunctious early UAW, UE was relatively staid in the steady character of its members and its orderly procedures—though also a young-minded union full of initiative and ambition. It was as if the rebellious youth of the Sixties were mated to the more sober but still purposeful ranks of organized industrial workers, in an amalgam preserving some at least of the qualities of both.

Helping to produce this encouraging phenomenon were the background of UE as an organization; the leeway it allowed rank-and-file activists; and the character of its field staff and local and international officers.

Unlike Steel and Textile, UE was not organized from on top by big CIO money and outside organizers under rules designed to insure centralized control. UE grew from the bottom up. It brought together preexisting independent and AFL unions, some of left inspiration, others definitely not. With little CIO aid, it grew into one of the largest strongest unions.

UE's leadership was a collective combining the young-minded but practical radicalism of people like Julius Emspak and James Matles with the reassuring stability and common-sense of people like Albert Fitzgerald. Unlike most big CIO unions, UE's top office could not—had it wanted—rule by arbitrary suppression of opposition. In the nature of its growth, UE was democratically constituted, with much local autonomy, and without large centrally controlled funds. Furthermore, as in early UAW, rival forces were too strong to permit of rigid top control. UE organizers, responsible to the international, had to respect local autonomies, but unlike the international reps of rightwing unions, they protected rather than suppressed progressive rank-and-file activities.

In the typical local of a rightwing union, the few members attending meetings were well known and closely watched by officers and "the clique." Anyone taking the floor was a marked man. What was his angle? Might he run for office? Should the clique enlist him? Or was he potential opposition? If he strayed from shop issues, he was suspect. If he talked of union struggle, labor solidarity, community affairs, political action, he was a "communist." Such men were dangerous. He would be checked on, watched; at the first false move, he'd be pounced upon.

In most UE locals, on the other hand, as in early UAW, there were active class-conscious—or at least labor-conscious—working members, who while putting job and wage concerns first, also wanted the union to promote general labor and progressive purposes. In UE, these members were not automatically marked for punishment, but protected in their rights.

I visited many rank-and-file UE activists on this trip. A few were communists, but most held differing ideas and were drawn together by common enthusiasm for the kind of union UE aspired to be. They were also drawn to the progressive consensus of the time which, in addition to traditional labor, libertarian, and social-welfare concerns, was crystallizing around opposition to the aggressions and repressions of the Cold War.

The UE organizers—directors, field representatives, staff people—were an exceptional group of men and women. They included leaders from the shops in their particular areas, and a more mobile group of troubleshooters with much verve and esprit de corps. They were relatively young—late twenties or early thirties, it mostly seemed. With the salary level low, and sticklish Organization Director Matles proverbially tight on expenses, most worked for the cause more than for what was in it for them.

UE had more World War II veterans on its staff than most unions. As a young union, it was not saddled with many staff oldtimers; and this war, like the Loyalist cause in Spain, had attracted crusading types. I met UE organizers with outstanding combat and commando records. They found outlet for their antifascism, social idealism, and pugnacity in organizing for UE.

The level of intelligence and education was high, though academic types need not apply, since a union organizer needed working experience and some rough-and-tumble in his background. He had to be a practical unionist close enough to the workers to meet their needs, not a starry-eyed "missionary"— usually doomed to disillusionment. Still, most UE organizers I met were more zealots than porkchoppers.

As to politics, the rightwing dubbed them all "communists" because they worked for UE, not the Carey faction out to split the union. If some were communists, they shared a common disposition to put UE first.

American unions all seemed to have a mind-your-own-business attitude toward the best meaning outsiders—due doubtless to the primacy here of union over political or other labor activities. This could reflect a democratic concern to serve their members' needs and wishes; or less creditably, a lack of concern for wider working-class interests. No union machine, right, center, or left, would let others butt in when it came to running their union. The UE, through its elected officers and its convention actions, made itself part of the progressive-to-left forces. Its organizers promoted progressive policies because they were UE policies.

In 1949 national CIO chartered a dual union headed by James B. Carey to break up the UE. Despite all efforts to infect the members with Cold War anticommunist hysteria, this split had to be engineered from the top down, not vice versa. For a dozen years UE leaders, like many other CIO leaders, had been persistently redbaited, but most members remained satisfied with UE as a strong, aggressive, progressive, and well-functioning union. The Carey faction had taken over only a minority of locals—due usually to local issues such as lay any leadership open to active opposition.

By 1949, the Taft Hartley law had given employers and

stooge union leaders a handy weapon against militant unions. ACTU and rightist factions were at the peak of their job-grabbing demands for a purge. Cold War hysteria was being promoted countrywide. When national CIO joined in, proclaiming an open season of raids and purges, ambitious local politicians in many UE locals saw their chance. Having built themselves up in many cases as lefts, or at least UE regulars, these split leaders held, or could grasp, the reins of control in their locals. At the opportune moment, they drove them in the direction government, employers, press, and all other establishment powers were bidding them go.

To move forward, a labor movement needs more than competent porkchoppers and well-organized workers. It needs some of the qualities shown by black and white youth in the Sixties—activism, inspiration, enthusiasm, broad social outlook. CIO had these yeasty ingredients in its rise; with its Cold War purge of the left, it eliminated them. CIO attracted radicals and put them to work. Writers, artists, students, contributed emotionally and intellectually. "Inspirational stuff" we'd say, contrasting it with the solid stuff of the practical organizer, the embryo porkchopper.

It wasn't impossible for one person to combine both the inspirational and the practical. In my youth, William Z. Foster seemed to fill that bill, as did John L. Lewis at his CIO peak. Harry Bridges was a rousing agitator with the staying power of the practical organizer and administrator. Ben Gold, who set New York needle workers afire in the early Twenties, became a most practical CIO union leader. The UE leaders and staff combined the inspirational and practical to an unusual degree.

As CIO grew older, the plain porkchopper became the rule. He was excessively job conscious and intolerant of opposition. He tended to be parochial and "economist." He had one solid virtue—the secret of his success: he was essentially practical and down-to-earth.

The porkchopper's opposite was the inspirational, intellectual, agitational leader. CIO produced no Eugene Debs. Its agitators were more wing-clipped than IWW's Big Bill Haywood,

Arturo Giovannitti, Joe Ettor, Elizabeth Gurley Flynn (though she lived to serve CIO too). But CIO too had its inspirationalists, caring more for the cause than for piecards they held briefly, if at all. These had many virtues, but the porkchopper's practicality about solid organization wasn't always one of them.

Between these two types, I found one little group who filled in some of the gaps. I visited many labor lawyers of regional fame and found surprisingly many to be good guys, and steadfast too. Lest I seem to absolve a profession in dire need of absolution, let me add the woods may also have been full of crooks, kooks, and conniving shysters; I didn't seek out that kind.

The labor lawyer had to be practical. He sold his counsel to the porkchopper, who measured results in dollars and cents. At the same time, union success often depended on a broad understanding of affairs; and the thoughtful lawyer might even supply some philosophy without extra fee. The best—and those I knew the best—were of the left, drawn to labor as a social force, a cause. They could have made more money in private or corporate practice. I meant to present some I met on this 1947-48 trip. But the list is long, and I wouldn't want to slight by omission or embarrass by inclusion. I revert to some I knew longer and better.

Lee Pressman was the labor lawyer as policy man—closest to CIO's two most important leaders. Comparison with his successor as CIO counsel, Arthur J. Goldberg—also an able legal and policy man—suggests that Pressman's policy line helped the organization more than himself, while the reverse might be said of Goldberg.

With Lewis, Pressman promoted the leftward policy line of CIO's spectacular rise. With Murray, he promoted the left-including unity that held CIO together with much of its early spirit. When the Cold War turned CIO to self-mutilation and submission, Pressman wanted no part of the change.

Goldberg had a gun for hire in the Cold War; he traveled far. He helped put through and rationalize the exclusion of CIO's left—and of most of CIO's old spirit. He left the organization diminished and domesticated. He traveled on, through Secretary of Labor and the Supreme Court, to become apologist for United States imperialism in the United Nations. Less successful in promoting himself, Pressman tired of a struggle that seemed to lead only into the wilderness. In 1950 he chickened out. But the Pressman I knew from 1936 to 1948 was no chicken; he was a scrappy, young rooster who helped herald a dawn that is still a-breaking.

John Abt I knew less well. He was to Hillman, in the high flights of his later leadership, what Pressman was to Lewis and Murray in their higher reaches. The Hillman of PAC, of FDR's postwar vision, of world labor unity, was partly Abt—who neither promoted himself nor chickened out of anything.

Harry Sacher was another one of the elect. Brilliant, charming, successful—I thought he'd play it as that kind do. But he stuck to his side when the cold blasts blew. He died young, still in its service.

Nathan Witt was a favorite of Caroline's. She loved his calm soothing manner, so sure and reasonable in his convictions. Secretary of the Wagner Act Labor Board during CIO's rise, he didn't desert labor to serve himself.

Other names crowd memory; I must stop playing favorites. But not before reverting to Maurice Sugar. "Maurice Sugar really was Mr. CIO in Michigan," Carl Haessler wrote me. "Any story of CIO without Sugar is imcomplete." Agreed—except that Sugar's influence radiated much further. We felt it in Washington. On this trip I found it still widely felt in CIO though, under the victorious Walter Reuther, Sugar was no longer UAW general counsel. Whatever brains conceived CIO, it was born in the labor struggles of the workers—notably those in Auto, for whom Sugar was counsel and advocate from the first. Attorney for unions since 1914, Sugar stood high in labor and progressive circles from long before CIO. His service to UAW capped a career marked by both legal talent and a deeply principled and philosophical attachment to the labor movement.

I met many leftwing unionists who didn't realize what Cold War anticommunism was doing to labor, and what it would lead to. This was just another of their many right-left fights, they figured. My notes reveal that none of the lawyers kidded themselves. Some quotes from several:

"The unions have become demoralized, defensive, defeatist. There's no fight-back political action. The labor demoralization is largely due to a national psychosis induced by the Cold War."

"The communist bogy and redbaiting are the worst checks on effective and united labor political action. A police-state thought control is beginning to terrorize liberals and progressives as well as radicals."

"I'm still active in liberal and progressive causes. But it's only too clear that reaction is in the saddle and riding hard; and things are going to get a whole lot worse."

In a nation of success-seekers and bandwagon-jumpers, it was impressive to find people like these—and lawyers at that— who foresaw the kind of period we were to enter in the Fifties, but who didn't drop out of the fight to run for cover or to join the other side.

Two threads of inquiry ran through my interviews—the impact of the Taft-Hartley law, and reactions to Henry A. Wallace's stand.

Taft-Hartley put labor in its place for the Cold War— a place of anticommunist subservience to government and corporation policy. It signaled the end of the union-organizing sweep begun by CIO. It set the terms under which big-business government would recognize and recompense labor's services. Around Henry Wallace rallied the resistance to the Cold War in all its implications.

In CIO the lines were drawn. In 1944—and briefly into the postwar—Wallace had symbolized CIO-PAC progressivism. When Truman switched from Big Three unity to Cold War, the CIO leaders followed suit. Wallace did not. He thus separated himself from the whole establishment, and was left with only a Gideon's army of peace-loving liberals, and the lefts CIO was purging.

At the start of my trip, in the fall of 1947, big Wallace meetings were being held in many cities. Leftwing unions supported them; rightwing unions opposed or kept hands off; some centrist leaders might give a shaky blessing. By the end of my trip, in the spring of 1948, Wallace's only official labor support was from the left.

Among working people, the black especially, and among liberals and peace-lovers, I found plenty of Wallace sentiment.

They turned out in large numbers to cheer his cause. But "sentiment" was a vague essence without organization to turn it into votes. And there was nothing vague about the organizational opposition. As the CIO leaders cracked down, it became as much as a porkchopper's job was worth to say a kind word for Wallace; while the rank-and-filer for him was hounded like any other "red."

When I was asked to return east to do labor publicity in the Wallace-for-President campaign, I was at first reluctant—lest my pessimism hurt more than help. But Caroline was deep in the campaign as a volunteer and insisted I was needed and could help. So off I went to Wallace headquarters in New York for the duration of the campaign.

The Henry Wallace of 1948 surprised me as did the John L. Lewis of 1935. A new engine in the old chassis.

The big, shy, shaggy, farmerish Vice President had seemed woolly-minded to me, a man of little stature or strength who rode into office on the coattails of the New Deal, and faded into the shadow of the driving, magnetic Roosevelt. The wartime flirtation between Wallace and CIO-PAC didn't impress me much. I felt the movement deserved a prophet more clear in ideology, more sharp in analysis, and with a more consistent sense of direction. When Wallace joined with Senator Claude Pepper in defending FDR's legacy against Truman's Cold War rape, my respect rose. But of the two, I thought of Wallace as the weaker sister. I didn't expect him to keep on ballooning like this, somewhere in his curiously assorted equipment he must soon find a parachute to drop down to his good farm earth.

Yet here in 1947-48 was Henry Wallace standing forth as national leader of the peace and freedom forces against the atomaniac imperialists—the only man in top politics with this much daring. As he barnstormed the country, Wallace rose to this role. In his opposition to the Cold War, there was little left of the old fuzzy Wallace. He spoke out sharp and clear. He did not evade the issues. He offered alternatives to the course of world domination on which the United States was embarking in the guise of a mission to save the world from communism.

Wherever I went, people were either for or against Wallace. They usually knew why. Huge numbers turned out and paid to hear him—some with emotion and enthusiasm, others from curiosity. Some frantically applauded, some pelted him. The press and all the ruling powers denounced him with fulsome and blackguardly slander. He was seldom ignored. Wallace did not disappoint the crowds. He didn't cop out. He took his stand, spoke out for it, and stuck to it—for the duration of the campaign anyhow.

Curtis D. MacDougall's monumental work on the campaign, *Gideon's Army*, leaves little more to be said. I can record only a few personal impressions—as for instance my wonder, as an old labor hack, at the intellectuals, artists, entertainers, writers, social workers, professional people of thought, of conscience, who gave the campaign its verve, its music, its emotion. They made it a movement, a cause, as no union porkchopper could. They weren't so expert in garnering votes.

MacDougall deplored the lack of professional politicians. It was felt. Here and there, Wallace had the support of some men like Congressman Vito Marcantonio—men of practical politics who had proved themselves at the polls. They were few. Success attracted the professional politician; failure relegated him to amateur status. The Henry Wallace campaign didn't look like a sure thing to the pros.

Also missing, in any numbers, were church leaders. The Wallace cause was peace-loving, antiracist, humanitarian, dogooder. Yet only a sprinkling of liberal churchmen supported it —in contrast to the stronger church support for peace, civil rights, and antipoverty movements in the Sixties. The Henry Wallace campaign was the key peace movement at a turning point time in history—when it seemed not inconceivable that the capitalist and socialist worlds might study the arts of peace rather than those of nuclear annihilation. Yet the established apostles of peace-on-earth-good-will-to-men withheld their support.

As to the reds around Wallace, of whom the redbaiting press made much: Communists everywhere supported the movement. They did much of the hard and thankless unpaid work, without seeking the public recognition that is one of its rewards. Lefts who took official part in the campaign were mostly conscripted—after pointing out that allegations against them might prove embarrassing. They tried to be inconspicuous and offered to resign when fingered or attacked. Far from trying to load the movement with their kind—as do most political, fraternal, church, and like groups—they cautioned against, or opposed, further left appointments.

The most serious lack was the lack of organized labor support. Had more been forthcoming, it might not have made up for other lacks, but it would have added much to the movement's prestige and morale.

PAC had given CIO unions some experience in political campaigns—in registration, precinct, election, work. But reaction, making CIO its favorite bogyman, had exaggerated this. It fell short of the experience of unions in countries with labor parties. On this trip, I found CIO unions largely back in the old AFL rut. Some left unions pushed registration and other PAC activity, but most of the rest put on little more than a surface show to impress old-party (chiefly Democratic) machines with which they made their deals in the time-honored way.

More labor support therefore—say, that of CIO—might not have added too impressively to the vote. The Wallace campaign would still have suffered third-party handicaps in getting on the ballot; the virulent hostility of the capitalist powers and their media; the sabotage of local union leaders unwilling to break ties with the old political machines. But more solid labor support would have added more working-class content to the movement. It would have contributed more of the porkchops practicality, organizational sense, and discipline that are trade unionism's strength.

Only the leftwing unions gave Wallace any official support —and not all of them emphatically. Leaders of 11 unions had shown Wallace sympathies by their votes in the CIO executive board. Each had problems in his own union. All were more confident at the start of the campaign than as it progressed. Most did not unduly overestimate Wallace's strength, though some underestimated the virulence of the reaction. They wanted chiefly to take a stand against the Cold War switch, with its dangers to peace, civil liberties, and their own union rights.

During the campaign, support of Henry Wallace increased a union's exposure to attack from the right. It became a defiance of "CIO policy"—once a protection for the left—at a time when the right was stepping up its raids anyhow, with the blessing of CIO top leaders. Under these circumstances, some left union leaders tried to pull in their horns—to stress an official neutrality, to avoid Wallace becoming an issue, to hedge and trim on support the optimists had hoped to give. In some cases, earlier-originated attacks became so damaging that pro-Wallace unions were in no position, financially or otherwise, to give the anticipated support.

The Wallace campaign was not to be blamed for the retreat of the CIO left; it was well under way long before. But continuing retreat during the campaign took much of the heart from that one small sector of organized labor on which Wallace could count. Even so, this was the strongest organizational support he got. Leftwing unionists built up the big Wallace rallies in most centers and brought out members and friends in large numbers. Their practical experience mobilized many for registration, signature collection, precinct work, house-to-house canvassing.

On election night, the gloom was so thick at Wallace headquarters it stung the eyes and nose and parched the throat like smog. As new returns brought less and less comfort to those who had looked for an impressive vote, people began to shun each other. It was painful to have to say or listen to anything. I retreated to a private home, where we could lick our wounds less publicly. I was disappointed . . . one always hopes against hope. I was not thrown, as were some optimists—including Wallace, apparently.

Many had anticipated a vote comparable to that for Robert M. LaFollette in 1924—between four and five million. But Wallace lacked LaFollette's labor and farm support and I hadn't thought that even with a successful campaign he could get more than two or three million. But as the campaign went on, Wallace was progressively losing votes. His small organized labor support kept dwindling, and he was losing ground with the rank and file, as perky little Harry Truman made his common-man pitch. Aping the Wallace tone on domestic issues, and soft-pedaling his own atomic imperialism, Truman won over many potential Wallace voters, who were reluctant to stray from the Democratic fold, and who saw Truman as at least a lesser evil than Tom Dewey and the Dixiecrats. I had therefore lowered my sights considerably. But admittedly, the 1,157,000 vote for Wallace wasn't much of a base on which to build radical hopes.

It was a disappointing campaign. It was not a disaster. The hopes it wrecked were of the card-castle kind. Their wreckage was not to be compared with the demolition under way—before, during, and after the campaign—of such a solid working-class structure as the CIO that was.

What was disastrous was that the United States was now officially launched on a bipartisan Cold War course with the appearance of a popular mandate. Every vote against it was a protest, a promise of resistance. Without this effort, few American progressives could have held up their heads. Those who put their hearts into this campaign could at least take pride that they had not slunk off without a fight. Like those Germans who resisted the advent of Hitlerism, the Americans who opposed Cold War imperialism were overwhelmed, almost obliterated. Perhaps they were not "smart" to throw their weak bodies, their strong minds, their breakable spirits, against the trampling onrush of reaction. But they did.

Chapter Twenty

IDENTIFIED COMMUNIST

Right after the Henry Wallace campaign, I escaped to California. Escapism it was. Ever since things soured in CIO, I had longed for sun, bright flowers, and sea—for peace of mind and a chance to write.

I felt delinquent—count one against peace of mind. But I'd been cut off from my whole past way of life. Most of my kind were also scattering, escaping, hunting a living. It was the Fifties —that decade of blank pages in radical history, of a blank new generation.

I managed to get by in my 1949-51 sitout—with my sun, sea, and bright flowers, if without peace of mind. I felt I'd salvaged my respectability in the nick of time. I was little perturbed, when after we settled in Corona Del Mar, two young men knocked on my door and said they were from the FBI.

Working for national CIO, I had not been intimidated by the political police. The FBI was cautious about harrying John L. Lewis and his immediate staff. Even Phil Murray stood up against such stuff—or said he did. I recall walking in on Murray once, when he was CIO president. He was red-faced, flustered. He burst out: "D'you know what Biddle (U.S. Attorney-General) had the nerve to ask me to do? Keep the FBI informed on our CIO people. I told him to go to hell."

Once severed from CIO, I became fair game. While away on my auto trip, I heard from Caroline the FBI had visited her in New York to ask questions about me. I brushed it off as probably concerned with a Taft-Hartley case I'd been involved in. The California visit I also assumed to be legitimate.

"Come in," I said. "What can I do for you men?"

The men came in, affable as door-to-door salesmen. One took out a notebook and made notes; the other led in the questioning. It related to the Alger Hiss case. The FBI men said they weren't concerned with labor activity or opinion, only possible acts of espionage. "Do you know Alger Hiss?" was the first question. I didn't. The men mentioned others in the news whom I didn't know personally, or knew only through CIO contact.

I had never known or heard of any activity even remotely connected with espionage. I couldn't conceive of any of my friends being in any way involved. But I also knew radicals were being slandered as potential spies.

Before the session was over, I felt less easy than when it started. I wondered if some questions hadn't strayed from the announced purpose. Green as I was about the FBI, I began to worry if I hadn't acted the innocent. When the men asked if I'd sign a transcript, I said I would not.

I consulted a lawyer. He confirmed that I'd acted the greenhorn. No matter how clear my own record, he said, my answers might serve some ulterior FBI purpose and possibly help to smear, frame, or blackmail somebody else. What then should I do, I asked, when the FBI called? "Say you will answer their questions only in the presence of your lawyer," he said.

I followed this advice thereafter every time—and there were many times—that FBI men called or phoned, asking to talk with me. In each case, it acted like a charm. The FBI men at once lost interest.

On the other hand, I was to hear of liberals, radicals, and ex-radicals who laid themselves open to much harassment by agreeing to "confidential" questioning. The purpose seemed to be to turn persons anxious to affirm their own legality into informers against radical friends. The FBI men might bring up some forgotten misdemeanor, make much of some slip or contradiction, or allege others had made charges against their victim. In one way or another, they made him feel threatened if he didn't "cooperate."

One businessman I knew was so sure of his respectability— and his right to show sympathy for some labor or progressive causes—that he agreed to talk freely with FBI men who came to his home. He had nothing to hide, he said. The FBI men came back again and again, each time extending their inquiries and trying to draw him in deeper.

The man was in a highly nervous condition when I knew him. When he realized what the FBI was up to, he tried to cease what it called his "cooperation." The FBI men became implicitly threatening and turned their attention to his family and friends. My friend, once so sure of himself, now seemed scared of shadows. He told me the FBI "kept bothering" him. When he started losing business clients, he was sure the FBI was behind it.

It was years later before I ran into such cases, or myself had more experiences with the FBI. My 1949-51 years in southern California were years of respectable innocence. Only later did I find out that, even then, informers were spying on me. Their tidbits about my personal friendships and my comings and goings were thrown up to me when I was haled before Congressional thought-control committees in 1952 and 1954. At the time, withdrawn as I was from major labor activity, I couldn't imagine I rated the attention. If I seemed to sniff stool pigeons, I thought little of it.

The labor movement withdrew from me more than I from it. If I ran into rightwing CIO officials who couldn't avoid me (or I them), they held out their hands as eagerly as to a leper. To lefts still wearing some shreds of their CIO coveralls, I was like Casper the Friendly Ghost. They shuddered at sight of a disembodiment also in store for themselves.

The CIO leaders were heading for Portland, Oregon, for their 1948 convention, when I headed for California. That was the first CIO convention I missed. I'd have traveled even further to miss it. It was, by all accounts, a great gloat for the right. A big Wallace vote or a Dewey victory might have made the CIO bosses bitter. The unexpected Truman triumph made them smug but seemingly all the more vindictive against the left. They took the election results as a mandate to turn a CIO which once opposed the Cold War into one of its foremost proponents.

It was the first CIO convention at which the leadership rode roughshod over a protesting left. No effort was made, as in the past, to compromise with the left for the sake of formal unity. The tactic seemed to be to make things so offensive for leftwing unions they'd have to stand up and be counted as an isolated minority—exposed to the expulsions to follow in 1949.

The proceedings note boos and catcalls when leftwing leaders tried to speak, cries of "Sit down," "Take a walk." Albert Fitzgerald of UE had to take the floor to denounce rightwingers' asides about "dirty Jews." Telltale to me were Murray's speeches. He formerly tried to uphold the dignity of top office with some show of evenhandedness. At Portland he let his spite show publicly—protesting the while that he was not given to "personal castigation." Like other orators on the right, Murray spoke as if Soviet policies were the issue. The left had repeatedly to protest that CIO was an American organization which should concern itself with United States policies, rather than those of foreign countries it could not influence.

Portland was a rehearsal for CIO's 1949 convention at Cleveland, where Murray and the same orators outdid even themselves in emotional redbaiting. They tried to make the Soviet Union, communism, Cold War, the issue in reading out of CIO 11 unions with up to a million members—20% of the CIO total, according to the figures of CIO Counsel Arthur J. Goldberg, legal deviser of the operation.

In his book on the later AFL-CIO merger, Goldberg wrote of the CIO purge of "the communists" as if it disposed of a minor nuisance, only briefly influential but quite out of place in the United States labor movement.

Yet radicals have always been active in the American working class. Each time they have gained strength in the unions, they have been thrown back by forces and tactics similar to those used against the CIO left—a combination, that is, of government, employers, and union bosses utilizing whatever red bogy was most hysteria-creating at the time.

Establishment theoreticians have always argued that this shows American workers are satisfied with the capitalist system and unwilling to listen to those who challenge their exploitation by an owning class and point to socialist goals. The frenzy with which each radical advance has been fought, however, suggests some fear that the workers just might listen, if given a chance. In each case, the frenzy has seemed out of proportion to the amount of red menace. The CIO case was no exception.

In my 1947-48 trip, I saw all the powers of the establishment mobilized against the CIO left, and beginning to drive it from pillar to post. By 1949, the media reported only defeats for the left—with shrill whistles of triumph from the steamroller that was crushing it. Why then so much emotion at Portland about battling a dwindling minority? Why did the CIO brass mobilize so massively at Cleveland to cannonade the left unions and drive them decimated across the border? Why the hopped-up passion of a life-and-death struggle with communism in the organizational excision of a "minor nuisance"?

Rightist reaction has always used an exaggerated hullabaloo about "communism" to serve its ulterior purposes. Liberals and ex-radicals like Reuther, Rieve, Baldanzi, Carey, Quill, Curran, who joined and prodded Murray against the left, did likewise. Then, after their frenzy had achieved its purpose, they mopped their fevered brows and said, "Nothing to it." They didn't want the anticommunism they stirred to carry so far, in fascist fashion, as to put themselves next in the line of fire.

As to the actual strength or weakness of the left in American unions in the Thirties-Forties, objective studies have yet to be made. The academic pattern so far has been to accept at face value the purpose-serving claims of victorious rightwing factions, regardless of their contradictions.

In their subjective reactions, union leaders I knew didn't seem to dismiss the radicalizing of labor as impossible, but took their stand against it as no wave-of-the-future for themselves. They took comfort, and nodded their heads, when theoreticians declared radicalism had no place in union attitudes. But for all their pooh-poohing, they never minimized left challenge and inclined to drastic measures against it.

In CIO, any radical with eyes open must have seen the limitations of left influence. I was surprised rightwing leaders took it so seriously. To me, as to Lewis, Hillman had seemed unduly afraid of it. Lewis, I thought, was more realistic. But in 1940, he set more stock on the left's support than its strength rated—perhaps because he had little other support. As to Murray, despite right pressure and his own conservatism, he sometimes conceded more to the left than it could command. I might have thought he was letting it bluff him, if I hadn't known he had inside information on per capita, loans, organizing aid, etc.; had rightwing informants in left unions; and was not the "simple man" he professed to be. Once Murray made his Cold War switch, he began using such information to pour scorn on the left; but more in bluster, it sometimes seemed, than in calm confidence of the left's weakness.

It was surprising how much effort and venom the CIO leaders put into their finally open war against the left. With all the government, employer, and opinion-controlling powers on their side, in a period of unprecedented persecution of radical dissenters, it seemed they could have ridden along, letting nature take its course. While the law, the bosses, the inquisitors, did the dirtier work, they might even—with tongue in cheek—have protested their own innocence and tolerance. But that was not the way it was.

There was gloating on the right; on the left, demoralization. I did what I could—a little here and there—defense committees for persecuted unionists, aid to stranded peapickers, liaison chores with unions, some peace talks, efforts to keep the Independent Progressive party alive after the Henry Wallace campaign, some fringe activities. But my heart was with the labor movement, and it was there I felt most disconnected.

It was much the same, not only in CIO, but everywhere that radicals or progressives once exerted much influence. The bravest and the best were in retreat—preparing camouflaged positions to hide from the blockbusters of redbaiting reaction. The weakest and worst became turncoats, informers.

This was aptly called the Time of the Toad. Stool pigeons of FBI and un-American committees came into the open to strut their stuff. Psychopathic "reds" became psychopathic redbaiters; others went to pieces. Former radicals wilted under inquisition, confessing, recanting, giving lists of erstwhile comrades and friends. A peculiar moral degradation was setting in.

The victims of inquisition didn't face racks, torture, death. American anticommunism had its jail terms, its fines at home;

its more extreme measures were for foreign fronts. Punishing enough for its purposes were the penalties of "exposure": Loss of jobs, wrecking of careers, blacklisting, possible mob or individual violence, social ostracism, family dislocation.

Those who wilted, who became turncoats or telltale traitors, or who just went to pieces, found it harder to justify their moral collapse than might victims of more dire physical persecution. They degraded themselves in the specious justifications they tried to devise. Terrorists and terrorized alike shared in the moral and intellectual degradation.

For all the subsequent anathemas on "McCarthyism," the whole establishment condoned or joined in the first Cold War persecutions of the left. The rot had set in, the stench filled the nostrils, long before the excesses of Senator Joseph McCarthy came to offend the rich, the respectable, and the powerful.

Among all the extreme cases, a minor one stuck in my craw.

I knew Dick little, but liked him. Maybe he reminded me of someone, or I just liked his style. He was a newspaperman, of the left in the Guild, as local CIO leader a Harry Bridges man. When I met Dick at CIO conventions, he was reserved, but our shared reactions—a slight grin or shrug or side glance, nothing so overt as a grin—seemed to say we were kindred spirits.

After my retreat to California, I was happy to run into Dick at a union convention and looked forward to letting myself go about CIO. A purgee—as I assumed he would be—Dick was reporting for a local paper. We had a drink and a bite and chewed the rag. He was friendly but didn't open up. Reserved as ever, I thought, and maybe picking up again the reporter's trick of trying not to let his sympathies show. But with me—after all. . . . His remarks, as I ran over them later in my mind, gave little clue to his feelings. Could it be that he didn't even care much any more?

Dick covered the 1948 CIO convention in Portland. I bought his paper just for his stories, hoping for some relief from the one-sided redbaiting in the rest of the press. Reading them, I felt I'd lost my kindred spirit. As a reporter, he might have had to play up the gloats of the triumphant right. But trying to read between the lines, I could find no trace of the Dick I thought I knew. For all the propaganda he may have to report, a canny newsman can delicately insert facts or quotes that enhance objectivity and tell a little about himself. Dick's stories were like all the rest. I concluded he was leaning over backward to keep his job; or the copydesk, wary of his leftist repute, was doing a job on his copy. Maybe both.

I was quite unprepared to read in the papers, some time later, that Dick had appeared as a prosecution witness to testify against Harry Bridges as a red, in one of the endless trials Bridges was subjected to.

Why had Dick done this? I gave up trying to find out. Friends simply speculated, as could I, that the FBI must have had something on him. Nobody was excited by what was now a common kind of occurrence. Friends just seemed unhappy about Dick. His reporting job had ended before he testified. I never heard tell of him again.

The Cold War had liquidated a personality.

I wasn't becoming liquidated myself—the sensation was more like shriveling and withering away. I didn't change my ideas or sympathies. But I lost confidence in doing anything effective about them. My side, the left, was losing ground so fast in the labor movement it seemed doomed.

At this low point, Johnny Steuben bustled into my life. With FBI agents trailing behind, he visited my California retreat toward the end of 1951 and asked me to become managing editor of *March of Labor*.

Johnny could be an engaging little guy. Like some others of conspicuously small stature, he could also be bumptious. When he had a purpose—which was most of the time—he went all-out to be engaging. His pitch for *March of Labor* was enticing, though I discounted most of it. Labor needed a militant left-wing organ, but most of all it needed more left wing.

I was nostalgic for the onetime spirit of CIO. Some of its leftwing unions survived—outside of CIO and with diminished reach. There must be others too in labor ranks who wanted to revive some of the impulses of early CIO. The magazine might help. Soon after Johnny left—with two cars trailing his—I was off to New York and my new job.

Steuben got little tribute when he died—too soon after a side-switching statement to be shriven by his old side, or hailed by the other side. The 1956 Hungarian events triggered his near-deathbed recantation. But a serious heart condition was at the root of his undoing.

When we worked together in Chicago, Johnny had a stroke and learned, for the first time, how weak was his heart. The shock changed his whole life and himself most of all. His physical decline coincided with his magazine's decline. He became extraordinarily embittered, against everyone and everything. Once tubby, he was just a wisp when last I saw him.

Before his stroke, Johnny was a different person—a cheerful, sociable, aggressive promoter. Then there was an earlier Johnny, the one I liked best, the Johnny of the Depression. When we ate together, we sometimes recalled hungrier times—I my boxcar days, and he the Johnny who organized for the Communist party in Youngstown, Ohio.

"We used to get so damned hungry!" he said. "We-ell, with me it wasn't so much hungry—I craved coffee. Sometimes we'd roll out of bed before daylight, on a shivery Ohio morning, and you know how late we stayed up! We couldn't wait for the bundle of *Daily Workers* to be delivered. We'd go to the railroad yards and get it right off the train, then go peddle some copies for our breakfast. Boy, oh bo-oy! That first nickel! That first cup of coffee!"

"Organizing for the party" covered plenty—unemployed demonstrations, eviction fights, picketings, sit-ins for black people's rights. The party organizer had to be alert to every grievance of a much aggrieved working class. But in a center like Youngstown, he must never forget where "the concentration" was. The party was out to get the steelworkers organized, as basic to unionizing other industries, an essential first step to eventual emancipation of the working class.

The old AFL Amalgamated Association let in few through its rusty creaky doors. The Trade Union Unity League started its Steel & Metal Workers Industrial Union more to fill a vacuum than to form a perfect union. With the New Deal, AFL federal unions and AA lodges began to sprout, and the lefts liquidated their TUUL union to bring militants into the mainstream. When CIO took over, they rejoiced and lined up with it at once.

Already a union organizer in fact, Johnny became one officially for the CIO Steel Workers Organizing Committee—with salary, expenses, and status. He found it hard to adjust to such sudden affluence. He didn't know how to spend like a porkchopper, let alone pad a swindle-sheet. He felt ashamed to take Pullman instead of overnight daycoach or bus. Normal union expenses seemed like robbing the working class. But Johnny made a good record with SWOC as an organizer.

After leaving Steel, Steuben was a pro as a union organizer. He became a local official of the AFL Hotel & Restaurant union in New York, when left influence was strong there. He wrote books on union strategy. He was a natural to organize and run a magazine like *March of Labor*. He threw himself into it phenomenally, excessively. The magazine's sure but desperately deferred death contributed to his own decline.

March of Labor was a sort of postscript to the CIO story.

Started after CIO drove its leftwing unions from the fold, MOL aimed to serve them and the left in other unions. It was not an official organ which was good for independence and reader interest, but bad for dependable support. Without union subsidy or advertising revenue, the magazine lived precariously. Friendly unions helped with convention resolutions, articles by leaders, subscription drives, bundle orders, group subscriptions. Most were on the defensive, with dwindling funds and expanding caution. They couldn't stick their necks out far for a neckout magazine; and the growing crackdown on all union leftism was undermining even this limited union support.

At its best, however, the venture had the warm glow of an Indian summer—the residual glow of the old CIO idea and those who warmed to it. Steuben tried to make *March of Labor* a group effort, a little movement in itself. It had its policy committees through which union leaders and activists conferred together, as once through the CIO apparatus. Johnny had many ideas to make the magazine itself an organizer.

To aid editorially, and spread the word to the intelligentsia and white-collardom, Johnny enlisted artists, cartoonists, writers, editors, photographers, copyreaders, layout men from commercial magazines and union offices. With honeyed talk, he drew these volunteers into his web. He put them on editorial committees that actually functioned. He had titles for all (make one phone call for him and you became "Liaison Officer for *March of Labor*"). Once assigned their commissions, titles, honors, emblems of rank, the experts were hooked. Johnny exploited them without mercy and without pay, other than pep talks.

These experts worked wonders with minimal resources against insuperable obstacles. They made the magazine unusually slick and lively for a labor publication. They produced whole issues on their own at times, with remarkable self-organization. In their company and that of our union boosters, one could live warmly again.

But no Indian summer can last long. Winter was well under way.

There was a distasteful side to working for *March of Labor*. Various snoops—working openly or undercover for the FBI and/or the House Un-American Activities Committee—hovered around, sniffing presumably for "communist conspiracy." The magazine had some communist inspiration and support—as had CIO and most steps since the Twenties toward union organization, unemployment insurance, black liberation, labor political action. This didn't make it a communist magazine. That wasn't its nature or function.

HUAC, however, had already put *March of Labor* on its index—and wanted only to pillory it and me—when it summoned me to the stand in 1954. I challenged the committee's right to infringe press freedom, citing the First Amendment to the Constitution; or to force me to incriminate myself under repressive and lying anticommunist laws, citing the Fifth.

The HUAC line was that the magazine was communist because it employed persons like me and carried articles by leaders of unions charged by CIO with being subject to communist influence. These unions determined their own policies under constitutions more democratic than most, and most of their leaders were not communists. HUAC, however, was content to continue describing as an "identified communist" anyone at whom one of its scruffy informers might ever have pointed a grubby finger.

HUAC did its little job on the near-dead body of a magazine from which by then I had been long disconnected, and called it a day.

FBI's surveillance was less overt than HUAC's "public exposure." It could have discovered as much as it did by diligently reading each issue of the magazine. It is the function of a publication to make public, and there was nothing secretive about ours. If FBI undercover agents weaseled into our office or homes or meetings of boosters, we had no counterespionage system to expose and drive them out. If we'd had one, I could have suggested several eager-beavers for countersurveillance.

There were those who wanted to establish "branches" in "key defense" industries—a tipoff to the FBI and gutterpress mentality that professed to believe communists intent on "sabotaging defense." Others became impatient for us to "do something"; snooped for names and addresses of our "contacts"; or cozied up to our personnel, inquisitive about the "inside" of what was all on the outside anyhow.

If the FBI's surveillance of our editorial operations was ostensibly under cover, its attentions to Johnny and myself were not the least covert. Johnny had an escort in most of his comings and goings. Once or twice, for kicks, he tried to dodge it. The FBI men got as sore as any worker with a beef. Johnny kidded they might be union-organizable.

In my case, FBI men kept tab on my southside Chicago home. It was a "rough shadow"—they tried to make me aware of it. They visited neighbors on each side of me, who duly reported the visits. Once, returning from work, I saw a pair of the deliberately conventional young men knocking at a door down my street. One waved and said, "How d'you do, Mr. De Caux?" He pronounced the name correctly—a tribute to FBI phonetic efficiency; few Americans did. I waved back, "Howdy, FBI." They grinned.

It was no grinning matter, for Caroline anyhow, when the FBI tried to involve our 11-year daughter. Shirley said an FBI man had approached her and asked if her parents were home when she came back from school at lunchtime. He said he'd phone the next day, if she were alone. We made a point of being home, and Caroline answered the phone when the man called. He identified himself as FBI in the familiar way and said he wanted to ask some questions. Caroline was not given to what is called "strong language"; she blistered his ears to a turn without a single cussword.

After my publicized "exposure" by HUAC, the FBI had to show it too was on the job. Early on a following morning, as I left the house for my car, I saw another car down the street with idling motor and two young men in it. It followed me to the trade school on the north side where I was studying linotype operation. It parked near me, and the men followed me into the school. As I sat at the machine, they came into the printshop and talked in unhushed voices to the instructor. Ostensibly asking questions about the school, they kept glancing toward me and in their talk mentioning names and places from my background. A cute performance.

For years after, the FBI kept tabs on me—at least every six months, more often if I moved, had visitors, or did anything out of routine. The checkups were mostly at home. But at work once in Los Angeles I noticed two of the unmistakably unobtrusive young men lounging at the open alley door of the printshop, and glancing at me each time I turned my head. I got up from my machine and walked toward them. One nudged the other, they grinned at me, and moved off—having let me know they knew where I worked.

Most often an FBI pair would come to my house when I was away and ask for me. After I got home, they'd phone and ask if I'd answer some questions. I always replied that I'd agree to grilling only in the presence of a lawyer of my own. After some time, the FBI men dropped house visits but continued periodical phone calls. I recall the last one:

The usual FBI identification. The always correct pronunciation of my name. A polite inquiry if I'm willing to talk about "past subversive associations." My routine response. I happen to say "my lawyer," not "a lawyer."

An eager: "Who's your lawyer?"

"I'll hire one."

A resigned: "All right, Mr. De Caux. We understand your point of view."

If that much understanding was achieved, after such prolonged dogging at the public expense, it was perhaps something.

The attentions bestowed on a red suspect had a cumulative effect—which helped demoralize many should-have-been radicals in the Fifties.

The first FBI visit was nothing much. One didn't really believe it. Like my liberal and Jewish friends in Berlin in 1925, one reflected on the civilization of one's country, its democratic institutions, strong labor movement. Must be some legitimate reason, a misunderstanding perhaps. . . .

It was even fun, in a way, when the Senate Internal Security Subcommittee summoned me in 1952. I had just started work on *March of Labor*, and the senatorial snoops hadn't known it. They sent the subpoena to my home in California; it reached me in New York only after much delay. My new job was not endangered; on it, such a summons was a status symbol.

I was cited for my previous connection with the Institute of Pacific Relations. I knew the probe hadn't been fun for Owen Lattimore. But in this net I was such a little fish I could see big holes to get through into the swim again. Committee Counsel Robert Morris was courteous, even consulted my convenience. Senator Watkins of Utah, who presided, was grayly sober. He didn't rant. He did his dirty job with dignified melancholy—like a Quaker voting appropriations for an aggressive imperialist war.

The proceedings were pregnant with manifest absurdities. I wrote them up hilariously for my own amusement and as an office joke. I was to laugh on the other side of my face when I got my next congressional subpoena.

The sleuthings and stoolings on *March of Labor* were unpleasant—especially after we moved from New York's more sophisticated behavior patterns to the hard-boiled crudities of Chicago. But one learned to live with them.

One started out feeling fine—with some Chicago equivalent of sun shining, birds chirping. Then one of those things happened. It made one queasy—more from disgust than fear. It might mean little; it could portend something. As in nightmare, one felt foreboding of ugly, formless squirm-things spawned when Power is bedded with a Lie. One felt fine no longer.

Harassment in itself did not demoralize; it could stimulate a militant. It did hamper organization. Once I sent a circular letter, in plain envelopes, to a long list of union contacts who had once actively supported projects like ours. It asked them to a meeting at the *March of Labor* office, or to phone in. Not one did either, except for one man personally reached. It reminded me of early CIO days—when employers did most of their own spying and intimidation. Organizers had to be devious to contact prospective members. Certainly the prospects would have disregarded a circular letter inviting them to show up at a union office.

Because my neck was already out, I could shrug off much that an employed worker, scared for his job, could not. Only after I was no longer with *March of Labor* did I personally feel the full effects of the intimidation.

When Richard M. Nixon was the wonder boy of redbaiting, red-hunting, and congressional inquisition, a well-known left-wing union leader ran into him on an airplane trip and found him cordial and easy to chat with. He asked how come. "We know who you are, what you stand for, where to find you," Nixon replied. "It's the hidden ones we're after."

So long as my name was on the masthead of *March of Labor*, they knew who, what, and where I was. When I had to find a job with a capitalist boss, and fit back with my family into the conventional patterns of American life, I became a hidden one, the quarry.

The FBI was mildly interested in my job-hunting, but didn't help place me where it could find me, nor try to block me from jobs, so far as I was aware. Just got tired, I guess, of waiting so long for me to get placed. In this period I had the experiences, earlier noted, of trying to find work in line with my labor

editorial qualifications. If this was hard after my severance from
CIO, it was impossible after *March of Labor*. As time went on,
I looked for odd jobs or anything at all.

It was a minor miracle when I finally landed a steady job—
as proofreader in a large, nonunion, magazine printing house.
Under pressure of its schedules, the company needed someone
at once; it showed little interest in the phony work record and
references I had to concoct. After weeks with no sign my past
had been investigated, I breathed freely again.

Only the generation of the Great Depression could fully appreciate the remoralization—ecstasy almost—of a steady job
after long unemployment. In our case, we had suffered less from
economic than from social insecurity. The feel of being radical
outcasts had been getting us down. A small sample:

Finding rentals unavailable and rents exorbitant, we wanted
to buy a house. When the broker learned I worked for *March of
Labor*, he was much disturbed. "It's not communistic, I hope,"
said he. "It's not communist, but it is of the left," I answered
honestly. The broker was a Nisci—one of those displaced from
California after Pearl Harbor. He shared some of the feelings of
the hunted. He cited some legalism about abetting reds. He expected trouble in getting a bank loan, was sure things would
break down at some point. His agitation gave us the jitters. Even
after the deal went through, our uneasiness lingered.

It was a great relief at last to land a respectable job we
could refer to for credit, standing, the credentials of daily American life. My morale shot up the more because this job gave me
scope for labor activity.

On-the-job solidarity was sometimes stronger in a nonunion
plant, I'd found, than under union conditions where grievance
handling could become routine. From the Twenties, I could recall the electric current that ran through ship, shop, or camp at
some clash, some defiance, of the boss by workers who had to
stand up for themselves without aid of union rep or contract.

In this case, I worked the night shift, when fellowship is
closer and fewer bosses are around. There was always one person
—not necessarily a foreman—who was known as a company
snoop. I saw a key skilled man, unafraid for his job, take on such
a stooge. His language exploded, he glared, he jostled, but didn't

strike a blow. The bosses' man tries to hush the other's voice. But all around the shop, the workers cocked their ears. They stopped their machines on any pretext, to hear better. Grins, winks, nudges, passed around. After the clash, the tough guy was a hero; the bosses' man drew tongue-in-cheek sympathy and double-edged cracks.

To talk of union in this nonunion shop was to risk one's job. To mention the word without damnation—in the john, say —was a conspiracy. If the subject of union came up within hearing of the office, some men would say: "A racket." "Wouldn't do us no good." "Won't let you guys in." "Out for theirselves, don't give a shit for us." Others would be stubbornly silent. None of the reactions necessarily revealed real feelings.

I contacted the Chicago Typographical Union to help organize the shop.

Talk about conspiracy! The union top shot dealt with me alone behind closed doors. He said I mustn't be seen coming to the union office. I must do nothing in the shop, at home, anywhere, to expose myself as a union sympathizer. The organizer would use my information on names, addresses, attitudes, only in contacting workers at their homes. Particularly in the shop must I be careful, not talk about the union, not show any interest. If the subject came up, I must keep out of the discussion or even, to keep clear of suspicion, express some antiunion sentiment.

The important thing, the union leader said, was that under no circumstances should I let myself get fired. I couldn't have agreed more heartily.

When the knock on the door came—after months of this rehabilitation—our family agitation was extreme. It was a subpoena to appear before the House Un-American Activities Committee in Washington, for a hearing on *March of Labor*. I hadn't been connected with the magazine for nearly a year. It had long since moved back from Chicago to New York, where its dying gasps were less and less frequent.

Could I somehow come through without losing my job? I

thought there was a fighting chance and began to plot the seemingly impossible—an undiscovered public appearance before HUAC.

Had the hearing been in Chicago, I'd have given up. Exposure, discharge, blacklist, would have been inevitable. If HUAC came to one's city, the only out was to dodge the subpoena. For years after, I had no telephone in my name, left no forwarding address when I moved. Each place of employment was a closely guarded secret—mentioned not even in family or among friends. At first I thought to dodge the FBI also, then concluded that was asking trouble from an outfit concerned chiefly with knowing my whereabouts. HUAC was the menace to my job, and I figured a local subpoena-server couldn't count on earning his pay by no more than calling the FBI.

In this 1954 case, however, the HUAC hearing was in Washington, and I was working in Chicago. Local hearings got a big splash. But a hearing in Washington, about a near-defunct labor magazine in New York, should rate no more than a routine wireservice squib in Chicago papers, I thought. Mention of my name might escape my employer's attention, or be passed off as error or coincidence, provided all evidence pointed to my being on the job continuously in Chicago at the time. Could I make the trip to Washington and back without being missed from the job?

It was fortunate I worked the night shift. By split-second timing I could work my shift Wednesday night, catch a plane to Washington, and return by afternoon plane after the hearing, to start my Thursday shift in Chicago at 4:30 P.M. Schooled in detective fiction, I gave close attention to every detail. Nothing about my clothes, habits, manner, must lead anyone to suspect I was not going home from work Wednesday night and coming from home Thursday afternoon exactly as I always did.

Every detail clicked, I thought—but one. If I quit work at the regular 1 A.M. time, I might miss my plane by minutes. Moreover, in leaving the shop with the rest of the shift, I might be seen heading for a taxi rather than the Elevated I normally took. I therefore fixed it with a foreman to punch me out at the regular time while I slipped out ten minutes early. It was a small and not unusual favor, but if anything came up, the strawboss mightn't confess his delinquency; whereas, if I begged off and punched out early, it could be a giveaway to the office.

It was a possible weak link. I agonized over it as I fidgeted sleeplessly in the plane. Everything else had seemed to work out perfectly.

In Washington, I had breakfast with my lawyer, who discussed my constitutional rights. Besides citing the First Amendment on press feeedom, I'd have to claim protection of the Fifth and answer no anticommunist questions, or I'd be required, under pain of jail and fine, to answer all related questions, inevitably designed to make me an informer against associates and friends. My chief concern was to protect my job, but the lawyer said they'd certainly ask about it and I'd have to answer.

Sure enough, committee counsel soon asked the question that could mean discharge and blacklist. I stalled, asking to keep my employer's name from the record—lest he be embarrassed, I said. Congressman Harold Velde (R., Ill.) was presiding inattentively, when not peacocking before some lady friends. At my feeble evasion he sprang to life with the look of a hunter out for the kill. He insisted I give full name, business, address of my employer, spell it out and repeat it. Velde's eagerness surprised me. Charitably I speculated he might have thought I was holding back on some juicy connection. Less charitably I concluded that anyone engaged in HUAC's persecution of individuals must have a strong streak of sadism.

With my job and employer's name in the record, I could only hope now that Chicago papers wouldn't print them—so I could keep my job long enough to quit voluntarily with a good reference. In this hope I was encouraged by the dullness of the hearing and the dearth of reporters. I was the only witness all morning and into a brief afternoon session. Some reporters spoke to chairman and counsel before the hearing, then disappeared. At the press table was only one man, bored, doodling, and lightly snoozing.

Besides Velde, there were Rep. Kit Clardy (R., Mich.) and Rep. Gordon Scherer (R., Ohio), who just seemed along for the ride; and Rep. Francis E. Walter, an aggressive inquisitor. Walter had been a New Deal Democrat enjoying labor support. With the Cold War, Walter became immigration specialist on keeping out and kicking out reds. He had personal reasons to spite me.

In 1953 *March of Labor* published a special issue demanding repeal of the McCarran-Walter immigration and nationality act. Under this act, thousands of unionists faced deportation for radical beliefs or associations; and famous foreigners, including Pablo Picasso, Maurice Chevalier, Graham Greene, Louis Aragon, were denied even brief entry into the United States. This issue was circulated widely and must have got under Walter's skin.

Walter came prepared with papers, from some 30 years back, relating to my immigration and naturalization. He was boorish, insulting, and peculiarly spiteful. Declaring I should have my naturalization revoked and be deported, Walter prompted Scherer to suggest and Velde to concur that the Justice Department should take action.

It did. I heard later from friends around the country visited by agents of U.S. Immigration inquiring about my past radical associations.

Unlike the Senate committee, HUAC was arrogant, hectoring, deliberately rude, and inconsiderate. Each time I started to snap back, I felt the cautioning glance of my lawyer, who had advised self-control under provocation, lest I risk extended persecution. When my anger tempted me to disregard him, my fear of publicity bringing job loss stopped me. The sure way to make a news story was to clash with the committee.

Once released from the hearing, I sped to the Washington airport with but minutes to spare. I congratulated myself on my self-control. The story shouldn't rate more than a squib in Chicago papers. All went smoothly on my return. At 4:30 P.M. I began my shift at the shop, in every detail exactly as I'd always done.

During the lunch break, I got a copy of the Chicago *Daily News.* On an inside page was an inconspicuous United Press story headed, "Chicagoan Defies Red Quiz." That much I had expected and, blessed break, it didn't give the name of my em-

ployer. With this I might be able to cope. It might escape
attention in the shop, where last names were never used and
only payroll clerks paid them attention. I had been continuously
on the job, and if confronted with the item, might plausibly
deny it referred to me.

Across the table from me, as I ate my lunch, was a printer
who always read the *Daily News* as he ate. He read it page by
page and column by column. By the time he came to the page
where my item was, I was in a sweat. I followed his eyes going
down column by column to the spot where my story was. His
eyes ran right past the item. He turned the page.

At end of shift, I left the shop with great relief. No one had
mentioned the news item. Others would likely pay it as little attention as had my lunch mate. At the El station, I bought the
other papers, to hunt through them on the way home for further
squibs. I started with the *Chicago Tribune*.

I didn't have to hunt; it was no squib. On the second page,
with my picture and sprawling over four columns, was a story exclusively about me, my life story and all. It was from Washington by the *Tribune's* redbait specialist, Willard Edwards, who
had evidently been the doodling, dozing reporter. It gave my
home address, the name, description, and address of my employer, and all possible identification of myself and my job.

That was that. I saw no point in going to work for the next
shift—thought I'd call the shop, let the boss speak first, then ask
him to mail my final paycheck. Caroline and I batted things
around. Friends looked in or phoned. I was uncertain and asked
their reactions.

A union printer friend made up my mind. A fellow left, he
had once worked in my shop. He was emphatic. I shouldn't slink
off, he said. I should go to work again as usual, and let the workers see the firing and know its reasons. "We've got to show them
what we're like," said he.

A mild person, who hated to stir up prejudice and shunned
personal confrontations, I climbed the long stairs to the shop as
to the scaffold.

First to pass me on the stairs, coming off shift, were black and Filipino workers in some sideline departments. Those I knew—and some I didn't—waved and smiled, seeming friendlier than usual. A good omen—my cup began to brim. In the locker room, no one paid me any attention, until . . .

"Lousy communist!"

I was standing at the urinal with back to the men coming and going. The harsh, grating voice may have said more. Those two words hit me so sharply I heard no others. I jerked my head around. The speaker was a compositor who'd always been friendly enough. He left the washroom as I turned. I pursued him. I didn't know why. My mind was numbed.

As the man circled through the plant to the composing room, the pressmen cleaning their machines turned to stare at my pursuit. I caught up with him as he joined a group of floormen and operators comparing notes at change of shift. My words tumbled out—like the pursuit, a reflex to the two words. My voice rose as I spoke of HUAC, and swore no one I knew should treat me like it had. Curious heads popped out of the front office.

The man said nothing. True, I gave him little chance. His mouth dropped open. The others were silent, too. I didn't wait. Having said my say, I went on into the proofroom.

There was only one galley proof, left from the day shift. The plant rumbled and clattered into full operation. No one brought me proofs. No one came in; and I didn't feel like going out. Only salesmen or clerks passed my open door—turning their heads to stare in at me. Printers who usually looked in to get off their feet all stayed away—as did the foreman.

I recalled the early days of the Newspaper Guild. A publisher who didn't want to run afoul of the Wagner act might keep a known or suspected unionist on the payroll but see that he got no assignments. The idea was to wear him down until he did something to excuse discharge.

For three hours I had no work and no company. Then— blessed advent—an old floorman came in. He was an American Legion member, with some opinions to match. But he also hated finks and bosslovers. I had an unverified hunch he'd been a union member, possibly still was. He brought a revise proof with two small corrections to read. He came in as always, with the same words: "I'm ti-i-ired, Len. My legs hurt."

The floorman sat on the edge of my table to rest his legs, as he always did. Then he got down and left without another word. That was my only human contact for the first half of the shift.

During the lunch break, I was still isolated. The men who usually ate in the shop, as did I, all went out for lunch. As they passed my door, none glanced in with a "Hi, there!" Eating my lonely lunch, I assumed I was the subject of a lunch-break bull session. I waited curiously for the return.

A linotype operator came in at once and sat down with me. He was young, white, a Korean War veteran. He just chatted, without diffidence or hesitation. He related my case to that of J. Robert Oppenheimer and others then in the news. He showed neither sympathy nor prejudice. But at such a time his talk was a tonic.

Next came the night foreman, who also sat down to chat. A politician, a diplomat, as a successful composing-room foreman needs to be, he was friendly and gabby, and told of a cousin who was once a communist.

All through the rest of the shift, printers came in one by one, as they saw a chance—to ask about the hearing or just to be friendly. The last to come was the comp who had said "lousy communist." A nervous, rather erratic person, he was visibly embarrassed.

"No hard feelings, Len?" he murmured, watching for my reaction. By now my feelings were mushy not hard. I laughed, held out my hand. "I didn't mean you, really I didn't," he kept repeating as he shook it.

The superintendent had come in after the foreman, to hear my story. Before I left, he came back and said I was a good worker, the shop needed me, he'd do all he could to keep me. The big boss would have the last word, and he was away, but I could keep on working till he returned.

It turned out to be a great night.

The next day was Saturday, and with a night's sleep to make up, I slept in till the afternoon. The super called. He sounded genuinely distressed.

"Can't tell you how sorry I am," he said, "but I've got to let you go. You can have it any way you like—quit, call it a layoff, a discharge, whatever's best for you. I can't wait till the boss returns. Customers have been calling in all day, and the salesmen are raising hell. They say I've got to fire you at once."

Down toppled the card-house of my rehabilitation. For a time I just gave up. Then shakily I tried to set up the cards again. Another printing plant advertised a job I just fitted. The super had said he'd give me a good reference. I gave his name. But the new boss knew someone else in my old firm who screamed "That communist!" The word got around to job agencies as well as bosses. I was on the blacklist.

On my old job I had noted the demand for linotype operators, and how independent they could be. With a sub rosa assist from my union contact, I had got into a linotype course at a public technical school. After the *Tribune* story and the FBI visit, I wasn't sure how I stood even there. The instructor, a gruff fellow, was not chatty. He may have known more than he let on. One day, out of a clear sky, he told me he'd read a book by Elmer Davis on civil liberties; he damned the redbaiters and redhunters.

After my firing, I studied floor composition as well as linotype. I went barnstorming in the sticks, learning a little more on each job before I was bounced. Like the boomer machinists I'd known in earlier days—boomer printers too—I went from town to town in the midwest and then in California. Eventually I could just walk into a printshop and say, "I'm an operator." If they needed one, they'd set me right down at the machine—not even asking my last name till payday.

At last I became competent enough to hold down a steady job and be admitted to the union. For the rest of my working life, I could enjoy union protection, some security, and more freedom of conscience than on any available writing job.

Chapter Twenty-one

SIXTIES

The Sixties were resurrection decade for any old left whose eyes could still see. From out of the tomb of the Fifties a new generation of radical youth stepped forth. It saw through many of the lies that cozened the people into submission. It rebeled against the supremacies of white over black, of rich over poor, of imperialist over colonial, of capitalist over worker, of age over youth, of man over woman.

To me, it was my own radical generation reincarnate. As we reacted against the First World War and responded to the Russian revolution, so it reacted against the Vietnam war and responded to black liberation and world struggle against imperialism.

One difference: To us, the rise of the working class clearly pointed the way. The first step must be workers' organization, to fight for the workers' needs, to form a base for advance to socialism. The radicals new-born in the Sixties saw unions and welfare, not as the workers fought to win them, but as capitalism sought to use them. They learned of the CIO uprising only from those who subdued it.

The CIO might seem to have betrayed its many radicals. Like earlier waves of working-class advance it broke on the capitalist shores and receded. But it was the greatest wave; and no wave has yet been the last.

CIO drew upon the dreams of the first radical union pioneers—upon the industrial unionism and socialism of Eugene Debs, upon the fighting spirit of the IWW, upon the union organizing of William Z. Foster and his communist and TUEL followers, upon the traditions of unions like the Machinists that were militant-to-class conscious up to the Twenties. Yet of all this that had gone before, few traces seemed left on the sand when the CIO wave was gathering force. The AFL was as smugly, narrowly business-unionist, as redbaiting and reactionary, as AFL-CIO in the Fifties.

At its crest, CIO drew into motion all those—yes, students too—who today reproach labor for lagging behind. Its strong left and progressive elements demonstrated the potentially leading role of the working class. Then the wave broke on the rocks of the Cold War. Anticommunism sucked back the waters, till no more seemed left of its radical surge than some foam on the beach.

The CIO left might seem to have failed. It was ruthlessly purged from most areas of influence in a period of fantastic, factitious antired hysteria. Seen in longer perspective, it succeeded phenomenally in exerting leadership within a labor movement carefully barred to radical influence. For more than a decade, the CIO left had a strong voice in top policy and throughout the ranks. It helped carry the labor struggle to heights of progressive purpose hardly matched before or since.

It is true that, once legalized and regulated by a capitalist state, unions can be used by corporations to discipline the workers, assuage the class struggle, and solve many personnel problems. But unions also provide the arena and offer the means for workers to rebel against their exploitation. Hence the stress placed by the CIO left on rank-and-file democracy—in face of strictures by top CIO leaders—so that their unions might reflect the workers' wishes, not bureaucratically obstruct them.

After the heyday of the CIO left, most unions relapsed into backward positions on broad issues—in contrast to the continuing solidarity and militancy of their members on understood wage issues. For this contrast, rightwing leaders were more to blame than the lethargy of the members. The CIO left showed that—provided it adequately served the economic interests of its members—an American union could just as well be left-led or progressive as right-led or conservative. Left-led unions were not confined to special groups but covered a broad cross-section of the workers.

A case could be made that left-led unions more closely reflected membership sentiment than did right-led unions, because their policies were adopted under more democratic procedures and under stress of much establishment opposition. Under a setup like that of the east coast longshoremen (ILA), dictatorial leaders could easily use henchmen for patrioteering antiradical stunts. But when the west coast longshoremen (ILWU), with far more rank-and-file democracy, adopted progressive-to-left policies running against the Cold War tide, these had to reflect argument, persuasion, conviction.

Impatient radicals have always felt frustrated by the stolidity of organized workers, who are preoccupied with making a living and whose unions were formed to function under capitalism, not to make the revolution as the IWW envisaged. Yet the class struggle continues in the most advanced of capitalist countries. Dramatic confrontations between workers and capitalists are not its only expression, though these have never ceased to occur and seem, if anything, to recur with increasing frequency and force. The struggle is also within the labor movement itself.

The struggle may lead at times to a sharp break with reactionary leaders and restrictive forms of organization, as in the first rise of CIO. It may take shape, as in the Sixties, in pressure from without by the most disadvantaged workers who have been neglected, excluded, or discriminated against; and by peace and radical forces to which labor has been slow to respond. In one way or another, from within or without, labor must be induced to move if any substantial social progress is to be achieved.

The CIO story shows that such movement can happen here.

INDEX